A Catalogue of English and Foreign Theology

Comprising the holy scriptures, in various languages, liturgies and liturgical works; A very choice collection of the Fathers of the Church, Councils and Ecclesiastical Historians; The Writings of the Nonjurors, and the Various Controversies Between the Roman Catholic and Protestant Churches. Together with the chief works of the Church of England divines, also, a few valuable manuscripts and works in miscellaneous literature

John Leslie

Alpha Editions

This edition published in 2020

ISBN : 9789354012136

Design and Setting By
Alpha Editions
email - alphaedis@gmail.com

As per information held with us this book is in Public Domain.
This book is a reproduction of an important historical work. Alpha Editions uses the best technology to reproduce historical work in the same manner it was first published to preserve its original nature. Any marks or number seen are left intentionally to preserve its true form.

INDEX.

	PAGE
The Holy Scriptures, in Various Languages	1
Translations of various portions of Scripture	6
Liturgies and Liturgical Works	8
English and Foreign Theology, including the Fathers of the Church	15
Bampton Lectures	29
Boyle Lectures	51
Concilia	83
Hulsean Lectures	154
Manuscripts	313
Moyer Lectures	204
Parker Society Publications	215
Psalms	231
Warburtonian Lectures	292
Appendix	309

₊ UNIVERSITIES and PUBLIC INSTITUTIONS, at home or abroad, supplied on liberal terms, and orders for new Publications promptly executed.

LIBRARIES, however extensive, or small collections of Books, purchased or exchanged, and Valuations made for testamentary and other purposes.

J. LESLIE'S CATALOGUE

OF

English and Foreign Theology,

MDCCCXLVI.

THE HOLY SCRIPTURES IN VARIOUS LANGUAGES.

1 BIBLIA SACRA POLYGLOTTA, complectantia Textus Originales, Hebraicum (cum Pentateucho Samaratino) Chaldaicum, Græcum; versionesque antiquas, Samaritanam, Græcam, Chaldaicam, Syriacam, Arabicam, Æthiopicam, Persicam, et Vulgatam Latinam, cum omnium Translationibus Latinis et apparatu, appendicibus tabulis, &c. edidit BRIANUS WALTONUS, 6 vols. *Lond.* 1657— E. CASTELLI, Lexicon Heptaglotton, Heb. Chald. Syr. Sam. Æthiop. Arab. et Pers. cum omnium Grammaticis, 2 vols. *ib.* 1669—together 8 vols. folio, *portraits and plates, fine copy, calf,* £30. ———

2 BIBLIA SACRA POLYGLOTTA textus Archetypos Versionesque præcipuas ab Ecclesia Antiquitus receptas complectantia; containing, the Hebrew Bible, *(with points)*, the Samaritan Pentateuch, the Syriac Testament; the Septuagint and Greek Testament; the Latin Vulgate; and the English Version, 4to. *calf, extra,* £3. 3s   *Lond.* ———

3 BIBLIA HEBRAICA, *(cum punctis)* cum Novo Domini Nostri Jesu Christi Testamento [Græcè]. Eorundem Latina interpretatio Xantis Pagnini Lucensis, Benedicti Ariæ Montani et quorundam aliorum collato studio, ad Hebraicam dictionem diligentissime expensa, &c., folio, *red morocco,* £1. 18s   *Aur. Allobr.* 1619

"Presented to his Royal Highness the Duke of Sussex, by H. R. H. the Prince of Capua, 1840."—*MS Note.*

4 ——— *(cum punctis)* correcta et collata cum antiquissimis MSS. et impressis, 2 vols. 8vo. *fine copy, old calf gilt,* 16s   *Amst.* 1661

5 ——— sine punctis; Versibus, Capitibus et Sectionibus interstincta, notisque Masoretarum quas Kri et Ktif appellant, instructa. Ad Leusdenianam editionem adornata, 12mo. *calf,* 8s   *ib.* 1701

6 ——— *cum punctis,* secundum ultimam editionem Jos. Athiæ, a Jo. Leusden denuo recognitam, recensita variisque notis illustrata ab E. Van der Hooght, *Best Edition, fine copy, bound* in 4 vols. *old calf, richly gilt,* £2. 2s   *ib.* 1705

7 ——— idem, recognita a Judah D'Allemand, 8vo. *blue morocco, gilt leaves,* £1. 11s 6d   *Lond.* 1822

The late Duke of Sussex's copy.

8 VETUS TESTAMENTUM Hebraicum, cum variis lectionibus; edidit Benj. Kennicott, S. T. P. 2 vols. folio, *calf,* £4. 14s 6d   *Oxonii,* 1776

9 THE HEBREW SCRIPTURES of the Old Testament, without points, after the Text of Kennicott, with the chief various readings, selected from his collation of Hebrew MSS., from that of De Rossi, and from the ancient Versions, with English Notes, critical, philological, and explanatory, by B. Boothroyd, 2 vols. in 1, 4to. *half bound, calf,* £1. 4*s* . *Pontefract*, ——

10 PSALMI, Proverbia, et Job, Hebraicè, 16mo. *calf*, 2*s* ——

11 PROVERBIA SALOMONIS, jam recens juxta Hebraicam veritatem translata, et Annotationibus illustrata, autore Sebast. Munstero, *Froben*, N. D.—Elia Levita Composita Verborum et Nominum Hebraicorum, edente S. Munstero, *Basil*. 1525, in 1 vol. 12mo. *calf*, 6*s* ——
From the Duke of Sussex's Library.

12 PROVERBIA, Job, Canticum Canticorum, Ruth, Threnodia, Ecclesiastes, et Esther, Hebraicè, 16mo. 3*s* 6*d*   *Antv. A.M.* 5326. *A.D.* 1566
From the Library of the late Duke of Sussex.

13 LIBRI JOSUE, Judicum, Samuelis, et Regum, Hebraicè, 16mo. *calf, neat, gilt leaves, with brass clasps*, 5*s*

14 JOEL Explicatus per Paraphrasin Chaldaicam Masorum Magnam et Parvam, necnon Obadias eodem fere modo illustratus authore J. Leusden, 12mo. *calf*, 4*s*   .   *Ult.* 1657

GREEK.

15 VETUS TESTAMENTUM Græcum, ex Versione Septuaginta interpretum, juxta exemplar Vaticanum Romæ editum, 2 vols. 12mo. *fine copy, old calf gilt*, 10*s* 6*d*   .   *Cantab. J. Field*, 1665

16 —— ex editione Septuaginta Interpretum. Summa cura edidit J. E. Grabe, 8 vols. 8vo. *plates, calf*, £1. 4*s*   *Oxonii*, 1707-9

17 —— juxta exemplar Vaticanum, cum Scholiis Romanæ editionis, variis MSS. codicum lectionibus, necnon fragmentis versionum Aquilæ, Symmachi et Theodotionis; edidit Lamb. Bos, 2 vols. in 1, 4to. *vellum*, £1. 10*s*   .   *Franeq.* 1709
"An elegant and accurate edition, which is deservedly esteemed."—*Horne.*

18 —— ex Versione Septuaginta interp. edidit cum var. lect. D. MILLII, 2 vols. 12mo. *calf*, 12*s*   *Amst.* 1725

19 —— ex editione Grabii, exemplaris Vaticani aliorumque MSS. codd. lectionibus variis necnon criticis dissertationibus illustratum; edidit J. J. BREITINGER, 4 vols. 4to. *calf*, £2. 5*s*—*fine copy, vellum,* £2. 10*s*   .   *Tiguri*, 1730-32
Michaelis pronounces this to be the best edition of the Septuagint, up to his time.

20 —— ex versione LXX. Interpretum, 3 vols. Libri Apocryphi, 1 vol.—Novum Testamentum, 1 vol.—together 5 vols. 8vo. *calf, neat*, £1. 18*s*   .   *Oxon.* 1805

21 —— ex versione Septuaginta interpretum. Accedunt varia lectiones e Codice Alexandrino necnon Introductio J. B. Carpzovii, 6 vols. 8vo. *new, in sprinkled calf, gilt*, £3. 3*s*   .   *ib.* 1817

22 —— juxta exemplar Vaticanum, ex editione Holmesii et Lamberti Bos, cum Novum Testamentum, Græcè, 4 vols. 18mo. *bds.* 12*s*
Glasg. 1822

23 DANIEL secundum LXX. ex Tetraplis Origenis Gr. et Lat. cum notis, dissertationibus, variis lectionibus, et de LXX. Interpretibus opusculis quibusdam, folio, *bds.* 16*s*—*calf*, 18*s* *Romæ*, 1773

[58, GREAT QUEEN STREET,

24 PSALTERIUM Davidicum Græco-Latinum, 16mo. *printed in red and black, neat*, 4s . Par. 1559
25 PSALMORUM Davidicorum Metaphrasis Græcis versibus contexta per Jac. Duportum, cui in oppositis paginis respondens accessit Paraphrasis poetica Latina, auctore Geo. Buchanano, 8vo. *calf*, 3s 1742
26 NOVUM TESTAMENTUM GRÆCUM. 2 vols. 18mo. *calf*, 5s 6d Camb. 1700
27 ———— 8vo. *front. calf*, 5s . Lond. 1728
28 ———— post priores Curcellæi, cum locis parall. et var. lect. [studio G. Von Maestricht] *best edition*, 12mo. *russia*, 6s Amst. ap. Wetstein, 1735
29 ———— textu per omnia Milliano, cum divisione, Pericoparum et interpuncturâ, J. A. Bengelii, 2 vols. 12mo. *calf*, 5s Oxon. 1742
30 ———— 12mo. *large paper, russia*, 6s Glasguæ, R. Urie, 1750
31 ———— cum lectionibus variantibus, nec non commentario pleniore ex scriptoribus veteribus Hebræis, Græcis et Latinis, opera et studio J. J. Wetstenii, 2 vols. folio, *fine copy in Dutch calf*, £6. 16s 6d Amst. 1751
32 ———— another copy, 2 vols. folio, *new in rich tree-marbled calf gilt*, £7. 17s 6d . ib. 1751
33 ———— juxta exemplar Millianum, typis J. Baskerville, 8vo. *interleaved and bound in* 2 vols. 4to. *half russia, and filled with a profusion of critical and explanatory notes and illustrations by the late Rev. T. Rennell, Vicar of Kensington, with some MS. memoranda by his great grandfather*, £1. 1s . Oxon. 1763
The prodigious quantity of notes and interlineations with which this copy abounds, would render it invaluable to any scholar engaged in a critical investigation of the Greek Testament.
34 ———— cum Scholiis theologicis et philologicis [cura — Hardy] 2 vols. 8vo. *hf. bd. calf*, 7s 6d . Lond. 1768
" A very useful companion to every biblical student."—*Dr. A. Clarke.*
35 ———— ex recensione J. J. Griesbachii, 2 vols. in 1, 8vo. LARGE PAPER, *russia, gilt leaves*, £1. 1s Cantabr. Nov-Angl. 1809
36 ———— cum Scholiis theologicis et philologicis, (cura E. Valpy,) 3 vols. 8vo. *calf, gilt leaves*, 18s . 1816
37 ———— aliud exemplar, 3 vols. 8vo. LARGE PAPER, *calf gilt*, £1. 11s 6d . . 1816
38 ———— Manuale, 32mo. *bds.* 3s—*calf*, 5s—*morocco, gilt leaves*, 7s Glasguæ, 1821
Printed on fine and thin laid writing paper.
39 ———— curante Jo. Fr. Boissonade, (" *an elegant edition*,") 2 vols. 24mo. *bds.* 5s . Par. 1824
40 ———— Græcè, juxta exemplar Millianum, 12mo. *bds.* 3s—*calf gilt*, 4s . . Oxon. 1825
41 ———— Græce, ex recensione J. Jac. Griesbachii, cum selecta lectionum varietate, 24mo. *bds.* 3s 6d—*calf*, 5s 6d Lond. 1829
42 THE NEW TESTAMENT, with English notes, critical, philological, and explanatory, (by E. Valpy) 3 vols. 8vo. *vellum, gilt leaves*, £1. 16s ib. 1831
43 ———— with English notes by the Rev. Edward Burton, D.D., 2 vols. 8vo. *calf extra*, £1. 8s .. Oxford, 1831

4   J. LESLIE'S CATALOGUE.

44 THE NEW TESTAMENT, the Greek and English Texts arranged in parallel columns, with marginal references, 12mo. *calf gilt*, 8s
Camb. 1836
45 QUATUOR Evangelia Græcè, textum receptum, signis distinctum ad instar Origenianæ recensionis, edidit J. White, S. T. P. 12mo. *hf. bd. russia*, 4s . *Oxonii*, 1798
46 CODEX Theodori Bezæ Cantabrigiensis, Evangelia et Acta Apostolorum complectens, quadritis literis Græco-Latinus ; edidit notasque adjecit Tho. Kipling, *fine paper*, 2 vols. imperial folio, *russia*, £3. 10s
Cantab. 1793

MODERN GREEK.

47 ΤΗΣ ΠΑΛΑΙΑΣ ΔΙΑΘΗΚΗΣ 'ΑΠΑΝΤΑ, royal 8vo. *splendidly bound in purple morocco, lined with crimson silk, gilt leaves*, £2. 2s
Lond. 1840
Presentation copy from the British and Foreign Bible Society to his late R. H. the Duke of Sussex.

LATIN.

48 BIBLIA cum summariorum apparatu, &c. **Black letter**, *with wood-cut initials*, 8vo. *rare, calf,* 18s . *Lugduni*, 1514
CONTENTS.—Various Tables—The books of Scripture with the Prologues of St. Jerome—Interpretationes nominum hebraicorum—Tota biblia compendiosissime per rithmos descripta. The present copy belonged to the late Duke of Sussex.

49 ——— Breves in eadem annotationes ex doctiss. interpretationibus, et Hebræorum commentariis, folio, *in the original stamped hogskin binding*, £1. 5s . *Par. R. Steph.* 1532

50 ——— Hebræa, Chaldæa, Græca, et Latina nomina virorum, &c. restituta, cum Latina interpretatione, &c. 2 vols. folio, *fine copy in old French olive morocco, arms on the sides*, £2. 10s
Par. ex Officina R. Stephani, 1540

51 ——— Sacra Vulgatæ Editionis, folio, *engraved title, new, in calf, very neat,* £2. 16s · *Lut. Par.* 1618
From the Library of the late Dr. Southey.

52 ——— Vulgatæ editionis, 6 vols. 32mo. *old red morocco, marbled and gilt leaves,* £1. 15s *Col. Agr.* 1647, &c.

53 ——— ex interp. Junii, Tremellii et Bezæ, *Lond.* 1661—Sternhold and Hopkins's Psalms, *ib.* 1664, in 1 vol. 12mo. *blue morocco, gilt leaves,* 12s . . ———

54 ——— ex Sebastiani Castellionis interpretatione, cum annotationibus ejusdem, folio, *new in calf, very neat,* £1. 11s 6d *Francof.* 1697

55 ——— ex Seb. Castellionis interpretatione, 4 vols. 12mo. *calf,* 10s
Lond. 1726

56 ——— Versio vetus Italica, et cætera quæcunque in Codd. MSS. et antiquis libris reperiri potuerunt, operâ P. SABATIER, 3 vols. folio, *fine copy, in rich calf gilt, (bound from sheets)* £6. 6s
Reims, 1743

57 ——— Vulgatæ editionis Sixti V. jussu recognita, et Clementis VIII. auctoritate edita, 8vo. *calf gilt*, 14s *Lugd.* 1830
——— idem, 8vo. *calf gilt*, 14s—*sewed*, 10s *Paris*, 1843
——— idem, small 8vo. *beautifully printed, in a small clear type, fine paper, sewed,* 12s—*calf, old style,* 16s—*morocco, gilt leaves,* 18s . . *Lugd.* 1845

60 SACROSANCTUS Evangeliorum Codex S. Eusebii Magni Episcopi et Martyris manu exaratus ex autographo Basilicæ Vercellensis ad unguem exhibitus, opera et studio J. A. Irici, 4to. *sewed*, 16*s*
Mediolani, 1748

FRENCH.

61 LA SAINTE BIBLE, avec l'explication du sens litteral et du sens spirituel tirée des SS. Peres et des auteurs Ecclesiastiques, par M. DE SACI, 34 vols. 8vo. *very fine copy, in rich old crimson morocco, full gilt, in beautiful preservation,* £12. 12*s* . *Par.* 1682, &c.
62 ———— another copy, 32 vols. 8vo. *old crimson morocco, gilt leaves,* £10. 10*s* . *ib.* 1740, &c.
" M. de Saci est celui de tous les Solitaires que l'on appelle de Port Royal, qui savait le mieux la langue et qui ecrivait le plus poliment en François."—*Dupin.*

63 PSEAUMES de David, en Latin et en François, selon la Vulgate: traduits par M. le Maitre de Saci, avec l'Office des Dimanches et des Festes, 2 vols. 18mo. *old green morocco, gilt leaves, neatly tooled*, 14*s*
ib. 1715
64 ———— mis en vers François, et revus par ordre du Synode Walon des Provinces-Unies, 12mo. *front. old red morocco,* 5*s* 6*d*
Londres, 1729
With musical notes throughout. After the Psalms are " La Forme des Prieres Ecclesiastiques, le Catechisme, Confession de Foi," etc.

65 NOUVEAU TESTAMENT, avec des Reflexions et Explications qui regardent la Vie interieure, 8 vols. 12mo. *calf*, £1. 5*s* *Cologne*, 1713

ENGLISH.

66 THE HOLY BIBLE, (with the Apocrypha) *engraved title, Cambridge*, (1629) Book of Common Prayer, *ib.* 1629. The whole Book of Psalmes, in meeter, *ib.* 1629, in 1 vol. folio, *old black morocco, gilt leaves*, £2. 12*s* 6*d* . ————
From the library of the late Duke of Sussex.

67 ———— containing the Old Testament and the New, newly translated, by his Majesties speciall command, black letter, *Lond. Rob. Barker*, 1639—The Book of Common Prayer, *ib. R. Barker*, 1636—The Whole Booke of Psalmes, collected into English meeter by T. Sternhold, J. Hopkins, &c. black letter, *ib. E. G. for the Comp. of Stationers*, 1641, in 1 vol. 4to. *fine copies, newly bound in calf extra, gilt leaves,* £2. 2*s* . ————

68 ———— with marginal references, and Sternhold and Hopkins's Psalms, folio, *maps and engraved title, fine copy, ruled with red lines, blue morocco, gilt leaves, and blind tooled,* £3. 3*s* *Amst.* 1679

69 ———— (with the Apocrypha and an Index) *Oxford, John Baskett*, 1715—The Book of Common Prayer, *ib.* 1715—The Whole Book of Psalms in metre, *Lond.* 1715, folio, *old blue morocco, richly gilt,* £1. 11*s* 6*d* . ————

70 ———— (with the Scotch metrical version of the Psalms) 2 vols. 18mo. *red morocco, richly tooled, gilt leaves*, 10*s* 6*d* *Edinb.* 1770

71 ———— containing the Old Testament and the New; with the Apocrypha, and Annotations, folio, *plates, russia neat,* £3. 3*s*
Birmingham, John Baskerville, 1772

6   J. LESLIE'S CATALOGUE.

72 THE HOLY BIBLE, with Notes by Anselm Bayly, LL.D., 3 vols. 8vo. *plates, calf, (the 3rd not uniform)* 18s . 1773-6
From the library of the Duke of Sussex. The present set consists of the Old and New Testaments in 2 vols.; the Apocrypha, and a duplicate copy of the New Testament is bound up in the third volume.

73 ———— containing the Old and New Testaments, and the Apocrypha, *with engravings by Charles Heath; and illustrated with upwards of 2160 additional plates by ancient and modern artists, including several extremely rare prints, drawings, &c.; handsomely bound in 9 vols.* folio, *rich blue morocco, embossed gilt edges, and full gilt backs by Mackenzie; enclosed in a mahogany box, divided into partitions for each volume, and lined with crimson velvet*—UNIQUE, £84. *Lond.* 1815

74 ———— with Notes, explanatory and practical, &c. prepared and arranged by Geo. D'Oyly, D.D. and Richard Mant, (now Bp. of Down and Connor) 3 vols. 4to. *large and fine paper, maps and plates, calf gilt, marbled edges,* £4. 10s   *Oxford,* 1817

75 ———— with explanatory Notes, practical observations, and copious marginal references by Thos. Scott, 6 vols. 4to. *maps, calf gilt,* £7. 7s . . 1828

76 ———— another copy, 3 vols. imp. 8vo. *calf,* £3.   1830

77 ———— with a Commentary, and critical Notes by Adam Clarke, LL.D., 6 vols. 4to. *calf gilt, marbled edges, very scarce,* £8. 8s 1836

78 ———— The Old Testament, with a Commentary, consisting of short Lectures for the daily use of Families, by the Rev. Cha. Girdlestone, 4 vols. 8vo. *bds.* £1. 16s . 1837, &c.

79 ———— The Septuagint Version of the Old Testament, according to the Vatican Text, translated into English by Sir L. C. L. Brenton, Bart, 2 vols. 8vo. *bds.* £1. 1s . 1844

TRANSLATIONS OF VARIOUS PORTIONS OF THE HOLY SCRIPTURES.

*** Harmonies of the Gospels, will be found under the names of their Compilers.

80 THE OLD TESTAMENT—A new and literal Translation of the Pentateuch of Moses, and of the Historical Books of the Old Testament, to the end of the Second Book of Kings, with Notes Critical and Explanatory, by the Rev. Julius Bate, 4to. *bds.* 8s . 1773

81 ———— The Book of Genesis in English-Hebrew, with an interlinear Translation and Notes, [by W. Greenfield] 8vo. *bds.* 5s   1828

82 ———— The Book of Job in English Verse, translated from the Hebrew, with Remarks, by Thos. Scott, 8vo. *calf gilt, marbled leaves,* 6s—*bds.* 3s 6d . . 1773

83 ———— The Book of Psalms, in Metre, close and proper to the Hebrew, smooth and pleasant for the Metre; newly translated by W. Barton, 12mo. *calf, scarce,* 5s . 1676

84 ———— A new and literal Version of the Book of Psalms, with a Preface and Notes, by the Rev. S. Street, 2 vols. 8vo. *bds.* 5s   1790

85 ———— The Book of Psalms, translated from the Hebrew, with Notes Explanatory and Critical, by Sam. Horsley, Bp. of St. Asaph, 8vo. *bds.* 12s . . 1845

[58, GREAT QUEEN STREET,

86 TRANSLATIONS — A new Translation of the Book of Psalms, from the original Hebrew, with Explanatory Notes, by Will. French, D.D. Master of Jesus College, and Geo. Skinner, M.A., *Camb.* 1830—A new Translation of the Proverbs of Solomon, by the same, *ib.* 1831, 2 vols. in 1, 8vo. *calf, very neat,* 9s

87 ——— Ecclesiastes, Proverbs, and Solomon's Song, translated from the Hebrew by Bernard Hodgson, LL.D., Principal of Hertford College, 3 vols. in 1, 4to. *calf,* 9s   *Oxford,* 1790, 88, 86

88 ——— A [poetical] version of Solomon's Song of Songs, together with the XLV. Psalm, by Joseph Stennett, 12mo. *old red morocco,* 3s   .   .   1700

89 ——— Solomon's Song, translated by Bernard Hodgson, 4to. *sewed,* 3s   .   .   1786

90 ——— The Song of Songs, which is by Solomon : a new Translation, with a Commentary and Notes, by T. Williams, 8vo. *bds.* 4s   1801
"This version is as literal as our language will admit, and is rendered in conformity with the authorized translation, whenever it was practicable. The notes are for the most part judiciously selected from the labours of all preceding Commentators, and give a *sober*, but practical and evangelical exposition of the allegory."—*Horne.*

91 ——— An Attempt towards an improved Version, a metrical Arrangement, and an Explanation of the Twelve Minor Prophets, by Will. Newcome, D.D. Bp of Waterford, 4to. *calf,* 12s   1785
From the library of the Duke of Sussex.

92 ——— Isaiah, a new translation, with a preliminary dissertation and notes, by Robert Lowth, Bp. of London, 4to. *calf,* 10s 6d   .   .   1779

93 ——— Lamentazioni di Geremia, tradotte da Evasio Leone Carmelitano, sm. 8vo. *bds.* 2s   .   *Parma,* 1800

94 ——— The text of the New Testament of Jesus Christ, translated out of the vulgar Latine by the Papists of the traiterous Seminarie at Rhemes, with arguments and annotations : whereunto is added, the translation commonly used in the Church of England ; with a confutation of all such arguments, glosses, and annotations, as contain manifest impiety of Heresie, Treason, and Slander, &c. by W. Fulke, D.D. folio, *calf,* £1. 10s   1601
"A valuable piece of ancient controversy and criticism, full of sound divinity, weighty arguments, and important observations."—*Rev. James Hervey.*

95 THE NEW TESTAMENT of our Lord and Saviour Jesus Christ, newly translated out of the Latin Vulgat, &c. together with annotations and marginal notes, by C. N. C. F. P. D. 8vo. *fine copy, calf,* 10s
[*Dublin ?*] 1718
The initials stand for the words *Cornelius* NARY *Consultissimæ Facultatis Parisiensis Doctor.* A full account of this translation will be found in Lewis's History, (8vo.) pp. 363—365.

96 A COMPENDIOUS HISTORY of the Old and New Testament, extracted from the Holy Bible, *and adorned with* 120 *copper cuts,* 12mo. 2s 6d   .   1726

97 THE NEW TESTAMENT, according to the antient Latin edition, with critical remarks upon the literal meaning in difficult places, from the French of Father Simon, by Will. Webster, 2 vols. in 1, *calf,* 10s 6d   .   .   1730

98 TRANSLATIONS.—Mr. Whiston's Primitive New Testament, according to the Greek part of the MS. of Beza at Cambridge, the imperfections of which copy are supplied from the vulgar Latin, 8vo. *calf, scarce*, 16s   *Stamford and London*, 1745

99 ——— A new translation of the New Testament, extracted from the paraphrase of P. Doddridge, D.D. with an introduction and notes [by Sam. Palmer], 2 vols. 12mo. 5s   .   1765

100 ——— The New Testament of our Lord and Saviour Jesus Christ, published in 1526; being the first translation from the Greek into English, by William Tyndale. Reprinted verbatim, with a Memoir of his life and writings by George Offor, 8vo. *port. bds.* 8s ———

101 ——— A new Version of St. Matthew's Gospel, with select notes, &c. by Daniel Scott, 4to. *bds.* 5s   .   1741

102 ——— A new translation of the Gospel of St. Matthew; with Notes by Gilbert Wakefield, 4to. *hf. bd. russia*, 8s   *Warrington*, 1782

103 ——— A new version of the Gospel according to Saint Matthew, with a literal Commentary, and an introduction to the reading of the Holy Scriptures, by Messieurs De Beausobre and Lenfant, 8vo. *bds.* 4s 6d   .   *Camb.* 1788

104 ——— Divers parts of the Holy Scriptures [the Gospels and Acts] done into English, chiefly from Dr. J. Mills's printed Greek copy, with notes and maps, [by —— Mortimer] sm. 8vo. *calf*, 4s   1761

105 ——— Actions of the Apostles: translated from the original Greek, by John Willis, D.D. (with notes) 8vo. *calf, a little wormed, scarce*, 3s 6d   .   1789

106 ——— The four Gospels, translated from the Greek, with preliminary dissertations and notes, by Geo. Campbell, D.D. 4 vols. 8vo. *calf*, 1l. 4s   .   *Aberdeen*, 1803-4

107 ——— another copy, 2 vols. 8vo. *bds.* 8s   1834

108 ——— A new Translation from the original Greek, of all the Apostolical Epistles, with a commentary and notes: to which is added, a Life of the Apostle Paul, by James Macknight, D.D., 4 vols. 8vo. *hf. bd.* 1l. 4s   .   1809

109 ——— another copy, with the Greek Text, a commentary and notes, &c. 6 vols. 8vo. *calf*, 1l. 18s   .   1816

110 ——— A paraphrastic translation of the Apostolical Epistles, with notes, by P. N. Shuttleworth, [afterwards Bp. of Chichester,] 8vo. *bds.* 5s 6d   .   *Oxford*, 1829

111 ——— the same, 8vo. *bds.* 8s   .   *Lond.* 1840

LITURGIES AND LITURGICAL WORKS.

112 LITURGIARUM ORIENTALIUM Collectio, in qua continentur Liturgiæ Copticarum Tres, S. Basilii, S. Gregorii Theologi, S. Cyrilli Alexandrini; Divi Marci, S. Jacobi, S. Joannis Evangelistæ, Matthæi Pastoris, S Joannis Patriarchæ, S. Ignatii, &c. *Gr.* et *Lat.* Accedunt Dissertationes de eorum origine et auctoritate, de Liturgiis Alexandrinis, de Linguâ Coptica, de Patriarcha Alexandrino, &c. opera et studio EUSEBII RENAUDOTII, 2 vols. 4to. RARE, *fine copy, calf,* £4. 4s   .   *Par.* 1706

113 ——— aliud exemplar, 2 vols. in 1, 4to. *calf*, £3. 13s 6d *ib.* 1706

114 ΤΡΙΩΔΙΟΝ ΨΥΧΩΦΕΛΕΣΤΑΤΟΝ, folio, *hf. bd. calf*, £1. 15s
Bononiæ, 1724
115 ΕΥΧΟΛΟΓΙΟΝ sive Rituale Græcorum, complectens ritus et ordines Divinæ Liturgiæ, Officiorum, Sacramentorum, etc. juxta usum Orientalis Ecclesiæ, Interpretatione Latina, æneis figuris, et observationibus illustratum, opera Jacobi Goar, folio, *fine copy, vellum, very scarce*, £5. 5s . *Venet.* 1730
116 ———— idem, folio. *calf*, £5. 5s . *Par.* 1647
117 'ΕΥΧΟΛΟΓΙΟΝ, (a collection of Greek Services and Prayers) *printed in red and black*, 4to. *hf. bd.* £1 5s *Romæ*, 1754
118 CODICES Sacramentorum nongentis annis vetustiores, nimirùm Libri III. Sacramentorum Romanæ Ecclesiæ ; Missale Gothicum, sive Gallicanum Vetus ; Missale Francorum ; Missale Gallicanum Vetus — Primùm prodeunt cura J. M. Thomasii, 4to. *calf, very scarce*, £1. 1s . . *Romæ*, 1680
From the Duke of Sussex's collection.
119 MURATORI (L. A.) Liturgia Romana Vetus tria Sacramentaria complectens, Leonianum scilicet, Gelasianum, et antiquum Gregorianum; accedunt Missale Gothicum, Missale Francorum ; duo Gallicana, et duo omnium vetustissimi Romanæ Ecclesiæ rituales libri, 2 vols. in 1, folio, *fine copy in vellum, scarce*, £2. 5s . *Venet.* 1748
120 ———— another copy, 2 vols. in 1, folio, *new in pannelled calf gilt, carmine edges*, £2. 16s . *ib.* 1748
121 [ALESII (ALEX.)] ORDO DISTRIBUTIONIS SACRAMENTI ALTARIS sub utraque specie, et Formula Confessionis faciendæ in Regno Angliæ, small 8vo. *excessively rare, fine copy, blue morocco, gilt leaves*, £10. 10s . . *Anno* 1548
This rare little volume purports to be a version of the Order of Communion, and has prefixed a Latin translation of Edward the Sixth's Proclamation. At the end is an address " Pio Lectori," signed A. A. S. D.—The only other copy known, is in the library of the Rev. W. Maskell.
122 ARTICULI de quibus convenit inter Archiepiscopos, et Episcopos utriusq; provinciæ, et clerum universum in synodo, Londini, A. D. 1562, secundum computationem Eccles. Ang. ad tollendam opinionum dissentionem, et consensum in vera religione firmandum. Æditi authoritate sereniss. Reginæ, 4to. *extremely rare, calf, very neat*, £2. 12s 6d *Lond. J. Day*, 1571
123 ———— idem, a reprint of the above, sm. 4to. *half bound, calf, neat*, 7s 6d . *Oxonii, (date torn off)* ———
124 ARTICLES to be enquired of in the visitation in the first year of the raign of our most dread sovereign ladie Elizabeth, 1559. ——Injunctions given by the Queenes Majestie, 1559, in one volume, 4to. *fine copy, calf, very neat*, 18s . *Lond.* 1600
125 ———— the same, *(title and last leaf mended)* sm. 4to. *calf, neat*, 14s . *ib.* 1600
126 LIBER Precum Eccles. Ang. Græcè et Latinè, 18mo. *wants title and part of the preface*, RARE, *red morocco, gilt leaves*, £2. 2s
Londini, apud Reg. Wolfius, [1569]
The Greek version was made by Whitaker, (see Churton's Life of Nowell, p. 144.) and the Latin, as it is supposed, by Walter Haddon. The present copy belonged to Bp. White Kennett, and has his autograph.

127 INJUNCTIONS giuen by the Queenes Majestie, A. D. 1559, 4to.
Black letter, *scarce*, 12s . 1559
128 NOWELLI (Alexandri) Catechismus sive prima Institutio Disciplinaque Pietatis Christianæ, Latinè explicata, FIRST EDITION, 4to. RARE, *blue morocco, gilt leaves,* £5. 5s
Londini in Off. Reginaldi Wolfii, 1570
129 RUDIMENTA Fidei Christianæ, sive Catechismus, cui adjunctus est Catechismus alius magis compendiarius, Gr. and Lat. 18mo. *calf, scarce,* 8s 6d . [*Par.*] 1575
130 CATECHISM, that is to say, an Instruction to be learned of every person before he be brought to be Confirmed, *Irish* and *English*, with Rules for reading the Irish language, 8vo. *sewed, scarce,* 4s 6d ——
131 LITURGIA : seu Liber Precum Communium &c. itemque Forma creandi, ordinandi, et consecrandi Episcopos, Presbyteros, et Diaconos. Epistolæ, Evangelia, et Psalmi inseruntur juxta Scb. Castellionis versionem, 12mo. *front. calf,* 3s . 1720
Translated by Tho. Parsell. It contains the form for the King's evil.
132 THE ANTIENT LITURGY of the Church of England, according to the uses of Sarum, Bangor, York, and Hereford, and the Modern Roman Liturgy, arranged in parallel columns ; by William Maskell, 8vo. *bds.* 9s 6d . 1844
133 THE TWO BOOKS of Common Prayer, set forth in the reign of Edward VI., compared with each other, and edited by the Rev. Edw. Cardwell, D. D. 8vo. *bds.* 8s . *Oxford*, 1841
134 —————— another copy, 8vo. *hf. bd. calf, gilt,* 8s 6d *ib.* 1841
135 THE TWO LITURGIES, A. D. 1549, and 1552 ; with other Documents set forth in the reign of King Edward VI. viz., The Order of Communion, 1548, the Primer, 1553, the Catechism and Articles, 1553. Catechismus brevis, 1553. Edited by the Rev. Jos. Ketley, 8vo. *bds.* 15s . . *Camb.* 1844
136 THREE PRIMERS put forth in the reign of Henry VIII. viz., a Godly Prymer, 1535, The Manual of Prayers, or the Prymer, in English, 1539, and King Henry's Primer, 1545. (Edited by Prof. Burton), 8vo. *bds.* 13s—*calf, gilt,* 16s *Oxford*, 1834
137 PRIMER (The) set furth by the King's majestie and his Clergie, to be taught, lerned, and red, Black letter, 8vo. *calf, rare,* 9s
reprint, London, 1546
138 THE BOOKS of Common Prayer, as used in the Church of England, from the time of Edward VI. to Charles II.; consisting of the First and Second Books of Edward VI. 1549 and 1552 ; the First of Q. Elizabeth, 1559 : King James's Book, as settled at Hampton Court, 1604 ; the Scotch Book of Charles I. 1637 ; and King Charles the Second's Book, as settled at the Savoy Conference, 1662 ; together 6 vols. small folio, *bound in parchment, gilt,* £18. 18s . 1845

This Collection of the Books of Common Prayer are uniformly reprinted in Black Letter, like the original editions. Their importance and value are well known ; but it is remarkable that in no public, or private, or collegiate library can the whole of these Books be found together. A limited number only has been reprinted : and may be subscribed for in sets, but not separately.

The Book of 1662 has been carefully collated with the Sealed Book in the Tower of London, and other copies of the Sealed Book have been occasionally consulted.

[58, GREAT QUEEN STREET,

139 THE COMMUNION SERVICE and Occasional Offices of the Church of England, beautifully printed in red and black, small folio, *bound in parchment, gilt*, £2. 15s . 1845
140 THE BOOKE of COMMON PRAIER noted, by John Merbecke as printed by Grafton, 1550, small 4to. *vellum*, £1. 15s 1844
This is a verbatim reprint with the Musical Notes without any alteration whatever, shewing what parts of the Service were chanted in the reign of Edward VI.
141 BOOK OF COMMON PRAYER, and Administration of the Sacraments, and other parts of Divine Service, for the use of the Church of Scotland, folio, RARE, *title inlaid, calf*, £5. 5s *Edin*. 1637
142 ———— and other Rites and Ceremonies of the Church of England, with the Psalter and Apocrypha, folio, *calf*, £1. 1s
Camb. Buck and Daniel, 1638
143 ———— with the Psalter, and the Form and Manner of Ordaining and Consecrating Bishops, Priests, and Deacons, small folio, 𝔅𝔩𝔞𝔠𝔨 𝔩𝔢𝔱𝔱𝔢𝔯, *calf*, £1. 11s 6d . *Lond*. 1662
144 ———— another copy, royal folio, *title ruled, old blue morocco, gilt leaves*, £1. 16s . *Oxford*, 1618
145 ———— with the Psalms paraphras'd, together with the Lives of the Apostles, and an account of the original of the Fasts and Feasts, &c. By W. Nicholls, D.D., 8vo. *calf*, 5s 6d 1709
146 ———— (with the Ordination Services), 8vo. *printed in black and red, old red morocco*, 4s 6d . *Oxford*, 1716
147 ———— English and French, 8vo. *calf*, 4s *ib*. 1717
148 ———— in eight languages, viz., English, French, Italian, German, Spanish, Greek ancient and modern, and Latin, 4to. *purple morocco, gilt leaves*, £1. 16s . 1821
149 THE LITURGY of the Church of Scotland, or John Knox's Book of Common Order; edited by the Rev. John Cumming, D. D., 12mo. *bds.* 5s . . 1840
150 THE ORDER of Daily Service, the Litany, and Order of the Administration of the Holy Communion according to the use of the United Church of England and Ireland; with the Ancient Musical Notation printed in red and black, with antique ornamental borders, edited by W. Dyce, Esq. 4to. *bds.* £2. 2s . 1843
151 ———— the same, *blue morocco, the sides richly tooled, and gilt leaves,* £3. 3s . . 1843
152 ———— the same, ON LARGE PAPER, *of which only a very few copies were printed*, royal 4to. *bds.* £4. 4s 1843
This volume contains the ancient music, as adapted to the first Prayer-book of Edward VI. by JOHN MARBECKE, together with the Litany-chant, and other portions of Gregorian Music, not included in his work; thus forming a complete choral book for the service of the English Church.
An explanatory introduction by the editor is prefixed. The volume is considered one of the most beautiful specimens of typography, which has appeared in the present day, and has therefore, a value independent of the interest attached to the musical portion of the work.
153 THE BOOK of Common Prayer, according to the use of the Church of England, with Notes, royal 8vo. *exquisitely printed in black and red, within ornamental borders, and illuminated and illustrated with engravings from the works of the great painters, rich crimson morocco, gilt leaves, and broad borders of gold,* £3. 3s 1845

154 THE BOOK of Common Prayer, German, von Dr. J. H. W. Küper, 24mo. *bds.* 4*s* . *Lond.* 1825
155 ———— Greek [interprete J. D.] 18mo. *calf*, 2*s* *Cantab.*
156 ———— Latin and modern Greek, 12mo. *calf*, 4*s* 6*d* *Lond.* 1823-20
157 ———— A brieff Discours off the troubles begonne at Franckford, Anno Domini, 1554, abowte the Booke of Common Prayer and Ceremonies, and continued by the Englishemen theyre, to thende off Q. Maries Raigne, 4to. *rare, £* 1575
158 ———— the same, reprinted from the black letter edition of 1575, with an Introduction, 8vo. *bds.* 6*s*—*large paper,* 10*s* 1846
159 CORPUS et Syntagma Confessionum Fidei, quæ en diversis Regnis et Nationibus, Ecclesiarum nomine fuerunt authenticè editæ; in celeberrimis Conventibus exhibitæ publicàque auctoritate comprobatæ, 4to. *vellum, very scarce,* £1. 1*s* *Genevæ,* 1654
160 L'ESTRANGE'S (Hamon) Alliance of Divine Offices, exhibiting all the Liturgies of the Church of England since the Reformation, as also the late Scotch Service-Book, with all their respective variations and annotations; to which is added, the Order of Communion set forth by Edward VI. *best edition,* folio, *calf, very scarce,* £1. 18*s* 1690
161 THE Original Services for the State Holidays, with documents relating to the same, collected and arranged by the Hon. and Rev. A. P. Perceval, 8vo. *bds.* 3*s* 6*d* . 1838
162 REFORMATIO Legum Ecclesiasticarum ex authoritate primum Regis Henrici VIII. inchoata; deinde per Regem Edovardum VI. provecta, adunctaque in hunc modum, atque nunc ad pleniorem ipsarum reformationem in lucem edita, 4to. RARE, *fine copy, new in calf, old style,* £1. 12*s* . 1640
163 ———— idem, 4to. *calf,* £1. 8*s* . 1641
164 BREVIARIUM Romanum, ex decreto Concilii Tridentini restitutum, Pii V. jussu editum, 4to. *calf, neat, from the library of the late Duke of Sussex,* . *Venetiis,* 1570

The above is a transcript of the title-page, but the whole of the volume, except the title, privilege, kalendar, &c. at the beginning, and the "Rubricæ generales" at the end, is of another edition. It is printed in black letter, and seems to be of about 1520. A portrait of Pope Pius V. is inserted.

165 ———— Romanum, ex decreto Sacrosancti Concilii Tridentini restitutum, cui accessit Kalendarium Gregorianum perpetuum, 8vo. *original binding, gilt sides,* £1. 5*s* *Par.* 1583
166 ———— Bituricense, 4 vols. 12mo. *old French red morocco, gilt leaves, with broad borders of gold,* £1. 16*s*
Avarici Biturigum, 1734
167 ———— Parisicnse, illustrissimi Caroli-Gaspar-Guillelmi de Vintimille Parisiensis Archiepiscopi autoritate editum, 4 vols. 4to. *old red morocco, gilt and marbled leaves,* £2. 2*s* *Paris,* 1736
168 ———— Romanum, ex decreto Concilii Tridentini restitutum, 4 vols. 12mo. *printed in black and red, calf, gilt leaves,* £1. 1*s*
Leodii, 1782
169 ———— ad usum Congregationis Sancti Mauri, Ordinis Sancti Benedicti in Gallia, 4 vols. 12mo. *calf,* 21*s* *Par.* 1787

[58, GREAT QUEEN STREET,

170 BREVIARIUM Romanum ex decreto Concilii Tridentini restitutum ; in quo Offici aNovissima Sanctorum ad hanc diem per summos Pontificis concessa accurate sunt disposita, 8vo. *calf, 10s 6d*
Venet. 1798
171 ——— Romanum, 4 vols. 18mo. *printed in red and black, plates, calf gilt,* £1. 16s . *Mechliniæ,* 1836
172 ——— aliud exemplar, complete in 1 vol. sm. 8vo. *sewed, 12s— calf gilt,* 15s . *Par.* 1838
173 ——— idem, *blue morocco, gilt and embossed leaves, the sides richly tooled in gold, &c.* £1. 1s . *ib.* 1838
174 ——— cum Officiis Sanctorum, 4 vols. 8vo. *printed in red and black, sprinkled calf gilt, marbled leaves,* £2. 15s *Mechl.* 1843
175 ——— Index in Breviarium Romanum, ad concionis formandas aptissimus ; authore Jo. Voello : accedit Index Biblicus, 18mo. *vellum,* 4s 6d . *Mogunt.* 1614
176 GRADUALE USUI CEDENS SUPERIORI ILBENSTADIO, royal folio, *beautifully executed in stencil, rubricated, the musical lines in colours, and ornamented title and capitals, the text and musical notation in very large character; a splendid volume in the original hogskin binding, with brass clasps and corners,* £4. 4s *circa* 1715
177 HORÆ Diurnæ Breviarii Romani, ex decreto S.S. Concilii Tridentini restituti, 24mo. *printed in red and black, sewed,* 6s—*calf gilt,* 8s 6d—*calf extra, gilt leaves,* 9s 6d *Mechl.* 1843
178 ——— 24mo. *calf super extra, gilt leaves, the sides richly tooled,* 10s 6d . *ib.* 1843
179 MISSALE sæcundum ritum Augustensis Ecclesie. Mandato et impensis Domini Othonis Cardinalis, episcopi Augustani novis typis elegantissime excusum, folio, 𝕭𝖑𝖆𝖈𝖐 𝖑𝖊𝖙𝖙𝖊𝖗, *rubricated, with spirited cuts ; but the Canon of the Mass (8 leaves) printed on vellum ; five leaves are wanting : in the original hogskin binding,* £2. 2s
Dilingæ, 1555
180 ——— Romanum, ex Decreto S. S. Concilii Tridentini restitutum Pii V. Pont. Max. jussu editum, *rubricated, Venetiis, apud Juntas,* 1578—PONTIFICALE ROMANUM, *ib. apud Juntas,* 1561—together 2 vols. folio, *blue morocco, gilt leaves, and blind tooled,* £6. 16s 6d

181 GREGORIUS (S. *Magnus*) Divinum Officium, sive Missa, cum interpretatione Græca Georgii Codini, 8vo. *fine copy, old red morocco, gilt leaves,* 7s . *Lutet.* 1595
182 MISSEL Romain, selon le reglement du Concile de Trent. *Latin and French,* 5 vols. 16mo. *ruled with red lines, old black morocco, lined with red, marbled and gilt leaves,* 21s *Par.* 1676
183 MISSALE Mixtum secundum regulam Beati Isidori, dictum Mozarabes; præfatione, notis, et appendice ab Alex. Lesleo, S. J. Sacerdote ornatum, 4to. *fine copy, vellum, scarce,* £1. 16s *Romæ,* 1755
184 MISSEL de Paris, Latin-François, avec Prime, Tierce, Sexte, et les Processions, 10 vols. 12mo. *fine copy, green morocco, gilt leaves,* £3. 3s . *Paris,* 1764
185 MISSALE Sacri Ordinis Cartusiensis, folio, *rubricated, plates, fine copy, calf gilt,* £2. 2s . *Gratianopoli,* 1771

14   J. LESLIE'S CATALOGUE.

186 MISSALE Parisiense, illustrissimi et reverendissimi Caroli—Gaspar—Guillelmi de Vintimille, Parisiensis Archiepiscopi, auctoritate, ac venerabilis ejusdem Ecclesiæ Capituli consensu editum, folio, *fine copy, calf, gilt leaves*, £1. 15s . *Paris*, 1777
187 ———— Bisuntinum, illustrissimi et reverendissimi Raymundi de Durfort, Archiepiscopi Bisuntini auctoritate editum, folio, *calf*, £1. 11s 6d . *Vesunt*. 1781
188 ———— Rhedonenense, illustrissimi et reverendissimi Francisci Bareau de Giræ Rhedonensis episcopi, auctoritate ac ejusdem ecclesiæ Capituli consensu editum, folio, *uncut*, £1. 10s
Paris, 1786
189 ———— Romanum, ex Decreto Concilii Tridentini restitutum, 8vo. *printed in red and black, sprinkled calf,* 12s   *Mechliniæ*, 1840
190 OFFICE de la Semaine Sainte, à l'usage de Rome, en Latin et en Francois, avec l'Explication des Céremonies de l'Eglise, 12mo. *ruled with red lines, fine copy, old French morocco, gilt and marbled leaves,* 7s 6d . *Par*. 1675
191 L'OFFICE des Chevaliers de l'ordre du St. Esprit, 12mo. *old red mor. tooled with the badge of the order,* 3s 6d   [*Par*.] 1740
192 OFFICIUM Pentaglotton B. Mariæ Virginis, *Lat. Gr. Ital. Gall. Hebr.* 12mo. *vellum,* 4s . *Neapoli*, 1741
193 THE DIVINE OFFICE for the Use of the Laity, 4 vols. 12mo. *calf,* 9s
N. P. 1763
194 MANUEL du Chrétien, contenant l'ordinaire de la Messe, le Psautier distribué, le Nouveau Testament, et l'Imitation de N. S. J. C. etc. 12mo. *old green morocco, richly tooled, gilt leaves,* 9s   s. L. 1751
195 PONTIFICALE Romanum, etc. folio, *rubricated, woodcuts, fine copy, old calf gilt,* £3. 3s . *Venetiis*, 1582
At the end is " Modus solennem professionem faciendi in Monasterio S. Magni in Kybach: sub Missa Pontificali." in M\NUSCRIPT very neatly written in red and black, on six leaves. This copy belonged to the late Duke of Sussex.

196 ———— Romanum, Clementis VIII. primum, nunc denuo Urbani VIII. auctoritate recognitum, 12mo. *printed in red and black, calf,* 5s 6d • . . *Lut. Par*. 1664
197 ———— Romanum, 12mo. *printed in red and black, fine copy,* 9s
Romæ, 1818
198 PSALTERIUM Romanum Decreto SS. Concilii Tridentini restitutum ; ex Breviario Romano PiiV. Pont. Max. jussu edito, et Clementis VIII. primùm, nunc dennò Urbani P.P. VIII. auctoritate recognito, royal folio, *rubricated, in the original binding, with brass knobs and clasps,* 18s . . *Antverpiæ*, 1655
199 RITUALE Romanum, Pauli V. Pont. Max. jussu editum, 8vo. *calf,* 5s
Par. 1679
200 ———— Carnotense, ad Romani formam expressum, Ferd. de Neufville Episcopi Carnotensis auctoritate editum, 4to. *calf,* 9s
Carnuti, 1689
201 ———— Cisterciense ex Libro usuum, Definitionibus Ordinis, et Cæremoniali Episcoporum Collectum, 8vo. *old calf gilt,* 6s
Parisiis, 1689
202 RITUEL du Diocese de Meaux, imprimé par autorité du Card. de Bissy, évèque de Meaux, *calf, marbled leaves,* 8s   *Par*. 1734

203 RITUALE Rothomagense, autoritate Nic de Saulx-Tavanes, Rothamagensis Archiepiscopi editum, 4to. *old calf gilt*, 12s   *Roth.* 1739
204 RITUEL du diocese d'Evreux, publié par l'autorité de P. J. C. de Rochechouart, évêque d'Evreux, 4to. *(wants two leaves) calf*, 4s   1741
205 RITUALE Bellovacense, illustrissimi ac Rev. F. J. de la Rochefoucauld episc. Bellovacensis auctoritate editum, 4to. *calf, gilt leaves*, 8s 6d   .   .   *Bellov.* 1783
206 LES Instructions du Rituel du diocese d'Alet, 12mo. *neat*, 3s
Lyon, 1678

*** FOR OTHER LITURGICAL WORKS, SEE THE RESPECTIVE AUTHORS.

MISCELLANEOUS ENGLISH AND FOREIGN THEOLOGY, PATRES ECCLESIASTICI, ETC.

207 ABBADIE (James) A Panegyric on our late Sovereign Lady Mary, Queen of England, &c. 4to. 1s   .   1695
208 ——— — (Dr. James), Accomplishment of Prophecy in the Character and Conduct of Jesus Christ, 12mo. *bds.* 1s 6d   1810
209 ABBOT (Robert, *Vicar of Cranbrook*), The Young Man's Warning-piece, or a Sermon at the burial of Wm. Rogers, Apothecary, with an history of his sinful life, and woful death, 18mo. *hf. bd.* 2s 1671
210 ABDIAS, *Babyloniæ primus Episcopus.* De Historia certaminis Apostolici libri decem, Julio Africano interprete, etc. 12mo. *neat*, 3s 6d
Par. 1566
211 ABENDANA'S (Isaac) Discourses of the Ecclesiastical and Civil polity of the Jews, 12mo. 2s   .   1706
A sensible and judicous selection from the works of Abendana.
212 ABERNETHIE (Tho.). A worthy Speech, wherein is discovered the villany and hellish plots wrought in the Pope's Courts against these our three Kingdomes, 4to. *sewed*, 4s 6d   .   1641
213 ABERNETHY'S (John) Discourses concerning the Being and natural Perfections of God, 2 vols. 1743—Sermons on various subjects, 4 vols. 1748-51—Scarce and valuable Tracts and Sermons, 1751—together 7 vols. 8vo. *fine copy, calf,* £1. 1s   .   ———
The works of this celebrated Presbyterian divine are held in considerable estimation, particularly his Discourses on the Divine Attributes.
214 ACCOUNT. A Scriptural and rational Account of the Christian Religion, particularly concerning Justification, 12mo. *calf,* 1s 6d 1695
215 ——— — of the Societies for the Reformation of Manners, 12mo. *sewed*, 1s   .   .   [1786]
216 ACTA Sanctorum Martyrum Orientalium et Occidentalium; Accedunt Acta S. Simeonis Stylitæ. Steph. Evodius Assemanus Archiep. Apamensis Chaldaicum Textum recensuit, Latine vertit, Admonitionibus, perpetuisque Adnotationibus illustravit, 2 vols. in 1, folio, *calf, very scarce,* £5. 5s   .   *Romæ,* 1748
217 ACTA SANCTORUM Christi Martyrum, Vindicata ab Odoacre Ilbachio, sive a Jacobo Laderchio, *front.* 2 vols. 4to. *calf,* £1. 5s   *ib.* 1723
LINCOLN'S INN FIELDS.]

218 ACTA SANCTORUM—Breves Notitiæ triplicis status Ecclesiastici, Monastici, et Secularis, excerptæ ex Actis Sanctorum Jan. Feb. et Martii, vulgatis ab Jo. Bollando, Godf. Henschenio, et Dan. Papebrochio, 12mo. *hf. bd. calf*, 4s . *Ant.* 1668

219 ADAM's (George) Exposition of some Articles of Religion, which strike at the tenets of the Arians, Socinians, Romanists, Lutherans, Calvinists, &c. 8vo. *calf*, 2s . 1752

220 ADAMS's (Tho.) Private Thoughts on Religion, with his Life and Character, 12mo. *bds.* 2s . 1822

221 ———— (Dr. W.) Sermons upon several subjects, 8vo. *bds.* 3s 6d
Shrewsbury, 1790

222 ADAMUS (Melchior) Vitæ Theologorum, jure-consultorum, politicorum, medicorum, atque philosophorum Germanorum et exterorum, folio, *calf*, 14s . *Franc. ad M.* 1706

223 ADDISON (Dr. L. *Father of the celebrated Joseph Addison*)—The present State of the Jews, wherein is contained an exact account of their customs, &c. 12mo. *calf*, 1s 6d . 1676

224 ———— The first State of Mahumedism, or an account of the author and doctrines of that imposture, 8vo. *calf*, 2s 6d
1679

225 ———— (Joseph). The Evidences of the Christian Religion, with several discourses against Atheism and Infidelity, 12mo. *calf*, 2s
Oxford, 1801

226 ———— the same, 12mo. *calf gilt*, 2s 6d *ib.* 1809

227 ADDRESS. A respectfull address to the Archbishops and Bishops on the necessity of Morning and Evening Service on Sunday, 8vo. *sewed*, 1s . . 1825

228 ———— A serious address to the Parochial Clergy on the increasing influence of the Methodists, by a Layman, 8vo. *sewed*, 1s 1806

229 ADEY's (Will.) Sixteen Discourses on several practical and important subjects, 8vo. *calf*, 2s . *Durham,* 1755

230 ———— another copy, 8vo. 3s . *Newcastle,* 1760

231 ADVICE from a Bishop, in a series of Letters to a young Gentleman, 8vo. *sewed*, 1s . 1759

232 ———— to the Clergy of every denomination and degree: with the evulgation of a late Congress held in Germany for the purpose of abolishing Christianity throughout Europe, 12mo. *bds.* 1s 6d . . 1786

233 ADVICE to a Parson, or the true art of preaching, in opposition to modern practice, a poem, by a person of Honour, 8vo. (*title supplied in MS.*) 1s 6d - 1691

234 AGOBARDUS (S. *Episc. Lugd.*) Opera: accesserunt binæ Epistolæ Leidradi, sm. 8vo. *new in calf, gilt*, 9s . *Par.* 1605

235 AGUESSEAU (Hen. Fra. d' *Chancellor of France*), Memoir of his life, and of his ordonnances for consolidating and amending certain portions of the French law: and an account of the Roman and Canon Law; by Charles Butler, Esq., 8vo. *bds.* 4s 1830

236 AIRAY's (Hen. *Prov. of Queen's Coll. Oxon.*) Lectures upon the whole Epistle to the Philippians, delivered in St. Peter's Church, in Oxford, 4to. *calf, extremely scarce*, £2. 10s 1618

[58, GREAT QUEEN STREET,

J. LESLIE'S CATALOGUE.

237 ALBERTI MAGNI (Ratisbonensis Episcopi) Opera Omnia, in lucem edita, Studio et Labore R. A. P. F. Petri Jamy, 21 vols. folio, *vellum, rare,* £18. 18*s* . *Lugduni,* 1651
238 AL-CORANUS Muhammedis, sive Lex Islamitica Muhammedis, ad optimorum Codd. fidem edita ex museo Abr. Hinckelmanni, *Arab.* 4to. *calf, scarce,* £1. 16*s* . *Hamb.* 1694
239 ———— Mohammedis filii Abdallæ pseudo-Prophetæ Fides Islamitica, i. e. Al-Coranus ex Idiomate Arabico : Latine versus per L. Marraccium ; cura Chr. Reineccii, sm. 8vo. *vellum,* 4*s Lips.* 1721
240 ALEGAMBE (Phil.) Bibliotheca Scriptorum Societatis Jesu, post catalogum P. Ribadeneiræ, folio, *hogskin, clasps,* 18*s* *Antv.* 1643
241 ALEXANDER's (A.) Key to part of the Hebrew Liturgy, 12mo. 2*s*
A. M. 5535
242 ———— (John). The Primitive Doctrine of Christ's Divinity, or a Specimen of a full view of the Ante-Nicene Doctrine, in an Essay on Irenæus, 8vo. *bds.* 4*s* . 1727

" The Rev. John Alexander was Minister of the Presbyterian Church in Plunket-Street, Dublin, from 1730 till his death, Nov. 1., 1743. He was a native of Londonderry, and nearest male heir to the Earldom of Stirling, on the demise of Henry, 5th Earl, in 1739. He was the author of an excellent work on Irenæus, and one of those men whose society was courted by the celebrated Dean Swift."—*Gent. Mag. Ap.* 1819, *p.* 290.

243 ———— A Paraphrase on I Cor. XV. with Notes. A Commentary on Romans VI. VII. and part of VIII., also a Sermon on Eccl. IX. 10. 4to. *sewed,* 3*s* . 1766
244 ALEXANDRI (Natalis) Theologia dogmatica et moralis, secundum ordinum Catechismi Concilii Tridentini, 10 vols. 8vo. *calf,* £1. 10*s*
Par. 1694
245 ———— Historia Ecclesiastica Veteris Novique Testamenti, ab orbe condito ad Annum Domini MDC., et in Loca ejusdem insignia Dissertationes Historicæ, Chronologicæ, Criticæ, Dogmaticæ, 8 vols. in 7, folio, *stamped hogskin, with clasps,* £4. 4*s Par.* 1730

" Inter Scriptores rerum Ecclesiasticarum P. Natalis Alexandrua principum fere locum obtinet."—*Prefatio.*

246 ALFORDI (Michael. *alias* Griffith) FIDES REGIA BRITANNICA, sive Annales Ecclesiæ Britannicæ, ubi potissimum Britannorum Catholica, Romana, et· Orthodoxa fides per quinque prima sæcula asseritur, 4 vols. folio, *fine copy, calf, scarce,* £5. 15*s* 6*d* *Leodii,* 1663
247 ALFRED, (*King*) The Will of King Alfred, *Anglo-Saxon, English, and Latin,* 4to. LARGE PAPER, *bds.* 7*s* *Oxford,* 1788
248 ———— The Anglo-Saxon Version from the Historian Orosius, by Alfred the Great, with an English translation, 8vo. *map, calf, scarce,* 18*s* . . 1773
249 ALLATIUS (Leo) Græcia Orthodoxa, in quo continentur Scriptores de processione Spiritus Sancti et aliis, *Gr. et Lat.* 2 vols. 4to. *vellum,* £1. 11*s* 6*d* . *Romæ,* 1652-59

CONTENTS.—Vol. I. Nicephorus Blemmida, Jo. Veccus, Patr. C. P., Petrus ep. Mediol., Georgius Pachymeres, Esaias Cyprius, Joannes Argyropulus, Gregorius Protosyncellus, Patr. C. P., Georgius Trapezuntius, Joannes Plusiadenus, Hilario Monachus, Niceta Byzantius, et de Gregorio Palama, Archiep. Thessal. Græcorum sententiæ.
Vol. II.—Jo. Veccus, Patr. C. P., Constantinus Meliteniota Chartophylax, Georgius Metochita Diaconus, Maximus Chrysoberga.

250 ALLATIUS (Leo) De Templis Græcorum recentioribus; de Narthece Ecclesiæ Veteris; necnon de Græcorum hodie quorundam opinationibus. *Col. Agr.* 1645.—Ejusdem de mensura temporum Antiquorum, et præcipue Græcorum Exercitatio, *ib.* 1645.—Ejusdem confutatio fabulæ de Joanna Papissa, ex MonumentisGræcis, *ib.* 1645. in one vol. 8vo. *vellum, clasps, very scarce*, 15s

251 ———— De ecclesiæ Occidentalis atque Orientalis perpetua consensione, libri tres. Ejusdem dissertationes de Dominicis et Hebdomadibus Græcorum, et de Missa Præsanctificatorum; cum B. NIHUSII, annotationibus de Communione Orientalium sub specie unica, 4to. *best edition, calf, neat,* 16s . *Colon. Agr.* 1648
The object of this learned work is to prove that the Latin and Greek Churches always believed in the same faith. Romanists consider this work of Allatius as his ablest performance, and, according to Mosheim, it is well known and valued by many learned Protestants.

252 A[LLEIN] (W[illiam]) of the State of the Church in future ages, 1684. —A discourse of occurrences prophetically represented in the II. Chapter of the Revelation, 1689, 2 vols. in 1, 12mo. *hf. bd. calf,* 4s

253 ———— The Christian's Justification stated, 12mo. *neat*, 2s 1678

254 ALLEN (William) Works, consisting of thirteen tracts on several subjects. With his Funeral Sermon by Bp. Kidder, and a preface concerning the author and his writings, by Bp. Williams, fol. *calf,* 12s . 1707

255 ALLESTRY (Richard) Eighteen Sermons, whereof fifteen preached before the King; the rest upon publick occasions, folio, *calf,* 6s 1669

256 ALLIACO (Petrus de) Libellus Sacrametalis, 4to. 𝕭lack letter, *fine copy, from the library of Mr. Heber, cf. very neat,* £1. 4s *Lovan.* 1481
This is the only edition noticed by Panzer. The author was one of the most learned of the Prelates assembled at the Council of Constance.

257 ALLIX (Peter) Dissertatio de Sanguine, D. N. J. C. ad Epist. CXLVI. —Dissertatio de Conciliorum quorumvis definitionibus—Dissertatio de Tertulliani Vita et Scriptis, 8vo. *calf,* 6s [*Par.* 1680?]

258 ———— Book of Psalms, with the Argument of each Psalm, and a Preface, *scarce*, 1701—NECTARII Patriarchæ Hierosolymitani Confutatio Imperii Papæ (curante J. Allix.) 1751, in 1 vol. 8vo. *calf,* 7s

259 ———— Dissertatio de Jesu Christi D. N. anno et mense Natali, 8vo. 3s 6d . 1707
An erudite work, in which the author endeavours to shew that the Messiah was born not in winter, but in the spring.

260 ———— The Judgment of the Ancient Jewish Church, against the Unitarians, 8vo. *calf,* 5s 6d . 1699

261 ———— new edition, 8vo. *bds.* 8s—*calf gilt*, 11s *Oxford*, 1821

262 ———— Reflexions upon the books of the Holy Scripture, to establish the truth of the Christian religion, 2 vols. in 1, 8vo. *calf,* 5s 6d
1688

263 ———— new edition, 8vo. *bds.* 8s—*calf gilt*, 11s *Oxford*, 1821

264 - ———— Remarks on the Ecclesiastical History of the Ancient Churches of the Albigenses, 8vo. *bds.* 7s—*cf. gilt*, 10s 6d *ib.* 1821

265 ———— Remarks on the Ecclesiastical History of the Ancient Churches of Piedmont, 8vo. *bds.* 7s—*calf gilt*, 10s 6d *ib.* 1821

[58, GREAT QUEEN STREET,

267 ALLWOOD (Philip). A Dissertation concerning the Chronological Numbers recorded in the Prophet Daniel, as compared with those in the Revelation of St. John, &c. 8vo. *sewed*, 1s 6d   1833
268 ALPHEN (Hieron. Van) Œconomia Catechesis Palatinœ, 4to. *vellum*, 7s   .   *Traj. ad Rh.* 1729
269 [ALSOP (Benj.)] Melius Inquirendum, or a sober Inquiry into the reasonings of the Serious Inquiry : (by Dr. Goodman) wherein the Inquirers cavils against the Non-Conformists are examined, &c. 8vo. *calf*, 4s   .   1679
270 —— ——— another copy 12mo. *calf*, 2s   .   1678
271 ALTAMURA (Ambrosius de) Bibliothecæ Dominicanæ incrementum ac prosecutio, folio, *vellum, very scarce*, 18s   *Romæ*, 1677
272 ALTHAM (Roger) Sermons on several occasions, 2 vols. 8vo. *calf*, 4s   1732
273 ALVA ET ASTORGA (Petrus de) Funiculi nodi indissolubilis de conceptu mentis et conceptu ventris, 4to. *vellum*, 6s   *Brux.* 1663
274 AMBROSE (Isaac) Works, viz. the Doctrine of Regeneration ; Looking unto Jesus ; and the Ministration of Angels, 8vo. *cf. gilt*, 8s   1829
275 AMBROSIUS (S. *Episc. Mediol.*) Expositio seu Explanatio in corpus evangelii sancti Luce evangeliste, small folio, black letter. *with woodcut capitals illuminated, very fine copy, half bound, russia*, £1. 16s
     Per Anthonium Sorg, incolam opidi Augustensis, 1476
     " Edition rare, et premiere de cet ouvrage."—*Santander*.
276 ——— ——— Opera ex editione Romana, S. Scriptura contextum ad faciliorem lectorum intelligentiam, ex ipsa S. Doctoris lectione, et ex LXX. interprete quos potissimum sequitur translatione erutum, complectente, 2 vols. folio, LARGE PAPER, *port. calf*, £2. 2s   .   1661
277 ——— ——— Opera, ad MSS. Codices Vaticanos, &c., studio et labore Monachorum ordinis S. Benedicti, 2 vols. folio, *calf, very scarce*, £8. 8s   .   *Paris*, 1686-90
278 ——— ——— aliud exemplar, 2 vols. folio, *very fine copy, new in sprinkled calf, gilt, carmine edges*, £10. 10s   .   *ib.* 1686-90
279 ——— ——— Opera, ad MSS. Codices Vaticanos, &c. studio et labore Monachorum ordinis S. Benedicti, 4 vols. folio, *hf. bd. vellum*, £5. 5s   .   *Venet.* 1748
280 ——— ——— Opera, studio et labore Monachorum ordinis S. Benedicti, 8 vols. in 4, 4to, *vellum*, £3. 13s 6d   *Venet.* 1781-82
281 AMES (W.) Bellarminus enervatus, 4 vols. in 1, 18mo. *vellum, scarce*, 7s 6d   .   *Amst.* 1658
282 ——— ——— Lectiones in omnes Psalmos Davidis, small 8vo. *neat*, 3s 6d   *ib.* 1635
283 ——— ——— Medulla Theologica, 18mo. *calf*, 2s 6d   *ib.* 1659
284 ——— ——— De conscientia et ejus jure vel casibus, 18mo. *calf*, 2s   *ib.*. 1631
285 ——— ——— Conscience, with the power and cases thereof, 4to. *hf. bd. calf, neat*, 4s   .   1643
     " An eminent Puritan, whose productions are not void of merit, considering the times in which they were written."—*Mosheim*.
286 AMMONIUS ALEXANDRINUS. Quatuor Evangeliorum consonantia, a Victore Capuano Episcopo translata, 12mo. *hf. bd. calf, neat*, 5s 6d
     Moguntiæ, Jo. Schoeffer, 1524

287 AMHURST (N.) Terræ filius; or the Secret History of the University of Oxford, 12mo. *hf. bd. calf*, 3s 6d . 1754

It was an ancient custom at Oxford in the public acts, for some person, who was called *Terræ-Filius* to mount the rostrum, and divert a large crowd from all parts with a merry oration, interspersed with secret history, raillery and sarcasm; as the occasions of the times supplied him with matter. Amhurst was expelled from St. John's College, Oxford, probably for his whig principles, *hinc illæ lachrymæ*; he made it his business to satirize the University.—*See Ralph's Case of Authors.*

288 AMPHILOCHII (S. *Iconiensis*,) Methodii Paterensis, et Andreæ Cretensis Opera omnia, *Gr. et Lat.* studio F. Combefis, folio, *calf*, £1. 15s . . *Paris.* 1644

289 AMYRALDUS (Moyses) A treatise concerning Religions, in refutation of the opinion which accounts all indifferent, 18mo. *calf*, 3s 1660

An eminent French Protestant Divine.

290 ANASTASIUS *Bibliothecarius.* Historia Ecclesiastica sive Chronographia tripertita; et Historia de Vitis Romanorum Pontificum, a B. Petro Apostolo ad Nicolaum I. Accedunt notæ Car. Annib. Fabroti, folio, LARGE PAPER, *fine copy*, *calf*, 18s *Par.* 1649

291 ———— Collectanea, studio et opera J. Sirmondi, 8vo. *vellum*, 3s *ib.* 1620

292 ANCYRANUS (Marcellus, [*i. e.* Jac. Boileau] Disquisitiones II. de Residentia Canonicorum; quibus accessit tertia, de tactibus impudicis, &c. 8vo. *calf*, 3s 6d . *ib.* 1695

293 ANDERSON (Christopher) The Annals of the English Bible, 2 vols. 8vo. *portrait of Tyndale, and fac-similes, cloth bds.* £1. 8s 1845

294 [ANDERSON (Henry)] An Inquiry into the natural Right of Mankind to debate freely concerning Religion, 8vo. *calf*, 4s 1737

295 ———— The Court Convert; or, a sincere sorrow for Sin, faithfully travers'd, [*a penitential poem*] 12mo. *calf*, 2s

Printed for the Author, ——

296 ———— (J. S. M.) The History of the Church of England, in the Colonies and Foreign Dependencies of the British Empire, Vol. I. (all yet published) 8vo. *bds.* 12s . 1845

297 ANDREWS'S (Dr. James) Key to Scripture Chronology, 8vo. *sewed*, 1s 1822

298 ———— (Lanc. *Bp. of Winchester*) The Morall Law expounded, that is, his work upon the Ten Commandements. With nineteen Sermons upon the Lord's Prayer, and seven on our Saviour's Tentations in the Wildernesse, folio, *portrait, hf. bd. calf*, £1. 1s 1642

299 ———— The pattern of Catechistical Doctrine at large; or, a learned and pious Exposition of the Ten Commandments, folio, *calf, scarce*, £1. 11s 6d . 1675

300 ———— Ninety-six Sermons on the Festivals and other subjects, with his Funeral Sermon by Bp. Buckeridge, folio, *portrait, calf*, £1. 10s . . *Lond.* 1635

301 ———— new edition, 5 vols. 8vo. *bds.* £2. 10s *Oxford*, 1841-4

302 ———— Nineteen Sermons concerning Prayer, with a Memoir of the Author, 8vo. *bds.* 3s 6d . 1830

303 ———— Private Prayers for every day in the week, translated from the Greek by Geo. Stanhope, D.D. 8vo. *2 portraits, calf*, 4s 1730

304 ANDREWS's (Lanc. Bp. *of Winchester*,) Devotions, translated from the Greek by Dean Stanhope, edited by Bp. Horne, 18mo. 2*s*
1778
305 ———— Devotions, translated by G. Stanhope, D.D. 24mo. *port. morocco*, 3*s* 6*d* – *calf*, 2*s* . 1830
306 ———— Devotions, translated from the Greek, and arranged anew, (Edited by the Rev. J. H. Newman), sm. 8vo. *bds.* 5*s*—*morocco, gilt leaves*, 5*s* . *Oxford*, 1842
307 ANNE DE S. BARTHELEMY. Histoire de la vie, vertus, et Miracles de la Venerable Mere Anne de S. Barthelemy, Compagne inseperable de la Sainte Mere Terese de Jesus. Traduite d'Espagnol par René Gaultier, 8vo. *neat*, 3*s* 6*d* . *Par.* 1633
308 ANNOTATIONES in Vetus Testamentum, et in Epistolam ad Ephesios. Incerto auctore, E. Bibl. Jo. Archiep. Ebor. in lucem erutæ, 8vo. *calf*, 3*s* . . *Cantab.* 1653

Found by Dr. Scattergood amongst the MSS. of Abp. Williams.

309 ANSALDUS (Castus Innocens) De authenticis Sacrarum Scripturarum apud SS. Patres lectionibus, libri duo, 4to. *hf. bd. vellum*, 6*s* [*Veronæ,*] 1747
310 ANSELMUS (S. *Archiep. Cant.*) Opera, nec non Eadmeri monachi Cantuar. Historia Novorum et alia opuscula : labore et studio Gabr. Gerberon, folio, LARGE PAPER, *very scarce, calf*, £3. 3*s* *Lut. Par.* 1675
311 ANTHEMS—A Collection of Anthems now performed in the Cathedral-Church, College, and St. Maurice-Church, in Winchester, 8vo. *calf*, 1*s* 6*d* . . *Winch.* 1765
312 ———— A collection of Anthems used in His Majesty's Chapels Royal, and most Cathedral Churches in England and Ireland. Published under the direction of Tho. Pearce, D.D. 8vo. *bds. very scarce*, 3*s* 6*d* . . 1795
313 ANTI-SOCINUS, hoc est, solida et exacta Confutatio omnium et singulorum Errorum, quos olim Ariani, Ebionitæ, Samosateniani, Pelagiani, et Tritheitæ, horribili audacia propugnarunt, small 8vo. *vellum*, 4*s* 6*d* . *Franc.* 1612
314 ANTONINI (S. *Archiep. Florentini*) Confessionale Domini Anthonini, sm. 4to. 𝔅lack letter, *fine copy, calf*, RARE, 12*s* *s. l.* 1487
315 ANTONIUS (Nic.) Bibliotheca Hispana vetus, sive Hispani scriptores qui ab Octaviano Auguste Ævo ad an. Christi 1500 floruerunt, cura Fra. Perezio Bayerio, qui prologum, auctoris vitam, et notulas adjecit, 2 vols. *portrait, Matriti*, 1788—Bibliotheca Hispana nova, sive Hispanorum Scriptorum qui ab an 1500 ad an. 1684 floruere notitia, 2 vols. *ib.* 1783-88—together 4 vols. folio, *fine copy, new in calf gilt*, £6. 6*s* . ——

These works contain much information respecting the History of Arabian Literature in Spain.

316 APHORISMS.—Moral and Religious Aphorisms, (collected from the writings of Dr. Jeffery and Dr. Whichcott,) sm. 8vo. *calf*, 2*s* *Norwich*, 1703

318 APOCRYPHAL NEW TESTAMENT, being all the Gospels, Epistles, and other pieces now extant, attributed in the first four centuries to Jesus Christ, His Apostles, and their companions, and not included in the New Testament by its compilers, 8vo. *hf. bd. calf, very scarce*, 12s . 1821
Edited by the celebrated W. Hone, and afterwards suppressed.

319 APOLINARIUS Interpretatio Psalmorum, versibus heroicis, Gr. et Lat. 12mo. *neat, 3s 6d* . *Par.* 1580

320 APOLOGIE pour les Saincts Peres de l'Eglise, defenseurs de la Grace de Jesus Christ, contre les erreurs qui leur sont imposées, dans la traduction du Traitté de la vocation des Gentils, attribué a S. Prosper, et dans les reflexions du traducteur – dans le livre de M. Morel, intitulé les veritables sentimens de S. Augustin, &c. et dans les ecrits de M. le Moine, 4to. *calf, 9s* *ib.* 1651

321 ———— pour la Morale des Reformez, ou defense de leur doctrine, pour réponse au livre de Mr. Arnaud, 8vo. *calf, 4s Quevilly*, 1675

322 APTHORP's (East) Letters on the prevalence of Christianity before its civil establishment : with Observations on [Gibhon's] Decline of the Roman Empire, 8vo. *russia, 7s 6d* . 1778
" The author has enriched his work with many learned remarks, and especially with a catalogue of civil and ecclesiastical historians, which the reader will find to be very useful."—*Bp. Watson*.

323 ———— Discourses on Prophecy, read in the Chapel of Lincoln's Inn, at the Warburtonian Lecture, 2 vols. 8vo. *fine copy, calf gilt*, 8s . 1784
A most excellent and highly esteemed work.

324 AQUINAS (S. Tho.) Questiones dignissime de anima, small folio, *very fine copy, vellum,* 12s . *s. l.* 1472

325 ———— Primum Scriptum super sententias, divinissime trinitatis misteria eleganter enodans, folio, **black letter**, *the initial letters are rubricated by hand; in the original binding, oak boards*, £1. 4s . *Colonie, Henr. Quentell*, 1480

326 ———— Summa Theologica, folio, *fine copy, stamped hogskin*, £1. 10s . *Lugduni*, 1738

327 ————— Catena Aurea ; a Commentary on the four Gospels, collected out of the works of the Fathers, and translated by Members of the University of Oxford, 7 vols. 8vo. *bds*. £3. 10s *Oxford*, 1845

328 ARCHER (James, *Priest of the Rom. Cath. Chapel, Duke St.*) Sermons on various moral and religious subjects, for Sundays and Festivals, 4 vols. 8vo. *bds. scarce*, 16s 1817-22

329 ARCUDIUS (Petrus) De concordia Ecclesiæ occidentalis et orientalis in septem Sacramentorum administratione, 4to. *calf*, 12s
Lut. Par. 1672
" Arcudius étoit très attaché aux sentimens et à la communion des Latins, et grand adversaire des Lutheriens et des Calvinistes. C'est dans cet esprit, qu'il a composé son Traité de la Concorde de l'Eglise Occidentale et Orientale, pour montrer que ces deux églises s'accordoient anciennement, non seulement dans la doctrine des sacremens, mais aussi dans leur administration. Son ouvrage des sacremens est estimable, et l'on y trouve beaucoup des passages assez bien recueillis."—*Dupin.*

330 A[RDERNE] (J[ames], D.D.) Directions concerning the matter and stile of Sermons, written to W. S. a young Deacon, 18mo. *calf*, 1s 6d . 1671

331 ARISTÆNETUS Epistolæ Græcæ, cum Latina interpretatione et notis, sm. 8vo. *bds. 2s* . *Par.* 1639
332 ARISTEUS. The ancient history of the Septuagint, written in Greek near two thousand years ago : Englished by Dr. John Donne, Dean of St. Paul's, 18mo. *calf, 3s* . 1685
333 ARNAULD (Antoine) Plaidoyé pour l'Université de Paris, contre les Jésuites, 1594, 12mo. *hf. bd. russia, 3s* . ———
334 ————— Justification de M. A. Arnauld, Docteur de Sorbonne, contre la censure d'une partie de la Faculté de Théologie de Paris, 2 vols. 12mo. *neat, 4s* . *Liege,* 1702
335 ————— Apologie pour M. Arnauld contre un libelle publié par les Jesuites, intitulé Remarques judicieuses sur la livre de la Frequente Communion, 4to. *old red morocco, gilt leaves,* 12s 1644
336 ————— L'Esprit de Mr. Arnauld, tiré de sa conduite, et des Ecrits de luy et de ses disciples, 2 vols. *neat, 4s* *Daventer,* 1684
337 ————— Histoire abregée de sa Vie et de ses ouvrages, 12mo. *port. neat, 2s 6d* . *Cologne,* 1695
338 ————— De la frequente Communion, où les sentimens des Peres, des Papes, et des Conciles touchant l'usage des Sacremens de Pénitence et d'Eucharistie sont fidellement exposez, 8vo. *calf, 7s 6d*
Lyon, 1739
339 ARNDTIUS (Jo.) De vero Christianismo libri IV. cura A. W. Boemii, —Accedit vita auctoris, 2 vols. 8vo. *calf, 4s 6d* *Lond.* 1708
The most esteemed work of all those written by this celebrated Protestant divine.

340 ARNOBIUS. Disputationes adversus Gentes, ex bibliotheca T. Canteri, 8vo. *vellum, 4s* . . *Antv.* 1582
With the autograph of Nic. Heinsius, 1634.

341 ————— Disputationes adversus Gentes, et ejusdem argumenti Dialogus : M. Minutii Felicis Octavius : G. Elmenhorst recensuit et notis illustravit, 8vo. *calf, 3s* . *Han.* 1603
342 ARROWSMITH (Joan.) Tactica sacra, sive de milite spirituali pugnante, vincente, et triumphante, dissertatio, 4to. *hf. bd. calf, neat, 5s*
Amst. 1700
Contains many ingenious remarks on those passages of Scripture which relate to scriptural warfare.

343 ARTICLES. An historical and critical Essay on the 39 Articles, wherein it is demonstrated that this clause, *the Church has power,* &c. is not a part of the Articles as they were established by that of Parliament 13 Elizabeth, 8vo. *calf, 3s* . 1724
344 ARTICLES de la Saincte Union des Catholiques François, 12mo. *fine copy, russia, gilt leaves, 4s 6d* . *s. l.* 1588
345 ARWAKER's (Edm.) Thoughts well Employ'd ; or the duty of self-observation, sm. 8vo. *front. 1s 6d* . 1695
346 ASCHAM's (Roger) English Works, containing I. A Report of the affairs of Germany. II. Toxophilus, or the Art of Shooting. III. The Schoolmaster, illustrated by Mr. Upton. IV. Letters to Queen Elizabeth and others, with Notes, and the Author's Life by James Bennet, 4to. *calf,* 12s . 1761
" In a word, his *Toxophilus* was a good book for young men, his *Schoolmaster* for old men, and his *Epistles* for all men."—*Dr. Sam. Johnson.*

347 ASHDOWNE (Wm.). An Essay explaining Jesus's true meaning in his Parables, 8vo. *sewed*, 1s 6d . *Canterbury*, 1780
348 ASHTON's (Tho.) Sermons on several occasions, 8vo. *portrait, calf*, 2s 6d— *bds*. 2s . 1770
349 ASKEW's (Egeon) Brotherly reconcilement, preached in Oxford for the union of some, and now published for the unitie of all in this Church and Common-wealth ; with an Apologie for the use of fathers and secular learning in Sermons, 4to. *fine clean copy, vellum*, 7s 6d— *calf*, 7s 6d . . *Lond*. 1605
350 ———— another copy, *the last leaf supplied in MS. and slightly stained*, 4to. *calf*, 4s 6d . *ib*. 1605
351 ASPINAL's (James) Sermons, doctrinal and practical, 3 vols. 8vo. *hf. bd. calf*, 7s 6d . 1822-27
352 ASPINWALL (Edward). An Apology, being a series of Arguments in proof of the Christian Religion, 8vo. *calf*, 2s . 1731
353 [ASPLIN's (Will.)] Alkibla. A disquisition upon Worshipping towards the East, 2 parts, 1731—The Anatomy of the Kebla; or a dissection of the defence of Eastward Adoration, lately published in the name of John Andrews, 1729 — A Letter to the Bp. of London, occasion'd by the abuse of a passage in his pastoral letter, 1730; in 1 vol. 8vo. *calf, neat*, 5s . ——
354 ASSEMANUS (Jos. Aloysius) Commentarius de Ecclesiis, earumque Reverentia et Asylo. Accesserunt tractatus Jos. de Bonis de Oratoriis Publicis, ac Fortunati à Brixia de Oratoriis domesticis, fol. *sewed*, £1. 8s . *Romæ*, 1766
355 ———— De catholicis seu patriarchis Chaldæorum et Nestorianorum Commentarius, 4to. *sewed, very scarce*, 24s *ib*. 1775
356 ———— (Jo. Sim.) Bibliotheca Orientalis Clementino Vaticana— Tomi 3, Pars 2—De Syris Nestorianis, folio, *sewed*, £1. 16s
ib. 1728
357 ———— De Syris Monophyticis Dissertatio, folio, *sewed*, 16s
ib. 1730
358 ———— De Sanctis Ferentinis in Tuscia, Bonifacio ac Redempto, episcopis ; deque Presb. et Martyre Eutychio Dissertatio, 4to. *neat, scarce*, 12s . *ib*. 1745
359 ———— Kalendaria Ecclesiæ Universæ, in quibus tum ex Codicibus, Tabulis, Pictis, Scriptis, Sanctorum Nomina, Imagines, et Festi per Annum dies Ecclesiarum Orientis et Occidentis, præmissis unius cujusque Ecclesiæ Originibus, 6 vols. 4to. *hf. bd*. £4.
ib. 1755
360 ———— aliud exemplar, 6 vols. 4to. *fine copy, new in vellum, by Mackenzie*, £4. 14s 6d . *ib*. 1755
361 ASSEMBLY's Annotations upon all the Books of the Old and New Testaments, *best edition*, 2 vols. folio, *calf*, £1. 11s 6d 1651
362 [ASTELL (Mrs. Mary)]. The Christian Religion as profess'd by a Daughter of the Church of England, 8vo. *calf*, 3s 1705

This book was suspected to be the work of Bp. Atterbury (see his Epist. Corresp. vol. i. p. 20, and vol. ii. p. 33.) The authoress is mentioned in No. 32 of the Tatler under the name of Madonella.

[58, GREAT QUEEN STREET,

363 [ASTELL (Mrs.)]. An Essay in defence of the Female Sex, &c. 8vo. *front. 2s 6d* . 1697
364 —————— another copy, 12mo. *front. 1s 6d* . 1696
365 ASSERIUS (*Menevensis*) Annales rerum gestarum Ælfredi Magni; recensuit Fra. Wise, royal 8vo. LARGE PAPER, *portraits by Vertue, fine copy, calf, gilt edges*, 18s . *Oxon.* 1722
366 ASTERIUS (S. *Episc. Amaseæ*) Homiliæ, Græcè et Latinè, Ph. Rubenio interprete—Ejusdem Rubenii Carmina et Epistolæ, etc. folio, *vellum*, 12s . *Antv.* 1615
With the autograph of Peter Burmann.
367 ATHANASIUS (S. *Archiep. Alex.*) Opera omnia, *Græcè et Latine,* 2 vols. folio, *calf,* £3. 3s . *Par.* 1627
368 —————— aliud exemplar, 2 vols. folio, *calf,* £2. 16s *ib.* 1627
From the library of his late R. H. the Duke of Sussex.
369 —————— Opera Omnia, *Gr. et Lat.* studio Monachorum Ordinis S. Benedicti, 3 vols. in 4, folio, *hf. bd. calf, uncut, neat, very scarce,* £10. 10s *Patavii,* 1777
370 —————— Opera Omnia, Græcè et Latine, cura et studio Monachorum Ord. S. Benedicti, *editio optima*, 3 vols. *Par.* 1698 — Collectio Nova Patrum et Scriptorum Græcorum (Athanasii, Eusebii et Cosmæ Ægyptii) *Editio Benedictina*, à B. de Montfaucon, 2 vols. *ib.* 1706— together 5 vols. folio, *remarkably fine copies, uniformly bound in rich calf gilt,* £18. 18s . ——
371 —————— Interpretatio Psalmorum, sive de titulis Psalmorum, *Gr. et Lat.* folio, *vellum,* £1. 11s 6d *Romæ,* 1746
372 —————— another copy, *bds.* £1. 5s . *ib.* 1746
373 —————— Historical Tracts (translated by the Rev. Miles Atkinson), with Notes, 8vo. *bds. 7s* . *Oxford,* 1843
374 ATHENAGORAS (S.) Legatio pro Christianis : ejusdem de Resurrectione Mortuorum, *Gr. et Lat.* cum Notis Variorum, cura Edv. Dechair, *best edition*, 8vo. *calf, 6s* . *Oxon.* 1706
375 —————— Apologeticks, I. for the Christian Religion—II. For the truth of the Resurrection, with a curious fragment of Justin Martyr on the Resurrection, and two other fragments, one attributed to Josephus, the other to Methodius, concerning the state of the Dead : done into English by David Humphreys, M.A., 8vo. *calf,* 6s . 1714
376 —————— another copy, 8vo. *calf, neat, 7s* . 1714
377 —————— the same, 8vo. *sprinkled calf gilt, 9s* 1714
378 ATKINSON'S (Miles) Practical Sermons, with a short Memoir of his Life, 2 vols, 8vo. *portrait, hf. bd. calf, marbled edges,* 7s 6d 1812
379 ATTERBURY'S (Fra. *Bp. of Rochester)* Sermons and Discourses on several subjects and occasions, 4 vols. 8vo. LARGE PAPER, *portrait, fine copy, rich blue morocco, gilt leaves,* £2. 10s 1723-34
380 —————— another edition, 4 vols. 8vo. *portrait, fine copy, new in pannelled calf gilt,* £1. 8s . 1730-34

"He has a peculiar force in his way. This art of his is used with the most exact and honest skill. He never attempts your passions till he has convinced your reason. All the objections which you can form are laid open and dispersed before he uses the least vehemence in his Sermon; but when he thinks he has your head, he very soon wins your heart, and never pretends to shew you the beauty of holiness, till he has convinced you of the truth of it."

381 ATTERBURY'S (Fra. *Bp. of Rochester*) Rights, Powers, and Privileges of an English Convocation stated and vindicated, in answer to Dr. Wake's authority of Christian Princes, &c. 8vo. *fine copy, calf,* 10s 6d . . 170⁞
382 ——— (Lewis) Sermons on select subjects, with a brief account of the Author, by E. Yardley, 2 vols. 8vo. *portrait*, 6s 1743
383 ATTERSOLL (Will.) A commentarie upon the Epistle of Saint Paule to Philemon, folio, *calf, scarce,* 16s 1633
384 AUBREY'S (John) Miscellanies, on Day - Fatality, Local - Fatality, Dreams, Apparitions, Marvels, Magick, Oracles, Second-Sight, &c. with some account of his Life, 8vo. *front. fine copy, new in calf gilt,* 7s . 1721
385 AUGUSTI (Jo. Chr. Gul.) Chrestomathia Patristica, ad usus eorum qui historiam dogmatum Christianorum accuratius discere cupiunt adornata, 2 vols. in 1, 8vo. *calf gilt,* 12s *Lips.* 1812
386 ——— Corpus librorum Symbolicorum qui in ecclesia Reformatorum auctoritate publicam obtinuerunt, 8vo. *calf,* 10s 6d
Elberfeld, 1827
387 AUGUSTINUS (S. Aurelius, *Hipponensis Episc.*) Opera omnia, per Theologos Lovanienses ex MSS. codicibus emendata, cum indicibus, &c. 12 vols. in 7, folio, *fine copy, old red morocco, gilt leaves,* £7. 7s . *Par.* 1586
388 ——— Opera omnia, cum Vita et Indice generali, studio Monachorum S. Benedicti, 11 vols. in 8, *best edition,* folio, *fine copy, calf.* £3. 13s *ib.* 1689-1700
389 ——— idem, 11 vols. in 8, *very fine copy, old French calf,* £14. 14s . . *ib.* 1689-1700
390 ——— aliud exemplar, cum Vita, Indice generale, et Appendix Augustiniana, 12 vols. in 9, folio, *calf,* £15. 15s *ib.* 1689-1700
391 ——— idem, 12 vols. in 9, folio, *vellum,* £10. 10s *Antverpiæ,*1700
392 ——— Opera omnia, ad Editionem Benedictinam expressa, 15 vols. imp. 8vo. *brown calf gilt, lettered contents,* £14. 14s *Par.*1836-40
393 ——— Lettre d'un Theologien à un de ses Amis sur un libelle qui à pour titre, Lettre de l'Abbé * * * aux PP. Benedictins sur le dernier tome de leur edition de S. Augustin, 12mo. *calf,* 1s 6d . 1699
394 ——— Retractio de agone Xpiano. Liber de Sermone dni in monte habito. 𝕭𝖑𝖆𝖈𝖐 𝖑𝖊𝖙𝖙𝖊𝖗, 4to. *fine copy, green morocco, gilt leaves, very neat,* £1. 10s [*Coloniæ, Ul. Zell, circa* 1468]
395 ——— Explication de S. Augustin et des autres Peres Latins sur le Nouveau Testament, 2 vols. 4to. *calf,* 12s *Par.* 1682
396 ——— Sermones inediti, cura et studio D. A. B. Caillau, folio, *sewed,* £1. 18s . *ib.* 1842
397 ——— Liber de Hæresibus ad Quod-Vult-Deum, una cum Gennadii Massiliensis Appendice. Edidit, notisque illustravit E. Welchman, 8vo. *vellum,* 2s 6d . *Oxon.* 1721
398 ——— De Civitate Dei libri XXII. post recensionem Monachorum, Ord. S. Benedicti, royal 8vo. *sewed,* 14s—*calf, neat,* 18s
Paris, 1838
399 ——— Of the Citie of God, with the learned Comments of J. L. Vives, Englished by J. H. folio, *calf neat,* £1. 1s 1610

[58, GREAT QUEEN STREET,

400 AUGUSTINE (S.) Of the Citie of God, with the learned Comments of J. L. Vives, Englished by J. H. folio, *fine copy, calf, very neat*, £1. 6s . 1620
401 ——— Confessiones (cura E. B. Pusey) 8vo. *bds*. 6s *Oxonii*, 1838
402 ——— Confessiones (cura E. B. Pusey) *Oxonii*, 1838—The same in English, revised from a former Translation by E. B. Pusey, D.D. with illustrations from S. Augustine himself, *Oxford*, 1840, in 1 vol. 8vo. *hf. bd. russia, very neat*, 15s . ——
403 ——— Les Confessions, traduites par le R. P. Ceriziers, 18mo. *vellum*, 3s . *Par*. 1659
404 ——— Sermons sur le Nouveau Testament, traduits per M. Du Bois, 4 vols. 8vo. *calf*, 18s . *ib*. 1700
405 ——— Livres de la maniere d'enseigner les principes de la Religion Chrestienne, de la Vertu de Continence et de Temperance, de la Patience, et Contre le Mensonge, 12mo. *neat*, 2s 6d *ib*. 1678
406 ——— Les Six livres de Saint Augustin contre Julien, defenseur de l'hérésie Pelagienne, 2 vols. sm. 8vo. *fine copy, old olive green morocco, gilt leaves*, 18s . *ib*. 1736
407 ——— Sermons on selected lessons of the New Testament (translated by the Rev. R. G. Macmullen) 2 vols. 8vo. *bds*. 18s
Oxford, 1844
408 ——— Pious Breathings, being the Meditations of St. Augustine, his Treatise of the Love of God, Soliloquies and Manual, with select Contemplations from St. Anselm and St. Bernard, translated by Dean Stanhope, 8vo. *new in calf gilt*, 8s 1745
409 ——— Commentarius brevis ad regulam S^{mi}. P. N. Angustini, authore F. Laurentio Landtmeter, 12mo. *neat*, 2s 6d *Lovanii*, 1621
410 ——— Les sentimens de S. Augustin sur la Grace, opposez à ceux de Jansenius, par le P. Jean Leporcq, *presentation copy*, 4to. *gilt leaves, crimson morocco, with a Cardinal's arms on the side*, 14s
Paris, 1682
411 ——— The judgment of St. Augustine concerning penal lawes against Conventicles, and for unity in Religion, delivered in his 48th Epistle to Vincentius, 4to. *sewed*, 4s 6d 1670
412 AURELIUS (Petrus) Opera, jussu et impensis Cleri Gallicani denuò in lucem edita, 3 vols. in 1, folio, *neat*, £1. 11s 6d *Par*. 1646

Continentur : Assertio Epistolæ Galliæ Antistitam, qua Libros Nicolai Smithæi et Danielis a Jesu damnarunt ; Responsio ad octo Causas Spongiæ præambulas ; Vindiciæ Censuræ Facultatis Theologiæ Parisiensis adversus Spongiam Læmelii ; Responsio ad Sirmondum de Canone Arausicano ; Anæreticus et Orthodoxus adversus Sirmondum.

413 AUSTIN (Benj.) The Presumptuous Man's Mirrour; or a Watch-bell to rouse up a secure Sinner out of his sleep of security, 16mo. *hf. bd. calf, neat*, 3s 6d . 1641
414 AVENAR's (John) The Enemy of Security, or a daily exercise of Godly Meditations, published in the German and Latine tongues, by the Right Reverend M. John Avenar, in English by Thomas Rogers, 18mo. *calf, neat*, 3s 6d . ——
415 AYLIFFE (John) The antient and present state of the University of Oxford, 2 vols. 8vo. *calf*, 10s 6d . 1714
Ordered to be burnt by the common hangman.

416 AYLIFFE (John) Parergon Juris Canonici Anglicani, or Commentary, by way of Supplement to the Canons and Constitutions of the Church of England, folio, *calf, scarce*, £1. 11s 6d   1726
417 AYLMER (Jo. *Bp. of Lond.*) Historical collections of his Life and Acts, by John Strype, 8vo. *portrait, calf,* 5s—*fine copy, old calf gilt,* 6s   1701
418 ———— another copy, *wanting the portrait*, 8vo. *calf*, 4s 6d   1701
419 BABINGTON (Gervase, *Bp. of Worcester*) Works, containing comfortable notes upon the five books of Moses, as also an exposition upon the Creed, the Commandements, the Lord's Prayer, with a conference between Frailtie and Faith, and three Sermons, folio, *rough calf, title inlaid,* £1. 1s   1622
420 ———— the same, folio, *with the rare portrait by Elstrack, fine tall, clean copy, calf,* £1. 8s   1637
421 ———— A very fruitfull exposition of the Commandements by way of Questions and Answeres, 18mo. Black letter, *cf. scarce*, 18s   1583
422 BACON (Fr. *Lord Verulam*). The Wisdom of the Ancients, done into English, by Sir A. Gorges, 18mo. 1s 6d   1619
423 ———— Cases of Treason, 4to. 2s   1641
424 ———— Essays, or Counsels Civil and Moral, and Wisdom of the Ancients, edited by B. Montague, 12mo. *bds*. 4s 6d   1836
425 ———— Novum Organum, or true suggestions for the interpretation of Nature, 12mo. *bds*. 3s 6d   1844
426 ———— (R.) Christ mighty in himself and members, revealed in some short expressions by way of Catechisme, 18mo. *front. calf, neat*, 4s 6d   1646
427 BADDELEY (Dr. Geo.) Several Discourses preached at St. James's, Westminster, 8vo. *bds*. 2s 6d   1766
428 BAGNALL-BAKER (Tho.) Anatomico-Theology; or a critical dissection of various Scriptures, 8vo. *bds*. 6s   1843
429 BAHRDTIUS (Car. Fr.) Observationes criticæ circa lectionem Codicum MSS. Hebr. 12mo. *sewed*, 1s 6d   *Lips*. 1770
430 BAIANISMUS redivivus in Scriptis Bellelli et Berti ordinis Eremitarum S. Augustini.—Jansenismus redivivus in scriptis Bellelli et Berti, in 1 vol. 4to. *calf*, 10s 6d   *s. l.* 1744
431 BAIL (Ludov.) De triplici examine ordinandorum, confessariorum, et Pœnitentium, 8vo. *neat*, 4s 6d   *Par.* 1668
432 BAKER's (Sir Richard) Meditations and Disquisitions upon the Lord's Prayer, upon the First Psalme, upon the One and Fiftieth Psalme, in one vol. 4to. *calf*, 4s 6d   1638
   From the library of the late Duke of Sussex.
433 ———— Theatrum Triumphans, or a Discourse of Plays, 12mo. 2s 6d   1670
434 BALEI (Joannis) Scriptorum Illustrium Majoris Britanniæ, quam nunc Angliam et Scotiam vocant : Catalogus ; à Japheto per 3618 annos, usque ad annum hunc Domini 1557, ex Beroso, Gennadio, Beda, Honorio, Bostono Buriensi, Frumentario, Capgravo, Bostio, Joanne Lelando, &c. atque aliis authoribus collectus, et IX Centurias continens ; folio, *vellum*, £1. 5s   *Basil, apud Joann. Operinum*, 1557
435 BALGUY (Th.) Discourses on various subjects, 8vo. *calf*, 3s 6d   *Winchester*, 1785

436 BALGUY (Th.) Discourses and Charges, with Advice to an unmarried Lady; edited by James Drake, 2 vols. 8vo. *bds.* 5s   *Camb.* 1822
Sensible and excellent discourses. His work on divine benevolence is a most able answer to ancient and modern sceptics.
437 BALTUS ( ) Défense des SS. Peres accusez de Platonisme, 4to. *front. fine copy, old gilt calf,* 14s   *Par.* 1711
438 BALUZII (Stephani) Miscellanea, novo ordine digesta, et non paucis ineditis Monumentis opportunisque Animadversionibus aucta, opera et studio J. D. Mansi, Archiep. Lucensis, 4 vols. folio, *fine copy, vellum,* £3. 10s   *Lucæ,* 1761-64
For a list of the contents of this work, see "*Dowling's Notitia Scriptorum,*" pp. 159-89.
439 BAMPTON LECTURE SERMONS, preached before the University of Oxford, on the following subjects, viz. To Confirm and Establish the Christian Faith, and to Confute all Heretics and Schismatics; upon the Divine Authority of the Holy Scriptures; upon the Authority of the Writings of the Primitive Fathers as to the Faith and Practice of the Primitive Church; upon the Divinity of our Saviour, and of the Holy Ghost; upon the Articles of the Christian Faith, as comprehended in the Apostles' and Nicene Creeds, &c. from the commencement in 1780 to 1844, inclusive, *(excepting the volume for* 1783 *and* 1829*)* 64 vols. 8vo. *fine copy, new in calf gilt,* £31. 10s
440 — 1780. BANDINEL (Dr. James) Eight Sermons, to which is added a Vindication of St. Paul from the charge of wishing himself accursed, 8vo. *calf,* 4s   1780
441 ———— another copy, 8vo. *calf gilt,* 5s   1796
442 — 1781. NEVE's (T.) Jesus the Saviour, &c. of Mankind, 8vo. *calf gilt,* 7s 6d   1781
443 — 1782. HOLMES's (R.) On the Prophecies and Testimony of John the Baptist, and parallel Prophecies of Jesus Christ, 8vo. *calf gilt,* 7s   1782
444 — 1784. WHITE's (Dr. Jos.) View of Christianity and Mahometanism, in their history, their evidence, and their effects, 8vo. *hf. bd. calf,* 6s—*calf gilt,* 7s   1785
445 ———— another copy, 8vo. *calf gilt,* 7s 6d   1811
446 ———— Facts relating to the Rev. Dr. White's Bampton Lectures, by R. B. Gabriel, D. D. 8vo. *sewed,* 1s 6d
With copious MS. Notes.
447 — 1785. CHURTON's (R.) on the Prophecies respecting the Destruction of Jerusalem, 8vo. *bds.* 5s   1785
448 — 1786. CROFT's (G.) on the Use and Abuse of Reason, Authority of the Fathers, Conduct of the Reformers, &c. 8vo. *calf gilt, very scarce,* 10s 6d   1786
449 — 1787. HAWKINS's (W.) on Scripture Mysteries, 8vo. *calf gilt,* 6s   1787
450 — 1790. KETT (Hen.) A representation of the Conduct and Opinions of the Primitive Christians, with remarks on certain assertions of Mr. Gibbon and Dr. Priestley, 8vo. *calf,* 4s 6d   *Oxf.* 1791
451 ———— another copy, with additions, 8vo. *calf gilt,* 5s 6d *ib.* 1792
452 — 1791. MORRES (Rob.) on Faith in general, 8vo. *calf, scarce,* 8s   *ib.* 1791

BAMPTON LECTURES — *continued.*

453 — 1792. EVELEIGH (Dr. John) on the Substance and History of the Christian Religion, with four Sermons before the University, 8vo. *calf,* 4s 6d—*calf gilt,* 5s 6d   Oxford, 1794

454 — 1793. WILLIAMSON (James). The truth, inspiration, authority, and end of the Scriptures considered and defended, 8vo. *calf,* 5s 6d   ib. 1793

455 — 1794. WINTLE'S (T.) Expediency, Prediction, and Accomplishment of the Christian Redemption illustrated, 8vo. *calf gilt,* 6s 1794

456 — 1796. GRAY (Robert). Sermons on the principles upon which the Reformation of the Church of England was established, 8vo. *calf gilt,* 6s 6d   .   1796

457 — 1797. FINCH'S (W.) on the Objections of Infidel Historians, and other Writers against Christianity, 8vo. *calf gilt,* 7s   1797

458 — 1798. HALL'S (C. H.) on the Fulness of Time, 8vo. *calf gilt,* 8s   .   1799

459 — 1799. BARROW'S (W.) on the Necessity or Credibility of the Christian Revelation, 8vo. *calf gilt,* 7s 6d   .   1799

460 — 1800. RICHARDS (Geo.) The divine Origin of Prophecy illustrated and defended, 8vo. *calf,* 6s   .   Oxford, 1800

461 — 1802. NOTT'S (G. F.) Religious Enthusiasm considered, 8vo. *calf gilt,* 8s   .   .   1803

462 — 1803. FARRER'S (J.) on the Mission and Character of Christ, 8vo. *calf gilt,* 7s   .   1804

463 — 1807. LE MESURIER (T.) The Nature and Guilt of Schism considered, with a reference to the Principles of Religion, 8vo. *calf gilt,* 6s   .   1808

464 — 1808. PENROSE'S (J.) Truth of Christianity proved from the Wisdom displayed in its Original Establishment, 8vo. *bds.* 5s 6d—*calf gilt,* 7s   .   .   1808

465 — 1809. CARWITHEN'S (J. B.) on the Brahminical Religion, and its Confirmation of the Truth of the Sacred History, 8vo. *calf gilt,* 6s   1810

466 — 1810. FALCONER'S (T.) Evanson's Dissonance of the Evangelists examined, 8vo. *calf gilt,* 6s—*russia gilt,* 7s   1811

467 — 1811. BIDLAKE'S (J.) on the Truth and Consistency of the Christian Religion, 8vo. *calf gilt,* 5s 6d   .   1813

468 — 1812. MANT'S (Bp.) Reply to the Charge that the Gospel is not preached by the National Clergy, 8vo. *calf gilt,* 7s   1816

469 — 1813. COLLINSON'S (J.) Key to the Writings of the principal Fathers of the Christian Church who flourished during the first Three Centuries, 8vo. *calf gilt,* 9s   .   1813

470 — 1819. MORGAN (H. D.) A compressed view of the Religious Principles and Practices of the Age, 8vo. *bds.* 5s 6d—*calf,* 7s   Oxford, 1819

471 — 1820. FAUSSET'S (G.) Claims of the Established Church to exclusive Attachment and Support, 8vo. *calf gilt,* 7s 6d   1820

472 — 1821. JONES'S (J.) Moral Tendency of Divine Revelation, 8vo. *calf gilt,* 7s   .   .   1821

473 — 1822 WHATELEY (Abp. Rd.) The Use and Abuse of Party-feeling in matters of Religion, 8vo. *bds.* 5s   Oxford, 1822

BAMPTON LECTURES—*continued.*

474 — 1828 HORNE (Tho.) The Religious Necessity of the Reformation asserted, and the extent to which it was carried in the Church of England vindicated, 8vo. *bds.* 5s *Oxford*, 1828
475 — 1836 OGILVIE (C. A.) The Divine Glory manifested in the Conduct and Discourses of our Lord, 8vo. *bds.* 5s *ib.* 1836
476 — 1838 WOODGATE (H. A.) The authoritative teaching of the Church shewn to be in conformity with Scripture, Analogy, and the Moral Condition of Man, 8vo. *bds.* 8s *ib.* 1839

477 BANCROFT'S (Abp.) Dangerous Positions and Proceedings published and practised within this Island of Great Britain, under pretence of Reformation, and for the Presbyterial Discipline, 8vo. *scarce*, 9s 1712
478 BAPTISTERY (The), or the Way of Eternal Life, [by the Rev. Isaac Williams.] Part IV. 8vo. *plates, bds.* 9s *Oxford*, 1844
479 BARBAULD (Anna Lætitia) Devotional Pieces compiled from the Psalms, and the Book of Job : with Thoughts on the Devotional Taste, on Sects, and on Establishments, 8vo. *calf gilt*, 2s 6d 1775
480 BARBEYRAC (Jean) Traité de la Morale des Peres de l'Eglise, où en défendant un article de la preface sur Puffendorf, contre l'Apologie de la Morale des Pere du P. Ceillier, on fait diverses reflexions sur plusieurs matieres importantes, 4to. *sewed, uncut*, 7s—*vellum*, 9s *Amst.* 1728
481 ———— the same, 4to. *fine copy, calf,* 10s 6d *ib.* 1728
482 ———— Recueil de discours sur divers matieres importantes, 2 vols. in 1, 12mo. *calf,* 4s . *ib.* 1731
483 BARBOSÆ (August.) Pastoralis Solicitudinis, sive de Officio, et Potestate Episcopi, &c. folio, *calf, scarce,* £1. 11s 6d *Lugduni,* 1650
484 BARDWELL'S (Wm.) Temples, Ancient and Modern ; or, Notes on Church Architecture, 8vo. LARGE PAPER, *plates, bds.* 14s 1837
485 BARECROFT (Dr. J.) Ars Concionandi ; or, an Instruction to Young Students in Divinity, 8vo. *calf,* 2s 6d . 1715
486 BAHRDT (Car. Fri.) Commentarius in Malachiam, cum examine critico Versionum Veterum, etc. Accedit Specimen Bibliorum Polyglottorum, 8vo. *bds.* 2s . *Lipsiæ,* 1768
487 BARKER (Peter) A judicious and painefull Exposition upon the Ten Commandements, in severall Sermons, 4to. *calf, neat,* 5s 1624
488 ———— A learned and familiar Exposition upon the Ten Commandments, second edition, 4to. *vellum,* 4s 6d 1633
489 BARLÆUS (Caspar.) Dissertatiuncula, in qua aliquot patriæ nostræ Theologorum ac Ecclesiastarum malesana consilia et studia reprehenduntur, 4to. 2s . *Lugd. Bat.* 1616
490 BARLANDUS (Adr.) Rerum gestarum a Brabantiæ Ducibus historia, conscripta usque in annum 1526, &c. 18mo. *neat,* 2s 6d *Lovanii,* 1566
491 BARLOW (John). An Exposition of the Second Epistle to Timothy, the First Chapter, 4to. *vellum, scarce,* 14s . 1625
492 ———— (Tho., Bp. of Linc.) Several miscellaneous and weighty Cases of Conscience, 8vo. *portrait by White, calf, scarce,* 9s 1692

LINCOLN'S INN FIELDS.]

493 BARLOW (Tho.) Traitté historique sur le sujet de l'Excommunication et de la deposition des Roys. [Translated from the English of Bp. Barlow.] 12mo. *green morocco, scarce,* 10s 6d
Par. 1681
From the library of the late Duke of Sussex.

494 ——————— (Dr. Will., *successively Bp. of Rochester and Lincoln*) A Sermon preached at Paule's Crosse, on the First Sunday in Lent, Martij 1, 1600 : with a short account of the late Earle of Essex, his Confession and Penitence before and at the time of his death, &c. 18mo. *hf. bd. calf neat, scarce,* 6s . 1601

495 BARNES (Joshua). The good old way ; or, three brief Discourses tending to the promotion of Religion, &c. small 8vo. *sewed,* 1s 6d
1703

496 BARONII (Card.) Annales Ecclesiastici ad annum 1198, 12 vols. folio, *portrait and engraved title, calf,* £8. 8s *Antverpiæ,* 1610

497 ——————— Annales Ecclesiastici, a Christo nato ad annum 1198, cum A. Pagi criticis et notis J. D. Card. Mansi, 19 vols. *Lucæ,* 1738-46 —Oderici Raynaldi Annales Ecclesiastici ab anno ad 1565, cum notis J. D. Mansi, 15 vols. *ib.* 1747-56—Annalium Ecclesiasticorum Baronii Apparatus, *ib.* 1740—Indices ad Annales Ecclesiasticos Baronii et Raynaldi, 3 vols. *ib.* 1757, *best editions,* together 38 vols. folio, *fine copy, vellum,* £45. . ———

" As an effort of literary labour, the work of Baronius largely demands our admiration. It still maintains a high rank among the works on Church history, and is one of the books which will never be superseded. It is a great repository of materials, and the student can never turn to it without advantage. It affords much which is absolutely indispensable to all who seek a well-grounded acquaintance with ecclesiastical history."—*Dowling's Study of Eccles. Hist.*

498 ——————— L'Abrége des Annales Ecclesiastiques de Cardinal Baronius, faict par Henri de Sponde, Evêque de Pamiez, mis en Francois et continué jusqu'à la fin de l'année 1635, par P. Coppin, 4 vols. in 3, folio, *old red morocco, gilt leaves,* £2. 2s *Par.* 1636-43

499 BARRADII (Sebast. *Soc. Jesu*) Commentaria in Concordiam et Historiam Evangelicam, 4 vols. *Moguntiæ,* 1601—NIC. SERARII, Opuscula Theologica, et Polemica, 3 vols. *ib.* 1611—together 7 vols. in 3, folio, *stamped hogskin, with clasps,* £1. 11s 6d ———

500 BARRE (M. De la) Historia Christiana Veterum Patrum, folio, *calf, very scarce,* £1. 11s 6d . *Par.* 1583
Contains Prochorus, Abdias, Linus, Palladius, Egesippus, Orosius, Bede, Gregory of Tours, and other ecclesiastical writers.

501 BARRINGTON'S (Shute, *Bp. of Durham*) Sermons, Charges, and Tracts, 8vo. *bds.* 4s 6d—*calf gilt,* 6s . 1811

502 BARROW'S (Isaac) Works, 3 vols. folio, *calf,* £1. 10s 1683-86
CONTENTS.—*Vol. I.* XXXII Sermons—An Exposition of the Lord's Prayer—A treatise of the Pope's Supremacy. *Vol. II.* Sermons, and Expositions on the Creed. *Vol. III.* XLV Sermons.

503 ——————— Works, published by Jo. Tillotson, Abp. of Canterbury, 3 vols. in 2, folio, *port. calf,* £1. 11s 6d . 1700

504 ——————— another copy, 3 vols. in 2, folio, *fine copy, calf,* £2. 2s
1722

[58, GREAT QUEEN STREET,

505 BARROW'S (Isaac) Works, with his Life by Abp. Tillotson, *best edition*, 3 vols. in 2, folio, *fine copy, calf, carmine edges, by Hayday, and portrait by Loggan*, £2. 12s 6d .. 1741
506 ———— Works, with his Life, a Summary of each Discourse, and Notes, by T. S. Hughes, 7 vols. sm. 8vo. *calf gilt*, £2. 2s 1830
507 ———— Works complete, including his Sermons and Latin Theological Treatises, Poems, &c. 8 vols. 8vo. *portrait, calf gilt*, £4. 4s
    Clarendon Press, 1830
508 ———— the same, 8 vols. 8vo. *new in calf gilt, lettered contents*, £5. 5s . . *ib.* 1830
509 ———— Sermons selected from his works, 2 vols. 8vo. *hf. bd. calf*, 14s . . *Oxford*, 1810
511 ———— another copy, 2 vols. 8vo. *bds.* 12s *ib.* 1812
512 ———— Sermons preached upon several occasions, 1678—Several Sermons against Evil-Speaking, 1678—Of the Love of God and our Neighbours, in several Sermons, 1680, 3 vols. 8vo. *portraits, calf*, 7s 6d . .
513 ———— The Duty and Reward of Bounty to the Poor, in a Sermon at the Spittal, 12mo. *portrait, calf*, 2s . 1680
514 ———— The Duty and Reward of Bounty to the Poor : in a Sermon at the Spittal, 1680—A Sermon upon the Passion, preached at Guild-Hall Chappel, 1678. In one vol. 12mo. *calf, neat*, 2s 6d

"No man that reads Dr. Barrow upon any subject which he has handled, need rack his invention for topics upon which to speak, or for arguments to make those topics good."—*Wotton*.

515 BARRUEL (l'Abbé) The History of the Clergy during the French Revolution, 3 parts in 1 vol. 8vo. *calf gilt*, 7s 6d 1794
516 ———— Du Pape, et de ses droits religieux, à l'occasion du Concordat, 2 vols. in 1, 8vo. *hf. bd. calf*, 4s 6d . *Par.* 1803
    From the library of the late Duke of Sussex.
517 BARRUFALDI (Hier.) ad Rituale Romanum Commentaria, *best edition*, folio, *hf. bd.* 14s . *Venetiis*, 1763
518 BARTON (Rd.) The Analogy of Divine Wisdom, 12mo. 1s 6d 1750
519 BARUH (Raphael) Critica Sacra examined ; or, an Attempt to shew that a new method may be found to reconcile the seemingly glaring variations in parallel passages of Scripture, 8vo. *sewed*, 2s 1775
520 BASILIUS (S. *Magnus Cæsareæ Archiep.*) Opera Omnia, *Gr. et Lat.* cum Appendice, 3 vols. folio, *fine copy, old red morocco*, £5. 15s 6d . *Paris.* 1618
521 ———— Opera Omnia, *Gr. et Lat.* 3 vols. folio, *hf. bd. calf*, £3. 3s
    ib. 1638
    From the library of the late Duke of Sussex.
522 ———— Opera Omnia, Editio Benedictina, *Gr. et Lat.* studio Jul. Garnier, 3 vols. folio, *fine copy, calf*, £9. 9s *ib.* 1721
523 ———— idem, 3 vols. folio, *fine copy, French calf*, £10. 10s
    ib. 1721
524 ———— Opera Omnia, editio postrema Veneta Latina, juxta novissimam interp. Parisiensem editam a J. Garnier, additis in fine notis selectis Frontonis Ducæi, F. Morelli, &c. 3 vols. folio, *fine copy, vellum*, £3. 10s . *Venet.* 1750

525 BASILIUS (S. *Magnus Archiep. Cæsareæ*) De vera atque incorrupta Virginitate, 4to. *hf. bd. calf*, 3s . *Mediol.* 1573
526 ———— Les Ascetiques, ou traittez spirituels de St. Basile le Grand, traduits et éclaircis par des remarques, par Godefroy Hermant, 8vo. *frontisp. calf,* 6s . *Paris,* 1673
527 ———— Sermons de S. Basile le Grand, avec les Sermons de S. Astere, evèque d'Amasée, traduits du Grec. 8vo. *calf,* 8s *ib.* 1691
528 ———— The Clergie's Honour ; or, the Lives of St. Basil the Great, Abp. of Neo-Cæsarea, and St. Chrysostom, Abp.of Constantinople, drawn by way of parallel, sm. 8vo. *calf,* 4s 1681
529 BASILII (*Seleuciæ Isauriæ Episcopi*) Orationes XLIV. Latine, notis illustravit C. D. Audomarius, 8vo. *fine copy, old French red morocco, gilt leaves,* 10s 6d . *Antverpiæ,* 1604
530 ———— De vita ac miraculis D. Theclæ Virginis Martyris Iconiensis libri duo.—Simeonis Metaphrastæ Logothetæ de eadem Martyre tractatus. P. P. Tiletanus è tenebris eruit, Latinè vertit, notisque illustravit, 4to. *fine copy, calf gilt, scarce,* £1. 4s
Antv. 1608
531 [BASIRE (Isaac)] The History of the Scotch and French Presbytery, wherein is discovered their designs and practices for the subversion of Government in Church and State. Written in French by an eminent divine of the Reformed Church, and now Englished, 8vo. *calf,* 10s . *Villa Franca,* 1660
From the library of the late Duke of Sussex.
532 BATES's (Ely) Rural Philosophy ; or, Reflections on Knowledge, Virtue, and Happiness ; chiefly in reference to a life of retirement in the Country, 8vo. *calf,* 3s . 1805

" As a companion in retirement I strongly recommend Bates's Rural Philosophy, which is a valuable specimen of the moral literature of the nineteenth century."
Bp. Burgess.

533 BATES's (Wm.) Works, with his Life and Funeral Sermon by Howe, *best edition,* folio, *fine copy, cal,* £1. 5s . 1723
534 ———— The four last things : viz. Death, Judgment, Heaven, Hell, practically considered in several discourses, 8vo. *calf,* 3s 1691
535 ———— A Funeral Sermon for the reverend, holy, and excellent divine, Mr. Rd. Baxter, with some account of his Life, 12mo. *portrait,* 2s . . 1692
536 ———— The Danger of Prosperity Discovered, in several sermons upon Prov. i. 27, 8vo. *port. calf,* 3s . 1685
537 ———— the same, 8vo. *portrait, presentation copy, red morocco, gilt leaves,* 8s 6d . 1685
538 ———— The Divinity of the Christian Religion proved by the Evidence of Reason and Divine Revelation, 8vo. *calf,* 2s 1677
539 ———— Spiritual Perfection unfolded and enforced, from 2 Cor. vii. 1, 8vo. *calf,* 4s . 1699
540 BATHER's (*Archd.* Edward) Sermons, chiefly practical, 2 vols. 8vo. *calf,* 8s . . 1827-29
541 BATHURST (Henry, *Bp. of Norwich*) Memoirs of his Life, by the Rev. Hen. Bathurst, LL.D., Archdeacon of Norwich, 2 vols. 8vo. *bds.* 6s
1837

[58, GREAT QUEEN STREET,

542 BATHURST's (Ralph, *Pres. Trin. Coll. Oxon.*) Life and Literary Remains, by Tho. Warton, 8vo. *port.* 5s . 1761
543 BATTY's (Adam) Twenty-six Sermons on various subjects, 2 vols. 8vo. *calf,* 4s 6d . 1739
544 BAXTER (Andrew) The Evidence of Reason in proof of the Immortality of the Soul, 8vo. *bds.* 4s . 1779
545 ———— An Inquiry into the Nature of the Human Soul; wherein the Immateriality of the Soul is evinced from the Principles of Reason and Philosophy, 3 vols. 8vo. *calf,* 12s 1745

"Containing the justest and most precise notions of God and the Soul, and is altogether one of the most finished of its kind."—*Warburton.*

546 ———— Matho; or, the Cosmotheori Puerilis, a Dialogue in which the first principles of Philosophy and Astronomy are accommodated to the capacity of young persons, 2 vols. 8vo. *calf,* 4s 6d 1740
547 BAXTER's (Richard) Practical Works, 4 vols. folio, *portrait and frontispiece, fine copy, hf. bd. russia,* £4. 14s 6d 1707
548 ———— Practical Works, with a Life of the Author, and a critical examination of his Writings by the Rev. W. Orme, 23 vols. 8vo. *portrait, hf. bd. calf, very neat,* £7. 17s 6d 1830
549 ———— Answer to Dr. Edw. Stillingfleet's Charge of Separation, 4to. *sewed,* 2s . 1680
550 ———— Methodus Theologiæ Christianæ, folio, *portrait and engraved title, calf,* 10s 6d . 1681
551 ———— Treatise of Self-denyall, 4to. *stained, and four leaves supplied in MS., scarce, calf,* 3s . 1660
552 ———— The Reasons of the Christian Religion, (*the preface neatly supplied in writing,*) 4to. *portrait, calf, neat,* 6s 1667
553 ———— the same, 4to. *portrait, fine copy, calf,* 8s 1667
554 ———— Certain disputations of right to Sacraments, and the true nature of visible Christianity, 4to. *calf,* 5s 1657
555 ———— Christian Directory; or, a Sum of Practical Theology, and Cases of Conscience, folio, *fine portrait by White, and engraved title, calf,* £1. 1s . 1678
556 ———— More Reasons for the Christian Religion, and No Reason against it, 18mo. 2s . 1672
557 ———— The Life of Faith, 4to. *portrait, calf,* 5s 6d 1670
558 ———— Poetical Fragments, 18mo. *port. bds.* 2s 1821
559 ———— A Call to the Unconverted to turn and live, 18mo. *calf,* 3s 1669
560 ———— Confession of his Faith, 4to. *calf,* 5s 1655
561 ———— The Divine Appointment of the Lord's Day proved, sm. 8vo. 2s . . 1671
562 ———— A Sermon of Repentance preached before the House of Commons, 4to. *hf. bd. neat,* 3s 6d . 1660
563 ———— Two Treatises: the first of Death, the second of Judgment, 12mo. 2s 6d . 1672
564 ———— Universal Redemption of Mankind stated and cleared, with a short account of Special Redemption, sm. 8vo. 3s 1694

564 BAXTER'S (Richard) The Cure of Church-Divisions: or directions for weak Christians, to keep them from being Dividers or Troublers of the Church, sm. 8vo. 3s 6d . 1670
565 ———— A Sermon of Judgment, preached at St. Pauls, 18mo. 2s 1655
566 ———— A Holy Commonwealth, or political Aphorisms, opening the true principles of Government, 8vo. *calf*, 4s 1659
567 ———— The safe Religion, or three disputations for the Reformed Catholike Religion against Popery, sm. 8vo. 3s 1657
568 ———— Directions and Persuasions to a Sound Conversion, 12mo. 3s . . 1658
569 ———— The Reformed Pastor; a discourse on the Pastoral Office: abridged by S. Palmer, 12mo. *bds. scarce*, 3s 1766
570 ———— The mischiefs of Self-Ignorance, and the benefits of Self-Acquaintance, opened in divers Sermons at Dunstan's West, 12mo. *calf*, 3s . . 1662
571 ———— Dialogues on Personal and Family Religion, with forms of Prayer: abridged by Benj. Fawcett, 18mo. *hf. bd. calf*, 1s 6d
Shrewsbury, 1776
572 BAYLY (Benj.) An Essay on Inspiration, 8vo. *calf*, 2s 1707
573 ———— the same, 8vo. *calf*, 2s . 1708
574 ———— Sermons on various subjects, 2 vols. 8vo. *port. calf*, 4s 6d
1721
575 BAYNE (Paul) A Commentarie upon the first and second chapters of St. Paul to the Colossians, 4to. *vellum, scarce*, 12s 1634
Bayne was successor to the celebrated Perkins, " And for the heavenly frame of his spirit; what it was, his incomparable writings will sufficiently demonstrate to all future generations."—*Clarke's Lives.*
576 BEAN'S (James) Family Worship; or a course of Morning and Evening Prayers, for every day in the month, 8vo. *bds.* 5s 6d 1833
577 ———— Parochial Instruction: or Sermons delivered from the pulpit at different times, 8vo. *hf. bd. calf*, 5s . 1817
578 ———— the same, 8vo. *calf*, 6s . 1823
579 BEARD'S (Thomas) Theatre of God's Judgements, collected out of Sacred, Ecclesiasticall, and Prophane Histories, 4to. *fine copy, calf, gilt leaves*, 10s 6d . 1612
Granger says ' Dr. Thos. Taylor was a joint compiler of this volume.'
580 BEATTIE'S (Dr. Jas.) Evidences of the Christian Religion briefly stated, 2 vols. in 1, 12mo. *calf, neat*, 2s 6d . 1786
581 ———— An Essay on the nature and immutability of Truth, in opposition to Sophistry and Scepticism, 8vo. *calf*, 2s 6d 1771
582 BEAUMONT (Christophe de, *Archevêque de Paris*) Instruction pastorale sur les atteintes données à l'autorité de l'église par les jugements des tribunaux séculiers, dans l'affaire des Jésuites, 8vo. *neat*, 3s 6d
1763
583 BEAUTIES OF ENGLAND AND WALES, or Delineations, Topographical, Historical and Descriptive, of each County, by Britton, Brayley, and Brewer, and Introduction by Brewer: together with the BEAUTIES OF SCOTLAND, by R. Forsyth, all on LARGE PAPER, *illustrated with several thousand additional plates, portraits, and numerous original autographs taken from Exchequer Documents, &c.*, 67 vols. roy. 8vo. *splendidly bound in red morocco, gilt leaves, &c.* by Mackenzie, £73. 10s . 1801-1818

[58, GREAT QUEEN STREET,

584 BEAUSOBRE (J. de) Histoire critique de Manichée et du Manicheisme, 2 vols. 4to. *fine copy, vellum,* £2. 12*s* 6*d*—another copy, 2 vols. 4to. *hf. bd. uncut, with MS. notes on the margin,* £2. 5*s Amst.* 1734-39
 "This work of Beausobre, of which I have made great use, contains not only a laboured history of the Manichees, but likewise several entertaining and useful digressions concerning the opinions of the Heathen philosophers, and the most early Christian sects. I wish some learned man might have sufficient license, and encouragement to give us a handsome edition of it in English."— LARDNER.
585 ———— A new version of the Gospel according to St. Matthew; with a literal Commentary on all the difficult passages, &c. Written originally in French, by Messieurs de Beausobre and Lenfant, 8vo. *bds.* 4*s* 6*d* . 1788
586 ———— another copy, 8vo. *calf,* 6*s* . 1823
587 BEAVEN (James) The doctrine of Holy Scripture and of the Primitive Church, on the subject of Religious Celibacy, &c., 2 parts, 8vo. *sewed,* 2*s* . 1840
588 BECKIUS (Matth. Frid.) Paraphrasis Chaldaica I. libri Chronicorum, hactenus inedita et multum desiderata; nunc vero e cod. MSC. ant. membr. Bibl. Rev. Ministerii Erfordiensis exscripta, 4to. *vellum,* 7*s* . *Aug. Vindel.* 1680
589 BECON (Thomas) The Reliques of Rome, contayning all such matters of Religion as have in times past bene brought into the Church by the Pope and his adherentes, 12mo. 𝔟𝔩𝔞𝔠𝔨 𝔩𝔢𝔱𝔱𝔢𝔯, *calf, rare,* 16*s*
 Lond. by John Daye, 1563
590 ———— His early works, being the treatises published by him in the reign of King Henry VIII. Edited by the Rev. John Ayre, royal 8vo. *bds.* 15*s* . *Camb.* 1843
591 BEDÆ (Venerabilis) Opera omnia, 8 vols. in 4, folio, *rough green calf,* £4. 10*s* . *Colon. Agrip.* 1612
592 ———— Opera omnia, *best edition,* 8 vols. in 4, folio, *fine large copy, hogskin, with clasps,* £5. 15*s* 6*d* . *ib.* 1688
593 ———— Historiæ Ecclesiasticæ gentis Anglorum libri quinque, una cum reliquis ejus operibus historicis, cura Jo. Smith, folio, *front. fine copy, new in marbled calf gilt,* £5. *Cantab.* 1722
 The best edition, with learned notes and dissertations. King Alfred's Saxon version is also inserted in this edition.
594 ———— Ecclesiastica Historia Gentis Anglorum Libri V. *Antverpiæ,* 1550—PLATYNA de Vitis Pontificum, (*wants one leaf in the index*) *Venet.* 1518—PONTANUS de Bello Neapolitano et de Sermone, *Neapoli,* 1509, in 1 vol. folio, *in the original oak boards, with clasps,* £1. 5*s* . ———
595 BEDE'S History of the Church of Englande, translated by Tho. Stapleton, *Antw.* 1565—A Fortresse of the Faith, which Protestants call Papistry, by Tho. Stapleton, *Antw.* 1565, *in one vol.* 4to. *calf, very rare,* £1. 11*s* 6*d* 1565
596 ———— The Ecclesiastical history of the English Nation, from the coming of Julius Cæsar, till 731. [Translated by Jo. Stevens.] with a Life of the author and notes, 8vo. *calf,* 18*s* 1723
597 ———— The Ecclesiastical history of the English Nation, collated with the original text, and revised, by J. A. Giles, LL.D. 8vo, *half bound, morocco, uncut,* 12*s* . 1845
598 ———— Biographical writings and Letters; translated by J. A. Giles, LL.D. 8vo. *hf. bd. morocco, uncut,* 10*s* 6*d* 1845
LINCOLN'S INN FIELDS.]

599 BEDE's (Venerable) Historical Works, 2 vols. 8vo. *hf. bd. morocco, uncut,* £1. 1s . . 1845
600 ——— The Complete Works of the Venerable Bede, in the original Latin, with a new English translation of the historical works, and a life of the author, by the Rev. J. A. Giles, D.C.L. &c. 12 vols. 8vo. *bds.* £5. 5s . 1843-44
601 BEDFORD's (Arthur) Scripture Chronology demonstrated by Astronomical calculations, &c., folio, *maps and plates, calf,* 14s 1730
"A very elaborate work, and displays much learning and research."—*Orme.*
602 ——— Hereditary Right of the Crown of England asserted, and the true English Constitution vindicated from the Misrepresentations of Dr. Higden's View and Defence, folio, *calf,* 7s 6d 1743
603 ——— A Serious Remonstrance in behalf of the Christian Religion, against the horrid blasphemies still used in the English Playhouses, 8vo. *calf, scarce,* 4s . 1719
604 BEDWELL's (Will.) Mohammedis Imposturæ: that is, a discovery of the manifold forgeries, and horrible impieties of the blasphemous seducer Mohammed; with a demonstration of the insufficiencie of his law, contained in the cursed Alkoran, sm. 4to. *sewed,* 2s 1615
605 BEE HIVE of the Romish Church (by Isaac Rabbotenu). a worke of all good Catholiks too be read and understoode, wherein the Catholike Religion is confirmed, and the Heretikes finely fetcht over the coales. Translated out of Dutch, by George Gilpin the Elder, 12mo. black letter, *vellum, rare,* 14s London, 1598
With the autograph of "White Kennett," Bp. of Peterborough.
606 BEESTON's (Edmund) Practical Sermons and Discourses upon several subjects, 8vo. *calf,* 3s 6d 1739
607 BEHMEN (Jacob) The four complexions: or, a treatise of consolatory instruction against the time of temptation, 12mo. *sewed,* 1s ———
608 BELGIC CONFESSION.—Ecclesiæ Belgicæ Confessio, Catechismus, Liturgia, et Canones, *Græcè,* 4to. *a very fine copy in russia, gilt leaves, from the library of Dr. Samuel Parr, with his autograph,* 18s Lugd. Bat. apud Elzivirios, 1648
609 [BELL (W.) D.D.] A defence of Revelation in general and the Gospel in particular, in answer to a book entitled the Morality of the New Testament, 8vo. *calf,* 3s . 1766
610 ——— An attempt to ascertain and illustrate the authority, nature, and design of the Lord's Supper, 8vo. *sewed,* 1s 6d 1781
611 BELLAMY's (D.) Family Preacher: consisting of practical discourses for every Sunday in the Year, &c., 2 vols. 8vo. *front. calf,* 5s 1754
"A truly valuable collection."
612 ——— The truth and safety of the Christian Religion, a series of Sermons at Kew and Petersham: with his paraphrase on the book of Job, 4to. *portrait, boards,* 5s 6d . 1789
613 BELLARMINUS (Rob. *Card.*) Disputationes de Controversiis Christianæ Fidei adversus hujus temporis Hæreticos, cum totius Operis recognitione ab eodem facta. Accedit Appendix Monumentorum Ecclesiasticorum ad Quæstiones Polemicas de recentioribus Erroribus perquam utilis, &c. 4 vols. 4to. *French calf gilt,* £7. 17s 6d
Romæ, 1832-40
614 ——— de Indulgentiis et Jubileo, &c., sm. 8vo. *nt.* 3s 6d Par. 1599

[58, GREAT QUEEN STREET,

615 BELLARMINUS (Rob. *Card.*) Vita Rob. Card. Bellarmini e Soc. Jesu, Italice scripta a Jac. Fuligatto, Latine reddita a Silv. Petra Sancta, 4to. *calf*, 5s . *Leodii*, 1626
616 BENEDICTUS (S.) Pratique de la Regle de S. Benoist, *Par.* 1700— La Regle du B. Pere S. Benoist, *ib.* 1729—Conduite pour la retraite du Mois, *ib.* 1700, in one vol. 12mo. *neat*, 2s 6d ———
617 ——— Pratique de la regle de S. Benoist, *Par.* 1700—Conduite pour la Retraite du Mois, *ib.* 1700—Regula Sanctissimi P. Benedicti, *ib.* 1681. In one vol. 12mo. *neat*, 2s 6d ———
618 BENGELIUS (———) Introduction to his Exposition of the Apocalypse, with a summary of the whole exposition. Translated from the High Dutch by J. Robertson, M.D. 8vo. *rough calf*, 2s 6d   1757
" I never quote this excellent writer, without admiring the abilities which have exalted him so much above all his predecessors in the critical knowledge of the New Testament."—*Michaelis.*
619 BENJOIN'S (George) Jonah, a faithful translation, from the original, with Philological and Explanatory Notes, and a Preliminary Discourse, proving the Genuineness, Authenticity, and the Integrity of the present Text, 4to. *bds.* 3s 6d—*hf. bd. calf*, 4s 6d *Camb.* 1796
620 ——— The integrity and excellence of Scripture, a vindication of Deut. vii. 2. 5. and xx. 16. 17., in answer to Tho. Paine and Dr. Geddes, 8vo. *bds.* 1s 6d . *ib.* 1797
621 BENNET (Benj.) Several discourses against Popery, 8vo. *calf*, 5s 1714
622 ——— The Truth, Inspiration, and Usefulness of the Scriptures asserted and proved in several discourses on 2d Tim. iii. 16., 8vo. *calf*, 3s 6d . . 1730
623 ——— A Memorial of the Reformation (chiefly in England) and of Britain's deliverances from Popery and arbitrary power, 8vo. *calf*, 5s 6d . 1721
624 ——— The Christian Oratory; or the devotion of the closet displayed, 8vo. *port. hf. bd. calf*, 5s 6d   1760
625 ——— (Dr. James) The Theology of the Early Christian Church, exhibited in quotations from the writers of the first three centuries, with reflections, 8vo. *bds.* 5s 6d . 1841
626 ——— (Tho.) Works, viz.: A Discourse of Schism, *Camb.* 1704— A defence of the discourse of Schism, in answer to Mr. Shepherd, *ib.* 1709—An answer to Mr. Shepherd's considerations of the Defence of the Discourse of Schism, *ib.* 1709—A brief History of the joint use of set forms of Prayer, with a Discourse of the gift of Prayer, *ib.* 1708—A Discourse of Joint Prayer, *ib.* 1708—A Confutation of Quakerism, *ib.* 1709—A Letter to Mr. B. Robinson, occasioned by his review of the case of Liturgies and their Imposition, *Lond.* 1710—A second Letter to Mr. B. Robinson, *ib.* 1710— The Rights of the Clergy of the Christian Church, *ib.* 1711—An Answer to the Dissenters Pleas for Separation; or, an Abridgement of the London Cases, *ib.* 1711—Directions for studying I. a general System of Divinity—II. The XXXIX. Articles, with S. Jerome's Epistle to Nepotianus, *ib.* 1715, together 7 vols. 8vo. *calf*, *neat*, £2. 2s . ———
627 ——— A Brief History of the joint use of precomposed set forms of Prayer, with a Discourse of the Gift of Prayer, 8vo. *calf*, 6s *Camb.* 1708

628 BENNET'S (Tho.) Works, viz.—A brief History of the joint use of precomposed Forms of Prayer, with a Discourse of the Gift of Prayer, *Camb.* 1708—A Discourse of Joint Prayer, *ib.* 1708—A Paraphrase on the Common Prayer, *Lond.* 1709—The Rights of the Clergy, *ib.* 1711—AConfutation of Popery, *ib.* 1714—A Confutation of Quakerism, *Camb.* 1709, together 3 vols. 8vo. *calf*, 15s
629 ———— A Confutation of Quakerism, 8vo. *calf*, 3s   *Camb.* 1705
630 ———— A Confutation of Popery, 8vo. *calf*, 4s 6d   *ib.* 1701
631 ———— A Paraphrase, with Annotations, upon the Book of Common Prayer, 8vo. *calf*, 6s . 1708
632 ———— the same, 8vo. *calf*, 6s . 1709
633 ———— An Answer to the Dissenters' Pleas for Separation; or, an Abridgement of the London Cases, 8vo. *calf*, 2s 6d   *Camb.* 1700
634 ———— An Answer to the Dissenters' Pleas, &c. 8vo. *fine copy, calf*, 3s 6d . . *ib.* 1707
635 ———— An Answer to the Dissenters' Pleas for Separation; or, an abridgement of the London Cases, *Camb.* 1701—A Confutation of Popery, *ib.* 1701, in one vol. 8vo. *calf*, 6s
636 ———— A Discourse of the ever-blessed Trinity in Unity, with an Examination of Dr. Clarke's Scripture Doctrine of the Trinity, 8vo. *calf*, 2s 6d . . 1718
637 BENOIST (Elie) Mélange de remarques critiques, historiques, philosophiques, theologiques, sur les deux Dissertations de M. Toland, intitulées L'Homme sans Superstition, et les Origines Judaiques, &c. 8vo. *old calf gilt*, 3s . *Delf*, 1712
638 ———— Adversus Epistolam Taco Hajo Van den Honert de Stylo Novi Test. amica expostulatio, *Delfis*, 1703—Abr. Boddens Epistola ad T. H. van den Honert, qua de occasione et editione libri memorialis E. Benoist quem falso inscripsit Memoires des Raisons, qui ont porté le Synode des Eglises Wallones des Provinces—Unies des Pais-Bas, &c. veriora narrantur, *Amst.* 1703. In one vol. 4to. *sewed*, 2s . . 1703
639 BENSON'S (George) History of the Life of Jesus Christ, taken from the New Testament, with Observations and Reflections, and the Life of the Author, 4to. *portrait, calf*, 8s . 1764
640 ———— (Martin) Sermons on various subjects, moral and theological, 8vo. *calf*, 3s . 1794
641 BENTHAM'S (Edw.) Sermon before the House of Commons, Jan. 30, 1749-50, *Oxford*, 1750—A Letter to a Young Gentleman at Oxford, 1749—A Letter to a Fellow of a College, 1749. In one vol. 8vo. *calf*, 2s 6d
642 BENTLEY'S (Dr. Richard) Remarks upon a late discourse of Freethinking, 8vo. *hf. bd. calf*, 2s 6d . 1737
643 ———— A Dissertation upon the Epistles of Phalaris, with an Answer to the Objections of the Hon. Charles Boyle, 8vo. *calf*, 4s
1699
644 ———— the same; to which is added, Dr. Bentley's Dissertation on the Epistles of Themistocles, Socrates, Euripides, &c. and the Fables of Æsop, *best edition*, 8vo. *calf*, 7s   1777
645 ———— A view of Dr. Bentley's Dissertation upon the Epistles of Phalaris, Themistocles, &c. 8vo. *calf*, 2s . 1698

J. LESLIE'S CATALOGUE. 41

646 BENTLEY (Dr. Rd.). Two Letters to Dr. Bentley, concerning his intended edition of the Greek Testament, with his Answer, 8vo. *sewed*, 1s . . 1717

647 BERAULT-BERCASTEL (———) Histoire générale de l'Eglise jusqu'au Pontificat de Grégoire XVI. La continuation (depuis l'an 1719 jusqu'à l'an 1843) par le Baron Henrion, 13 vols. 8vo. *sewed*, £2. 18s . 1843-44

648 BERENS's (Edw., *Archd. of Berks*) Village Sermons on the chief Articles of Faith, on the Christian Character, and on some of the Relative Duties, 12mo. *bds*. 3s . 1837

649 ———— Twenty-six Village Sermons, 12mo. *bds*. 5s 1840

650 BERINGTON's (S.) Dissertations on the Mosaical Creation, Deluge, Building of Babel, and Confusion of Tongues, 8vo. *calf*, 4s 1750
The production of a Roman Catholic writer, and displays considerable research.

651 BERKELEY's (Geo. *Bp. of Cloyne*) Three Dialogues between Hylas and Philonous in opposition to Sceptics and Atheists, 8vo. *calf*, 2s 1725

652 ———— another copy, 8vo. *hf. bd. calf*, 1s 6d 1776

653 ———— A Treatise concerning the principles of Human Knowledge, and three Dialogues between Hylas and Philonous, 1734— The Analyst; or a Discourse addressed to an infidel Mathematician, 1734—A Defence of Free-thinking in Mathematics, 1735—in 1 vol. 8vo. *calf*, 5s . ——

654 ———— Alciphron; or the Minute Philosopher, 2 vols. 1732—A Miscellany, containing several Tracts on various subjects, 1752— Six Tracts on Tar-water, by Bp. Berkeley and others, 1744, &c. 4 vols. 8vo. *fine copies, old calf gilt*, 16s . ——

655 ———— Alciphron, or the Minute Philosopher, 2 vols. 8vo. *calf, neat*, 6s . . *Lond.* 1732
This masterly work is written in a series of seven dialogues on the model of Plato, a philosopher of whom the author is said to have been very fond; and it professes to be " an apology for the Christian Religion, against those who are called Freethinkers," whom he pursues through the various characters, of atheist, libertine, enthusiast, scorner, critic, metaphysician, fatalist, and sceptic. The Rev. John Ryland, says of it that " it is such a glorous defence of revelation, as every man of taste will wish if possible to read at once." It should be observed that his first English work, called " an Essay towards a new Theory of Vision," and first published in 1709, is reprinted at the end of the second volume of this, for reasons which he has given in the fourth dialogue. Of this Essay Dr. Reid observes, " that it was the first attempt that ever was made to distinguish the immediate and natural objects of sight, from the conclusions we have been accustomed to draw from them; and of all the author's works this seems to do the greatest honour to his sagacity."

656 BERNARD (James, *of Leyden*) on the Excellence of the Christian Religion, translated from the French, with the life of the Author, and notes by the translator, Mr. Bernard of Doncaster, 8vo. *calf*, 5s 6d . *York*, 1793

657 BERNARDUS (S.) Melliflui devotique doctoris Sancti Bernardi Opus preclarum suos complectens Sermones de tempore, de Sanctis, et super Cantica Canticorum, ceteraque universa ejus opuscula—Domini quoque Gilleberti Abbatis de Hoilanda in Anglia super Cantica Sermones, folio, **black letter**, *fine copy, in antique calf*, £2. 2s
Paris. 1517
From the Library of the late Dr. Southey.

658 BERNARDUS (S. *Claræ Vallensis Abbatis*) Opera Omnia, *Editio Benedictina*, edidit J. Mabillon, 2 vols. folio, *best edition, very neat*, £3. 13s 6d . *Paris*, 1719
659 ———— Four Homilies upon the Incarnation of our Lord Jesus Christ, commonly called super Missus est, 12mo. *bds. 2s Edinb.* 1843
660 BERNINO (Domenico) Historia di tutte l'heresie, 4 vols. folio, *vellum*, £2. 12s 6d . *Roma*, 1705-9

With the autograph of " Robert Southey, Edinburgh, Oct. 1805."

661 BERRIMAN'S (Will.) Christian Doctrines and Duties, explained and recommended in fifty-nine Sermones, 3 vols. 8vo. *calf*, 8s 1751-63
662 BERTHEAU (Charles, *Pasteur de l'Eglise Françoise de Londres*) Sermons sur divers textes de l'Ecriture Sainte, 2 vols. 8vo. *calf*, 6s *Amst.* 1712-30
663 BERTOLD (Frater) Horalogium Devotionis, 𝔅lack letter, *curious woodcuts*—— De vita et beneficiis salvatoris Jhesu Cristi devotissime meditationes cum gratiarum actione, 𝔅lack letter, 2 vols. in 1, 16mo. *red morocco, gilt leaves*, 18s
[*Coloniæ, Iliskyrchen, circa* 1482]
664 BERTRAM, or *Ratramn*. The Book of Ratramn the Priest and Monk of Corbey, on the body and blood of the Lord, *English* and *Latin;* to which is added, the Saxon Homily of Ælfric, 12mo. 2s 6d
Oxford, 1838
665 BERTUS (Jo. Laur.) Theologia historico-dogmatico-scholastica, seu libri de theologis disciplinis, 10 vols. in 5, folio, *hogskin, with clasps*, £2. 12s 6d . *Monachii*, 1750

This author was one of the most learned of the Augustine order; he was Prefect of the celebrated Anglican Library at Florence, and subsequently Professor of Theology at Pisa. His system of Theology was attacked by the Jesuits, as reviving the errors of Jansenius; but on his reply, which forms the two last volumes, the author establishes the difference between the doctrines of Augustine and Jansenius.

666 BESSE (Pierre le) Conceptions Theologiques sur le Caresme, preschées a Paris en l'Eglise de St. Severin l'an 1602, 8vo. *neat*, 4s
Cambray, 1618
667 BEST (Hon. Sam.) Pietas Domestica ; Family Prayers and Discourses for Sundays and Holydays, 12mo. *bds.* 4s 1843
668 ———— Parochial Sermons on subjects engaging the attention of the Day, 12mo. *bds.* 3s . 1836
669 ———— Parochial Ministrations, 12mo. *bds.* 3s 1839
670 BETHELL (Chr. *Bp. of Bangor*) A general view of the Doctrine of Regeneration in Baptism, 8vo. *bds.* 9s . 1845
671 BEVERIDGE'S (Wm. *Bp. of St. Asaph*) Works, with a Memoir of the author, and critical examination of his Writings, by Tho. H. Horne, 9 vols. 8vo. *portrait, calf gilt, very scarce*, £6. 16s 6d 1824
672 ———— Theological Works, comprising his Sermons and Discourse upon the XXXIX Articles, 7 vols. 8vo. *bds.* £3. 17s
Oxford, 1844-6
673 ———— Ecclesia Anglicanum Ecclesia Catholica ; or, the Doctrine of the Church of England consonant to Scripture, Reason, and Fathers, in a Discourse upon the XXXIX Articles, *new edition*, 8vo. *bds.* 8s . *ib.* 1846

674 BEVERIDGE (Wm. Bp. of St. Asaph) A Sermon, concerning the excellency of the Common Prayer, 18mo. 2s 6d 1683
675 ———·—— Sermons on the Ministry and Ordinances of the Church of England, 12mo. bds. 2s 6d . Oxford, 1842
676 ———— Sixteen Discourses, abridged from his works by the Rev. G. H. Glasse, with a Supplement, 8vo. bds. scarce, 5s 6d 1805
677 ———— Private Thoughts upon Religion, 18mo. 1s 1710
678 ———— Private Thoughts on Religion, portrait, 1709—The great necessity and advantage of public Prayer and frequent Communion, portrait, 1708, in 1 vol. 8vo. calf, neat, 4s 6d ——
679 ———— ΣΥΝΟΔΙΚΟΝ, sive Pandectæ Canonum SS. Apostolorum et Conciliorum ab Ecclesia Græca receptorum; necnon Canonicarum SS. Patrum Epistolarum : Gr. et Lat. 2 vols. fol. RARE, calf, £8. 8s. Oxon. 1672
680 ———— Codex Canonum Ecclesiæ Primitivæ Vindicatus ac illustratus, 4to. calf, scarce, 14s . Lond. 1678
"Eoque sententiam suam de Ætate Canonum, uti adpellantur, Apostolicorum contra adversarium quendam defendet."—Walch.
681 BEZA (Theod.) Ad Nic. Selnecceri et Theologorum Jenensium calumnias responsio, 12mo. sewed, 4s 6d Genevæ, 1571
682 ———— Tractatus pius et moderatus de vera Excommunicatione et Christiano Presbyterio, contra Th. Erastum, 4to. vellum, 2s 6d ib. 1590
683 ———·—— Poemata varia, 18mo. calf, 3s 6d ib. 1592
684 BIBLIOTHECA Patrum Ascetica, sive selecta Veterum Patrum de Christiana ac Religiosa perfectione Opuscula, studio ac labore D. C. Chantelou, 5 vols. 4to. calf, £1. 11s 6d Par. 1661-3
685 BIBLIOTHECA Veterum Patrum et Auctorum Ecclesiasticorum ; per MARGARINUM DE LA BIGNE collecti ; editione quarta, nunc præter multorum librorum accessionem, qui in Catalogis asterisco notantur, duobus tomis Græco-Latinis aucta, qui Græcos auctores utraque Lingua editos complectuntur, 12 vols. in 9, folio, fine copy, hf. bd. calf, £6. 6s . ib. 1624
686 ———— MAGNA BIBLIOTHECA VET. PATRUM, et antiq. Scriptorum Ecclesiasticorum, primo quidem a M. De la Bigne composita; postea studio Doctissimorum Coloniensium Theolog. ac Professor. aucta; nunc vero additione ducentorum circiter Authorum tam Græcorum, qui in editione Coloniensi, quam Latinorum qui in Parisiensibus desiderabantur, locupletata, et accuratissimè emendata, &c. 17 vols. in 15, folio, fine copy, calf, £14. 14s ib. 1654
687 ———— MAXIMA BIBLIOTHECA VETERUM PATRUM et antiq. Scriptorum Ecclesiasticorum, primo a M. de la Bigne in lucem edita, deinde celeb. in Universitate Coloniensi studio aucta et disposita, ed. PHILL. DESPONT, cum Indice locorum S. Scripturæ, a Simeone a S. Cruce, 28 vols. in 23, folio, hogskin, with clasps, £35. ib. 1677, &c.
688 ———— Collectio Selecta S.S. Ecclesiæ Patrum; complectens exquitissima Opera tum dogmatica et moralia, tum apologetica et oratoria; accurantibus D. Caillau, Missionum Gallicarum Presbytero, &c. 12 vols. 8vo. sewed, £1. 16s ib. 1829
Contains the Apostolic Fathers, also Irenæus, Minucius Felix, Clemens Alexandrinus, Hippolytus, Tertullian, Origen, &c. with copious Indexes.

689 BIBLIOTHEQUE Portative des Peres de l'Eglise, par M. Tricolet, 9 vols. 8vo. *calf,* £1. 16s . *Par.* 1758
690 BIBLIOTHECA Fratrum Polonorum quos Unitarios vocant ; viz.— F. Socini, Jo. Crellii, Jonæ Sclichtingii, et Jo. Lud. Wolzogenii, Opera, quæ omnia simul juncta totius Novi Testamenti explicationem complectantur, 8 vols. folio, *vellum,* £5. 5s
Irenopoli [*Amst.*] 1656
691 BICKERSTETH (Edw.), The Christian Hearer : designed to shew the importance of hearing the Word, &c. 12mo. *calf gilt,* 4s 1826
692 —————— the same, 12mo. *morocco, gilt leaves,* 5s 1829
693 —————— A Treatise on Prayer, 12mo. *morocco, gilt leaves,* 6s 1830
694 —————— the same, 12mo. *bds.* 4s 6d . 1834
695 —————— A Treatise on the Lord's Supper, 12mo. *morocco, gilt leaves,* 6s . . 1830
696 —————— The Christian Student, designed to assist Christians in general in acquiring Religious Knowledge ; with lists of books, 12mo. *calf gilt,* 7s . . 1832
697 BIDDULPH's (Theoph.) Plain and Practical Sermons, 3 vols. 12mo. *bds.* 3s 6d . *Bristol,* 1835—*Lond.* 1838-39
698 —————— (Tho. T.) Practical Essays on the Morning and Evening Services, and on the Collects, in the Liturgy of the Church of England, 3 vols. 8vo. *hf. bd. calf,* 10s . 1822
699 BILSON (Tho. *Bp. of Winchester*), The perpetual Government of Christ's Church, with a biographical notice by the Rev. Robert Eden, 8vo. *hf. bd. calf, neat,* 10s 6d *Oxford,* 1842
700 BILSTONE's (John) Thirteen Sermons before the University of Oxford, 8vo. *calf,* 2s . *ib.* 1749
701 —————— Grace considered in its Operations, &c., a Sermon before the University, *Oxford,* 1756—A Fast Sermon, *ib.* 1758—A Sermon at St. Martin's, Oxford, on the day of the interment of Tho. Rowney, Esq. 1759—The Nature and Excellence of Christian Zeal, a Sermon, 1761—A Sermon at the Consecration of Chislehampton Church, 1763—The Ignorance of the Jewish Church, as to the extent of their Institution, a Sermon before the University of Oxford, 1763, in one vol. 8vo. *calf,* 2s
702 BINGHAM's (Joseph) Origines Ecclesiasticæ ; or, the Antiquities of the Christian Church, 10 vols. 8vo. *maps, calf,* £2. 12s 6d
1708
703 —————— Origines Ecclesiasticæ, *new edition,* with Two Sermons, and Two Letters on the Nature and Necessity of Absolution, and an enlarged analytical Index, 2 vols. imp. 8vo. *bds.* £1. 10s
1845
704 —————— Works, viz. Origines Ecclesiasticæ, Scholastical History of Lay-Baptism, the French Churches' Apology for the Church of England, Discourses, &c. 2 vols. folio, *maps, calf, fine copy,* £3. 13s 6d . . 1726
705 —————— Works, *new edition,* with all the Quotations at length, in the original languages, and a Memoir of the Author, revised and corrected by the Rev. J. R. Pitman, 9 vols. 8vo. *maps, cloth bds.* £4. 14s 6d - *calf gilt,* £6. 6s . 1844

706 BINGLEY (Will., *Quaker*) A Faithful Warning once more to the Inhabitants of England, 4to. *sewed*, 1s . 1690
707 BIOGRAPHY. THE ANNUAL BIOGRAPHY AND OBITUARY, from the commencement in 1817 to the end of 1836, 21 vols. 8vo. *hf. bd. calf gilt*, £5. 5s . 1817-37
708 ———— British Biography; or, an accurate Account of the Lives and Writings of Eminent Persons in Great Britain and Ireland, from Wickliff to the present time, 10 vols. 8vo. *portraits, calf*, £1. 16s . . 1773
709 ———— A Select Collection of Biographies, comprising the Life of Alfred the Great, by Bicknell, 1777—Annual Necrology for 1797-8—R. Bathurst, by Warton, *port.* 1761—Edm. Burke, by Bisset, 2 vols. 1800—H. Blair, by Hill, 1807—Sir Wm. Blackstone, 1782—Jo. Calvin, by Mackenzie, *port.* 1809—Catherine II. of Russia, *port.* 2 vols. 1799—Catherine II., by Castera, *port.* 1800—T. A. D'Aubigne, 1772—Edward the Black Prince, *port.* 1776—N. Ferrar, by Peckard, *port.* 1790—Frederick II., by Latrobe, 1788—Benj. Franklin, 1793—James Hervey, by Ryland, *port.* 1790—Henry Prince of Wales, by Birch, 1760—D. Hume, by Ritchie, 1807—Jo. Jortin, by Disney, 1792—Leland, Hearne, and Wood, *portraits*, 2 vols. 1772—S. Medley, *port*, 1800—Mary Queen of Scots, by Whitaker, 3 vols. 1790—Metastasio, by Burney, *port.* 3 vols. 1795—Philip II. of Spain, by Watson, 3 vols. 1779—Pope Pius VI. 2 vols. 1799—Peter the Great, by Stæhelin, 1788—Philip King of Macedon, by Leland, 2 vols. in 1, 1806—Rob. Robinson, by Dyer, *port.* 1796—Scipio Africanus, and Epaminondas, 2 vols. 1787—Servetus, by Chaufepie, 1771—Suworow, by Anthing, *port.* 2 vols. 1799—A. A. Sykes, by Disney, 1785—Dr. J. Swift, by Sheridan, *port.* 1787—Thuanus, by Collinson, 1807—Abp. Tillotson, by Birch, 1753—Is. Watts, by Gibbon, 1780—together 47 vols. 8vo. *uniformly bound in calf, marbled leaves*, £5. 15s 6d . V. Y.
710 BIRD'S (Cha. Smith) Defence of the Principles of the English Reformation from the Attacks of the Tractarians, 8vo. *bds.* 5s 1843
711 BIRD'S (Edw.) Fate and Destiny inconsistent with Christianity, or the Horrid Decree of absolute Election and Reprobation fully detected, 8vo. *calf*, 2s . 1726
712 ———— (Geo.) Hints for the revival of Scriptural Principles in the Anglican Church, 8vo. *bds.* 4s . 1842
713 BISCOE'S (Richard) History of the Acts of the Holy Apostles, confirmed from other authors, and considered as full evidence of the Truth of Christianity; being the substance of Sermons at the Boyle Lecture in 1736-7-8, 8vo. *calf gilt*, 12s Oxford, 1829
714 BISHOP.—The Reformed Bishop desiring union; or, XIX. Articles humbly proposed by a well-wisher of the peace of the Church, 8vo. *calf*, 3s . . 1689
715 BISHOP'S (Sam.) Sermons, chiefly upon practical subjects, 8vo. *bds.* 2s 6d . . 1798
716 ———— (Wm.) Village Sermons on Personal and Relative Duties, the Sacrament, &c. 2 vols. 12mo. *bds.* 3s Oxford, 1828

717 BISSE's (Tho.) Beauty of Holiness in the Common Prayer: four Sermons at the Rolls Chapel, 8vo. *calf*, 3s 1716
718 ——————— another copy, 8vo. 1s 6d . 1717
719 ——————— another copy, with the Christian use of the World, a Sermon, 1707—A Sermon before the University of Oxford, 1712—An Assize Sermon, 1711—The merit of Building Churches, a Sermon, 1712—A Sermon before the University of Oxford, 1713—A Sermon before the University of Oxford, 1708—REEVES' (William) Funeral Sermon on the Queen, 1714—An Assize Sermon, 1713—Three Sermons before the Queen, 1713 - BURSCOUGH's (William) Sermon at the Consecration of Richard Bp. of Gloucester, 1715—The Revolution recommended to our Memories, a Sermon, 1715—A Sermon before the House of Commons, May 29, 1716—A Sermon before the King, May 29, 1715—BENTLEY (Richard) A Sermon before the King, 1717—A Sermon on Popery, preached before the University of Cambridge, Nov. 5, 1715, *Camb.* 1715, in 1 vol. 8vo. *calf*, 5s . . v. Y.
720 ——————— Decency and Order in Publick Worship recommended, in three Discourses, 8vo. *sewed*, 1s 6d . 1723
721 ——————— another copy, LARGE PAPER, 8vo. *calf*, 3s 6d 1723
722 BLACKBURNE's (Fra., *Archd. of Cleveland*) Considerations on the present state of the Controversy between the Protestants and Papists of Great Britain and Ireland, 8vo. *bds.* 2s—*calf*, 3s 1768
723 ——————— another copy, 8vo. *red morocco*, 6s 1768
724 BLACKALL's (Ofspring, *Bp. of Exeter*) Works, consisting of Eighty-seven practical Discourses on the Sermon on the Mount; his Sermons at Boyle's Lecture, and several others; with a preface giving some account of the author, by Abp. Dawes, 2 vols. folio, *portrait, calf*, 15s . . 1723
725 ——————— Practical Discourses upon our Saviour's Sermon on the Mount, 8 vols. 8vo. *portrait, calf*, 12s . 1717
"His manner of preaching was so *excellently easy, clear, judicious, substantial, pious, affecting,* and upon all accounts *truly useful and edifying*, that he universally acquired the reputation of being one of the best preachers of his time."
Abp. Dawes.
726 BLACKMORE's (Sir Rich.) Redemption: a divine poem in six books, 8vo. *calf*, 2s 6d . 1722
727 ——————— Essays upon several subjects, 2 vols. 8vo. *calf*, 4s 1716-17
728 ——————— Just Prejudices against the Arian Hypothesis, 8vo. *sewed*, 1s 6d . . 1721
729 ——————— (R. W.) Doctrine of the Russian Church, being the Primer or Spelling Book, the Catechisms, and a Treatise on the Duty of Parish Priests; translated from the Slavono-Russian originals, 8vo. *bds.* 10s 6d . 1845
730 BLACKWALL's (A.) Sacred Classics defended and illustrated, 2 vols. 12mo. *portrait, calf*, 4s . 1737
731 BLACKWALL (Ant.) Auctores sacri classici defensi et illustrati, sive critica sacra Novi Testamenti. Chr. Wollius ex Anglico Latine vertit, observationibus locupletavit, et Hermeneuticam N. F. dogmaticam adjunxit, 4to. *portrait, calf, neat*, 5s 6d *Lips.* 1736
732 BLACKWOOD (Christopher) A treatise concerning Deniall of Christ, 4to. *hf. bd. calf, neat*, 4s . 1648

733 BLAIR's (Hugh) Sermons, with his Life by James Finlayson, D.D. 5 vols. 8vo. *tree marbled calf gilt*, £1. 11s 6d 1777-1801
734 ———— Companion to the Altar, chiefly selected from his works, 24mo. 1s 6d . 1826
735 ———— (James) Sermons and Discourses on our Saviour's Divine Sermon on the Mount, with a Paraphrase on the whole, and a recommendatory Preface by Dr. Waterland, *best edition*, 4 vols. 8vo. *fine copy, rich calf gilt, in the Montagu style*, £2. 5s 1740
736 ———— (John) Lectures on the Canon of the Scriptures, comprehending a dissertation on the Septuagint version, 4to. *bds.* 3s 6d 1785
738 BLAKE's (Thomas) Works: viz. Vindiciæ Fœderis; or, a Treatise of the Covenant of God with Mankind, and the Covenant Sealed, or a Treatise of the Sacraments of both Covenants, 2 vols. 4to. *calf*, 7s 6d 1653-55
739 BLAKEWAY (Rob.) An Essay towards the Cure of Religious Melancholy, 8vo. 1s 6d . . 1717
740 BLAND's (Dr. M.) Annotations on the Gospels of St. Matthew and St. Mark, 2 vols. in 1, 8vo. *bds.* 4s 6d, *pub. at* £1. 2s *Camb.* 1828-29
741 BLOMFIELD's (Cha. James, *Bp. of London*) Sermons at St. Botolph Bishopsgate, 8vo. *hf. bd. calf*, 6s . 1830
742 ———— A Dissertation upon the Traditional Knowledge of a Promised Redeemer which subsisted before the Advent of our Saviour, 8vo. *bds. scarce*, 6s . *Camb.* 1819
743 BLUNT's (Gregory) Six more Letters to Granville Sharp, Esq. on his Remarks upon the uses of the Article in the Greek Testament, 8vo. *sewed*, 1s 6d . 1803
744 ———— Discourses upon some of the Doctrines and Articles of the Church of England, 12mo. *bds.* 3s . 1835
745 ———— Two Discourses on the Trial of the Spirits, 12mo. *sewed*, 1s 1834
746 ———— An Introduction to a course of Lectures on the Early Fathers, 8vo. *sewed*, 1s 6d . *Camb.* 1840
747 BOETHIUS (A. M. S.) Consolationis Philosophiæ libri V. et Opuscula Sacra, cum notis variorum, 8vo. *calf, fine copy*, 6s *Lugd. Bat.* 1671
748 BOLTON's (Rob.) Discourse about the state of true happinesse, delivered in certaine Sermons in Oxford, and at St. Paul's Crosse, 1636 —Instructions for a right comforting afflicted Consciences, 1635. *in one* vol. 4to. *calf*, 7s . ————
748* ———— Works, comprising, The four last things, Death, Judgment, Heaven, and Hell—Assize Sermons—Notes on the Funeral of his Patron, Sir Augustine Nicolls—An Account of his Life and Death by E. B.—Funeral Sermon by Nic. Elstrack, 1639—Meditations of the Life to Come—A Cordial for Christians in the time of Affliction, 1640—Some General Directions for a Comfortable Walking with God, 1639, 4to. *calf, fine port. by Payne*, 10s 6d ————
749 BOLSWAERT—Some Meditations and Prayers selected from the Way of Eternal Life, in order to illustrate and explain the pictures by Boetius a Bolswaert; translated from the Latin, and adapted to the use of the English Church, by the Rev. Isaac Williams, 8vo. *plates, cloth bds.* 10s—*morocco, gilt leaves*, 15s *Oxford*, 1845

750 BONA MORS: or the Art of dying happily in the congregation of Christ crucified, and of His condoling Mother; with the Rosary of our Blessed Lady, 24mo. *front.* 2s (1749)
751 BONA (D. Joannis, *Cardinalis*) Opera Omnia (de Rebus Liturgicis, Manuductio ad Cœlum, Horologium Asceticum, &c.) Acced. Opuscula Posthumo de Præparatione ad Mortem, folio, *(six leaves supplied in MS.) half bound,* £1. *Antverpiæ,* 1739
752 ———— Opera (Rerum Liturgicarum Libri duo et Epistolæ), cum Notis et Observationibus D. Roberti Sala. Adjiciuntur inediti duo singulares Ritus Ecclesiarum Vercellensis et Augustæ Prætoriæ; nonnullæ item Dissertationes adversus Misoliturgos aliosque Pseudo-criticis, etc., *best edition,* 4 vols. in 2, folio, *fine copy, in stamped hogskin,* £6. 6s *Augustæ Taurinorum,* 1747-55
753 ———— Epistolæ Selectæ aliæque Eruditorum sui temporis Virorum ad eumdem scriptæ, una cum nonnullis ipsius Analectis collegit, digessit, brevibusque notis illust. D. R. Sala, folio, *hf. bd.* £1. 11s 6d *ib.* 1755
754 BONAR (Arch.) Sermons, chiefly on Devotional Subjects, 2 vols. 8vo. *bds.* 7s 6d *Edinb.* 1815
755 BONAVENTURÆ (Sancti) Opera Omnia, 7 vols. in 4, folio, *portrait, fine copy, in stamped hogskin,* £5. 5s *Lugduni,* 1668

" Albertus Magnus, Thomas Aquinas, and J. *Bonaventuræ*, were each of them possessed of an inquisitive turn of mind, a sublime and penetrating genius, accompanied with an uncommon talent for souuding the most hidden truths, and treating with facility the most abstruse subjects."— *Mosheim.* " J. Bona-ventura, called the *Seraphic* Doctor, was the second of two great lights which illumined this age."— *Clarke.*

756 BONEFIDIUS (Enimuudus) Juris Orientalis, libri III. *Græce et Latine* 12mo. *calf,* 4s . [*Par.*] *H. Stephanus,* 1573
757 BONIFACIUS (S. *Archiep. Mogunt.*) Opera quæ extant omnia; edidit J. A. Giles, LL. D. 2 vols. 8vo. *bds.* £1. 1s 1844
758 BONNELL (James, *Esq. Accomptant General of Ireland*). Life and Character of, by Will. Hamilton, Archdeacon of Armagh, with his Funeral Sermon by Edward, Bp. of Killmore, 8vo. *port. old blue morocco,* 4s *Dublin,* 1703
759 ———— Harmony of the Holy Gospels digested in one history, reformed and improved by James Bonnel, 8vo. *calf,* 3s 1705
760 BONS (L. de) Sermons, sur divers textes de l'écriture sainte, 8vo. *calf,* 2s 6d *Lausanne,* 1774
761 BOOK of the Fathers: containing the Lives of celebrated Fathers of the Christian Church, and the Spirit of their Writings, 8vo. *bds.* 5s 6d 1837
762 BOONE'S (T. Cha.) Book of Churches and Sects; or, the opinions of all denominations of Christians differing from the Church of England, traced to their source, by an exposition of the various trans-lations and interpretations of the Sacred Writings, 8vo. *hf. bd. calf,* 6s 1826
763 BOS (Lambertus) Exercitationes philologicæ, in quibus Novi Fœderis loca nonnulla illustrantur, &c. 8vo. *vellum,* 4s *Fran.* 1713

[58, GREAT QUEEN STREET,

764 Bos (Lamb.) Exercitationes philologicæ, &c. *Fran.* 1713—Observationes Miscellanea ad loca quædam Novi Fœderis, &c. *ib.* 1707, in *one* vol. 8vo. *vellum,* 5*s*
—— aliud exemplar, *Fran.* 1713 — Animadversiones ad Scriptores quosdam Græcos, &c. *ib.* 1715—Observationes Miscellaneæ ab loca quædam Novi Fœderis, &c. *Leovardiæ,* 1731, 3 vols. in 1, 8vo. *neat,* 6*s*

766 Bosius (Jac.) Crux triumphans et gloriosa, *Antv.* 1617—Pauli Sherlogi Hiberni Antiquitatum Hebraicarum dioptra, in duos libros tributa—I. Orbem Conditum, et memorabilium sub lege naturæ doctrinam continet—II. De Opere sex dierum, *Lugduni,* 1651 *in one* vol. folio, *vellum,* £1. 5*s*

767 Bossuet (J. B. *Evêque de Meaux.*) Collection Complette de ses Sermons, Panégyriques, et Oraisons Funèbres, 19 vols. 12mo. *French calf gilt,* £2. 15*s*   *Par.* 1808

768 ——— Défense de la Tradition des Saints Peres, 2 vols. 12mo. *calf,* 8*s*   *ib.* 1763

769 ——— Recueil des Oraisons Funèbres, 18mo. *hf. bd. calf, uncut,* 2*s* 6*d*   *ib.* 1774

770 ——— Traité de l'amour de Dieu, ouvrage posthume composé eu Latin par J. B. Bossuet, Evêque de Meaux ; donné avec la traduction Françoise par J. B. Bossuet, Evêque de Troyes, 12mo. *nt.* 3*s ib.* 1736

771 ——— Lettres et Opuscules, 2 vols. 12mo. *neat,* 4*s*   *ib.* 1748

772 ——— Iustruction sur les estats d'oraison, où sont exposée les erreurs des faux mystiques de nos jours, 8vo. 4*s* 6*d*   *ib.* 1697

773 ——— Abrégé du célèbre ouvrage de M. Bossuet intitulé, Défense de la Déclaration de l'Assemblée générale du Clergé de France de 1682, par M. L'Abbé Coulon, 8vo. *sewed,* 4*s*   *Londres,* 1813

774 - ——— History of the Variations of the Protestant Churches, 2 vols. 8vo. *bds.* 7*s* 6*d*   *Dublin,* 1829

775 Bouhours ( ) Pensées Ingenieuses des Peres de l'Eglise, 12mo. *neat,* 4*s*   *Par.* 1700

776 Boullier (David Renaud) Sermons sur divers textes de l'Ecriture Sainte, 8vo. *vellum,* 5*s*   *Amst.* 1748

777 ——— (Jacques Renaud) Sermons sur divers textes de l'Ecriture Sainte, 4 vols. 8vo. *calf, neat,* 8*s*   *ib.* 1803-4

778 Bourdaloue (Père) Sermons pour le Carême, l'Avent, les Dimanches, et les Fêtes des Saints, et sur les Mysteres ; Exhortations et Instructions Chretiennes; Retraite Spirituelle, à l'usage des Communautés Religieuses ; Pensées sur divers sujets de Religion et de Morale ; et Table générale des Matières, 19 vols. 12mo. *hf. bd. calf,* £1. 14*s*   *Par.* 1716-1802

779 ——— Pensées sur divers sujets de Religion et de Morale, 3 vols. 12mo. *hf. bd. calf, neat,* 8*s*   *ib.* 1802

780 ——— Œuvres, viz.—Sermons pour l'Avent : Sermons pour le Caresme, 3 vols. : Sermons pour les Dimanches, 4 vols. : Sermons pour les Festes de Saintes, 2 vols. : Sermons sur les Mysteres, 2 vols. : Exhortations et Instructions Chretiennes, 2 vols. Retraite Spirituelle : Pensées, 2 vols. Together 18 vols. 12mo. *fine copy, calf,* £2 2*s*   *Toulouse,* 1787

781 ——— Œuvres, 6 vols. 8vo. *sewed,* £1. 11*s* 6*d*   *Par.* 1844

782 BOURDALOUE (Pere) Sermons sur divers sujets, 18 vols. 12mo. *old calf gilt*, £1. 18s . *Par.* 1726, &c.
783 BOURGOING (François) Paraphrase, ou briefve explication sur le Catechisme, receu en l'Eglise reformée, 24mo. *vellum*, 3s 6d *Lyon*, 1564
784 BOURIGNON (Antoinette) Œuvres, *savoir*, Traité de l'Aveuglement des hommes et de la lumière née en ténèbres – du Nouveau Ciel et du Règne de l'Antè Christ—Traité de la solide Vertu—le Renouvellement de l'Esprit Evangélique—l'Innocence reconnue et la Vérité découverte, &c. 19 vols. 12mo. *calf, very scarce*, £1. 16s
Amst. 1686
" L'esprit de cette fille bizarre était vif, pénétrant, son style facile, et son éloquence entrâinante."—*Biog. Univer.*
785 BOURN's (Samuel, *of Norwich*) Discourses on the Principles and Evidences of Natural Religion, 4 vols. 8vo. *calf*, 14s   1768
786 BOWER's (Archibald) History of the Popes, from the foundation of the See of Rome, to the present time, 7 vols. 4to. *bds.* £2. 8s
1750, &c.
787 ———— another copy, 7 vols. 4to. *calf*, £3. 3s   1748-66
From the library of the Duke of Sussex.
788 BOWLES (Oliver) de Pastore Evangelico tractatus, 4to. *calf, scarce,* 7s . 1649
" Liber ob utilia ac pia precepta, in eo pro ministris Ecclesiæ proposita, laudatur."
Walch.
789 ———— (Wm. Lisle) Days departed, or Banwell Hill; a Lay of the Severn Sea : including the tale of the Maid of Cornwall, or Spectre and Prayer-Book, 12mo. *bds. scarce*, 2s . 1829
790 ———— The plain Bible, and the Protestant Church in England, 8vo. *sewed*, 1s 6d . 1818
791 BOWNDES' (Nich.) Doctrine of the Sabbath, 4to. *hf. bd. calf, neat,* 7s . . 1595
Dedicated to Robert Devereux, Earl of Essex. On the back of the title is a large wood-cut of his arms and quarterings.
792 BOWYER's ( ) Conjectures on the New Testament, collected from various authors, as well in regard to words as pointing, 8vo. *calf*, 4s
1772
793 BOYD's (H. S.) Select passages of the writings of St. Chrysostom, St. Gregory Nazianzen, and St. Basil, 8vo. *bds.* 6s   1813
794 BOYLE's (Hon. Rob.) Christian Virtuoso : shewing that by experimental Philosophy, a man is rather assisted, than indisposed, to be a good Christian, &c. 12mo. *calf*, 1s 6d   *In the Savoy*, 1690
795 ———— The Martyrdom of Theodora, and of Didymus, sm. 8vo. *calf*, 2s . . 1687
796 ———— A free Discourse against Customary Swearing, 8vo. *calf,* 2s
1695
797 ———— Some considerations about the reconcileableness of Reason and Religion ; by T. E. a lay-man [Boyle] ; to which is annexed, a discourse of Mr. Boyle, about the possibility of a Resurrection, 12mo. *calf*, 2s . 1675
798 ———— Some considerations touching the style of the Holy Scriptures, 1661—Some motives and incentives to the love of God, 1663, 2 vols in 1, 12mo. *calf*, 4s ——
799 ———— the same, 1668 and 1665, 2 vols in one, 12mo. *calf*, 4s ——

800 BOYLE's (Hon. Rob.) Some motives and incentives to the love of God, 12mo. 2s . *In the Savoy*, 1692
801 ———— Considerations touching the style of the Holy Scriptures; with his life by the Rev. F. Elwin, 12mo. *bds.* 2s 1821
802 ———— Dr. Bentley's dissertations on the Epistles of Phalaris, and the Fables of Æsop examined, by the Hon. Charles Boyle, 8vo. *calf*, 5s . 1699
803 BOYLE LECTURES; in Defence of Natural and Revealed Religion, preached at the Lecture founded by the Hon. Robt. Boyle, between the years 1691 and 1780, by Bentley, Harris, Bradford, Stanhope, Williams, Gastrell, Hancock, Whiston, Turner, Butler, Woodward, Ibbot, Leng, Gurdon, Burnett, Berriman, Owen, Stebbing, Worthington, &c. 3 vols. 4to. and 21 vols. 8vo. *the original editions, uniformly bound, calf, very neat,* £3. 13s 6d . ———
804 ———— the same, from 1692 to 1732, collected in 3 vols. folio, *calf*, £3. 10s . . 1739
805 ———— another copy, 3 vols. folio, *new, in tree marbled calf gilt,* £4. 10s . 1739
806 ———— A defence of Natural and Revealed Religion: being an Abridgment of the Sermons preached at Boyle's Lecture, with a general Index, by G. Burnet, 4 vols. 8vo. *calf*, 18s 1737
807 ———— 1692. BENTLEY's (Rich.) Eight Sermons, (in confutation of Atheism) to which are added three Sermons, 8vo. *calf*, 5s *Camb.* 1735
808 ———— another copy, 8vo. *hf. bd. calf, uncut,* 5s *Oxford*, 1809

"The first Boyle Lectures preached. In this the author successfully applied Sir Isaac Newton's Principia to demonstrate the being of God, and altogether silenced the Atheists, who in this country have since that time for the most part sheltered themselves under Deism."—*Chalmers.*

809 ———— 1695-6. WILLIAMS's (John, *Bp. of Chichester*) Twelve Sermons concerning the possibility, necessity, and certainty of Divine Revelation, with three other Sermons, 8vo. *calf,* 3s 6d 1708
809*———— another copy, 8vo. *calf, neat,* 4s 6d 1708
810 ———— 1697. GASTRELL (Fra. *Bp. of Chester)* The certainty and necessity of Religion in General, or the first grounds and principles of Human Duty established, sm. 8vo. *calf,* 3s 1697
811 ———— 1698. HARRIS (Jo.) The Atheistical objections against the being of a God, and his Attributes, considered and refuted, 4to. *calf,* 3s . 1698
812 ———— 1701-1702. STANHOPE (DR. GEORGE) The truth and excellence of the Christian Religion asserted against the Jews, Infidels, and Hereticks, 4to. *calf,* 3s 6d . N. D.
813 ———— 1704. CLARKE (Dr. Sam.) A demonstration of the Being and Attributes of God, in answer to Hobbs, Spinoza, &c. 8vo. *fine copy, old red morocco,* 5s 1706
814 ———— 1707. WHISTON (Will.) The Accomplishment of Scripture Prophecies, eight Sermons, 8vo. *calf*, 2s 1708
815 ———— 1708. TURNER (Dr. John), The wisdom of God in the Redemption of Man, vindicated from the chief objections of modern Infidels, 8vo. *fine copy, old calf gilt*, 3s 1709

816 BOYLE LECTURES—1711-12. DERHAM'S (W.) Physico-Theology; or a Demonstration of the Being and Attributes of God from his works of Creation, being the substance of XVI Sermons, 2 vols. 8vo. *calf,* 4s 6d . 1713
817 ———— another copy, 2 vols. 8vo. *plates, calf,* 7s 6d 1798
818 ———— 1721-22. GURDON (Brampton) The pretended difficulties in Natural and Revealed Religion no excuse for Infidelity; sixteen Sermons, 8vo. *old calf gilt, fine copy,* 4s 1723
819 ———— 1730, 31, 32. BERRIMAN'S (Will.) The gradual revelation of the Gospel, from the time of Man's Apostacy, set forth in 24 Sermons, 2 vols. 8vo. *calf,* 7s 6d 1733
820 ———— 1739-41. TWELLS's (Dr. L.) XXIV Sermons at the Lecture founded by the Hon. R. Boyle, and VIII at the Lecture founded by Lady Moyer, &c. 2 vols. 8vo. *calf,* 5s—*sewed,* 4s 1743
821 ———— 1747-49. STEBBING's (Dr. Henry) Christianity justified upon the Scripture foundation, 8vo. *calf,* 4s . 1750
822 ———— 1766, 67, 68. WORTHINGTON's (Dr. Wm.) Evidence of Christianity deduced from facts, and the testimony of sense, throughout all ages of the Church to the present time, 2 vols. 8vo. *bds.* 6s
———— 1769
823 BOYS's (John, *Dean of Canterbury*) Exposition of the Dominical Epistles and Gospels used in our English Liturgie, 4to. *calf, scarce,* 16s . . 1615
824 BRADBURY (Chas.) A Cabinet of Jewels opened to the curions, 12mo. 2s . . 1757
825 ———— (Tho.) The power of Christ over Plagues and Health, &c. in ten Sermons, with an account of the Anti-Arian Lecture, 1752—Six Sermons on Hebr. vi. 12,1743—The Duty and Doctrine of Baptism, in thirteen Sermons, 1749, *in one vol.* 8vo. *calf,* 4s ——
826 BRADFORD's (Sam.) Twelve Sermons on various occasions, including his Boyle Lectures, *in one vol.* 4to. *calf, neat,* 4s 1697-1716
827 BRADLEY's (Cha.) Parochial Sermons, 8vo. *hf. bd. calf,* 5s 1827
827* ———— Sermons preached in the Parish Church of High Wycombe, 8vo. *calf,* 7s . 1819
828 BRADNEY's (Joseph) Contemplations of an ancient Layman on the Christian System, 12mo. *calf,* 2s 1812
829 BRADWARDINUS (Tho. *Archiep. Cant.*) de Causa Dei, contra Pelaginm, et de Virtute Causarum, ad suos Mertonenses, opera et studio Hen. Savilii, *Lond.* 1618—Chr. Becmani Exercitationes theologicæ contra F. Socinum,V. Smalcium, etc. *Amst.* 1644, *in one vol.* folio, *vellum,* £2. 15s . ——
That scarce and curious work, "Bradwardinus de Causa Dei," has been accused by modern Romanists, "as holding out the same doctrine which has since been termed Protestantism."

830 BRAGGE's (Francis) Works, consisting of Discourses on the Miracles and Parables, Sermons, &c. 5 vols. 8vo. *bds.* £1. 5s—*calf gilt, new,* £2. 8s . . *Oxford,* 1833
831 ———— Practical Observations on the Miracles, 2 vols. 1719—Practical Discourses on the Parables, with Prayers annexed to each, 2 vols. 1722—Practical Treatise on the regulation of the Passions, 1708 – together 5 vols. 8vo. *old calf gilt, fine copy,* £1. 5s ——

[58, GREAT QUEEN STREET,

J. LESLIE'S CATALOGUE. 53

832 BRAGGE's (Francis) Practical Discourses upon the Parables of our Blessed Saviour, with Prayers, 8vo. *calf, 4s* 1702
833 ———— (Robert) Church Discipline according to its ancient standard, 8vo. *calf, 4s 6d* . 1739
834 ———— A brief Essay concerning the Soul of Man, 1725—A Letter concerning the Soul and Knowledge of Brutes, from a Gentleman in the Country to his friend, 1721—*in one vol.* 8vo. *hf. bd. 2s* ——
835 BRAIS (Steph. de) Epistolæ S. Pauli ad Romanos Analysis paraphrastica, notis eruditissimis illustrata. Præfixa est, Epistola commendatoria T. H. Van den Honert, 4to. *vellum, 7s 6d*
Lugd. Bat. 1734
836 BRAKENRIDGE's (Dr. Will.) Sermons on several subjects, 8vo. *bds. 2s* 1764
837 BRAMHALL's (John, Abp. of Armagh) Works, (with a copy of the Records touching Abp. Parker's Consecration, as also the copy of an old MS. in C. C. C. Cambridge, on the same subject, and a life of the author) folio, *hf. bd. calf, very scarce, £3. 16s Dublin,* 1677
838 ———— another copy, folio, *hf. bd. calf, slightly stained, £2. 18s*
ib. 1677
839 ———— Works, *new edition*, with a Life of the Author, vols. 1 to 4, (*all yet published*) 8vo. *bds. £2. 2s* *Oxford,* 1842
840 ———— A fair Warning to take heed of the Scottish discipline, 4to. *sewed, very scarce,* 10s . 1649
841 ———— His Vindication of himself and the Episcopal Clergy from the Presbyterian charge of Popery, 12mo. *calf, 5s* 1672
842 ———— An Answer to M. de la Militiere's impertinent Dedication to his "Victory of Truth," with Notes, and a Memoir of the Abp. by Geo. Ingram, B.D. 12mo. *bds. 4s* . 1841
843 BRANDT's (Gerard) History of the Reformation and other Ecclesiastical Transactions, in and about the Low Countries, from the beginning of the Eighth Century, down to the Synod of Dort, 4 vols. folio, *portraits, calf gilt, £5. 10s* . 1720-23
844 ———— the same, 4 vols. in 2, folio, *portraits, fine copy, in rich calf gilt, £5. 15s 6d* . 1720-23
845 ———— another copy, 4 vols. in 2, *hf. bd. calf, uncut, £5. 5s*
1720-23
One of the most interesting and authentic ecclesiastical histories extant.
846 BRAY's (Dr. Tho.) Bibliotheca Parochialis, or a Scheme of such Theological and other heads as seem requisite to be perused by the Clergy, &c. 8vo. *calf, 6s* . 1707
847 ———— Publick Spirit, illustrated in the Life and designs of Dr. Bray, 8vo. *calf, 2s 6d* . 1745
848 BREBEUF (M. de) La defence de l'Eglise Romaine sur la Separation des Calvinistes, 12mo. *front. neat, 3s 6d* *Par.* 1664
849 BRETSCHNEIDER (Car. Gottl.) Lexici in Interpretes Græcos Vet. Test. Maxime Scriptores Apochryphos Spicilegium, 8vo. *bds. 3s*
Lips. 1805
850 BRETT's (Tho.) Remarks on Dr. Waterland's Review of the Doctrine of the Eucharist, 8vo. *calf, 4s* 1738

LINCOLN'S INN FIELDS.]

851 BRETT's (Tho.) Collection of the principal Liturgies used by the Christian Church in the celebration of the Holy Eucharist, with a Dissertation upon them, shewing their usefulness and authority, 8vo. *calf*, 14s . . 1720
852 ———— new edition, 8vo. *bds. scarce*, 10s 6d—*calf gilt*, 14s 1838
853 BREVIATES. Spiritual Breviates; or short Compendiums of Faith and Practice for the Visitation of the Sick, 12mo. *bds.* 2s 6d 1839
854 BREVINT's (Dr. Dan.) The Christian Sacrament and Sacrifice, by way of Discourse, Meditation, and Prayer, upon the Holy Communion, 12mo. *hf. bd. calf, neat*, 4s 6d . 1739
855 ———— Saul and Samuel at Endor, or the New Waies of Salvation and service which tempt Men to Rome, &c. 8vo, *calf*, 5s
Oxford, 1674
856 ———— another copy, 8vo. *calf*, 7s . 1674
857 BREWSTER's (John) Meditations for the Aged, adapted to the progress of Human Life, 8vo. *bds.* 3s . 1814
858 ———— Meditations for Penitents, with an Assize Sermon, 8vo. *bds.* 3s 6d . . 1817
859 ———— The Meditations of a Recluse, chiefly on Religious subjects, 8vo. *bds.* 2s 6d . . 1816
860 ———— Sermons for Prisons, with Prayers for the use of Prisoners in Solitary Confinement, 12mo. *sewed*, 1s 6d 1790
861 ———— Practical Reflections on the Ordination Services for Deacons and Priests, 8vo. *bds.* 4s 6d . . 1817
862 BRIDGES's (Cha.) Christian Ministry; with an Inquiry into the causes of its Inefficiency, 8vo. *bds.* 7s 1835
863 ———— Exposition of Psalm CXIX: as illustrative of the character and exercises of Christian experience, 12mo. *calf, neat*, 6s 1843
864 BRIDGWATER (Jo.) Concertatio Ecclesiæ Catholicæ in Anglia, adversus Calvinopapistas et Puritanos sub Elizabetha Regina, parts 1 and 2, in 1 vol. 4to. *calf*, 10s 6d . *Aug. Trev.* 1589
Published under the name of Aquapontanus.
865 BRIGHT's (George) Six Sermons before Queen Mary, 8vo. *calf*, 4s 6d
Lond. ————
866 BRIGHTMAN's (Tho.) Revelation of Saint John illustrated, with Analysis and Scholions; also a comfortable Exposition of the last part of Daniel, 4to. *calf*, 7s . *Amst.* 1644
867 BRINSLEY's (John) Stand Still; or, a Bridle for the Times, a Discourse delivered to the Church of God at Great Yarmouth, anno 1643, 4to. *hf. bd. calf, neat*, 3s 6d . 1647
868 ———— Two Treatises—I. A Groan for Israel; II. The Spiritual Vertigo, 12mo. *calf*, 3s . 1655
869 ———— Two Treatises—I. Three Sacred Emblems of the Son of Man; II. Tears for Jerusalem, 12mo. 2s 6d . 1656
870 BRITISH REFORMERS, consisting of the Writings of the British Reformers, viz. Wiclif, Becon, Bradford, Tindal, Frith, Barnes, Hooper, Ridley, Philpot, Fox, Bale, Coverdale, Jewel, Knox, Latimer, Edward VI., and others, 12 vols. 12mo. *portraits, bds.* £1. 10s . . 1831, &c.

[58, GREAT QUEEN STREET,

871 BRITISH CRITIC, Quarterly Theological Review, and Ecclesiastical Record, 27 vols. 8vo. *hf. bd. calf, and one part sewed*, £2. 10s
1827-41
871*BROGDEN'S (James) Illustrations of the Liturgy and Ritual of the United Church of England and Ireland, being Sermons and Discourses, selected from the Works of Eminent Divines, who lived during the Seventeenth Century, 3 vols. 8vo. *cloth bds.* £1. 7s 1842
872 BROKESBY'S (Fra.) History of the Government of the Primitive Church, 8vo. 4s . . 1712
873 —————— another copy, 8vo. *calf, (from the library of the late Duke of Sussex,)* 4s 6d . 1712
874 —————— another copy, 8vo. *new in calf gilt*, 6s 1712
875 —————— A View of the Elections of Bishops in the Primitive Church. By a Presbyter of the Church of Scotland, 8vo. *calf*, 4s
Edinb. 1728
876 BROMLEY'S (Rob. Ant.) Inquiry into the Necessity of Preparation for the Lord's Supper, 12mo. *calf*, 2s 6d . 1772
877 BROOKE'S (Z.) Examination of Dr. Middleton's Free Inquiry into the Miraculous Powers of the Primitive Church, 8vo. *tree marbled calf, gilt leaves*, 7s . *Camb.* 1750
878 —————— another copy, 8vo. *hf. bd. calf*, 3s *ib.* 1750
879 BROOKSBANK'S (Cha.) Prize Dissertation on the Doctrine of Faith in the Holy Trinity, read in the Divinity School, Oxford, 8vo. *sewed*, 2s 6d . . 1840
880 BROUGHTON'S (Hugh) Replie upon the R. R. Th[omas Bilson, Bishop of] Winton, for Heads of his Divinity in his Sermon and Survey; how he taught a perfect truth, that our Lord went hence to Paradise; but adding, that he went thence to Hades, and striving to prove, that he injurieth all learning and Christianitie, [*Amst.*] 1605—The Familie of David, for the Sonnes of the Kingdome, with a Chronicle unto the Redemtion. *Hebrew and English, Amstel.* 1605, *in one vol.* 18mo. *sewed, rare*, 14s ——
The first tract is dedicated to Prince Henry: the other to Queen Anne.
881 —————— (John) Psychologia; or, an Account of the Rational Soul, 8vo. *calf*, 3s 6d . 1703
882 BROWNRIG (Ralph, *Bp. of Exeter,*) A Sermon in the Temple-Chappel at his Funeral, with an Account of his Life and Death, by Dr. Gauden, 8vo. 4s . 1660
883 BROWN'S (John, *of Haddington,*) Dictionary of the Holy Bible, 2 vols. 8vo. *fine copy, old calf gilt, neat*, 7s 6d *Edinb.* 1778
884 —————— Compendious History of the British Churches in England, Scotland, Ireland, and America, with an introductory Sketch of the History of the Waldenses, and an historical Account of the Secession; and the Life of the Author, 2 vols. 8vo. *bds.* 7s
Edinb. 1823
885 —————— (John, *Vicar of Newcastle,*) Sermons on various subjects, 8vo. *calf*, 2s 6d . 1764
886 —————— Essays on the Characteristics (of the Earl of Shaftesbury,) 8vo. *calf*, 3s . . 1751

887 BROWN'S (Tho.) Legacy for the Ladies; or, Characters of the Age, with a Comical View of London and Westminster, and the character of Mrs. Brown by Dr. Drake, 8vo. *calf*, 5s   1705
888 ———— (Sir Tho.) Christian Morals; published by Jo. Jeffery, D.D., Archdeacon of Norwich, 12mo. *calf*, 3s   *Camb.* 1716
889 ———— Certain Miscellany Tracts, sm. 8vo. *scarce*, 3s 6d   1684
890 ———— Religio-Medico; together with a Letter to a Friend on the Death of his intimate Friend, and Christian Morals, edited by Henry Gardiner, M. A., 12mo. *bds.* 6s   .   1845
891 ———— (Tho., M.D.) Inquiry into the Relation of Cause and Effect, 8vo. *bds.* 6s   .   1835
892 ———— (Dr. Will. Laurence) Essay on the Existence of a Supreme Creator, 2 vols. 8vo. *bds.* 7s 6d   *Aberdeen*, 1816
893 ———— An Essay on the Folly of Scepticism, &c. 8vo. *bds.* 2s   1788
894 BROWNE (Isaac Hawkins) De Animi Immortalitate, a poem, edited by the Rev. Peter Hall, 12mo. *bds.* 1s 6d   *Salisbury*, 1833
895 ———— (J. H.) Strictures on some parts of the Oxford Tracts, a Charge to the Clergy of the Archdeaconry of Ely, 8vo. *bds.* 3s 6d   1838
896 ———— (Peter, *Bp. of Cork*) A Discourse of Drinking Healths, wherein the great evil of this custom is shewn, 8vo. 3s 6d   1716
897 ———— A Letter in answer to a book [by Toland] entitled, Christianity not Mysterious, 8vo. *calf*, 2s   .   1697
898 ———— another copy, sm. 8vo. 1s 6d   1703
899 ———— (Simon) A Defence of the Religion of Nature, and the Christian Revelation, against a book [by Tindal] entitled, Christianity as Old as the Creation, 8vo. *calf*, 3s 6d   1732

" On the deaths of his wife and only son, the author lost his reason, and thought himself deprived of a rational soul, yet in this state of mind he composed several works, and particularly two of merit against Woolston and Tindal."

900 ———— Sermons on several subjects, 8vo. *calf*, 4s   1722
901 ———— (Tho.) The Story of the Ordination of our first Bishops in Queen Elizabeth's reign at the Nag's Head Tavern in Cheapside examined, and proved to be an absurd fable, 8vo. *calf, scarce*, 16s   1731
902 BROXOLME (Cha.) The Good Old Way; or, Perkins improved, in a plain exposition of those depths of Divinity contained in his Six Principles, 12mo. *calf*, 5s 6d   .   1657
903 BRUNO (S., *Episc. Signiensium*) Opera, aucta et adnotationibus illustrata a Bruno Bruni, 2 vols. folio, *vellum*, £3. 3s *Romæ*, 1789-91
904 BRUNSWICK'S (Anthony Ulrick, *Duke of*) Fifty Reasons or Motives why the Roman Catholick, Apostolic Religion, ought to be preferred to the sects this day in Christendom, and which induced his most Serene Highness to abjure Lutheranism, &c. 18mo. 2s   *Antwerp*, 1741
905 [BRUYS (———)] Histoire des Papes, depuis St. Pierre, jusqu'à Benoit XIII. inclusivement, 5 vols. 4to. *calf*, £1. 18s   *A la Haye*, 1732-34

906 BRYANT's (Jacob) Treatise upon the Authenticity of the Scriptures and the Truth of the Christian Religion, 8vo. *calf*, 4s 6d
Lond. 1792
907 ——— another copy, 8vo. *hf. bd. calf*, 4s *Camb.* 1793
908 ——— the same, 8vo. *bds.* 3s . 1810
  " An excellent book for popular instruction."
909 BRYCE's (James, *Clergyman of the Ch. of Scotland at Fort William*) Sermons, 8vo. *bds.* 4s . 1818
910 BUCELINUS (Gabriel) Annales Benedictini quibus potiora Monachorum ejusdem ordinis merita ad compendium referuntur, folio, *vellum, engraved title*, 10s 6d . *Aug. Vindel.* 1656
911 BUCERUS (M.) Præfatio in quartum tomum Postillæ Lutheranæ, continens Summam doctrinæ Christi, &c. 12mo. *very rare, bds.* 3s
s. l. 1527
912 ——— Novissima Confessio de Cœna Domini, 12mo. *bds.* 3s
Lips. 1562
913 BUCHANAN's (Claudius) Memoir of the Expediency of an Ecclesiastical Establishment for British India, 4to. LARGE PAPER, *bds.* 3s 6d
1805
914 ——— (Geo.) Rerum Scoticarum Historia, 8vo, *vellum*, 5s
Franc. 1594
915 BUCHERUS (Sam. Frid.) Antiquitates Biblicæ ex Novo Test. selectæ, 4to. *vellum*, 7s . *Vitemb.* 1729
916 BUCK's (Cha.) Young Christian's Guide ; or, Directions to the Believer on his first entrance into the divine life, 12mo. *neat*, 2s 1826
917 BUCKLER's (Wm.) Catechism compiled from the Book of Common Prayer, 12mo. *hf. bd. calf*, 1s 6d . 1807
918 BUDDEUS (Jo. Fra.) De Atheismo et Superstitione, sm. 8vo. *calf gilt*, 5s—*vellum*, 3s 6d . *Jenæ*, 1717
919 ——— Institutiones theologiæ moralis variis observ. illustratæ, 4to. *vellum*, 6s . *Lips.* 1719
920 ——— Theses theologicæ de Atheismo et Superstitione, variis observ. illustratæ, quibus suas annot. adjecit Jo. Lulofs, 4to. *half bound, calf, uncut*, 8s . *Lugd. Bat.* 1767
921 BUHLE (Jo. Gottl.) Calendarium Palestinæ Œconomicum, 4to. *sewed*, 1s 6d . . *Gott.* 1785
922 BULKLEY's (Cha.) Discourses on various subjects; and Sermons on public occasions, 2 vols. 8vo. *calf, neat*, 4s 1752-61
923 BULL's (Geo. *Bp. of St. David's*) Some important points of Primitive Christianity maintained and defended in several Sermons and other Discourses, 3 vols. 8vo. *calf*, 12s . 1713
924 ——— new edition, 8vo. *bds.* 10s 6d *Oxford*, 1840
925 ——— the same, with his Life by Nelson, and a History of the Controversies in which he was engaged, 4 vols. 8vo. *calf*, 14s—*fine copy, calf*, 16s . 1713-14
926 ——— another copy, 3 vols. 8vo. *calf gilt*, £1. 1s *Oxford*, 1816
927 ——— Judicium Ecclesiæ Catholicæ trium primorum Seculorum de necessitate credendi quod D. N. Jesus Christus sit verus Deus, assertum contra Simonem Episcopium, &c. 8vo. *calf*, 2s 6d
Oxon. 1694

928 BULL's (Geo. *Bp. of St. David's*) Harmonia Apostolica; or, Two Dissertations on the Doctrine of St. James on Justification by Works; and on the agreement of St. Paul with St. James; with the Examen Censuræ ; or an Answer to certain Strictures, &c. with an Apology for the Harmony, in answer to T. Tully, D.D., in his Justificatio Paulina, 2 vols. 8vo. *bds.* 16*s* *Oxford,* 1842-43
929 ———— English Theological Works, 8vo. *bds.* 10*s* 6*d* *ib.* 1844
930 ———— Works, complete, collected and revised by the Rev. E. Burton, with the Life of Bp. Bull, by Nelson, 8 vols. 8vo. *calf gilt,* £4. 10*s* . . *ib.* 1827
931 ———— Opera Omnia, in quibus duo præcipui Catholicæ Fidei Articuli, de S. Trinitate et Justificatione, orthodoxè ac solidè explanantur et confirmantur, edente J. E. Grabe, folio, *portrait, calf,* £1. 1*s* . . *Lond.* 1721
932 ———— idem, LARGE PAPER, folio, *portrait, calf,* £1. 10*s ib.* 1721
933 ———— idem, LARGE PAPER, folio, *portrait, calf,* £1. 8*s ib.* 1703
934 ———— idem, CHARTA MAXIMA, folio, *portrait, calf,* £1. 18*s ib.* 1703
935 ———— Life, by Robert Nelson, Esq., 18mo. *morocco, gilt leaves,* 6*s* . *Oxf.* 1840
936 BULLARIUM PRIVILIGIORUM AC DIPLOMATUM ROMANUM PONTIFICUM USQUE AD CLEMENT XII. 1740, AMPLISSIMA COLLECTIO, cui accessere Pontificum omnium Vitæ, Notæ, et indices, opera et studio C. Cocquelines, *best edition,* 36 vols. in 34, *Romæ,* 1739-45 —BULLARIUM ROMANUM Pontificum Continuatio, complectens Constitutiones, Literas, Epistolas ad Principes et alios, atque Alloqnutiones, collegit A. Barberi ; cum Summariis, Annotationibus, Indicibusque instruxit Comes Alex. Spetia, 9 vols. (*all yet published*) *ib.* 1835-45, together 45 vols. folio, bound in 43, *vellum,* £45. . . ———

The remaining portion of the Continuation to this important work is now in the course of publication, and may be had at 2*s* 6*d* each Fasciculus.

937 ———— Magnum Romanum, a Leone Magno usque ad Benedictum XIV, (1757). Editio novissima cum Rubricis, Scholiis, et Indicibus locupletissimis, 19 vols. in 14, folio. *vellum,* £9. 9*s Luxemburgi,* 1727-58
938 ———— à Leone Magno usque ad Innocentium X. Accedunt Vitæ omnium Pontif. cum Rubricis, Summariis, Scholiis et Indicibus locupletissimis, edente L. Cherubino, 4 vols. folio, *portraits, calf,* £2. 2*s* . *Lugduni,* 1655
939 ———— Ordinis Fratrum Minorum S. P. Francisci Capucinorum, seu Collectio Bullarum, Brevinm, Decretorum, Rescriptorum Oraculorum, &c. quæ à Sede Apostolica pro Ordine Capucino emanarunt variis Notis et Scholiis elucubrata à P. F. Michaele a Tugio, 7 vols. in 5, folio, RARE, *fine copy, vellum,* £5. 5*s Romæ,* 1740-52
940 ———— Collectionis Bullarum S. S. Basilicæ Vaticanæ, à Sancto Leone Magno ad Benedictum XIV. productus, Notis auctus et illustratus. Accedit Dissertatio de Abbatia Sancti Salvatoris ad Montem Magellæ, 3 vols. folio, *fine copy, vellum,* £3. 3*s ib.* 1747-52

[58, GREAT QUEEN STREET,

941 BULLERUS (Dav. Rinaldus) Dissertationum Sacrarum Sylloge, 8vo. calf, 2s . Amst. 1750
942 BULLINGER (Hen.) Novi Testam. Historia Evangelica sigillatim per quatuor Evangelistas descripta, unà cum Actis Apostolorum, omnibusque Apostolicis Epistolis, explicata Commentariis Heinrychi Bullingeri, 3 vols. folio, rare, fine clean copy, vellum, £4. 4s
Tiguri, 1554, &c.
943 BULLOCK's (Tho.) Reasoning of Christ and his Apostles in the defence of Christianity considered in seven Sermons, at Hackney, 8vo. calf, 2s 6d . 1725
944 ——— another copy, 8vo. hf. bd. calf, 2s 6d 1728
945 [BULTEAU (Louis)] Abrégé de l'histoire de l'ordre de S. Benoist, où il est parlé des Saints, des hommes illustres, de la fondation, et des principaux évenemens des Monasteres, 2 vols. 4to. calf, scarce, £1. 15s . . Paris, 1684
946 BUNCLE's (John, Esq.) Life, by Thomas Amory, Gent. 3 vols. 12mo. bds. 9s . 1825
947 BUNDY's (Rich.) Sermons on several occasions, with a course of Lectures on the Church Catechism, 2 vols. 8vo. calf, 5s 1740
948 ——————— Sermons on several occasions, with a course of Lectures on the Church Catechism, ; and select Sermons on some of the most important points of the Christian Religion, 3 vols. 8vo. calf, 6s
1750
949 BUNYAN's (John) Pilgrim's Progress, with original Notes by the Rev. Tho. Scott, sm. 4to. plates designed by T. Stothard, red morocco, broad borders of gold, gilt leaves, £1. 1s 1840
950 BURDER's (Henry Foster) Lectures on the Essentials of Religion, personal, domestic, and social, 8vo. bds. 3s 6d 1825
951 BURGES's (Sir J. B., Bart.) Reasons in favour of a new Translation of the Holy Scriptures, 8vo. bds. 3s 6d . 1819
952 BURGESS' (Tho. Bp. of Sarum) Vindication of 1 John, v. 7, from the objections of M. Griesbach, 8vo. bds. 4s 1823
953 ——— Greek Original of the New Testament asserted : in answer to a recent publication entitled Palæoromaica, 8vo. sewed, 1s 6d . . 1823
954 BURNABY's (Dr. Andrew) Six occasional Sermons, 8vo. hf. bd. calf, 1s 6d . . 1777
955 BURNET's (G. Bp. of Sarum) Vindication of the Authority, Constitution, and Laws of the Church and State of Scotland, in four Conferences, 12mo. calf, rare, 4s 6d Glasgow, 1673
956 ——— Royal Martyr and the dutiful Subject, in two Sermons, 4to. sewed, 2s . . 1675
957 ——— History of the Rights of Princes in disposing of Ecclesiastical Benefices and Church-lands, relating chiefly to the pretensions of the Crown of France to the Regale, &c. 8vo. calf, 4s 1682
958 ——— History of the Reformation of the Church of England, 6 vols. 8vo. portraits, calf gilt, £2. 12s 6d Lond. 1820
959 ——— another copy, 7 vols. 8vo. calf gilt, £4. Oxford, 1829

960 BURNET's (Gilb. *Bp. of Sarum*) Abridgment of the History of the Reformation of the Church of England, 8vo. *calf, 5s*   1682
961 ——— ——— The Letter writ by the last Assembly General of the Clergy of France to the Protestants, inviting them to return to their Communion, translated and examined, 1683— Jo. Calvini Defensio sanæ et orthodoxæ doctrinæ de Sacramentis, *R. Steph*. 1555—A Dialogue between two Protestants, in answer to a Popish Catechism called, a Short Catechism against all Sectaries, &c. [by Jo. Rawlet] 1686, *in one vol*. 8vo. *calf, 4s*
962 ——— ——— Collection of eighteen Papers relating to the affairs of Church and State during the reign of James II. 4to. *calf, 4s 6d*   1689
963 ——— ——— Discourse of the Pastoral Care, 8vo. *calf, 3s*   1692
964 ——— ——— Four Discourses delivered to the Clergy of the Diocess of Sarum, 8vo. *calf, 4s 6d*   .   1694
965 ——— ——— Essay on the Memory of the late Queen, small 8vo. *portrait, calf, 2s*   .   .   1695
966 ——— ——— Reflections on a Pamphlet entitled, Some Discourses upon Dr. Burnet and Dr. Tillotson, occasioned by the late Funeral Sermon of the former upon the latter, 8vo. *calf, 2s 6d*   1696
967 ——— ——— Exposition of the Church Catechism, for the use of the Diocese of Sarum, 8vo. *calf, 3s*   .   1710
968 ——— ——— Some Sermons preach'd on several occasions; and an Essay towards a new Book of Homilies, in seven Sermons, 8vo. *calf, 3s 6d*   .   .   1713
969 ——— ——— History of his own Time, 2 vols. folio, *calf, 18s*   1724-34
970 ——— ——— another copy, with his Life by Thomas Burnet, and Notes, 4 vols. 8vo. *calf gilt*, £1. 15*s*   .   1818
971 ——— ——— another copy, with the suppressed passages, and Notes by the Earls of Dartmouth and Hardwicke, Speaker Onslow, Dean Swift, and other Annotations, 6 vols. 8vo. *calf gilt*, £3. 3*s*
Oxford, 1833
972 ——— ——— Abridgment of Bp. Burnet's History of his own Times, (*portrait inserted*) 1724—A Character of the Right Rev. Bp. Burnet, with a true copy of his last Will and Testament, &c. 1715, *in one vol.* 8vo. 3*s* 6*d*
973 ——— ——— Exposition of the XXXIX Articles, folio, *fine copy, calf, 10s 6d*   .   1737
973*——— ——— another copy, 8vo. *hf. bd. calf, 6s*   *Oxford*, 1805
974 ——— ——— another copy, 8vo. *bds. 4s—calf, neat, 5s 6d*   1826
974*——— ——— another copy, 8vo. *bds. 8s—calf gilt, 11s 6d Oxford*, 1830
975 ——— ——— Lives, Characters, and an Address to Posterity; with five hitherto unpublished Letters by Anne, Countess Dowager of Rochester, upon her son's last illness and conversion: edited with notes, &c., by John Jebb, Bp. of Limerick, 12mo. *calf gilt, 6s*   1833
976 ——— ——— (G. *Vicar of Coggeshal, and Minister of Clerkenwell*), Practical Sermons, 2 vols. 8vo. *calf, 5s*   .   1747
977 ——— ——— (Tho.) Telluris theoria sacra, orbis nostri originem et mutationes complectens, 4to. *calf, 2s 6d*   .   1689

From the library of H. R. H., the Duke of Sussex.

[58, GREAT QUEEN STREET,

978 BURNET (Tho.) De statu mortuorum et resurgentium liber, accessit epistola circa libellum de Archæologiis Philosophicis, 4to. LARGE PAPER, *fine copy, very scarce, old blue morocco, gilt leaves*, 9s 1720
With the autograph of Archdeacon Wrangham.
979 ———— De statu mortuorum et resurgentium tractatus ; adjicitur appendix de Futurâ Judæorum restauratione, 8vo. *port. calf*, 4s 6d
1728
980 ———— Traité de l'état des morts et des résuscitans ; traduit du Latin par Jean Bion, 12mo. *fine copy, old red morocco, gilt leaves*, 8s . . *Rotterdam*, 1731
981 ———— de Fide et Officiis Christianorum, liber posthumus, 8vo. *port. calf*, 2s . 1773
982 ———— The Faith and Duties of Christians, translated by Mr. Dennis, 8vo. *calf*, 2s 6d . . 1733
983 BURNS' (Rob.) Plurality of Offices in the Church of Scotland examined, with a particular reference to the case of Dr. M'Farlane, principal of the University of Glasgow, 12mo. *bds.* 2s 6d
Glasgow, 1824
984 BURROUGH's (Edw.) Measure of the Times : and a full and clear description of the Signes of the Times, &c. sm. 4to. *sewed*, 1s 6d 1657
985 ———— (Dr. Hen.) Lectures on the Church Catechism, Confirmation, and the nature of Religious Vows, 8vo. *sewed*, 1s 6d *Camb.* 1773
986 ———— (Jerem.) Jerusalem's Glory breaking forth into the world, being a Scripture Discovery of the New-Testament-Church, in the latter days, 18mo. *port.* 2s . 1697
987 BURROW's (Dr. E. J.) Summary of Christian Faith and Practice, confirmed by references to Holy Scripture, compared with the Liturgy, &c. 3 vols. 12mo. *half bound, calf*, 6s 1822
988 ———— A Letter to the Rev. W. Marsh, on the nature of certain Principles denominated Evangelical, 8vo. *sewed*, 1s 1819
989 ———— (Robert, LL.D.) Meletemata Darringtoniana, an Essay upon Divine Providence, 8vo. *calf*, 3s . 1726
990 BURTHOGGE's (Rd. M.D.) Causa Dei, or an Apology for God, 12mo. 2s
1675
991 BURTON's (Dr. Edw. *Regius Professor of Divinity*) Lectures on the Ecclesiastical History of the first Century, 8vo. *bds.* 8s
Oxford, 1831
992 ———— Lectures upon the Ecclesiastical History of the first three Centuries, 8vo. *bds.* 15s . *ib.* 1845
993 ———— An attempt to ascertain the Chronology of the Acts of the Apostles and of St. Paul's Epistles, 8vo. *sewed*, 2s *ib.* 1830
994 ———— Testimonies of the Ante-Nicene Fathers, to the Doctrine of the Trinity, and of the Divinity of the Holy Ghost, 8vo. *bds.* 8s 6d . . *ib.* 1831
995 ———— Sermons preached before the University of Oxford, 8vo. *hf. bd. calf gilt*, 8s *ib.* 1832
996 ———— Theological Works, 5 vols. 8vo. *calf gilt*, £2. 10s
ib. 1837
997 ———— (Robert) Anatomy of Melancholy, 2 vols. 8vo. *calf gilt*, £1. 1s . . 1837

LINCOLN'S INN FIELDS.]

998 Burton's (Will.) Certaine Questions and Answeres, concerning the Attributes of God, 1602—An exposition of the Lordes Prayer, 1602—God wooing his Church, set foorth in three godlie Sermons, 1602—David's Evidence; seaven Sermons on Psalme 41, 1602—Conclusions of peace betweene God and Man, 1602—The rowsing of the Sluggard, in seven Sermons, 1602—Ten Sermons on Matth. vi., whereunto is annexed the Anatomie of Belial, 1602—David's thanksgiving for the arraignment of the man of the earth, 1602. *in one* vol. 4to. *calf,* 10*s* 6*d*

So complete a collection of the works of Will. Burton is seldom to be met with.

999 Bury (Rich. de, *Bp. of Durham*). Philobiblion Richardi Dunelmensis, sive de Amore Librorum, et Institutione Bibliothecæ tractatus pulcherrimus ; cui accessit, appendix de Manuscriptis Oxoniensibus : opera et studio T[homæ] I[ames]. *The appendix,* (4 *leaves*) *wanting,* 4to. *green vellum,* 7*s* 6*d*   *Oxon.* 1599

1000 ——— —— Account of the Life and Writings of the Rev. Alban Butler, 8vo. *bds.* 4*s*   1799

1001 Butler's (Alban) Lives of the Fathers, Martyrs, and other principal Saints, collected from original Monuments and Authentic Records, 2 vols. imp. 8vo. *portraits and plates, bds.* £1. 7*s*   *Dublin,* ——

1002 ——— —— (Cha.) Historical Memoirs of English, Irish, and Scottish Catholics, since the Reformation, 4 vols. 8vo. *bds.* £1. 12*s*   1822

1003 ——— —— Vindication of "The Book of the Roman Catholic Church," against the Rev. Geo. Townsend's "Accusations of History against the Church of Rome ;" with notice of some charges brought against "The Book of the Roman Catholic Church," by Dr. Philpotts, the Rev. John Todd, the Rev. S. Isaacson, the Rev. J. B. White, Dr. Southey, &c. 8vo. *bds.* 6*s*   1826

1004 ——— —— Memoir of the Life of Henry-Francis d'Aguesseau, Chancellor of France ; and of his ordonnances, &c. : and an account of the Roman and Canon Law, 8vo. *bds.* 4*s*   1830

1005 ——— —— Reminiscences of C. Butler, Esq.; with a Letter to a Lady on Ancient and Modern Music, &c., 2 vols. 8vo. *bds.* 10*s*   1824-27

1006 ——— —— Horæ Biblicæ, being a connected Series of Miscellaneous Notes on the original Text, early Versions, and printed editions of the Old and New Testament, &c. 2 vols. 8vo. *bds.* 4*s* 6*d*   *Oxford,* 1799-1807

1007 ——— —— Horæ Biblicæ ; being a Series of Notes on the Text and Literary History of the Sacred Books of the Jews, Christians, Mahometans, Hindus, &c. 2 vols. 8vo. LARGE PAPER, *calf,* 8*s*   1807

1008 ——— —— (Joseph, *Bp. of Durham*) Analogy of Religion, Natural and Revealed, to the constitution and course of Nature, with a Charge, and a preface by Samuel Halifax, Bp. of Gloucester, 8vo. *calf,* 5*s*   1798

1009 ——— —— another edition, 8vo. *calf,* 6*s*   1809

1010 ——— —— another copy, 12mo. *calf gilt,* 3*s* 6*d*   1819

1011 ——— —— Works, containing his Analogy of Religion, and Sermons, 2 vols. 8vo. *hf. bd. russia,* 9*s*   *Oxford,* 1807

1012 ——— —— (John, *Bp. of Hereford*) Select Sermons, with two Charges, 8vo. *hf. bd. calf,* 3*s* 6*d*—*bds.* 2*s* 6*d*   *Hereford,* 1801

[58, GREAT QUEEN STREET,

1013 BUTT'S (Geo.) Sermons, 2 vols. 8vo. *bds.* 4s   *Kidderminster,* 1791
1014 BUXTORFII (J.) Concordantiæ Bibliorum Hebraicæ, folio, *calf,*
£1. 15s   .   *Basil.* 1632
1014* ———Thesaurus Grammaticus Linguæ Sanctæ Hebrææ, sm. 8vo. *neat,* 3s   .   *ib.* 1620
1015 - ——— Tiberius, sive Commentarius Masorethicus Triplex Historicus, Didacticus, Criticus ad illustrationem Operis Biblici Basiliensis conscriptus, 4to. *vellum,* 8s   .   *ib.* 1665
1015*——— Doctor Perplexorum; ad dubia et obscuriora Scripturæ loca rectius intelligenda veluti Clavem continens, 4to. *calf,* 7s
   ib. 1629
1016 ———— Anticritica, seu Vindiciæ Veritatis Hebraicæ adv. Lud. Capelli Criticam Sacram, 4to. *vellum,* 12s   *ib.* 1653
1017 ———— Liber Cosri, continens Colloquium seu disputationem de religione inter Regem Cosareorum, et R. Isaacum Sangarum, *Hebr. et Lat.* 4to. *vellum,* 6s   .   *ib.* 1660
1018 ———— Tractatus de punctorum vocalium et accentuum in libris Vet. Test. Hebr. origine, antiquitate, et authoritate: oppositus Arcano Punctationis revelato Ludov. Cappelli, 4to. *calf,* 4s 6d
   ib. 1648
1019 ——— ——idem, 1648—Liber Cosri, 1660, *in one* vol. 4to. *vellum,* 8s   . .   *ib.* 1648-60
1020 BYFIELD'S (Nich.) Exposition upon the Epistle to the Colossians, folio, *calf,* 18s   .   1617
1021 ———— Commentary upon the three first Chapters of the first Epistle Generall of St. Peter, folio, *calf,* 18s   1637
1022 BYTHNERI (Vict.) Lyra Prophetica, Davidis Regis; sive Analysis Critico-practica Psalmorum, 4to. *calf,* 14s   1653
1023 CABASILA (Nic.) De Divino Altaris Sacraficio. Maximi de Mystagogia, hoc est, de introductione ad Sacra Ecclesiæ Mysteria—Divi Chrysostomi et Divi Basilii Sacrificii, seu Missæ ritus, ex Sacerdotali Græco, Gentiano Herveto interprete, *Venet.* 1548—S. Maximi Mystagogia, *Gr. et Lat.* opera Dav. Hoeschelii Augustæ, 1599, 2 vols. in one, 12mo. *calf,* 4s 6d   .   ———
1024 CADOGAN'S *(Hon. and Rev.* W. B.*)* Discourses, short observations on the Lord's Prayer, and Letters, with Memoirs of his Life by R. Cecil, 8vo. *portrait, calf,* 3s 6d   .   1798
1025 CÆREMONIALE Episcoporum, jussu Clementis VIII., novissimè reformatum, 4to. *vellum,* £1. 1s   *Romæ,* 1600
1026 ——— Episcoporum jussu Clementis VIII. Pont. Max. reformatum; omnibus Ecclesiis, præcipue autem Metropolitanis, Cathedralibus, et Collegiatis perutile ac necessarium, folio, *rubricated, fine copy, plates, French calf, gilt leaves,* £2. 15s   *Par.* 1633
1027 ———— idem, nunc denuò Innocentii Papæ auctoritate recognitum, folio, *rubricated, fine copy, with plates, hf. bd. morocco, uncut,* £1. 16s   *Antverpiæ,* 1713
1028 CAILLARD (Gaspar *Pasteur à Dublin*) Sermons sur divers textes de l'Ecriture Sainte, 2 vols. 8vo. *calf,* 5s 6d   *Dublin,* 1728—38
1029 CALAMY'S (Benj.) Sermons on several occasions, 8vo. *calf,* 3s 6d 1690
1030 ———— (Edm.) Saints' Transfiguration, a Sermon at the funeral of Dr. Samuel Bolton, 4to. 2s   .   1655

1031 CALAMY'S (Edm.) Art of Divine Meditation, in several Sermons on Gen. xxiv. 63, sm. 8vo. 2s . 1680
1032 ――――― Godly Man's Ark, or, City of Refuge in the day of his distress, discovered in several Sermons, 18mo. 2s 6d 1682
1033 ――――― Practical Discourse concerning Vows: with a special reference to Baptism, and the Lord's Supper, 8vo. *calf*, 2s 1697
1034 CALASIO (Marius de) Concordantiæ Sacrorum Bibliorum Hebraicorum, edidit. Gul. Romaine, 4 vols. folio, *fine copy, new in calf, very neat*, £6. 6s . Lond. 1747-9
This copy belonged to the late Dr. Van Mildert, Bp. of Durham, and has his book plate.
1035 ――――― ― another copy, 4 vols. folio, *old calf gilt*, £5 *ib.* 1747-49
" This work is infinitely useful to those who study the Holy Scriptures. In it the Hebrew passages are translated into Latin, ranged in two columns; and in the margin are the differences of the Vulgate and the Septuagint likewise. In the beginning of every article we see all the significations of the same word disposed in order; and at the end, the combinations of the Hebrew with other Oriental languages."—*Calmet*.

1036 CALDERWOOD's (David) True History of the Church of Scotland, from the beginning of the Reformation unto the end of the reign of James VI. fol. *calf*, £1. 5s . 1678
Calderwood was a Presbyterian.—" This abstract (says Nicolson) is in high esteem with the men of its author's principles."

1037 CALMET's (Aug.) Dictionary of the Bible, with the Biblical Fragments, by the late Charles Taylor, *illustrated with maps, and 502 copper-plate engravings, and much enlarged*, 5 vols. 4to. *calf gilt*, (pub. at £10. 10s in *bds*.) £6. 16s 6d . 1838
" An invaluable treasury of Biblical lore, and a stupendous monument of literary industry."—*Horne*.

1038 CALOVII (Ab.) Biblia Illustrata, in quibus simul annotata H. Grotii exhibentur, 4 vols. folio, *fine copy, from the late Duke of Sussex's Library, vellum*, £3. . Franc. 1672
" This learned and elaborate work, besides the immense information it contains on every Biblical topic, furnishes a full antidote to the Socinian glosses and perversions. The sentiments of the author are evangelical, and the work is highly extolled by Walch and other continental writers."

1039 CALVINUS (Joannes) Opera Omnia, 9 vols. folio, *best edition, fine copy, portrait, vellum*, £14. 14s Amst. 1671-67
1040 ――――― Institutio Christianæ Religionis. Præmissa est Vita ejusdem Calvini, authore Theod. Beza, folio, *calf*, 15s Lug. Bat. 1654
1041 ――――― Institutio Christianæ Religionis, cum brevi annotatione curâ A. Tholuck, 2 vols. 8vo. *vellum*, 10s Berolini, 1834
1042 ――――― Institutionis Christianæ Religionis Epitome, per Gul. Launeum, 12mo. *hf. bd.* 7s 6d . Lond. 1584
1043 ――――― in Novum Testamentum Commentarii, curavit A. Tholuck, 7 vols. 8vo. *fine copy, calf gilt*, £2. 10s—*vellum*, £2.
Berolini, 1833-34
1044 ――――― in Librum Geneseos Commentarius, curâ E. Hengstenberg, 8vo. *vellum*, 11s . *ib.* 1838
1045 CALVIN's (John) Sermons upon the Epistle of S. Paule to the Ephesians, translated out French by Arthur Golding, 𝔅𝔩𝔞𝔠𝔨 𝔩𝔢𝔱𝔱𝔢𝔯, 4to. *calf, neat*, £1. 11s 6d .

[58, GREAT QUEEN STREET,

1046 CALVIN's (John) Prayers and Collects translated from his Annotations on Ezechiel, by the Rev. Edward Murray, 12mo. *bds. 2s Lond.* ——
1047 CALVINISM. Calvinismus bestiarum Religio: et Appellatio pro Dominico Baune Calvinismi damnato, a P. P. de Bellis: per R. P. A. Riviere, 18mo. *calf*, 4s . *Lugd.* 1630
1048 ——————— Le Calvinisme convaincu de nouveau de dogmes impies: ou la Justification du livre du renversement de la morale par les erreurs des Calvinistes, contre M. le Fevre et M. le Blanc, 12mo. *neat*, 3s . *Cologne*, 1682
1049 CALVÖR (Casp.) Ritualis Ecclesiastici; Origines ac causas Rituum, quos Ecclesia, Evangelica cum primis, in Vitæ Ingressu, Progressu, Egressu frequentat, evolvens; subnexo Usu ac Abusu, &c. 2 vols. 4to. *plates, vellum, £1. 11s 6d* . *Jenæ*, 1705
1050 CAMBRIDGE.—A History of the University of Cambridge, its Colleges, Halls, and Public buildings, 2 vols. 4to. LARGE PAPER, *coloured plates, red morocco, gilt leaves, with joints, and green silk linings, £3. 10s* . 1815
1051 ——————— An Address to the Members of the Senate, on the attention due to Worth of Character from a Religious Society; with a view to the Election of a High Steward, 8vo. *sewed*, 1s 1764
1052 CAMDENI (Wm.) Anglica, Normannica, Hibernica, Cambrica, Normannica à veteribus scripta, folio, *fine copy, red morocco, tooled borders, and gilt edges by Mackenzie, £3. 13s 6d* *Franc.* 1603
1053 CAMERONIS (Jo.) Myrothecium Evangelicum, hoc est Novi Test. loca quamplurima ab eo, aliorum labores aptè et commodè vel illustrata, vel explicata, vel vindicata. Quibus adjectum est L. Capelli Spicilegium, &c. 4to. *vellum*, *Genevæ*, 1632
 This valuable work exhibits the knowledge which the Author possessed of the Greek language, and particularly of the idiom of the New Testament. It was never inserted in any edition of Cameron's collected works.
1054 CAMFIELD's (Benj.) Theological Discourse of Angels and their Ministeries, sm. 8vo. *hf. bd. calf, scarce*, 4s 1678
1055 CAMPBELL's (Arch.) Discourse proving that the Apostles were no Enthusiasts, &c., 8vo. *sewed*, 1s 6d . 1730
1056 ——————— Necessity of Revelation: or, an Inquiry into the extent of Human Powers with respect to matters of Religion, 8vo. *calf*, 4s 6d 1739
1057 ——————— (Dr. Geo.) Lectures on the Pastoral Character; edited by James Fraser, D.D., 8vo. *bds.* 2s 6d 1811
1058 ——————— Lectures on the Pastoral Character: and Lectures on Systematie Theology and Pulpit Eloquence, 2 vols. 8vo. *calf gilt*, 7s 6d . 1811-24
1059 ——————— Dissertation on Miracles, containing an Examination of the Principles advanced by D. Hume, Esq., 8vo. *calf gilt*, 7s 6d 1823
1060 ——————— (T.) History of the Old Testament, digested according to the order of time, connected with Profane History, and illustrated with Notes, 2 vols. folio, *fine copy, old calf gilt*, £1. 8s 1738
1061 CANISIUS (Petrus) Authoritatum Sacræ Scripturæ et SS. Patrum quæ in Summa Doctrinæ Christianæ citantur et ipsis Catechismi Verbis subscriptæ sunt; 3 vols. 4to. *scarce, neat*, £1. 4s
 Ven. Ex bibl. Aldina, 1571
1062 CANNON's (T.) Calvinist and Lutheran's Family Library, or the Church of England's Foundation, designed to revive the Doctrines of the Old and New Testament, 8vo. *calf, scarce*, 6s ——

1063 CANONES SS. APOSTOLORUM Conciliorum Generalium et Provincialium; S. Patrum Epistolæ Canonicæ; quibus præfixa est, Photii Constant. Patriarchæ Nomocanon; omnia Commentariis amplissimis THEOD. BALSAMONIS Antioch. Patriarchæ explicata; et de Græcis conversa G. Herveto interprete, folio, *fine copy, calf, scarce*, £1. 15s . *Par.* 1620

1064 ———— JOANNIS ZONARÆ Monachi in Canones SS. Apostolorum et S. Conciliorum, tam Œcumenicorum quàm Provincialium, Commentarii, Græce et Latine, cum Annotationibus. Adjectum est Concilium Constantinopolitanum sub Menna Patriarcha, una cum Constitutionibus Apostolorum, utraque Lingua erutam, folio, *calf, scarce,* £1. 10s . *ib.* 1618

1064*CANONICÆ et reverentissimæ Expostulationes apud SS. DD. NN. Pium, divinâ providentiâ Papam VII. de variis Actis ad Ecclesiam Gallicanam spectantibus, 8vo. *sewed*, 1s 6d *Lond.* 1803

1065 CAPITULA sive Constitutiones Ecclesiasticæ per Archiepiscopum, Episcopos, et reliquum Clerum Cantuariensis Provinciæ in Synodo inchoata Londini Octobris 1597 sm. 4to. *bds*. 7s 6d 1597

1066 CARDALL's (P.) Gospel-Sanctuary: or, God's Name recorded in places of Publick Worship, 8vo. *calf*, 2s . 1740

1067 CARDWELL's (Dr. Edw.) Synodalia, a collection of Articles of Religion, Canons, and proceedings of Convocations in the province of Canterbury, from 1547 to 1717, with Notes, 2 vols. 8vo. *bds*. 19s *Oxford*, 1842

1068 ———— Documentary Annals of the Reformed Church of England; a collection of Injunctions, Declarations, Orders, Articles of Inquiry, from 1546 to 1716, 2 vols. 8vo. *bds*. 15s *ib.* 1839

1069 CAREME. Traité des Dispenses de Carême, dans lequel on decouvre la fausseté des prétextes qu'on apporte pour les obtenir, 2 vols. 12mo. *neat*, 4s 6d . *Par.* 1710

1070 CARLETON's (Geo.) Sermons at the Royal Chapel of Whitehall, 8vo. *calf*, 2s 6d . 1736

1071 CAROLUS BORROMÆUS (S.) Doctrina et praxis de Pœnitentia, &c. integre representato S. Præsulis textu, per Herm. Damen. 12mo. *neat*, 3s . *Lovanii*, 1711

1072 CARR's (Geo. *Senior Clergyman of the English Episcopal Congregation in Edinburgh,*) Sermons, with some account of the Author, 2 vols. 8vo. *calf, marbled leaves*, 5s *Edinb.* 1787

1072*———— another copy, 2 vols. sm. 8vo. *calf*, 5s *ib.* 1791

1073 CARRIERES (Pere De) Commentaire litteral sur le Nouveau Testament de Nostre Seigneur Jesus-Christ, inseré dans la traduction Françoise avec le texte Latin à la marge, 5 vols. 12mo. *fine copy, old red morocco, with the royal arms of France on the sides, gilt and marbled leaves,* £1. 10s *Reims*, 1710

1074 CARRINGTON's (James) Theory of Christianity, in twelve plain Discourses, or, the Articles of the Christian Faith, 8vo. *calf*, 2s 1748

1075 CARTARI (Vincenzo) Le Imagini de i Dei degli Antichi, nelle qual isi contengono gl' Idoli, Riti, Ceremonie, ed altre cose appartementi alla religione degli Antichi, 8vo. *woodcuts, calf*, 4s 6d *Lione*, 1581

1076 CARTER's (Benj.) Sixteen Discourses on practical subjects, 8vo. *calf*, 2s 6d . 1729

1077 ———— (Bezaleel) Sermon of God's Omnipotencie and Providence, 12mo. *hf. bd. calf neat*, 3s . 1615

1078 CARTER'S (John) The Nail and the Wheel, two Sermons in the Green-yard at Norwich, 4to. *hf. bd. neat*, 3s 6d 1647
1079 CARTWRIGHT'S (Tho.) Confutation of the Rhemists' translation, Glosses, and Annotations on the New Testament, so farre as they containe manifest impieties, heresies, idolatries, &c. folio, *calf*, £1. 16s . 1618
From the library of the late Duke of Sussex.
1080 CARY'S (Henry) Testimonies of the Fathers of the first four Centuries to the Doctrine and Discipline of the Church of England, as set forth in the XXXIX Articles, 8vo. *bds*. 7s *Oxford*, 1835
1081 CARYOPHILUS (Jo. Matth.) Refutatio pseudo-christianæ Catechesis, editæ a Zach. Gergano, Græco. *Græce et Lat*. 4to. *calf, scarce*, 8s
Romæ, 1631
1082 CASALIUS (Jo. Bapt.) De Antiquis Romanorum Ritibus—De Veteribus Sacris Christianorum ritibus, sive apud Occidentales, sive Orientales Catholica in Ecclesia probatis, etc. *in one vol*. 4to. *plates, calf*, 14s . *Franc. et Han*. 1681
1083 CASAUBONI (Isaaci) ad Frontonem Ducæum S. T. Theologum Epistola; in qua de Apologia disseritur communi Jesuitarum nomine ante aliquot menses Lutetiæ Parisiorum edita, 4to. *hf. bd. calf*, 4s
Lond. 1611
1084 CASAUBON'S (Meric) Treatise proving Spirits, Witches, and Supernatural Operations, by pregnant instances and evidences, 8vo. *neat*, 3s 6d . . 1672
1085 [CASE'S (———)] Historical Epitome of the Old and New Testaments; in which the events are arranged in Chronological order, 12mo. *calf gilt*, 2s 6d . 1820
1086 CASES. A collection of Cases and other Discourses, lately written to recover Dissenters to the Communion of the Church of England, by some Divines of the City of London, 2 vols. 4to. *calf*, 12s 1685
1087 ——— another copy, consisting of the original editions of twenty-five Tracts, including three which are not in the collected editions, *a scarce and valuable collection*, 4to. *calf*, 18s 1683-84
1088 ——— An Answer to the Dissenters' pleas for Separation, or an Abridgment of the London Cases, (by Thomas Bennet) 8vo. *calf*, 3s . *Camb*. 1701
1089 CASSAN'S (Stephen Hyde) Sermons designed to correct some of the principal Doctrinal Errors of the present times, &c. 8vo. *calf, gilt leaves*, 5s 6d . 1827
1090 CASSIANUS (Joannes) Opera Omnia, cum Commentariis Alardi Gazæi, folio, *vellum*, £1. 4s *Lipsiæ*, 1733
1091 ——— (S. Johannes, *Heremita*) Duodecem libri de Institutis Cenobiorum et de octo principalium Viciorum remediis. Item, Viginti quatuor Collationes Sanctorum Patrum, folio, 𝔅lack letter, *brown calf*, £1. 5s *Apud Venetias*, 1491
Saint John the Hermit, commonly called Cassian, "ranks among the greatest masters of the monastic life. His works are written with a clearness and simplicity excellently calculated to inspire the heart with virtuous dispositions."
Chalmers.
1092 CASSIODORUS (Magnus Aurelius) Opera Omnia, Notis et Observationibus illustrata, opera et studio J. Gareti, *Monachi Benedictini*, 2 vols. in 1, folio, *calf*, £1. 16s *Rotomagi*, 1679
1093 ——— idem, 2 vols. in 1, folio, *calf gilt*, £2. 8s *Venetiis*, 1729
LINCOLN'S INN FIELDS.]

1094 CASSIODORUS (*Senator*) Complexiones in Epistolas, Acta Apostolorum et Apocalypsin; opera S. Chandler, 12mo. *calf*, 3s *Lond.* 1722

From the Sussex Library.

1095 CASTELLI (Edmundi) Lexicon Heptaglotton; Hebraicum Chaldaicum, Syriacum, Samaritanum, Æthiopicum, et Arabicum, conjunctim; et Persicum separatim. Cui accessit brevis et harmonica Grammaticæ omnium præcedentium Linguarum delineatio, 2 vols. in 1, royal folio, *portrait, fine copy, stamped hogskin binding, the edges bound with brass*, £5. *Lond.* 1669

1096 CASTELLIO (Seb.) Dialogi IV. de Prædestinatione, Electione, Libero Arbitrio, Fide. Ejusdem Opuscula quædam lectu dignissima, 12mo. *calf*, 4s 6d . *Goudæ*, 1613

1097 CASWALL'S (H.) Prophet of the 19th Century, or the Rise, Progress, and Present State of the Mormons, or latter-day Saints; to which is appended, an Analysis of the Book of Mormon, 8vo. *frontispiece, bds.* 5s . 1843

1098 CATALANI (Josephi) Sacrosanta Concilia Œcumenica Prolegomenis et Commentariis illustrata; 4 vols. *Romæ*, 1736-49—Sacrarum Cæremoniarum, sive Rituum Ecclesiasticorum S. Romanæ Ecclesiæ Lib. III.; 2 vols. *ib.* 1750- Rituale Romanum Benedicti Papæ XIV. jussu editum, et auctum, perpetuis Commentariis exornatum, 2 vols. *ib.* 1757—together 8 vols. folio, RARE, *uncut*, £6. 6s ———

1099 ————— the same, 8 vols. in 6, folio, *rich calf gilt*, £10. ———

1100 CATCOTT'S (A. S.) Sermons, 8vo. *calf*, 3s—*calf gilt*, 5s 1753

1101 ————— (Alexander) Treatise on the Deluge, 8vo. *best edition, plates, calf*, 9s—*fine copy*, 10s 6d . 1768

1102 CATECHISM. A Dialogue between two Protestants (in answer to a Popish Catechism, called a short Catechism against all Sectaries) plainly shewing that the Members of the Church of England are no Sectaries, but true Catholics, 8vo. *calf*, 2s 6d 1686

1103 CATENÆ LI Patrum in Octateuchum et libros Regum, opera NICEPHORI HIER. THEODOKI, Græcè, 2 vols. in 1, roy. folio, *rich calf gilt*, £2. 12s 6d . *Lipsiæ*, 1772-3

1104 CATENÆ PATRUM in Psalmos, Gr. et Lat. à B. Corderio digesta, et commentario illustrata, 3 vols. folio, *fine copy, vellum*, £3. 3s *Antverpiæ*, 1643

1105 CATENA AUREA in quinquaginta Davidicos Psalmos Doctorum Græcorum, interprete Dan-Barbaro Electo Patriarcha Aquileiensi, folio, *old calf gilt, gilt leaves, fine copy*, 18s *Venet.* 1569

1106 ————— Sexaginta quinque Græcorum. Patrum in S. Lucam. Gr. et Lat. annotationibus illustrata a B. Corderio, folio, *fine copy, new in half calf gilt, very neat*, 18s *Antv.* 1628

1107 ————— Græcorum Patrum in Beatum Job, collectore Niceta Heracleæ Metropolita, *Gr. et Lat.* opera et studio Patr. Junii, folio, *calf*, 18s *Lond.* 1637

From the late Duke of Sussex's Collection.

1108 CATENÆ Patrum Græcorum in Evangelia S. Matthæi et S. Marci ad fidem Codd. MSS. edidit T. A. Cramer. S. T. P. 8vo. *bds.* 12s *Oxon.* 1841

1109 ————— in S. Lucæ et S. Joannis, ed. S. T. Cramer, 8vo. *bds.* 12s *ib.* 1841

1110 CATENÆ in Acta SS. Apostolorum e Cod. Nov. Coll. descripsit, edidit J. A. Cramer, S. T. P. 8vo. *bds.* 10s 6d *Oxonii,* 1838
1111 ———— in S. Pauli Epistolam ad Romanos, ed. J. A. Cramer, 8vo. *bds.* 12s 6d . *ib.* 1844
1112 ———— in S. Pauli Epistolas ad Corinthios, ed. J. A. Cramer, 8vo. *bds.* 12s 6d . *ib.* 1841
1113 ———— in S. Pauli Epp. ad Galatas, Ephesios, Philippenses, Colossenses, Thessalonicenses, ed. J. A. Cramer, 8vo *bds.* 12s 6d *ib.* 1842
1114 ———— in S. Pauli Epistolas ad Timotheum, Titum, Philemona, et ad Hebræos, ad fidem Codd. MSS. edidit J. A. Cramer, S. T. P. 8vo. *bds.* 12s 6d . *ib.* 1843
1115 ———— in Epistolas Catholicos, accesserunt Œcumenii et Arethæ Commentarii in Apocalypsin, 8vo. *bds.* 12s 6d *ib.* 1843
1116 CATENA AUREA; a Commentary on the four Gospels, collected out of the Works of the Fathers, by S. Thomas Aquinas, 8 vols. 8vo. *bds.* £3. 17s . *Oxford,* 1841-45
1117 CATHARINA (S. *da Siena.*) Epistole devotissime, folio, *fine large clean copy, vell.* £1. 16s *Venetia, in Casa de Aldo Manutio Romano,* 1500
One of the rarest and most beautiful of the productions of the Aldine press, scarcely ever found clean or perfect. The present copy is in the finest possible condition, but unfortunately wants one leaf, containing a woodcut of S. Catherine. Sir M. M, Sykes' copy, indifferent and imperfect, sold for £5. 10s.
This book is one of the "TESTE DI LINGUE."
1118 CATTENBURGH (Adr. à) Bibliotheca Scriptorum Remonstrantium, 12mo. *calf,* 2s 6d . *Amst.* 1728
1119 CATTERMOLE'S (Rich.) Literature of the Church of England, indicated in selections from the writings of eminent Divines, with Memoirs of their Lives, and Historical Sketches of the times in which they lived, 2 vols. 8vo. *bds.* 14s 1844
1120 CAUSES of the Decay of Christian Piety, by the author of the Whole Duty of Man, 8vo. *old blue morocco, gilt leaves,* 7s 1683
1121 CAUSSINUS (Nic.) Symbolica Ægyptiorum Sapientia, 8vo. *calf,* 3s *Par.* 1634
1122 ———— Symbolica Ægyptiorum Sapientia, *Par.* 1647— Lan. Pignorii Mensa Isiaca, quâ Sacrorum apud Ægyptios ratio et simulacra subjectis tabulis æneis simul exhibentur et explicantur. Accessit ejusdem Anthoris de Magna Deum Matre discursus, nec non J. P. Thomasini Manus ænea, et de vita rebusque Pignorii dissertatio, *Amst.* 1670, *in one vol.* 4to. *vellum,* 8s 1647-70
1123 CAVALIERUS (Jo. Mich.) Opera omnia Liturgica, seu Commentaria in authentica Sacræ Rituum Congregationis Decreta ad Romanum præsertim Breviarium, Missale, et Rituale quomodolibet attinentia, 5 vols. in 1, folio, *port. hogskin binding, with clasps,* £1. 14s *Venet.* 1758
1124 ———— aliud exemplar, 5 vols. in 1, folio, *vellum,* £1. 11s 6d *Augustæ,* 1764
1125 CAVE'S (Will.) Primitive Christianity; or, the Religion of the ancient Christians in the first ages of the Gospel, 3 parts in 2 vols. 8vo. *front.* LARGE PAPER, *fine copy, very scarce, old red morocco, gilt leaves,* 18s . 1673
1126 ———— Primitive Christianity; or the Religion of the ancient Christians, in the first ages of the Gospel, 8vo. *frontispiece, calf,* 5s *—fine copy,* 6s . 1714

1127 CAVE's (Will.) Primitive Christianity, or the Religion of the ancient Christians, in the first ages of the Gospel, 8vo. *frontispiece, calf,* 5s 6d . . 1728
1128 —————— Chartophylax Ecclesiasticus quo prope M. D. Scriptores Ecclesiastici, tam Minores, quam Majores, tam Catholici, tam Hæretici, eorumque Patria, Ordo, Secta, Munera, Ætas et Obitus; Editiones Operum, etc. indicantur. Accedunt P. Colomesii Paralepomena, etc. 8vo. *calf,* 5s . 1685
1129 —————— Historia Literaria Scriptorum Ecclesiasticorum, a Christo Nato usque ad Sæculum XIV. Accedunt ab aliis manibus Appendices duæ, ab ineunte Sæc. XIV. ad Annum usque MDXVII. 2 vols. in 1, folio, *vellum,* £2. 10s *Basil.* 1741-45
1130 —————— aliud exemplar, 2 vols. folio, *old calf gilt,* £2. 5s *ib.* 1741-45
1131 —————— Antiquitates Apostolicæ; or, the History of the Lives, Acts, and Martyrdoms of the Holy Apostles, and the two Evangelists, SS. Mark and Luke, folio, *plates, calf,* 12s 1677
1132 —————— another copy, folio, *calf,* 12s . 1684
1133 —————— Apostolici; or, the History of the Lives, Acts, Death, and Martyrdoms of those who were contemporary with, or immediately succeeded the Apostles, as also the most eminent of the Primitive Fathers for the first 300 years, &c. folio, *plates, hf. bd. calf,* 18s 1677
1134 —————— Ecclesiastici; or, the History of the Lives, Acts, &c. of the most eminent Fathers of the Church, that flourished in the fourth century, folio, *hf. bd. calf,* 18s . 1683
1135 —————— Apostolici, and Lives of the most eminent of the Primitive Fathers of the first four centuries, *best edition,* 2 vols. in 1, folio, *plates, calf, (slightly stained in the margin)* £1. 16s 1706
1136 —————— Dissertation on the Government of the Ancient Church, by Bishops, Metropolitans, and Patriarchs, 8vo. *calf,* 4s 6d —*fine copy, calf,* 5s . . 1683
1137 C[AWDREY] (D.) The Account audited and discounted; or, a Vindication of the Three-fold Diatribe, of Superstition, WillWorship, and Christmas Festivall, against Dr. Hammond's manifold Paradiatribes, 12mo. 3s . 1658
1138 CEILLIER (Dom. Remy) Histoire Générale des Auteurs Sacrés et Ecclésiastiques; qui contient leur Vie, le Catalogue, la Critique, le Jugement, la Chronologie, l'Analyse, et le dénombrement des différentes éditions de leurs ouvrages : ce qu'ils renferment de plus interessant sur le Dogme, sur la Morale, et sur la Discipline de l'Eglise ; l'Histoire des Conciles tant généraux que particuliers, et les Actes choisis des Martyrs, avec une table des matiéres par E. Roudet, 25 vols. 4to. *old French calf gilt, very scarce,* £13. 13s *Par.* 1729-82
1139 CEREMONIES.—An Appendix to a foregoing Sermon concerning the Ceremonies of the Church of England, 4to. *sewed,* 4s *Camb.* 1636
1140 —————— Twelve general Arguments, proving the Ceremonies imposed upon the Ministers of the Gospel in England by our Prelates, are Unlawful, 4to. *sewed,* 2s . 1660

1141 CENSURA TEMPORUM—The Good or Ill Tendencies of Books, Sermons, Pamphlets, &c. impartially considered, in a Dialogue between Eubulus et Sophronius. 2 vols. in 1, 4to. *calf*, 5s 1709-10
By Sam. Parker, of Trin. Coll. Oxon, author of the "Bibliotheca Biblica," to the 5th vol. of which is prefixed some account of him by Dr. Thomas Hayward. The present copy of the Censura contains all that was ever published.

1142 —————— another copy, Vol. I. only, for 1708, 4to. *calf*, 2s 6d
                                                                    1709
1143 —————— another copy, wanting the last number ; 1709. The Monthly Catalogue, being a general Register of Books, &c. for 1727-28. (*incomplete*) *in one vol*. 4to. 6s

1144 CERRI (Urbano) Account of the State of the Roman Catholick Religion throughout the World, with a Discourse on the State of Religion in England, written in French in the time of K. Charles I., and a Dedication to the present Pope, by Sir Richard Steele, 8vo. *calf*, 2s 6d   .   .   1715

1145 CEVENNES.—A Cry from the Desart : or, Testimonials of the miraculous Things lately come to pass in the Cevennes, *very scarce*, 1707—The Prophetical Warnings of John Lacy, Esq. pronounced under the Operation of the Spirit, 1707—Warnings of the Eternal Spirit, by the mouth of his servant John, surnamed Lacy, the second part, 1707—The third and last part, 1707—A Relation of the Dealings of God with his unworthy servant John Lacy, since the time of his professing himself inspired, 1708—An Answer to several Treatises lately published on the subject of the Prophets, by Sir Rich. Bulkeley, Bart., *in one vol*. small 8vo. *calf, very scarce*, 5s

1146 CHALONER (Edw.) Credo Ecclesiam Sanctam Catholicam ; the Authoritie, Universalitie, and Visibilitie of the Church handled and discussed, 4to. *very scarce, hf. bd. calf, neat*, 7s 6d   1625
From the library of the Duke of Sussex.

1147 —————— Six Sermons, *Oxford*, 1629. VII Sermons by Bp. Laney, 1669—Asheton's (W.) Danger of Hypocrisie, a Sermon, 1673—Pelling's (E.) True March of the Beast, a Sermon on Nov. 5, 1682, *in one vol*. 4to. *calf*, 6s

1148 CHALLONER (Rd.) The Catholick Christian instructed in the Sacraments, Sacrifice, Ceremonies, and Observances of the Church : by way of Question and Answer, 12mo. *red morocco, marbled leaves*, 8s 6d   .   1737

1149 —————— A Short Daily Exercise, with Devotions for Mass, &c. abridged from the Garden of the Soul, 12mo. 2s   1770

1150 —————— Think well on't : or, Reflections on the Truths of the Christian Religion for every day in the month, 18mo. 1s 6d 1785

1151 —————— The Garden of the Soul ; or, Manual of Spiritual Exercises, 12mo. 2s   .   1830

1152 CHALMERS' (Dr. Tho.) Application of Christianity to the Commercial and Ordinary Affairs of Life, in a series of Discourses, 8vo. *bds.* 3s 6d   .   .   *Glasg*. 1820

1153 —————— Sermons preached in St. John's Church, Glasgow, 8vo. *bds*. 5s   .   .   *ib*. 1823

LINCOLN'S INN FIELDS.]

1154 CHALMERS's (Dr. Tho.) Christian and Civic Economy of Large Towns, 3 vols. 8vo. *bds. 9s* . *Glasg.* 1821
1155 ——— Evidence and Authority of the Christian Revelation, 8vo. *bds. 3s 6d* . . *Edinb.* 1824
1156 ——— On the Use and Abuse of Literary and Ecclesiastical Endowments, 8vo. *bds. 3s 6d* . *Glasg.* 1827
1157 ——— Sermons preached in the Tron Church, Glasgow, 8vo. *bds. 4s 6d* . . *ib.* 1828
1158 ——— Series of Discourses on the Christian Revelation, viewed in connection with the Modern Astronomy, 8vo. *bds. 4s* *ib.* 1830
1159 ——— Lectures on the Establishment and Extension of National Churches, 8vo. *bds. 3s* . 1838
1160 CHANDLER's (Samuel) The Witnesses of the Resurrection of Jesus re-examined, and their Testimony proved entirely consistent, 8vo. 1s

1161 ——— Vindication of the Antiquity and Authority of Daniel's Prophecies, and their application to Jesus Christ, 8vo. *bds.* 2s 1728
1162 ——— Case of Subscription to Explanatory Articles of Faith, as a Qualification for admission into the Christian Ministry, calmly and impartially reviewed, 8vo. 1s . 1748
1163 ——— Sermons, with a brief Account of his Life by Thomas Amory, 4 vols. 8vo. *bds. 7s* . 1769

There is such a fulness and variety of thought upon almost every subject which Dr. Chandler treats, as is very rarely to be met with.

1164 ——— Review of the History of Man after God's own heart, 8vo. *bds. 3s* . . 1762
1165 ——— (Dr. Thos.) Free Examination of the Critical Commentary on Abp. Secker's Letter to Mr. Walpole, with a copy of Bp. Sherlock's Memorial, 8vo. *bds.* 2s . 1774
1166 ——— Discourse on the Nature and Use of Miracles, 8vo. *calf, neat, 3s* . 1728
1167 ——— History of Persecution—I. Amongst the Heathen—II. Under the Christian Emperors—III. Under the Papacy and Inquisition—IV. Amongst Protestants, with Remarks on Dr. Rogers's Vindication of the Civil Establishment of Religion, 8vo. *bds. 3s 6d* . . 1736
1168 CHAPEAVILLE (Jo.) Tractatus de Necessitate et modo ministrandi Sacramenta tempore pestis, 18mo. *neat*, 3s 1637
1169 CHAPMAN's (Jo.) Eusebius: or, the Christian's Defense against a late Book [by Morgan] entitled the Moral Philosopher, 2 vols. 8vo. *calf*, 5s . *Camb.* 1739-41
1170 ——— Miscellaneous Tracts relating to Antiquity, 8vo. *hf. bd. calf*, 4s . . 1742
1171 CHAPPELOW's (Leonard) Commentary on the Book of Job; in which is inserted the Hebrew text and English translation, with paraphrase, 2 vols 4to. *fine copy, calf,* 9s *Camb.* 1752

The author of this esteemed work was a disciple of Schultens, and contributed materially to the advancement of Oriental literature in England.

[58, GREAT QUEEN STREET,

1172 CHARLES I.—WORDSWORTH'S (Dr. Christopher, *late Master of Trinity College, Cambridge*) Who wrote Icôn Basilikè? considered and answered, 1824—Documentary Supplement to "Who Wrote Icôn Basilikè," including recently discovered Letters and Papers of Lord Chancellor Hyde, and of the Gauden family, 1825—King Charles the First, the author of Icôn Basilikè, further proved, in a Letter to the Abp. of Canterbury, in reply to the objections of Dr. Lingard, Mr. Todd, Mr. Broughton, the Edinburgh Review, and Mr. Hallam, 1828—*in one vol.* 8vo. *bds.* 5s

1173 CHARLES'S (Joseph) Dispersion of the Men of Babel considered, and the principal cause inquired into; with Observations on the Sibylline Writings, and on Newton's Dissertation on the Prophecies, 2 vols. 8vo. *bds.* 5s . 1769

1174 CHARLESWORTH'S (J.) Practical Sermons, selected and abridged from various authors, 2 vols. 8vo. *bds.* 3s 1788-9

1175 ———— Five Sermons on the Presence of God, Christian Contentment, &c. with Practical Discourses, 8vo. *bds.* 2s 1801

1176 CHATELAIN (Henri) Sermons sur divers textes de l'Ecriture Sainte, 6 vols. in 3, 8vo. *port. old calf gilt*, 18s *Amst.* 1759-60

1177 CHAUFEPIÉ (Samuel de) Sermons sur divers textes de l'Ecriture Sainte, 2 vols. 8vo. *hf. bd. calf*, 6s . *ib.* 1808

1178 CHEKE (Sir John)—Life of Sir John Cheke, Kt., first Instructor, afterwards Secretary of State to K. Edw. VI.; by John Strype, with a Treatise of Superstition by the same learned Knight, 8vo. *calf*, 5s 6d . . 1705

1179 CHEMINAIS (Pierre R., *de la Comp. de Jesus*) Sermons sur divers textes, 3 vols. 12mo. *calf*, 6s . *Par.* 1741

1180 ———— autre exemplaire, 2 vols. 12mo. *calf gilt*, 7s *Avignon*, 1757

1181 ———— le même, 4 vols. 12mo. *calf*, 8s *Par.* 1764

1182 CHEVALLIER'S (T.) Translation of the Epistles of Clement of Rome, Polycarp, and Ignatius; and of the Apologies of Justin Martyr and Tertullian, with an Introduction and Notes, 8vo. *bds.* 13s
Camb. 1833

1183 CHEYNE'S (George, M.D.) Philosophical Principles of Religion, Natural and Revealed, 2 parts in 1 vol. 8vo. *calf*, 2s 6d 1715

1184 CHILLINGWORTH'S (W.) Religion of Protestants a safe way to Salvation, made more generally useful by omitting personal contests; with an addition of some genuine pieces of Mr. Chillingworth's never before printed, 4to. *calf*, 6s . 1687
Published by Dr. Jo. Patrick at the request of the London clergy, who esteemed it a most effectual preservative againt Popery.

1185 ———— Works, containing his Religion of Protestants, Nine Sermons before the King, Letter to Mr. Lewgar, Nine additional Discourses, and an Answer to some Passages in Rushworth's Dialogues, folio, *calf*, 16s—*fine copy, calf*, 18s 1742

1186 ———— Works, *new edition*, 3 vols. 8vo. *calf gilt*, £1. 11s 6d— *bds.* £1. 1s . *Oxford*, 1838

1187 ———— An Historical and Critical Account of his Life and Writings, (by P. Des Maizeaux), 8vo. *calf*, 5s 1725

1188 ———— Some Account of his Last Days, by W. L. Bowles, 8vo. *sewed*, 1s . *Salisb.* [1836]

1189 CHILLINGWORTH (W.)—Infidelity Unmasked; or, the Confutation of a Book published by Mr. W. Chillingworth under this title, The Religion of Protestants, &e. 4to. *calf, 8s* *Gant*, 1652
1190 CHISHULL'S (Edm.) Charge of Heresy maintained against Mr. Dodwell's Epistolary Discourse concerning the Mortality of the Soul, 8vo. *calf, 2s 6d* . 1706
1191 CHOHELETH; or, the Royal Preacher, a Poem, 4to. *hf. bd. calf, 4s* 1765
1192 CHRIST's Appearance the second time for the Salvation of Believers; with an Epistle giving an Account of the author's Opinion about the Thousand Years, 12mo. *sewed*, 1s 6d . 1829
1193 CHRISTMAS.—Christ's birth misse-timed; evidencing by Scripture that Jesus Christ was not born in December; by R. S. 4to. *sewed*, 1s 6d . . 1649
1194 CHRISTIAN REMEMBRANCER: (The) a Monthly Magazine and Review, vols. 1 – 3, 8vo. *bds. 7s 6d* . 1841-42
1195 CHRISTIAN YEAR: (The) Thoughts in verse for the Sundays and Holidays throughout the year, 32mo. *morocco, gilt leaves, 5s—bds. 3s 6d* . . *Oxford*, 1845
1196 ————— the same, 8vo. *bds. 8s—new,* 10s 6d *ib.* 1840
1197 CHRONICON Saxonicum; seu Annales Rerum in Angliâ præcipuè gestarum ad Annum 1654; cum indice rerum chronologico, Latinè et Anglo-Saxonicè, cum notis Edmundi Gibson, 4to. *fine copy, russia, gilt leaves, and joints,* 24s . *Oxonii,* 1692
From the library of the late Bp. Van Mildert.
1198 CHRYSOLOGUS (S. Petrus) Sermones in Evangelia de Dominicis et festis Solemnioribus. Quibus accesserunt, S. Maximi Homiliæ Hyemales et Æstivales, 4to. *vellum, 7s* *Col. Agr.* 1579
1199 CHRYSOSTOMUS (S. Joannes, *Archiep. Constant.*) Opera Omnia, *Græcè et Latinè,* studio B. de Montfaucon, 13 vols. folio, *vellum, £26.—calf, neat, £28.* . *Paris.* 1718-38
1200 ————— aliud exemplar, 13 vols. folio, *slightly stained, new in calf, very neat, £30.* . *ib.* 1718-38
1201 ————— Opera Omnia, *Græcè,* edente HENRICO SAVILLE, 8 vols. folio, *calf, rare, £14. 14s* *Etonæ, in Coll. Regali,* 1613
1202 ————— Homiliæ ad Populum Antiochenum *Græcè* opera Jo. Harmari, 12mo. *calf, 4s* . *Lond.* 1590
1203 ————— Homiliæ in Matthæum, textum emendavit, lect. var. adnotationibus et indicibus instruxit F. Field, 3 vols. 8vo. *bds. £2. 2s* . . *Cant.* 1839
1204 ————— Homelies ou Sermons, qui contiennent son Commentaire sur l'Evangile de S. Matthieu, avec des exhortations, où les principales regles de la Vie et de la Morale Chrestienne sont expliquées; traduits par Paul Antoine de Marsilly, 3 vols. 4to. *old calf gilt,* 12s . *Par.* 1664-65
1205 ————— Homiliæ V. e Codice Manuscripto Biblioth. Regiæ Dresdensis, nunc primum edidit et Latine reddidit G. T. Becher, 8vo. *sewed, 2s* . *Lipsiæ,* 1839
1206 ————— Homelies ou Sermons sur la Genese, 2 vols. 8vo. *old red morocco, gilt leaves,* 14s . *Paris,* 1702

1207 CHRYSOSTOMUS (S. Joannes) Epistola ad Cæsarium Monachum; cui adjunctæ sunt, Tres Epistolicæ Dissertationes, authore J. Basnage, 12mo. *neat, 3s* . *Rot.* 1687
1208 —————— Abregé de S. Jean Chrysostome sur l'Ancien Testament, 12mo. *old calf gilt, 4s—vellum, 5s 6d* . *Par.* 1688
1209 —————— Abregé de S. Jean Chrysostome sur le Nouveau Testament, 2 vols. 8vo. *brown calf, 12s—vellum, 10s 6d* *ib.* 1670
1210 —————— Homelies ou Sermons sur l'Epistre de S. Paul aux Romains, 8vo. *brown calf, neat, 7s* . *ib.* 1675
1211 —————— Commentary on the Epistle to the Galatians, and Homilies on the Epistles to the Ephesians, translated with Notes and Indices, by the Rev. J. H. Newman, 8vo. *bds. 8s* - *Oxford,* 1840
1212 —————— De Sacerdotio libri VI. Gr. et Lat. accessere Dissertationes de Dignitate Sacerdotali, item S. Chrysostomi Vita, præfationemque adjecit T. Hughes, 8vo. *calf, 8s* *Cant.* 1710
1214 —————— idem, accessit S. Gregorii Nazianzeni Oratio Apologetica, opera S. Thirlby, 8vo. *calf, 8s* . *ib.* 1712
1215 —————— Of the Priesthood, translated by the Rev. Jo. Bunce, 8vo. *hf. bd. calf, 8s—calf, 8s 6d* . 1759
1216 —————— another copy, 8vo. *calf extra, 12s* . 1759
1217 —————— Opera Selecta, *Græce et Latine.* Præfatus est, et Annotationem subjecit Jo. Van Voorst, 2 vols. in 1, 8vo. *sprinkled calf gilt, 10s 6d* . *Lugd. Bat.* 1827-30
1218 —————— Sentences et Instructions Chrestiennes, tirées de ses œuvres, par le Sieur de Laval, 2 vols. 12mo. *old red morocco, gilt leaves, 9s* . *Par.* 1682
1219 —————— Les Panegyriques des Martyrs, traduits, avec un abregé de la Vie de ces mêmes Martyrs, par le R. P. de Bonrccueil, 8vo. *old calf gilt, 7s* . *ib.* 1735
1220 —————— another copy, 8vo. *brown calf, neat, 8s 6d* *ib.* 1735
1221 —————— A Companion for the Sincere Penitent; or, a Treatise on the Compunction of the Heart; translated from the Greek, with Devotions, and a Preface, by Jo. Veneer, 8vo. *front. calf, 4s* 1728
1222 —— —— ACTA S. JOANNIS CHRYSOSTOMI, Episc. Constantinopolitani Eccles. Doctoris, Commentario illustrata a Joanne Stiltingo, folio, *calf, (from the late Duke of Sussex's collection), £1. 5s* *Antverpiæ,* 1753
1223 CHURCH'S (Hen.) Good Man's Treasury, or, a Treatise wherein severall points of Divinity are handled in order, 12mo. *calf, 3s 6d* 1636
1224 CHURCH OF ENGLAND. The order and forme for Church-Government by Bishops and the Clergie of this Kingdome, voted in the House of Commons, July 16, 1641, with the Queene's Answer to the House of Commons, concerning her intended Voyage, 4to. *hf. bd. 2s* . . 1641
1225 —————— The Churches thank-offering to God, her King, and the Parliament, for rich and ancient Mercies; her Yeares of Captivity; her first Yeare of Jubilee, &c., 4to. *scarce, bds. 5s 6d* 1641
1226 —————— A Serious and Compassionate Inquiry into the Causes of the present Neglect and Contempt of the Protestant Religion and Church of England, 8vo. *front. calf, 2s 6d* . 1674

1227 CHURCH. A Vindication of the Answer to some late papers concerning the Unity and Authority of the Catholick Church, and the Reformation of the Church of England, 4to. *hf. bd. calf, very neat,* 4s . . 1687
1228 ———— An Answer to a late pamphlet entitled, " The Judgment and Doctrine of the Clergy of the Church of England, concerning one special branch of the King's Prerogative, viz., in dispensing with the Penal Laws," 4to. *hf. bd. calf, very neat,* 5s 1687
1229 ———— A Defence of the Doctrine and Practice of the Church of England, against some modern innovations, 1712—An Answer to the exceptious made against the Bp. of Oxford's Charge, by Mr. L. and Dr. Brett, 1713—The Christian Eucharist no proper Sacrifice, in answer to Mr. Johnson, 1714, *in one* vol. 8vo. *calf,* 4s ——
1230 CHURCH OF ROME. Doubts concerning the Roman Infallibility, 4to. 2s . 1688
1231 CHURCHILL'S (James, *of Henley*) Essay on Unbelief: describing its Nature and Operations, 12mo. *calf,* 2s 6d Oxford, 1811
1232 CHURCHMAN Armed against the Errors of the Time; a Collection of Tracts in defence of the Doctrines and Discipline of the Church of England, 3 vols. in 2, 8vo. *calf, marbled leaves,* 14s 1814
1232* ———— another copy, 3 vols. 8vo. *bds.* 9s . 1814
1233 CHURCHMAN'S Companion: a Help to Scripture Knowledge, for the Family Circle, and the Closet, 12mo. *bds. gilt leaves,* 1s 6d 1843
1234 CHYTRÆUS's (David) Postil, or orderly disposing of certeine Epistles usually red in the Church of God, uppon the Sundayes and Holydayes throughout the Ycere; translated by Arthur Golding, 4to. *title wanting, hf. bd. calf,* 9s . Lond. 1577
1235 ———— Libellus de Morte et Vita Æterna; cui additæ sunt, Imagines Mortis, illustratæ epigrammatis D. Georgii Æmylii, sm. 8vo. *vellum,* 7s . Witeb. 1590
   The book contains a series of wood-cuts representing the *Dance of Death,* after Hans Holbein.
1236 CIACONII (ALPHONSI) VITÆ ET RES GESTÆ PONTIFICUM ROMANORUM et S. R. E. Cardinalium, ab initio nascentis Ecclesiæ usque ad Clementem IX. 4 vols. in 2, *Romæ,* 1677—GUARNACCI (M.) Vitæ et Res Gestæ Pontificum Romanorum, &c. à Clementi X usque ad Clementem XII. 2 vols. in 1, *ib.* 1751—*Additis Pontificum recentiorum Imaginibus, et Cardinalium Insignibus, plurimisque æneis figuris, cum Indicibus locupletissimis,* together 6 vols. in 3, royal folio, *extremely scarce, hf. bd,* £8. 8s . ——
1237 ———— idem, 6 vols. in 5, folio, *vellum,* £7. 17s 6d 1677-1751
1238 ———— aliud exemplar, 6 vols. folio, *hf. bd. morocco,* £8. 18s 6d 1677-1751
1239 CIRUELUS (Petrus) Expositio libri Missalis peregregia; de Arte Predicandi; de Arte Memorandi, et de Correctione Kalendarii, folio, 𝕭lack letter, *vellum, wormed,* 10s *In Universitate Complutensi,* 1528
1240 CLAGETT'S (Will.) Paraphrase with Notes upon the sixth Chapter of St. John, with a Discourse on Humanity and Charity, 1693 —BENNET'S (Tho.) Discourse of Schism, 1702—A Defence of the same, against Mr. Shepherd, 1703—An Answer to Mr. Shepherd's Considerations on the Defence, &c., 1703, *in one* vol. 8vo. *calf,* 4s . . ——

[58, GREAT QUEEN STREET,

1241 CLAGETT'S (Will.) Discourse concerning the Operations of the Holy Spirit, with a confutation of some part of Dr. Owen's book upon that subject, &c. 8vo. *calf, neat,* 4s—*calf, very neat,* 4s 6d   1680
1242 ———— Sermons, 4 vols. 8vo. *calf, neat,* 12s   1704-20
Abp. Sharpe says that he should not hesitate to give Dr. Clagett a place amongst the most celebrated writers of the Church of England.

1243 CLAPHAM'S (Sam.) Sermons, selected and abridged chiefly from minor authors, with translations from celebrated French preachers, 2 vols. 8vo. *hf. bd. calf,* 8s   1830
1244 CLARENDON'S (Edw. Hyde, *Earl of*) History of the Rebellion and Civil Wars in England, imp. 8vo. *bds.* £1.   Oxford, 1839
1245 CLARK'S (N.) Complete Body of Divinity, consonant to the Church of England, 2 vols. 8vo. *calf,* 4s 6d   1718
1246 CLARKE'S (Adam) Concise View of the Succession of Sacred Literature, in a Chronological arrangement of Authors and their Works, &c. 2 vols. 8vo. *bds.* 16s   1830
1247 ———— (E. W.) Church-Yard-Stile; being XII Sermons adapted to the Mechanical and Agricultural Population, 8vo. *bds.* 4s 1835
1248 ———— (John) Holy Oyle for the Lampes of the Sanctuarie, or Scripture phrases alphabetically disposed for the use of such as desire to speake the language of Canaan, more especially the Sonnes of the Prophets, 4to. *calf,* 6s   1630
1249 ———— another copy, 4to. *vellum,* 4s   1630
1250 ———— (Richard) Spiritual Voice to the Christian Church and to the Jews, 1760—A Second Warning to the World by the Spirit of Prophecy, 1760—A Voice of Glad-Tidings to Jews and Gentiles, 1763—The Gospel of the Daily Service of the Law, &c., 1767, 4 vols. 8vo. *hf. bd. calf,* 6s
1251 ———— (Sam.) Marrow of Ecclesiastical History, contained in the Lives of the Fathers, Schoolmen, Reformers, and Modern Divines; whereunto is added, the Life of Gustavus Ericson, King of Sweden, and of some other eminent Christians. 2 vols. 4to. *many portraits, calf, very scarce,* 16s   1654-62
1252 ———— Paraphrase on the Gospel of St. Matthew, 8vo. *calf,* 3s 6d   1701
1253 ———— (Sam. D. D.) Sermons on several subjects and occasions, edited by John Clarke, D.D. Dean of Sarum, with his Life by Bp. Hoadley, *best edition,* 8 vols. 8vo. *portrait, fine copy, calf gilt, old style,* £1. 15s   1756
1254 ———— another copy, with his Letters to Dodwell, in answer to his Discourse against the Immortality of the Soul; and the Scripture Doctrine of the Trinity, together 12 vols. 8vo. *port. fine copies, calf,* £1. 11s 6d   1731-32
1255 ———— Answer to Dr. Clarke and Mr. Whiston concerning the Divinity of the Son, and of the Holy Spirit; with a summary of the chief Writers of the three first Ages, by H. E. 8vo. *calf,* 2s 6d   1729
1256 ———— Three practical Essays on Baptism, Confirmation, and Repentance, 8vo. *calf,* 3s   1730

1256 *CLARKE (Dr. Sam.) Forty Sermons on doctrinal and practical subjects, selected from the works of Dr. Samuel Clarke, by S. Clapham, 8vo. *bds. 3s* . 1806
1257 CLARKSON's (David) Sermons and Discourses on several Divine Subjects, folio, *calf, scarce,* £1. 1s . 1696
1258 ——— (Tho.) Portraiture of Quakerism, 3 vols. 8vo. *calf gilt, 6s* 1806
1259 CLAUDE's ( ) Historical Defence of the Reformation, in answer to a book intituled, Just Prejudices against the Calvinists; translated by T. B., 4to. *calf, neat, 7s 6d* . 1683
1260 ——— Reponse generale au nouveau livre de M. Claude, 12mo. *neat, 2s 6d* . *Par.* 1671
1261 CLAYTON's (Rob. Bp. *of Clogher)* Vindication of the Histories of the Old and New Testaments, in a series of letters: to which is prefixed, an Essay on Spirit, wherein the Doctrine of the Trinity is considered, 1759—Some Thoughts on Self-love, innate Ideas, Freewill, Taste, &c., 1763—A Defence of the Essay on Spirit, 1753—A Speech made in the House of Lords in Ireland, for omitting the Nicene and Athanasian Creeds out of the Liturgy, 1774—Letters between the Bishop and Mr. W. Penn, on Baptism, 1756—3 vols. 8vo. *calf, 6s* .
1262 CLEMENS *(Alexandrinus)* Opera Omnia, *Græcè (a beautiful specimen of Greek typography), Florentiæ,* 1550—Justini Martyris Opera, *Græcè,* EDITIO PRINCEPS, *Lutetiæ, ex off. R. Stephani,* 1551. *In one* vol. folio, *fine large copies, calf gilt, gilt leaves,* £1. 15s
1263 CLEMENTIS ALEXANDRINI Opera Omnia, *Gr. et Lat.* recognita et illustrata per Jo. Potterum, Episc. Oxon. 2 vols. in 1, folio, *best edition, very scarce, fine copy, rich cf. gilt,* £7. 17s 6d *Oxon.* 1715
1264 ——— aliud exemplar, 2 vols. folio, *new in calf gilt, old style,* £4. 4s . *Venet.* 1757
1265 ——— idem, 2 vols. in 1, folio, *calf gilt,* £3. 15s *ib.* 1757
1266 ——— aliud exemplar, 2 vols. folio, *vellum,* £3. 3s *ib.* 1757
1267 CLEMENTIS Romani ad Corinthios Epistola prior, *Gr. et Lat.* notis illustravit Pat. Junius. 4to. *vellum,* 4s 6d—*sewed,* 3s *Oxon.* 1633
1268 ——— idem, 4to. *large paper, half bound, vellum,* 6s *ib.* 1633
1269 ——— idem, *Oxon.* 1633—Hexameron Ægidii Columnæ, *Patav.* 1549—Eutychii Ægyptii Patriarchæ Alexandrini Ecclesiæ suæ Origines, ed. Jo. Seldenus, *Arab. et Lat.* 1642—Gennadii Patr. Constant. Defensio quinque capitum quæ in Œcumenica Florentina Synodo continentur, *Rom.* 1579, *in one* vol. 4to. *vellum,* 9s V. Y.
1270 ——— Epistola prior, cum notis Patr. Junii, ed. J. J. Maderus, 4to. *bds. 4s 6d* . *Helmst.* 1654
1271 ——— Epistolæ duæ ad Corinthios, *Gr. et Lat.* recensuit et notas adjecit P. Colomesius: accedit Tho. Brunonis Dissertatio de Therapeutis Philonis, &c. 12mo. *calf,* 5s *Lond.* 1687

From the Sussex Library.

[58, GREAT QUEEN STREET,

1272 CLEMENTIS Rom. Epistolæ duæ, *Græce et Lat.* cum notis variorum, præfatione de usu Patrum ac Dissertationibus Hen. Wottoni, 8vo. *fine copy, calf,* 9s . *Cant.* 1718
From the library of the Duke of Sussex.
1273 ——— aliud exemplar, 8vo. *vellum,* 10s 6d *ib.* 1718
1274 ——— idem, LARGE PAPER, roy. 8vo. *calf gilt,* 16s *ib.* 1718
1275 ——— De rebus gestis, peregrinationibus, atque concionibus, Sancti Petri, ad Jacobum Hierosolymarum episcopum. Ejusdem Clementis Vita, *Græcè.*—Alexander Aphrodisæus, *Græcè.*—Callimachi Cyrenæi Hymni, *Græcè, Par.* 1549, *in one* vol. 4to. *sewed,* 5s
1276 ——— First Epistle to the Church at Corinth, 12mo. *sewed,* 1s
Aberdeen, 1768
1277 ——— First Epistle to the Church at Corinth, 12mo. *bds.* 2s
Dundee, 1803
1278 CLEMENTIS XI. (*Pontifex Maximus*) Homiliæ hactenus habitæ ad Pop. Rom. Græcæ e Latinis factæ, labore Jo. Sagvens. *Gr. et Lat.* 8vo. *vellum,* 4s 6d . *Tolosæ,* 1606
1279 CLEMENT'S (Benj.) Sermons on several subjects and occasions, 2 2 vols. in 1, 8vo. 3s . *Wolverhampton,* ———
1280 CLERGYMAN'S (The) Assistant, being a collection of Statutes, Ordinances, and Forms, relating to the rights and duties of the Clergy, 8vo. *bds.* 7s 6d . 1828
1281 CLERICUS (Dav.) Quæstiones Sacræ in quibus multa Scripturæ loca : accesserunt Diatribæ Steph. Clerici, edidit Jo. Clericus, 12mo. *calf,* 2s 6d . . *Amst.* 1685
1282 CLINTON'S (Hen. Fynes) Fasti Hellenici ; the Civil and Literary Chronology of Greece, from the earliest accounts to the Death of Augustus, 3 vols. 4to. *hf. bd. calf,* £3. 13s 6d *Oxford,* 1834
1283 CLUBBE'S (Jo.) Miscellaneous Tracts, 2 vols. 12mo. *neat,* 4s 1771
1284 CLUTTERBUCK'S (J.) Brief Explanation of the obscure Phrases in the Book of Psalms, 8vo. 4s . 1702
1285 COADE'S (G.) Letter to a Clergyman on his Sermon on the 30th of January, 12mo. *hf. bd. uncut,* 2s . 1747
1286 ——— another edition (published anonymously) 12mo. 1s 6d
1760
1287 [COBBIN'S (Ingram)] Account of the Reformed Church of France, 8vo. *neat, scarce, not printed for sale,* 5s 1819
1288 COCCEI (Jo.) Opera omnia theologica, exegetica, didactica, polemica, philologica, *best edition,* 12 vols. in 11, folio, *vellum,* £5. 10s
Amst. 1701
Cocceius was Professor of Divinity at Leyden, and according to Mosheim " a man of vast erudition, ardent piety, and uncommon application to the Scriptures."
1289 COCHLÆUS (Jo.) Ad semper victricem Germaniam Παράκλησις : ut pristinæ Constantiæ fidei et virtutis memor, insolentissima Lutheranorum factione abdicata, in errores se abduci non patiatur, 12mo. *calf,* 7s 6d . *Urb. Agrip.* 1524
1290 ——— Historia Hussitarum ; Tractatus duorum Bohemorum de septem Sacramentis et de Cæremoniis Ecclesiæ ; et Philippica de Caroli V. ordinatione, quæ vulgo Interim dicitur, folio, *calf, very rare,* 18s . *Moguntiæ,* 1549

1291 COCHLÆUS (J.) Commentaria de Actis et Scriptis Martini Lutheri, folio, *very rare, vellum*, 14s
Apud S. Victorem prope Moguntiam, 1549
1292 ———— Septiceps Lutherus, ubique sibi, suis scriptis contrarius, in visitationem Saxonicam æditus, small 8vo. *vellum*, 7s 6d
Par. 1564
1293 COCKBURN's (John) Inquiry into the nature of Christian Faith, in several Essays, 8vo. *calf*, 2s . 1697
1294 ———— (G. A.) First Chapters on the Church of England, her Clergy, Liturgy, Articles, and Temporalities, 12mo. *bds*. 3s 6d 1842
1295 [COCKBURNE's (Rob.)] Historical Dissertation on the Books of the New Testament; with a History of the Methods by which these Sacred Writings have been preserved and conveyed down to us, 8vo. (Vol. 1, *all published*) *calf, scarce*, 4s *Privately printed*, 1755
" A work of more merit than fame."—*Townson's Four Gospels*.
1296 COCKMAN's (Dr. Tho. *Univ. Coll. Oxon.*) Select Theological Discourses, 2 vols. 8vo. LARGE PAPER, *portrait, calf*, 4s 1750

" If we go beyond the surface we shall find a bottom, sound and solid ; just and great sentiments, clear and distinct ideas, strong and weighty reasons, supporting the fundamentals of our religion in faith and practice."—*Silvester.*

1297 CODEX THEODORI BEZÆ Cantabrigiensis, Evangelia et Acta Apostolorum complectens, quadritis literis Græco-Latinus ; edidit notasque adjecit Tho. Kipling, *fine paper*, 2 vols. imp. folio, *russia*, £3. 10s . *Cantab.* 1793
1298 CODINUS (Geo. *Curopalata*) de Officiis et Officialibus Magnæ Ecclesiæ et Aulæ Constantinopolitanæ, *Gr. et Lat.* studio Jac. Gretseri, folio, *vellum*, £1. 10s *Par.* 1625
1299 COKAYN's (Geo.) Flesh Expiring, and the Spirit inspiring in the new earth ; a Sermon before the House of Commons, 4to. *sewed*, 2s . 1648
1300 COLBATCH's (John) Case of Proxies payable to Ecclesiastical Visitors, *Camb.* 1741—Reasons for altering the method of letting Church and College Leases, *ib.*1739—*in one vol.* 8vo. *calf*, 3s ——
1301 COLERIDGE's (Derwent) Scriptural Character of the English Church, considered in a series of Sermons, 8vo. *bds*. 6s 1839
1302 ———— Practical Advice to the Young Parish Priest, 12mo. *bds.* 2s . . 1834
1303 ———— (S. T.) Specimens of his Table Talk, 12mo. *port. bds.* 5s 1836
1304 ———— (W. H., *Bp. of Barbados*) On the right Hearing of God's Word, a Sermon, 4to. *sewed*, 1s 6d *Barbados*, 1832
1305 ———— A Primary Charge addressed to the Clergy of the Diocese of Barbados, in 1830 and 1831, 4to. *sewed*, 1s 1834
1306 ———— A Charge addressed to the Clergy of the Diocese of Barbados in 1834, 4to. *sewed*, 1s . 1834
1307 ———— Address delivered at the City of Caracas, 26 Feb. 1834, at the Consecration of a Chapel and Burial Ground, 4to. 1s 6d
Winchester, [1834]
1308 COLES's (Elisha) Practical Discourse of God's Sovereignty ; with a recommendatory preface by W. Romaine, 8vo. *calf*, 3s 1794

[58, GREAT QUEEN STREET,

1309 COLLECTIO NOVA Patrum et Scriptorum Græcorum, viz. Eusebii Commentarii in Psalmos, S. Athanasii Opuscula, Cosmæ Indicopleustæ Christianorum opinio de Mundo, sive Topographia Christiana, et Eusebii Commentaria in Hesaiam, *Gr. et Lat.* studio Bern. de Montfaucon, 2 vols. folio, *calf*, £3. 3s   Par. 1707

1310 COLLIBER's (Sam.) Free Thoughts concerning Souls, &c. 8vo. *calf*, 3s   .   .   1734

1311 ——— Impartial Enquiry into the Existence and Nature of God, 8vo. *calf*, 2s   .   .   1735

1312 COLLIER's (Jeremy) Ecclesiastical History of Great Britain to the end of the reign of Charles II.; with an Account of Religion in Ireland, 2 vols. folio, *front. fine copy, calf*, £4. 10s   1708-14

1313 ——— A Defence of Dramatic Poetry : being a Review of Mr. Collier's View of the Immorality of the Stage, 8vo. (*two leaves wanting*) 1s 6d   .   1698

1314 COLLINGES's (John) Cordial for a Fainting Soule, 4to. *calf*, 9s 1652

1315 ——— Several Discourses concerning the Actual Providence of God, 4to. *calf*, 8s   .   1678

" What Collinges hath written on Providence is well performed."
                                                            Cotton Mather.

1316 ——— Intercourses of Divine Love between Christ and his Church, metaphorically expressed by Solomon in the first and second chapters of the Canticles, opened in several Sermons, 2 vols. 4to. *calf, neat*, 12s   .   1683-76

1317 [COLLINS's (Ant.)] Historical and Critical Essay on the 39 Articles, wherein it is demonstrated that this clause, *The Church has power, &c.* is not a part of the Articles as they were established by Act of Parliament, &c. 8vo. *calf*, 2s   .   1724

1318 ——— the same, with a Discourse on Free Thinking, 1713—A Philosophical Inquiry concerning Human Liberty, 1718—A Letter to Mr. Henry Dodwell, containing some Remarks on a (pretended) Demonstration of the Immateriality and Natural Immortality of the Soul, in Mr. Clark's Answer to his late Epistolary Discourse, &c. 1709—A Reply to Mr. Clark's Defence of his Letter to Mr. Dodwell, with a Postscript relating to Mr. Milles's Answer to Mr. Dodwell's Epistolary Discourse, 1709—Reflections on Mr. Clark's Second Defence of his Letter to Mr. Dodwell, 1711—An Answer to Mr. Clark's Third Defence of his Letter to Mr. Dodwell, 1711—An Essay concerning the Use of Reason in Propositions, the evidence whereof depends upon Human Testimony, 1711, *in one* vol. 8vo. *calf*, 6s   .   ——

1318* ——— Discourse of the Grounds and Reasons of the Christian Religion, 1737—A Letter to the author of the Discourse of the Grounds and Reasons of the Christian Religion, in answer to Mr. Green's Letters, &c., with a Postscript occasioned by Dr. Lobb's Brief Defence, &c., *in one* vol. 8vo. *calf*, 4s 6d   1737

1319 COLLINSON's (J.) Observations on the History of the Preparation for the Gospel, and its early Propagation; from the Dedication of Solomon's Temple to the end of the first Christian century, 8vo. *bds.* 4s   .   .   1830

1320 COLLYER's (David) Sacred Interpreter; or, a Practical Introduction towards a beneficial reading of the Holy Bible, 2 vols. 8vo. *maps, calf*, 6s . 1732
1321 ——— the same, 2 vols. 8vo. *plates, bds.* 6s 1821
1322 ——— another copy, 2 vols. *hf. bd. morocco*, 7s 6d 1815
1333 ——— another copy, 8vo. *.hf bd. calf gilt*, 9s   *Oxford*, 1831
1324 COLOMESIUS (Paulus) Observationes Sacræ: accedunt ejusdem Paralipomena de Scriptoribus Ecclesiasticis, et passio S. Victoris Massiliensis ab eodem emendata, 12mo. *calf*, 3s   *Lond.* 1688
1325 COMBEFIS (Franc.) Historia Hæresis Monothelitarum, sanctæque in eam Sextæ Synodi Actorum, Vindiciæ, diversorum item Antiqua ac Medii Ævi, tum Historiæ Sacræ, tum Dogmatica, Græca Opuscula, &c. folio, *calf, scarce*, £1. 5s . *Par.* 1648
1326 ——— Christi Martyrum Lecta Trias, Hyacinthus Amastrensis, Bacchus et Elias, Novi-martyres, Agarenico pridem mucrone sublati, 8vo. *calf*, 4s . . *ib.* 1666
1327 ——— Bibliotheca Patrum Concionatoria, hoc est anni totius Evangelia, festa Dominica, S. Deiparæ, illustriorumque Sanctorum Solennia; Patrum Symbolis, tractatibus, panegyricis, &c. illustrata ac exornata, 7 vols. royal folio, *new in rich calf gilt*, £12. 12s
    Venetiis, 1749
1328 COMBER'S (Tho.) Companion to the Temple; or, a Help to Devotion in the use of the Common Prayer, folio, *calf*, £1. 4s   1701
1329 ——— new edition, with the Occasional Offices; a History of Liturgies, and other Works, 7 vols. 8vo. *bds.* £2. 2s—*calf gilt*, £3. 6s . . *Oxford*, 1841
1330 ——— Historical Vindication of the Divine Right of Tithes, with a Discourse concerning Excommunication, 2 parts, 4to. *calf*, 6s
    1685
1331 ——— Life and Writings, with an Account of his Literary Correspondence, by Thomas Comber, 8vo. *portrait, tree-marbled calf gilt*, 6s . . 1799
1332 COMMON PLACE-BOOK to the Holy Bible: wherein the substance of Scripture respecting Doctrine, Worship, and Manners is reduced to its proper head, &c., 4to. *calf*, 4s . 1725
1333 COMMON PRAYER.—The Book of Common Prayer, and Administration of the Sacraments, and other parts of Divine Service, for the use of the Church of Scotland, folio, RARE, *fine copy, calf*, £5. 15s 6d . *Edinb.* 1637
1334 ——— (The Book of,) according to the use of the Church of England, together with the XXXIX. Articles, *English* and *Irish;* to which is added, the Elements of the Irish Language, 8vo. *calf, scarce*, 7s 6d . *Lond.* ——
1335 ——— An Account of all the Proceedings of the Commissioners of both Perswasions appointed for the Review of the Book of Common Prayer, 4to. *hf. bd. calf*, 5s 6d . 1661
1336 COMPLETE Body of Divinity, extracted from the best Ancient and Modern Authors, thick folio, *calf*, 9s . 1729

1337 COMPANION for the Sick-Room, being a Compendium of Christian Faith and Practice, chiefly compiled from the Writings of Divines of the Holy Catholic Church ; and Devotions for the Sick-Room, and for Times of Trouble, compiled from Ancient Liturgies, &c. 2 vols. in 1, 12mo. *bds. 6s* . 1843
1338 CONANT's (John, D.D., *Rector of Exeter Coll. Oxon.*) Life, by his son John Conant, LL.D., now first published by the Rev. W. Stanton, 8vo. *bds. 2s* . 1823
1339 CONCILIA SACROSANCTA ad Regiam Editionem exacta, ab initiis Christianæ ad annum 1645 : cum Apparatu, opera et studio P. LABBÆI et G. COSSARTII, 18 vols. folio, *fine copy, calf, £15. 15s*
Par. 1671
1340 ———— CONCILIA GERMANIÆ, quæ R. P. Joannis Mauritii Archiepisc. Pragensis, sumptu, J. F. Schannat magna ex parte primum collegit, dein P. JOSEPHUS HARTZHEIM, continuavit et prelo dedit, P. Hermannus Scholl, *S. J.* evolvit, auxit, ac Notis illustravit, et Opus ejusdem Morte interruptum absolvit Ægidius Neissen *S. J.* Accedit Index quintuplex, opera et studio A. A. Hesselmanni, 11 vols. folio, RARE, *hf. bd. £8. 8s Coloniæ*, 1759-90
1341 ———— PALLAVICINO (Sforza) Istoria del Concilio di Trento, illustrata con Annotazioni da Francesco Zaccaria, *best edition*, 6 vols. in 3, 4to. *fine copy, new in vellum, £4. 4s In Faenza*, 1792
1341* ———— VON DER HARDT (Herm.) Magnum Œcumenicum Constantiense Concilium de Universale Ecclesiæ Reformatione, Unione et Fide, 6 vols. in 3, folio, *calf, £2. 10s Franc.* 1700
1342 ———— WILKINS (DAV.) CONCILIA MAGNA BRITANNIÆ ET HIBERNIÆ, à Synodo Verolamiensi 446 ad Londinensem, 1717— Accedunt Constitutiones et alia ad Historiam Ecclesiæ Anglicanæ spectantia, 4 vols. fol. EXTREMELY RARE, *fine copy, calf, £24*. 1717
1343 ———— Collectio Conciliorum Hispaniæ, diligentia Garsiæ Loaisa elaborata, ejusque vigiliis aucta, folio, *the Colbert copy, in old French red morocco, gilt leaves, £2. 2s Madriti*, 1593
1344 ———— Statuta Concilii Florentini, 4to. *fine copy, vellum, 6s*
Florent. 1564
1345 CONCILIUM Romanum in S. Lateranensi Basilica celebratum, anno Jubilæi 1725, a Benedicto Papa XIII. 12mo. *nt. 3s 6d Brux.* 1726
1346 CONCLAVE, in quo Fabius Chisius, nunc dictus Alexander VII. summus Pontifex creatus est ; Urbani VIII. Confirmatio Bullæ Gregorii XV. de electione Romani Pontificis ; Nomina et Tituli Cardinalium nunc viventium ; Bulla, quæ die Cœnæ Dominicæ promulgari solet ; Matthæ Palmerii, de Captivitate Pisarum Historia—De Vita Innocentii X—De Cardinalium Origine, auctoritate et factionibus ; etc. 12mo. *vellum, 5s Sleswici*, 1656
1347 CONCLAVES (Histoire des) depuis Clement V. jusqu'à present, enrichie de plusieurs Memoires, qui contiennent l'Histoire du Pape et des Cardinaux d'aujourd'hui, et celles des principales Familles de Rome ; où l'on apprend quantité de particularités de cette cour, 2 vols. 12mo. *frontispiece, calf, 4s Cologne*, 1694
1348 ———— autre exemplaire, augmentée du Conclave de Clement XI, et d'un Traité de l'Origine des Cardinaux et des Legats, 2 vols. 12mo. *plates, vellum, 7s 6d* . *ib.* 1703

1349 CONCORDANCE.—The Fort-royal of Holy Scriptures; or, a New Concordance of the chief heads of Scripture common-placed, by J. H. 12mo. *new in sprinkled calf gilt*, 7s . 1655
1350 CONDREN Idée du Sacerdoce et du Sacrifice de Jesus Christ, 12mo. *neat*, 2s . . *Par*. 1697
1351 CONEY's (Tho.) Devout Soul; or, an Entertainment for a Penitent; consisting of Meditations, Poems, Hymns, and Prayers, 8vo. *calf*, 2s 6d . . 1722
1352 ——— Twenty-five Sermons; to which is annexed, a short Character of Dr. Geo. Hooper, late Bp. of Bath and Wells, 8vo. *calf*, 3s . . 1730
1353 CONFESSEURS.—Conduite des Confesseurs, dans la Tribunal de la Pénitence, selon les instructions de S. Charles Borromée et la doctrine de S. François de Sales : imprimée par l'ordre de l'Evêque de Bayeux, 12mo. *neat*, 3s 6d . *Par*. 1760
1354 CONFESSIO AUGUSTANA. Concordia pia et unanimi concensu repetita : Confessio Fidei et Doctrinæ Electorum, Principum, et ordinum Imperii, atque eorundem theologorum, qui Augustanam Confessionem amplectuntur, etc. sm. 8vo. *front. hf. bd.* 7s
Lips. 1756
1355 CONFESSION of Faith, together with the larger and lesser Catechisms of the Assembly of Divines, 12mo. *calf*, 2s 6d 1688
1356 ——— idem, Latine, 12mo. *calf*, 4s *Cantab*. 1656
1357 ——— The Orthodox Confession of the Catholic and Apostolic Eastern Church, faithfully translated, 8vo. 3s 1762
1358 CONRINGII (Herm.) Opera Omnia, continens Varia Scripta ad Historiam et Jus Publicum Imperii Germanici spectantia, etc. 7 vols. folio, *fine copy, vellum*, £4. 4s *Brunsvigæ*, 1730
1359 CONTI (Le Prince de) Lettres, ou l'accord du libre arbitre avec la grace de Jesus Christ, 18mo. *hogskin*, 2s 6d *Cologne*, 1689
1360 CONVERSATION (A) on the advance which we have made in Christian Charity, or why is it not enough for a Man to be Sincere? 18mo. *bds.* 1s 6d . . 1837
1361 CONVERSION. Idée de la Conversion du Pécheur, ou Explication des qualitez d'une vraie pénitence, etc. 2 vols. in 1, 12mo. *neat*, 3s 6d
s. l. 1732
1362 CONVOCATION. A Letter from a Minister in the Country to a Member of the Convocation, 4to. *sewed*, 2s 6d 1689
1363 ——— Remarks from the Country upon the two Letters relating to the Convocation, and Alterations in the Liturgy, 4to. *sewed*, 2s 6d . 1689-90
1364 COOKE's (John, *of Canterbury*) Thirty-nine Sermons, 2 vols. 8vo. *calf*, 5s . . 1729
1365 ——— Preacher's Assistant, containing a Series of the Texts of Sermons and Discourses published either singly or in volumes, by Divines of the Church of England and by the Dissenting Clergy, from the Reformation to the present time, 2 vols. 8vo. *calf*, 18s— *bds.* 14s *Oxford*, 1783

" I refer the reader to this, as a useful catalogue, from which he may select such writers of Sermons as he may think fit for his Library ; for where all are equally good, it would be presumptuous in me to attempt to particularize the best."
Bp. Watson.

[58, GREAT QUEEN STREET,

1366 COOPER's (Edw.) Practical and Familiar Sermons, 12mo. *hf. bd.* 2s 6d . 1809
1367 ———— (Oliver St. John) Manual of Orthodox Divinity, 8vo. *bds.* 1s . 1806
1368 ———— (Wm. *Archd. of York*) Discourses on various subjects, 2 vols. 8vo. *calf*, 5s . 1795
1369 ———— (Wm. *of Boston, N. E.*) Doctrine of Predestination unto Life, explained and vindicated in four Sermons, 12mo. *hf. bd. calf*, 2s . 1765
1370 COPLESTONE's (Bp.) Inquiry into the Doctrines of Necessity and Predestination, with Notes, and an Appendix on the XVIIth Article of the Church of England, 8vo. *hf. bd. calf*, 8s . 1821
1371 ———— Sermon preached before the Members of Oriel College, Oxford, upon the Commemoration Festival held June 26, 1826, to celebrate the completion of five hundred years, from the foundation of the College, 4to. 1s 6d *Oxford*, 1826
1372 COPUS (Alanus) [*i. e.* Nicholas Harpsfelde] Dialogi sex contra Summi Pontificatus, Monasticæ vitæ, Sanctorum, Sacrarum Imaginum oppugnatores, et Pseudomartyres, 4to. *fine copy, in the original hogskin binding*, 25s—*calf*, 25s *Antv.* 1566
1373 ———— aliud exemplar, 4to. *blue morocco, gilt leaves*, £1. 16s *ib.* 1573

The 5th and 6th of these dialogues relate chiefly to England. The present copies contains the rare folded plate of the miraculous cross in perfect preservation.

1374 CORAH. Hieragonisticon; or Corah's Doom, being an Answer to two Letters of Inquiry into the Grounds of the Contempt of the Clergy, 12mo. 2s 6d . 1672
1375 CORDERIUS (Balth.) Expositio Patrum Græcorum in Psalmos, 3 vols. folio, *vellum*, £3. 3s *Ant.* 1643
1376 CORNISH's (Hubert Kestell) Book of Family or Private Prayer, 18mo. *morocco, gilt leaves*, 6s *Oxford*, 1841
1377 CORTES (Hernando). The Despatches of Hernando Cortes, the Conqueror of Mexico, addressed to the Emperor Charles V. and translated by G. Folsom, 8vo. *bds.* 8s *New York*, 1843
1378 COSENS' (Dr. Jo.) Sermons on useful and important subjects, 2 vols. 8vo. *bds.* 4s . 1793
1379 COSTARD's (G.) Dissertation upon II Kings, x. 22, translated from the Latin of Rabbi C., 8vo. *sewed*, 1s *Lond.* N. D.
1380 ———— Some Observations tending to illustrate the Book of Job, 8vo. *sewed*, 1s . *Oxford*, 1747
1381 [COSIN's (J.) *Bp. of Durham*] — An Apologie of, and for sundrie proceedings by Jurisdiction Ecclesiasticall, 4to. *poor copy*, 7s 1591

A note upon the title states that "only about 40 copies were printed."

1382 ———— Scholastical History of the Canon of the Holy Scripture, 4to. *calf*, 14s . 1672
1383 ———— another copy, 4to. *calf*, 12s 1683
1384 ———— A Collection of Private Devotions, in the practice of the ancient Church, called the Hours of Prayer, 24mo. *bds.* 5s 6d 1841
1385 ———— Works, now first collected, 2 vols. 8vo. *bds.* 16s *Oxford*, 1843-45

1386 [COSIN'S (J.) *Bp. of Durham*] HISTORY OF POPISH TRANSUBSTANTIATION, to which is premised and opposed, the Catholic Doctrine of the Holy Scripture, the Ancient Fathers, and the Reformed Churches, about the Sacred Elements and presence of Christ in the blessed Sacrament of the Eucharist. Also, an Account of a Conference held at York House, Feb. 1625, between Dr. White (Dean of Carlisle) Dr. Cosin, Dr. Buckeridge (Bp. of Rochester), and Bishop Morton, on several Questions respecting the Doctrine and Discipline of the Church of England, particularly such as had been discussed in the Writings of Bp. Montague; now first printed from Dr. Cosin's own narrative, preserved in the Bodleian Library at Oxford, 12mo. *bds. 6s Lond.* 1840

> This reprint of Dr. Cosin's valuable work on Transubstantiation is much improved by having the references verified, and the quotations given at full length. The hitherto unpublished tract on Church Discipline will be found extremely interesting. A copious Memoir of the Author (by the Rev. J. S. Brewer, of Queen's Coll. Oxon.) is prefixed.

1387 ―――― le même, en *François*, d'après la premiere édition d'Amsterdam, 1689, qui fut traduite du Latin, 12mo. *bds. 4s Laus.* 1820

1388 COTELERIUS (J. B.) S. S. Patrum qui temporibus Apostolicis floruerunt, Barnabæ, Clementis, Hermæ, Ignatii Polycarpi Opera, edita et inedita, vera et supposititia, Græce et Latine; unà cum Clementis, Ignatii, Polycarpi, Actis et Martyriis. Accesserunt in hac nova editione, Notæ integræ aliorum virorum Doctorum, item Guil. Beveregii Codex Canonum Primitivæ Ecclesiæ Vindicatus, Jac. Usserii Dissertationes Ignatianæ, et J. Pearsonii Vindiciæ Epistolarum S. Ignatii; recensuit et notulas aliquot adspersit Joannes Clericus, 2 vols. in 1, folio, *fine copy, new in calf gilt,* £7. 7s
Antverpiæ, 1698

1389 ―――― aliud exemplar, access. Notæ H. Menardi et Notæ et Opuscula aliorum Virorum doctorum [recensuit J. Clericus] 2 vols. folio, *calf,* £7. 7s . *ib.* 1700

1390 ―――― idem, editio nova, auxit, recensuit, et notulas suas et aliorum adspersit J. Clericus, *best edition,* 2 vols. folio, *vellum,* £8. 8s― *calf, neat,* £8. 18s 6d . *Amst.* 1724

1391 ―――― aliud exemplar, 2 vols. folio, *fine copy, new in calf gilt,* £10. 10s . *ib.* 1724

1392 COTES's (Digby) Fifteen Sermons on several occasions, 8vo. *calf, 3s*
Oxford, 1721

1393 COTTON'S (John, D.D., *of Boston, N. E.*) Pouring out of the Seven Vials, or an Exposition of Revelation xvi. 4to. *calf, 4s 6d*   1642

1394 ―――― Christ the Fountaine of Life: or sundry choice Sermons on part of the 5th chapter of the I. Epist. of St. John, 4to. *calf,* 5s 6d . 1651

1395 ―――― Practical Commentary, or an Exposition upon the first Epistle Generall of St. John, folio, *calf,* £1. 5s   1656

1396 ―――― (Dr. Henry) Memoir of a French Translation of the New Testament, in which the Mass and Purgatory are found in the Sacred Text: together with Bishop Kidder's Reflections on the same, 8vo. *sewed, scarce, 2s 6d* . 1827

[58, GREAT QUEEN STREET,

1397 COTTON's List of Editions of the Bible, and parts thereof in English, from 1505 to 1820; with an Appendix containing specimens of Translations and Bibliographical descriptions, 8vo. *bds.* 4s 6d
Oxford, 1821
1398 ———— Typographical Gazetteer, 8vo. *bds.* 8s *ib.* 1831
1399 COUNSEL and Directions, Divine and Moral, in plain and familiar Letters from a Divine to his Nephew, soon after his admission into a College in Oxford, 8vo. *calf,* 2s 1685
1400 COURAYER's (P. F. le) Defence of the Validity of the English Ordinations, and of the Succession of the Bishops in the Church of England, translated by D. Williams, 8vo. *calf,* 9s 1725
From the library of the late Duke of Sussex.
1401 ———— Dissertation on the Validity of the English Ordinations, and of the Succession of the Bishops of the Anglican Church, 8vo. *bds.* 7s . Oxford, 1844
1402 ———— Memoires ou Dissertation sur la Validité des Ordinatious des Anglois, pour servir de Réponse au livre du R. Pere Le Courayer, par M. E. Fennell, 2 vols. in 1, 8vo. *calf,* 7s 6d *Par.* 1726
1403 ———— La Defense des Ordinations Anglicanes refutée par le Pere Hardouin, 2 vols. 12mo. *fine copy, old French red morocco, gilt and marbled leaves,* 16s . *ib.* 1727
1404 ———— Nullité des Ordinations Anglicanes, ou refutation du livre [de Courayer] intitulé Dissertation, etc. 2 vols. 12mo. *calf,* 8s
ib. 1725
1404* ———— le même, 2 vols. 12mo. *sewed,* 7s *ib.* 1730
1405 ———— Justification de l'Eglise Romaine sur la réordination des Anglois Episcopaux : ou réponse à la Dissertation [de Courayer], et a la Défence de la Dissertation sur la Validité des Ordinations Angloises ; par Theodoric de S. René, 2 vols. 12mo. *old green morocco, marbled and gilt leaves, scarce,* 21s *Par.* 1728
1406 ———— A Declaration of my last Sentiments on the different Doctrines of Religion; published in French by W. Bell, D.D. A faithful translation, with an Account of Dr. Courayer, [by Dr. John Calder,] 12mo. *hf. bd.* 3s 6d . 1787
1407 COURTENAY's (Reginald) Future States, their Evidences and Nature considered on principles Physical, Moral, and Scriptural; with the design of shewing the Value of the Gospel Revelation, 8vo. *bds.* 10s 6d . . 1843
1408 COVEL's (John) Account of the present Greek Church, with some Reflections on their Doctrine and Discipline, particularly on the Eucharist, and the rest of their Sacraments, compared with Goar's Notes on the Greek Ritual, folio, *calf, scarce,* £1. 6s *Camb.* 1722
1409 ———— another copy, LARGE PAPER, folio, *calf,* £1. 11s 6d
ib. 1722
1410 COVERDALE's (Miles, *Bp. of Exeter*) Letters of the Martyrs : collected and published in 1564, with a Preface by Miles Coverdale, and Introductory Remarks by the Rev. Edw. Bickersteth, 12mo. *portrait, bds.* 5s . 1837
1411 ———— Writings and Translations, edited by the Rev. George Pearson, 8vo. *bds.* 14s . *Camb.* 1844

1412 COVERDALE (Miles, *Bp. of Exeter*) A Spiritual and most Preciouse Perle, teachynge all men to love and embrace ye Crosse, as a most swete and necessarye thinge unto the soule; what comfort is to be taken thereof; where and howe bothe consolacion and aide in al manner of Afflyccions is to bee sought; and agayne, howe all men should behave themselves therin, accordyng to the Word of God, 12mo. *bds. very scarce,* 3s—*large paper,* 4s 6d
1550. Reprinted, 1812

> This tract is usually supposed to have been written by Edward Seymour, Duke of Somerset, and Protector, during the short reign of Edward VI. who was his nephew; but it is, in fact, the production of *Otho Wormulerus*, and was first translated into the English language, from the original German of that author, by MYLES COVERDALE.
> When the "Protector" sank beneath the violence of party, and was committed to the Tower, a manuscript copy of the "Spiritual Pearl" afforded so much genuine consolation to his hours of melancholy privacy and political disgrace, that, on his release, he caused it to be printed, and prefixed that recommendatory address which does so much honour to his principles and understanding. The firm sense and soundness of general religious opinion contained in the work, caused the edition published by the Duke to be eagerly procured by all parties, and copies have recently sold for as much as TEN GUINEAS.

1413 ———— Memorials of the Right Reverend Father in God, Myles Coverdale, sometime Lord Bishop of Exeter, with divers matters relating to the Promulgation of the Bible, 8vo. *portrait, bds.* 6s
1838
1414 Cox's (Sir Richard) Inquiry into Religion, and the use of Reason in reference to it, in several Discourses, 8vo. *calf,* 3s   1713
1415 ———— (Robert) Narratives of the Lives of the more eminent Fathers of the three first centuries, with copious quotations from their Writings, &c. 8vo. *calf, neat,* 5s   .   1817
1416 COXE's (R. C.) Practical Sermons, 12mo. *bds.* 2s   1834
1417 CRABB'S (Hab.) Sermons on practical subjects, with a Discourse of Massillon, translated from the French, and Memoirs of the Author by the Rev. H. Worthington, jun., 8vo. *bds.* 3s 6d   Camb. 1796
1418 CRADOCK'S (Sam.) Harmony of the four Evangelists, and their text methodized, folio, *neat,* 8s   .   1688

> The author was a Nonconformist. The above work was revised by Dr. Tillotson, afterwards Abp. of Canterbury, by whom it was preserved from destruction during the great fire of London.

1419 ———— Apostolical History, containing the Acts, Labours, and Miracles of the Holy Apostles, from Christ's Ascension to the Destruction of Jerusalem, folio, *calf,* 10s 6d   1672

> With the autograph of "*Sarah Churchill,*" probably the celebrated Duchess of Marlborough.

1420 ———— Brief and plain Exposition, with Paraphrase, of the whole Book of the Revelation, 8vo. *calf,* 4s   .   1696
1421 CRAIG's (Dr. Wm.) Essay on the Life of Jesus Christ, 18mo. 2s 6d
Glasgow, 1769
1422 CRANFIELD'S (Tho.) Harmony of the Gospels, from the Resurrection to the Ascension of our Lord and Saviour Jesus Christ, folio, *bds.* 3s 6d   .   Dublin, 1795

[58, GREAT QUEEN STREET,

1423 CRANMER (George) Concerning the New Church Discipline, an excellent Letter to Mr. R. H. sm. 4to. *sewed*, 3s ———
1424 ——— —— (Tho. *Abp. of Cant.*) Writings and Disputations relative to the Sacrament of the Lord's Supper. Edited by the Rev. J. E. Cox, roy. 8vo. *bds.* 15s . *Camb.* 1844
1425 ——— —— Life, by the Rev. Henry John Todd, 2 vols. 8vo. *2 portraits, bds.* 12s—*calf gilt*, 18s . 1831
1426 CRANTZ's (David) History of Greenland, including an Account of the Mission carried on by the United Brethren in that Country, with Notes, 2 vols. 8vo. *bds.* 7s 6d 1820
1427 CRAVEN's (Dr. Wm.) Jewish and Christian Dispensations compared with other Institutions, 8vo. *bds.* 3s *Camb.* 1813
1428 ————— Continuation of a Discourse on the Jewish and Christian Dispensations, &c., 8vo. *sewed*, 1s . *ib.* 1800
1429 ————— Sermons on the Evidence of a Future State, 8vo. *sewed*, 1s 6d . . *ib.* 1783
1430 CRELLIUS (J.) Ethica Aristotelica, ad sacram literarum normam emendata. Ethica Christiana, seu explicatio virtutum et vitiorum quorum in sacris literis sit mentio. Cui accedit, Catechesis Ecclesiarum Polonicarum a J. Crellio, J. Schlichtingio, M. Ruaro, et A. Wissowatio recognita, notisque illustrata, 4to. *calf,* 5s *Cosmopoli,* 1681
1431 CRENII (Tho.) Animadversiones Philologicæ et Historicæ, 8vo. *calf*, 3s . . *Oxon.* 1699
1432 CRESSY's (R. F. S.) Church-History of Brittany, from the beginning of Christianity to the Norman Conquest, shewing that the present Roman Catholick Religion hath from the beginning been professed in this Island, folio, *very scarce, some leaves in the preface mended, and slightly stained, hf. bd. calf,* £1. 16s 1668
1433 CRISP's (Stephen, *Quaker*) Scripture-Truths demonstrated in XXXII Sermons, 3 vols. in 1, 12mo. *calf,* 5s 6d . 1707
1434 ——— —— (Tobias, D.D.) Christ alone exalted ; being his complete Works, containing 42 Sermons, with Notes and the Doctor's Life, by Dr. Gill, 2 vols. 8vo. *portrait*, 12s . 1791
1435 CRITICI SACRI, SIVE DOCTISSIMORUM VIRORUM in S. S. BIBLIA ANNOTATIONES ET TRACTATUS, *best edition*, 9 vols. folio, *fine copy, vellum,* £8. 8s . *Amst.* 1698
1436 ——— —— idem, 9 vols. *Amst.* 1698—Thesaurus Theologico-Philologicus, sive Sylloge Dissertationem elegantiorum ad selectiora et illustriora Novi Test. Loca, a Theologicis Protestantibus in Germania separatim diversis Temporibus conscriptarum secundum ordinem N. T. Librorum digesta, 2 vols. *ib.* 1702—Thesaurus Novus Theologico-Philologicus, sive Sylloge Dissertationum Exegeticarum in V. et N. Test. ex Musæo Th. Hasæi et Conradi Ikenii, 2 vols. *ib.* 1732, together 13 vols. folio, *very fine copy, vellum,* £13. 13s . ———
1437 ——— idem, 13 vols. *Amst.* 1698, L. Cappelli Critica Sacra, *Amst.* 1689, Lud. De Dieu, Critica Sacra, sive Animadversiones in Loca quædam V. et N. Testamenti, *ib.* 1693, together 15 vols. folio, *best editions, fine set in vellum,* £15. 15s ———

1438 CROESIUS (Ger.) Historia Quakeriana, sive de vulgò dictis Quakeris, ab ortu illorum, usque ad recens natum Schisma, 12mo. *vellum*, 3s
Amst. 1695
1439 CROFTON's (Zech.) Saints' Care for the Church Communion, in sundry Sermons at St. James's, Duke's Place, 12mo. *half bound*, 4s 6d . . 1671
1440 CROMBIE's (Dr. Alex.) Natural Theology; or Essays on the Existence of the Deity, &c. 2 vols. 8vo. *bds*. 9s 1829
1441 CROSS' (Nicholas) Cynosura; or a Saving Star that leads to Eternity, discovered amidst the Celestial Orbs of David's Psalms; by way of paraphrase upon the Miserere, folio, *calf*, 8s 1670
1442 CROSTHWAITE's (J. C.) Sermons on practical subjects, 12mo. *bds*. 6s 6d . . 1840
1443 ———— Communio Fidelium; an Historical Inquiry into the mode of distributing the Holy Communion, prescribed by the Church of England and Ireland, 18mo. *bds*. 1s 6d Oxford, 1841
1444 CROWLEY's (Robert) Confutation of XIII. Articles, whereunto Nicolas Shaxton, late Bishop of Salisburye, subscribed, and caused to to be set forthe in print the yere of our Lorde 1546, when he recanted in Smithfielde, at London, at the burning of mestres Anne Askue, 16mo. 𝔅𝔩𝔞𝔠𝔨 𝔩𝔢𝔱𝔱𝔢𝔯, *calf*, £2. 2s London, [1548]
From the library of the late Duke of Sussex.
1445 CROXALL's (Dr. Sam. *Archd. of Salop*) Scripture Politics: being a View of the Original Constitution and subsequent Revolutions in the Government of that People, out of whom the Saviour of the World was to arise, 8vo. *calf*, 2s 6d . 1735
1446 CRUDEN's (Alex.) Complete Concordance to the Holy Scriptures of the Old and New Testament, with a Concordance to the Apocrypha, and a Life of the Author, 4to. *portrait, calf*, 16s 1805
1446*———— another copy, with the Life of the Author by Alex. Chalmers, 4to. *portrait, calf*, £1. 5s 1838
1447 CRUWYS's (H. S.) Enquiries into the Archetype of the Septuagint Version, its Authenticity, and different editions, 8vo. *sewed*, 1s 1774
1448 CUDWORTH's (Ralph) True Intellectual System of the Universe, wherein all the Reason and Philosophy of Atheism is confuted, and its impossibility demonstrated, folio, *frontispiece, calf*, £1. 4s 1678
"An immense magazine of learning and research... It contains the greatest mass of learning and argument that ever was brought to bear on Atheism."—*Orme*.
1449 CUJACII (Jacobi) Opera Omnia, edente C. A. Fabroto, *best edition*, 11 vols. folio, *hf. bd. uncut, scarce*, £5. 15s 6d Neapoli, 1758-83
1450 CULENS (Hen.) Thesaurus Locorum Communium de quo Nova et Vetera proferuntur, 8vo. *neat*, 3s . Antv. 1622
1451 CUMBERLAND's (Rd. *Bp. of Peterborough*) Treatise of the Laws of Nature, made English by John Maxwell, with an Introduction and Appendix by the Translator, 4to. *calf*, 7s [1727]
1452 ———— Essay towards the Recovery of the Jewish Measures and Weights, comprehending their Monies compared with ours of England, sm. 8vo. *fine copy, calf gilt*, 5s 1686
This work, which displays great sagacity, learning, and research, was attacked by Bernard, but highly extolled by Le Clerc.

[58, GREAT QUEEN STREET,

1453 CUMBERLAND'S (Richard) Calvary; or the Death of Christ, a Poem in eight books, 4to. LARGE PAPER, *plates, (Hayley's copy) hf. bd. russia, 5s 6d* . 1792
1454 —— —— another copy, 2 vols. 12mo. *plates, calf,* 3s 1800
1455 CUMMING'S (John, *Minister of the Scots' Church in London*) Grounds of the present Differences among the London Ministers, 8vo. *calf,* 3s 6d . . 1720
1456 CUNNINGHAM'S (J. W.) Velvet Cushion, 8vo. *bds. 2s* 1814
1457 —— —— — (J. W. *Vicar of Harrow)* Sermons, 8vo. *bds.* 4s 1822
1458 CUNINGHAME'S (Wm.) Septuagint and Hebrew Chronologies, tried by the Test of their internal Scientific Evidence; also on the Great Epochs which terminate in 1838, and appear to shew the approach of the End, 8vo. *bds.* 2s 6d 1838
1459 CUROPALATA, de Officialibus Palatii Constantinopolitani, et Officiis magnæ Ecclesiæ; ed. Jul. Pacius, 12mo. *calf, rare,* 5s *Lugd.* 1588
1460 CUSTOS (Raphael) Πατρολογια, id est Descriptio S. Patrum Græcorum et Latinorum qui in Augustana Bibliotheca visuntur æri incisa, folio, *sewed,* 7s 6d . *Aug. Vind.* 1624
1461 CYPRIANUS (S.) Opera, cum adnotationibus Jac. Pamelii, fol. *calf,* 15s . *Paris,* 1616
1462 —— —— Opera, ad vetustissimorum exemplarium fidem emendata diligentia Nic. Rigaltii, cum ejusdem annotationibus. Accedunt M. Minucii Felicis Octavius de Idolorum Vanitate; Arnobius adversus Gentes; Julius Firmicus Maternus de errrore profanarum religionum; Commodiani instructiones adversus Gentium Deos, cum Rigaltii notis, etc. folio, *calf,* £1. 1s . *ib.* 1666
1463 —— —— idem, folio, *fine copy, calf,* £1. 4s *ib.* 1666
1464 —— - —— Opera, recognita et illustrata per Jo. Fell, Oxon. Episcopum. Accedunt Annales Cyprianici per Jo. [Pearson] Cestriensis, Episc. folio, *calf, very scarce,* £2. 2s *Oxon.* 1682
1465 —— —— Opera, recognita et illustrata per Jo. Fell, Oxon. Episc. —Accedunt Annales Cyprianici per Jo. Pearson, et Dissertationes Cyprianicæ Henrici Dodwelli, folio, *calf,* £2. 2s *Amst.* 1700
1466 —— —— Opera, studio et labore St. Baluzii, *Editio Benedictina,* folio, *calf,* £4.—*vellum, calf back,* £4. *Paris.* 1726
1467 —— —— idem, LARGE PAPER, royal folio, *fine copy, tree marbled calf extra,* £5. 5s . *ib.* 1726
1468 —— —— idem, folio, *vellum,* £2. 2s *Venet.* 1728
1469 —— —— aliud exemplar, folio, *fine copy, vellum, neat,* £2. 10s *ib.* 1728
1470 —— —— Dissertationes Cyprianicæ H. Dodwelli, folio, *calf,* 12s

1471 —— —— Les Œuvres de Saint Cyprien, traduites par M. Lombert, avec des remarques, et une nouvelle Vie de S. Cyprien, etc. 4to. *calf,* 9s . . *Paris,* 1672
1472 —— —— autre exemplaire, 2 vols. in 1, 4to. *calf,* 8s *Rouen,* 1716
1473 —— —— De la singularité des Clercs, ou de l'obligation où sont les Ecclesiastiques de vivre separez des femmes, 12mo. *neat,* 3s *Par.* 1718

1474 CYPRIAN. (S.) Sermons, avec quelques Epistres, et une Oraison des Martyrs, sm. 8vo. *neat, 3s 6d*   *Par.* 1565
1475 ———— The genuine Works of St. Cyprian, with his Life by his own Deacon Pontius : done into English, with a Dissertation upon the case of Heretical and Schismatical Baptism at the Council of Carthage, by Nath. Marshall, folio, *hf. bd. calf*, £1. 11s 6d   1717
1476 ———— another copy, *with the frontispiece, calf*, £1. 16s   1717
1477 ———— Works, containing his Treatises, Epistles, and the Works of St. Pacian; translated, with Notes and Indices, (by the Rev. Cha. Thornton) together with the Life and Times of St. Cyprian by G. A. Poole, 3 vols. 8vo. *bds* £1. 10s   *Oxford*, 1840, &c.
1478 ———— The Treatises of St. Cyprian and his Epistles, translated with Notes (by the Rev. C. Thornton,) 2 vols. 8vo. *bds.* 16s   *ib.* 1840-44
1479 ———— Life and Times of Saint Cyprian, by G. A. Poole, M.A. 8vo. *bds.* 8s .   *ib.* 1840
1480 CYRILLI ALEXANDRINI, Opera Omnia, Græcè et Latinè, curâ AUBERTI, *editio optima*, 7 vols. folio, *extremely rare, calf*, £15. 15s   *Par.* 1638
1481 ———— in XII Prophetas, *Gr. et Lat.* cum notis et indice, folio, *hf. bd.* 18s .   *Ingolst.* 1607
1481* ———— (S. *Hierosol. Episc.*) Opera, Gr. et Lat. cum notis edidit Tho. Milles, folio, *calf*, £1. 1s .   *Oxon.* 1703
1482 ———— Opera, *Editio Benedictina*, Græcè et Latinè, ab A. A. Touttée, folio, *calf*, £3. 3s .   *Paris.* 1720
1482* ———— Hierosolymitani, et Synesii Cyrenensis Episc. Opera, Græcè et Latinè, studio et opera Joan. Prevotii, folio, *neat*, £1. 10s   *Par.* 1631
1483 ———— Liber de Sacrosancta Trinitate, *Græce*, Latine versus et Scholiis passim declaratus a Jo. Wegelino, *Aug. Vind.* 1604—S. MAXIMI Mystagogia, *Græce*, cum interpretatione Latina Davidis Hoeschelii, (*sheet C in the Latin part wanting*) *Aug.* 1599, 2 vols. in 1, sm. 8vo. *calf, neat, 7s 6d*
1484 ———— (*Patr. Const.*) L'Imposture de la pretendue Confession de Foy de Cyrille, Patriarche de Constantinople, 12mo. *fine copy, old French red morocco, gilt leaves by De Rome*, 8s   *Par.* 1629
1485 D'ACHERY (L.) Spicilegium, siveCollectio veterum aliquot Scriptorum, qui in Galliæ Bibliothecis diliterant; editio accuratior per F. De la Barre, 3 vols. *Par.* 1723 — MABILLON (I.) Vetera Analecta, sive Collectio Veterum aliquot Operum et Opusculorum omnis generis, cum ejusdem Itinere Germanico, Annotationibus et aliquot Disquisitionibus; cui accessere Mabillonii Vita et aliquot Opuscula, scilicet Dissertatio de Pane Eucharistico, Azymo et Fermentato. Subjungitur Opusculam Eldefonsi Hispaniensis Episcopi de eodem Argumento; et Eusebii Romani ad Theophilum Gallum Epistola de Cultu Sanctorum ignotorum, *ib.* 1723—together 4 vols. fol. *fine copy, vellum*, £8. 18s 6d
1486 DAILLE's (J.) Apologie for the Reformed Churches, wherein is shewed the Necessitie of their Separation from the Church of Rome, 12mo *hf. bd. calf, very neat*, 4s 6d .   *Camb.* 1653

1487 DAILLE (Jean) De la Creance des Peres sur le fait des Images, sm. 8vo. *calf, 4s* . *Geneve,* 1641
1488 ———— Melange de Sermons, 2 vols. in 1, 12mo. *vellum, 12s* *Amst.* 1658
1489 ———— XLIX Sermons upon the whole Epistle to the Colossians, translated by F. S. folio, *calf, 15s* . 1672
1490 ———— Treatise concerning the Right Use of the Fathers in the Decision of the Controversies that are at this day in Religion, 4to. *neat, 7s 6d* . 1651
1491 ———— another copy, 4to. *calf, 9s* . 1675
1492 — ———- de duobus Latinorum ex Unctione Sacramentis, Confirmatione, et Extrema ut vocant Unctione disputatio, 4to. *sewed, uncut, 5s* . *Genev.* 1659
1493 DALE (Ant. Van) Dissertationes de origine ac progressu Idolatriæ et Superstitionum : de vera ac falsa Prophetia, &c. 4to. *calf, 6s* *Amst.* 1696
1494 DALHUSIUS's (J. H.) Salvation of Protestants asserted and defended, 4to. *hf. bd. calf, very neat, 3s 6d* . 1689
1495 DALRYMPLE's (Sir D. Lord *Hailes*) Remains of Christian Antiquity, with explanatory Notes, Vol. 2, containing the Trial of Justin Martyr and of his Companions, 12mo. *uncut, 2s 6d* *Edin.* 1778
1496 ———— - Vol. 3, containing a History of the Martyrs in Palestine, 12mo. *uncut, 2s 6d* . *ib.* 1780
1497 — ———- Disquisitions concerning the Antiquities of the Christian Church, 12mo. *new in calf gilt, 8s 6d* *Glasgow,* 1783
1498 DALTON's (W.) Explanatory and Practical Commentary on the New Testament, 2 vols. 8vo. *bds. 15s* *Dublin,* 1838
1499 DAMASCENUS (S. Joannes) Opera Omnia, Gr. et Lat. edidit cum Notis Mich. Le Quien, *best edition,* 2 vols. folio, *calf,* £4. *4s* *Paris.* 1712
1500 ———— Orationes tres Apologeticæ, cum vita ejus, *Græce,* sm. 8vo. *vellum, 7s 6d* . *Romæ,* 1553
1501 ———— Adversus Sanctarum Imaginum oppugnatores orationes tres : Petro Francisco Zeno interprete, sm. 8vo. *calf, gilt leaves, 8s* *Venet.* 1554
1502 DAMASI Papæ (Sancti) Opuscula, et Gesta, cum Notis M. M. Sarazanii iterum collecta, nunc vero primum aucta, et illustrata Diatribis duabus ; I. de Gestis Liberii Exulis ; II. an Damasus faverit aliquando Maximo Cynico adversus Gregorium Nazianzenum et Nectarium ? Accedunt ejusdem Opuscula Apocrypha (cura A. Merendæ) BEST EDITION, folio, *uncut,* £1. *Romæ,* 1754
1503 ———— idem, folio, *fine copy, tree marbled calf gilt,* £1. *10s* *ib.* 1754
1504 DAMIANI (B. Petri Cardinalis) Opera Omnia, studio D. Constantini Cajetani. Accessit Regula Petri de Honestis Clerici Ravennatis antehac inedita, 4 vols. in 1, folio, *calf,* £1. *4s* *Par.* 1663
1505 ———— idem, 4 vols. in 2, folio, *portrait, vellum,* £1. *11s 6d* *Venetiis,* 1743
1506 ———— aliud exemplar, 4 vols. 4to. *port. sewed,* £1. *8s* *Bassano,* 1783
1507 ———— idem, 4 vols. in 2, 4to. *vellum,* £2. *ib.* 1783

1508 D'ANDILLY (Arnauld) Œuvres, *savoir;* Vies de plusieurs Saints Illustres, de divers siécles — Histoire des Juifs, écrite par Flavius Joseph, traduite sur l'original Grec, 2 vols.—Œuvres Diverses, contenant l'Histoire de l'Ancien Testament, et les Confessions de S. Augustin, &c. together 4 vols. folio, *calf,* £1. 11s 6d *Par.* 1664

1509 ———— Histoire de l'Ancien Testament, 4to. *calf,* 5s 6d
ib. 1675

1510 DANIEL secundum Septuaginta ex Tetraplis Origenis Græcè, cum Versione Latina, nunc primum editus e singulari Christiano Codice Annorum supra DCCC. &c. folio, *bds. uncut,* 16s —*calf,* 18s
Romæ, 1772

1511 DANIEL, an improved Version attempted; with a preliminary Dissertation and Notes, by Tho. Wintle, 4to. *hf. bd. calf,* 12s 1807

"A very valuable translation, executed on the same plan as Bp. Lowth's version of Isaiah, and Dr. Blayney's of Jeremiah."—*Horne.*

1512 DANIEL'S (Jo.) Ecclesiastical History of the Britons and Saxons, 8vo. *hf. bd. calf, neat, scarce,* 7s 6d . 1815

1513 DANISH MISSIONARIES—Thirty-four Conferences between them and the Malabarian Bramans, concerning the Truth of the Christian Religion: translated out of High Dutch by Mr. Philipps, 8vo. *calf,* 4s 6d . . 1719

1514 DART's (J.) History and Antiquities of the Cathedral Church of Canterbury, and the once adjoining Monastery, 61 *fine plates,* folio, *calf gilt,* £1. 5s . . 1726

1515 DAUBENY'S Eight Discourses on the Connection between the Old and New Testament, considered as two parts of the same Divine Revelation, and demonstrative of the great Doctrine of Atonement, 8vo. *calf,* 4s . . 1802

1516 D'AUBIGNE'S (J. H. M.) History of the Great Reformation of the Sixteenth Century, in Germany, Switzerland, &c., translated from the French, with the author's latest corrections and additions, 3 vols. 8vo. *calf gilt,* £2. 2s . 1843

1517 ———— A Voice from the Alps; or, a brief Account of the Evangelical Societies of Paris and Geneva; edited by the Rev. Edw. Bickersteth, 12mo. *bds.* 2s 6d 1838

1518 DAVENANT (Jo., *Bp. of Sarum*) Expositio Epistolæ D. Pauli ad Colossenses, folio, *calf,* 15s . *Cantab.* 1630

1519 ———— idem, 4to. *vellum,* 10s . *Amst.* 1646

Bp. Davenant was one of the English Divines who attended the Synod of Dort. This exposition is the substance of lectures read by the author while Lady Margaret Professor at Cambridge.

1520 DAVIDSON'S (Dr. Sam.) Lectures on Biblical Criticism, 8vo. *bds.* 6s
Edinb. 1839

1521 ———— Sacred Hermeneutics developed and applied; including a History of Biblical Interpretation from the earliest of the Fathers to the Reformation, 8vo. *bds.* 9s . *ib.* 1843

1522 DAVIES's (Edward) Celtic Researches, on the Origin, Traditions, and Language of the Ancient Britons, with some introductory sketches on Primitive Society, royal 8vo. *new in calf gilt,* 14s
1804

[58, GREAT QUEEN STREET,

1523 Davies's (E.) Mythology and Rites of the British Druids, ascertained by National Documents, &c., royal 8vo. *calf gilt*, 10s 6d 1809
1524 ——— (Sir Jo., *Attorney Gen. to Q. Eliz.*) The Original, Nature, and Immortality of the Soul, a Poem, 12mo. 1s 6d 1714
1525 ——— (Sam. *Pres. of the College in New Jersey*) Sermons on important subjects, with some occasional Sermons, and Memoirs of the author by Drs. Gibbons and Finley, 4 vols. 8vo. *hf. bd. calf, scarce*, 18s . . 1824
1526 ——— (Tho.) Faith and Practice of a Christian, explained and enforced, in sixteen Discourses, 8vo. *calf*, 2s 6d 1720
1527 Davy's (Wm.) System of Divinity, in a course of Sermons on the Being, Nature, and Attributes of God, and on some of the most important Articles of the Christian Religion, &c. 6 vols. in 3, 12mo. *calf*, 12s . Exeter, 1785-86
1528 ——— System of Divinity, &c. Vol. 1, 8vo. (*imperfect*) *bds. very rare*, 5s . Lustleigh, Devon, 1795
This work was printed by [the author] himself, "*pro bono publico.*" He struck off 40 copies of the former part, but only 14 of the remainder.
1529 Dawson's (John) Greek-English Lexicon of the New Testament, with an Outline of Greek Grammar, by W. C. Taylor, LL.D., 8vo. *bds.* 6s . . 1841
1530 ——— (Dr. Tho.) Suspiria Sacra; or, the Church of England's Memorial; with an Admonition to Jesuits, 8vo. *sewed*, 2s 1718
1531 Dean's (Rd.) Essay on the Future Life of Brutes, 2 vols. 12mo. *hf. bd. uncut*, 2s 6d . 1768
1532 Debia's (James, *Preb. of Lincoln*) Account of the Religion of the Muscovites, 12mo. 2s . 1710
1533 Dechamps (Steph.) de Hæresi Janseniana, ab Apostolica Sede merito proscripta Liber III., folio, *calf*, 18s *Par.* 1728
1534 Declaration of the true state of the Secluded Members' Case, 4to. *sewed*, 2s . . 1660
1535 Defense de la Discipline qui s'observe dans le Diocese de Sens, touchant l'imposition de la Penitence Publique pour les Pechez Publics, 8vo. 3s . *à Sens*, 1673
1536 Deism.—The Principles of Deism truly represented and set in a clear light, in two Dialogues between a Sceptick and a Deist, 8vo. *hf. bd. interleaved*, 3s . 1726
1537 De la Cour (M. du Bois) An excellent Discourse, proving the Divine Original of the Five Books of Moses; with a second part, against Simon and Spinosa, by W. L. 12mo. 2s 6d 1682
1538 Delany's (Dr. Patrick) Sermons and Discourses on Social Duties, upon Doctrines and Duties more peculiarly Christian, and on other subjects, 3 vols. 8vo. *rich calf gilt, old style*, 18s 1706-54
1539 ——— Doctrine of Abstinence from Blood defended, 8vo. *sewed*, 1s 6d . . 1734
1540 ——— Reflections upon Polygamy, and the Encouragement given to it in the Old Testament, 8vo. *calf*, 3s . 1737
1541 De la Rue (———) Sermons pour l'Avent, et le Carêsme, 4 vols. 8vo. *old French calf gilt, scarce*, 16s *Par.* 1719
1542 ——— another copy, 4 vols. 12mo. *calf extra, gilt leaves*, by C. Lewis, £1. 1s . Toulouse, 1782

1543 DE LAUNE's (Tho.) Plea for the Non-Conformists, 4to. *hf. bd.* 3s 6d
   1684
1544 ——— (Dr. Wm., *Pres. St. John's Coll. Oxon.*) Twelve Sermons
   upon several subjects and occasions, 8vo. *calf,* 2s 6d   1728
   " His sermon on original sin is much esteemed."—*Biog. Brit.*
1545 DELECTUS Actorum Ecclesiæ Universalis, seu Nova Summa Conciliorum, Epistolarum, Decretorum SS. Pontificum, Capitularium, &c. quibus Ecclesiæ Fides et Disciplina nita solent, cum Notis ad Canones, 2 vols. folio, *vellum,* £1. 10s   *Lugduni,* 1706
1546 DEL RIO (Mart.) Florida Mariana, sive de Laudibus S. Virg. Deiparæ Panegyrici XIII. sm. 4to. *vellum,* 4s 6d   *Antv.* 1598
1547 DELUSION.—The general Delusion of Christians touching the Ways of God's revealing Himself to, and by the Prophets, 8vo. *calf,* 3s 6d
   1713
1548 D'EMILLIANE's Frauds of Romish Monks and Priests, set forth in eight Letters, sm. 8vo. *calf,* 3s   .   1691
1549 DEMETRIUS PEPANUS Opera, *Gr. et Lat.* curâ Bern. Stephanopoli: accedit Præfatio Jo. Chr. Amadutii, 2 vols. 4to. *sewed, scarce,* £1. 16s   .   .   *Romæ,* 1781
   Dedicated to Henry Benedict, Duke of York, and Cardinal, whose arms are upon the title pages.
1550 DEMONIACKS.—An Account of the Demoniacks, and of the Power of casting out Demons, both in the New Testament, and in the four first centuries, by W. Whiston, 8vo. 1s 6d   1737
1551 ——— An Enquiry into the Meaning of Demoniacks in the New Testament, 8vo. 1s 6d   .   1737
1552 ——— An Examination of the Enquiry into the Meaning of Demoniacs in the New Testament, by Samuel Pegge, 8vo. 1s   1739
1553 ——— A Dissertation on the Gospel Demoniacks, by A. Young, LL.D. 8vo. 1s 6d   .   1760
1554 ——— Demoniacal Possessions; reasons for the Credibility of their Reality, not only as recorded, but as exhibited, in the New Testament, 12mo. *bds.* 2s   .   1817
1555 DERHAM's (W.) Physico and Astro-Theology; or, a Demonstration of the Being and Attributes of God, from His Works of Creation, 2 vols. 8vo. *calf, fine copy,* 6s   .   1754-58
   " Works which bespeak as much the philosopher as the divine."
1556 DERODON (Dav.) La Lumiere de la Raison opposée aux tenebres de l'Impieté, sm. 8vo. *fine copy, old olive-green morocco, gilt leaves by De Rome,* 7s 6d   .   *Genève,* 1665
1557 ——— Funeral of the Mass; or, the Mass dead and buried, without hope of Resurrection; translated out of French, sm. 8vo. *calf, neat,* 6s   .   *Dublin,* 1685
   From the collection of the Duke of Sussex.
1558 DE SAINCTES (Claude) de Rebus Eucharistiæ Controversis, folio, *calf,* 16s   .   1755
1559 DESIRÉ (Artus) Les Combatz du fidelle Papiste pelerin Rommain, contre l'apostat Antipapiste, tirant a la Sinagogue de Geneve, Maison Babilonique des Lutheriens. Ensemble la description de la Cité de Dieu, assiegée des Hereticques, 18mo. *woodcuts, scarce and curious, calf,* 7s 6d   .   *Rouen,* 1552

[58, GREAT QUEEN STREET,

1560 [DESLANDES (Fra. Boureau a)] Philological Essay ; or, Reflections on the Death of Free-Thinkers, with the Characters of the most eminent persons that died pleasantly and unconcerned, 8vo. *calf, scarce*, 2s . . 1713
1561 DEVOTIONS.—Private Devotions for several occasions, ordinary and extraordinary, 8vo. *calf*, 1s . 1706
1562 DIBDIN'S (T. F.) Bibliomania ; or, Book Madness, a Bibliographical Romance, *new and improved edition*, with Preliminary Observations, and a Key to the Characters, royal 8vo. *plates, bds*. £1. 5s 1842
1563 DICK'S (John) Essay on the Inspiration of the Holy Scriptures, 12mo. 2s . *Edinb.* 1800
1564 DICKSON'S (David) Short Explanation of the Epistle of Paul to the Hebrews, 12mo. *calf, scarce*, 4s 6d
Aberdene, by Edward Raban, 1635
1565 ———— the same, *fine clean copy, hf. bd. calf, neat*, 6s *ib.* 1635
1566 ———— another copy 12mo. *hf. bd, calf*, 4s 6d *Camb.* 1649
1567 DIDYMUS ALEXANDRINUS, de Trinitate libri III. *Lat. et Gr.* Notis illustrati a Jo. Aloysio Mingarellio, fol. *sewed, very scarce*, £1. 16s
Bonon. 1769
1568 DIGBY'S (Will.) Twenty-one Lectures on Divinity, 8vo. *calf*, 4s 6d
Dublin, 1787
1569 DILHERRUS (Jo. Mich.) in Canticum Canticorum Annotationes, cura J. C. Sagittarii, 12mo. *vellum*, 2s *Vratisl.* 1680
1570 DILLON'S (Dr. R. C.) Sermons, 8vo. *bds.* 5s 1831
1571 DIMOCK'S (H.) Critical and Explanatory Notes on Genesis, Exodus, Isaiah, Jeremiah, Ezekiel, Daniel, and the Minor Prophets, &c., and Remarks on the XXXIX Articles, 4to. *sewed*, 4s 6d 1804
1572 ———— Eight Sermons on the Nativity, Personal Character, Death, Resurrection, and Ascension of Christ, with Notes, several Hebrew Odes, literally translated, and Miscellaneous Observations, 4to. *bds.* 3s . . 1806
1573 DIODATI'S (John) Pious and learned Annotations upon the whole Bible, 4to. *hf. bd. calf, portrait and engraved title by Hollar*, 14s
1648
" Diodati was an eminent Italian divine and reformer in the early part of the 17th century ; his annotations are properly *scholia*, rather practical than critical, but containing many useful hints ; a considerable portion of them was introduced into the Assembly's Annotations."—*Horne.*
1574 DIONYSII AREOPAGITÆ, Opera, cum Scholiis S. Maximi et Paraphrasi Pachymeræ a B. Corderio Latine interpretate et notis illustrata, 2 vols. folio, *vellum*, £2. 2s *Antv.* 1634
1575 ——— — aliud exemplar, 2 vols. folio, *vellum*, £2. 2s
Lutet. Par. 1644
1576 ——— idem, 2 vols. folio, *vellum*, £2. 10s – *hf. bd. vellum*, £2. 2s
Venet. 1755-56
1577 ———— Opera ; in eadem Maximi Scholia, G. Pachymeræ Paraphrasis, M. Syngeli Encomium, *Græce*, sm. 8vo. *calf, a few leaves at the end damaged*, 3s *Par.* 1562
From the Library of the late Duke of Sussex.
1578 DISCOURSES (Four) on Obedience to the Supreme Powers ; of the Laws of Nations ; of the Power of the Magistrate in matters of Religion ; and of the Liberty of the Press, 8vo. *calf*, 2s 1709

1579 D'ISRAELI's (I.) Amenities of Literature 3 vols. 8vo. *bds.* 15s 1842
1580 ———— Miscellanies of Literature, royal 8vo. *bds.* 10s 6d 1840
1581 DISSERTATIONES.—De Locis Theologicis Dissertationes decem, Theologi Lovaniensis, 3 vols. 12mo. *calf*, 6s *Insulis Fland.* 1737
1582 DISTEMPER (The New), or the Dissenters' usual Pleas for Comprehension, Toleration, and the Renouncing the Covenant, considered and discussed, sm. 8vo. *front. calf*, 2s . 1680
1583 DITTON's (Humphrey) Discourse concerning the Resurrection of Jesus Christ, 8vo. *calf*, 3s 6d . 1727
1584 DOCTRINE of the Bible ; or, Rules of Discipline, briefly gathered by way of Question and Answer, 18mo. . 1709
1585 [DOD's (Charles)] Church History of England, from the year 1500 to the year 1688, chiefly with regard to [Roman] Catholicks : being a complete Account of the Divorce, Supremacy, Dissolution of Monasteries, and first attempts for a Reformation, under King Henry VIII. ; the unsettled state of the Reformation under Edward VI. ; the Interruption it met with from Queen Mary ; with the last hand put to it by Queen Elizabeth ; together with the various fortunes of the Catholick Cause, during the Reigns of James I., Charles I. and II., and James II., particularly the Lives of the eminent Catholicks, Cardinals, Bishops, Inferior Clergy, Regulars and Laymen, also a critical Account of the Works of the learned, and the Trials of those who suffered for Religion, &c. ; with the Foundation of all the English Colleges, and Monasteries abroad; to the whole is prefixed a general History of Ecclesiastical Affairs, under the British, Saxon, and Norman periods, 3 vols. folio, *a remarkably fine copy, new in calf*, £8. 8s *Brussels,* 1737
1586 DOD (Jo.) and Rob. CLEAVER. Ten Sermons tending chiefly to the Fitting of Men for the Worthy Receiving of the Lord's Supper ; whereunto is added, a plaine and learned Metaphrase on the Epistle to the Colossians, 4to. *hf. calf, neat*, 3s 6d 1611
1587 ———— — A plaine and familiar Exposition of the Ten Commandments, with a Short Catechism, 4to. *calf*, 4s 6d 1622
1588 DODD's (Will. LL.D.) Practical Discourses on the Miracles of our Blessed Lord and Saviour Jesus Christ, 4 vols. 8vo. *best edition, fine copy, rich calf gilt, old style*, £1. 11s 6d 1768
1589 ———— —— another copy, 4 vols. 8vo. *bds.* 14s 1809
1590 ————— Commentary on the Old and New Testament ; in which are inserted the Notes of John Locke, Daniel Waterland, D.D., the Earl of Clarendon, &c., *with the Preliminary Dissertations,* 3 vols. folio, *calf*, £2. 12s 6d . 1770

The name of Locke in the title page of this book is an error. The notes attributed to him were written by his friend, the celebrated Dr. Cudworth.

1591 ———— —— Sermons to Young Men, 3 vols. 12mo. 4s 6d 1771
1592 DODDRIDGE's (Philip) Family Expositor ; or, Paraphrase and Version of the New Testament, with Critical Notes and a Life of the Author by And. Kippis, 6 vols. 8vo. *portrait, calf gilt*, £1. 11s 6d 1821
1593 ———— —— Sermons and Religious Tracts, 3 vols. 12mo, *calf*, 5s 1761

[58, GREAT QUEEN STREET,

1594 DODDRIDGE'S (Dr. Ph.) Ten Sermons on the Power and Grace of Christ, and on the Evidences of his glorious Gospel, 8vo. *calf*, 3s . 1741
1595 ———— another copy, 12mo. *calf*, 2s . 1776
"I have received the very valuable present of your Ten Sermons, which I have read with much pleasure and improvement; they are excellent."
Bishop Warburton, in a Letter to Dr. D.
1596 ———— Sermons to Young Persons, 12mo. *calf*, 1s 6d 1743
1597 ———— the same, 12mo. *calf*, 2s . 1760
1598 ———— Course of Lectures on the principal subjects in Pneumatology, Ethics, and Divinity, with Notes, &c. by A. Kippis, 2 vols. 8vo. *calf*, 7s . . 1794
"And *first*, as an universal storehouse, necessary to him in the conduct of his theological pursuits, Doddridge's Lectures."—*Bp. of Durham's Charge.*
1599 ———— Leading Heads of XXVII Sermons preached at Northampton, in 1749, 8vo. 2s . *Northampton*, 1824
1600 ———— Lectures on Preaching, and the several branches of the Ministerial Office, 12mo. *sewed*, 1s 1807
1601 ———— Rise and Progress of Religion in the Soul, 12mo. *calf gilt, very neat*, 4s . . 1834
1602 DODSON'S (John) Twelve Discourses, 8vo. *bds.* 2s 1728
1603 DODWELL'S (Henry) Separation of Churches from Episcopal Government, as practised by the present Non-Conformists, proved Schismatical, sm. 4to. *calf, very scarce*, 10s 6d 1679
1604 ———— Two Letters of Advice—I. For the Susception of Holy Orders. II. For Studies Theological; with a Catalogue of the Christian Writers of the three first Centuries, 1680—A Discourse concerning Sanchoniathon's Phœnician History, 1681—*in one vol.* 8vo. *calf*, 4s . ——
1605 ———— another copy, 8vo. *calf*, 3s 6d 1691
1606 ———— An Epistolary Discourse, proving from the Scripture and the first Fathers, that the Soul is naturally Mortal, but Immortalized by the pleasure of God, by Union with the Divine Baptismal Spirit, 8vo. *fine copy, calf*, 5s . 1706
1607 ———— another copy, 8vo. *calf*, 3s . 1706
1608 ———— Occasional Communion fundamentally destructive of the Discipline of the Primitive Catholic Church, 8vo. 3s 1705
1609 ———— Treatise concerning the Lawfulness of Instrumental Music in Holy Offices, 8vo. *calf*, 4s 6d . 1706
1610 ———— Scripture Account of the Eternal Rewards or Punishments of all that hear the Gospel, &c. 8vo. *calf*, 4s 1708
1611 ———— Christianity not founded on Argument; and the true Principle of Gospel-evidence assigned, 1743—Remarks on the same, by Jo. Leland, D.D., 1744—A second Letter, containing Remarks, &c. by the same, 1744, *in one vol.* 8vo. *hf. bd. calf*, 3s ——
1612 ———— Dissertationes in Irenæum, accedit Fragmentum Philippi Sidetæ de Catechistarum Alexandrinorum successione, 8vo. *calf, very scarce*, 10s 6d . *Oxon.* 1689
Written at the persuasion of Bp. Fell.

LINCOLN'S INN FIELDS.]

1613 DODWELLI (H.) de Parma Equestri Woodwardiana Dissertatio. Accedit Tho. Neli, Dialogus inter Reginam Elizabetham et Rob. Dudleium, Comitem Leycestriæ et Academiæ Oxoniensis Cancellarium, in quo de Academiæ Ædificiis præclare agitur, edidit Tho. Hearne, 8vo. *plates, fine copy, calf,* 12s . *Oxon.* 1713
Rare, having been suppressed. The plates represent the principal buildings of Oxford as they appeared in the reign of Elizabeth.

1614 ———— (Will.) Practical Influence of the Doctrine of the Holy Trinity represented, a Sermon before the University of Oxford, 1745—An Assize Sermon at Oxford, 1750, *in one vol.* 8vo. *hf. bd. calf,* 1s

1615 ———— Full and final Reply to Mr. Toll's Defence of Dr. Middleton's Free Inquiry, with an Appendix, and a Preface on the Credibility of Miracles, 8vo. *calf,* 3s . 1751

1616 DOLEMAN'S (R.) Conference about the next Succession to the Crown of England, *with the Genealogical Table,* 8vo. *calf, scarce,* 8s 1681
By R. Parsons, the Jesuit. This book was so rigorously suppressed, that it was made high treason, even to possess a copy, and the printer is said to have been hung, drawn, and quartered.

1617 DOMINICANS. Apologie des Dominicains Missionnaires de la Chine, on rèponse au livre du Père Le Tellier, Jesuite, intitulé, Défense des Nouveaux Chretiens ; et à l'Eclaircissement du P. Le Gobien, &c. 12mo. *calf,* 4s . *Cologne,* 1700

1618 DONE'S (Dr. Wm. Stafford, *Archd. of Bedford*) Sermons before the Hon. Societies of the Inner and Middle Temple, 8vo. *calf,* 3s 6d
1786

1619 DONNE'S (Dr. John) Devotions ; with two Sermons—I. On the Decease of Lady Danvers, Mother of George Herbert. II. Death's Duel, his own Funeral Sermon, to which is prefixed his Life by Izaak Walton, sm. 8vo. *front. bds.* 6s . 1840

1620 ———— Selections from his Works, 18mo. *bds.* 2s 6d *Oxford,* 1840

1621 DOOLITTLE'S (Tho.) Treatise concerning the Lord's Supper, 18mo. *port.* 2s . . 1697

1622 ———— The Lord's Last Sufferings shewed in the Lord's Supper, being a second part to a former Treatise, 18mo. 2s 1682

1623 DOPPING (Anth. *Episcopus Midensus*) Tractatus de Visitationibus Episcopalibus, 18mo. 1s 6d . *Dubl.* 1696

1624 DORMAN'S (Wm.) Twelve Sermons at the Rolls Chapel, 8vo. *calf,* 3s . . 1744

1625 DORN (Jo. Chr.) Bibliotheca Theologica Critica, secundum singulas Diviniorae Scientiæ partes, 2 vols. 12mo. *hf. bd. calf, uncut,* 6s
Franc. 1721

1626 DORRINGTON'S (Theoph.) Discourse on Singing in the Worship of God, 8vo. 3s 6d . . 1704

1627 ———— Family Instruction for the Church of England, offered in several Practical Discourses, 8vo. *portrait, hf. bd. calf,* 3s 1705

1628 DORT.—Actes du Synode National tenu a Dordrecht 1618 et 1619, mis en François par R. J. de Neree, 4to. *vellum,* 5s 6d
Leyden, 1624

1629 DOUESPE (Sam. de la) Sermons sur divers textes de l'Ecriture Sainte, 8vo. 4s . *A la Haye,* 1752

[58, GREAT QUEEN STREET,

1630 DOUGHTÆI (Jo. *Preb. of Westminster*) Analecta Sacra, sive Excursus Philologici breves super diversis Vet. et Novi Testamenti locis. Subjiciuntur Nortoni Knatchbul Animadv. in libros Novi Test. 8vo. *calf*, 3s . *Amst.* 1693
1631 DOUGHTY'S (John) Ten Discourses in the Parish Churches of St. James, Clerkenwell, and St. Ann and Agnes, Aldersgate, 8vo. *calf,* 2s . 1761
1632 [DOUGLAS'S (Jo. *Bp. of Sarum*)] Criterion ; or, Miracles Examined, with a view to Expose the Pretensions of Pagans and Papists, &c. 8vo. *calf*, 5s—*fine copy, rich calf gilt,* 8s 6d 1754
1633 ———— the same, 8vo. *interleaved with writing paper, russia, neat,* 8s 6d . 1807
1634 ———— another copy, 8vo. *bds.* 4s 6d *Oxford,* 1832
1635 ———— the same, *new,* 8vo. *bds.* 5s 6d *ib.* 1832
1636 D'OULTREMAN (Philippe) Le Pedagogue Chrestien, ou la Maniere de Vivre Chrestiennement, 12mo. *neat,* 3s *S. Omer,* 1633
1637 DOWARS' (Wm.) Hint to the Spiritually Learned, or the Spiritual Mariner inspected, &c. in two Sermons, 8vo. *sewed,* 1s 1775
1638 DOWLING (J. G.) Notitia Scriptorum S. S. Patrum, aliorumque Veteris Ecclesiæ Monumentorum quæ in Collectionibus Anecdotorum post annum 1700, editis continentur, 8vo. *bds.* 7s 6d *Oxonii,* 1839
1639 ———— Sermons preached in the Parish Church of St. Mary-de-Crypt, Gloucester, 12mo. *bds.* 5s . 1841
1640 DOWNAME'S (Geo. *Bp. of Derry*) Abstract of the Duties commanded, and Sinnes forbidden in the Law of God, sm. 8vo. *scarce, vellum,* 4s—*calf, (title stained)* 3s 1620
1641 ———— another copy, sm. 8vo. *vellum,* 3s 1625
1642 DOWNE'S (John) Sermons on various subjects, 2 vols. 8vo. LARGE PAPER, *calf,* 4s 6d . *Sheffield,* 1761
" The author's style is clear and manly, his manner animated, his sentiments just, and often striking."
1643 DOWNSIDE DISCUSSION. The authenticated Report of the Discussion which took place in the Chapel of the Roman Catholic College of Downside, near Bath, 1834—Subjects: the Rule of Faith, and the Sacrifice of the Mass—Protestant Speakers : Rev. E. Tottenham, Rev. Jo. Lyons.—Roman Catholic Speakers: Rev. T. J. Brown, Rev. T. M. Macdonnell, Rev. Fra. Edgeworth, 8vo *hf. bd. calf, neat,* 6s . 1836
1644 DROIT. Histoire du Droit public Ecclesiastique François, par Mons. D. B., 2 vols. *Londres,* 1751—Histoire du Droit Canonique, et du gouvernement de l'Eglise, par M * * Avocat au Parlement, *Paris,* 1720—together 3 vols. 12mo. *old calf gilt, uniform,* 6s ————
1645 DROUVEN (R. H.) de Re Sacramentaria contra Hæreticos Libri X. cum Notis et Additionibus J. E. Patuzzi, 2 vols. in 1, folio, *neat, scarce,* £2. 2s *Par.* 1756
1646 DRUMMOND'S (Sir W.) Œdipus Judaicus, *plates, privately printed, very scarce; with MS. notes by the author,* 1811—Remarks on Sir. W. Drummond's Œdipus Judaicus, by G. D'Oyly, B.D. 1813—Remarks on additional Letters to the Rev. G. D'Oyly, by Vindex, Biblicus, and Candidus : by Q. R. 1814—2 vols. 8vo. *hf. bd. morocco gilt, uncut,* £2. 15s . ————

1647 DRUMMOND's (Rob. *Abp. of York*) Sermons on public occasions, and a Letter on Theological Study, with Memoirs of his Life, by [his Son] G. H. Drummond, 8vo. *portrait, bds.* 2s 6d
Edinb. 1803

1648 DRUSIUS (Jo.) Ad loca difficiliora Josuæ, Judicum, et Samuelem Commentarius, *Franck.* 1618—De Sectis Judaicis Commentarius, etc. *Arnhem.* 1619—2 vols. 4to. *calf,* 6s 1618-19

1649 ———— Commentarius in Prophetas Minores XII. 4to. *vellum, neat,* 6s . *Amst.* 1627

1650 ———— Nova Versio et Scholia in Jobum, *Amst.* 1636—Annotationes in Coheleth. *ib.* 1635, *in one vol.* 4to. *vellum,* 7s 1636-35

"Drusius was the most noted critic, linguist, and theologist of his day, and well versed in the Rabbins, and hath given great light to a large part of the Scriptures."—*Walch.*

1652 DRYSDALE (Dr. John) Sermons, with his Life by A. Dalzel, 2 vols. 8vo. *calf,* 5s . *Edinb.* 1793

1653 DU BARTAS's (Saluste, *Sieur*) Divine Weekes and Workes, translated by Josuah Sylvester, 4to. *calf,* 4s 6d . [1608]

1654 DU CANGE (Car. du Fresne, *Dom.*) Glossarium ad Scriptores Mediæ et Infimæ Græcitatis, 2 vols. in 1, folio, *rellum,* £2. 8s *Lugd.* 1688

1655 ———— Glossarium ad Scriptores Mediæ et Infimæ Latinitatis, 3 vols. folio, *calf,* £2. 10s . *Lutet. Par.* 1688

1656 ———— Glossarium ad Scriptores Mediæ et Infimæ Latinitatis, 6 vols. *Par.* 1733-36—CARPENTIER (D. P.) Glossarium Novum ad Scriptores Medii Ævi, cum Latinos tum Gallicos, 4 vols. *ib.* 1766— together 10 vols. folio, *best editions, fine copy, new, in rich calf gilt, by Mackenzie,* £18. 18s

1657 DUCHÉ (Jacob, *Rector of Ch. Ch. and St. Peter's, Philadelphia*), Discourses on various subjects, 2 vols. 8vo. *frontispieces after West, calf, fine copy,* 7s . *Lond.* 1779

These sermons "have great spirit and warmth; and at times are in the strain of our old Divines."

1658 DUGUET (l'Abbé) Traité des Devoirs d'un Evesque, 12mo. *sewed,* 2s
Pavie, 1791

1659 ———— Explication du livre des Pseaumes, 5 vols. in 8, 12mo. *fine copy, old French calf gilt,* £1. 1s *Par.* 1733-39

1660 ———— Traité de la Croix de N. S. Jesus Christ, ou Explication du Mystére de la Passion de N. S. Jesus-Christ, selon la concorde, 9 vols. in 12, 12mo. *fine copy, old French calf gilt,* £1. 10s
ib. 1733

Concerning the Exposition of Duguet, it has been said, that they have the rare quality of presenting evangelical morality with that proper dignity, austerity, and amiableness which belongs to them, and his Treatises have been pronounced to be worthy of a place with the works of Rochefoucault and La Bruyere.

1661 DUGDALE ET DODSWORTH MONASTICON ANGLICANUM; SIVE PANDECTÆ CŒNOBIORUM BENEDICTINORUM, CLUNIACENSIUM, CISTERCIENSIUM, CARTHUSIANORUM, A PRIMORDIIS AD EORUM USQUE DISSOLUTIONEM; 3 vols. folio, *plates by Hollar, red morocco, gilt leaves, and broad gold borders by Mackenzie,* £18. 18s 1655-73

1662 DUGDALE'S (Sir William) Monasticon Anglicanum, or the History of the Ancient Abbies, Monasteries, Hospitals, Cathedrals and Collegiate Churches, with their dependencies, in England and Wales, &c., with a Catalogue of the Bishops of the Dioceses, to the year 1717; and large additions by Captain John Stevens, 3 vols. folio, *plates, calf gilt backs*, £7. 17s 6d   1718-23

1663 ———— MONASTICON ANGLICANUM, A HISTORY OF THE ABBEYS, AND OTHER MONASTERIES, HOSPITALS, FRIARIES, AND CATHEDRAL AND COLLEGIATE CHURCHES, IN ENGLAND AND WALES, AND ALL SUCH SCOTCH, IRISH, AND FRENCH MONASTERIES AS WERE IN ANY MANNER CONNECTED WITH THE RELIGIOUS HOUSES IN ENGLAND; A NEW EDITION, GREATLY ENLARGED AND IMPROVED, AND CONTINUED FROM LEIGER BOOKS, CHARTULARIES, ROLLS AND OTHER NATIONAL DOCUMENTS, BY MESSRS. CALEY, ELLIS, AND BANDINEL; *illustrated with 250 copper-plates, including Facsimiles of all Hollar's Engravings, and a multitude of wood-cuts*, 8 vols. folio, *hf. bd. morocco, uncut, gilt tops*, £31. 10s   1846

It would be quite out of place, as well as unnecessary, to dwell at any length upon the value of this imperishable monument of the indefatigable industry of the original compiler. To the ANTIQUARY and HISTORIAN the Monasticon affords the most ample information respecting our venerable and wealthy Religious Houses. A receptacle for a mass of biographical and historical information, its value is greatly enhanced by the numerous AUTHENTIC CHARTERS preserved in its pages. In this particular, the labours of SIR HENRY ELLIS and the REV. DR. BANDINEL have enriched the work from LEIGER BOOKS, CHARTULARIES, ROLLS, AND OTHER NATIONAL DOCUMENTS, and thus rendered it indispensable to those professional men, who on questions respecting REAL PROPERTY, practise in the highest Courts of the Country, the PRIVY COUNCIL, and the COURT OF CHANCERY.

To the CLERGY the work possesses an interest, not only of an Antiquarian and Historical character, but one which has a more solid claim to their notice. By its means they are frequently enabled to settle, without employing the costly machinery of the Law, disputed questions respecting the property of the Church; and a reference to the very copious Index, added by the editors to the work, will show at once that there is scarcely a single parish which is not mentioned in its pages.

Thus the CLERGY, the LAWYER, the ANTIQUARY, the HISTORIAN, the ARCHITECT, and the TOPOGRAPHER, as well as the POSSESSOR OF REAL PROPERTY, and the DESCENDANT OF A NOBLE LINE OF ANCESTORS, will find the Monasticon Anglicanum one of the most interesting and indispensable works, that has ever issued from the press of this country.

1664 DU MOULIN (Pierre, *le fils*) Traitté de la Paix de l'Ame, et du Contentement de l'Esprit, sm. 8vo, *vellum*, 3s   *Charenton*, 1661

1665 ———— Treatise on Peace of Soul, and Content of Mind, translated from the French, with Notes, by John Scrope, D.D. 2 vols. 8vo. *neat*, 5s   *Salisbury*, 1765

1666 DUNLOP'S (Wm.) Preface to an edition of the Westminster Confession lately published at Edinburgh; being an Account of the ends and uses of Creeds and Confessions of Faith, &c. 1724—An Essay towards explaining the History and Revelations of Scripture, &c. by Jeremiah Hunt, D.D., Part 1, 1734, *in one* vol. 8vo. *bds. uncut*, 6s

1667 DUNS SCOTUS (Joannes) Super primum Sententiarum—Frater Rufinus ordinis Cordiferorum emendavit, 𝕭𝖑𝖆𝖈𝖐 𝖑𝖊𝖙𝖙𝖊𝖗, folio, *fine copy, calf*, 15s   *Venetiis*, 1472

1668 Duppa's (Brian, Bp. of Winchester) Holy Rules and Helps to Devotion; to which is added, the Soul's Soliloquy, and a Conference with Conscience, a Sermon, 18mo. *morocco, gilt leaves,* 5s 6d
1817
From the library of the Duke of Sussex.

1669 Dupuis Traitez concernant l'histoire de France : sçavoir la Condemnation des Templiers, avec quelques actes : l'histoire du Schisme, les Papes tenans le siege en Avignon : et quelques Procez criminels, 12mo. *portrait, neat,* 2s . *Par.* 1685

1670 Du Pin (L. Ellies) Nouvelle Bibliothéque des Auteurs Ecclesiastiques, contenaut l'histoire de leur Vie, le Catalogue, la critique, et la chronologie de leurs Ouvrages, &c. 20 vols. in 8, 4to. *calf,* £4. 14s 6d . *Paris,* 1690-1715

1671 —————— Ecclesiastical History of the first XVI. Centuries of the Church, or Bibliotheca Patrum ; containing the Authors of the several Books of the Old and New Testament, and the Lives and Writings of the Primitive Fathers, determining the genuine and the spurious ; with an Abridgment and Catalogue of their Works, and a Compendious History of the Councils (translated by W. Wotton, and Digby Cotes), *best edition,* 3 vols. folio, *fine copy, sprinkled calf gilt, in the old style,* £6. 6s *Dublin,* 1723

1672 —————— Compendious History of the Church, from the beginning of the World to the present time, 4 vols. 12mo. *calf,* 10s 1706

1673 —————— Complete Method of studying Divinity ; or, a regular course of Theological Studies, with a Catalogue of the most important Theological Questions, and of the most eminent Authors that have wrote on each, 8vo. *calf,* 3s 6d—*fine copy, calf,* 4s 6d
1720

1674 Duport (Jacobus) Metaphrasis libri Psalmorum Græcis versibus contextu, 4to. *fine copy, portrait of Charles II., vellum,* 5s 6d
Cantab. 1666

1675 Dupré's (John) Sermons on various subjects, 8vo. *calf,* 2s 6d—*bds.* 2s . . *Oxford,* 1782

1676 Durand's (F. J.) Sermons on various subjects, selected, abridged, and translated from his Année Evangélique, by Rich. Munkhouse, D.D., 8vo. *bds.* 3s—*calf,* 5s . 1802

1677 —————— another copy, 8vo. *hf. bd. russia, neat,* 4s 1802
From the library of the late W. Wilberforce, Esq.

1678 —————— another copy, 8vo. *hf. bd. calf gilt,* 5s 1802

1679 Durand de Maillane (———) Les Libertez de l'Eglise Gallicane, prouvées et Commentécs, suivant l'ordre des articles dressés par P. Pithou, 5 vols. 4to. *fine copy, old French calf, marbled leaves,* £1. 10s . . *Lyon.* 1771

'680 Durandi (Gul.) Rationale Divinorum Officiorum, 4to. 𝕭lack letter, *calf, neat,* 16s . *Lugduni,* 1540

1681 —————— Speculi Reperto, quatuor Librorum Speculi utriusq. Juris acutissimi Domini Guilielmi Durandi Repertorium, sm. 4to. *vellum, rare,* 7s . . *ib.* 1554

1682 Durantus (Jo. Steph.) de Ritibus Ecclesiæ Catholicæ, sm. 8vo. *vellum,* 10s 6d . . *Par.* 1632

[58, GREAT QUEEN STREET

1683 DURANTUS (Jo. Steph.) Libri tres de Ritibus Ecclesiæ Catholicæ, 4to. *calf, scarce,* 15s—*fine copy, calf,* 16s   *Lugduni,* 1675
1684 ———— idem, 4to. *rich calf gilt, old style,* £1. 1s   *ib.* 1675
   Fleury says that this treatise was written by Danet, Bp. of Lavaur, a member of the Council of Trent, and that Durant, who became possessor of the Bishop's library, revised it, and published it with his own name.
1685 DUREL'S (John) View of the Government and Public Worship of God in the Reformed Churches beyond the Seas, wherein is shewed their Conformity and Agreement with the Church of England, 4to. *calf, scarce,* 10s 6d   1662
1686 DURER'S (Albert) Passion of our Lord Jesus Christ, edited by Henry Cole, sm. 4to. *stamped calf, gilt leaves,* 18s   1844
   This beautiful little volume contains 37 plates, 35 of which were taken from the original wooden blocks of Albert Durer, now deposited in the British Museum. The binding is an adaptation of a German binding of the XVth century.
1687 DURHAM'S (James) Dying Man's Testament to the Church of Scotland; or, a Treatise concerning Scandal, 18mo. *calf,* 2s 6d   *Edinb.* 1680
1688 ———— Practical Exposition of the X. Commandments, 4to. *calf, neat,* 4s   1675
1689 DU VAL (Anthoine) Mirouer des Calvinistes et Armure des Chrestiens, pour rembarrer les Lutheriens et nouveaux Evangelistes de Geneve, sm. 8vo. *calf,* 4s 6d   *Par.* 1562
1690 DUVALLIUS (Andr.) de Suprema Romani Pontificis in Ecclesiam potestate, 4to. *calf, scarce,* 12s   *ib.* 1614
1691 DU VEIL'S (Dr. C. M.) Literal Explanation of the Acts of the Apostles, translated from the Latin, with a translation of a learned Dissertation about Baptism for the Dead, by Frid. Spanhemius, 8vo. *calf,* 4s   1685
1692 EATON'S (John) Honey-Combe of Free Justification by Christ alone, 4to. *calf, scarce,* 6s   ·1642
1693 ECCLES'S (Sam.) Sixteen Sermons on different ojects, most of them preached before the University of Oxford, 8vo. *calf,* 2s 6d   1755
1694 ECCLESIÆ Smyrnensis Epistola de Martyrio S. Polycarpi, cum Lectionis varietate Maxime ex Eusebio, curante D. J. T. Danzio, 4to. *sewed,* 1s 6d   *Jenæ,* 1818
1695 ECCLESIASTICAL COMMISSION.—A Discourse concerning the Ecclesiastical Commission opened in the Jerusalem Chamber Oct. 10, 1689, 4to. *sewed,* 1s 6d   1689
1696 EDGE'S (W. J.) Earnest Appeal to the Readers and Admirers of [Taylor's] "Ancient Christianity," 8vo.   1840
1697 EDWARDS'S (John) Thoughts concerning the several Causes and Occasions of Atheism, especially in the present Age, 8vo. 1s 6d   1695
1698 ———— Demonstration of the Existence and Providence of God, from the Contemplation of the visible structure of the Greater and the Lesser World, 8vo. *calf,* 2s 6d   1696
1699 ———— Discourse concerning the Authority, Stile, and Perfection of the Books of the Old and New Testament, 3 vols. 8vo. *calf,* 8s   1696, &c.

1700 EDWARDS'S (John) Socinian Creed; or, a brief Account of the professed Tenets and Doctrines of the Foreign and English Socinians, 8vo. *calf, 2s 6d* . 1697
1701 ———— Free Discourse concerning Truth and Error, especially in matters of Religion, 8vo. *hf. bd. 2s 6d* . 1701
1702 ———— The Preacher: a Discourse concerning the Offices and Employments of that Character in the Church, 3 vols. 8vo. *port. calf, 8s* . . 1705-9
1703 ———— Theologia Reformata; or, the Body and Substance of the Christian Religion, comprised in Discourses upon the Apostles' Creed, the Lord's Prayer, and the Ten Commandments, &c. 2 vols. —Discourses on those Graces and Duties which are purely Evangelical, and not contained in the Moral Law, &c., together 3 vols. folio, *portrait, calf, very scarce,* £2. 5s 1713-26
From the library of the late Duke of Sussex.
1704 ———— (Jonathan, *Princ. Jesus Coll. Oxon.*) Preservative against Socinianism, *four parts, Oxon.* 1698—The Exposition by my Lord Bp. of Sarum upon the Second Article of our Religion Examined, *Lond.* 1702, *in one* vol. 4to. *calf, 7s* . ——
1705 ———— Sermons on various subjects, 12mo. *hf. bd.* 3s 1795
1706 ———— Works, complete, with Memoirs of his Life by Williams and Parsons, 8 vols. royal 8vo. *fine paper, calf gilt, marbled edges,* £5. 5s . . 1806
1707 ———— (Thomas) Gangræna; or, a Catalogue and Discovery of many of the Errours, Heresies, Blasphemies, and Pernicious Practices of the Sectaries of this time, three parts in 1 vol. 4to. *very rare, calf,* £1. 11s 6d . 1646
1708 ———— Discourse of Praying in the Spirit; or, against Extemporary Prayer, 8vo. *calf, 2s 6d* . 1703
1709 ———— (Timothy) Paraphrase with Annotations on the Epistles of St. Paul to the Romans and Galatians, 4to. *bds. 4s* 1752
1710 EGLISE.—De l'Eglise du Pape, 8vo. *calf, 2s 6d* Genève, 1783
1711 ELEONOR.—La Vie de l'Imperatrice Eleonor, mere de l'Empereur Regnant, 12mo. *neat,* 2s . *Brux.* 1724
1712 ELLESBY'S (James) Caution against Ill Company, &c. 12mo. 1s 6d 1705
1713 ELLIS'S (Clem.) Gentile Sinner; or, England's Brave Gentleman characterized in a Letter to a Friend, 12mo. 3s 6d Oxford, 1664
1714 ———— (Dr. John) Knowledge of Divine Things from Revelation, not from Reason or Nature, 8vo. *calf,* 5s 1743
1715 ———— another copy, 8vo. *calf,* 5s 6d . 1771
1716 ELLYS'S (Anth. *Bp. of St. Davids*) Tracts on the Liberty, Temporal and Spiritual, of Protestants in England, 4to. *russia,* 7s 1767
1717 [———— (Sir Richard, *Bart.*)] Fortuita Sacra: quibus subjicitur Commentarius de Cymbalis, 8vo. *calf, neat,* 5s *Rotterodami,* 1727
1717* ———— another copy, 8vo. *calf extra, gilt leaves,* 8s *ib.* 1727
The learned author of the *Fortuita Sacra* was a Dissenter; Dr. Andrew Gifford was his chaplain. It consists of critical essays on various difficult texts of the New Testament, which the author illustrates from the Mischna and other books of Jewish tradition. The term *Fortuita* is used to denote that these explanations casually presented themselves.

[58, GREAT QUEEN STREET,

1718 ELLYS's (Tobias) Kingdom of God Opened, and proved to be a Kingdom of Grace and Glory, &c. 8vo. *portrait of King Charles II.* 2s . Oxford, 1683
1719 ELRINGTON's (Thos. D.D. *Provost of Trinity Coll. Dublin*) Validity of English Ordination Established, in Aswer to the Rev. P. Gandolphy's Sermon on St. John, ch. x. v. 1, 8vo. *bds. scarce,* 2s 6d *Dublin*, 1818
1720 [ELSLEY's ( )] Annotations on the Four Gospels, and the Acts of the Apostles, 3 vols. 8vo. *hf. bd. calf,* 16s 1812
1721 ELSMERE's (Dr. Sloane) Sermons on several important subjects, 2 vols. *calf,* 5s . 1767
1722 ELSNER (Jac.) Observationes Sacræ in Novi Fœderis libros quibus plura illorum Libr. loca et Auct. potiss. Græcis et Antiquitate exponantur et illustrantur, 2 vols. 8vo. *fine copy, russia, gilt leaves,* 14s . *Traj. ad Rh.* 1720-28

" One of the most valuable books of sacred criticism. Grotius and other commentators, have incidentally applied the productions of the classic writers to the elucidation of the Bible; but no one has done so much in this department as Elsner, Raphelius, and Kypke."—*Harwood.*

1723 ENGLISH HISTORICAL SOCIETY. A complete set of the Publications of the Society, 16 vols. royal 8vo. LARGE PAPER, *extremely scarce, bds.* £14. 14s . 1838-45

CONTENTS:—BEDÆ (VEN.) Historia Ecclesiastica Gentis Anglorum, et recensuit J. Stevenson—BEDÆ Opera Historica minora, recensuit J. Stevenson— GILDAS, de Excidio Britanniæ, recensuit J. Stevenson—KEMBLE (J. M.) Codex Diplomaticus Ævi Saxonici, 3 vols.—NENNIUS, Historia Britonum, recensuit J. Stevenson —RICARDUS DIVISIENSIS, Chronicon de rebus gestis Ricardi primi, nunc primum typis mandatum curante J. Stevenson— ROGERUS DE WENDOVER, Chronica, sive Flores Historiarum, nunc primum edidit H. O. Coxe, 4 vols. - Appendix, in qua lectionum varietas additionesque, quibus Chronicon ampliavit et instruxit Matthæus Parisiensis—TRIVETUS (NIC.) Annales sex Regum Angliæ, qui a comitibus Andegavensibus originem traxerunt (1136-1307) recensuit Tho. Hog — WILLELMUS MALMESBIRIENSIS, Gesta Regum Anglorum, atque Historia Novella, recensuit T. D. Hardy, 2 vols.

1724 ———— KEMBLE (J. M.) Codex Diplomaticus Ævi Saxonici, 2 vols. 8vo. *very scarce, bds.* £2. 2s . 1839-40
1725 ———— NENNIUS Historia Britonum, recensuit J. Stevenson, 8vo. *bds. scarce,* 7s 6d . 1838
1726 ———— RICARDUS DIVISIENSIS Chronicon de rebus gestis Ricardi primi : nunc primum typis mandatum, curante J. Stevenson, 8vo. *bds. scarce,* 7s 6d . 1838
1727 ——— ——— WILLELMUS MALMESBIRIENSIS Gesta Regum Anglorum, et Historia Novella; recensuit T. D. Hardy, 2 vols. 8vo. *bds.* 18s . . 1840

1728 ENCHIRIDION Theologicum Anti-Romanum, containing Bp. Taylor's Dissuasive from Popery, and his Treatise on the Real Presence— Barrow on the Pope's Supremacy, and Miscellaneous Tracts on the points at issue between the Churches of England and Rome, 3 vols. 8vo. *calf gilt, £2.* - *Oxford,* 1836-7
1729 ENFIELD's (Wm.) Sermons for the use of Families, 2 vols. 12mo. *3s*
            1769-71
1730 ——— Sermons on practical subjects, with Memoirs of the Author by J. Aikin, M.D., 3 vols. 8vo. *calf, neat, 7s 6d*   1798
1731 ——— Prayers for the use of Families, 8vo. *bds. 2s*   1812
1732 ENGLISH Presbyterian Eloquence, or Dissenters' Sayings, Ancient and Modern, 8vo. *sewed, 1s 6d* . 1720
1733 ENOCH.—The Book of the Prophet Enoch : an Apocryphal production, now first translated from an Ethiopic MS. in the Bodleian Library, by Rd. Laurence, Abp. of Cashel, 8vo. *calf gilt, 7s*
            Oxford, 1833
1734 ENTICK's (John) Evidence of Christianity asserted and proved from facts, as authorized by Sacred and Prophane History, 8vo. *calf, scarce, 3s* . . 1729
1735 EPHRAEM (S. Syri) Opera omnia, *Syriace, Græce, Latine,* edente J. S. ASSEMANNO, *best edition,* 6 vols. folio, *fine copy, new in calf gilt, scarce,* £14. 14s   *Romæ,* 1737-46
1736 ——— Opera, *Græce,* e Codicibus MSS. Bodleianis, (cura Ed. Thwaites) folio, *calf,* 15s . *Oxon.* 1709
1737 ——— idem, LARGE PAPER, royal folio, *fine copy, calf, (from the late Duke of Sussex's collection)* £1. 5s   *ib.* 1709
1738 EPIPHANIUS (S. *Constantiæ Episcopus*) Opera Omnia, Græce et Latine, ed. Dion. Petavius, cum indicibus, etc. 2 vols. folio, *calf,* £3. 3s . *Coloniæ,* 1682
1739 ——— Ad Physiologum: Ejusdem in die festo Palmarum Sermo: Gr. et Lat. D. Consali Ponce de Leon interpretis et scholiastæ bimestre otium, 8vo. *plates,* RARE, *fine copy, red morocco, gilt leaves, by Roger Payne,* 16s . *Antv.* 1588
    Marked in a recent catalogue £1. 11s 6d.
1740 EPISTLE of Comfort to the Reverend Priests, and to the Honourable, Worshipfull, and others of the lay sort, restrayned in endurance for the Catholike Faith, small 8vo. *vellum, rare,* 8s
            Printed with licence, 1605
1741 EPITAPHS.—A Collection of Epitaphs and Monumental Inscriptions: with an Essay on Epitaphs, by Dr. Johnson, 2 vols. in 1, 8vo. LARGE PAPER, *calf gilt, marbled leaves,* 14s   1806
1742 ERASMUS (Desiderius) Opera Omnia, emendatiora et auctiora ex recensione Jo. Clerici, 10 vols. in 11, folio, *with portraits of all the Reformers, fine copy, old calf gilt,* £10. 10s
            Lugd. Bat. 1703-6
1743 ——— in Novum Testamentum Paraphrasis, 7 vols. in 6, sm. 8vo. *black morocco,* £1. 4s   *Lugduni et Basileæ,* 1544, &c.
1744 ——— in Acta Apostolorum Paraphrasis, sm. 8vo. *hf. bd.* 4s
            [*Basileæ.*] 1548

J. LESLIE'S CATALOGUE. 109

1745 ERASMUS (Des.) Colloquia, cum notis variorum, accurante C. Schrevelio, 8vo. *fine copy, old calf gilt,* 6s   *Lugd. Bat.* 1664
1746 ———— Colloquia, 18mo. *fine copy, red morocco, gilt leaves,* 15s
    Amst. 1679
1747 ———— Epistolæ Selectiores, cum præfatione J. E. Kappii, 8vo. *portrait, vellum,* 4s .   *Wratisl.* 1752
1748 ———— Ecclesiastæ, sive de Ratione Concionandi libri quatuor; recensuit F. A. Klein, 8vo. *sewed,* 5s   *Lipsiæ,* 1820
1749 ———— Ecclesiastes, or the Preacher; an Essay on the Duties of a Public Religious Instructor, chiefly taken from a Latin Treatise by Erasmus: with a prefatory Address to Patrons of Livings, &c. 12mo. 2s—*sewed,* 1s 6d .   1797
1750 ———— Paraphrase upon the Newe Testamente, 2 vols. folio, 𝔟𝔩𝔞𝔠𝔨 𝔩𝔢𝔱𝔱𝔢𝔯, *the titles supplied in MS.* £3. 3s
    London, Edw. Whitchurche, 1548-49

The first volume of this Commentary was translated by Nicholas Udall, the second by Coverdale, John Olde, and Leonard Coxe. The paraphrase upon the Apocalypse, was written by Leo Jude, and translated by Edmund Allen. This work was set forth by authority, and commanded to be placed in all parish churches.

1751 ———— Moriæ Encomium; or, a Panegyrick upon Folly; with fifty cuts designed by Hans Holbein, 8vo. *new in morocco, old style, gilt leaves,* 18s .   1709
1752 ———— The Life of Erasmus (by Dr. John Jortin) 2 vols. 4to. *portrait, calf,* 16s .   1758-60
1753 ———— His Life, with Historical Remarks on the state of Literature between the Tenth and Sixteenth Centuries, by Cha. Butler, Esq. 8vo. *bds.* 4s .   1825
1754 ERSKINE'S (John) Theological Dissertations, 1765—HOWE'S (J.) Abridgment of his Discourse on Self-Dedication, and the Temper of Jesus towards his Enemies, by B. Grosvenor, D.D., with the Lives of the Authors [by J. Archdeacon], *Camb.* 1785—WESLEY'S (John) Duty and Advantages of Early Rising, [a Sermon] *ib.* 1785; *in one vol.* 12mo. *hf. bd. calf,* 2s 6d .   ———
1755 ESSAY on the Necessity of Revealed Religion, 18mo. *calf,* 2s
    Oxford, 1796
1756 ESSAYS on the Church, by a Layman, 12mo. *bds.* 3s   1838
1757 ———— written in the Intervals of Business, 12mo. *bds.* 3s   1842
1758 ———— on the Original of Funeral Sermons, Orations, and Odes, occasioned by two Funeral Discourses on the Death of Dame Mary Page, 8vo. 1s . .   1729
1759 ESSEX, (Arthur *Earl of*) An Enquirie into, and Detection of, the Barbarous Murther of the late Earl of Essex, 4to. *sewed,* 2s 6d
    1684
1760 ESTIUS (Gul.) Historiæ Martyrum Gorcomiensium, majori numero Fratrum Minorum; qui pro Fide Catholica à perduellibus interfecti sunt anno Domini, 1572, small 8vo. *fine copy, old red morocco, richly tooled, with gilt leaves, and the arms of Pope Clement VIII. on the sides,* 15s .   *Duaci,* 1603

1761 EUCHARIST.—Traditio Ecclesiæ de Sanctissimo Eucharistiæ Sacramento, ex SS. Patribus, &c. collecta, small 4to. *with fine portraits of the four principal Fathers of the Western Church, fine copy, old French calf gilt, marbled and gilt leaves,* 8s *Par.* 1659

1762 EUSEBIUS (*Pamphilus*) de Evangelica Preparatione, a Geo.Trapezuntio Græco in Latinum traductus, *illuminated initial letters, Venetiis*, 1497 —LACTANTII Firmiani Opera—Jo. Chrysostomus de Eucharistia, et in eandem materiam Lau. Vallæ Sermo : Philippi Adhortatio ad Theodosum : et Tertulliani Apologeticus, *curious initial letters engraved on wood; the first printed in red ink, Venetiis,* 1502 —2 vols. in 1, folio, *fine copies, in the original oak boards,* 14s
1497-1502
From the library of the late Duke of Sussex.

1763 ———— Evangelica Præparatio et Demonstratio, Græcè ; 2 vols. in 1, folio, FIRST EDITION, *fine copy, vellum,* 18s
Lutetiæ R. Stephanus, 1544-45

1764 ———— de Demonstratione Evangelica, *Gr. et Lat.* cum notis, folio, *calf,* £1. 4s . *Paris,* 1628

1765 ———— Præparatio et Demonstratio Evangelica, *Gr. et Lat.* notis illust. F. Vigerus, [et R. Montacutii] 2 vols. folio, *old calf gilt, neat,* £2. 10s . *Coloniæ,* 1688

1766 ———— aliud exemplar, 2 vols. folio, *vellum,* £1. 18s *ib.* 1688
1767 ———— idem, 2 vols. folio, *rough calf,* £2. 8s *Paris,* 1628
1768 ———— Thesaurus Temporum, opera ac studio J. J. Scaligeri, folio, LARGE PAPER, *fine copy, old morocco, gilt leaves,* £1. 16s
Lugd. Bat. 1606
" Amplissimo viro Jac. Tumerio Regio Consiliario in Consistorio sanctiore Jos. Scal. D.D.—*Autograph note on title.*

1769 ———— Sacrosanctus Evangeliorum Codex S. Eusebii Magni Episc. et Martyris, manu exaratus ex Autographo Basilicæ Vercellensis ad unguem exhibitus ; nunc primum in lucem prodit opera et studio J. And. Irici Tridinensis, cum ejusdem Præfatione, Notis, &c. 4to. *sewed,* 16s . *Mediolani,* 1748

1770 ———— Eclogæ Propheticæ, e Codice MS. Bibl. Cæs. Vindob. nunc primum edidit Tho. Gaisford, 8vo. *bds.* 10s *Oxonii,* 1842

1771 ———— Historiæ Ecclesiasticæ libri decem Ejusd. de vita Imp. Constantini libri IV. *Gr. et. Lat.* ed. Hen. Valesius, folio, *calf,* 18s
Paris, 1659

1772 ———— Historiæ Ecclesiasticæ libri decem, recensuit Edv. Burton, S. T. P., 2 vols. 8vo. *bds.* £1. 1s *Oxon.* 1838

1773 ———— Socratis, Sozomeni, Theodoriti, Evagrii, Philostorgii, et Theodori, Historiæ Ecclesiasticæ, Græce et Latinè, Notis illustravit Hen. Valesius, 3 vols. folio, *vellum,* £3. 16s *Par.* 1678

1774 ———— Ancient Ecclesiastical Histories of the first six hundred years after Christ, by Eusebius, Socrates, and Evagrius ; whereunto is added, Dorotheus, Bp. of Tyre, of the Lives and Ends of the Prophets, Apostles, and LXX. Disciples ; translated by Meredith Hanmer, D.D. Hereunto is added, Eusebius his Life of Constantine, with Constantine's Oration to the Clergy, folio, *hf. bd. calf,* 18s . . 1633

1775 EUSEBIUS'S Ecclesiastical History to the Year 324, with a Description of the Martyrdom of those who suffered for the cause of Christ, translated by the Rev. C. F. Cruse, 8vo. *bds.* 5s 6d 1838
1776 ———— Greek Ecclesiastical Historians of the first six centuries, viz.—Eusebius's Life of Constantine, Oration, his Ecclesiastical History, Socrates Scholasticus's History, Sozomen's Narrative, Theodoret's Ecclesiastical History, and Evagrius's Ecclesiastical History, 6 vols. 8vo. *bds.* £2. 2s   1843-45
    Any volume may be had separately.
1777 EVANGELICAL HISTORY of our Lord Jesus Christ Harmonized; explained, and illustrated, by a Society of Gentlemen, 2 vols. 8vo. *fine copy, old calf gilt, broad tooled borders,* 5s   1757
1778 EVANS'S (A. B.) Plain Sermons on the Relative Duties of the Poor, 12mo. *bds.* 1s 6d   1822
1779 ———— Sermons on the Christian Life and Character, 8vo. *bds.* 4s 6d   1832
1780 ———— (Caleb) Christ Crucified; or, the Scripture Doctrine of the Atonement illustrated and defended, in four Discourses, 12mo. *bds. scarce,* 2s   Bristol, 1789
1781 [———— (John)] Case of Kneeling at the Holy Sacrament stated and resolved, 4to. *sewed,* 1s   1683
1782 ———— Sermons preached on various occasions, 19 tracts in 1 vol. 8vo. *hf. bd. uncut,* 3s 6d   1707-30
1783 ———— Practical Discourses concerning the Christian Temper, with the Life of the Author, by Jo. Erskine, D.D., 2 vols. 12mo. *calf,* 3s   1802
1784 ———— (Rob. Wilson) The Church of God, in a series of Sermons, 8vo. *bds* 4s 6d   1832
1785 ———— Rectory of Valehead, 12mo. *bds.* 2s 6d   1839
1786 ———— Bishoprick of Souls, 12mo. *bds.* 3s   1842
1787 EVANSON'S (Edw.) Letter to thé Bp. of Lichfield on the Prophecies of the New Testament, and the Grand Apostacy, 8vo. *sewed,* 1s   1777
1788 EXODUS.—A Corrected Translation, with Notes, by Will. Hopkins, 4to. *bds.* 5s   1784
1788*FABER'S (G. S.) Dissertation on the Prophecies that have been fulfilled, are now fulfilling, or will hereafter be fulfilled, relative to the 1260 years; the Papal and Mahommedan Apostacies; the Reign of Antichrist, and the Restoration of the Jews, 2 vols. 8vo. *calf,* 7s   1808
1789 ———— Practical Treatise on the ordinary Operations of the Holy Spirit, 8vo. *calf,* 3s   1813
1790 ———— Sermons on various subjects and occasions, 2 vols. 8vo. *hf. bd. calf, neat,* 6s   1816-20
1791 ———— Christ's Discourse at Capernaum fatal to the Doctrine of Transubstantiation, 8vo. *bds.* 6s   1840
1792 ———— Inquiry into the History and Theology of the Ancient Vallenses and Albigenses, 8vo. *bds.* 6s   1838
1793 ———— Dissertation on the Mysteries of the Cabiri; or, the Great Gods of Phoenicia, Samothrace, Egypt, Troas, Greece, and Italy, 2 vols. 8vo. *bds.* 14s   1803

1794 FABRICIUS (Jo. Alb.) Delectus Argumentorum et Syllabus Scriptorum qui Veritatem Religionis Christianæ adversus Atheos, Judæos, etc. asseruerunt. Præmissa sunt Eusebii Procemium et capita priora Demonstrationis Evangelicæ, quæ in editionibus hactenus desiderantur, 4to. *calf, 9s—vellum, 9s* *Hamb.* 1725

    " This performance, very valuable in itself, is yet more so on account of the Procemium etc., of Eusebius's Demonst. Evang. which are wanting in all the editions of that work, and were supposed to be lost, but are here recovered by Fabricius, with a Latin translation."

1795 ———— (Steph.) Sacræ Conciones in S. Prophetarum quos minores vocant, Libros, folio, *vellum*, £1. 8s *Bernæ*, 1641

1796 FAITH.—An impartial Enquiry into the True Nature of that Faith which is required in the Gospel; by Philalethes Cestriensis, 8vo. *calf, 2s* . 1746

1797 FALKNER (Wm.) Libertas Ecclesiastica, or a Discourse vindicating the lawfulness of those things which are chiefly excepted against in the Church of England, especially in its Liturgy and Worship, 8vo. *calf, 4s* . 1674

1798 ———— Christian Loyalty : or a Discourse concerning Supremacy in Causes Ecclesiastical, &c., 8vo. *calf, 2s 6d* 1679

1799 FAMILY CHAPLAIN; a complete course of Sermons upon the Festivals and Fasts, selected from the celebrated Discourses of Abps. Tillotson and Secker, Bps. Stillingfleet, Atterbury, Conybeare, and Warburton, Drs. Swift, Littleton, Hole, Waterland, Clarke, Fothergill and Brown, and others, 2 vols. 8vo. *fine copy, calf, 8s* 1775

1800 FARINGTON's (Wm.) Sermons on several important occasions, 8vo. *bds. very scarce, 5s* . *Warrington*, 1769

    These Sermons were in reality composed by the Rev. Edw. Owen, who succeeded Mr. Farington in the Rectory of Warrington.

1801 FARMER's (Hugh) Dissertation on Miracles, designed to shew that they are Arguments of a Divine Interposition, and absolute Proof of the Mission of a Prophet, 8vo. *calf, 4s 6d* 1771

1802 ———— another copy, *large paper, old calf gilt, 7s 6d* 1771

1803 ———— The general Prevalence of the Worship of Human Spirits in the Antient Heathen Nations, asserted and proved, 8vo. *bds. 4s 6d —calf, 6s* . 1783

1804 ———— Inquiry into the Nature and Design of Christ's Temptation in the Wilderness, 8vo. *calf, 2s 6d* . ——

1805 ———— (Rich.) Sermon at Paul's Crosse, 4to. *1s 6d* 1629

1806 FARQUHAR's (John) Sermons on various subjects, corrected by G. Campbell, D.D., and A. Gerard, D.D., 2 vols. 12mo. *old calf gilt, neat, 2s 6d* . 1772

1807 ———— the same, 8vo. *bds. 2s 6d* . 1792

1808 FARRER's (John) Sermons on the Parables, 8vo. *bds. 4s* 1809

1809 FARROW's (Benj.) Practical Exposition of the Catechism of the Church of England, 8vo. *neat, 2s* 1708

1810 FAWCETT's (Benj.) Sacred Almoner, in two Discourses, 1757—The Grand Inquiry, am I in Christ or not? explained and recommended, 1756—FORDYCE's (James) Delusive and persecuting Spirit of Popery, a Sermon, 1758; *in one* vol. 12mo. *hf. bd. 2s* ——

[58, GREAT QUEEN STREET,

1811 FATHERS OF THE ENGLISH CHURCH; or, a Selection from the Writings of the Reformers, and Early Protestant Divines of the Church of England, viz., Tindal, Frith, Hamilton, Joy, Barnes, Lancelot Ridley, Bp. Latimer, Abp. Cranmer, Bp. Nicholas Ridley, Clement, Philpot, Rogers, Turner, Bp. Hooper, Bradford, Saunders, and Bp. Jewell. Edward VIth's Catechism, Dean Nowell's Catechism, Abp. Parker's Prefaces to the Bible, and various Tracts, annexed to the Geneva Bible, Liturgy, &c. &c. Edited by Legh Richmond, 8 vols. 8vo. *scarce, calf, £5. 5s*   *Lond.* 1807-12

1812 FAWCETT's (James) Sermons before the University of Cambridge, 8vo. *calf, 5s* . *Camb.* 1794

1813 FEATLEY's (Daniel) Clavis Mystica: a Key opening divers difficult and mysterious Texts of Holy Scripture, in Seventy Sermons, fol. *calf, 15s* . . 1636

1814 ——— Ancilla Pietatis: or the Hand-maid to Private Devotion, 18mo. *5s 6d* . . 1656

1815 ——— another copy, sm. 8vo. *calf, 4s* . 1675
From the Duke of Sussex's Library.

1816 FEBRONIUS (Justinus, *i. e. Bp. Hontheim*), de Statu Ecclesiæ et legitima potestate Romani Pontificis, ad reuniendos dissidentes in Religione Christianos compositus, cum Defensionibus, 4 tom. 4to. *calf, £1. 10s* . *Bullioni,* 1765-74
This work, denying the Supremacy of the Pope, was written by Bp. Hontheim under the assumed name of Febronius, and caused a great sensation. Four Papal bulls condemnatory of the book having been published, Hontheim, in 1778, compelled to retract, suppressed it.

1817 ——— Traité du Gouvernment de l'Eglise et de la puissance du Pape, traduit du Latin par L. D. L. S. Membre de l'Académie de B., 3 vols. 12mo. *neat, 7s 6d* . *Venise,* 1767

1818 FELIBIEN (Michel) Histoire de l'Abbaye Royale de Saint-Denys en France, contenant la Vie des Abbez qui l'ont gouvernée depuis onze cens ans; les Hommes Illustres qu'elle à donnez à l'Eglise et à l'Etat, &c. folio, *maps and plates, fine copy, calf, £1. 16s*
Par. 1706

1819 FELL's (Jo. *Bp. of Oxon.*) Paraphrase and Annotations upon all the Epistles of St. Paul, (done by several eminent men at Oxford, corrected by Bp. Fell), 8vo. *calf, 6s*   *Oxford,* 1684

1820 ——— another copy, 8vo. *calf, 7s 6d* . 1702

1821 FELLOWES's (W. D.) Visit to the Monastery of La Trappe, in 1817: with notes taken during a tour through various parts of France, 8vo. *coloured engravings, morocco, gilt leaves, 6s*   1818

1822 FELTHAM's (Owen) Resolves, Divine, Moral, and Political, sm. 8vo. *brown calf, very neat, 8s 6d* . 1840

1823 FELTON's (Dr. Hen.) Sermons on the Creation, Fall, and Redemption of Man, &c., 8vo. *calf, 3s* . 1748

1824 FÉNELON (Fr., *Archevêque de Cambrai*), Œuvres complètes, 5 vols. 8vo. *sewed, £1. 8s* . *Paris,* 1838
"Ces 5 volumes en contiennent réelement 18 des anciennes editions en 8vo."

1825 ——— Œuvres Spirituelles, 4 vols. 12mo. *old calf gilt,* 12s
s. l. 1767

1826 ——— Private Thoughts upon Religion, in several letters to the Duke Regent of France, 12mo. *calf,* 2s   1719

1827 FENELON's (Abp.) Pastoral Letter concerning the Love of God; with a circular Letter by Bp. Bull, his Visitation Sermon, and his Charge; published by Robert Nelson, Esq., 12mo. *calf*, 1s 6d 1715

1828 ———— Dialogues concerning Eloquence in general; and particularly that kind which is fit for the Pulpit, translated by W. Stevenson, 8vo. *calf*, 2s 6d . 1722

1829 ———— Histoire de sa Vie, 12mo. *port. hf. bd.* 3s *La Haye*, 1723

1830 ———— Histoire de Fénelon, composée sur les MSS. originaux, par M. le Card. De Bausset, 4 vols. 8vo. *port. French marbled calf*, £1. 8s . *Versailles*, 1817

1831 FENNER's (Wm.) Treatise of the Affections; or the Soule's pulse, whereby a Christian may know whether he be living or dying, &c. 12mo. 3s 6d . 1642

1832 ———— Christ's Alarm to drowsie Saints: or Christ's Epistle to His Churches, 4to. *calf*, 4s 6d . 1650

1833 FENTON's (Tho.) Annotations on the Book of Job, and the Psalms, 8vo. *calf*, 4s 6d . 1732

1834 FERGUSON's (James) Brief Exposition of the First and Second Epistles of Paul to the Thessalonians, 12mo. *calf, neat, rare*, 7s 6d *Glasgow*, 1675

1835 ———— (Robert) Justification onely upon a Satisfaction: or, the Necessity and Verity of the Satisfaction of Christ, asserted against the Socinians, 12mo. *calf*, 4s . 1668

1836 FERRARIUS's (James Alex.) Epistles to the two Brethren of Wallenburgh, concerning the Usefulness and Necessity of the Roman Catholic Faith, wherein the Ambition and Avarice of the Church of Rome are lively demonstrated, 12mo. *morocco, gilt leaves*, 7s 6d . 1673

1836*———— another copy, 12mo. *title supplied in MS. calf*, 4s 1673
'From the library of the late Duke of Sussex.

1837 FERRERIUS (Zach.) Hymni Novi Ecclesiastici, novis Ludovici Vicentini ac Lautitii Perusini characteribus in lucem traditi, 4to. *sewed, title stained*, 8s . *Romæ*, 1523

1838 ———— idem, 4to. *calf*, 10s 6d . *ib.* 1523
Printed in Italic characters.

1839 FERUS's's (Jo.) Doctrine and Dominion of the Crosse; in an Historical Narration and Spiritual application of the Passion of Jesus, turned into English by Henry Pinnell, 4to. *calf*, 6s 1659

1840 FIDDES's (Rich.) Practical Discourses on several subjects, 8vo. *calf*, 2s . 1713

1841 ———— the same, folio, LARGE PAPER, *calf*, 18s 1720

1842 ———— Body of Divinity, wherein are explained the Principles of Natural and Revealed Religion, 2 vols. LARGE PAPER, royal folio, *calf*, £1. 11s 6d . 1718

1843 ———— Life of Cardinal Wolsey, folio, *portraits, calf*, 12s 1724
This work brought on him the charge of being popishly affected.

1844 FIELD (Richard) Of the Church, five books, *first edition*, 4to. *hf. bd. calf, neat, scarce*, £1. 8s . 1606

1845 ———— third edition, much enlarged, folio, *fine copy, calf gilt, old style*, £3. 10s . *Oxford*, 1635

[58, GREAT QUEEN STREET,

1846 FIENUS (Tho.) de Viribus Imaginationis tractatus, 18mo. *calf*, 1*s* 6*d*
   Lond. 1657
1847 FILMER's (Sir Rob.) Discourse whether it be Lawful to take Use for Money, published by Sir Roger Twisden, with his Preface, 18mo. *calf*, 1*s* 6*d* . . 1678
1848 FINCH's (Geo.) Sketch of the Romish Controversy, with a Supplement, 2 vols. 8vo. *bds.* £1. 4*s* . 1831-36
   Privately printed, and very scarce.
1849 FIRMIN's (Giles) Real Christian: or a Treatise of Effectual Calling, 4to. *calf*, 4*s* . . 1670
1850 FISHER's (Ambrose) Defence of the Liturgie of the Church of England, in a dialogue between Novatus and Irenæus, 4to. *calf*, 7*s* 1630
1851 FISHERI (Jo. *Episc. Roffensis*) Assertionis Lutheranæ Confutatio, 4to. *original wooden boards*, 15*s* . *Colon.* 1525
1852 ———— de Veritate Corporis et Sanguinis Christi in Eucharistia, adversus Johannem Oecolampadium, folio, *fine clean copy, new in brown calf gilt*, £1. 1*s* . *Coloniæ*, 1527
1853 FISHER's (Bp.) Funeral Sermon of Margaret, Countess of Richmond and Derby, Mother to K. Henry VII. and Foundress of Christ's and St. John's Coll. Cambridge, 8vo. *front. calf*, 6*s* 1708
1854 FITZ SIMON (Henr.) Britannomachia Ministrorum in plerisque et Fidei Fundamentis, et Fidei Articulis dissidentium, 4to. *vellum, rare*, £1. 5*s* . *Duaci,* 1614
1855 FLAVEL's (John) Divine Conduct; or the Mystery of Providence, 8vo. *calf*, 2*s* 6*d* . 1786
1856 FLECHIER (Esprit, *Evéque de Nismes*) Panegyriques et autres Sermons, 2 vols. 12mo. *port. calf*, 4*s* *Brusselles,* 1696
1857 ———— Recueil des Oraisons Funebres, 12mo. *port. calf*, 3*s*
   Par. 1734
1858 ———— the same, 12mo. *calf*, 2*s* 6*d* . *ib.* 1747
1859 ———— the same, 12mo. *calf*, 3*s* 6*d* . *ib.* 1749
1860 ———— the same, 12mo. *hf. bd. uncut*, 2*s* 6*d* *ib.* 1785
1861 [FLEETWOOD's (Bp.)] Account of the Life and Death of the Blessed Virgin, according to Romish Writers, 4to. 1*s* 6*d* 1687
1862 ———— Relative Duties of Parents and Children, Husbands, and Wives, Masters and Servants, considered in 16 Sermons, with three more on Self-Murther, 8vo.*calf*, 2*s* 6*d* 1705
1863 ———— another copy, 8vo. *calf*, 2*s* 6*d* . 1716
1864 ———— Reflections on Dr. Fleetwood's Essay upon Miracles, [by the Rev. J. Gilbert] 8vo. *calf*, 2*s* 6*d* 1706
1865 ———— Reasonable Communicant, or an Explanation of the Doctrine of the Sacrament of the Lord's Supper, from the Communion Service, 18mo. 1*s* . 1724
1866 ———— another copy, 18mo. 1*s* . 1748
1867 ———— Reasonable Communicant, 1767—A Short Office for the Holy Communion, collected from Abp. Tillotson, Bp. Fleetwood, and others, N. D. *in one vol.* 12mo. 1*s* 6*d* ———
1868 ———— Seventeen Sermons upon several occasions, 8vo. *calf*, 3*s* ———
   Fleetwood, surnamed "Silver-toogue;" his Sermons are recommended by Bishop Cleaver.

1869 [FLEMING's (Robert)] Fulfilling of the Scripture, or, an Essay shewing the exact Accomplishment of the Word of God, &c. 12mo. *fine copy, calf, neat*, 5s . 1671
1870 ———— another copy, 12mo. *calf*, 3s ——
"An elaborate work, which is in fact a view of the operations of Providence in preserving the Church through all the vicissitudes of Ecclesiastical History."
Chalmers.
1871 ———— Mirrour of Divine Love unvailed, in a poetical Paraphrase of the Song of Solomon, with several other Poems, &c. 12mo. *calf*, 5s . 1691
1872 ———— Discourse of Earthquakes, 12mo. *calf*, 3s 1693
1873 ———— Confirming Work of Religion; or its great Things made Plain, 12mo. *very scarce*, 4s . 1693
1874 ———— Discourses on several subjects, viz—the Rise and Fall of the Papacy; God's Dwelling with Men; the Ministerial Office; and Religion as it centers in the Lord Jesus Christ, 8vo. *portrait, calf, scarce*, 7s 6d . 1701
"Fleming's work very remarkably anticipated the French Revolution, and its results, nearly a century before they took place. K. Geo. III. was desirous of seeing it, but it could only be found in Dr. Williams's library in Red Cross Street, from which the King borrowed it."—*MS. Note.*
1875 ———— Christology : a Discourse concerning Christ, 3 vols. 8vo. *portrait, calf*, 15s . . 1705-8
"This work is now rather uncommon. Many ingenious thoughts occur in the Christology, and many passages of Scripture are placed in a new light."—*Orme.*
1876 ———— History of Hereditary Right, from Cain to Nero, 8vo. *calf*, 3s . . 1717
1877 FLETCHER's (Giles, LL.D.) Israel Redux; or the Restauration of Israel, exhibited in two short Treatises—the first contains an Essay upon some probable grounds that the present Tartars near the Caspian Sea, are the Posterity of the Ten Tribes of Israel, by G. Fletcher, LL.D.; the second, a Dissertation concerning their ancient and successive State, &c. by S[amuel] L[ec], 18mo. *calf*, 4s 1677
1878 ———— (John, *of Madeley)* Vindication of the Rev. Mr. Wesley's Last Minutes, &c. 1788 —A second Check to Antinomianism—A third Check to Antinomianism, in a Letter to [Sir Richard Hill] the Author of Pietas Oxoniensis, 1775, *in one vol.* 12mo. *calf*, 3s . . ——
1879 FLEURY (Claude) Histoire Ecclesiastique, avec la Continuation (jusqu'à 1595) par J. C. Fabre et Goujet, et la Table générale des matiéres, par Etienne Rondet, *best edition*, 37 vols. 4to. *fine copy, old French calf gilt*, £8. 18s 6d *Par.* 1691-1774
1880 ———— another copy, 37 vols. 4to. *fine copy, calf*, £9. 9s
ib. 1722-58
1881 ———— Histoire du Christianisme, augmentée de Quatre Livres (les Livres CI. CII. CIII. CIV.) comprenant l'Histoire du Quinzième Siecle, publiés pour la premiere fois d'après un Manuscrit de Fleury appartenant à la Bibliothèque Royale, &c. 6 vols. royal 8vo. *calf gilt*, £4. 4s — *sewed*, £2. 12s 6d *ib.* 1836
1882 ———— Ecclesiastical History from 381 to 456, translated, with Notes by the Rev. J. H. Newman, 3 vols. 8vo. *bds.* £1. 16s
Oxford, 1842-4
Either of the volumes may be had separately.

[58, GREAT QUEEN STREET,

1883 FLEURY (Claude) Catechisme Historique, contenaut en Abrégé, l'Histoire Sainte, et la Doctrine Chretienne, 12mo. *neat, 2s 6d*
Brux. 1778
1884 ——————— another copy, 12mo. *calf, 3s* *St. Malo,* 1805
1885 ——————— Short History of the Israelites, with an Account of their Manners, Customs, &c. translated by Ellis Farneworth, 8vo. *bds. 4s* . . 1756
" This translation was not made by the person to whom the title-page attributes it, but by Tho. Bedford, son of the celebrated Hilkiah."
See Nichols's Lit. Anec. ii, 392.
1886 FLORUS (L. Annæus) Res Romanæ, cum notis J. G. Grævii, 8vo. *plates, fine copy, old calf gilt, 5s* *Traj. Bat.* 1680
1887 FLUDD'S (Robert, *Doctor of Physick*) Mosaicall Philosophy, grounded upon the essential Truth of Eternal Sapience, folio, *cuts, fine copy, calf extra, gilt leaves,* £1. 1s . 1659
1888 FOIX (Paul de, *Archivesque de Tolose*) Lettres escrites au Roy Henry III. 4to. LARGE PAPER, *calf,* 4s *Paris,* 1628
1889 FONTENELLE Entretiens sur la Pluralité des Mondes; avec les Dialogues des Morts, 12mo. *calf,* 2s *ib.* 1769
1890 ——————— Nouveaux Dialogues des Morts, 12mo. *calf,* 1s 6d
Amst. ———
1891 ——————— An Answer to his History of Oracles, in which Mr. Van-Dale's System is confuted, and the Opinion of the Fathers vindicated, translated from the French, 8vo. *calf,* 2s 1709
1892 [FORBES's (Duncan)] Reflexions on the Sources of Incredulity with regard to Religion, 12mo. *calf,* 1s 6d *Edinb.* 1750
1893 ——————— another copy, 12mo. *bds.* 1s *ib.* 1752
1894 ——————— Letter to a Bishop, containing some important Discoveries in Philosophy, Theology, &c. 1747—Reflexions on the Sources of Incredulity, 1750, *in one vol.* 12mo. *calf,* 2s 6d ———
1895 FORBESIUS (Jo., *à Corse*) Instructiones historico-theologicæ, de Doctrina Christiana et vario rerum statu, ortisque erroribus et controversiis, a temporibus Apostolicis usque ad Sæc. XVII. folio, *calf,* 12s . . *Amst.* 1644
From the collection of the late Duke of Sussex.
" His historico-theological instructions is a work universally admired, and considered one of the best of the kind ever published."—*Chalmers.*
1896 ——————— Opera omnia, 2 vols. in 1, folio, *vellum, scarce,* £1. 11s 6d
Amst. 1703-2
1897 ——————— another copy, 2 vols. folio, *calf,* £1. 11s 6d *ib.* 1703
1898 FORBES'S (Patrick, *of Corse*) Exquisite Commentarie upon the Revelation of St. John, 4to. *hf. bd. scarce, 7s 6d* 1613
1899 FORD (Simon) Ambitio Sacra: conciones duæ habitæ ad Academicos Oxonienses pro forma Bacc. in Theol. 4to. 1s *Oxon.* 1650
1900 ——————— Primitiæ regiminis Davidici, or the First-Fruits of David's Government, an Assize Sermon, 4to. 2s 1654
1901 ——————— (Steph.) Gospel Church; or, God's Holy Temple opened, sm. 8vo. *hf. bd. calf, neat, scarce,* 5s 1675
1902 [FORDYCE'S (James)] Sermons to Young Women, 2 vols. 12mo. *calf,* 3s . . 1766
1903 ——————— the same, 2 vols. 12mo. *fine copy, old calf gilt,* 4s 1768

1904 FORDYCE's (Dr. James) Addresses to Young Men, 2 vols. 12mo. *calf*, 3s . . 1777
1905 FORMBY'S (H.) Visit to the East, comprising Germany and the Danube, Constantinople, Asia Minor, Egypt, and Idumea, 12mo. *cuts, bds*. 6s . . 1843
1906 FORMEY (J. H. Sam.) Sermons sur divers textes de l'Ecriture Sainte, 2 vols. in 1, 8vo. *hf. bd. calf*, 6s *Leide*, 1772
1907 ―――― Ecclesiastical History, from the birth of Christ to the present time, with an Appendix, giving an Account of the people called Methodists, by the translator, [the Rev. Rd. Dodd] 2 vols. in 1, 8vo. *tree marbled calf gilt*, 8s 6d . 1766
  The translator was the brother of the unfortunate Dr. Wm. Dodd.—See Gent.'s Mag. 1811, pt. 1, p. 606.
1908 FORMULÆ Congregationum in Quarta Generali Congregatione; confectæ et approbatæ, in sexta, et septima recognitæ, et auctæ, sm. 8vo. *vellum*, 4s 6d . *Romæ*, 1616
1909 FORMULARIES of Faith, put forth by Authority during the reign of Henry VIII., viz. Articles about Religion, 1536- The Institution of a Christian Man, 1537—A Necessary Doctrine and Erudition for any Christian Man (edited by Bp. Lloyd). 8vo. *bds*. 7s—*calf gilt*, 10s . . *Oxford*, 1825
1910 FORSTER's (Chas.) Discourses, principally on subjects of Scripture History, 8vo. *calf extra, gilt leaves*, 9s 1823
1911 FOSTER's (James) Sermons on various subjects, 2 vols. 8vo. *calf*, 4s 1736-37
  " His talent for preaching was eminent and extraordinary. To his lectures resorted persons of every rank, station, and quality, and thither curiosity might probably have drawn Pope himself, who in the epilogue to his Satires, has taken occasion to praise him in the following lines:—
  " ' Let modest Foster, if he will ; excel
  Ten Metropolitans in preaching well.' "—*Chalmers*.
1912 ―――― (John) Essays, in a series of Letters upon various subjects, 8vo. *bds*. 4s . 1826
1913 FOTHERBY's (Martin, *Bp. of Salisbury*) Atheomastix, clearing foure truthes against Atheists and Infidels, folio, *calf*, 6s 1622
1914 FOTHERGILL's (Dr. Geo.) Sermons on several subjects and occasions, 8vo. *calf*, 5s . *Oxford*, 1761
1915 ―――― (Dr. Tho.) Five Sermons on public occasions, 8vo. *calf*, 2s *ib.* 1766
1916 FOULIS's (Henry) History of Romish Treasons and Usurpations; together with a particular Account of many gross Corruptions and Impostures in the Church of Rome, folio, *fine copy, calf, scarce*, 16s 1671
1917 ―――― another copy, folio, *calf*, 14s 1681
1918 FOWLER's (Edw. *Bp. of Glouc.*) Discourse upon occasion of the Death of Queen Mary, 12mo. *neat*, 1s 6d 1695
1919 ―――― Design of Christianity, 8vo. *calf*, 1s 6d 1676
1920 ―――― Libertas Evangelica ; or, a Discourse of Christian Liberty, 8vo. *front*. 2s 6d . 1680
1921 ―――― Reflections upon the late Examination of the Discourse of the Descent of the Man Christ Jesus, &c. 8vo. 1s 1706

[58, GREAT QUEEN STREET,

1922 Fox's (John) Acts and Monuments of matters most special and memorable happening in the Church, with an Universal History of the same, 3 vols. folio, BEST EDITION, *title and portrait inlaid, calf,* £3. 10s . . 1684
1923 ———— another copy, LARGE PAPER, *with two brilliant impressions of the Portrait by Sturt, richly bound in blue morocco, gilt leaves, with broad borders of gold, by Mackenzie,* £15. 15s 1684
1924 ———— another copy, black letter, 3 vols. folio, *hf. bd. calf, vellum sides,* £2. 15s . 1632
1925 ———— Abridgement of the Booke of Acts and Monuments of the Church, by Timothe Bright, black letter, 4to. *russia, neat,* 16s
1589
1926 ———— (Sam.) Monks and Monasteries; being an Account of English Monasticism, 12mo. *bds.* 5s . 1845
1927 FOXES and Firebrands; or, a Specimen of the Danger and Harmony of Popery and Separation, 3 vols. in 2, sm. 8vo. *scarce,* 12s
Dublin, 1682, *Lond.* 1689
Attributed by some to Dr. Nelson, by others to Sir James Ware. From the library of the late Duke of Sussex.
1928 FRANCE.—La Politique du Clergé de France, 18mo. *vellum,* 3s
La Haye, 1682
1929 FRANCILLON (Jacob) Histoire de la Passion de Notre Seigneur Jesus Christ, 8vo. *fine copy, calf gilt,* 3s *Geneve,* 1779
1930 FRANCIS (Paulus de) Orationes Selectæ in Sacello Apostolico habitæ, tom. I., 3 partes, 4to. *calf,* 5s *Romæ,* 1606
1931 FRANCIS's (Ann) Poetical Translation of the Song of Solomon, from the original Hebrew, with a Preliminary Discourse and Notes, Historical, Critical, and Explanatory, 4to. *calf,* 3s 1781
1932 FRANCK's (Aug. Herman) Guide to the Reading and Study of the Holy Scriptures; translated, with notes, &c. by Wm. Jacques, 8vo. *hf. bd. calf,* 4s . . 1813
1933 FRANCKLIN's (Tho.) Sermons on the Relative Duties, 8vo. *calf,* 2s 6d—*bds.* 2s . . 1765
1934 ———— Sermons on various subjects, 3 vols. 8vo. *bds.* 6s 1790
1935 FRANÇOIS (———) Preuves de la Religion de Jesus Christ, contre les Spinosistes et les Deistes, 8 vols. 12mo. *fine copy, old olive green morocco, gilt leaves,* £1. 10s *Par.* 1754, &c.
1936 ———— (John) Four Discourses on the Liturgy of the Church of England, Burial Service, Baptism, and on Confirmation, 12mo. *sewed,* 1s . . *Norwich,* 1776
1937 FRANCOIS DE PAULE (S.) Le Thresor de ses Œuvres Spirituelles, recueilly de divers autheurs par J. J. Courvoisier, 18mo. *neat,* 2s 6d
ib. 1646
1938 ———— La Vie de S. F. de Paule, fondateur de l'ordre des Minimes, par le R. P. Giry, 12mo. *front. neat,* 2s 6d *Brus.* 1738
1939 FRANKE's (A. H.) Nicodemus; or, a Treatise against the Fear of Man, 18mo. *calf,* 1s 6d . 1706
1940 FRASER's (Peter) Sermons on the Lives of some of the first Promulgators of Christianity, and on miscellaneous subjects, 8vo. *hf. bd. calf,* 4s 6d . 1829

1941 FREE's (Dr. John) Sermons preached before the University of Oxford, 8vo. *calf, 2s 6d* . 1750
1942 FREEMAN's (Sir George, K.B.) Golden Remains, being choice Discourses on select subjects, 12mo. *calf, 3s* 1682
1943 FRERE's (John) Doctrine of Imposition of Hands; or, Confirmation, 8vo. *bds. 4s 6d* . 1845
1944 FRITH (John) A Disputacion of Purgatorye made by Jhon Frith, whiche is devided in to thre bokes. The fiyrst boke is an answere unto Rastell. The second boke answereth unto Sir Thomas More. The thyrde boke maketh answere unto my Lorde of Rochestre, black letter, N. D.—An other boke against Rastel, named the Subsedye or Bulwark to his fyrst boke, made by Jhon Frithe, presoner in the Tower, black letter, N. D., *in one* vol. 12mo. *with MS. notes, very rare, calf,* £1. 1s . ———

> An extremely rare and interesting volume, and for writing which, the author was imprisoned in the Tower, and soon after suffered martyrdom. Hall in his Chronicle, states, that Frith " was after divers and sondry examinations, brought unto the consistory in Paule's Church in London, before divers bisshopes, where after much disputyng for that he woulde not yielde nor submit himselfe to theim, they condemned him, and delivered hym to the secular power to be brent as an heretike."

1945 FROMONDI (L.) Commentaria in S. Scripturam, Epistolas Catholicas, Acta Apostolorum, Apocalypsin et Cantica Canticorum, 2 vols. in 1, folio, *calf,* £1. 10s . *Rothomagi,* 1710

> Fromond was professor of Sacred Literature at Louvain, and the intimate friend, successor, and executor of Jansenius. His works, most of which were condemned at Rome, are uncommon; Des-Cartes had a high opinion of this author's writings.

1946 FRY's (John) Short History of the Church of Christ, from the close of the Sacred Narrative to our own times, 8vo. *bds. 4s 6d* 1825
1947 FULKE's (Dr. Wm.) Defense of the sincere and true Translation of the Holie Scriptures into the English tong, against the manifold cavils of Gregorie Martin of Rhemes, sm. 8vo. *vellum, 7s 6d* Lond. 1583
1948 ——— new edition; edited by the Rev. C. H. Hartshorne, 8vo. *bds.* 10s 6d . Camb. 1843
1949 FULLER's (Tho.) Church History of Britain, from the birth of Jesus Christ untill the year 1648; with the History of the University of Cambridge, and of Waltham Abbey, *with all the plates, and map, and Index,* folio, *fine copy, blue morocco extra, gilt leaves,* £4. 14s 6d . . 1665
1950 ——— another copy, folio, *with the Index, but wanting the two plates of Lichfield Cathedral, and one of the seals of the Mitred Abbeys,* 1655—Appeal of Injured Innocence, *(imperfect at the end)* 1659, *in one* vol. folio, *calf,* £2. 18s . ———
1951 - ——— new edition, edited by the Rev. J. S. Brewer, 6 vols. 8vo. *bds.* £3. 3s . Oxford, 1844
1952 ——— Worthies of England, folio, *fine copy, portrait, calf,* £3. 3s . . 1662

[58, GREAT QUEEN STREET,

1953 FULLER'S (Tho.) Holy and Profane State, folio, *plates, calf, neat,* 14s
Camb. 1642
1954 ———— new edition, 12mo. *bds.* 6s—*calf gilt,* 8s 6d Lond. 1840
1955 ———— Historie of the Holy Warre, folio. *curious engraved title by W. Marshall, new in calf gilt,* £1. 1s Camb. 1640
1956 ———— new edition, sm. 8vo. *brown calf, very neat,* 8s 6d—*bds.* 6s . 1840
1957 ———— Comment on the first Eleven Verses of the Fourth Chapter of St. Matthew's Gospel, concerning Christ's Temptations, 12mo. *scarce,* 6s . 1652
1958 ———— Memorials of the Life and Works of Thos. Fuller, D.D., by the Rev. Arthur Russell, 12mo. *portrait, bds.* 6s 1844
1959 ———— (Tho. M.D.) Gnomologia: Adagies and Proverbs; Wise Sentences and Witty Sayings, 12mo. 3s . 1732
1960 FULLWOOD (Dr. Fr.) Roma Ruit; the Pillars of Rome broken: wherein all the pleas for the Pope's authority in England are answered, 8vo. *portraits of Charles I. and II. calf,* 4s 1679
1961 FUR PRÆDESTINATUS: sive, Dialogismus inter quendam Ordinis Prædicantium Calvinistam et Furem ad laqueum damnatum habitus, 18mo. *vellum,* 7s . Lond. 1651
1962 ———— new edition, 8vo. *bds.* 4s 6d . *ib.* 1813

Fur Prædestinatus was published anonymously, and has generally been ascribed to the pen of Abp. Sancroft; it is therefore made a prominent article in the life of that distinguished Prelate, published by Dr. D'Oyly. This however is a mistake. The tract was in existence many years before Sancroft was capable of producing such a composition. It was first published and circulated in Holland, in the early part of the 17th century, when the controversy respecting Predestination was warmly agitated between the Calvinists and Arminians in the United Provinces; and was generally thought to have been the production of Henry Statius, a man of some note amongst the Remonstrants, &c.

1963 GALATINUS (P.) de Arcanus Catholicæ Veritatis. Item, Jo. Reuchlinus de Cabala, folio, *bds.* 6s . Franc. 1612
1964 GALE'S (Dr. John) Sermons upon several subjects, with his Life, 4 vols. 8vo. *port.* 7s 6d . 1726
"Distinguished by the utility and importance of their subject, strength and clearness of reasoning, and masculine unaffected eloquence."—*Theol. Mag.*
1965 ———— (Theophilus) The Court of the Gentiles: or a Discourse touching the original of Human Literature, both philologie and philosophie, from the Jewish Church, 4 parts in 2 vols. 4to. *calf,* £2. 2s . Oxon. 1677
1966 ———— the same, 4 vols. 4to. *hf. bd. calf,* £1. 15s *ib.* 1672, &c.
"This learned and elaborate work, the object of which is to trace all human learning, philosophy, and religion, to the ancient Scriptures, and the Jewish Church, is now in great repute. The latter parts, particularly the last, are scarce."—*Lowndes.*
1967 GALE (Thos.) RERUM ANGLICARUM SCRIPTORES VETERES, Vol. 1 and 3, *hf. bd. uncut, rare,* £5. 15s 6d 1684-91
CONTENTS.— Vol. I. Ingulfi Croylandensis Historia—Petri Blesensis Continuatio —Chronica de Msilros—Annales Burtonensis—Historia Croylandensis Continuatio.—Vol. III. Gildæ Historia et Epist.—Eddii Stephani Vita, S. Wilfridi Eboracensis—Nennii Hist. Britonum—J. Asserii Chronicon—Higdeni Polychronicon—W. Malmesburiensis de Antiq. Glastoniensis Ecclesiæ, et Lib. V. de Pontificibus—Historia Ramesiensis—Hist. Eliensis—Chronica Joannis Wallingford—J. Fordun Scoti Chronicon—F. Alcwini de Pontificibus et S. Ecclesiæ Eboracensis Pnema, &c.

1968 GALENUS (Matthæus) Origines Monasticæ, seu de prima et vera Christianæ Monastices origine, 4to. *calf, rare,* 12s *Dilingæ,* 1563

1969 GALFREDUS MONUMETENSIS Historia Britonum, edidit J. A. Giles, LL.D. 8vo. *bds.* 8s . 1844

1970 ———— the same, translated by A. Thompson, Esq., revised by J. A. Giles, 8vo. *hf. bd. morocco, uncut,* 9s 6d 1842

1971 GALLONIUS (Ant.) de SS. Martyrum Cruciatibus liber, 18mo. *plates, vellum,* 4s . *Antv.* 1668

1972 GALLAWAY (John Cole) Seventeen Sermons on various subjects, 8vo. *hf. bd. calf,* 2s 6d—*sewed,* 2s . 1785

"Calculated beyond the ordinary run of Christian Sermons to instruct and edify."
Christian Observer.

1973 GALLOWAY's (Joseph) Brief Commentaries upon such parts of the Revelation and other Prophecies as refer to the present times, 8vo. *scarce, calf,* 3s 6d . 1802

1974 GAMBART (M. A.) Le Missionnaire Paroissial, ou sommaire des Exhortations familieres sur le Symbole des Apôtres. &c., 12mo. *vellum,* 2s . *Par.* 1676

1975 GARBUTT's (Rd.) Demonstration of the Resurrection of our Lord Jesus Christ; and therein of the Christian Religion, 18mo. 2s 1669

1976 GARNETT's (John, *Bp. of Clogher*) Dissertation on the Book of Job, to which is prefixed an Introductory Discourse, with a short analysis of the whole book, 4to. *calf,* 3s 6d 1751

1977 ———— Dissertation on the Book of Job, with Four Sermons at Cambridge and Whitehall, 1749—An Essay towards a new Version of the book of Job. with a Commentary; by Thomas Heath, 1756, *in one* vol. 4to. *calf,* 10s 6d ——

1978 GARNONS's (Jo.) Sermons on various subjects, 2 vols. 8vo. *bds.* 4s 1792

1979 GARRICK's (David) Mode of Reading the Liturgy of the Church of England with Notes, and a Preliminary Discourse on Public Reading, by Rd. Cull, 8vo. *bds.* 3s 6d . 1840

1980 GASTON's (Hugh) Scripture Account of the Faith and Practice of Christians, 8vo. *calf, scarce,* 4s . 1764

1981 GASTRELL's (Fra. *Bp.*) Certainty of the Christian Revelation, and the Necessity of believing it, 8vo. *calf,* 2s 6d . 1699

1982 ———— Some Considerations concerning the Trinity: together with a Defence of them against the objections of [Dr. Gastrell] Dean of St. Paul's, 1698—[Bp. Gastrell's] Remarks upon Dr. Clarke's Scripture Doctrine of the Trinity, 1714, *in one* vol. 8vo. *calf,* 3s . . ——

1983 GATAKERI (Thomæ) Opera critica. Dissertatio de N. Instrumenti Stylo. Cinnus sive Adversaria Miscellanea. Adversaria Miscellanea Posthuma. Marci Antonini Imperatoris de Rebus suis Libri XII. Commentario perpetuo explicati. Opuscula varia; 2 vols. folio, *hf. bd. vellum,* £1. 5s . *Traj. ad Rhen.* 1698

1984 GATTON's (Benj.) Eighteen Sermons on several occasions, 8vo. *cf.* 2s *Oxf.* 1732

1985 GAUTIER (Pierre Boudet, *Pasteur de l'Eglise Prot. François de Bristol*,) Sermons sur divers textes de l'Ecriture Sainte, 2 vols. in 1, 8vo. *hf. bd. neat*, 4s 6d . 1792
1986 [GEDDES's (Dr. Alex.)] Modest Apology for the Roman Catholics of Great Britain, 8vo. *bds.* 3s 6d . 1800
1987 ———— Memoirs of the Life and Writings of the Rev. Alex. Geddes, LL.D., by John Mason Good, 8vo. *portraits, bds.* 2s 6d 1803
1988 ———— (Dr. Michæl) Miscellaneous Tracts, containing the History of the Expulsion of the Moriscoes out of Spain: and of the Wars of the Commons of Castile; A View of the Spanish Cortes—An Account of the Manuscripts and Reliques found in the Mountains of Granada, 1588—A View of the Inquisition of Portugal—A Spanish Protestant Martyrology—Dissertation on the Papal Supremacy—Discovery of some gross mistakes in the Roman Martyrology—Essay on the Canons of the Council of Sardica—On the Adoration of Images, Praying to Angels and Saints, Purgatory, the Doctrine of the Seven Sacraments, &c.—A View of all the Orders of Monks and Friars in the Roman Church, &c. 3 vols. 8vo. *calf,* 12s . . 1702-6
1989 ———— the same, together with several Tracts against Popery, including the Life of Don Alvaro de Luna, 4 vols. 8vo. *calf,* 16s 1730-15
1990 GEE's (Edw.) Treatise of Prayer, and of Divine Providence as relating to it, sm. 8vo. *neat,* 3s 6d . 1653
1991 GELASII Cyziceni Commentarius Actorum Nicæni Concilii, cum Corollario Theodori Presbyteri, de Incarnatione Domini, Gr. et Lat. cum notis Rob. Balforei, Scoti, sm. 8vo. *rare, vellum,* 9s *Lutetiæ,* 1599
1992 GELL's (Robert) Essay towards the Amendment of the last English translation of the Bible, folio, *hf. bd. calf,* 10s 6d 1659
1993 ———— Remains, or several Scriptures of the New Testament opened and explained, in sundry pious and learned Notes and Observations thereupon, 2 vols. in 1, folio, *calf,* 16s 1676

This curious work consists of a number of discourses on particular passages, full of allegorical and cabalistic illustrations, along with some ingenious and solid criticisms. The author was for some time Chaplain to Abp. Laud.

1994 GEORGII (F. A.) Alphabetum Tibetanum Missionum Apostolicarum Commodo editum. Præmissa est Dissertatio, qua de vario Literarum ac Regionis Nomine, Gentis Origine, Moribus, Superstitione et Manichæismo fuse disseritur: Beausobrii Calumniæ in S. Augustinum aliosque Ecclesiæ Patres refutantur; thick 4to. *plates, fine copy, calf gilt,* £1. 16s . *Romæ,* 1762
1995 ———— Fragmentum Evangelii S. Johannis Græco-Copto-Thebaicum Sæc. XIV. Additamentum ex vetustissimis Membranis Lectionum Evangelicarum Divinæ Missæ. Cod. Diaconici Reliquiæ et Liturgica alia Fragmenta veteris Thebaidensium Ecclesiæ ante Dioscorum in Latinam versa et notis illustrata, 4to. *scarce, fine copy, new in calf gilt, uniform with the above,* £1. 11s 6d *ib.* 1789
1996 GERARD's (Dr. Alex.) Dissertations on subjects relating to the Genius and Evidences of Christianity, 8vo. *calf,* 3s *Edinb.* 1766

1997 GERARD'S (Dr. Alex.) Pastoral Care, 8vo. *calf gilt*, 3s 1799
1998 ———— (Drs. Alex. and Gilbert) Compendious View of the Evidences of Natural and Revealed Religion; being the Substance of Lectures at Aberdeen, 8vo. *bds*. 2s 6d . 1828
1999 ———— (Dr. Gilbert) Institutes of Biblical Criticism, or heads of Lectures on that subject at Aberdeen, 8vo. *scarce, rich calf gilt*, 18s . . *Edinb*. 1808

* Of general and elementary treatises, there is none which is more to be recommended than the Institutes of Dr. Gerard."—*Bp. Marsh*.

2000 GERBERTUS (Martinus, *Abbas Monast. S. Blasii in Silva Nigra*), Historia Nigræ Silvæ, ordinis S. Benedicti Coloniæ, 3 tom. 4to. *with plates of Charters, &c., calf*, £1. 15s
  Typis ejusdem Monasterii, 1783-88
2001 ———— de Cantu et Musica Sacra a prima Ecclesiæ Ætate usque ad præsens tempus, 2 vols. *Typis San-Blasianis*, 1774—*Ejusd*. Scriptores Ecclesiastici de Musica Sacra potissimum, ex Variis Italiæ, Galliæ, et Germaniæ Codicibus Manuscriptis collecti, 3 vols. *ib*. 1784, together 5 vols. 4to. *plates, bds. rare*, £5. 10s ——
2002 ———— de Cantu et Musica Sacra, 2 vols. 4to. *fine paper, plates, calf*, £2. 2s . . *ib*. 1774
2003 ———— aliud exemplar, *fine paper*, 2 vols. 4to. *new in calf gilt, carmine edges*, £2. 18s . *ib*. 1774
2004 ———— Iter Alemannicum accedit Italicum et Gallicum, sm. 8vo. *bds*. 10s . *ib*. 1773
2005 GERDESII (Dan.) Specimen Italiæ Reformatæ, una cum Syllabo Reformatorum Italorum, 4to. *calf*, 5s *Lugd. Bat*. 1765
2006 ———— Motuum Ecclesiasticorum in Civitate Bremensi, 1547-61, *Gron. & Brem*. 1756—Meletemata Sacra, sive Isagoge et Exegesis in Cap. XV. Epist. I. ad Corinthios. *Gron. & Brem*. 1759, *in one vol*. 4to. *vellum, neat*, 8s 1756-9
2007 ———— Introductio in Historiam Evangelii Secolo XVI. passim per Europam renovati Doctrinæque Reformatæ; accedunt varia Monumenta Pietatis et Rei Literariæ, 4 vols. in 2, 4to. *vellum, neat*, £1. 11s 6d *Groning*. 1744-52

" Learned and accurate, containing much important matter, and many valuable documents."—*Scott's continuation of Milner*. The work is illustrated with the portraits of the most eminent Reformers, including many English.

2008 GEREE (J.) Vindiciæ Pædo-baptismi; or a Vindication of Infant Baptism, in answer to Mr. Tombs, 4to. 1s 6d 1646
2009 GERMON (Barth.) de Veteribus Hæreticis Ecclesiasticorum Codicum Corruptoribus, sm. 4to. (*with the autograph of Cæsar de Missy*) 7s 6d . . *Paris*, 1713
2010 GESNERI (J. M.) Thesaurus Linguæ Latinæ, 4 vols. folio, *fine copy, vellum*, £2. 12s 6d *Lipsiæ*, 1749

Foreign scholars generally prefer Gesner's Thesaurus to the Lexicon of Facciolati, as the latter omits many scientific terms contained in the former. It was a great favourite with the late Dr. Goodall, Provost of Eton, and, perhaps, scarcely any book in his library was more consulted.

2011 GERSON (Joannis) Opera Omnia novo ordine digesta : quibus accessere Henrici de Hassia, Petri de Alliaco, Joannis Brevicoxæ, Joannis de Varenis Scriptorum coætaneorum, ac insuper Jacobi Almaini et Joannis Majoris Tractatus, partim editi partim inediti; necnon Monumenta omnia ad causam Joannis Parvi pertinentia, opera et studio L. E. Dupin, 5 vols. in 3, folio, *stamped hogskin binding*, £4. 4s . *Antverpiæ*, 1706
2012 ———— idem, 5 vols. in 4, folio, *calf gilt*, £4. 4s *ib.* 1706

" From the time of St. Bernard," says Dupin, " the Church never had an author of greater reputation, more profound knowledge, more solid piety, than Gerson. His style is harsh and careless ; yet he is methodical, reasons well, and exhausts his subjects. He founds his conclusions upon principles drawn from Scripture, or natural reason. He defends the truth upon all occasions, with an admirable and undaunted courage. He suffered a cruel persecution for a righteous cause, and died in exile for maintaining it with vigour. Many of his books are excellent, and divines cannot profit more than by reading them diligently."

2013 GESTE's (Edmund, *Bp. of Salisbury*) Life and Character, by Henry Geast Dugdale, Esq. 8vo. 2 *ports. bds. 7s 6d* 1840
2014 GIBBES's (Charles) XXXI Sermons upon several subjects, 4to. *calf*, 4s . 1677
2015 GIBERT (J. P.) Corpus Juris Canonici, per regulas naturali ordine digestas, et cum Prolegomenis ad Jus Canonicum in se et universim consideratum, 3 vols. folio, *calf*, £2. 10s *Lugduni*, 1737
2016 GIBSON's (Edmund, *Bp. of London*) Codex Juris Ecclesiastici Anglicani : or the Statutes, Constitutions, Canons, Rubricks, and Articles of the Church of England, methodically digested, with a Commentary, &c. BEST EDITION, 2 vols. folio, *fine copy, new in calf, blind tooled, very scarce*, £6. 6s . *Oxford*, 1761
2017 ———— PRESERVATIVE AGAINST POPERY, in select Discourses upon the principal heads of Controversy between Protestants and Papists, written and published by the most eminent Divines of the Church of England, chiefly in the reign of James II, vols. 1 & 2, folio, *calf*, £3. 16s . 1738
2018 ———— the same, *complete*, 3 vols. folio, *fine copy, calf*, £11. 11s 1738
2019 ———— another copy, *(from the Duke of Sussex's library)* 3 vols. folio, *calf*, £12. 12s . 1738
2020 ———— Holy Sacrament explained, with Prayers and Meditations, 12mo. 1s 6d . 1705
2021 ———— Five Pastoral Letters to the People of his Diocese, 12mo. *calf*, 2s . 1751
2022 ———— the same, 12mo. *calf*, 2s . 1760
2023 GIL's (Alexander) Sacred Philosophie of the Holy Scripture, laid downe as Conclusions on the Apostles Creed, folio, *calf*, 9s 1635
2024 GILBERT's (Richard) Parent's School and College Guide ; or Liber Scholasticus : being an Account of all the Fellowships, Exhibitions, &c. at the Universities, and also of such Schools, &c. as have University advantages connected with them, 12mo. *bds. 7s* 1843
2025 GILDAS de Calamitate, Excidio, et Conquestu Britanniæ, EDITIO PRINCEPS, 12mo. *fine copy, scarce, 7s 6d* [1525]

2026 GILDAS.—The Works of Gildas and Nennius, translated from the Latin by J. A. Giles, LL.D., 8vo. LARGE PAPER, *hf. bd. morocco, uncut*, 16s . . 1841

2027 GILDON'S (C.) Deist's Manual: or a Rational Enquiry into the Christian Religion, 8vo. *calf,* 3s . . 1705
" Mr. Gildon justified suicide when he wrote the preface to Blount's Oracles of Reason, and this work is the best apology for the author's conversion from Deism to Christianity."—*Leland.*

2028 GILBERTUS Sermones super Cantica Canticorum, folio, *large and fine copy, calf, neat,* £1. 11s 6d   *Per Nicolaum Florentie,* 1485

2029 GILL'S (Dr. John) Complete Body of Doctrinal and Practical Divinity, or a System of Evangelical Truths, deduced from the Sacred Scriptures, 3 vols. royal 8vo. *calf,* 14s . 1796

2030 GILLY'S (W. S.) Horæ Catecheticæ; or an Exposition of the Duty and Advantages of Public Catechising, 8vo. *bds.* 2s 6d   1828

2031 GILPIN'S (Bernard) Life, collected from the Life written by Bishop Carleton, &c. by William Gilpin, *plates*—Whiston's Memoirs of Dr. Sam. Clarke, 1730, *in one vol.* 8vo. *hf. bd. calf,* 4s 6d   ——

2032 ——— (Will.) Exposition of the New Testament, 4to. *bds.* 5s— *calf,* 8s . . 1790

2033 ——— the same, 2 vols. 8vo. *calf,* 5s . 1798

2034 ——— another copy, 2 vols. 8vo. *bds.* 5s   1811
" A justly-admired and ably executed work."—*Horne.*

2035 ——— Lectures on the Catechism of the Church of England, 8vo. *calf,* 2s 6d . . 1781

2036 ——— Lives of the Reformers, 2 vols. 8vo. *hf. bd. calf gilt,* 7s . 1809

2037 GILSON'S (David) Sermons on Practical subjects, 8vo. *hf. bd. calf,* 3s —*bds.* 2s . . 1788

2038 GIRDLESTONE'S (Cha.) Devotions for Family Use, 12mo. *bds.* 2s . 1835

2039 ——— Course of Sermons for the Year, 2 vols. 12mo. *bds.* 8s . . 1836

2040 ——— Farewell Sermons, preached in the Parish Church of Sedgley, 12mo. *bds.* 2s . 1837

2041 ——— (Wm.) Observations on the Visions of Daniel, and on part of the Book of the Revelation of St. John, 8vo. *hf. bd. calf, neat,* 4s 6d   *Oxford,* 1820

2042 GISBORNE'S (Thos.) Works, viz.:—An Inquiry into the Duties of Men in the Higher and Middle Classes of Society in Great Britain, 2 vols. 1795—The Principles of Moral Philosophy investigated, and applied to the Constitution of Civil Society, 1798—A Familiar Survey of the Christian Religion, &c. 1810—Sermons, 3 vols. 1814—An Inquiry into the Duties of the Female Sex, 1816— together 8 vols. 8vo. *calf gilt, neat,* £1. 11s 6d   ——

2043 ——— Principles of Moral Philosophy, investigated and applied to the Constitution of Civil Society, 8vo. *calf,* 2s   1789

2044 ——— Inquiry into the Duties of Men in the Higher and Middle Classes of Society in Great Britain, 8vo. *calf,* 4s 6d   *Dublin,* 1795

2045 ——— Essays on the Recollections which are to subsist between Earthly Friends reunited in the World to Come, &c. 12mo. *bds.* 3s . . 1822

2046 GISBORNE'S (Thos.) Familiar Survey of Christian Religion, and of History as connected with Christianity, 8vo. *calf, 3s* 1806
2047 ——— the same, 8vo. *calf, 5s 6d* . 1816
2048 GLADSTONE'S (W. E.) State in its relations with the Church, 8vo. *bds. 4s 6d* . . 1839
2049 ——— another copy, with additions, 2 vols. 8vo. *bds. 10s* 1841
2050 GLANVIL'S (Jos.) Discourses, Sermons, and Remains, collected and published by A. Horneck, with his Funeral Sermon by Jos. Pleydell, 4to. *calf, neat, 4s* . 1681
2051 GLASS' (Jo.) Testimony of the King of Martyrs concerning his Kingdom, 12mo. *scarce, 2s* *Edinb.* 1776
2052 GLASSE'S (Geo. Hen.) Sermons on Christian Faith and Hope, and the Consolations of Religion, 8vo. *bds. scarce, 6s* 1798
2053 GLEIG'S (Geo. *Bp.*) Sermons preached at the Episcopal Chapel, Stirling, 8vo. *bds. 3s* *Edinb.* 1803
2054 GOD'S Judgments upon the Gentile apostatized Church; against the modern Hypotheses of some eminent Apocalyptical Writers, with a Discourse of St. Ephrem Syrus, concerning Antichrist and the End of the World, and Dr. Grabe's Opinion of the Scripture Prophecies concerning the Church of Rome, 8vo. *calf, 4s* 1713
2055 GODEFROY (Ant.) La Conduite Canonique de l'Eglise pour la reception des Filles dans les Monasteres, 18mo. *neat, 2s 6d* *Brux.* 1669
2056 GODOLPHIN (John) Repertorum Canonicum; or an Abridgment of the Ecclesiastical Laws of this Realm, 4to. *calf, 12s* 1680
2057 ——— — Holy Arbor, containing a Body of Divinity: or the Sum and Substance of Christian Religion, collected from many Orthodox labourers in the Lord's Vineyard, folio, *calf, 7s* 1651
2058 GODWIN'S (Fra. *Bp. of Hereford*) Annales of England; containing the reignes of Henry VIII., Edward VI., Queen Mary, translated by Morgan Godwyn, folio, *fine copy, hf. bd. calf, neat, 8s* 1630
2059 ——— — Catalogue of the Bishops of England, with a briefe History of their Lives, 4to. *vellum, scarce, 7s 6d* 1601
2060 ——— De Præsulibus Angliæ Commentarius, omnium Episcoporum necnon et Cardinalium ejusdem gentis nomina, tempora, seriem, atque actiones maxime memorabiles ab ultima Antiquitate repetita complexus. Recoguovit Gul. Richardson, S. T. P., folio, LARGE PAPER, *portrait, fine copy, calf,* £1. 16s *Cantab.* 1743
2061 ——— (Wm.) Sketches of History, in six Sermons, 12mo. *calf, 2s* . . 1784
2062 ——— (Tho.) Moses and Aaron: Civil and Ecclesiastical Rites used by the ancient Hebrewes observed and opened, 1655 — Romanæ Historiæ Anthologia: an English Exposition of the Roman Antiquities, 1658; *in one* vol. 4to. *calf, 4s* 1655-8
2063 GOLDIE'S (Geo.) Sermons, 8vo. *bds. 2s* *Edinb.* 1805
2064 GOMARUS (Franciscus) Opera Theologica Omnia, folio, *vellum, 18s* *Amst.* 1664

2065 GOMEZ (Alvari) Musa Paulina, hoc est Epistolæ Pauli Apostoli cantatæ per Alvarum Gomez, atque Elegis Versibus interpretatæ. Accedit ejusdem Epistola ad Clementem VII. Pont. Max., sm. 4to. *olive morocco, gilt leaves, by Charles Lewis*, £2. 10s
Compluti in Ædibus M. de Eguia, 1529
Extremely rare; this copy cost the late Mr. Heber £6. 3s 3d.—See his MS. Note.

2066 GONZALEZ (Thyrsus) Pretiosa Sensa, et cœlestia lumina, monita, ac documenta Ven. P. Ludovici de Ponte, Soc. Jesu. 18mo. *neat*, 2s 6d
Pragæ, 1691

2067 GOOD WORKES, if they be well handled; or, certaine Projects about Maintenance for Parochial Ministers, Provision for, and Election of Lecturers, the Erection and Endowment of new Churches about London, sm. 4to. 2s . 1641

2068 GOODMAN'S (J.) Penitent Pardoned; or, a Discourse of the Nature of Sin, and the Efficacy of Repentance, under the Parable of the Prodigal Son, 4to. *calf, plates*, 2s . 1689

2069 ——— another copy, 8vo. *frontispiece, calf*, 3s 1707

2070 ——— Serious and Compassionate Inquiry into the Causes of the present Neglect and Contempt of the Protestant Religion and the Church of England, &c., 8vo. *front. calf*, 2s 6d ——

2071 ——— the same, with his Winter-Evening Conference between Neighbours, 1684—*in one* vol. 8vo. *calf*, 4s 6d ——

2072 ——— Winter-Evening Conference between Neighbours, 8vo. *calf*, 2s 6d . . 1692

2073 ——— the same, 8vo. *calf*, 2s 6d . 1720

2074 [GORDON'S (———)] INDEPENDENT WHIG; or, a Defence of Primitive Christianity, and of our Ecclesiastical Establishment, against the exorbitant Claims and Encroachments of Fanatical and Disaffected Clergymen, 4 vols. 12mo. *calf*, 5s 1735-47

2075 ——— Independent Whig, 8vo. *calf*, 2s 6d 1722

2076 ——— (Sir Adam, *Bart.*) Sermons on several subjects and occasions, 2 vols. 8vo. *portrait, calf*, 4s 6d 1790
From the library of Bp. Tomline, with his book-plate.

2077 ——— another copy, 8vo. *calf, neat*, 5s 6d 1790

2078 ——— Discourses on several subjects, being the substance of the Homilies of the Church of England, rendered in a modern style, 2 vols. 8vo. *portrait, calf*, 6s—*bds*. 4s 6d 1795

2079 ——— another copy, 2 vols. 8vo. *bds*. 7s 6d 1817
Recommended by Bp. Tomline.

2080 ——— Collection of Sermons on several subjects and occasions, particularly on the Festivals and Fasts, 8vo. *bds*. 3s 1796

2081 ——— (John) Famous Bull or Constitution Unigenitus, put forth by Clement XI. against Father Quesnel's Translation of the New Testament, &c.; the whole impartially related in Memoirs of John Gordon, who was 13 years in the Scots College at Paris, but being accused of teaching the principles condemned in the Bull, he made his escape to Scotland, where he renounced Popery before the Presbytery of Edinburgh, &c. 12mo. *front. neat*, 5s 6d ——

[58, GREAT QUEEN STREET,

2082 GORDON's (Hunter) Present State of the Controversy between the Protestant and Roman Catholic Churches, 12mo. *bds.* 1s 6d 1837
2083 GOUGE's (Tho.) Principles of Christian Religion explained to the capacity of the meanest, &c. 12mo. 2s 1684
2084 GOURDAN (Simon) Sacrifice perpétuel de Foi et d'amour au très-saint Sacrement, 12mo. 2s . *Par.* 1776
2085 GRABE (Jo. Ern.) Spicilegium SS. Patrum, ut et Hæreticorum seculi I. et II., 2 vols. in 1, 8vo. *calf, neat, old style,* 15s
Oxon, 1698-99
2086 ———— idem, LARGE PAPER, 2 vols. royal 8vo. *vellum, gilt backs,* £1. 5s . . *ib.* 1698-99
2087 ———— aliud exemplar, 2 vols. in 1, *calf, old style,* 14s *ib.* 1714
2088 ———— Dissertatio de variis Vitiis LXX. Interpretum Versioni ante B. Origenis ævum illatis, &c. 4to. 4s *ib.* 1710
2089 GRAHAM (Mrs. Isabella *of New York*) The Power of Faith, exemplified in her Life and Writings, 8vo. *calf, neat,* 2s 1816
2090 GRANCOLAS (————) Histoire de la Communion sous une seule Espece, 12mo. *calf,* 5s . *Pnr.* 1696
2091 GRANT's (Dr. Alex., *Minister of the Eng. Episc. Chapel at Dundee*) Sermons on various subjects and occasions, 2 vols. 8vo. *calf,* 3s 6d
Dundee, 1800
2092 GRAVERUS Redivivus, hoc est Prælectiones Academicæ in Augustanum Confessionem, cum Supplemento ex Islebicis Alberti Graveri modernis Adversariis denuò opposita, thick 12mo. *vellum,* 5s
Jenæ, 1665
2093 GRAVES's (John, *Dean of Ardagh*) Works, containing his Essay on the Apostles and Evangelists, Lectures on the Pentateuch, Prælectiones, Proofs of the Trinity, Sermons, &c. with a Memoir of his Life by R. H. Graves, D.D. 4 vols. 8vo. *portrait, bds.* £1. 6s—*calf gilt,* £2. . ———— 1841
2094 ———— Lectures on the four last Books of the Pentateuch, designed to shew the Divine Origin of the Jewish Religion, chiefly from Internal Evidence, 8vo. *bds.* (pub. at 14s) 7s 1839
2095 ———— Essay on the Character of the Apostles and Evangelists, designed to prove that they were not Enthusiasts; with a Dissertation on the Cure of the Blind Man near Bethsaida, by James Drought, D.D. 8vo. *bds.* 3s 6d . *Dublin,* 1820
2096 GRAY's (Andrew) Mystery of Faith opened up; or, some Sermons concerning Faith, &c. 18mo. 3s . *Glasgow,* 1774
2097 ———— (Robert, *Bp. of Bristol*) Connection between the Sacred Writings and the Literature of Jewish and Heathen Authors illustrated, 2 vols. 8vo. *calf, neat, marbled leaves,* 9s—*bds.* 6s
1819
2098 ———— another copy, 8vo. *tree-marbled calf gilt,* 10s 6d 1816
" Indispensably necessary to the Biblical Student who cannot command access to *all* the classic authors."—*Horne.*
2099 ———— Key to the Old Testament and Apocrypha, 8vo. *calf gilt, marbled leaves,* 10s . 1841
2100 ———— Key to the Old Testament and Apocrypha, with Bp. Percy's Key to the New Testament, 8vo. *calf, neat, marbled leaves,* 10s . . 1825

2101 GREEN's (Sam.) Sermons on various important subjects, moral and theological, 8vo. *bds*. 2s . 1786
2102 ———— (Will.) Poetical parts of the Old Testament, and other poetical pieces, newly translated from the Hebrew, with Notes, 4to, *bds*. 5s . *Cambridge*, 1781
2103 GREGENTIUS (*Archiep. Tephrensis*) Disputatio cum Herbano Judæo, nunc primum Græcè edita, cum interpretatione N. Gulonii, sm. 8vo. *vellum*, 4s . *Par*. 1586
2104 GREGG's (T. D.) Protestant Ascendancy vindicated, and National Regeneration through the Instrumentality of a National Religion urged ; in a series of Letters to the Corporation of Dublin, 12mo. *bds*. 2s 6d . *Dublin*, 1840
2105 GREGORIE (————, Ancien Evêque de Blois) Essai historique sur les libertés de l'Eglise Gallicane, et des autres Eglises de la Catholicité, pendant les deux derniers siècles, 8vo. *hf. bd. calf, uncut*, 4s *Par*. 1818
2106 GREGORIUS (S. II. *Pontifex Agrigentinorum*) Libri decem Explanationis Ecclesiasticæ, *Gr. et. Lat.* cum vita ejusdem Pontificis, folio, *fine copy, calf, very scarce*, £1. 11s 6d *Venet*. 1791
2107 ———— (*Hieromonachus*) Synopsis Dogmatum Ecclesiæ, Neo-Græcè, 12mo. *bds*. 4s 6d . *Venet*. 1669
2108 ———— (S. MAGNUS) Opera omnia, studio et labore Monachorum Ordinis S. Benedicti, 4 tom. folio, *calf*, £6. 6s *Paris*. 1705
2109 ———— idem, 4 vols. folio, *fine copy*, LARGE PAPER, *calf*, £8. 18s 6d . . *ib*. 1705
2110 ———— Ex omnibus ejus operibus flores : H. Scutteputæo Concinnatore, et ejusdem D. Gregorii Concordia quorundam locorum Sacræ Scripturæ, 24mo. *vellum*, 4s . [*ib*.] 1572
2111 ———— De Cura Pastorali liber, 32mo. *sewed*, 2s *ib*. 1826
2112 ———— Les Morales de S. Gregoire Pape sur le livre de Job, 3 vols. 4to. *portrait, calf*, £1. 1s *ib*. 1666-69
2113 ———— Morals on the Book of Job, by S. Gregory the Great ; translated, with Notes and Indices, 3 vols. 8vo. *bds*. *Oxford*, 1845
2114 ———— The Dialogues of S. Gregorie, surnamed the Greate, with a short Treatise of sundry Miracles wrought at the Shrines of Martyrs, taken out of S. Augustine : together with a notable Miracle wrought by S. Bernard : also a shorte Relation of divers Miracles, wroughte at the Shrines of certaine Martirs, especially St. Steune, the Protomartyr of Christe's Church, &c. translated by P. W. 12mo. RARE, *fine copy, calf extra*, 10s 6d *Paris*, 1608
2115 ———— (S. NAZIANZENUS) Opera, *Gr. et Lat.* Jac. Billius cum MSS. contulit, emendavit, interpretatus est, &c. cum multis Gregorii Epistolis nunquam antehac editis ex interpr. Fed. Morelli, 2 vols. folio, *calf*, £2. 15s . *Lut. Par*. 1609
2116 ———— idem, 2 vols. folio, *calf*, £2. 18s *Paris*, 1630
2117 ———— aliud exemplar, 2 vols. folio, £2. 10s *Coloniæ*, 1690
2118 ———— Opera omnia, Gr. et Lat. studio Monach. Benedictinorum et D. A. B. Caillau, *best edition*, 2 vols. folio, *fine copy, new in calf gilt*, £6. 16s 6d . *Paris*, 1778-1842

[58, GREAT QUEEN STREET,

2119 GREGORIUS (S. NAZIANZENUS) Opera omnia, Gr. et Lat. studio Monach. Benedictinorum et D. A. B. Caillau, 2 vols. folio, *hf. bd. vellum, uncut, gilt tops*, £5. 15s 6d   *Par.* 1778-1842
The first volume only was edited by the Benedictines, their labours being interrupted by the Revolution. The second was edited by M. Caillau.

2120 —————— Due Orationi, in una de le quali, si tratta quel che sia Vescovado, et quali debbiano essere i Vescovi ; Nel' altra, de l'Amor verso i Poveri ; et il primo Sermone di S. Cipriano sopra l'Elemosina ; fatte in lingua Toscana dal Commendatore Annibal Caro, 4to. *green morocco, gilt leaves, and broad borders of gold*, 10s 6d   *In Venetia, appresso Aldo Manutio*, 1569
With the Aldine anchor upon the title.

2121 —————— in Julianum Invectivæ duæ, cum Scholiis, *Græcè*. Edidit R. Montagu, 4to. *calf*, 6s   *Etonæ*, 1610

2122 —————— another copy, *much stained, calf*, 3s   *ib.* 1610

2123 —————— (S. EPISC. NYSSENUS) Opera omnia, *Gr. et Lat.* 2 vols. folio, *very scarce, calf*, £4. 10s   *Paris*, 1615

2124 —————— Oratio Catechetica, Græce et Latine ; edidit J. G. Krabingerus : accedit ejusdem Gregorii Oratio funebris in Meletium, episc. Antioch. 8vo. *sewed*, 4s   *Monac.* 1835

2125 —————— (S. NEOCÆS. sive THAUMATURGI) Macarii Ægypti, et Basilii Seleuciæ Isauriæ Episcopi Opera omnia, *Gr. et Lat.* accessit Jo. Zonaræ Expositio Canonicarum Epistolarum, folio, *Gr. et Lat. very scarce, calf*, £4.   *Paris*, 1622

2126 —————— idem, *with Dedication to Merico de Viq*, folio, *calf*, £4. 4s   *ib.* 1622

2127 —————— aliud exemplar, folio, *fine copy*, LARGE PAPER, *neat*, £4. 10s   *ib.* 1622

2128 GREGORY'S (John) Works, in two parts : the first containing Observations upon several Passages of Scripture ; the second, his Posthuma, being divers learned Tracts upon various subjects, 4to. *calf*, 4s   1671

2129 —————— another copy, 4to. *calf*, 4s 6d   1684
" The miracle of his age for critical and curious learning."—*Ant. à Wood.*

2130 —————— (Dr. G.) History of the Christian Church, from the earliest period to the present time, 2 vols. 8vo. *frontispieces, bds.* 6s —*calf, neat*, 10s 6d   1795

2131 —————— Sermons ; with Thoughts on the Composition and Delivery of a Sermon, 8vo. *bds.* 2s 6d   1787

2132 —————— Essays, Historical and Moral, 8vo. *calf*, 2s   1788

2133 GRENADE (Louis de) La Guide des Pecheurs, composée en Espagnol, trad. par M. Girard, 8vo. *neat*, 4s   *Par.* 1668

2134 GRESLEY'S (W.) Ecclesiastes Anglicanus ; being a Treatise on the Art of Preaching, as adapted to a Church of England Congregation : contained in a series of Letters to a Young Clergyman, 8vo. *bds.* 6s   1835

2135 —————— Portrait of an English Churchman, 12mo. *bds.* 5s 6d   1838

2136 —————— another copy. 12mo. *bds.* 5s   1840

2137 —————— the same, 12mo. *bds.* 4s   1841

2138 GRESLEY'S (Wm.) Bernard Leslie; or, a Tale of the last Ten Years, 12mo. *bds*. 3*s* . 1842
2139 ———— Siege of Lichfield, 18mo. *sewed*, 1*s* 1843
2140 ———— Church-Clavering; or, the Schoolmaster, 12mo. *bds*. 2*s* 6*d* . 1843
2141 ———— Charles Lever; or, the Man of the XIXth Century, 18mo. *cuts, bds*. 2*s* . 1841
2141*GRESWELL'S (Wm.) Popular View of the Correspondency between the Mosaic Ritual and the Facts and Doctrines of the Christian Religion, in nine Discourses, 8vo. *bds*. 4*s* . 1834
2142 GRETSERI (Jac.) Defensio Controversiarum Rob. Bellarmini adversus Whitackerum, Junium, Danæum, Sutlivium, Hunnium aliosque Sectarios, 2 vols. folio, *calf, wooden boards*, £1. 16*s*
Ingolst. 1607-9
2143 ———— de Jure et more Prohibendi Expurgandi, et abolendi libros hæreticos et noxios, adversus Fr. Junium, Jo. Pappum, etc. 4to. *vellum*, 7*s* . *ib*. 1603
2144 GRETTON'S (F. E.) Introduction to the Translation of English Poetry into Latin Elegiacs and Hexameters, 2 vols. 12mo. *bds*. 2*s* 6*d* . . 1838
2145 GREY'S (Dr. Richard) New and easy Method of Learning Hebrew without Points; to which is annexed, the Book of Proverbs, divided according to the metre, with notes, &c. 8vo. *calf*, 3*s* 6*d* 1738
2146 GRIESBACHII (Jo. Jac.) Symbolæ Criticæ ad supplendas et corrigendas Variarum N. T. Lectionum Collectiones. Accedit multorum N. T. Codicum Græcorum descriptio et examen, 2 vols. 8vo. *bds. scarce*, 10*s* . *Halæ*, 1785
2147 GRIMAUD (Gilbert) La Liturgie Sacrée, où toutes les parties et Ceremonies de la Saint Messe sont expliquées, avec leurs Mysteres et Antiquitez, et un Traité particulier de l'Eau-benite, du Painbenit, des Processions, et des Cloches, 4to. *frontispiece, calf*, 9*s*
Lyon, 1666
2147*———— autre exemplaire, 3 vols. 18mo. *calf*, 14*s* *Par*. 1678
2148 GRINDAL'S (Edm., *Abp. of Cant*.) Remains, edited by the Rev. William Nicholson, 8vo. *bds*. 12*s* *Camb*. 1843
2149 GRINFIELD'S (E. W.) Sketches of the Danish Mission on the Coast of Coromandel, 12mo. *bds*. 1*s* 6*d* . 1831
2150 GRONOVIUS (Jac.) Exercitationes Academicæ de Nece Judæ, et Cadaveris Ignominia, 4to. *vellum*, 4*s* 6*d* *Lugd. Bat*. 1702
2151 GROSE'S (John) Sermons on various subjects, 8vo. *bds. scarce*, 5*s*
1812
2152 GROSER'S (Wm.) Six Lectures on Popery, 12mo. *bds*. 2*s* 6*d* 1825
2153 GROSSETESTE'S (Robert, *Bp. of Lincoln*) Life, by Samuel Pegge, LL.D., with an Account of the Bishop's Works, &c. 4to. *fine clean copy, sewed, uncut, rare*, £2. 12*s* 6*d* . 1793
2154 GROSVENOR'S (B.) Health, an Essay on its Nature, Value, Uncertainty, Preservation, and best Improvement, 12mo. 1*s* 6*d* 1716
2155 GROTIUS (Hugo) de Veritate Religionis Christianæ, 18mo. *calf*, 2*s* 6*d*
Amst. 1674
2156 ———— de Veritate Religionis Christianæ, 18mo. *calf*, 2*s* 6*d*
ib. 1675

[58, GREAT QUEEN STREET,

2157 GROTIUS (Hugo) de Veritate Religionis Christ. 8vo. *calf*, 3s
Oxon. 1700
2158 ———— de Veritate Religionis Christianæ, cui accessere Jo. Clerici notæ, &c. 12mo. *bds*. 3s . *ib.* 1817
2159 ———— de Veritate Religionis Christianæ, cui accessere Jo. Clerici notæ, et libri duo de Eligenda inter Christianos dissentientes sententia, 12mo. 2s 6d . *ib.* 1820
2160 ———— de Veritate Religionis Christianæ, with the notes of the Author, Le Clerc, and others, translated into English, 12mo. 2s 1821
2161 ———— de Veritate &c. &c., 12mo. *bds*. 3s Oxon. 1827
2162 ———— Baptizatorum Puerorum Institutis: et Eucharistia: una cum ejusdem Adnotationibus ad Decalogum et ad Sermonem Christi in Monte habitum, 8vo. *calf*, 2s 6d . *ib.* 1706
2163 ———— His Arguments for the truth of Christian Religion, rendered into plain English verse, 8vo. *calf*, 3s . 1686
2163* ———— The Truth of Christian Religion, in six books; translated, with the addition of a seventh book, against the present Roman Church, by Symon Patrick, Bp. of Ely, 8vo. *calf*, 3s 1700
2164 ———— The truth of the Christian Religion, in Six Books, with Notes by Le Clerc; to which is added, a seventh Book concerning what Christian Church we ought to join ourselves to, by Le Clerc. Done into English by John Clarke, D.D. Dean of Sarum, 8vo. *calf*, 4s—*hf. bd. russia*, 3s 6d 1767
2165 ———— the same, 8vo. *calf*, 3s 6d . 1777
2166 ———— another copy, 8vo. *calf*, 3s . 1743
2167 ———— the same, 8vo. *bds*. 3s . Oxford, 1823
2168 ———— Vie de Grotius, avec l'histoire de ses ouvrages, &c. par M. de Burigny, 2 vols. 12mo. *calf*, 5s 6d Par. 1752
2169 ———— The Life of H. Grotius, with a critical account of his Works, written originally in French by M. De Burigny. 8vo. *calf*, 3s 6d . . 1754
2170 ———— His Life, with brief Minutes of the Civil, Ecclesiastical, and Literary History of the Netherlands, by Charles Butler, Esq., 8vo. *bds*. 4s . . 1826
2171 GROVE's (Hen.) Sermons and Tracts, being his Posthumous Works, 4 vols. 8vo. *port.* 6s . 1741
2172 ———— Works, viz., Sermons, Discourses, Tracts, Poems, System of Moral Philosophy, &c. 12 vols. 8vo. *calf, neat,* £1. 5s 1742-49

"Resembles Watts; not equally poetical, but yet more nervous. He has many judicious and new thoughts, which are disposed in a manner quite peculiar, and expressed with force and elegance."—*Doddridge.*

2173 GRUEBER (Rupert.) de Privilegiis Religiosorum, opus posthumum, cum additionibus Eusebii Amort, 4to. *hf. bd. calf, new,* 14s
Aug. Vind. et Herbip. 1747
2174 GUARNACCI (Marius) Vitæ et res gestæ Pontificum Romanorum et S. R. E. Cardinalium, a Clemente X. usque ad Clementum XII. 2 vols. in 1, folio, *fine copy, many portraits and other plates, old calf gilt, very scarce,* £3. 3s . Romæ, 1751
A continuation of Ciacconi's Lives of the Popes.

2175 [GUENÉE (M. l'Abbé)] Lettres de quelques Juifs Portugais, Allemands et Polonais à M. de Voltaire ; avec un petit Commentaire extrait d'un plus grand, 3 vols. 8vo. *neat, 9s*   *Par.* 1781

2176 —————— Letters of certain Jews to M. de Voltaire, containing an Apology for their own people and for the Old Testament, with a short Commentary, &c. Translated by the Rev. Philip Lefanu, D.D. 2 vols. 8vo. *scarce, calf,* 15s   *Dublin,* 1777

" These letters," says Bp. Watson, " contain an elegant answer to the various objections to revealed religion, which Voltaire has borrowed from our English Deists."

2177 GUIBERTUS (*Abbas*) Opera omnia, una cum Appendice ad librum III. de vita ipsius, &c. *Editio Benedictina,* a L. d'Achery, folio, *calf,* £1. 16s   *Lut. Par.* 1651

2178 GULIELMI (Alverni *Episcopis Parisiensis,*) Mathematici perfectissimi, eximii Philosophi, ac Theologi præstantissimi Opera omnia, *best edition,* 2 vols. folio, *calf,* £2. 10s   *Par.* 1674

2179 GUILLERMUS, Postilla super Epistolas et Evangelia, 𝔅lack letter, *wood-cuts, Basil.* 1513—Passio Domini nostri Jesu Christi secundum seriem quattuor Evangelistarum, per fratem Danielem Agricolam, 𝔅lack letter, *wood-cuts, Basil.* 1513 ; *in one* vol. 4to. *neat, scarce,* 10s 6d   1513

2180 GUNNING's [Peter] Paschal or Lent Fast, apostolical and perpetual, wherein the judgment of Antiquity is laid down, 8vo. *bds.* 9s   *Oxford,* 1845

2181 GUTHRIE's (Wm.) Christian's Great Interest; with his Life, by W. Dunlop, &c. 12mo. *neat,* 2s   1733

2182 GYLES's (J. F.) Essay on the Authenticity of the New Testament, with an account of the ancient Versions, and some of the principal Greek MSS., 8vo. *bds.* 2s 6d   1812

2183 HABERTI (Isaaci) ΑΡΧΙΕΡΑΤΙΚΟΝ, seu Liber Pontificalis Ecclesiæ Græcæ, Gr. et Lat. notis et observationibus illustratus, folio, *scarce, fine copy, new in calf gilt,* £4.   *Par.* 1643

2184 ————— Theologiæ Græcorum Patrum Vindicatæ circam universam materiam Gratiæ, cum perpetua collatione Scripturæ, Conciliorum, Doctrinæ S. Augustini, S. Thomæ, et Scholæ Sorbonicæ, folio, *very scarce, neat,* £1. 11s 6d   *ib.* 1646

2185 HACKET's (John, *Bp. of Lichfield*) Century of Sermons, upon several remarkable subjects ; with his Life by Thos. Plume, D.D., folio, *scarce, portrait by Faithorne, calf,* £1. 16s   1675

2186 ————— (John) Select and Remarkable Epitaphs, of illustrious and other persons, 2 vols. 12mo. *calf,* 10s 6d   1757

2187 HACKMANNUS (Dithmar) Præcidanea Sacra, sive Animadversionum Philologico-criticarum ad textum originalem Veteris Testamenti, tom 1, (the only volume published) exhibens Gen. Exod. Levit. 8vo. *vellum,* 4s 6d   *Lugd. Bat.* 1735

2188 HAKEWIL's Libertie of the Subject, against the pretended power of Impositions, 4to. *hf. bd.* 3s   1641

2189 HAKEWILL (Dr. George) Scutum Regium, id est adversus omnes Regicidas et Regicidarum Patronos, ab initio mundi usque ad Interritum Phocæ Imp. A. D. 610. Ecclesiæ Catholicæ Consensus orthodoxus, sm. 8vo. *vellum,* 8s   *Lond.* 1612

[58, GREAT QUEEN STREET,

2190 HAKEWILL's (Dr. George) King David's Vow for Reformation of himself, his Family, his Kingdom, in twelve Sermons upon Ps. 101. sm. 4to. *engraved title, calf, very scarce*, 12s   1622
From the library of the late Duke of Sussex.
2191 ———— Apologie of the Power and Providence of God in the Government of the World, folio, *calf*, 6s . 1627
2192 ———— another copy, folio, *calf*, 8s   *Oxford*, 1630
21 93 ———— best edition folio, *engraved title, fine copy, old calf*, £1. 10s . *ib*. 1635
2194 HALE's (Sir Matthew) Contemplations Moral and Divine, in two parts, 8vo. *portrait, calf, neat*, 6s . 1689
2195 ———— Contemplations, Moral and Divine, in two parts, 8vo. *calf*, 4s 6d—*fine copy, calf*, 6s . 1711
2196 ———— Contemplations, &c., with a third part, and his Life by Bp. Burnet, 2 vols. 8vo. *portraits, calf*, 10s 6d   1705
2197 ———— Three Epistles to his Children, with directions concerning their observation of the Lord's Day, and the Author's Life, 12mo. 1s 6d . . 1759
2198 ———— Life and Death, by Gilbert Burnet, D.D., sm. 8vo. *port. calf*, 2s . . 1682
2199 ———— (John, *of Eton*) Tract concerning the Sin against the Holy Ghost, 8vo. *neat*, 2s 6d . 1677
2200 ———— Several Tracts: viz. I. Concerning the Sin against the Holy Ghost. II. Of the Lord's Supper. III. Paraphrase on St. Matthew's Gospel. IV. Of the Power of the Keys. V. Of Schism. VI. Miscellanies: with his Letter to Abp. Laud. sm. 8vo. *portrait, calf*, 3s . 1721
2201 ———— Discourse of the several Dignities, and Corruptions of Man's Nature, since the Fall, 8vo. *neat*, 2s   1720
2202 ———— Golden Remains of the Ever Memorable Mr. John Hales of Eaton College, 4to. *frontispiece, portrait inserted, calf*, 8s 1673
2203 ———— Golden Remains, with Sermons and Miscellanies, also Letters and Expresses, concerning the Synod of Dort, 8vo. *calf*, 3s 6d . . 1688
2204 ———— Works, [Edited by Lord Hailes] 3 vols. 12mo. *calf, scarce*, 16s . . *Glasgow*, 1765
2205 ———— the same, vols. 1 and 2, *bds.* 4s   *ib.* 1765
2206 ———— (Dr. Wm.) Dissertations on the principal Prophecies representing the Divine and the Human Character of our Lord Jesus Christ. 8vo. *hf. bd. calf*, 4s 6d . 1808
2207 ———— Faith in the Holy Trinity, the Doctrine of the Gospel, and Sabellian Unitarianism shewn to be "the God-denying Apostacy," 2 vols. 8vo. *bds.* 6s—*calf, neat, marbled leaves*, 9s 1818
2208 ———— another copy, 2 vols. 8vo. *calf*, 7s   1818
2209 ———— Dissertations on the principal Prophecies representing the Divine and Human Nature of our Lord Jesus Christ, 1808— Graves's (Dr. Richard, *Dean of Ardagh*), Select Scriptural Proofs of the Trinity, arranged in Four Discourses, with Notes and Illustrations, 1819—2 vols. in 1, 8vo. *hf. bd, calf, neat, uncut*, 5s

2211 HALES' (Dr. Wm.) New Analysis of Chronology and Geography, History and Prophecy; in which their Elements are attempted to be explained, harmonized, and vindicated, 4 vols. 8vo. *calf gilt*, £3. 10s . . 1830

"This work ought to have a place in the library of every biblical student who can procure it. Not only is it the most elaborate system of Chronology extant in our language, but there is scarcely a difficult text in the sacred writings which is not illustrated."—*Horne.*

2212 HALL'S (John) Explanatory Discourses on the Epistles for every Sunday in the year, and the principal Festivals, 2 vols. 8vo. *bds.* 9s
1839

2213 ———— (John, *Bp. of Bristol*) Jacob's Ladder : or, the devout Soul's Ascension to Heaven, 18mo. *bds.* 1s . 1764

2214 HALL'S (Joseph, *Bp. of Norwich*) Common Apologie of the Church of England, against the unjust Challenges of the over-just Sect, commonly called Brownists, 4to. *hf. bd. calf, neat*, 5s 1610

2215 ———— Occasional Meditations, by Ios. Exon. set forth by R. H. 12mo. *hf. bd. calf, neat*, 3s . 1631

2216 ———— ΑΥΤΟΣΧΕΔΙΑΣΜΑΤΑ, vel Meditatiunculæ Subitaneæ, éq; re natâ subortæ, 18mo. *vellum, scarce*, 5s . 1635

2217 ———— Enoch : or, a Treatise on the Manner of Walking with God : translated by Henry Brown, M.A., 12mo. *sewed, very scarce*, 2s 6d . *Oxford*, 1768

2218 ———— Christ Mystical ; or the Blessed Union of Christ and his members ; also, an Holy Rapture, or, a patheticall Meditation of the Love of Christ ; also, the Christian laid forth in his whole disposition and carriage, 18mo. 2s . 1647

2219 ———— Horæ Subsecivæ, Observations and Discourses, 8vo. *vellum*, 4s . . 1620

Commonly attributed to Bp. Hall. A MS. note upon the fly-leaf says that it is certainly *not* by Bp. Hall, but probably by Sir Grey Brydges, Lord Chandos, who died 1621.

2220 ———— Contemplations on the History of the New Testament, with his Life and Hard Measure, the whole revised by Wm. Dodd, LL.D., 2 vols. 12mo. *port. bds.* 5s . 1777

2221 ———— Contemplations on the Sacred History, altered from his Works, by G. H. Glasse, 4 vols. 12mo. *hf. bd. calf*, 10s
Gloucester, 1793

2222 ———— Works, (containing his Meditations on the Old and New Testaments, Sermons, Epistles, &c.) folio, *title and some leaves mended, calf*, 18s . 1628

2223 ———— Works, 3 vols. in 2, folio, *rough calf*, £3. 3s   1647, &c.

2224 ———— Works, revised and corrected, with considerable additions, the Author's Life by himself, and a Translation of all his Latin pieces, by the Rev. Peter Hall, 12 vols. 8vo. *bds.* (pub. at £7. 4s) £5. . *Oxford*, 1837-9

2225 ———— the same, 12 vols. 8vo. *calf gilt extra*, £7.   *ib.* 1837-9

2226 ———— Select Works, containing his Contemplations on the Old and New Testaments, with his devotional and practical pieces, and some account of his Life and Sufferings, arranged and revised by Josiah Pratt, B.D., 5 vols. 8vo. *hf. bd. calf*, £1. 11s 6d   1811

2228 HALL's (Jos. *Bp. of Norwich*) Death's Alarum, or the Presage of approaching Death, given in his Funeral Sermon, by John Whitefoote, M.A. sm. 8vo. *hf. bd.* 2s . 1656
2229 ——— another copy, *with the scarce portrait* [*by Faithorne*] 2s 6d . 1656
2230 ——— ——— The Shaking of the Olive-Tree ; the remaining Works of that incomparable Prelate, with some specialities of Divine Providence in his Life, noted by his own hand, and his Hard Measure, 4to. *calf,* 6s . . 1660
2231 ——— ——— Bishop Hall, his Life and Times, with an Appendix, containing some of his unpublished Writings, his Funeral Sermon, &c. by the Rev. John Jones, 8vo. *port. bds.* 4s 6d 1826
2232 ——— ——— (Robert) Reply to the Rev. Joseph Kinghorn, being a further Vindication of the practice of Free Communion, 8vo. *bds.* 3s . *Leicester,* 1818
2233 HALLET's (Joseph, Jun.) Defence of a Discourse on the Impossibility of proving a Future State by the Light of Nature, with an Answer to the Rev. Mr. Grove, 8vo. 1s 6d 1731
2234 ——— ——— Collection of Notes on some Texts of Scripture, and of Discourses on various subjects, 3 vols. 8vo. *calf, neat,* 14s 1729-36
2235 HALLIER (Franc.) de Sacris Electionibus et Ordinationibus ex antiquo et novo Ecclesiæ usu, 3 vols. folio, *vellum, very scarce,* £3. 13s 6d
Romæ, 1740

" C'est son chef d'œuvre. Cet ouvrage lui valut une pension de la part du clergé de France, il est clair et methodique."—*L'Abbé Fetler.*

2236 HALLOWS's (Dan.) Worthy Communicant, with Prayers, Meditations, and Hymns, 12mo. *neat,* 1s 6d . 1727
2237 HALLYWELL's (Hen.) Account of Familism, as it is revived and propagated by the Quakers, 1673—The sacred Method of saving Humane Souls by Jesus Christ, 1677—Melampronœa, or a Discourse of the Polity and Kingdom of Darkness ; with a solution of the chief Objections against the being of Witches, 1681—The Excellency of Moral Vertue, &c. 1691, *in one vol.* 12mo. *calf, neat,* 3s . . ———
2238 HALUS (Aulus) de Adventu in Hispanias S. Jacobi Zebedæi filii, cognomento Majoris, Apostoli, Carmen Heroicum, illustratum á Jo. Tamayo Salazar, 4to. *vellum,* 7s . *Matriti,* 1648
2239 HALYBURTON's (Tho.) Natural Religion insufficient ; and Revealed necessary, to Man's Happiness in his present state, 4to. *calf,* 7s 6d
Edinb. 1714
2240 ——— ——— Memoirs of his Life, 12mo. *neat,* 3s *ib.* 1715
2241 HAMERSLEY's (Rd. *Barber-Chyrurgeon in Walsall*) Advice to Sunday Barbers, against Trimming on the Lord's Day, 12mo. *very curious and scarce,* 2s . . 1706
2242 HAMILTON (Fra. *Prior Cœnobii Scotorum Herbipoli*) de Sanctorum Invocatione Demonstratio duplex, 4to. *scarce,* 5s 6d
Wiceburgi, 1596
2243 HAMMOND (H.) Of Fraternal Admonition, or Correction, 4to. 1s 6d
1647

2244 HAMMOND'S (Dr. Henry) Works, containing his various Treatises in Defence of the Church of England, against the Romanists and other adversaries—Annotations on the Psalms and New Testament—Practical Catechism, Sermons, Discourses, &c. 4 vols. folio, *fine copy, rich calf gilt, very scarce,* £8. 8s *Lond.* 1684

2245 ———— Power of the Keyes, 1647—A brief Vindication of three Passages in the Practical Catechisme, 1648—Of Fraternal Admonition, or Correption—The larger Treatise concerning Tithes, by Sir H. Spelman, with other Tracts, by the same author, 1647—Of the Lawes of Ecclesiasticall Polity, the 6th and 8th books, by Richard Hooker, 1648—Cyrilli Patr. Const. Confessio Christianæ Fidei, *Gr. et Lat. Genev.* 1633, *in one vol.* 4to. *calf*, 9s

2246 ———— Power of the Keyes: or, of Binding and Loosing, 1651—A View of some Exceptions made by a Romanist to Viscount Falkland's Discourse of the Infallibility of the Church of Rome, 1650—A Vindication of Dr. Hammond's Addresse from the exceptions of Eutactus Philodemius, with a Reply to Mr. Jo. Goodwin's Ὑβριστοδίκαι, as far as it concerns Dr. Hammond, 1650—A View of some Exceptions to the Practicall Catechisme, etc. *in one vol.* 4to. *old red morocco, gilt leaves,* 6s 6d 1650-51

2247 ———— Mysterium Religionis recognitum; an Expedient for composing Differences in Religion, 4to. 1s 6d 1649

2248 ———— Dissertationes quatuor, quibus Episcopatus jura ex S. Scripturis et primitiva antiquitate adstruuntur, contra sententiam D. Blondelli, etc. 4to. *calf,* 5s . 1651

2249 ———— Letter of Resolution to six queries of present use in the Church of England, 18mo. *calf,* 3s 6d 1653

2250 ———— Profitable Directions both for Priest and People, in two Sermons preached before these evil times, sm. 8vo. 2s 6d 1657

2251 ———— Paraphrase and Annotations upon the Psalms, folio, *calf, gilt back,* 14s . 1659

2252 ———— Paraphrase and Annotations upon the Books of the Psalms; also on the ten first Chapters of the Proverbs, folio, 15s 1683

"Dr. Hammond's notes are exceedingly valuable, and contain many learned observations that had escaped preceding Commentators."—*Horne.*

2253 ———— Collection of Discourses chiefly practicall, with the Life of the Author, (by Bp. Fell) folio, *calf, fine copy,* £1. 1s 1674

2254 ———— second edition, folio, *calf,* £1. 1s 1684

2255 ———— Collection of Discourses in Defence of the Church of England, folio, *very scarce, hf. bd.* £1. 16s 1684

2256 ———— Paraphrase and Annotations upon all the Books of the New Testament, folio, *calf, gilt back, title ruled with red lines,* £1. 10s . 1671

2257 ———— another copy, folio, *calf,* £1. 5s 1671

2258 ———— *best edition,* folio, £1. 10s . 1703

2259 ———— new edition, 4 vols. 8vo. *cloth bds.* £1. 10s *Oxford,* 1845

2260 ———— Supplement to Dr. Hammond's Paraphrase on the New Testament, by Mons. Le Clerc, 4to. *calf,* 5s 6d 1699

Doddridge remarks, that Dr. Hammond "finds the Gnostics everywhere, which is his principal fault. Many (says he) of Le Clerc's animadversions on those places are very good."

[58, GREAT QUEEN STREET,

2261 HAMMOND's (Dr. H.) Practical Catechism, whereunto is added, the Reasonableness of Christian Religion, 8vo. *calf*, 4s 6d   1691

2262 ———— Parænesis, or Seasonable Exhortatory to all true Sons of the Church of England, 18mo. *bds*. 2s — *morocco, gilt leaves*, 5s   *Oxf.* 1841

2263 ———— (*Capt*. Charles) Persecutio Undecima, the Churches eleventh Persecution ; or, a briefe of the Persecution of the Protestant Clergy of the Church of England, begun 1641, 4to. *scarce*, 4s 6d . *Reprinted*, 1682

"Afflictions do a Christian no more harm than persecutions do the Church, which always purify, purge, and strengthen it: and as an ancient divine expresses it, 'God's vines are always the better for bleeding.'"—*Mason*.

2264 ———— (Will. And.) Definitions of Faith, and Canons of Discipline, of the six Œcumenical Councils, with the remaining Canons of the Code of the Universal Church, translated with Notes, to which is added, the Apostolical Canons, 8vo, *bds*. 7s 6d   *Oxford*, 1843

2265 HANAPE. — THE ENSAMPLES OF VERTUE AND VICE, GATHERED OUTE OF HOLYE SCRIPTURE, BY NICHOLAS HANAPE PATRIARCHE OF JERUSALEM; VERY NECESSARYE FOR ALL CHRISTEN MEN AND WOMEN TO LOOK UPON, Englished by Thomas Paynell, 12mo. 𝔅𝔩𝔞𝔠𝔨 𝔩𝔢𝔱𝔱𝔢𝔯, *rare*, £2. 2s   *Imprented at London, by Jhon Tisdale*, 1561

Dedicated "to the most noble, most excellent, and mooste vertuous Lady Elizabeth, Queene of Englande, Fraunce, and Irelande."
From the late Duke of Sussex's library.

2266 HANCOCK's (W.) Hear the Church : ten Discourses on some of the principal Articles of the United Church of England and Ireland, 12mo. *bds*. 2s . . 1832

2267 H[ANMER's] (J[onathan]) View of Antiquity, presented in a short but sufficient Account of some of the Fathers, during the first 300 years after Christ, 8vo. *calf*, 6s . 1677

"This Book was answered in 'Remarques on the State of the Church of the first Centuries, with Animadversions on J. Hanmer's View of Antiquity by A. S. [Abednego Seller] 8vo. 1680.'"

2268 HARDT (Herm. Von der) Magnum Œcumenicum Constantiense Concilium de Universali Ecclesiæ Reformatione, Unione, et Fide, 6 vols. in 3, folio, *portraits and plates, neat*, £3. 3s   *Franc.* 1700

2269 HARDY's (Nath.) Justice Triumphing : or the Spoylers Spoiled, a Sermon at St. Paul's, Nov. 5, 1646, 4to. 1s 6d   1656

2270 ———— Sad Prognostick of approaching Judgment; or the Happy Misery of good Men in bad Times, a Sermon, 4to. 1s 6d . . 1658

2271 HARE's (Fra. *Bp. of Chichester*) Scripture vindicated from the Misinterpretations of the Bp. of Bangor, [Hoadley] in his Answer to the Dean of Worcester's Sermon concerning Church Authority, 8vo. *calf*, 2s . 1721

2272 ———— Works, (viz. Sermons ; Scripture Vindicated, in reply to Bp. Hoadly ; Epistola Critica ; Political Tracts, &c.) 4 vols. 8vo. *calf, neat*, 8s . . 1746

2273 ———— (Julius Cha.) Victory of Faith, and other Sermons, 8vo. *bds*. 5s , *Camb.* 1840

2274 HARENBERGUS (Jo. Chr.) Otia Gandershemensia Sacra, exponendis Sacris Litteris et Historiæ Ecclesiasticæ dicata, complexa XIII. Observationes, 8vo. *calf*, 5s . *Traj.* 1740

2275 HARINGTON's (E. C.) Brief Notes on the Church of Scotland, from 1555 to 1842, 8vo. *bds.* 4s *Exeter*, 1843

2276 ———— Object, Importance, and Antiquity of the Rite of Consecration of Churches, 8vo. *bds.* 7s . 1845

2277 HARMER's (Tho.) Observations on divers Passages of Scripture, placing many of them in a light altogether new, by means of circumstances mentioned in books of Voyages and Travels into the East, 4 vols. 8vo. *calf*, 16s . 1776

2278 ———— the same, edited, with additions, by Adam Clarke, LL.D., BEST EDITION, 4 vols. 8vo. *portrait, bds.* 18s 1816

2279 HARMONY of the Confessions of the Faith of the Christian and Reformed Churches, which purelie professe the Holy Doctrine of the Gospel, sm. 8vo. *vellum, rare, imprint torn off*, 12s 1586

2280 HARPSFELDI (Nicolai) Historia Anglicana Ecclesiastica, ad nostra tempora deducta. Adjecta Narratione de Divortio Henrici VIII., et de ejusdem ab Ecclesiæ discessione, scripta ab Ed. Campiano nunc primum edita studio Richardi Gibboni, folio, *calf, scarce*, £2. 2s . *Duaci*, 1622

2281 HARRIS's (Dr. T. M.) Natural History of the Bible, 12mo. *plates, bds.* 2s . . 1825

2282 ———— (Wm.) Self-dedication, Personal and Sacramental, briefly explained and enforced, 12mo. *calf*, 1s 6d . 1717

2283 ———— Funeral Sermon on Mrs. Bathshua Barker, 1719—On Mr. Pickard, 1720—On the Rev. Dan. Mayo, 1733—Two Sermons against Lukewarmness, and a Discourse on false Zeal, 1732— Funeral Sermon on the Rev. Jo. Billingsley, 1722—On the Prince, 1708—Two Sermons on the Reasonableness of Believing in Christ, &c., 1729—Discourse on Transubstantiation, 1735—Funeral Sermon on the Rev. Jo. Evans, D.D., 1730—On the Rev. Sam. Harvey, 1729; *in one* vol. 8vo. *bds.* 3s 6d . ——

2284 —— —— Funeral Discourses, 8vo. *calf*, 3s . 1736

2285 HARRISON's (W.) Sermons on the Commandments, 12mo. *bds.* 3s 1841

2286 HARVEST's (Geo.) Collection of Sermons on various subjects, 8vo. *bds.* 2s—*hf. bd.* 2s 6d . 1754

2287 HAVENSII (R. P. Arnoldi) Historica Relatio XII. Martyrum Cartusianorum Ruræmondæ, Anno 1572. Accedunt ejusdem Exhortatio ad Cartusianos et Historia Martyrii octodecim Cartusianorum ANGLORUM *sub Rege Anglia* HENRICO VIII. A.D. 1535, 1537, et 1541; sm. 8vo. *plate, blue morocco, gilt edges, very rare*, £1. 8s *Permissu Superiorum*, 1608

2288 HAWEIS's (J. O. W.) Sketches of the Reformation and Elizabethan Age, taken from the Contemporary Pulpit, sm. 8vo. *bds.* 6s 1844

2289 HAWKINS's (Dr. Edw. *Provost of Oriel Coll.*) Discourses upon some of the principal Objects and Uses of the Historical Scriptures of the Old Testament, 8vo. *bds.* 2s 6d *Oxford*, 1833

2290 HAYNE's (Tho.) General View of the Holy Scriptures: or, the Times, Places, and Persons of the Holy Scriptures, folio, *scarce,calf*, 6s 1640

2291 HAY's (Peter) Vision of Balaam's Asse, wherein he did perfectly see the present Estate of the Church of Rome. Written by P. Hay, Gentleman of North Britaine, for the Reformation of his Countrymen, specially of Francis, Earle of Errol, 4to. *calf, neat,* 4s . 1616

2292 ———— (Wm.) Religio Philosophi : or the Principles of Morality and Christianity, illustrated from a View of the Universe, &c., 8vo. *calf,* 2s 6d . . 1753

2293 [HAYES's (Cha.)]Vindication of the History of the Septuagint from the Misrepresentations of Scaliger, Dupin, Hody, Prideaux, &c.. 8vo. *sewed,* 2s 6d . 1736

2294 HEARNE's (Tho.) Ductor Historicus, or a short System of Universal History, &c., 2 vols. 8vo. *front. calf,* 5s . 1724

2295 HEBER's (Reg. *Bp. of Calcutta*) Hymns written and adapted to the Weekly Church Service of the Year, 8vo. *bds.* 4s 6d 1827

2296 HECKFORD's (Wm.) Succinct Account of all the Religions, and various Sects in Religion that have prevailed in the World, 8vo. *bds.* 3s . 1791

2297 HEIDEGGERI (Jo. Hen.) Enchiridion Biblicum, 12mo. *calf,* 4s
Tiguri, 1703

2298 HEINSIUS (Dan.) Aristarchus Sacer, sive ad Nonni in Johannem Metaphrasin Exercitationes, 8vo. *calf,* 3s 6d *Lugd. Bat.* 1627

2299 HELE's ( ) Select Offices of Private Devotion, 12mo. *bds.* 2s 1832

2300 HELP to a National Reformation ; containing an Abstract of the Penal Laws against Profaneness and Vice, &c., with an Account of the Progress of the Reformation of Manners in England and Ireland, &c. 12mo. 2s . 1720

2301 HEMMERLIN (FELICIS) VARIE OBLECTATIONIS OPUSCULA ET TRACTATUS, contra validos Mendicantes, contra Anachorites, Beghardes, Baginasque silvestres, Lollhardorum Descriptio, &c. *s. l. et a.—* Felicis Malleoli, vulgo Hemmerlein, de Nobilitate et Rusticitate Dialogus, de Levitensium Ortu, Nomine, Confederatione, Moribus, &c. *s. l. et a.—*Roderici Episcopi Zamorensis Speculum Vitæ Humanæ *Argentinæ, J. Prys,* 1507, 3 vols. in 1, folio, *in the original binding, with clasps,* £1. 18s . ———

The variety of the works of Hemmerlein, is attested by a host of bibliographers. Speaking of the first work, Freytag pronounces it, " INTER RARISSIMOS PRIMI ORDINIS LBIROS," and the second he considers, " RARIOR SUPERIORE LIBRO." Fabricius for years hunted for the second in vain ; and at last was indebted to his friend Vockerode for a sight of it. In the " Bibliotheca Mediæ et infimæ Latinitatis," he tells us, " *Hic liber ante annum* M.D. *excusus* RARISSIME PROSTAT. *In Helvetiæ profecto ac vicinis Helvetiæ urbibus, utut adsidue requisitus fuerit, reperiri non potuit.*"

2302 HENDY's (A. D.) Three Sermons on Practical Subjects, with an Essay on the Utility of Classical Learning, in Subserviency to Theological Studies, 8vo. *bds.* 2s . *Oxford,* 1808

2303 HENLEY's (Sam.) Dissertation upon the controverted passage in St. Peter and St. Jude, concerning the Angels that sinned, &c., 8vo. 1s 6d . . 1778

2304 HENRY's (Matth.) Works, with an Account of his Life, and a Sermon on his Death, both by the Rev. Wm. Tong, folio, 18s 1726

2307 HENRY's (Philip) Life, by his Son Matthew Henry, abridged, 18mo, bds. 1s 6d
2308 HENRICI VIII. *Angliæ &c. Regis.* Assertio Septem Sacramentorum adversus Mart Lutherum. Cui subnexa est, ejusdem Regis Epistola Assertionis ipsius contra eundem defensoria. Accedit quoque Johan. [Fisher] Roffen. Episcopi contra Lutheri Captivitatem Babylonicam Assertionis Regiæ Defensio, 18mo. RARE, *calf,* £1. 5s
Par. 1562
2309 ———— idem, 18mo. *russia, neat,* £1. 8s *ib.* 1562
Upon the title is written, "*Robert Southey, Como, June* 1817, *from Walter Savage Landor.*"
2310 HENSHALL's (Sam.) Saxon and English Languages, reciprocally illustrative of each other; the impracticability of acquiring an accurate knowledge of Saxon Literature through the medium of Latin phraseology; and a new mode suggested of radically studying the Saxon and English Languages, 4to. *hf. bd. calf,* 7s 1798
2311 HENSHAWE's (John, *Bp. of Peterborough*) Meditations, Miscellaneous, Holy, and Humane, in two parts; with a third part by Rd. Kidder, Bp. of Bath and Wells, 18mo. *bds.* 2s 6d
Oxford, 1841
2312 HERBERT's (Geo.) Temple; Sacred Poems, and Private Ejaculations, 12mo. *bds.* 5s . 1844
2313 ———— Remains, containing his Priest to the Temple, Letters, Orations, and Life, 12mo. *bds.* 5s . 1844
2314 HERESBACHIUS (Conrad.) Psalmorum Davidicorum simplex et dilucida Explicatio; Vulgata translatio cum Græca LXX. versione ad Hebraicam veritatem collata, et scholiis eruditis illustrata. Cum præfatione Jo. Sturmii, 8vo. *vellum,* 5s . *Basil.* 1578
2315 HERICOURT (Louis de) les Loix Ecclesiastiques de France dans leur ordre naturel, et une Analyse des livres de Droit Canonique conferés avec les usages de l'Eglise Gallicane, folio, *calf,* 12s *Paris.* 1748
2316 HERLE's (Cha.) Wisdome's Tripos, or rather its Inscription, Detur Sapienti, in three Treatises. I. Of Worldly Policy. II. Of Morall Prudence. III. Of Christian Wisdome, 18mo. *calf,* 3s 1655
2317 HERMANT Histoire des Conciles, 4 vols. 12mo. *neat,* 8s
Rouen, 1695-99
2318 HERODOTUS Historiarum libri IX. *Gr. et Lat.* Editionem curavit, et suas itemque L. C. Valckenarii notas adjecit P. Wesselingius, &c. folio, LARGE PAPER, *plates, fine copy, russia, gilt leaves, bound by Hering,* £3. 10s . *Amst.* 1763
2319 ———— aliud exemplar, Codicem Sancrofti Manuscriptum, denuo contulit reliquam, Lectionis Varietatem, commodius digessit, Annotat. Var. adjecit Tho. Gaisford, S. T. P. 2 vols. 8vo. *fine copy, vellum, marbled edges, and full gilt backs,* £1. 1s
Oxonii, 1840
2320 HERPORT's (Anthony) Essay on Truths of importance to the Happiness of Mankind, wherein the Doctrine of Oaths is impartially considered, translated from the German, 8vo. *calf,* 5s 6d 1768
" This book was publicly burnt by the authorities at Berne, the author was imprisoned in his own house, and died a martyr to the truth."
2321 HERRING's (Tho. *Abp. of Cant.*) VII. Sermons on Public occasions, 8vo. *calf,* 3s 6d . 1763

[58, GREAT QUEEN STREET,

2322 HERRING's (Tho. *Abp. of Cant.*) Letters to William Duncombe Esq., from 1728 to 1757, with Notes and an Appendix, 12mo. *bds.* 2*s* . 1777
2323 HESKETH's (Henry) Dangerous, and almost Desperate State of Religion, represented in a Discourse upon Ez. xxxvii. 3, 4to. 1*s* 6*d* 1679
2324 HETT's (Wm.) Discourses on several Subjects and Occasions, 2 vols. 8vo. *hf. bd. calf, marbled leaves*, 4*s* 6*d* . 1818
2325 HEWLETT's (Jo.) Sermons on different subjects, 8vo. *bds.* 2*s* 1786
2326 ——— Sermons on different subjects, 2 vols. 8vo. *calf.* 6*s* 1786-91
2327 ——— Sermons on different subjects, 8vo. *hf. bd. cf.* 2*s* 6*d* 1788
2328 ——— Sermons on different subjects, 2 vols. 8vo. *hf. bd. calf,* 4*s* 1789
2329 ——— Manual of Instruction and Devotion on the Sacrament of the Lord's Supper, 12mo. *bds.* 2*s* [1815]
2330 ——— (J. P.) Sermons adapted for Parochial and Domestic use, 8vo. *portrait,* 3*s* . 1821
2331 HEY's (Dr. John) Lectures in Divinity, delivered in the University of Cambridge, 4 vols. 8vo. *calf,* £1. 11*s* 6*d* Camb. 1796
2332 ——— (———) The Sincere Christian instructed from the Written Word, 2 vols. 12mo. *bds.* 2*s* . Edinb. 1793
2333 HEYLIN's (Peter) Aërius Redivivus; or, the History of the Presbyterians from 1536 to 1647, folio, *calf,* 18*s* 1672
2334 ——— Theologia Veterum; or, the Summe of Christian Theologie, contained in the Apostles' Creed, folio, *calf,* 15*s* 1673
2335 ——— Historical and Miscellaneous Tracts—I. Ecclesia Vindicata; or, the Church of England Justified, &c.; II. The History of the Sabbath; III. Historia Quinquarticularis; or, a Historical Declaration of the Judgment of the Western Churches, and more particularly of the Church of England, in the five controverted points reproached with the name of Arminianism; IV. The Stumbling-block of Disobedience and Rebellion; V. A Treatise de Jure Paritatis Episcoporum; with the Life of the Author, folio, *calf, very scarce,* £2. 2*s* . 1681
2336 ——— Historia Quinq-Articularis Exarticulata: or, Animadversions on Dr. Heylin's Quinquarticular History; by Henry Hickman, B. D. sm. 8vo. *hf. bd. vellum,* 3*s* 1674
2337 ——— Theologo-Historicus; or, the True Life of the most reverend divine, and excellent historian, P. Heylin, D.D., Sub-Dean of Westminster; written by his Son-in-law, John Barnard, D. D., with an Answer to Mr. Baxter's false Accusations, 12mo. *front. calf,* 7*s* 6*d* . 1683
2338 ——— (Dr. John) Select Discourses on the Principal Points of Natural and Revealed Religion, with Lectures on the first ten chapters of St. Matthew, 2 vols. 8vo. *bds.* 4*s* 6*d* 1793
2339 HICKES (Geo.) Institutiones Grammaticæ Anglo-Saxonicæ et Mœso-Gothicæ, 4to. *calf,* £1. 1*s* . Oxon. 1689
2340 ——— Two Treatises; one of the Christian Priesthood, the other of the Dignity of the Episcopal Order, &c. 8vo. *calf,* 12*s* 1707

2341 HICKES's (Geo.) Two Treatises of the Christian Priesthood, and of the Dignity of the Episcopal Order; with a Treatise by Is. Casaubon of the Liberty of the Church, and Mr. Hughes's Preliminary Dissertations to St. Chrysostom de Sacerdotio, 2 vols. 8vo. *calf*, £1. 8s . . 1711

2342 ———— Spirit of Enthusiasm Exorcised; in a Sermon before the University of Oxford; with the History of Montanism, by a Lay-Gentleman, and the New Pretenders to Prophecy examined, by N. Spinckes, 8vo. *calf*, 7s - *calf*, *neat*, 8s . 1709

2343 ———— Three short Treatises: viz. A Modest Plea for the Clergy, a Sermon of the Sacerdotal Benediction, and a Discourse on Tithes, 8vo. *calf*, 7s . 1709

2344 ———— Gentleman Instructed in the Conduct of a Virtuous and Happy Life, with a Word to the Ladies, 8vo. *calf*, 4s 6d   1732

2345 ———— Volume of Posthumous Discourses; published by N. Spinckes, 8vo. *calf*, 7s 6d . 1726

2346 ———— another copy, *new in sprinkled calf gilt, red edges, (the title a little soiled)* 9s . 1726

2347 HICKMAN's (Cha., *Bp. of Derry*) Sermons at St. James's Westminster, 2 vols. 8vo. *port. calf*, 4s   1718-24

2348 ———— another copy, 2 vols. 8vo. *calf*, 3s   1743

2349 HIERONYMUS (S. Eusebius) Opera, studio et labore Jo. Martianay et Ant. Pouget, Monachorum Ord. S. Benedicti, 5 vols. folio, *calf, scarce*, £11. 11s . *Par.* 1693-1706

2350 HILARIUS (S., *Pictav. Episc.*) Opera, folio, *calf*, 14s   *ib.* 1631

2351 ———— aliud exemplar, folio, *calf*, 16s   *ib.* 1652

2352 ———— Opera, studio et labore Monachorum Ordinis S. Benedicti, folio, *vellam*, £2. 16s . *ib.* 1693

2353 ———— Opera, studio et labore Monach. Ord. S. Benedicti, castigata, aucta, atque illustrata, 2 vols. folio, LARGE PAPER, *new in tree-marbled calf gilt*, £3. 3s . *Veronæ*, 1730

2354 HILDEBERTUS, (*Turon. Archiep.*) Opera, accesserunt Marbodii Redonensis Episcopi Opuscula; studio et labore Ant. Beaugendre, Monachi Ord. S. Benedicti, folio, *calf*, £1. 18s   *Paris.* 1708

2355 HILDERSAM's (Arth.) Doctrine of Fasting and Prayer, and Humiliation for Sinne, in sundry Sermons, 18mo. *neat*, 4s 6d   1636

2356 HILDESLEY's (Mark, *Bp. of Sodor and Mann*) Memoirs, by the Rev. Weeden Butler, 8vo. *hf. bd. calf gilt*, 6s—*bds.* 5s   1799

2357 HILDROP's (Dr. John) Miscellaneous Works, viz.—An Essay for the better regulation of Free-Thinking; an Essay on Honour; Free Thoughts upon the Brute Creation; a modest Apology for the antient and honourable Family of the Wrongheads; a Proposal for Revising the Ten Commandments; Contempt of the Clergy; Life of Simon Shallow, Esq. 2 vols. 12mo, *calf*, 4s   1754

2358 HILL's (Dr. Geo.) Theological Institutes, 8vo. *hf. bd. russia*, 3s   *Edinb.* 1803

2359 [———— (Dr. Henry)] Account of the Growth of Deism in England, with other Tracts, 8vo. *calf*, 3s . 1709

2360 ———— (Sam.) Rights, Liberties, and Authorities of the Christian Church, asserted against all oppressive Doctrines and Constitutions, 8vo. *calf*, 3s 6d . 1701

[58, GREAT QUEEN STREET,

2361 HILL's (Sam.) Thorough Examination of the False Principles advanced in [Tindal's] Rights of the Christian Church, 8vo. *calf*, 3s
1708
2362 HILLERUS (Matthæus) Onomasticum Sacrum, in duas partes distinctum. In priori Nominum Propriorum quæ in Sacris Literis leguntur, Origo, Analogia, et sensus declaratur: in posteriori juxta ordinem literarum digesta nomina explicantur, &c. 4to. *vellum*, 5s
Tubingæ, 1706
Dr. Parr's copy, with his book-plate.
2363 HINCHLIFFE's (Jo. *Bp. of Peterb*.) Sermons, 8vo. *calf*, 2s 6d 1796
2364 HINCMARUS, (*Archiep. Remensis*.) Opera, cura et studio Jac. Sirmondi, 2 vols. folio, *calf*, £3. 3s *Lut. Par*. 1645
2365 HINGESTON's (James) Discourses upon the Two Covenants; or, an Enquiry into the Origin and Progress of Religion, Natural and Revealed, 8vo. *calf, scarce*, 3s . 1771
2366 HISTOIRE Abrégé chronologique de l'Histoire Ecclésiastique, 3 vols. 12mo. *old calf gilt*, 14s . *Par*. 1768
2367 ——— Generale de l'Eglise, depuis la Prédication des Apôtres jusqu'à Pontificat de Grégoire XVI. renfermant, par ordre chronologique, l'Histoire des Eglises d'Orient et d'Occident, les Souverains Pontifes, les Conciles généraux et particulier, les Schismes et les Hérésies, les Institutions d'Ordres Religieux, les Auteurs Ecclesiastiques, &c.; publication dont les neuf premiers volumes contiennent le texte rectifié de Berault-Bercastel, et les quatre derniers la continuation, dépuis l'an 1719, jusqu'à l'an 1840, par M. Le Baron Henrion, 12 vols. 8vo. *sewed*, £2. 18s *ib*. 1840
2368 ——— de la Sainte Larme de N. Seigneur J. C. comme et par qui elle fut apportée au Monastere de la Sainte Trinité de Vendôme, ou elle est conservée, &c. 18mo. *calf*, 2s 6d
Vendosme, [1656?]
2369 HISTORIÆ Anglicanæ, circa tempus Conquestûs Angliæ à Gulielmo Notho, Normannorum Duce, selecta Monumenta. Excerpta ex magno volumini, cui titulas est "Historiæ Normannorum Scriptores Antiqui" à doctiss. Viro And. Duchesne, cum notis plurimis, Anglico Sermone ad illustrandum textum, conscriptis, à Francisco Maseres, 4to. *bds*. 14s . *Lond*. 1807
2370 HITTORPII (Melchiori) de Divinis Catholicæ Ecclesiæ Officiis ac Ministeriis variis vetustorum aliquot Ecclesiæ Patrum ac Scriptorum Libri, folio, *calf, very neat*, £1. 16s *Coloniæ*, 1568
"Liber utilissimus."—*Grævius*. This rare and very uncommon work, edited by the learned Melchior Hittorp, contains, besides the Ordo Romanus per totius anni circulum, and the Missæ Exposito, *ten* very early authors on the Offices of the Church, which are no where else to be found; as the work appears not to be so well known as it deserves, we have stated the contents below.—I. Ordo Romanus, de Missæ et Reliquiis per annum officiis.—II. B. Isidorus Hispal. Episc. de Ecclesiasticis Officiis.—III. Albini Flacci Alcuini liber de officiis divinis.—IV. Amalarii Treverensis Episc. Officiales.—V. H. Rabanus Maurus de Institutione Clericorum.—VI, Walafrid Strabo de exordiis et incrementis rerum Ecclesiasticarum.—VII. Bernonis Augiensis Abbatis, de rebus ad Missæ Officium pertinentibus libellus.—VIII. Micrologus de Ecclesiasticis observationibus.—IX. B. Juonis Carnotensis de rebus Ecclesiasticis, Sermones.— X. Hildeberti Cenomanensis de Mysterio Missæ Carmen.—XI. Radulphi de Rivo de observantiæ canonum Liber.—XII. Missæ exposito brevis, ex antiquis libris excerpta.

2371 HOADLEY'S (Benj. Bp. of Winchester) Reasonableness of Conformity to the Church of England, represented to the Dissenting Ministers, 8vo. *calf*, 1s 6d . 1703
2372 ———— Brief defence of Episcopal Ordination, 8vo. *calf*, 2s 6d 1707
2373 ———— Original and Institution of Civil Government discussed, with an Answer to Dr. Atterbury's Charge of Rebellion, 8vo. *calf*, 2s 6d . . 1710
2374 ———— Plain Account of the Nature and End of the Sacrament of the Lord's Supper, with Forms of Prayer, 8vo. *old blue morocco, gilt leaves*, 5s 6d . 1735
2375 ———— Sermons, 2 vols. 8vo. *calf*, 4s 6d 1754-55
2376 [HOARD (———)] God's Love to Mankind manifested, by disproving his absolute Decree for their Damnation, 12mo. 6s 1673
2377 H[OARE] (J.) Index Biblicus Multijugus; or, a Table to the Holy Scriptures, 12mo. *calf, very scarce*, 4s 6d 1672
2378 HOBART (Henry, Bp. of New York) The Early Life and Professional Years of Bp. Hobart, by John M'Vicar, D.D.; with a Preface containing a History of the Church in America, by W. F. Hook, D.D. 8vo. *bds*. 5s 6d . Oxford, 1838
2379 HOBBES's (Tho.) True Ecclesiastical History, from Moses to the time of Martin Luther, in verse, from the Latin, 8vo. *calf*, 4s 1722
2380 ———— Mr. Hobbs's State of Nature considered, in a Dialogue between Philantus and Timothy; with Five Letters from the author of the Grounds of the Contempt of the Clergy, 8vo. *calf*, 3s 6d . . 1672
2381 ———— A brief View and Survey of the dangerous and pernicious Errors to Church and State in Mr. Hobbes's book entitled Leviathan, by Edward [Hyde], Earl of Clarendon, 4to. *calf*, 2s Oxon. 1676
2382 HOBSON'S (Tho. *Queen's Coll. Oxon.*) Christianity the Light of the Moral World, a Poem, 4to. *sewed*, 1s . 1745
2383 HOCKIN'S (Tho.) Discourse of the Nature of God's Decrees, 8vo. *calf*, 2s 6d . . 1684
2384 HODGE'S (John) Sermons on the Principal Evidences of the Christian Religion, and the chief Objections made to it, 8vo. *calf*, 2s 6d 1758

"His arguments are laid down in a plain but judicious manner, and shew the author to be no mean defender of Christianity."

2385 ———— (Dr. Walter) Elihu; or, an Inquiry into the principal Scope and Design of the Book of Job, 8vo. *calf*, 4s 1751
2386 ———— Christian Plan; with other Theological Pieces, and an Oration before the University of Oxford, 8vo. *calf*, 3s 1755
2387 HODGSON'S (Bernard, LL.D.) Proverbs of Solomon, translated from the Hebrew, 4to. *sewed*, 3s . Oxford, 1788
2388 ———— (Chr.) Account of the Augmentation of Small Livings by the Governors of the Bounty of Queen Anne, &c. 8vo. *bds*. 6s 1826
2389 HODGSON'S (Chr.) Instructions for the Use of Candidates for Holy Orders, and of the Parochial Clergy, 8vo. *bds*. 12s 1845

2390 HODSON's (Archd. George) Morning Discourses at Christ Church, Birmingham, 8vo. *bds.* 2s 6d . 1832
2391 ———— (Septimus) Sermons on the Present State of Religion in this Country, &c. 1792—Eveleigh's (Dr. John) Eight Sermons at the Lecture founded by the Rev. J. Bampton, 1792, 2 vols. in 1, 8vo. *calf,* 5s
2392 HODY's (H.) History of English Councils and Convocations, and of the Clergy's sitting in Parliament, with an Account of our ancient Laws, 8vo. *calf, very scarce,* £1. 4s . 1701
2393 ———— Contra historiam Aristeæ de LXX. Interpretibus Dissertatio ; in qua probatur illam a Judæo aliquo confictam fuisse ad conciliandam authoritatem Versioni Græcæ, *Oxon.* 1685— Smith (Tho.) Miscellanea, in quibus continentur Tractatus Varii de Ecclesia Orientali, *Lond.* 1686—Usserius (Jac. *Archiep. Armach.*) Opuscula duo, alterum de Episcoporum et Metropolitanorum Origine; alterum de Asia proconsulari; accedit Appendix de Antiquâ Ecclesiæ Britannicæ libertate et privilegiis, *Lond.* 1687—*in one* vol. 8vo. *vellum,* 8s
2394 HOFMANN (Car. Gottl.) Institutiones Theologicæ Exegeticæ, 12mo. *interleaved, numerous MS. notes, bds.* 3s *Vitemb.* 1754
2395 HOFMANNUS (Jo. Jac.) Lexicon Universale, Historiam Sacram et Profanam, Chronologiam, Geographiam, Genealogiam, Mythologiam, &c. explanans, 4 vols. folio, *vellum,* £3. 3s *Lugd. Bat.* 1698
2396 HOLBEIN (Hans) Todentanz in 53 getreu nach den Holzschnitten lithographirten Blättern. Herausgegeben von J. Schlotthauer : mit erklärendem Texte, small 8vo. *morocco extra, uncut, gilt top,* 10s 6d . *München,* 1832
2397 HOLDEN's (Geo.) Dissertation on the Fall of Man; in which the literal sense of the Mosaic Account is vindicated, 8vo. *bds.* 3s 6d 1823
2398 ———— Authority of Tradition in Matters of Religion, 12mo. *bds.* 3s . . 1838
2399 HOLDSWORTH's (Dr. Winch.) Defence of the Doctrine of the Resurrection of the same Body, 8vo. *calf,* 3s . 1727
2399*HOLE's (Matthew) Practical Discourses on the Liturgy of the Church of England, edited by the Rev. J. A. Giles, 4 vols. 8vo. *bds.* £2. 2s—*calf gilt,* £2. 12s 6d *Lond.* 1837
2400 HOLLAND's (Ph.) Sermons on practical subjects, 2 vols. 8vo. *bds.* 4s *Warrington,* 1792
2401 HOLLEBEEK (Ewald.) Dissertatio Theologica de Optimo Concionum genere, *Lugd. Bat.* 1779—Ravius (J. E.) Dissertationes Sacræ Antiquariæ, de Nube Gloriosa super Arcam Fœderis, et de Libamine facto in sacra mensa, *Traj. ad Rh.* 1760—*in one* vol. 8vo. *hf. bd.* 3s 6d
2402 HOLLIS's (Lord Denzill) Remains ; being a second Letter to a Friend concerning the Judicature of Bishops in Parliament, 8vo. *calf,* 5s . 1682
2403 HOLLOWAY's (Benj.) Letter and Spirit ; or, Annotations upon the Holy Scriptures according to both, 8vo. *hf. bd. calf,* 2s 6d *Oxford,* 1753

2404 [HOLMES (——)] Enchiridion Clericum; or, the Preacher's Guide, [in verse] 2 parts, I. The Art of getting up Sermons; II. Delivery and Canting, 8vo. *hf. bd. very scarce,* 5s   1812

2405 HOLSTENIUS (Lucas) Collectio Romana Bipartita, veterum aliquot Historiæ Ecclesiasticæ monumentorum, 8vo. *old red morocco, gilt leaves,* 10s 6d   .   *Romæ,* 1662

2406 HOLSWORTH'S (Richard) Valley of Vision; or, a Clear Sight of sundry Sacred Truths, in twenty-one Sermons, 4to. *very scarce, calf,* 6s   .   .   1651

2407 HOLTZFUS (Bartholdus) Tractatus theologicus de Prædestinatione, Electione et Reprobatione Hominum, 8vo. *marbled calf extra, gilt leaves,* 12s   .   *Lugd. Bat.* 1756

2408 HOME'S (James) Scripture History of the Jews and their Republick, 2 vols. 8vo, *calf, scarce,* £1. 10s   .   1737

2409 ———— (Nathaniel) Peasants Price of Spiritual Liberty; in three Sermons, 4to. 2s   .   1642

2410 HOMILIES.—Certaine Sermons appointed by the Queene's Maiestie, to be declared and read by all Parsons, Vicars, and Curates, every Sunday and Holy day in their Churches; 2 vols. in 1, 4to. 𝔅lack 𝔩etter, *slightly wormed, hf. bd. calf,* 10s 6d   *Lond.* 1582

2411 ———— another edition, 2 vols. in 1, 4to. 𝔅lack 𝔩etter, *slightly wormed, original binding,* 16s   .   *n. pl.* 1587

2412 ———— Vol. 2, (the same edition as the preceding,) *fine clean copy, in the original binding, (a part of the last leaf wanting,)* 8s   .   .   1587

2413 ———— another edition, folio, 𝔅lack 𝔩etter, *hf. bd. calf, neat,* 8s   1640

2414 ———— another edition, folio, 𝔅lack 𝔩etter, *neat,* 7s   1673

2415 ———— another edition, 8vo. *calf,* 8s   .   1816

2416 ———— another edition, with the Thirty-nine Articles, *in one* vol. 12mo. *hf. bd. calf,* 4s   .   1827

2417 ———— another edition, 8vo. *bds.* 8s—*calf gilt,* 11s 6d   *Oxford,* 1832

2418 HOMILY.—An English-Saxon Homily on the Birth-Day of St. Gregory, anciently used in the English-Saxon Church; giving an Account of the Conversion of the English from Paganism to Christianity; translated into modern English, with Notes, &c. by Eliz. Elstob, 8vo. LARGE PAPER, *fine copy, front. calf, neat,* 12s   1709

" Mrs. Elstob's present to A. Prowse."—*MS. Note.*

2419 ———— An Anglo-Saxon Homily on St. Gregory's Day. with an English translation by Elizabeth Elstob; a new edition, with a Preface, containing some Account of Mrs. Elstob, 8vo. *bds.* 7s   1839

2420 ———— A Testimony of Antiquity concerning the Sacramental Body and Blood of Christ; written in the old Saxon tongue before the Conquest; being a Homily appointed to be spoken at Easter; together with the two Epistles of Ælfrie on the same subject, 8vo. *hf. bd.* 5s 6d   .   .   1736

2421 HOMMEY (Jacobus) Supplementum Patrum, complectens multa SS. Patrum, Conciliorum, Scriptorumque Ecclesiasticorum Opera, notis et dissertationibus illustrata, 8vo. *calf,* 12s Par. 1686
2422 HONE's (Rd. B.) Lives of Eminent Christians, 4 vols. 12mo. *port. bds. 9s* . . 1842-43

    The volumes contain the lives of Abp. Usher, Hammond, Evelyn, Bp. Wilson, B. Gilpin, P. de Mornay, Bp. Bedell, Horneck, Bp. Ridley, Bp. Hall, Boyle, Bradford, Abp. Grindal, and Sir M. Hale.

2423 —— —— (William) Every-Day Book, and Table Book, 3 vols.— The Year Book, 1 vol,, together 4 vols. 8vo. *numerous woodcuts, calf gilt, marbled leaves,* £1. 18s 1830-41
2424 HOOK's (W. F.) Last Days of our Lord's Ministry, a course of Lectures delivered in Trinity Church, Coventry, 1832—Two Sermons on the Church and the Establishment, 1834—Five Sermons preached before the University of Oxford, 1837, *in one vol.* 8vo. *hf. bd. calf gilt,* 8s . ——
2425 ———— Call to Union, on the principles of the English Reformation, a Sermon at the primary Visitation of the Bishop of Ripon, with Notes and an Appendix, 8vo. *sewed,* 2s 1838
2426 ———— Sermons on various subjects, 8vo. *bds.* 10s 1841
2427 HOOKER's (Richard) Lawes of Ecclesiastical Politie, eight bookes, folio, *engraved title, calf,* 12s . N. D.

    Although the title expresses VIII. Books, only *five* appeared in this edition.

2428 ———— Workes, (with his Life by Bp. Gauden) folio, *engraved title, hf. bd. calf,* 12s . 1662
2429 ———— Works, with the Life of the Author by Isaac Walton, folio, *engraved title and port. hf. bd. calf,* 16s 1705
2430 ———— Works, with the Life of the Author by Isaac Walton, folio, *fine copy, engraved title and port. calf,* £1. 4s 1723
2431 ———— Works, containing eight books of the Laws of Ecclesiastical Polity, and several other Treatises; with an Index, and the Life of the Author by Isaac Walton, 3 vols. 8vo. *hf. bd. calf,* 18s Oxford, 1793
2432 ———— Works, with his Life by Isaac Walton, a new edition, with Additions and Notes, arranged by the Rev. John Keble, 3 vols. 8vo. *tree-marbled calf gilt, old style,* £1. 16s *ib.* 1841
2433 ———— new edition, 3 vols. 8vo. *bds.* £1. 11s 6d—*calf gilt,* £2. 2s . *ib.* 1845
2434 ———— the same, without the Notes, 2 vols. 8vo. *bds.* 12s *ib.* 1845
2435 ———— Faithful abridgment of his Works, with an Account of his Life, 8vo *calf,* 5s . 1705

    Zouch, in his edition of Walton's Lives, says that this abridgment is a publication of great merit. The life is abridged from Walton.

2436 ———— Divine Service, the Sacraments, &c. being selections from the fifth book of the Ecclesiastical Polity, [by the Rev. John Keble] 18mo. *bds.* 2s 6d . Oxford, 1845
2437 HOOLE's (Sam.) Sermons at St. Albans, Wood Street, 8vo. *calf,* 2s 6d . . 1786

2438 HOOPER'S (Geo. Bp. of Bath and Wells) Works, folio, calf, 12s
Oxford, 1757
2439 ———— Works, folio, new in tree-marbled calf gilt, £1. 1s
ib. 1757
Containing a discourse on Lent, an enquiry into ancient measures, several other discourses, and eight sermons.
2440 ———— (John, Bp. of Gloucester) Early Writings of John Hooper, DD., Lord Bp. of Gloucester and Worcester, Martyr, 1555, comprising the Declaration of Christ and His Office—Answer to Bp. Gardiner—Ten Commandments—Sermons on Jonas—Funeral Sermon, &c. edited by the Rev. Sam. Carr, M.A., 8vo. bds. 10s
Camb. 1843
2441 HOPKINS'S (Ezechiel, Bp. of Londonderry) Works, containing the Vanity of the World; Exposition on the X Commandments; Exposition on the Lord's Prayer, and several Sermons and Discourses, folio, portrait inserted, calf, £1. 1s . 1701
2442 ———— Discourses, or Sermons on several Scriptures, 8vo. 2s
1691
2443 ———— Death disarmed of its Sting, with a Discourse of Redemption from the Curse of the Law, 8vo. calf, 3s 6d 1712
2444 ———— another copy, 8vo. portrait, calf, 4s 1712
2445 ———— Doctrine of the two Sacraments; the Way of Salvation; and a Sermon against Rebellion, 8vo. calf, 4s In the Savoy, 1712
2246 ———— another copy, 8vo. portrait, calf, 4s 1712
"The writings of Bp. Hopkins are eminent for the combination of clear statements of doctrinal and practical truth, with an eloquent application of it to the conscience and heart."—*Christian Observer.*
2447 ———— (Dr. Sam.) Treatise on the Millennium, 12mo. calf, 2s
Edin. 1806
2448 ———— (Dr. William) Seventeen Sermons, with a Preface, containing a short account of his Life, by G. Hickes, D.D., 8vo. calf, 3s . 1708
2449 [———— (Will. an Arian)] Tractarian Controversy reviewed; wherein an humble attempt is made to put a final period to this Controversy, 8vo. calf, 3s . 1760
2450 ———— Exodus, a corrected translation, with Notes, Critical and Explanatory, 4to. bds. 4s 6d . 1784
2451 HOPWOOD'S (Hen.) Elisha's Staff in the Hand of Gehazi, and other Sermons, 12mo. bds. 1s 6d . 1844
2452 HORÆ DIURNÆ, new edition, 24mo. beautifully printed in red and black, calf gilt, 7s—calf extra, 8s—vellum, gilt leaves, 9s
Mechliniæ, 1843
2453 ———— Breviarii Leodiensis, 2 vols. 18mo. old morocco, gilt leaves, in leather cases, 14s . Leodii, 1756
2454 HORLER'S (Joseph) Apology for the Ministers of Jesus Christ, and a Vindication of the Gospel, from the Misrepresentations of Tho. Chubb, 8vo. calf, 2s . ——
2455 [HORNBY'S (Cha.)] Caveat against the Whigs, in a short Historical View of their Transactions and Contrivances against the established Government in Church and State, since the Restoration, 4 parts in 1 vol. 8vo. calf, 3s 6d . 1711-13

2456 HORANTIUS (F.) Locorum Catholicorum, tum Sacræ Scripturæ, tum etiam antiquorum patrum, pro orthodoxa et vetere fide retinenda, Lib. VII. in quibus præcipua Institutionis Calvini, capita, apertissimè confutantur, sm. 8vo. RARE, *fine copy, calf, gilt leaves,* 12s
Par. 1566

"Ce livre, rarissime, inconnu de Brunet, et imprimé deux ans apres la mort de Calvin, refute toutes les erreurs contenues dans son livre de *l'Institution Chretienne*, qui devint la base de la croyance religieuse appellée de son nom Calvinisme. Cet ouvrage qu'on croiroit, par la beauté de son execution, sorti des presses des Elzevirs, à paru environ un siècle avant leur execution comme imprimeurs. L'exemplaire ci-joint a en outre le merite d'etre de la plus belle conservation."—*MS. Note.*

2457 HORBERY's (Matth.) Enquiry into the Scripture Doctrine concerning the duration of future Punishment, 8vo. *calf,* 4s 6d   1744

2458 HORNE's (Geo. *Bp. of Norwich*) Works, with Memoirs of his Life, Studies, and Writings, by William Jones, M.A. 6 vols. 8vo. *port. calf,* £1. 16s   .   1809

2459 ———— Commentary on the Book of Psalms, 2 vols. *Oxford,* 1794—Discourses on several subjects and occasions, 4 vols. *ib.* 1795 —Sixteen Sermons on various occasions, *ib.* 1795, together 7 vols. 8vo. *calf, uniform,* £1. 10s   .   ——

2460 ———— Discourses on several subjects and occasions, 5 vols. 8vo. *port. calf,* 15s   .   .   1799

2461 ———— Discourses, 2 vols. 8vo. *hf. bd. calf,* 9s   1831

2462 ———— Discourses, 2 vols. 8vo. *bds.* 15s   1845

2463 ———— Commentary on the Book of Psalms, 8vo. *bds.* 10s 6d   1843

2464 ———— Considerations on the Life and Death of St. John the Baptist, 12mo. *calf,* 2s   .   *Oxford,* 1777

2465 ———— the same, 12mo. *calf,* 2s 6d   .   *Lond.* 1806

2466 ———— (T. H.) Compendious Introduction to the Study of the Bible, 12mo. *maps, hf. bd. calf,* 6s   .   1827

2467 ———— Introduction to the Critical Study and Knowledge of the Holy Scriptures, *ninth edition,* much enlarged, 5 vols. 8vo. *bds.* £3. 3s   .   1845

2468 ———— Scripture Doctrine of the Trinity, briefly stated and defended, 12mo. *hf. bd. calf,* 2s 6d   .   1826

2469 ———— Romanism contradictory to the Bible; or the peculiar Tenets of the Church of Rome contrasted with the Holy Scriptures, 12mo. *hf. bd. calf, neat,* 1s   .   1827

2470 ———— Protestant Memorial, for the Commemoration of the fourth day of October, 1835, the third Centenary of the Reformation, &c. 8vo. *bds.* 2s   .   1835

2471 HORNECK's (Dr. Anth.) Crucified Jesus: or a full Account of the Nature, End, Design, and Benefits of the Lord's Supper, with Directions, Prayers, &c. 8vo. *calf,* 2s 6d   .   1680

2472 ———— Happy Ascetick: or, the Best Exercise, with Prayers, and a Letter concerning the Holy Lives of the Primitive Christians, 8vo. *with the rare frontispiece by Hogarth, calf,* 6s   .   .   1699

2473 ———— another copy, 8vo. *new in calf gilt,* 10s   1724

2474 HORNECK'S (Dr. Anth.) Great Law of Consideration, 8vo. *frontispiece, calf,* 2s 6d . 1702
2475 ———— another copy, 8vo. *frontispiece, calf,* 3s 1711
2476 ———— the same, 8vo. *calf,* 3s . 1729
2477 ———— Several Sermons upon the 5th of Matthew, with the Life of the Author, by Richard Kidder, Bp. of Bath and Wells, 2 vols. 8vo. *port. calf,* 7s 6d . 1706
2478 HORSLEY'S (Sam. *Bp. of St. Asaph*) Nine Sermons on the Evidence of our Lord's Resurrection, and other subjects, with a Dissertation on the Prophecies of the Messiah dispersed among the Heathen, 8vo. *calf, neat,* 5s 6d . 1815
2479 ———— Charge delivered to the Clergy of the Archdeaconry of St. Albans, 4to. *sewed,* 1s . 1783
2480 ———— Enjoyments of the Future Life, and the true notion of Christian Purity, a Sermon at the Chapel of the Magdalen Hospital, 4to. *sewed,* 1s . . 1795
2481 ———— Critical Disquisition on the XVIIIth Chapter of Isaiah, 4to. *sewed,* 2s 6d 1799
2482 ———— Sermons, 2 vols. 8vo. *cloth bds.* 18s 1829
2483 ———— Charges, 8vo. *cloth bds.* 9s . 1830
2484 ———— Biblical Criticism on the first fourteen Historical Books of the Old Testament, also on the first nine Prophetical Books, and translations by the Author never before published, together with copious Indexes, 2 vols. 8vo. *cloth bds.* £1. 10s 1844
2485 ———— Book of Psalms, translated from the Hebrew; with notes Explanatory and Critical, 8vo. *cloth bds.* 12s 1845
2486 ———— HOSEA, translated, with notes, and a Sermon on Christ's descent into Hell, 4to. *calf,* 10s 1804

" The preface contains a treasure of Biblical criticism."—*Horne.*

2487 ———— Works, viz. Sermons, Charges, Book of Psalms, translated from the Hebrew; Biblical Criticism on the first fourteen Historical Books of the Old Testament, also on the first nine Prophetical Books; together 6 vols. 8vo. *calf extra, lettered contents,* £4. 10s 1829-45
2488 HORSTIUS (J. M.) Septem Tubæ Sacerdotales, sive selecti Septem SS. Patrum tractatus; J. Chrysostomi, Hieronymi, Prosperi, Gregorii, P. Damiani, Bernardi, et P. Blesensis; quibus de novo addita est, Tuba Octava, SS. Salviani et Vincentii Lirinensis, cum notis St. Baluzii, 4to. *calf, rare,* 18s . *Lugd.* 1693
2489 HORT'S (Josiah, *Bp. of Kilmore*) Sermons on practical subjects, 8vo. *calf,* 3s . 1757
2490 HOTTINGERUS (Jo. Hen.) Thesaurus Philologicus, seu Clavis Scripturæ, 4to. *calf,* 4s . *Tiguri,* 1649
2491 HOUARD Coutumes Anglo-Normandes, publiés en Angleterre, depuis l'onzième jusqu'a quatorzième siecle, 4 vols. 4to. *French calf,* £2. 2s *Rouen,* 1776
2492 HOUDRY (Vincentius) Bibliothecæ Concionatoria, Ethices Christianæ præcipua, continens Argumenta ordine alphabetico digesta, 4 tom. folio, *vellum,* £2. 2s . *Venet.* 1742

2493 Hough's (John, *Bp. of Worcester*) Sermons and Charges, with his Life by Will. Russell, B.D., 8vo. *bds.* 4s   *Oxford*, 1821
2494 Houghton's (Pendlebury) Sermons, 8vo. *calf*, 3s   1790
2495 Howard's (Cha. *Esq. of Greystock*, [*afterwards Duke of Norfolk*]) Thoughts, Essays, and Maxims, chiefly Religious and Political, 12mo. *bds.* 2s   1768
2496 ———— (Henry, *Dean of Lichfield*) Scripture History of the Old Testament, 12mo. *bds.* 2s 6d   1840·
2497 ———— Scripture History of the New Testament, 12mo. *bds.* 2s   1841
2498 ———— (Leonard) Sermons on several occasions, 8vo. *calf*, 2s 1742
2499 Howe's (Jo.) Living Temple: or, a designed improvement of that notion that a Good Man is the Temple of God, 2 vols. 8vo. *port. calf*, 8s   1702
2500 ———— (John) Office and Work of the Holy Spirit, in every Age, &c., considered in several Sermons, 2 vols. 8vo. *calf*, 6s   1726
2501 ———— Prosperous State of the Christian Interest before the end of Time, by a plentiful effusion of the Holy Spirit, considered in XV. Sermons, 8vo. *calf*, 2s 6d   1726
2502 Howel's (Laurence) Complete History of the Holy Bible, and of the Occurrences from the days of Malachi, to the Birth of our Blessed Saviour, with notes, 3 vols. 8vo. *plates, fine copy, calf gilt, old style, carmine edges*, 18s   1725
2503 ———— (James) Epistolæ Ho-Elianæ. Familiar Letters, Domestic and Forren, upon emergent occasions, 4to. *fine frontispiece by Marshall, calf*, 4s 6d   1645
2504 ———— Epistolæ Ho-Elianæ: Familiar Letters, domestic and foreign, 8vo. *front. calf, fine copy*, 9s   1726
2505 ———— another copy, 8vo. *new in calf gilt, old style*, 12s   1737
"Howell's Letters (unquestionably his best work) throw considerable light upon the history of those distracted times, and abound with excellent moral, political, and religious sentiments, and are equally enlivened by numerous anecdotes."— *Orthodox Churchman's Magazine*, Vol. V.
2507 Howie's (John) Biographia Scoticana: or, a brief Historical Account of the Lives of the most eminent Scots Worthies, &c. *frontisp.* 8vo. *calf*, 6s   *Glasgow*, 1781
Chiefly relating to such as suffered death on account of their religious opinions, from 1527 to 1688.
2508 Howlett's (Jo. Hen.) Instructions in Reading the Liturgy, 8vo. *bds.* 4s 6d   1826
2509 Hozie (Stanislas, *Evesque de Varme en Pouloigne*). Des Sectes et Heresies de nostre temps: traicté composé premierement en Latin, et nouvellement mis en François, sm. 8vo. *calf*, 4s 6d   *Par.* 1561
From the library of the late Duke of Sussex.
2510 Hudleston's (Wm.) Divine Truths Vindicated in the Church of England, 8vo. *front. calf*, 5s   1733
The author was once a Benedictine Missionary Priest, but conforming to the Church of England, became Vicar of Tirley or Trinley, Gloucestershire.
2511 Huet's (Pierre Dan. *Bp. of Avranches*) Philosophical Treatise concerning Human Understanding, 8vo. *portrait*, 2s   1729
2512 ———— (Theod.) Sermons sur divers textes du l'Ecriture Sainte, 2 vols. 8vo. *old calf gilt*, 4s   *Amst.* 1732-34

2513 HUET (Theodore) Sermons sur divers textes de l'Ecriture Sainte, 3 vols. 8vo. *vellum, 8s*   *Amst.* 1734-38

2514 HUETIUS (Pet. Dan. *Episc. Abrincensis*) Demonstratio Evangelica, 4to. *portrait, calf, neat, 6s* . *Lips.* 1703
"A work written in the purest Latinity, and diverging into an amazing range of learning."—*Butler.*

2515 HUG's (Jo. Leonard) Introduction to the Writings of the New Testament, translated by D. G. Wait, LL.D., 2 vols. 8vo. *hf. bd. calf gilt, 12s* . . 1827

2516 HUGO (Herm.) Pia Desideria, Emblematis, elegiis et affectibus SS. Patrum illustrata, 18mo. *numerous spirited wood-cuts, old green morocco, gilt leaves,* 12s—*calf gilt,* 10s   *Antv.* 1628

2517 ———— Pia Desideria, 12mo. *plates, fine copy, olive morocco, gilt leaves, 9s* . . *ib.* 1632
Much of this curious work is taken from the emblems of And. Alciatus. Francis Quarles borrowed extensively both from the text and the plates of Hugo.

2518 HUGO DE SANCTO CHARO, (*Card.*) Opera omnia, sc. Commentarii in omnes libros Veteris et Novi Testamenti, 8 vols. in 4, folio, *fine copy, hogskin, clasps, £4. 4s* . *Venetiis,* 1703

2519 HULL's (W. W.) Disuse of the Athanasian Creed advisable in the present state of the United Church of England and Ireland, 8vo. *bds. 2s 6d* . . 1831

2520 HULSEAN LECTURE. 1821. FRANKS (J. C.) On the Evidences of Christianity as they were stated and enforced in the Discourses of our Lord, 8vo. *bds.* 6s . *Camb.* 1821

2521 ———— 1825. FRANKS (J. C.) On the Apostolical Preaching and Vindication of the Gospel, as exhibited in the Acts, the Epistles of St. Peter, and the Epistle to the Hebrews, 8vo. *bds.* 6s *Camb.* 1823

2522 ———— 1826. CHEVALLIER (T.) On the Historical Types contained in the Old Testament, 8vo. *bds.* 6s . 1826

2523 ———— 1833. ROSE's (Henry J.) Law of Moses reviewed in connection with the Character of the Jews; with a Defence of the Book of Joshua, against Prof. Leo of Berlin, 8vo. *bds.* 5s *Camb.* 1834

2524 ———— 1838. PARKINSON's (Rd.) Constitution of the Visible Church of Christ considered, 8vo. *bds.* 5s . 1839

2526 ———— 1843. MARSDEN's (J. H.) Examination of certain Passages in our Lord's Conversation with Nicodemus; eight Sermons before the University of Cambridge, 8vo. *bds. 8s 6d* 1844

2527 ———— 1844. MARSDEN's (J. H.) Evils which have resulted at various times from a Misapprehension of our Lord's Miracles, 8vo. *bds. 6s* . . 1845

2528 ———— 1845. TRENCH's (R. C.) Fitness of Holy Scripture for Unfolding the Spiritual Life of Man, 8vo. *bds.* 5s *Camb.* 1845

2529 HUMAN SOULS Naturally Immortal; translated from a Latin MS. by S. E.; with a recommendatory Preface by Jeremy Collier, 12mo. *sewed, 1s 6d* . 1707

2530 HUME's (John) Jachin and Boaz; or, the stedfast and unwavering Christian, 8vo. *old blue morocco, gilt leaves,* 3s 1676

2531 ———— Sermons upon religious and practical subjects, 8vo. *bds.* 1s 6d . . *Edinb.* 1775

2532 HUME's (Wm.) Sacred Succession; or, a Priesthood by a Divine Right, 8vo. *calf,* 4s 6d . 1710
2533 HUNARRY's (Levek) Five lookes over the professors of the English Bible, wherein is shewed the infinite indiscreet invention, of inconsiderate, inveterate dissention, about the exaltation of the propagation of that Gospel, which we all say, we doe professe to believe, 4to. RARE, *hf. bd. morocco,* 7s 6d . 1642
2534 HUNT's (Dr. Jeremiah) Sermons on various subjects, published by Geo. Benson, D.D.; with the Funeral Sermon by N. Lardner, D.D., 4 vols. 8vo. *calf,* 8s . 1748-49
2535 —————— (Tho.) Argument for the Bishops' Right in Judging in Capital Causes in Parliament, 8vo. *calf,* 2s 6d 1682
2536 —————— Apology for the Government of England, introduced upon a Question of the Bishops' Right of Judging in Capital Causes in Parliament; with Two Discourses on the Necessity and Lawfulness of the Bill of Exclusion, for shutting out a Popish Successor, 8vo. *calf,* 4s . . 1686
2537 —————— Observations on several Passages in the Book of Proverbs, with two Sermons, 4to. *calf,* 5s *Oxford,* 1775
2538 —————— Observations on several Passages in the Book of Proverbs, with two Sermons, *Oxford,* 1775—The Posthumous Works of Conyers Middleton, D.D, 1753; *in one* vol. 4to. *calf,* 6s ———
2539 HUNTER's (Dr. Henry) Sacred Biography; or, the History of the Patriarchs: being a Course of Lectures at the Scots Church, London Wall, 6 vols. 8vo. *calf gilt,* 18s 1792-95
2540 ————— another copy, 5 vols. 8vo. *bds.* 10s 1807
2541 HUNTINGFORD's (G. J., *Bp. of Glouc.*) Call to Union with the Established Church, addressed to English Protestants; being a compilation of passages from various authors, 8vo. *bds.* 2s 6d
Winchester, 1800
2542 ——— ——— Thoughts on the Trinity, 8vo. *sewed,* 1s 1804
2543 —— ——— (Tho.) Testimonies in proof of the Separate Existence of the Soul in a state of Self-Consciousness between Death and the Resurrection, 8vo. *bds.* 2s 6d . 1829
2544 HUNTINGTON's (Rev. Jedidiah, M.D.) Poems, 12mo. *bds.* 3s
New York, 1843
2545 [HURD's (Rd., *Bp. of Worc.*)] Moral and Political Dialogues between divers eminent persons of the past and present age, 8vo. *calf,* 2s 6d . . 1759
2546 - ——— Sermons preached at Lincoln's Inn, between 1765 and 1776; with a Discourse on Christ's Driving the Merchants out of the Temple, 8vo. 2s 6d . 1776
2547 ————— the same, 8vo. 2s 6d . 1777
2548 ————— the same, with additions, 3 vols. 8vo. *bds.* 6s 1785
2549 HURLY's (Tho., *late a Priest of the Church of Rome*) Brief Account of his Conversion, 1766—FINCH's (Dr. R. P.) Hints for the Right Improvement of the Fast, 1779, and other Tracts, in 1 vol. 12mo. 2s 6d . ———

2550 Hussey's (Dr. Chr.) Twenty Sermons on various subjects, 8vo. *calf*, 2s 6d . . 1755

2551 Hutchinson's (Fra., *Bp. of Down aad Connor*) Defence of the Antient Historians, with a particular Application to the History of Ireland and Great Britain, and two Sermons, 8vo. *vellum, scarce*, 7s 6d . . Dublin, 1734

2552 ———— (H. M.) Reasons for Conservatism, as exhibited in a brief Statement of the Character of the Civil Constitution, and Church of England, 8vo. *bds*. 4s 6d . 1840

2553 ———— (Roger) Works, containing, the Image of God, or Layman's Book; Sermons on the Lord's Supper, &c. edited by John Bruce, 8vo. *bds*. 12s . Camb. 1842

2554 Hutton's (J. H.) Horæ Ecclesiasticæ : Practical Essays on the Documents of the United Church, 12mo. *hf. bd*. 1s 6d 1807

2555 Huyshe's (Francis) Specimen of an intended publication, which was to have been entitled, "A Vindication of them that have the rule over us, for not having cut out 1 John v. 7, 8, from the Authorized Version," being an Examination of Porson's Letter to Travis, 8vo. *bds*. 2s 6d . 1827

2556 Hyperius (Andreas) de Theologo, seu de Ratione Studio Theologici, libri IIII., sm. 8vo. *calf*, 4s . Basil. 1582

2557 ———— Practise of Preaching, otherwise called the Pathway to the Pulpit ; conteyning an excellent Method how to Frame Divine Sermons, and to Interpret the Holy Scriptures according to the capacitie of the vulgar people ; Englished by Iohn Ludham : hereunto is added, an Oration concerning the Lyfe and Death of the same Hyperius, sm. 4to. black letter, *very rare, new in stamped calf*, 9s . London, Tho. East, 1577

A few leaves at the beginning mended.

2558 Hymni Ecclesiastici novo cultu adornati, auctore Mart. Claire, 12mo. *vignettes, fine clean copy, blue morocco, gilt leaves, tooled*, 15s
Par. 1676

2559 Ignatius (S. Episc. Antioch.) Epistolæ genuinæ et suppositiæ, *Gr. et Lat*. cum XII. Exercitationibus in eundem Ignatium, auctore N. Vedelio, 4to. *calf*, 5s . Genevæ, 1623

2560 ———— Epistolæ genuinæ S. Ignatii, quæ nunc primum lucem vident ex Bibl. Florentina. Adduntur S. Ignatii Epistolæ, quales vulgo circumferuntur. Adhæc S. Barnabæ Epistola. Accessit universis translatio vetus. Edidit et notas addidit J. Vossius, *Gr. et Lat*. 4to. *calf, neat*, 6s — *vellum*, 5s 6d Amst. 1646

2561 ———— Epistolæ VII. genuinæ, *Gr. et Lat*. (Ed. C. Aldrich.) 8vo. *scarce, calf*, 8s . Oxon. 1708

2562 ———— Epistolæ genuinæ, *Gr. et Lat*. cum annotationibus Jo. Pearsoni, Episc. Cestriensis, et Tho. Smithi ; accedunt Acta genuina Martyrii S. Ignatii, Epistola S. Polycarpi ad Philippenses, et Smyrnensio Ecclesiæ Epistola de S. Polycarpi Martyrio, best edition, 4to. large paper, *calf*, 12s . *ib*. 1709

[58, GREAT QUEEN STREET,

2563 IGNATIUS.—The Ancient Syriac Version of the Epistles of St. Ignatius to St. Polycarp, the Ephesians and the Romans; together with Extracts from his Epistles: edited, with an English Translation and Notes, also the Greek Text of these three Epistles, corrected according to the authority of the Syriac Versions, by W. Cureton, M. A., 8vo. *bds.* 10s 6d . 1845

2564 IGNATIUS LOIOLA (S.) De Vita et Moribus ejus, libri III. auctore J. P. Maffeio, 12mo. *portrait, calf, 3s*   *Duaci,* 1621

2564* ———— Exercitia Spiritualia, cum sensu eorumdem explanato, et Directorium auctore P. J. Diertens, 2 vols. 12mo. *sewed, 9s*   *August. Taurin.* 1838

5265 ILBACHIUS (Odacris) Acta Sanctorum Christi Martyrum Vindicata ab Odacre Ilbachis sive a Jacobo Laderbachio, 2 vols. 4to. *calf,* £1. *5s* . . *Romæ,* 1723

2566 INCIDENTS of the Apostolic Age in Britain, sm. 8vo. *bds. 6s*   1844

2567 INDEX Librorum Expurgatorum, illustrissimi Gasparis Quiroga Card. et Archiep. Toletani, generalis inquisitoris, jussu editus, 4to. *calf, very rare, 6s* . *Salmuri,* 1601

"This was edited by Mornay du Plessis, who exposes with convincing evidence the fact, and the dishonesty of attacking the most distinguishing and important doctrines of the Bible, and ancient Christian writers through the sides of the Indexes, which do little more than verbally repeat them."—*Mendham.*

2568 ———— Indices Expurgatorii duo, Testes Fraudum ac Falsationum Pontificiarum; quorum prior jussu Philippi II. atq; Albani Ducis consilio concinnatus est in Belgio, anno 1571; posterior editus jussu G. Guiroga, Card. et Arch. Tolet. anno 1571. Additus est Index Librorum Prohibitorum cum registris confectis per Patres a Tridentino Synodo delectos, &c., sm. 8vo. *vellum, 8s Hanov.* 1611

2569 INDEX Librorum Prohibitorum usque ad annum 1681 — Eidem accedit Appendix [usque ad Febr. 1753.] sm. 8vo. *bds. 6s*   *Romæ,* 1704

2570 ———— Librorum Prohibitorum Benedicti XIV. jussu recognitus, atque editus, 8vo. *front. neat, 7s 6d* . *ib.* 1758

2571 ———— Librorum Prohibitorum Benedicti XIV. jussu recognitus, 8vo. *neat, 4s* . *ib.* 1770

2572 ———— Librorum Prohibitorum a Sixto V. Papa confectus et publicatus: at verò a successoribus ejus suppressus. Edente Jos. Mendham, 4to. LARGE PAPER, *bds. 7s 6d*   1835

2573 ———— Librorum Prohibitorum, juxta exemplar Romanum, editum anno 1835, 12mo. *sewed, 5s*   *Mechliniæ,* 1838

2574 ———— An exact Reprint of the Roman Index Expurgatorius, edited, with a preface, by Rd. Gibbings, A. D. 12mo. *bds. 7s 6d*   *Dublin,* 1837

2575 ———— An Index of Prohibited Books, by command of Gregory XVI. in 1835; being the latest specimen of the Literary Policy of the Church of Rome, by the Rev. Jos. Mendham, 12mo. *portrait of Pope Gregory, bds. 3s* . 1840

2576 INDIANS.—The Agreement of the Customs of the East-Indians with those of the Jews and other ancient People, 8vo. *plates, calf,* 2s 6d . . 1705

2577 INETT's (Dr. John) Origines Anglicanæ ; or, a History of the English Church, beginning where Bp. Stillingfleet has ended his History of the British Church, 2 vols. in 1, folio, *calf, very scarce,* £3. 3s
Lond. 1704— Oxf. 1710
2578 INFALLIBILITY.—Doubts concerning the Roman Infallibility, 4to. *sewed,* 2s . . 1688
2579 INGELO's (Dr. Nath.) Sermons preached at St. Paul's, April 17, 1659, 12mo. 1s 6d . 1659
2580 ——— Discourse concerning Repentance, 8vo. *neat,* 2s 1677
2581 INGRAM's (Geo.) Popish Doctrine of Transubstantiation refuted, and the Catholic Doctrine of the Real Presence vindicated, 8vo. *bds.* 5s . . 1840
2582 ——— True Character of the Church of England, as exhibited in her Antiquity, Orders, and Liturgies, 8vo. *bds.* 5s 1838
2583 INNES's (Dr. Alex.) Twelve Sermons on several occasions, 8vo. *calf,* 2s . . 1726
2584 INQUISITION.—Histoire de l'Inquisition et son Origine, 12mo. *neat,* 2s 6d . *Cologne,* 1693
2585 IRELAND's (Dean) Paganism and Christianity compared, in a course of Lectures to the King's Scholars at Westminster, 8vo. *hf. bd. calf,* 4s 6d—*bds.* 3s 6d . 1809
2586 IRENÆI (S. Episc.) Opera Omnia, Græce et Latine, *Editio Benedictina,* novis fragmentis Gr. aucta, studio Renati Massuet, folio, *calf, scarce,* £4. 10s . *Par.* 1710
2587 ——— idem, editio nova, cui accedunt Fragmenta a Pfaffio inventa ; necnon S. Maffæi Epistolæ duæ de Fragmentorum eorundem auctore cum Pfaffii Responsis; denique Fr. F. M. Leoni in Maffæi et Pfaffii Controversiam Epistolæ tres, 2 vols. folio, *very scarce, vellum,* £7. . *Venet.* 1734
2588 ——— Fragmenta Anecdota, *Gr. et Lat.* Dissertationibus duabus de Oblatione et Consecratione Eucharistiæ, illustravit, denique Liturgia Græca J. Grabii, et Dissertatione de Prejudiciis Theologicis ; ed. C. M. Pfaffius, 8vo. *calf,* 9s *Hagæ Com.* 1715
2589 IRONS's (Wm. J.) Parochial Lectures on the Holy Catholic Church, 8vo. *bds.* 2s 6d . . 1837
2590 ——— Parochial Lectures on the Apostolical Succession, (second series) 8vo. *bds.* 4s 6d . 1837
2591 ISAIAH, A new Translation ; with a Preliminary Dissertation and Notes, by Robert Lowth, Bp. of London, 4to. *calf,* 10s 6d 1779

" A sublime and admirably executed version."—*Horne.*

2592 ISENBERG and KRAPF. . Journals of the Rev. Messrs. Isenberg and Krapf, Missionaries of the Church Missionary Society, detailing the proceedings in Shoa and other parts of Abyssinia in 1839-42; with a Geographical description of Abyssinia, &c. by J. M'Queen, Esq. *and two maps,* 8vo. *bds.* 6s 1843
2593 ISHAM's (Dr. Z.) Divine Philosophy, containing the Books of Job, Proverbs, and Wisdom, with Explanatory Notes, 8vo. *calf,* 4s 1706

[58, GREAT QUEEN STREET,

2594 ISIDORUS (S. *Pelusiota*) de Interpretatione Divinæ Scripturæ Epistolarum libri IV. folio, *vellum*, £1. 1s

2595 —————— de Interpretatione Divinæ Scripturæ Epistolarum libri V. Gr. et Lat. folio, *calf*, BEST EDITION, £1. 15s   *Ex Officina Commeliniana*, 1606   *Par.* 1638

"Isidorus Pelusiota has left us numerous short epistles, which display more piety, ingenuity, and judgment, than the larger volumes of some others."

2596 —————— Le Combat des Chrestiens, avec sa Vie, 12mo. *calf, 2s*   *ib.* 1676

2597 ISIDORI (Hispalensis Episcopi) Opera, e Vetustis exemplaribus emendata, nunc denuo diligentissime correcta, atque aliquibus Opusculis, Appendicis loco aucta J. Griel, 2 vols. folio, *frontispiece, calf, very scarce*, £5. 5s   *Matriti*, 1778

2598 —————— idem, recensente Faustino Arevalo, 7 vols. 4to. *portrait, fine copy, vellum,* £6   *Romæ*, 1797-1803

"One of the brightest ornaments of the Church of Spain. His works, still extant, display his extensive learning, and amply account for the admiration with which he was regarded by his contemporaries."—*Dowling.*

2599 ITTIGIUS (L. Tho.) Bibliotheca Patrum Apostolicorum, Græco-Latina, qua continentur Epistolæ, etc. S. Clementis, S. Ignatii, et S. Polycarpi: cum est, Dissertatio de Patribus Apostolicis, sm. 8vo. *neat,* 8s 6d   *Lipsiæ*, 1699

2600 —————— idem, 8vo. *vellum,* 8s   *ib.* 1699

2601 —————— de Bibliothecis et Catenis Patrum Tractatus, sm. 8vo. *vellum, scarce,* 12s   *ib.* 1707

2602 —————— de Hæresiarchis primi et secundi seculi Dissertatio, cum Appendice, 2 vols. in 1, 4to. *scarce, vellum,* 10s 6d   *ib.* 1690-96

2603 —————— aliud exemplar, 4to. *scarce, vellum,* 12s   *ib.* 1703

Bishop Tomline considered this the best work on the heresies of the Apostolic age.

2604 IVES (le Pere) Les Progres de l'Amour Divin; l'Amour Naissant, l'Amour Souffrant, 2 vols. in 1, 24mo. *neat,* 2s 6d   *Par.* 1643

2605 —————— (Cornelius) Sermons composed for a Country Congregation, 8vo. *bds.* 2s   *Oxford*, 1832

2606 IZACKE's (Rd.) Remarkable Antiquities of the City of Exeter, 8vo. *map and cuts of arms, calf,* 4s   1681

2607 JABLONSKI (M.) Thorn Affligée, ou relation de ce qui s'est passé dans cette ville depuis le 16 Juillet, 1724 : traduite de l'Allemande par M. C. L. de Beausobre, 12mo. *plates, calf gilt, marbled leaves,* 6s   *Amst.* 1726

2608 JACKSON's (Tho. Pres. C. C. C. Oxon.) Works, with his Life by Edward Vaughan, and edited by Barnabas Oley, M.A. *best edition,* 3 vols. folio, *old calf, very scarce,* £6. 6s—*fine copy,* £7. 7s 1673

2609 —————— Works, *new edition,* with his Life, &c. 12 vols. 8vo. *bds.* £4. 14s 6d—*calf gilt,* £6. 6s   *Clarendon Press,* 1844

"Corpus Christi College may glory that it had Bp. Jewell, Dr. John Reynolds, and Dr. Tho. Jackson of that foundation ; the third famous for his most excellent Exposition of the Creed, and for his other treatises; all such as have given greatest satisfaction to men of the greatest learning."—*Walton's Life of Hooker.*

2611 [JACKSON's (Francis)] Occasional Letters on several subjects, 8vo. *calf, scarce*, 4s . . 1745
2612 ——— (*John*) Reply to Dr. Waterland's Defence of his Queries, wherein is contained a full state of the whole Controversy, 8vo. *calf*, 3s . 1722
2613 ——— Defense of Human Liberty, in Answer to the principal Arguments which have been alledged against it; and particularly to Cato's Letters, 8vo. *calf*, 2s 6d . 1725
2614 ——— Chronological Antiquities: or the Antiquities and Chronology of the most ancient Kingdoms, from the Creation for 5000 Years, 3 vols. 4to. *calf*, 16s . 1752
2615 ——— (Lawrence) Examination of a Book, entitled, "The True Gospel of Jesus Christ asserted," by Tho. Chubb, and also of his Appendix on Providence, with a Dissertation on Episcopacy, 8vo. *calf*, 3s . 1739
2616 JACOBSON (Wm.) S. Clementis Romani, S. Ignatii, S. Polycarpi, quæ supersunt: accedunt S. Ignatii et Polycarpi Martyria, recensuit, adnotationes, variorum et suis illust. 2 vols. 8vo. *bds.* £1. 1s
Oxonii, 1840
2617 JACOMB's (Dr. Tho.) Treatise of Holy Dedication, both Personal and Domestick, 8vo. *fine copy, old blue morocco, gilt leaves*, 7s 6d . 1668
2618 ———— another copy, 8vo. *calf*, 4s . 1668
Addressed to the citizens of London after the Great Fire.
2619 JAMES's (Dr. John) Comment upon the Collects, 12mo. *bds.* 3s . 1840
2620 ———— Christian Watchfulness in the Prospect of Sickness, Mourning, and Death, 12mo. *bds.* 5s 6d 1843
2621 ———— (Tho.) The Jesuites Downfall, threatened against them by the Secular Priests for their wicked lives, accursed manners, heretical doctrine, and more than Matchiavellian Policie; together with the Life of Father Parsons, an English Jesuite, small 4to. *rare, hf. bd. calf*, 9s . *Oxford*, 1612
2622 ———— Two short Treatises against the Order of Begging Friars, compiled by that famous Doctour of the Church, John Wicliffe, and faithfully printed according to two ancient Manuscript copies, *Oxford*, 1608 — An Apologie for John Wicliffe, shewing his Conformitie with the now Church of England, with Answere to the slanderous objections of Father Parsons and others, *wants a few leaves at the end, ib.* 1608—in 1 vol. sm. 4to. *hf. bd. rare*, 12s .
2623 ——————— Bellum Papale, sive Concordia discors Sixti V. et Clementis VIII. circa Hieronymianam Editionem S. Bibliorum, 4to. *bds.* 7s 6d . 1600
2624 ——— idem, 12mo. *calf*, 8s 1678
2625 ——————— Treatise of the Corruption of Scripture, Councils, and Fathers, by the Prelats, Pastors, and Pillars of the Church of Rome for maintenance of Popery. 8vo. *fine copy, calf, scarce*, 14s . . 1688

[58, GREAT QUEEN STREET,

2626 JAMESON (Will.) Nazianzeni Querela et Votum Justum ; the Fundamentals of the Hierarchy examined and disproved, 4to. *calf, 2s*
Glasgow, 1697
2627 ———— Spicilegia Antiquitatum Ægypti atque ei Vicinarum Gentium, sm. 8vo. *vellum, 4s 6d* . *Glasguæ,* 1720
2628 ———— ( ) Critical and Practical Exposition of the Pentateuch, with notes, and two Dissertations on the Mosaic History of the Creation, and on the Destruction of the Seven Nations of Canaan, folio, *hf. bd. calf, 10s* . 1748

This copy belonged to Dr. Magee, Abp. of Dublin, and has his autograph on the title.

2629 ———— another copy, fol. *calf, 12s* 1748
2630 ———— (Dr. John) Vindication of the Doctrine of Scripture, and of the Primitive Faith, concerning the Deity of Christ, in answer to Dr. Priestley's History of Early Opinions, &c. 2 vols. 8vo. *calf, neat, 9s* . *Edinb.* 1794
2631 JANSENIUS (Cornelius, *Episc. Iprensis*). Augustinus, seu Doctrina S. Augustini de humanæ Naturæ Sanitate, ægritudine, medicina, adversus Pelagianos et Massilienses, 3 tom. in 1, folio, *calf, £1. 10s*
Rothom. 1652

" This celebrated work of Jansenius gave such a wound to the Romish Church, as neither the power nor wisdom of its pontiffs, will ever be able to heal. The doctrine of Augustine concerning man's natural corruption, and the nature and efficacy of that Divine grace which alone can efface this unhappy stain, is here unfolded at large, and illustrated, for the most part, in Augustine's own words."
—*Mosheim*. It was condemned by a bull of Urban VIII., confirmed by Innocent X. and Alexander VIII.

2632 ———— Augustinus Europæus perperam dictus in ferali famosarum suarum Pentade per Augustinum triumphatus, damnatus, priusquam natus atque Apostolico fulmine ictus, opera et studio Ph. Van Wavre, 8vo. *neat, scarce, 6s* *Antv.* 1709
2633 JANSENISM. La secrete Politique des Jansenistes, et l'estat present de la Sorbonne de Paris, decouverts par un Docteur, 18mo, *stamped calf, 4s 6d* . *Troyes,* 1667
2634 ———— Réponse a la Bibliotheque Janseniste, avec des remarques sur la Refutation des Critiques de M. Bayle, et des Eclaircissemens sur les Lettres de M. de Saleon, Eveque de Rhodes à M. Bossuet, Eveque de Troies. *Nanci,* 1740—Le vraie Doctrine de l'Eglise, sur les Excommunications injustes : opposé a la doctrine de la Bulle Unigenitus, *title wanting*. 2 vols. in 1, 12mo. *neat, 3s 6d* ————
2635 JAQUELOT ( ) Sermons sur divers textes, 2 vols. 12mo. *calf, neat, 3s 6d* . *Amst.* 1710
2636 ———— another copy, 2 vols. 12mo. *calf, 4s* *ib.* 1732
2637 ———— another copy, 2 vols. 12mo. *hf. bd. calf, neat, 4s*
Geneve, 1767
2638 JASHER. The Book of Jasher : with Testimonies and Notes, translated into English from the Hebrew, by Flaccus Albinus Alcuinus, who went a pilgrimage into the Holy Land and Persia, where he discovered this volume in the city of Gazna, 4to. *bds. rare, 9s—hf. bd. calf, 10s 6d* . *Bristol,* 1829

A clumsy forgery, by one Jacob Ilive, originally published in 1751. Of this edition the above is an unacknowledged reprint.

2639 JASHER (The Book of), with " Bibliographical Notes on the same by T. H Horne, B.D." 4to. *bds.* 12*s*   1829—1833

2640 JAY's (Will.) Sermons, 2 vols. 8vo. *bds.* 10*s* 6*d*   1830

2641 JEBB's (Jo. *Bp. of Limerick*) Sacred Literature; comprising a review of the Principles of Composition laid down by Bp. Lowth, &c. 8vo. *calf gilt,* 10*s*   1820

2642 ——— —— Practical Theology : comprising Discourses on the Liturgy and Principles of the Church of England and Ireland ; Critical and other Tracts ; and a Speech in the House of Peers, 2 vols. 8vo. *hf. bd. calf,* 12*s*   1830

2643 ——— ——— Practical Theology, &c. 2 vols. 8vo. *bds.* 12*s*   1837

2644 ——— —— Divine Economy of the Church, 18mo. *bds.* 3*s* 6*d*   1840

2645 JEFFERY's (Dr. John, *Archd. of Norw.*) Complete collection of his Sermons and Tracts, 2 vols. 8vo. *portrait, calf,* 4*s* 6*d*   1751

2646 ——— —— (Tho.) Christianity the perfection of all Religion, Natural and Revealed, wherein some of the principal Prophecies relating to the Messiah in the Old Testament, are shewn to belong to him in the literal sense, 8vo. *calf,* 2*s*   1728

2647 ——— —— Christianity the perfection of all Religion, 1728—The true Grounds and Reasons of the Christian Religion, [in answer to Collins], 1725—A Review of the Controversy between the Author of a Discourse of the Grounds and Reasons of the Christian Religion [Collins] and his Adversaries, 1726, 3 vols. in 2, 8vo. *calf,* 5*s* 6*d*

2648 JELLINGER's (Chr.) Three Treatises. I. The Spirituall Merchant. II. The unvaluable Worth of Man's Soul. III. The Usurer cast : whereunto is added, a Latin and English Disputation against the Popish Mass, 12mo. *neat,* 3*s*   1676

2649 JENKS's (Benj.) Prayers and Offices of Devotion for Families, and for particular Persons, 12mo. 1*s* 6*d*   1792

2650 ——— ——— Submission to the Righteousness of God, or the Necessity of trusting to a better Righteousness than our own, 12mo. *neat,* 1*s* 6*d*   1755

2651 JENKINS's (Henry) Liturgy of the Church of England explained, with a brief Memoir of the Apostles, &c. in a series of familiar letters, 12mo. *sewed,* 1*s* 6*d*   1823

2652 ——— —— (Dr. Robert) The Reasonableness and Certainty of the Christian Religion, 2 vols. 8vo. *calf,* 5*s*   1721

" Dr. Jenkins's work," says Mr. Orme, " is now less attended to than it deserves. It contains a very considerable portion of correct and useful information, it shews that the author was a man both of learning and research on the antiquity, the inspiration, the style, the canon, the various readings, the chronology, and the obscurity of the Scriptures ; his reasonings and statements are well deserving of attention. It possesses considerable merit."

2653 ——— —— (Robert C.) Plea for Christian Peace and Unity, and against the prevailing Spirit of Controversy, 12mo. *bds.* 1*s* 6*d* 1843

2654 JENKYN's (Will.) Exposition of the Epistle of Jude, 2 vols. 4to. *calf, scarce,* 16*s*   1652-54

" The work of a most rigid Presbyterian and Non-Conformist divine."—*Lowndes.*

2655 JENNINGS's (Dr. David) Jewish Antiquities ; or a Course of Lectures on the three first books of Godwin's Moses and Aaron ; with a Dissertation on the Hebrew Language, 2 vols 8vo. *calf,* 7*s* 6*d* 1766

[58, GREAT QUEEN STREET,

2656 JENNINGS'S (Dr. David) Jewish Antiquities, 2 vols. 8vo. *calf*, 8s—
calf, neat, 9s . 1808
2657 ———— another copy, 8vo. *calf neat*, 8s *Edinb.* 1808
2658 ———— (John) Two Discourses : the first, of Preaching Christ, the second, of particular and experimental Preaching : with a Preface by the Rev. Isaac Watts, 8vo. 1s . 1723
2659 JEPHSON'S (Alex.) Discourse concerning the Religious Observation of the Lord's Day, 8vo. *calf*, 2s 6d . 1738
2660 JESSE (Wm.) on the Scriptures, intended to encourage the Study of the English Translation of the Bible ; with a Visitation Sermon, 8vo. *bds.* 2s 6d . 1799
2661 JESUITS. Canones Congregationum Generalium Soc. Jesu, cum aliis nonnullis ad praxim pertinentibus, 12mo. *vellum, scarce*, 6s
Romæ, 1581
2662 ———— Constitutiones Soc. Jesu, cum earum Declarationibus, 8vo. *vellum, scarce*, 9s . *ib.* 1583
2663 ———— La Verité defendue pour la Religion Catholique en la cause des Jesuites, contre le Plaidoyé d'Antoine Arnaud, par Francois des Montaignes, *Liege*, 1596—Plaidoyé de M. Ant. Arnauld pour l'Université de Paris, contre les Jesuites, *Par.* 1594—Plaidoyé sur lequel a esté donné contre les Jesuites, l'arrest du 16 Oct. 1597, inseré à la fin d'iceluy, *ib.* 1597, *in one* vol. sm. 8vo. *vellum*, 4s —
From the Library of Colbert.
2664 ———— Historia Societatis Jesu, (Pars I.) authore Nic. Orlandino. —Pars II. auctore Fra. Sacchino, 2 vols. sm. folio, *calf*, 14s
Col. Agr. 1615-21
The two first parts of a History of the Society of Jesuits by Orlandinus, Sacchinus, Passinua, Juvencus, and Cordara. A complete set is of the utmost rarity.
2665 ———— MIRÆUS (Aubertus) de Congregationibus Clericorum in Communi Viventium, ut Theatinorum, Societatis Jesu, Barnabitarum, Somaschæ, Oratorii, Doctrinæ Christianæ, et aliorum, 12mo. *vellum*, 4s 6d . *Coloniæ*, 1632
2666 ———— Index Generalis in omnes Libros Instituti Soc. Jesu, 12mo. *vellum*, 5s . *Antv.* 1635
2667 ———— Alph. de Vargas Relatio ad Reges et Principes Christianos de Stratagematis politicis Societatis Jesu, 12mo. *vellum*, 3s 1641
2668 ———— Bullæ, Decreta, Canones, Ordinationes, Instructiones, Epistolæ, &c. quæ instituti Societatis Jesu impressioni Antverpiensi accesserunt ab anno 1636, 12mo. *neat*, 4s *Antv.* 1665
2669 ———— Anatomia Societatis Jesu ; seu Probatio Spiritus Jesuitarum. Item, Arcana Imperii Jesuitici, Instructione secretissima pro Superioribus ejusdem, et Deliciarum Jesuiticarum Specimina, &c. 4to. *sewed*, 6s . 1668
2670 ———— Le Cabinet Jesuitique, contenant plusieurs pieces tres curieuses, &c., 12mo. *front. calf*, 2s 6d *Cologne*, [*Amst.*? 1674]
2671 ———— Elogia Societatis Jesu, sive Propugnaculum Pontificum, Conciliorum, Cardinalium, Antistitum, necnon Imperatorum, Regum, Principum et aliorum Virtute, Religione, omnique Literatura illustrium (etiam Hæreticorum) testimoniis quà expressis verbo, quà scripto consignatis constructum a P. Christ. Gomez. ejusd. Soc. 4to. *uncut, very scarce*, 12s . *Antverp.* 1677

2672 JESUITS. Le Jesuite Secularisé, 12mo. *sewed, uncut,* 1s 6d
Cologne, [*Amst.?*] 1683
2673 ———— Les Enluminaires du fameux Almanach des PP. Jesuites, intitulé la Deroute des Jansenistes, 12mo. *front. calf,* 2s 6d
Liege, 1683
2674 ———— Le Jesuite Défroqué, ou les Ruses de la Societé, 18mo. *hf. bd. vellum,* 2s Rome, [*Amsterdam?* 1683]
2675 ———— Corpus Institutorum Societatis Jesu, 2 thick vols. 4to. *calf, scarce,* £1. 16s . Antv. 1702
2676 ———— La Morale des Jesuites, extraite fidelement de leurs livres, par un docteur de Sorbonne, 3 vols. 12mo. *calf,* 6s
Suivant la copie imprimée à Mons, 1702
2677 ———— Artes Jesuiticæ in sustinendis pertinaciter Novitatibus damnabilibusque Sociorum laxitatibus. Clementi XI. denuntiatæ. 12mo. *vellum,* 3s . Salisburgi, 1703
2678 ———— Artes Jesuiticæ in sustinendis pertinaciter novitatibus laxitatibusque Sociorum S. D. N. Clementi XI. denuntiatæ. [Auctore Hen. de S. Ignatio, Presb.] 12mo. *calf,* 3s Argent. 1710
2679 ———— Tuba altera majorem clangens sonum, ad Papam Clementem XI. Imperatorem, Reges, Principes, &c. de necessitate longè maxima reformandi Societatem Jesu, 12mo. *calf,* 4s *ib.* 1714
2680 ———— JOUVENCI (Joseph) Recueil de pieces touchant l'Histoire de la Compagnie de Jesus, 12mo. *calf,* 5s Liége, 1716
2681 ———— Secreta Monita Societatis Jesu, *Latin* and *English,* 18mo. *calf, very scarce,* 4s 6d . [1723?]
2682 ———— A Parallel of the Doctrine of the Pagans, with the Doctrine of the Jesuits, and that of the Constitution Unigenitus issued by Pope Clement XI. (Translated by Steph. Whatley.) 8vo. *calf, fine copy,* 4s . 1726
2683 ———— Procès contre les Jésuites, pour servir de suite aux Causes Celèbres, 12mo. *sewed,* 1s 6d . Brest, 1750
2684 ———— Problême Historique, qui des Jesuites, ou de Luther et Calvin, ont le plus nui a l'Eglise Chrétienne? 2 vols. 12mo. *cf.* 7s 6d
Utr. 1758
2685 ———— Nouvelles interessantes au sujet de l'attentat commis le 3 Sept. 1758, sur la personne sacrée du Rois de Portugal, 12mo. *neat,* 2s . . 1759
2686 ———— Observations sur la conduite du Ministre de Portugal dans l'Affaire des Jesuites, 12mo. 2s . Avignon, 1760
2687 ———— Les Jesuites criminels de Leze-Majesté, dans la theorie et dans la pratique, 12mo. *calf,* 4s 6d Haye, 1760
2688 ———— Reflections d'un Portugais sur le Mémorial présenté par les Peres Jesuites à Clement XIII. 12mo. *nt.* 2s 6d Lisbonne, [1760?]
2689 ———— Histoire generale de la Naissance et du Progrès de la Compagnie de Jesus, 4 tom. 12mo. *calf,* 8s 1761
2690 ———— Appel à la Raison des écrits et libelles publiés par la passion, contre les Jesuites de France, 12mo. *neat,* 2s 6d *Brux.* 1762
2691 ———— Compte rendu des Constitutions des Jésuites, par M. L. R. de Caradduc de la Chalotais, Procureur général du Roi au Parlement de Bretagne, 12mo. *calf,* 2s . 1762
2692 ———— another edition, 12mo. *calf,* 2s 1762

[58, GREAT QUEEN STREET,

2693 JESUITS. L'Apologie des Jesuites convaincue d'attentats contre les loix divines et humains, 3 vols. 12mo. *hf. bd. 4s* 1763
2694 ———— Compte Rendu des Constitutions des Jésuites, par M. J. P. F. de Bipert de Monclar, Procureur général du Roi au Parlement de Provence, 12mo. *calf, 3s* 1763
2695 ———— Histoire impartiale des Jesuites dépuis leur établissement jusqu'à leur premiere expulsion, 2 vols. 12mo. *calf, 6s* 1768
2696 ———— Histoire Religieuse, Politique et Littéraire, de la Compagnie de Jésus, composée sur les documents, inédits et authentiques par J. Crétineau-Joly, 5 vols. 8vo. *portraits, and facsimiles of documents, sewed,* £2. 2s . *Par.* 1845
2697 JESUP'S (————) Lives of Picus (Prince of Mirandula) and Pascal; with a Parallel between those two Christian Worthies, 8vo. *calf, 2s* 1723
2698 JEWELL'S (John, Bp. *of Sarum*) Works: with a brief Discourse of his Life, folio, Black letter, *a few leaves of the dedication slightly stained, calf, neat,* £3. 10s . 1609
2699 ———— another copy, *wanting the dedication and life,* folio, *calf,* £2. 10s . . 1609
2700 ———— Defense of the Apologie of the Churche of Englande, conteininge an Answeare to a certaine booke lately set foorthe by M. Hardinge, and entituled, A Confutation, &c. whereunto there is also newly added, an Answeare unto another like Booke by the said M. Hardinge, entituled, A Detection of sundrie foule Errours, folio, Black letter, *calf, title stained,* £1. 8s 1570
2701 ———— Defence of the Apologie of the Church of England, &c. folio, Black letter, *neat, fine copy, but imperfect at the end,* 15s 1611
2702 ———— Apologia Ecclesiæ Anglicanæ, 18mo. *hf. bd. calf, 2s 6d* *Lond.* 1626
From the library of the late Duke of Sussex.
2703 ———— idem, Græcè versa, interprete I. S[mith], 18mo. *calf, 2s* *Oxon.* 1614
2704 ———— Apologia Ecclesiæ Anglicanæ, 18mo. *calf, 4s Cant.* 1683
2704* ———— Apologia Ecclesiæ Anglicanæ; nuper recensuit, et notas addidit A. C. Campbell, 12mo. *hf. bd. 2s 6d—bds. 2s* *Pontefract,* 1812
2705 ———— Apologia Ecclesiæ Anglicanæ, 12mo. *bds. 2s* *Cantab.* 1818
2706 ———— Apology of the Church of England, translated by Tho. Cheyne, 8vo. *5s—calf neat, 6s*—another copy, *new in sprinkled calf gilt, 9s* . 1719
2707 ———— Apology for the Church of England, translated and illustrated with copious notes, by the Rev. S. Isaacson, 8vo. *port. bds. 5s* . . 1829
2708 ———— Apology of the Church of England; and an Epistle to Seignior Scipio concerning the Council of Trent; translated, with notes, 12mo. *calf, old style, 8s—bds. 5s* *Camb.* 1839
2709 ———— Two Treatises—I. On the Holy Scriptures—II. On the Sacraments, 12mo. *calf, old style, 8s 6d* *Oxford,* 1840

2710 JOANNIS (Fr. *Parisiensis Prædicatoris*) Determinatio de Modo Existendi Corpus Christi in Sacramento Altaris; [ed. P. Allix.] *Lond.* 1686—ALLIX (P.) de Messiæ duplici Adventu, Dissertationes duæ adversus Judæos, *ib.* 1701; *in one* vol. 12mo. *bds.* 3s 6d ——

2711 JOHNSON'S (John) Clergyman's Vade-Meeum; or, an Account of the ancient and present Church of England, the Duties and Rights of the Clergy, and of their Privileges and Hardships; containing also the Canonical Codes of the Primitive and Universal Church; and the Canonical Codes of the Eastern and Western Churches, translated at large from the original Greek, with explanatory notes, 2 vols. 12mo. *rough calf,* 9s . 1715

2712 ———— another copy, 2 vols. 12mo. *new in calf gilt, old style,* 14s . . 1715

2713 ———— fifth edition, enlarged, 2 vols. 12mo. *calf,* 11s 1723

2714 ———— sixth edition, corrected, 2 vols. 12mo. *calf,* 12s 1731

2715 ———— the same, 2 vols. 12mo. *fine copy, calf,* 13s 1731

2716 ———— Vol. 1, 12mo. *calf,* 4s . 1709

2717 ———— Life, by Dr. Tho. Brett, and Posthumous Tracts, viz.— The Primitive Communicant, a Sermon at Canterbury School Feast; and an Explanation of Daniel's Prophecy of the LXX. Weeks; with an Appendix, containing Letters by Dr. Geo. Hickes, Robert Nelson, and Mr. Johnson, 8vo. *hf. bd. calf,* 7s—*calf,* 8s 1748

2718 ———— (Samuel) Jovian; or, an Answer to Julian the Apostate, [by Dr. Geo. Hickes], 8vo. *calf,* 5s 6d 1683

2719 ———— Second Five Years Struggle against Popery and Tyranny, being a Collection of Papers published by him during his last imprisonment of five years and ten days, 8vo. *calf,* 2s—*old blue morocco,* 5s 6d . 1689

2720 ———— Scripture-Doctrine of Christ's Divinity, considered in six Sermons, 8vo. *calf,* 2s 6d . 1729

2721 ———— Laodicean Age; or, an Attempt to Prove that Christ's Seven Epistles to the Seven Churches in Asia, are to be understood in a Mystical and Prophetical sense, &c. 8vo. *calf,* 2s 6d 1734

2722 ———— XXXVI. Discourses, doctrinal and practical, upon the most important points of the Christian Religion, 2 vols. 8vo. *calf,* 5s . . 1740

2723 ———— Works, folio, *hf. bd.* 8s 6d . 1713

2724 ———— another copy, folio, *hf. bd.* 9s 1713
Contains the author's Life of Julian the Apostate, for which he was imprisoned, and fined 500 marks; together with his miscellaneous papers written during his five years' imprisonment.

2725 ———— (Dr. Samuel) Prayers and Meditations, published by Geo. Strahan, A.M., 8vo. *bds.* 2s 6d . 1785

2726 ———— another copy, 8vo. *calf,* 4s 6d 1807

2727 ———— Dictionary of the English Language, abridged from Todd's enlarged 4to. edition, by Alex. Chalmers, 8vo. *calf gilt,* 15s 1837

2728 JOHNSTONE'S (John) Way of Life, set forth in several Sermons before the Queen Dowager, 8vo. *bds.* 9s 1841

2729 JONAH, a faithful Translation, with Notes, &c. by Geo. Benjoin, 4to. *bds*. 5s . *Camb*. 1796
2730 ——— the same, 4to. *hf. bd. calf*, 5s 6d *ib*. 1796
2731 JONES's (Jeremiah) New and Full Method of Settling the Canonical Authority of the New Testament, 3 vols. 8vo. *calf*, 18s
Oxford, 1798
2732 [——— (John, *Vicar of Alconbury*)] Free and Candid Disquisitions relating to the Church of England, and the means of advancing Religion therein, 8vo. *calf*, 2s 6d 1750
2733 ——— (Dr. Rob.) Sermons on the Ten Commandments, 8vo. *bds*. 2s . . 1818
2734 ——— (Tho. *of Creaton*) Scripture Directory ; or, an Attempt to assist the Unlearned Reader to understand the General History of the Old and New Testament, 12mo. *bds*. 1s 6d 1813
2735 ——— another copy, 12mo. *hf. bd. calf*, 2s 6d 1821
2736 ——— (Dr. Walter) XVII. Sermons upon several subjects, 8vo. *calf*, 2s 6d . . 1741
2737 ——— (Will.) Commentary upon the Epistles to Philemon and the Hebrews, together with a compendious Explication of the Second and Third Epistles of Saint John, folio, *fine copy, scarce, calf*, 16s . . 1635
2738 ——— (Will. *of Nayland*) Theological, Philosophical, and Miscellaneous Works, with his Life, 12 vols. 8vo. *fine copy, port. calf gilt*, £5. 5s . 1801
2739 ——— Theological and Miscellaneous Works, with his Life by Stevens, 6 vols. 8vo. *portrait, new in calf gilt*, £3. 1810
2740 ——— Zoologia Ethica: a Disquisition concerning the Mosaic Distinction of Animals into clean and unclean, 8vo. *sewed*, 1s 6d
1771
2741 ——— Letters from a Tutor to his Pupils, 18mo. *morocco, gilt leaves*, 5s . *Oxford*, 1841
2742 JORTIN's (Dr. John) Works, viz. Life of Erasmus ; Discourses concerning the Truth of the Christian Religion, and Remarks on Ecclesiastical History ; Sermons on different subjects, and Dissertations —Miscellaneous Observations upon Authors, ancient and modern ; Tracts, Philological, Critical, and Miscellaneous, and Memoirs of the Life and Writings of Dr. Jortin, by Dr. Disney, &c. in all 22 vols. 8vo. *calf, lettered contents*, £5. . v. y.
From the library of the late Duke of Sussex.
2743 ——— Six Dissertations upon different subjects, 8vo. *calf*, 3s
1755
2744 ——— Sermons on different subjects, 7 vols. 8vo. *portrait, fine copy, calf*, £1. 11s 6d . 1787

"In these sermons good sense and sound morality appear, not indeed dressed out in the meritricious ornaments of a florid style, but in all the manly force and simple graces of natural eloquence. They will always be read with pleasure and edification"—*Knox's Essays*.

2745 ——— Discourses concerning the Truth of the Christian Religion ; and Remarks on Ecclesiastical History, 3 vols. 8vo. *port. bds*. 15s . . 1805

2746 JOSEPHUS (Flavius) Antiquitates Judaicæ, et Historia de Bello Judaico, *Gr. et Lat.* edente Edv. Bernard, folio, *calf*, 16*s* *Oxon.* 1700

2747 ——— —— Opera omnia, Græcè et Latinè, cum notis edidit Jo. Hudson, 2 vols. folio, *calf, gilt backs*, £1. 8*s*   *ib.* 1720

2748 ——— —— Opera omnia, Græce et Latine, accedunt notæ var. et Daubuz de Testimonio Josephi de Jesu Christi, Brinch Examen Chronologiæ Josephicæ, Noldius de Vita, &c. Herodum, &c. recensuit S. Havercampus, 2 vols. folio, *calf gilt, slightly wormed,* £1. 16*s*   .   *Amst.* 1726

2749 ——— —— de Bello Judaico Lib. VII. Ad fidem Codicum emendavit, variis lectionibus instruxit, et notis partim aliorum partim suis illustravit Edvardus Cardwell S.T.P., 2 vols. 8vo. *calf gilt,* £1. 1*s*   .   *Oxonii,* 1837

2750 ——— —— Histoire des Juifs, traduite par M. Arnauld d'Andilly— Histoire de la Guerre des Juifs contre les Romains ; Réponse à Appion ; Martyre des Machabées ; et sa Vie etc. traduit par M. Arnauld d'Andilly, 2 vols. folio, *fine copies, old red morocco, gilt leaves,* £3. 13*s* 6*d*   *Paris,* 1667-68

These volumes belonged to the great Colbert, and have his arms on the sides. They came from the library of the late Bishop of St. David's.

2751 ——— —— The Jewish History, being an Abridgment of Sir R. L'Estrange's Josephus, with a Continuation by J. Crull, M.D. 2 vols. 8vo. *plates, calf,* 4*s* 6*d*   .   1708

2752 ——— —— Genuine Works, translated, with three Dissertations concerning Jesus Christ, John the Baptist, James the Just, God's Command to Abraham, &c. translated by Wm. Whiston, 6 vols. 12mo. *calf,* 9*s*   .   *Edinb.* 1777

2753 ——— —— another copy, 4 vols. 8vo. *portrait, calf gilt, marbled leaves,* £1. 4*s*   .   .   1818

2754 ——— —— another copy, 4 vols. 8vo. *calf,* £1. 4*s*   1806

2755 JOUX (Pierre de) Prédication du Christianisme, ou Vérités de la Religion Chretienne, exposées dans une suite de Sermons et Prières, 4 vols. 8vo. *vellum,* 12*s*   *Genève,* 1803-4

2756 JULIAN. The Arguments of the Emperor Julian against the Christians, translated from the Greek fragments preserved by Cyril, Bishop of Alexandria, with extracts from the other Works of Cyril, relative to the Christians, by Thomas Taylor, 8vo. *hf. bd. morocco, uncut,* 5*s* 6*d*   .   .   1809

"*Very rare ; all the copies except two or three were destroyed.*"—*MS. Note.*

2757 JUNGENDRES (Seb. Jac.) Specimen Philologicum de Veterum Gentilium et Judæorum Theologia Mythica, 1728—Disquisitio in Notas characteristicas Librorum a typographiæ incunabulo ad An. 1500 impressorum, *Norib.* 1740—Ikenius (C.) Tractatus Talmudicus de Cultu quotidiano Templi, *Brem.* 1736—H. Grotii Defensio Fidei Catholicæ de Satisfactione Christi ; præmissa auctoris Vita etc. per Joach. Lange, *Lips.* 1730, *in one vol.* 4to. 3*s* 6*d*   ———

2758 JUNILIUS, (*Episc. Africanus*) In priora aliquot Geneseos Capita valde doctus et utilis Commentarius, *Basil.* 1538—Philonis Judæi Questionum et Solutionum in Genesin, de Mundo, de Nominibus Hebraicis, &c. *ib.* 1538, *in* 1 *vol.* 4to. *hf. bd. calf,* 4*s*   ———

[58, GREAT QUEEN STREET,

2759 JUNII (FRANCISCI) Etymologicon Anglicanum; ex autographo descripsit et accessionibus permultus auctum, edidit Edw. Lye. Præmittuntur Vita Auctoris et Grammatica Anglo-Saxonica, folio, *portrait, calf,* £1. 15*s* . *Oxonii,* 1743
2760 ———— Sacrorum Parallelorum libri tres, 4to. *calf,* 4*s*
Heidelb. 1588
2761 JURDAIN (Ignatius). The Life and Death of Mr. Ignatius Jurdain, one of the Alderman of Exeter, who departed this life July 15, 1640, drawn up and published by Ferd. Nicolls, 4to. 2*s* 1654
2762 JURIEU (Pierre) Abrégé de l'Histoire du Concile de Trente, 2 vols. 18mo. *front. calf,* 2*s* . *Amst.* 1683
2763 [————] Lettres Pastorales addressées aux fideles de France, qui gemissent sous la captivité de Babylon, 4to. *calf,* 3*s* 6*d*
Rotterdam, 1686
2764 ———— The Accomplishment of the Scripture Prophecies, or the approaching Deliverance of the Church, 8vo. *calf,* 4*s* 6*d* 1687
2765 ———— Plain Method of Christian Devotion, laid down in Discourses, Meditations, and Prayers; translated and revised by Wm. Fleetwood, Lord Bishop of Ely, 12mo. *calf,* 2*s* [1759]
2766 JUSTINI (S. Martyris) Opera, item Athenagoræ Atheniensis, Theophili Antiocheni, Tatiani Assyrii, et Hermiæ Philosophi tractatus aliquot, Gr. *et Lat.* folio, *portrait, old red morocco, arms on the sides,* £1. 11*s* 6*d* . *Paris.* 1636
2767 ———— Opera omnia; necnon TATIANI adversus Græcos Oratio, ATHENAGORÆ Legatio pro Christianis, S. THEOPHILI libri ad Autolycum, HERMIÆ Irrisio Gentilium philosophorum et Acta Martyrii Justini, Gr. et Lat. studio P. Maran, Mon. Benedict. folio, *best edition, calf,* £3. 13*s* 6*d* . *ib.* 1742
2768 ———— cum Tryphone Judæo Dialogus, *Græcè*; cum J. Langi versione *Lat.* Annexis Annotationibus Langi et Kortholti; edita à Sam. Jebb, 8vo. *calf,* 8*s*—*tree-marbled calf gilt,* 10*s* 6*d* 1719
2769 ———— Opera, Græce et Latinè, recensuit Prolegomenis Adnotatione ad Versione instruxit, Indicesque adjecit J. C. Otto; Præfatus est L. F. Baumgarten-Crusius, 2 vols. 8vo. *sewed,* 16*s* *Jenæ,* 1842
2770 ———— idem, 2 vols. in 1, 8vo. *calf gilt,* £1. 1*s* *ib.* 1842
2771 ———— Apologia Prima, edited, with a corrected Text and English Introduction and Notes by the Rev. W. Trollope, M.A. 8vo. *bds.* 7*s* 6*d* . *Camb.* 1845
2772 ———— Apologia Prima pro Christianis ad Antoninum Pium, Gr. et Lat.; edita à J. E. Grabe, *Oxon.* 1700—Apologia Secunda pro Christianis, Oratio Cohortatoria, Oratio ad Græcos, et de Monarchia Liber, Gr. et Lat.: Edita ab H. Hutchin, *ib.* 1703—2 vols. in 1, 8vo. *tree-marbled calf extra,* 12*s* . ————
2773 ———— Apologia pro Christianis, Gr. et Lat. Annotationes adjecit Carolus Ashton, 8vo. *tree-marbled calf extra,* 12*s* *Cantab.* 1768
2774 ———— Apologiæ duæ, et Dialogus cum Tryphone Judæo, Gr. et Lat. curâ Thirbii, folio, *calf,* £1. 1*s* *Lond. Bowyer,* 1772
Bishop Van Mildert's copy.
2775 ———— Some account of the Writings and Opinions of Justin Martyr, by John [Kaye] Bp. of Lincoln, 8vo. *bds.* 6*s* *Camb.* 1829
2776 ———— new edition, 8vo. *bds.* 7*s* 6*d* *ib.* 1840

2777 JUSTIN Martyr's Dialogue with Trypho the Jew, translated with Notes, by Hen. Brown, 2 vols. 8vo. *calf, scarce*, £1. 8s
Oxford, 1755
2778 JUSTINIANUS (Fabianus) de Sacra Scriptura, ejusque Usu ac Interpretibus Commentarius, 8vo. *vellum, 7s 6d*   *Romæ*, 1614
2779 KAYE's (Jo., *Bp. of Lincoln*) Ecclesiastical History of the Second and Third Centuries, illustrated from the writings of Tertullian, 8vo. *hf. bd. calf*, 10s 6d   *Camb.* 1826
2780 ———— Account of the Writings and Opinions of Clement of Alexandria, 8vo. *cloth bds.* 12s   1835
2781 KEACH's (Benjamin) Poems, viz.—War with the Devil; or, the Young Man's Conflict with the Powers of Darkness, *front*. 1676—The Glorious Lover; a Divine Poem, 1679—Sion in Distress; or, the Groans of the Protestant Church, 1681—Distressed Sion relieved, *front*. 1689—together 4 vols. 12mo. *uniform in calf*, 14s

2781* ———— War with the Devil, 12mo. *calf, neat*, 3s   1718
2782 —— —— Sion in Distress; or, the Groans of the Protestant Church, 12mo. *hf. bd. calf*, 4s 6d   1682
2783 [KEBLE's (Jo.)] Memorials and Communications addressed to his late Majesty's Commissioners of Inquiry into the State of the Established Church, from the Cathedral and Collegiate Churches of England and Wales, 8vo. *bds.* 3s 6d   1838
2784 ———— Primitive Tradition recognized in Holy Scripture, a Sermon; with a Postscript, and Catena Patrum, 8vo. *hf. bd. calf, neat*, 5s 6d   1839
2785 KEELING's (Barth.) Eight Discourses on the Harmony of the three first Evangelists, in their Accounts of the Malefactors crucified with our Blessed Lord, &c. 8vo. *sewed*, 1s 6d   *Oxford*, 1773
2786 KEITH's (Alex.) Signs of the Times, as denoted by the fulfilment of Historical Predictions traced down from the Babylonish Captivity to the present time, 2 vols. 12mo. *hf. bd. red morocco, uncut, gilt tops*, 7s   *Edinb.* 1832
2787 ———— (Rob.) History of the Affairs of Church and State in Scotland from the beginning of the Reformation to 1568, vol. 1, (*all published*), folio, *fine copy, calf, scarce*, £1. 10s   *ib.* 1734
2788 KELLETT's (Edw.) Tricœnium Christi: the Threefold Supper of Christ in the night that he was betrayed, folio, *frontispiece by W. Marshall, calf*, 10s   1641
2789 KELSEY's (Jos.) Sermons upon various occasions, 8vo. *calf*, 2s 6d   1703
2790 KEMPIS (Thomæ à) Opera Omnia, ad Autographa ejusdem emendata, et aucta; opera ac studio Henrici Sommalii, 3 vols. in 1, 8vo. *vellum, scarce*, 14s   *Coloniæ*, 1680
2791 ———— Christian's Pattern; in a Treatise of the Imitation of Jesus Christ, translated, with Meditations and Prayers, by S. Smith, D.D. 8vo. *plates, calf*, 4s 6d   1738
2792 ———— the same, translated by Geo. Stanhope, D.D. 8vo. *plates, calf*, 3s 6d   1742
2793 ———— another copy, 8vo. *hf. bd. russia*, 5s   1809

2794 KEMPIS's (Thomas à) Works, viz.—Christian's Pattern, translated by Stanhope, and the Sighs of a Penitent Soul; a Short Christian Directory; of Spiritual Exercises; of Spiritual Entertainments; translated by Geo. Hickes, D.D., wtth the Author's Life, 2 vols. 8vo. *plates, calf, 8s* . 1759-1710

2795 ——— Meditations, with Prayers, on the Life and Loving-kindness of our Lord Jesus Christ, translated by H. Lee, LL.B. 8vo. *neat, 4s 6d* . . 1760

2796 KEN (Tho., Bp. *of Bath and Wells*) A short Account of his Life, by W. Hawkins, Esq.; with a small specimen in order to a publication of his Works, 8vo. *fine portrait by Vertue, calf, neat, 4s* 1713

2797 KENNEDY's (Rann.) Cuhrch of England Psalm-Book; or, Portions of the Old and New Versions, 8vo. *bds. 2s* *Birm.* 1821

2798 ——— Thoughts on the Music and Words of Psalmody, as at present in use in the Church of England, 8vo. *bds. 2s* 1821

2799 KENNETT's (B.) Brief Exposition of the Apostles' Creed, according to Bp. Pearson, 8vo. *calf, 3s 6d* . 1705

2800 ——— the same, 8vo. *calf, 2s 6d* 1721

2801 ——— Essay towards a Paraphrase of the Psalms in English Verse; with a Paraphrase on the 3rd Chapter of the Revelations, by Basil Kennett, 8vo. *3s* . 1706

2802 ——— Sermons to a Society of British Merchants in Foreign Parts (Leghorn), 8vo. *calf, 3s* . 1715

2803 ——— (White, Bp. *of Peterb.*) Ecclesiastical Synods and Parliamentary Convocations in the Church of England, historically stated, and vindicated from the misrepresentations of Mr. Atterbury, 8vo. *old calf gilt, 9s* . 1701

2804 ——— Case of Impropriations, and of the Augmentation of Vicarages and other insufficient cures, stated by history and law, from the first usurpation of the Popes and Monks to Her Majesty's royal bounty, 8vo. *calf, 7s 6d* . 1704

2805 ——— Sermon at the Funeral of William, Duke of Devonshire, with some Memoirs of the Family of Cavendish, 8vo. *calf, 2s 6d* 1708

2806 [———] Bibliothecæ Americanæ Primordia; an Attempt towards laying the Foundation of an American Library, in several Books, Papers, and Writings, humbly given to the Society for the Propagation of the Gospel, 4to. *calf, 4s* . 1713

2807 ——— Register and Chronicle, Ecclesiastical and Civil: containing Matters of Fact delivered in the words of the most authentic Books, Papers, and Records, from the Restoration of King Charles II. Vol. I. (*all ever published*), folio, *fine copy, calf, £2.5s* . . 1728

2808 KENNEY's (A. H.) Principles and Practices of Pretended Reformers in Church and State, 8vo. *hf. bd. calf, uncut, 4s* 1819

2809 KENNICOTT (Benj.) Dissertatio Generalis in Vetus Testamentum Hebraicum; cum Variis Lectionibus, ex Cod. MSS. et impressis, folio, *bds. 8s* . . *ib.* 1780

2810 KENNICOTT's (Benj.) State of the Printed Hebrew Text of the Old Testament considered ; a Dissertation in two parts: Pt. I. compares 1 Chron. xi. with 2 Sam. v. and xxiii. ; and Pt. II. contains Observations on seventy Hebrew MSS. 8vo. *calf, 5s Oxford,* 1753

2811 ——— another copy, *interleaved with numerous Manuscript Notes by the late Dr. Jenkinson, Bp. of St. David's,* 2 vols. 8vo. *hf. bd. vellum, uncut,* 18s . *ib.* 1753

2812 ——— Annual Accounts of the Collation of Hebrew MSS. of the Old and New Testament, begun in 1760, and completed in 1769, *Oxf.* 1770—Two Dissertations, I. on the Tree of Life; II. on the Oblations of Cain and Abel, *ib.* 1747—A Letter to the Rev. Mr. Kennicott, in which his Defence of the Samaritan Pentateuch is examined, &c. by T. Rutherforth, D.D., *Camb.* 1761 ; *in one* vol. 8vo. *hf. bd. calf,* 8s .

From the library of the late Duke of Sussex.

2813 KENWRICK's (George) Surest Guide to Eternity; or, a Body of Divinity extracted from the Old and New Testament : in words of Scripture only, 8vo. *calf,* 3s . *Oxford,* ——

2814 KETT's (Hen.) History the Interpreter of Prophecy; or, a View of Scripture Prophecies and their Accomplishment, 2 vols. 8vo. *hf. bd. calf,* 7s . *ib.* 1799

2815 KETTLEWELL's (John) Works ; with an Account of his Life and Times, 2 vols. folio, *portrait, calf, neat, very scarce,* £2. 10s
1719

2816 ——— — The Measure of Christian Obedience, or, a Discourse shewing what obedience is necessary to a Regenerate State, &c., 4to. *calf, neat,* 4s . 1681

2817 ——— Help and Exhortation to Worthy Communicating, with suitable Devotions, 12mo. *calf,* 1s 6d . 1683

2818 ——— Help and Exhortation to Worthy Communicating, or a Treatise describing the Meaning, &c. of the Holy Sacrament, *portrait, calf,* 4s . 1706

2819 ——— the same, 8vo. *portrait, calf,* 4s . 1717

2820 ——— The great Evil and Danger of Profuseness and Prodigality, 18mo. 1s . . 1717

2821 K[EYWORTH] (T.) and J[ONES] (D.) Principia Hebraica, comprising a Grammatical Analysis of 564 Verses from the Psalms, and a concise Hebrew Grammar, 8vo. *bds. scarce,* 7s 6d 1817

2822 KIDDER's (Rd. *Bp. of Bath and Wells*) Commentary on the Five Books of Moses, 2 vols. 8vo. *calf,* 7s . 1694

" A learned and valuable work, though now not to be met with."—*Horne.*

2823 ——— Demonstration of the Messias, in which the Truth of the Christian Religion is proved, especially against the Jews, 3 vols. 8vo. *old calf gilt,* 15s . 1684-1700

2824 ——— best edition, folio, *calf,* £1. 1s 1726

2825 ——— another copy, folio, *calf, slightly stained,* 16s 1726

2826 KILLINBECK's (John) Eighteen Sermons on Practical subjects, 8vo. *calf, wormed,* 2s . *Nottingham,* 1717

2827 KING's (Edward) Morsels of Criticism, tending to illustrate some few passages in the Holy Scriptures, upon Philosophical Principles, 2 vols. 4to. *hf. bd. calf, uncut, neat*, 10s   1718-1800
2828 ———— Remarks on the Signs of the Times, with a Supplement, 4to. *calf*, 4s   . 1798-99
2829 ———— (Hen. *Bp. of Chich.*) Poems and Psalms: edited by the Rev. J. Hannah, 12mo. *bds.* 7s 6d   . *Oxford*, 1843
2830 ———— (J. *of Hull*) Sermons on important subjects, with a Sermon preached at his Funeral, by the Rev. J. Stillingfleet, 8vo. *calf*, 3s 6d   . *York*, 1782
2831 [———— (Peter, *Lord Chancellor,*)] Enquiry into the Constitution, Discipline, Unity, and Worship of the Primitive Church, 8vo. *calf, neat*, 4s 6d   . [1720]
*2832 ———— History of the Apostles' Creed; with Critical Observations on its several Articles, 8vo. *calf*, 4s 6d   . 1719
2833 [———— (Wm. *Abp. of Dublin*) State of the Protestants of Ireland, under the late King James' Government, 4to. *calf*, 5s   1691
2834 ———— another copy, 8vo. *calf*, 4s   *Cork*, 1768
 "This copious history is so well received, and so universally acknowledged to be as truly as it is finely written, that I refer my readers to the account of those matters, which is fully and faithfully given by that learned and zealous prelate."—*Burnet's Own Times*.
2835 ———— Discourse on Predestination, with Notes by Richard Whately, M.A., 8vo. *bds.* 4s   . 1821
2836 KIRBY's (Wm.) Seven Sermons on our Lord's Temptation; grounded on those of Bp. Andrews, with another from the same Author on the Passion, 8vo. *hf. bd. calf*, 4s 6d   *Ipswich*, 1829
2837 KIRWAN's (W. B. *Dean of Killala*) Sermons, with a Sketch of his Life, 8vo. *portrait, calf*, 5s 6d   . 1816
2838 KNATCHBULL (Norton) Animadversiones in libros Novi Testamenti, 12mo. *calf*, 1s 6d   . *Oxon.* 1677
 From the collection of the late Duke of Sussex.
2839 ———— Annotations upon some difficult Texts in all the Books of the New Testament, 8vo. *calf*, 4s   . *Camb.* 1693
2840 ———— another copy, 8vo. *calf*, 3s 6d   *ib.* 1693
 From the Library of the late Duke of Sussex.
2841 [KNIGHT's (Sam.)] True Doctrine of the most Holy and Undivided Trinity, vindicated from the misrepresentations of Dr. Clarke, with a Letter to the Rev. Dr. by Robert Nelson, 8vo. *bds.* 2s   1714
2842 ———— the same, with additions, 8vo. *calf*, 3s   1714-15
2843 KNOWLES (Dr. Tho.) The Passion; or, a Descriptive and Critical Narrative of the Incidents as they occurred on each day of the week in which Christ's Sufferings are commemorated: with Reflections, 12mo. *bds.* 2s   . 1780
2844 KNOX's (John) History of the Reformation of the Church of Scotland, folio, *calf*, 18s   . 1644
2845 ———— Liturgy of the Church of Scotland; or, Book of Common Order, as prescribed by the General Assembly, and used by the Churches of Scotland from 1564 to 1611. Edited by the Rev. John Cumming, D.D., 12mo. *bds.* 5s   1840

2846 KNOX's (Vicesimus) Sermons chiefly intended to promote Faith, Hope, and Charity, 8vo. *calf*, 3s 6d . 1796

2847 —————— Considerations on the Nature and Efficacy of the Lord's Supper, 12mo. *bds. 1s* . 1799

2848 KOECHERUS (Jo. Chr.) de Idolatria Literaria liber singularis, sm. 8vo. *bds. 3s* . *Hanov.* 1738

2849 KOERNERUS (Jo. Got.) Epitome Controversiarum Theologicarum, sm. 8vo. *hf. bd. 2s* . *Lips.* 1769

2850 KORAN ; (The) commonly called the Alcoran of Mohammed; translated from the original Arabic, with Notes and a Preliminary Discourse, by George Sale, 2 vols. 8vo. *calf gilt, 14s* 1825

2851 KRAZER (P. A.) de Apostolicis, necnon Antiquis Ecclesiæ Occidentalis Liturgiis, illarum Origine, Progressu, Ordine, Die, Hora, et Lingua, cæterisque Rebus ad Liturgiam Antiquam pertinentibus, Liber singularis, 8vo. *fine copy, calf extra, 12s*
Augustæ Vind. 1786

2852 KUEN (Mich.) Collectio Scriptorum rerum historico-monastico-ecclesiasticarum variorum Religiosorum Ordinum, 6 vols. in 5, folio, *rare, plates, calf, £2. 10s* . *Ulmæ*, 1755-65

The present copy came from the library of the late Duke of Sussex. Amongst other interesting pieces contained in the Monasticon Germanicum are Germania Canonico Augustiniana, ordine Alphabetico cooscripta ; Myræi Origines Carthusianorum Monasteriorum per orbem universum ; Ejusdem Origines Benedictinæ, &c.

2853 KUINOEL (Chr. Theoph.) Commentarius in libros Novi Testamenti historicos, 4 vols. 8vo. *sewed*, 14s *Lipsiæ*, 1824-37

2854 KYPKE (Geo. Dav.) Observationes Sacræ in Novi Fœderis libros, ex auctoribus potissimum Græcis et Antiquitatibus, 2 vols. in 1, 8vo. *old calf gilt, 7s* . *Wratisl.* 1755

2855 LABBE (Phil.) Eruditæ Pronuntiationis Catholici Indices, *Lond.* 1821 —Lud. KUSTERUS de vero Usu Verborum mediorum, eorumque differentiâ a verbis activis et passivis, operâ Edwardi Leedes, *ib.* 1822 ; *in one* vol. 12mo. *calf gilt, 3s* ——————

2856 LA CENE's Essay for a New Translation of the Bible, translated by Ross, *best edition*, 8vo. *calf*, 5s . 1727

2857 LA CROZE (M. V.) Histoire du Christianisme des Indes, 2 vols. 12mo. *front. old calf gilt,7s 6d* *La Haye*, 1758

2858 LACTANTIUS (L. C. F.) Divinarum Institutionum libri septem : Ejusdem de Ira Dei liber I. ; de Opificio Dei liber I. : Epitome in libros suos; Phœnix ; Carmen de Dominica Resurrectione ; et Tertulliani liber apologeticus, cum indice, sm. 8vo. *fine copy, green morocco, gilt leaves*, 16s
Venetiis, in œdibus hœredum Aldi, &c. 1535

2859 —————— Epitome Divinarum Institutionum ad Pentadium Fratrem ; emendavit Jo. Davisius, 12mo. *calf*, 3s 6d *Cant.* 1718

" A well published book."—*Harwood.*

2860 —————— Divinarum Institutionum Liber V. sive, de Justitia, accurante D. Dalrymple de Hailes, Eq. 12mo. *new in calf gilt, 6s—bds. 3s* . *Edinb.* 1777

2862 LACTANTIUS (L. C. F.) de Mortibus Persecutorum ; accesserunt Passiones SS. Perpetuæ et Felicitatis, S. Maximiliani, et Felicis, 18mo. *calf, 2s 6d* . *Oxon.* 1680

2863 ————— de Mortibus Persecutorum, cum notis S. Baluzii et variorum, ed. P. Bauldri, 8vo. *fine copy, russia, marbled leaves*, 12s *Traj. ad R.* 1692

2864 ————— the same, 8vo. *fine copy, neat,* 9s *ib.* 1693
Both from the library of the late Duke of Sussex.

This treatise, although commonly ascribed to Lactantius, is believed to have been written by Lucius Cecilius. Nic. Le Nourry, edited an edition under that name in 1710.—Vide, the following number.

2865 ————— Liber ad Donatum Confessorem de Mortibus Persecutorum, hactenus Lucio Cœlio Firmiano Lactantio adscriptus; ed. Nic. le Nourry, 8vo. *calf,* 6s . *Par.* 1710

2866 ————— Opera omnia, cum selectis Variorum Commentariis, opera et studio S. Gallæi, 8vo. *calf,* 8s *Lugd. Bat.* 1660

2867 ————— Opera, ad fidem MSS. recognita et Commentariis illustrata a Tho. Spark, 8vo. *calf,* 8s . *Oxon.* 1684
From the library of the late Duke of Sussex.

2868 ————— Opera omnia, sm. 8vo. *old calf gilt,* 6s *Cantab.* 1685
2869 — - — Opera omnia, cum Notis Variorum et J. L. Bünemanni, 2 vols. 8vo. *hf. bd. vellum, neat,* 12s *Lipsiæ,* 1739
From the library of the late Duke of Sussex.

2870 ————— Opera omnia, cum Notis Variorum cura J. B. Le Brun et N L. Dufresnoy, *best edition,* 2 vols. 4to. *calf,* £1. 11s 6d
. . *Paris.* 1748
2871 ————— another copy, 2 vols. 4to. *French calf,* £1. 16s *ib.* 1748
2872 ————— Opera omnia; accesserunt Arnobii Afri libri VII. adversus Gentes, necnon Minutii Felicis Octavius, 8vo. *vellum,* 6s
Vesontione, 1838

2873 ————— A relation of the Death of the Primitive Persecutors; Englished by Gilbert Burnet, D.D., to which he hath made a large preface concerning Persecution, 18mo. *calf,* 2s *Amst.* 1687

2874 ————— another copy, 18mo. *calf,* 3s 6d *Glasgow,* 1766

2875 LADY's Religion; in two Letters from the Hon. Lady Howard, by a divine of the Church of England; with a Letter to a Lady on the death of her Husband, by the Editor, 12mo. 1s 1748

2876 LAGET (Guillaume) Sermons sur divers sujets importants, 8vo. *calf extra, gilt leaves,* 7s 6d . *Geneve,* 1773

2877 LAICK's (Wm.) The Scots Episcopal Innocence: or the juggling of that party with the late King, &c., together with a Catalogue of the Scots Episcopal Clergy turn'd out for their Disloyalty and other enormities since the Revolution, 1694—An Answer to the Scotch Presbyterian Eloquence, with a Continuation of the same, 1693, *in one* vol. 4to. *scarce and curious, hf. bd.* 7s 1694

2878 LAMBE's (Cha.) Sermons on several occasions; many of them preached in the height of the late Rebellion, 8vo. *calf,* 2s 6d 1717

2879 LAMONT (Jean de) Sermons de la Hierarchie de l'Eglise, 8vo. *fine copy, blue morocco, gilt leaves,* 10s 6d . *Par.* 1682
2880 LAMPE (Frid. Adolph.) Exercitationum Sacrarum δωδεκας, quibus Psalmus XLV. perpetuo Commentario explanatur, 4to. *vellum,* 6s *Bremæ,* 1715
2881 ——— Commentarius Analytico-Exegeticus tam literalis quam realis Evangelii secundum Joannem, 3 vols. 4to. *vellum,* £1. 18s *Basil.* 1725-7
2882 ——— another copy, 3 vols. 4to. *vellum,* £2. 2s *Amst.* 1724-6

"This is unquestionably the most copious work on St. John's Gospel, that ever was published; every thing which the learned author could possibly collect, in order to illustrate the Evangelist, being here concentrated."—*Horne.*

2883 ——— Meditationum Exegeticarum Opera Anecdota, quibus sistuntur Commentarius in Psalmos Graduum, itemque Fragmenta in Apocalypsin, et in Ecclesiasten Annotationes, recensuit Dan. Gerdes, 4to. *vellum,* 5s . *Gron.* 1741
2884 ——— Delineatio Theologiæ Activæ; accedunt Rudimenta Theologiæ Elenchticæ, 4to. *bds.* 5s *Traj. ad Rh.* 1745
2885 LAMY (Bernardus) Apparatus Biblicus, ad intelligenda Sacra Biblia, 12mo. *calf,* 1s . *Lugd. Bat.* 1711
2886 LANCASTER'S (Peter) Chronological Essay on the Ninth Chapter of Daniel: or, an interpretation of the Prophecy of the Seventy Weeks, 4to. *bds.* 3s 6d . 1722
2887 [LANGFORD'S (Dr. Wm.)] Familiar Discourses upon the Apostles' Creed, the Lord's Prayer, and the Litany, 8vo. *bds.* 2s 1809
2888 LANFRANCUS (S. *Archiep. Cant.*) [Opera omnia, a L. Dacherio, notis illustravit, folio, *calf,* £1. 18s *Lut. Par.* 1648
2889 ——— editio altera, folio, *vellum,* £1. 8s *Venet.* 1745
2890 LANGIUS (Joach.) Historia Ecclesiastica Vet. Testamenti, cum Isagoge Exegetica in Libros Sacros, 4to. *vellum,* 6s *Hal. Magd.* 1718
2891 ——— Gloria Christi et Christianismi Apocolyptico-prophetica, necnon Anti-Sociniana et Anti-Judiaca, exhibens Commentarium Apocalypticum, &c., 2 vols. in 1, folio, *vellum,* 16s *Amst.* 1740

"Præstantissimum illud est, atque inter optimos Apocalypseos Commentarios referri debet."—*Walch.*

2892 LAPIDE (Corn. à.) Commentaria in libros Vet. ac Nov. Testamenti, 10 vols. folio, *vellum,* £7. 7s *Antverpiæ,* 1648, &c.
2893 ——— Commentaria in Acta Apostolorum, Epistolas Canonicas, et Apocalypsin, folio, *old calf gilt,* £1. 5s *ib.* 1627
2894 LARDNER'S (Dr. Nathaniel) Sermons upon various subjects, 8vo. *calf,* 4s . 1751
2895 ——— Fides Historiæ Evangelicæ, sive Facta quæ ex occasione in Novo Testamento commemorantur, Veterum Scriptorum testimoniis confirmata. Præfationem, &c. præmisit Jo. Chr. Wolfius, sm. 8vo. *calf,* 3s . *Bremæ,* 1733
2896 ——— Collection of Ancient Jewish and Heathen Testimonies to the Truth of the Christian Religion, with notes, 4 vols. 4to. *calf,* £1. 10s . 1764

2897 LARDNER's (Dr. Nath.) Credibility of the Gospel History, 17 vols. 1741-60—Sermons, 2 vols. 1751-60—Tracts, viz. Counsels of Prudence, for the use of Young People, Vindication of our Saviour's Miracles—Caution against Conformity to this World, 1739—Remarks on Ward's Dissertations upon several passages of Scripture —The Case of the Demoniacs, &c., together 20 vols. 8vo. *old calf gilt, excepting the volume of Tracts which is hf. bd. uncut, but uniform in the back*, £2. 10s

2898 ——— —— Works, with his Life by A. Kippis, DD., 11 vols. royal 8vo. *calf*, £4. 4s . 1788

"This edition, on which uncommon care was bestowed, has of late become scarce and dear."—*Chalmers.*

2899 ————— Works, new edition, 10 vols. 8vo. *rich sprinkled calf gilt, lettered contents*, £5. 5s . 1838

2900 [LASCELLES's (Rowley)] Letters of Yorick, or, a good humoured Remonstrance in favour of the Established Church, 3 vols. 8vo. *calf*, 4s 6d . *Dublin*, 1817

Presentation copy to the Bp. of Lincoln, to whom the work is dedicated.

2901 LATHBURY's (Tho.) State of Popery and Jesuitism in England, from the Reformation to the period of the Relief Bill in 1829, and the Charge of Novelty, Heresy and Schism against the Church of Rome substantiated, 12mo. *bds.* 5s . 1838

2902 ——————— History of the Nonjurors: their Controversies and Writings; with Remarks on some of the Rubrics in the Book of Common Prayer, 8vo. *bds.* 14s . 1845

2903 LATIMER's (Hugh, *Bp. of Worcester.*) Fruitfull Sermons, 4to. *the last leaf supplied in MS. calf*, 10s 6d *Lond.* 1635

2904 ———— Sermons on various subjects, with his Life, 2 vols. in 1, 8vo. *hf. bd. calf, neat*, 8s . 1788

2905 ———— another copy, with a Memoir of the Bishop, by J. Watkins, 2 vols. 8vo. *portrait, calf gilt*, £1. 1s—*bds.* 13s 1824

2906 LAUD's (Wm. *Abp. of Canterbury*) Relation of the Conference betweene Wm. Laud, then Bp. of St. Davids, and Mr. Fisher, [John Perse] the Jesuit; with an answer to such objections as A. C. takes against it, folio, *calf*, 9s . 1686

2907 ———— *new edition*, 8vo. *bds.* 7s *Oxford*, 1839

2907* ———— Liturgy, Episcopacy, and Church Ritual: three Speeches, 18mo. *bds.* 3s 6d . *ib.* 1840

2908 ———— The Life and Times of Abp. Laud, by J. P. Lawson, M. A., 2 vols. 8vo. *portrait, calf gilt*, 15s *Lond.* 1829

2909 ———— The Life of William, now Lord Archbishop of Canterbury, examined, &c. by Mr. Robert Bayley, a learned Pastor of the Kirk of Scotland, *portrait inserted*, 1643—A large Supplement of the Canterburian Self-Conviction, N. P. 1641—The Archbishop's Speech at his Martyrdom, N. D.—His Speech or Funerall Sermon preached by himself on the Scaffold, 1644; *in one vol.* 4to. *hf. bd. calf*, 12s

2910 LAUDER's (Wm.) Essay on Milton's Use and Imitation of the Moderns in his Paradise Lost, 8vo. *calf, scarce, 4s* 1750

2911 LAUDES DIURNÆ: The Psalter and Canticles in the Morning and Evening Service of the Church of England: set to the Gregorian tones, by Robert Redhead, with a Preface on Antiphonal Chanting, by the Rev. F. Oakeley, 12mo. *bds. 4s* . 1843

2912 LAUNOII (Joannes) Opera omnia, Ineditis Opusculis aliquot, Notis, Auctoris Vita, &c. aucta. Accessit Tractatus de varia Launoii librorum fortuna, 10 vols. folio, *fine copy, hogskin,* £5. 5s
Coloniæ Allobr. 1731, *&c.*

His works were collected by the Abbé Grauet; they discover great learning, and extensive knowledge of ecclesiastical affairs. He strenuously defends the liberties of the Gallican Church, and shews much penetration and skill in criticism.

2913 —— —— Veneranda Romanæ Ecclesiæ circa Simoniam traditio, 8vo. *calf, 4s* . *Par.* 1675

2914 LAURENCE's (John) Christian Morals and Christian Prudence, 8vo. *calf, 3s* . . 1717

2915 LAURENTIUS JUSTINIANUS (S. *Protopatriarcha Venetus*) Opera omnia, cum Vita Auctoris, folio, *frontispiece, calf, neat,* £1. 8s
Venetiis, 1721

2916 LAVINGTON's (Geo. Bp. *of Exeter*) Enthusiasm of Methodists and Papists considered; with Notes, &c. by the Rev. R. Polwhele, 8vo. *hf. bd. calf, scarce, 6s* . 1820

2917 LAW's (Edm., Bp. *of Carlisle*) Considerations on the State of the World with regard to the Theory of Religion, 8vo. *calf,* 2s 6d
Camb. 1745

2918 —— —— Considerations on the Theory of Religion, with two Discourses and an Appendix, 8vo. *calf, 4s* *ib.* 1755

2919 —— —— the same, 8vo. *calf,* 4s 6d *Lond.* 1759

2920 —— —— the same, 8vo. *calf, 5s* . *Camb.* 1765

2921 —— —— another copy, 8vo. *tree-marbled calf extra,* 8s
Carlisle, 1784

2922 —— —— (Edward) Sermons preached in the British Chapel, St. Petersburg, 8vo. *bds.* (pub. at 10s 6d) 2s 6d—*calf gilt,* 5s 6d
1827

2923 —— —— (Wm.) Reply to Bp. Hoadley's Answer to the Committee of Convocation, 8vo. *sewed,* 1s . 1719

2924 —— —— The Way to Divine Knowledge; being several Dialogues, preparatory to the new edition of the Works of Jacob Behmen, 1752—An Epistle concerning Law's Spirit of Prayer, and the Bishop of London's Appendix, 1752—The Grounds and Reasons of Christian Regeneration, offered to the Consideration of Christians and Deists, 1750—An Earnest and Serious Answer to Trapp's Discourse on the Folly, Sin, and Danger, of being Righteous overmuch, 1741—Remarks upon the Fable of the Bees, 1726—in 2 vols. 8vo. *old red morocco, gilt leaves, and borders of gold,* 6s

2925 —— —— Case of Reason; or, Natural Religion fairly and fully stated, in Answer to [Tindal's] Christianity as Old as the Creation, 8vo. *sewed,* 1s . . 1731

2926 LAW's (Wm.) Remarks on the Fable of the Bees (by B. Mandeville), with an Introduction by the Rev. F. D. Maurice, and an Appendix, 12mo. *bds. 3s* . *Camb.* 1844

2927 LAWMIND's (John) Putney Projects; or, the Old Serpent in a new forme, presenting to the view of all the well affected in England, the serpentine deceit of their pretended friends in the Armie, 4to. *sewed, 2s* . . 1647

2928 LAWRENCE's (Edw.) Parents' Groans over their Wicked Children: several Sermons on Prov. xvii. 25, 12mo. *calf, 1s 6d* 1681

2929 ——— (Henry) Our Communion and Warre with Angels; being certain Meditations on that subject, particularly on Eph. vi. 12, &c. 4to. *hf. bd. calf, 5s 6d* . 1646

2930 ——— (William) Marriage by the Morall Law of God vindicated against all Ceremonial Laws of Popes, &c. *engraved title,* 1680—The Right of Primogeniture in Succession to the Kingdoms of England, Scotland, and Ireland, 1681—The two great Questions whereupon the peace and safety of His Majestie's person and of all his Protestant Subjects next under God depend, 1681; in 1 vol. 4to. *calf, 18s* . . 1680-81

<small>The second treatise supports the claims of the Duke of Monmouth: the third was intended to promote the exclusion of the Duke of York. They are all very scarce and curious. The present copies came from the library of the late Duke of Sussex.</small>

2931 LAWSON's (Dr. John) Occasional Sermons on various subjects, 8vo. *bds. 2s* . . 1764
" A volume of excellent sermons."—*Dr. Loveday.*

2932 LAYMAN's (A) Account of his Faith and Practice as a Member of the Episcopal Church, with Family Devotions, 18mo. *bds.1s 6d* 1836

2933 [LEAKE's (John)] Scholar's Manual, being a Collection of Meditations, Reflections, and Reasonings, with suitable Devotions, 8vo. *calf, 2s 6d* . . 1733

2934 LE BLANC (Thomas) Psalmorum Davidicorum Analysis; adjungitur Commentarius amplissimus, 6 vols. in 3, folio, *calf, £2. 5s*
Col. Agrip. 1726

2935 LE BRUN (Pierre) Explication de la Messe, contenant les Dissertations historiques et dogmatiques sur les Liturgies de toutes les Eglises du Monde Chretien, 4 vols. 8vo. *bds. £1. 11s 6d*
Par. 1726

2936 ——— Histoire critique des Pratiques Superstitieuses, qui ont seduit les Peuples, et embarrassé les Sçavans, 3 vols. 12mo. *neat, 7s 6d* . . *ib.* 1732

2937 LE CLERC (—) Twelve Dissertations out of M. Le Clerk's Genesis, done out of Latin by Mr. Brown; with a Dissertation concerning the Israelites' Passage through the Red Sea, 8vo. *calf, 3s* 1696

2938 ——— Treatise of the Causes of Incredulity, 12mo. *1s* 1697

2939 ——— Free and Important Disquisitions concerning the Inspiration of the Holy Scriptures, 8vo. *hf. bd. calf, 2s 6d* 1750

2940 LECTURES on the Miracles, selected from the New Testament, 8vo. *bds. 3s* . 1823

2941 ——— on the Parables, selected from the New Testament, 8vo. *bds. 3s* . . 1824

2942 LE COINTE (—) Sermons choisies, 8vo. *calf,* 3s 6d   *Genève,* 1783
2943 LEE'S (Hen.) Free Enquiry into the Meaning of the most excellent name Jesus, 12mo. 2s 6d
2944 ——— the same, LARGE PAPER, 8vo. *calf,* 3s 6d   N. D.
2945 ——— (Dr. Sam.) Grammar of the Hebrew Language, comprised in a series of Lectures, 8vo. *bds.* 8s   1844
2946 ——— Lexicon, Hebrew, Chaldee, and English, 8vo. *bds.* 14s   1844
2947 LEGER (Jean) Histoire generale des Eglises Evangeliques des Vallees de Piemont, ou Vaudoises, folio, *plates, calf,* £1. 10s *Leyde,* 1669

"Quæ historia non solum propter fidem auctoris, sed etiam ob ipsas res, memorabiles ac diligenter memoratas, meritò singularem estimationem tueter ac lectione digna."—*Walch.*
"Liber præstans ac rarus"—*Bauer Bib. Rar.*

2948 LEIGH'S (Edward) Critica Sacra, in two parts—the first containing Observations on all the Primitive Hebrew Words of the Old Testament; the second, containing Observations on all the Greek Words of the New Testament, folio, *portrait, calf,* 10s   1662
2949 ——— Critica Sacra, duabus partibus, quarum prima continet Observationes Philologicas et Theologicas in omnes radices Vet. Testamenti — Secunda continet Observationes in omnes Græcas voces Novi Testamenti, ab Hen. à Middorch in Latinum sermonem conversa, folio, *vellum,* 8s   *Amst.* 1679
2950 ——— (Wm.) Short Inquiry into Revealed Religion, in five Sermons, 12mo. *bds.* 2s   *Bath,* 1794
2950*LEIGHTON'S (Rob. *Abp. of Glasgow*) Sermons, 8vo. *calf, scarce,* 4s   1692
2951 ——— Practical Commentary upon the First Epistle of St. Peter, and other Expository Works; with a Life of the Author, by the Rev. J. N. Pearson, 8vo. *portrait, bds.* 6s — *calf gilt,* 9s 6d   1835
2952 ——— Select Works, with some Letters never before printed, 8vo. *portrait,* 6s   1758
2953 ——— Select Works, 2 vols. 8vo. *portrait, bds.* 7s   1823
2954 ——— Whole Works: with the Life of the Author by the Rev. J. N. Pearson, 2 vols. 8vo. *portrait, bds.* 16s   1835
2955 LEIGHTONHOUSE'S (Walter) Twelve Sermons preached at the Cathedral Church at Lincoln, 8vo. *calf,* 3s   1697
2956 ——— another copy, 8vo. 2s
2957 LE JEUNE (*dit le Père Aveugle*) Le Missionnaire de l'Oratoire, ou Sermons pour l'Avent, le Carême et les Fêtes, 13 vols. in 6, 8vo. *fine copy, French calf gilt,* £3. 13s 6d   *Lyon,* 1825
2958 LELAND'S (John) Works, viz.—Answer to [Tindal's] Christianity as Old as the Creation, 2 vols.—Divine Authority of the Old and New Testament asserted, 2 vols.— View of the Principal Deistical Writers, 2 vols.—together 6 vols. 8vo. *uniformly bound in treemarbled calf extra,* £2. 12s 6d   1733-66
2959 ——— Answer to a late Book [by Tindal] entitled, Christianity as Old as the Creation, 2 vols. 8vo. *calf,* 9s   *Dublin,* 1733
2960 ——— Remarks on a late Pamphlet [by Dodwell] entitled Christianity not founded on Argument, 2 parts in 1 vol. 8vo. *hf. bd. calf,* 2s 6d   1744

[58, GREAT QUEEN STREET,

2961 LELAND's (Dr. John) Divine Authority of the Old and New Testament asserted, 2 vols. 8vo. *calf, 6s* 1739-40
2962 [————] Forms of Devotion for the use of Families, &c. 1758— [DUCHAL's (Dr. —)] Short Explanation of the End and Design of the Lord's Supper, 1758—2 vols. in 1, 12mo. *calf, 2s 6d* ———
2963 ———— Advantage and Necessity of the Christian Revelation shewn from the state of Religion in the ancient Heathen World, 2 vols. 4to. *portrait, calf*, 10s 1764
2964 ———— View of the principal Deistical Writers that have appeared in England, in the last and present Century, 2 vols. 8vo. *calf*, 10s . 1766
2965 ———— the same, 2 vols. 8vo. *old calf gilt*, 12s 1766
2966 ———— View of the principal Deistical Writers, &c.; with an Appendix, containing a View of the present times with regard to Religion and Morals, by W. L. Brown, D.D., 2 vols. 8vo. *hf. bd. calf, neat, uncut*, 10s 6d . 1798
   It is a well known fact that King George III. at the age of 15 or 16 purchased about 50 copies of this useful work for presents.
2967 ———— (Dr. Tho.) History of Ireland, from the Invasion of Henry II., with a preliminary Discourse on the antient State of that Kingdom, 3 vols. 4to. *calf*, £1. 10s . 1773
2968 ———— Sermons on various subjects, 3 vols. 8vo. *calf, neat*, 14s . *Dublin*, 1788
2968* ———— another copy, (*a sheet wanting in the Life of the Author*) 3 vols. 8vo. *calf, neat*, 7s . *ib*. 1788
   " The peculiar character which pervades and colours his discourses, seems to be that of a strong earnestness, and an intense effort to persuade, and impress conviction."
2969 ———— (Joan.) Cygnea Cantio, sm. 4to. *woodcut title, bds.* 10s 6d . N. D.
   Dedicated to King Henry VIII.
2969* ———— Assertio inclytissimi Arturii Regis Britanniæ, (*dedicated to Henry VIII.*) sm. 4to. *bds. slightly stained in the margins*, 7s 6d . . *Lond.* 1544
   A curious tract on King Arthur and the Knights of the Round Table.
2970 ———— Laudatio Pacis, sm. 4to. *bds.* 5s *ib.* 1546
2970* ———— Genethli Acon illustrissimi Eäduerdi Principis Cambriæ, (a Poem on Edward VI. when Prince of Wales) sm. 4to. *title mended*, 10s . . *ib.* 1543
2971 LE MAIRE (——) Le Sanctuaire fermé aux profanes, ou la Bible, defendue au Vulgaire, 4to. 5s 6d *Paris*, 1651
2972 LEMOINE's (Abr.) Treatise on Miracles, 8vo. *calf*, 3s 1747
2973 LE MOYNE (le Pere) La Gallerie des Femmes Fortes, 2 parts. in 1 vol. 12mo. *portraits, fine copy, red morocco, gilt leaves*, 8s *Par.* 1665
2974 ———— (Steph.) Varia Sacra, seu Sylloge Variorum Opusculorum Græcorum ad rem ecclesiasticum spectantium, 2 vols. 4to. *vellum*, 8s . . *Lugd. Bat.* 1785
2975 LEMPRIERE's (F. D.) Lectures upon the Collects of the Book of Common Prayer, according to the use of the United Church of England and Ireland, *first series*, 8vo. *bds.* 12s 1845

2976 LEMPRIERE's (F.) Universal Biography, containing a copious account of the Lives of Eminent Persons of all Ages and Countries, 4to. *calf, marbled leaves,* 18s 1808
2977 LENFANT (Jacques) Histoire du Concile de Pise, et de ce qui s'est passé de plus mémorable depuis ce Concile jusqu'au Concile de Constance, 2 vols. in 1, 4to. *portraits, calf,* 8s *Amst.* 1724
2978 LENSÆUS (Jo.) de Una Christi in terris Ecclesia, sm. 8vo. *neat,* 3s 6d *Lovanii,* 1587
2979 ―――― de Verbo Dei non scripto, seu de Traditionibus Ecclesiasticis, contra Scholasticam Antonii Sadeelis de Verbo Dei scripto Dissertationem, sm. 8vo. *vellum,* 5s *Antv.* 1591
2980 ―――― Christianæ Pietatis Summarium, contra varias ætatis nostræ hæreses, sive de virtutibus tribus Fide, Spe, et Charitate, sm. 8vo. *neat,* 3s *Lovanii,* 1599
2981 LEONIS MAGNI, Opera Omnia, accedunt S. Hilarii Opuscula, Vita, et Apologia, 2 vols. in 1, folio, *hogskin, clasps,* £2. 2s *Lugd.* 1700
2982 ―――― Opera, post recensionem P. Quesnelli, emendata et ineditis aucta, præfationibus, admonitionibus illust. curantibus Fratribus Ballerinüs, 3 vols. folio, *calf gilt,* £4. 4s *Venetiis,* 1753-57
2983 ―――― Sermons de S. Leon Pape, surnommé le Grand, 8vo. *old green morocco, with the arms of a Princess of France on the sides, gilt leaves,* 10s 6d *Paris.* 1698
2984 LEO X. Vie et Pontificat de Léon X. par W. Roscoe, ouvrage traduite de l'Anglais par P. F. Henry, 4 vols. 8vo. *portrait and plates of medals, French calf gilt,* 14s *ib.* 1808
2985 LE PLAT (Judocus) Monumentorum ad Historiam Concilii Tridentini amplissima Collectio, 7 vols. 4to. *vellum,* £4. 14s 6d *Lovanii,* 1781-87
2986 ―――― idem, 7 vols. *ib.* 1781-87—Canones et Decreta Concilii Tridentini juxta exemplar authenticum, cum serie variantium Lectionum, Constitutionibus ex antiq. jure desumptæ et per Conc. spcciatim innovatæ Regulis de Libris prohibitis, indicibus etc. studio J. Le Plat, *Ant.* 1779—together 8 vols. 4to. *calf gilt,* £5. 10s ――
2987 LEPORCQ (Jean) Les Sentimens de Saint Augustin sur la Grace, opposez à ceux de Jansenius, 4to. *presentation copy, red morocco, gilt leaves, arms on the sides,* 14s *Paris.* 1682
2988 LE QUIEN (Michel) Nullité des Ordinations Anglicanes, ou refutation du livre [du Pere Courayer] intitulé, Dissertation sur la Validité des Ordinations des Anglois, 2 vols. 12mo. *calf,* 8s *ib.* 1725
From the library of the late Duke of Sussex.
2989 LE ROUX (Seb.) Concorde des Quatre Evangelistes, 8vo. *fine copy, old French red morocco, gilt leaves, with arms on the sides,* 12s *ib.* 1699

"Présenté par l'auteur a Monsieur le Comte de Meslay, Seigneur d'Andeville, etc."—*Note on Title.*

2990 [LESLIE's (Cha.)] Snake in the Grass: or Satan transformed into an Angel of Light, discovering the deep subtilty which is couched under the pretended simplicity of the Quakers, 8vo. *frontispiece, calf,* 2s 6d 1698
2991 ――――― the same, *(frontispiece wanting)* 8vo. *calf,* 2s 1698

2992 LESLIE's (Charles) Theological Works, 2 vols. folio, *calf*, £1. 16s
        1721
2993 ———— new edition, 7 vols. 8vo. *bds.* £2. 12s 6d—*calf gilt*, £3. 13s 6d . *Clarendon Press*, 1832
2994 [————] History of Sin and Heresie, in some Meditations upon the Feast of St. Michael and all Angels, 1698—Primitive Heresie revived in the Faith and Practice of the Quakers, 1698—A Discourse shewing who are now qualified to administer Baptism and the Lord's-Supper, 1698—A Discourse proving the Divine Institution of Water-Baptism, &c. 1697—Satan Disrobed from his disguise of Light, or the Quakers last shift laid open, 1698—The new Association of those called Moderate-Church-Men, with the Moderate-Whigs and Fanaticks, to undermine and blow up the present Church and Government, 2 parts, 1702-3—*in one vol.* 4to. *calf*, 5s . . V. Y.
2995 ———— Defence of a Book intituled, The Snake in the Grass; in Reply to G. Whithead, J. Wyeth, &c. 8vo. *calf*, 3s   1700
2996 [————] Essay concerning the Divine Right of Tythes, 8vo. *calf*, 2s . . 1700
2997 ———— Sermon preached at Chester, against Marriages in different Communions: and the same subject farther prosecuted by Hen. Dodwell, 8vo. *calf*, 3s . 1702
2998 ———— Finishing Stroke, being a Vindication of the Patriarchal Scheme of Government, wherein Mr. Hoadly's Examination of this scheme is fully considered, 8vo. *calf*, 2s 6d   1711
2999 ———— the same, 8vo. *calf*, 2s 6d . 1716
3000 ———— Scourge, in Vindication of the Church of England, 12mo. *calf*, 2s . . 1717
3001 ———— Case of the Regale and of the Pontificate stated, in a Conference concerning the Independency of the Church upon any power on earth, in the exercise of her purely spiritual power and authority, 8vo. *bds.* 4s 6d . 1838

    The above Treatise on the Regal and Papal Supremacy, was published in the year 1702, when the principles of the Ecclesiastical and Civil Powers had been thrown into confusion by the Revolution of 1688. Its object is to fix the respective limits of these several authorities, and to exhibit the true theory of their combined operation in the so-called union of Church and State.

    It is hoped that its present republication may serve as an antidote to the false opinions which still prevail on this vital question, and at this moment threaten to bring the gravest practical evils upon the Church of England.

    The Treatise, which has become very scarce in its separate form, is reprinted from the Oxford edition of Leslie's Theological Works, and being complete in itself, it is given alone, without the Preface or Supplement, which have a special reference to the controversy of the day.

3002 [————] View of the Times, their Principles and Practices, 6 vols. 12mo. *port.* 6s . 1750
    Necessary to complete the folio edition of Leslie's works.
3003 ———— Short and Easy Method with the Jews; wherein the Certainty of the Christian Religion is demonstrated, 12mo. 1s
        1825
3004 ———— The Case stated between the Church of Rome and the Church of England, 8vo. *calf*, 3s . ——

3005 Less' (Godfrey) Authenticity, uncorrupted Preservation, and Credibility of the New Testament; translated from the German by Roger Kingdon, 8vo. *bds.* 3s—*calf gilt,* 6s   1804

3006 L'Estrange's (Hamon) Alliance of Divine Offices, exhibiting all the Liturgies of the Church of England, since the Reformation; also the late Scotch Service Book, with all their respective Variations, and Annotations upon them all; together with the Order of the Communion set forth 2 Edward VI. *best edition,* folio, *calf, scarce,* £1. 18s   .   .   1690

3007 ——— —— Some important Duties and Doctrines of Religion proved from the Scriptures, with occasional Thoughts on Deism, &c. 8vo. *calf,* 2s 6d   .   .   1739

3008 ——— —— (Roger) Relapsed Apostate; or, Notes upon a Presbyterian Pamphlet entitled, "A Petition for Peace," 4to. 2s   1641

3009 ——— —— Interest Mistaken; or, the Holy Cheat; proving from the practises of the Presbyterians, that the design of that people is to enslave both King and People, &c. 12mo. *neat,* 2s 6d   1662

3010 ——— —— Dissenters' Sayings, in requital for L'Estrange's Sayings, published in their own words, 2 parts, 4to. *sewed,* 1s 6d   1681

3011 ——— —— third edition, 2 parts, 4to. 1s 6d   1681

3012 ——— —— Character of a Papist in Masquerade, in answer to the Character of a Popish Successor, 4to. *hf. bd. calf,* 3s 6d   1681

3013 ——— —— Casuist Uncased, in a Dialogue between Richard and Baxter, with a Moderator between them for quietnesse sake, 4to. *sewed,* 1s 6d   .   1681

3014 Letsome's (Sampson) Preacher's Assistant, a Series of Texts of all the Sermons and Discourses published since the Restoration, and an Historical Register of all the Authors, with Lists of the Bishops of England and Ireland, &c. 2 vols. 8vo. *old blue morocco, gilt leaves,* 10s   .   .   1753

3015 ——— —— another copy, 2 vols. in 1, 8vo. *calf,* 8s   1753

3016 Lette (Ger. Jo.) Observationes Philologico-criticæ in Deboræ et Mosis Cantica, sm. 8vo. *sewed,* 4s 6d   *Lugd. Bat.* 1748

3017 Letters.—Five Letters concerning the Inspiration of the Holy Scriptures; translated out of French, 12mo. *calf,* 2s   1690

3018 ——— to a Sick Friend, containing Observations on the Removal of Sickness and Preservation of Health, by J. M. sm. 8vo. *calf,* 1s 6d   .   .   1682

3019 ——— —— Written by eminent Persons in the XVII. and XVIIIth centuries; to which are added, Hearne's Journeys to Reading, and to Whaddon Hall; and Lives of Eminent Men by John Aubrey, Esq. Now first published from the originals in the Bodleian Library, and Ashmolean Museum, 3 vols. 8vo. *bds.* 8s   1813

3020 Lewis's (John) Apology for the Clergy of the Church of England, in a particular examination of a book, entitled "The Rights of the Christian Church, &c." 8vo. *calf,* 2s 6d   1711

3021 ——— —— History of the Rise and Progress of Anabaptism in England; with some Account of Dr. Wiclif, and a Defense of him from a false charge of denying Infant Baptism, 8vo. *hf. bd. calf,* 4s   1738

3022 LEWIS's (John) Complete History of the several Translations of the Holy Bible into English, both in MS. and in Print, 8vo. *best edition, calf, 9s* . . 1739
3023 ———— History of the Life and Sufferings of John Wicliffe, D.D., *portrait inserted*, 1723—The Life of Reynold Pecock, S.T.P., Lord Bishop of St. Asaph and Chichester, being a sequel to the Life of Dr. John Wiclif, 1744, 2 vols. 8vo. *fine copies, calf extra, gilt leaves by C. Lewis*, £1. 1s
3024 ———— (Tho.) Origines Hebrææ: the Antiquities of the Hebrew Republick, 4 vols. 8vo. *calf, neat*, 15s   1724-25
3025 ———— Origines Hebrææ, *new edition*, 3 vols. 8vo. *bds.* £1. 4s —*calf gilt*, £1. 10s . Oxford, 1835
3026 ———— the same, *new*, 3 vols. 8vo. *tree-marbled calf gilt*, £1. 16s . *ib.* 1835

"A laborious compilation from the most distinguished writers, whether Jews or Christians, on the manners and laws of the Hebrews."—*T. H. Horne.*

3027 ———— Inquiry into the Shape, the Beauty, and Stature of the Person of Christ, and of the Virgin Mary, 8vo. *hf. bd. mor.* 5s   1735
3027*LEX FORCIA; being a Sensible Address to the Parliament, for an Act to Remedy the foul Abuse of Children at Schools, especially in the Great Schools of this Nation, sm. 4to. *hf. bd.* 2s 6d   1698
3028 LIBERTY.—The true Liberty and Dominion of Conscience, vindicated from the usurpations and abuses of Opinion and Persuasion, 8vo. *calf*, 2s 6d . 1677
3029 LIENHART (S.) de Antiquis Liturgiis et de Disciplina Arcani, Tractatus Historico-dogmaticus, ad commonstrandam perpetuam Ecclesiæ Catholicæ Fidem de S. Eucharistiæ Mysterio, 8vo. *hf. bd. calf*, 7s . Argent. 1829
3030 LIGHTFOOT's (John, *Master of Cath. Hall, Camb.*) Whole Works, edited by J. R. Pitman, A.M., 13 vols. 8vo. *portrait, calf gilt, scarce*, £6. 6s . . 1825
3031 LIMBORCH (Phil. à) Commentarius in Acta Apostolorum et in Epistolas ad Romanos et ad Hebræos, folio, *hf. bd. uncut*, 9s
   Rott. 1711
3032 ———— Complete System or Body of Divinity, abridged by John Riles, 8vo. *neat*, 4s   Macclesfield, 1807
3033 LINDSEY's (Theoph.) Sequel to the Apology on Resigning the Vicarage of Catterick, 8vo. *bds.* 2s   1776
3034 LINGARD's (Dr. John) History and Antiquities of the Anglo-Saxon Church, containing an account of its Origin, Government, Doctrines, Worship, Revenues, and Clerical and Monastic Institutions, 2 vols. 8vo. *bds.* £1. 4s . 1825
3035 LIVES of those Eminent Antiquaries John Leland, Thomas Hearne, and Anthony à Wood, with an account of their respective writings, 2 vols. 8vo. *large paper, calf*, £1. 4s   Oxford, 1772
3036 ———— of Dr. Edward Pocock, by Dr. Twells, Dr. Z. Pearce, Bp. of Rochester, and of Dr. Tho. Newton, Bp. of Bristol, by themselves; and of the Rev. Philip Skelton, by Burdy, 2 vols. 8vo. *bds.* 6s . 1816

3037 LLANDAFF. The Liber Landavensis, Llyfr Teilo, or the ancient Register of the Cathedral Church of Llandaff; with an English Translation and Notes, by the Rev. W. J. Rees. Published for the Welsh MSS. Society, royal 8vo. *scarce, plates, cloth bds.* £1. 1s
Llandovery, 1840

3038 LLEWELYN's (Dr. Tho.) Historical Account of the British or Welsh versions and editions of the Bible, 8vo. *very scarce, the last few leaves mended,* 5s 6d . 1768

3039 LLOYD's (David) State-Worthies: or, the Statesmen and Favorites of England, from the Reformation to the Revolution, 2 vols. 8vo. *calf,* 12s . . 1766

3040 ———— (Pierson) Sermons on several occasions, preached at Westminster Abbey, and St. Margaret's Westminster, 8vo. *calf,* 2s . . 1765

3041 ———— another copy, 8vo. LARGE PAPER, *calf,* 3s 1765

3042 LOBBETIUS (Jacobus) Opera omnia, (Quæstiones in Evangelia et in Festa; Opuscula Moralia; Conciones, &c.) 7 vols. in 2, folio, *hogskin,* £2. 2s . *Leodii,* 1668-72

3043 [LOCKE's (Jo.)] Reasonableness of Christianity, as delivered in the Scriptures, sm. 8vo. *calf,* 2s . 1695

3044 ———— Paraphrase and Notes on the Epistles of St. Paul to the Galatians, Corinthians, Romans, and Ephesians; with an Essay for the understanding of St. Paul's Epistles, by consulting St. Paul himself, 4to. *calf,* 4s . 1707

3045 ———— History of our Saviour, Jesus Christ, containing in order of time, all the Events and Discourses recorded in the Four Evangelists, &c. 8vo. *calf,* 2s 6d . 1721

3046 ———— Essay concerning Human Understanding, 2 vols. 8vo. *portrait, calf,* 4s 6d . 1748

3047 ———— Reasonableness of Christianity as delivered in the Scriptures, sm. 8vo. *calf,* 2s . 1695

3048 ———— Reply to the Bp. of Worcester's Answer to his Letter, concerning some passages relating to the Human Understanding, &c., 8vo. *calf,* 1s 6d . 1697

3049 ———— Account of Mr. Locke's Religion, out of his own writings, and in his own words [by John Martin, B.D.] 8vo. *calf,* 2s 6d 1700

3050 LOCKMAN's (Jo.) History of the cruel Sufferings of the Protestants and others, by Popish Persecutions, in various Countries, in Question and Answer, 12mo. *bds.* 3s 1760

3051 LOCKYER's (Nic.) Baulme for bleeding England and Ireland, or Seasonable Instructions for Persecuted Christians, in several Sermons, sm. 8vo. *calf,* 4s 6d . 1643

3052 LOESCHERUS (Val. Ern.) de Causis Linguæ Ebrææ libri III. *Franc.* 1706. — Jo. Abr. Kromayerus de Usu Linguæ Arabicæ in addiscenda Ebræa, &c. *ib.* 1707, *in one* vol. 4to. *vellum,* 5s
1706-7

3053 ———— Prænotiones Theologicæ, contra Naturalistarum et Fanaticorum omne genus, 4to. *calf,* 5s 6d *Vittemb.* 1708
The late Bp. Van Mildert's copy, with his book-plate.

3054 ———— Stromateus, sive Dissertationes Sacri et literarii argumenti, 4to. *vellum,* 5s . *ib.* 1724

[58, GREAT QUEEN STREET,

3055 LOGAN's (John) Sermons, including a complete detail of the Service of a Communion Sunday, according to the usage of the Church of Scotland, 2 vols. 8vo. *calf*, 4s 6d . *Edin.* 1800
3056 [LONG's (Tho.)] Vindication of the Primitive Christians, in point of Obedience to their Prince, against the Calumnies of a Book entitled, the " Life of Julian," as also the Doctrine of Passive Obedience cleared, in defence of Dr. Hicks, 8vo. *calf*, 3s 6d 1683
3057 ————— History of the Donatists, 8vo. *hf. bd. calf, scarce*, 5s 1677
3058 ————— Compendious History of all the Popish and Fanatical Plots and Conspiracies against the Established Government in Church and State, in England, Scotland, and Ireland, from the first year of Queen Elizabeth to 1684, sm. 8vo. *neat*, 5s 1684
3059 LONGUEVAL (Jacques) Histoire de l'Eglise Gallicane, depuis l'etablissement de la Religion jusqu'en 1559, 18 vols. 4to. *old calf gilt, very scarce*, £6. 6s . *Paris.* 1730

" *L'Histoire de l'Eglise Gallicane*, est un chef-d'œuvre. L'intérêt, l'utilité y fixent tour-à-tour l'esprit du lecteur que l'historien soit captiver par un mélange de méthode, de clarté, de critique, d'élégance. Tous les objets sonts préséntés sous un jour qui side autant le jugement que la mémoire. On aime à y voir les événements racontés sans enthousiasme, et dévelloppés avec impartialité."
L'Abbé Sabatier.

3060 LORENZANA (Franciscus de, *Archiep. Toletanus*) SS. PP. Toletanorum quotquot extant Opera, nunc primum simul edita, ad Codices MSS. recognita, nonullis notis illustrata, 3 vols. folio, *Spanish binding, extremely rare, fine copy*, £3. 3s *Matriti*, 1782-93

CONTENTS:—Tom. I. Montanus ; S. Eugenius IV. ; S. Ildephonsus.—Tom. II. S. Julianus ; S. Eulogius—Tom. III. Roderici Ximenii de Rada Historia de Rebus Hispaniæ ; Historia Romanorum ; Historia Ostrogothorum, Hunnorum, Vandalorum, etc. ; Historia Arabum ; Appendix I. Series Regum Hispaniæ; Synopsis Conciliorum Toletanorum ; Catalogus Præsulum Toletanorum.—II. Blazii Ortizii Descriptio Templi Toletani.
This work is a desideratum in almost all the public libraries in this country. It is not mentioned by Brunet, nor in the Nouvelles Recherches, a great portion of which was furnished by the intelligent M. Salva. In Spain it is of the greatest rarity, and very few copies have occurred for sale in this country.

3061 LORTIE's (Andr.) Practical Sermons upon several subjects, 8vo. *calf*, 2s . . 1720
3062 LOVEDER's (Tho.) Practical Discourses on various subjects, 8vo. *calf*, 2s . . 1756

The author was originally the Minister of a Presbyterian Meeting-house at Newington Green, but afterwards Rector of Little Stambridge, Essex.

3063 LOWE's (T. H.) Essay on the Absolving Power of the Church, with especial reference to the Offices for the ordering of Priests, and the Visitation of the Sick, 8vo. 1s 6d *Oxford*, 1825
3064 LOWMAN's (Moses) Considerations on Mr. Foster's Discourse on the Jewish Theocracy, 8vo. 1s . 1744
3065 ————— Rational of the Ritual of the Hebrew Worship, 8vo. *fine copy, calf*, 7s . . 1748
3066 LOWTH (Rob. *Ep. Lond.*) de Sacra Poesi Hebræorum Prælectiones Academicæ, cum notis J. D. Michaelis, 2 vols. 8vo. *bds.* 6s *Oxonii*, 1810

3067 LOWTH (Rob. *Ep. Lond.*) de Sacra Poesi Hebræorum Prælectiones Academicæ, cum notis J. D. Michaelis et aliorum : edidit E. F. C. Rosenmüller, 8vo. *port. autograph of Robert Southey, bds. 9s*
Oxonii, 1821
3068 ———— another copy, 8vo. *sprinkled calf gilt, 12s*   *ib.* 1821
3069 ———— Lectures on the Sacred Poetry of the Hebrews, translated by G. Gregory, with the Notes of Michaelis and others, 2 vols. 8vo. *calf, 12s*   .   1787
3070 ———— Lectures on the Sacred Poetry of the Hebrews, translated by G. Gregory, with Notes by Michaelis and others, 2 vols. 8vo. *portrait, hf. bd. calf, 12s*   .   1816
3071 ———— another copy, 2 vols. 8vo. *sprinkled calf gilt, 18s*   1816
3072 ———— (Will.) Commentary upon the Prophet Isaiah, 4to. *calf, 3s 6d*   .   1714
3073 ———— Directions for the Profitable Reading of the Holy Scriptures, 12mo. *calf, 1s 6d*   .   1712
3074 ———— another copy, 12mo. *calf, 2s*   .   1769
3075 LOYOLA (Ignatius), The Enthusiasm of the Church of Rome, demonstrated in some Observations upon the Life of Ignatius Loyola, (by H. Wharton, D.D.) 4to. *2s*   1688
3076 ———— Ignatii Loyola, Exercitia Spiritualia, cum sensu eorumdem explanato et directorium, additis tribus appendicibus, auctore P. Ignatio Diertens, 2 vols. 12mo. *sewed, 9s*   *August. Taur.* 1838
3077 LUCAS (*Tudensis Episcopus*) de altera Vita, fideique controversiis adversus Albigensium errores; notis illustrati a Jo. Mariana, 4to. *uncut, 4s 6d*   .   *Ingolst.* 1612
3078 ———— (Dr. R.) Practical Christianity ; or, an Account of the Holiness which the Gospel enjoins, &c. sm. 8vo. *new in marbled calf gilt, 6s*   .   1693
3079 ———— Fifteen Sermons on Death and Judgment, and a Future State, 8vo. *calf, 3s*   .   1716
3080 ———— Plain Man's Guide to Heaven, 12mo. *sewed, 1s*   1720
3081 ———— Sermons on several occasions and subjects, 5 vols. 8vo. *port. calf, scarce, 15s*   .   1722-35
3082 ———— XXIV Sermons on several occasions, 2 vols. 8vo. *calf, 4s*   .   1735
3083 ———— Enquiry after Happiness, 2 vols. 8vo. *calf, 5s*   1734-35

"Lucas's style is sometimes exceedingly free, sometimes grand and solemn, and generally very expressive. His most valuable works are his Enquiry after Happiness, and his Practical Christianity."—*Doddridge.*

3084 LULLIN (Amadée) Sermons sur divers textes de l'Ecriture Sainte, 2 vols. 8vo. *hf. bd. uncut, 5s*   Genève, 1761-67
3085 LUMPER (Gottf.) Historia Theologico-Critica de Vita, Scriptis, atque Doctrina SS. Patrum, aliorumque Scriptorum Ecclesiasticorum trium primorum Sæculorum, 13 vols. 8vo. *vellum, £3. 13s 6d*
Aug. Vind. 1783-99
3086 LUPUS (B. Servatus, *Abbas Ferrariensis*) Opera, curâ Steph. Baluzii, 8vo. *calf, 9s*   *Par.* 1664
3087 LUTHER'S (Martin) Commentarie upon the Epistle of S. Paule to the Galatians, 4to. 𝔅lack letter, *hf. bd. scarce, 12s*   1588

3088 LUTHER'S (Martin) Commentary upon the Epistle to the Galatians, with an account of the Life of the Author, 8vo. *calf, 7s*
Paisley, 1786
3089 ———— Commentary on the Psalms, called Psalms of Degrees; with an Historical Account of the Monastic Life, particularly in England, 8vo. *bds. 8s* . 1819
3090 ———— On the Bondage of the Will, written in Answer to the Diatribe of Erasmus on Free-Will, tránslated by the Rev. Henry Cole, 8vo. *calf, marbled edges, 8s* 1823
3091 ———— Historia de Vita et Actis ejus, conscripta a P. Melancthone, *Witeb.* 1549—De Resurrectione Mortuorum in XV. cap. I. Cor. Homiliæ Christianissimæ, *Franc. anno* XLVI.—Jona Propheta cum Annotationibus, *Argent.* 1526—3 vols. in 1, sm. 8vo. *calf, 6s* . ——
3092 LUZANCY'S (H. de) Remarks on several late Writings of the Socinians, &c. 8vo. *calf, 2s* . 1696
3093 ———— Considerations concerning the Trinity, and the Ways of managing that Controversie: together with a Defence against the Objections of the Dean of St. Paul's, 1698—Remarks on several late Writings by the Socinians, 1696—*in one rol.* 8vo. *calf, 3s 6d* . . ——
3094 LUZERNE (C. G. Evèque de Langres) Dissertation sur les Eglises Catholiques et Protestantes, 2 vols. in 1, 12mo. *bds. 3s*
Par. 1816
3095 LYDIUS (Balth.) Waldensia, id est Conservatio Veræ Ecclesiæ, demonstrata ex confessionibus, cum Taboritarum, tum Bohemorum, sm. 8vo. *very rare, hf. bd. 8s* . Roterd. 1616
3096 ———— (Jac.) Florum sparsio ad Historiam Passionis Jesu Christi, 12mo. *plates, vellum, 2s 6d* Traj. ad Rh. 1701
3097 LYE (Edw.) Dictionarium Saxonico et Gothico-Latinum. Accedunt fragmenta Versionis Ulphianæ, &c., edidit Owen Manning, 2 vols. folio, *hf. bd. calf, £4. 14s 6d* . 1772
3098 LYNDEWODE (Guillelmus) Provinciale seu Constitutiones Anglie, cum Summariis, atq; in istis annotationibus, politissimis caracteribus impresse, 𝔅lack letter, *wood-cut title, Antverpie,* 1525—Constitutiones legitime seu Legatine regionis Anglicane, cum interpretatione Jo. de Athon; necnon et Constitutiones provinciales ab Archiepiscopis Cantuariensibus edite, 𝔅lack letter, *wood-cut titles, In inclyta Parrhisiorum Academia,* 1504—in 1 vol. folio, *fine copies, in the original stamped binding, wooden boards,* £2. 10s ——
3099 ——·—— Provinciale Angliæ continens Constitutiones, Provinciales XIV. Archiepisc. Cantuariensium, cum Summariis atque Annotationibus; cui adjiciuntur Constitutiones Legatinæ D. Othonis et D. Othoboni, cum Annotationibus Jo. de Athona, *best edition,* folio, *calf, scarce, £1. 16s* . Oxon. 1679
3100 LYON'S (C. J.) History of St. Andrews, Episcopal, Monastic, Academic, and Civil, 2 vols. 8vo. *plates, bds. 16s* Edinb. 1843
3101 LYRA APOSTOLICA, 18mo. *calf gilt, 4s 6d* Derby, 1838
3102 MABILLON (Jo.) de Liturgia Gallicana libri III.; accedit Disquisitio de Cursu Gallicano, 4to. *calf, 12s* ib. 1729
" Hic liber in Actis Eruditorum et Dupinii Bibliotheca, verbosius laudatur."
Koecheri Bibl. Symbol.

3103 MABILLON (Jo.) Annales Ordinis S. Benedicti Occidentalium Monachorum Patriarchæ, ia quibus non modo Res Monasticæ, sed etiam Ecclesiasticæ Historiæ non minima pars continetur, 6 vols. folio, *fine copy, calf, full gilt backs*, £7. 17s 6d   *Paris.* 1703-39

"This work ought not to be considered as a mere compilation of memoirs relating to monastic history, but as a valuable collection of aucient ecclesiastical monuments; which being illustrated by learned notes, throw great light on the most obscure part of the History of the Church."—*Le Long.*

3104 MACARIUS's (S.) Primitive Morality; or, the Spiritual Homilies of St. Macarius the Egyptian, done out of Greek [by Dr. Tho. Haywood], 8vo. *calf*, 10s 6d   1721

3105 [MACDONALD'S (A.)] Twenty-eight Miscellaneous Sermons, 8vo. *bds.* 2s 6d   1788

3106 ——— Twenty-nine Miscellaneous Sermons, 8vo. *bds.* 2s 6d   1793

3107 [MACKENZIE'S (James)] Essays on Retirement from Business, on Old Age, and on the Employment of the Soul after Death; with Meditations on various subjects, 12mo. *bds.* 1s 6d   1812

3108 MACKNIGHT'S (Dr. James) Harmony of the Four Gospels, with a Paraphrase and Notes, 2 vols. 8vo. *bds.* 14s   1809

3109 ——— another copy, 2 vols. 8vo. *bds.* 10s   1822

3110 ——— Translation of the Apostolical Epistles—*Vide No.* 108.

3111 MACLAINE'S (Dr. A.) Discourses delivered in the English Church at the Hague, 8vo. *bds.* 3s   1799

3112 M'NEILE'S (Hugh) Miscellaneous Sermons, selected from "The Pulpit," 8vo. *bds.* 3s   1834

3113 ——— Lectures on the Church of England, 8vo. *bds.* 3s   1840

3114 MACRAY'S (W. D.) Manual of British Historians to A.D. 1600; containing a Chronological Account of the Early Chronicles and Monkish Writers, their printed works and unpublished MSS., 8vo. *hf. bd. morocco, uncut,* 9s   1845

3115 MACROBIUS (Aur. Theod.) Opera, accedunt Notæ J. Pontanii, J. Meursii, J. Gronovii, 8vo. *calf, neat,* 7s   *Lugd. Bat.* 1670

3116 ——— aliud exemplar, 8vo. *calf,* 6s   *Lond.* 1694

3117 MADRIGAL (Alph. de) Brevis Tractatus de Episcopis, Parochis, Prædicatoribus, Confessoribus, Sacerdotis, Clericis, &c. 4to. *calf,* 4s   *Neap.* 1608

3118 MAGDEBURGENSES CENTURIATORES. Historia Ecclesiastica, integram Ecclesiæ Christianæ conditionem indè à Christo ex Virgino nato, juxta Sæculorum seriem, exponens, jam olim per Studiosos ac Pios aliquot Viros, in urbe Magdeburgica, et alibi, diligenter congesta; 3 vols. folio, *fine copy, new in cf.* £5. 15s 6d *Basil.* 1624

3119 MAGEE'S (Wm. *Abp. of Dublin*) Discourses and Dissertations on the Scriptural Doctrines of Atonement and Sacrifice, 3 vols. 8vo. *calf,* 18s   1816

3120 ——— another copy, 3 vols. 8vo. *bds.* 18s   1832

3121 MAILLANE (Durand de) Libertez de l'Eglise Gallicane, prouvées et commentées suivant l'ordre et la disposition des Articles dressés par M. Pierre Dupuy, 5 vols. 4to. *fine copy, French calf,* £1. 10s   *Lyon,* 1771

[58, GREAT QUEEN STREET,

3122 MAILLANE (Durand de) Dictionnaire de Droit Canonique et de Pratique bénéficiale, 6 vols. 8vo. *sewed*   *Lyon*, 1787
3123 MAITLAND'S (Captain) History of the Beast of the Apocalypse, 8vo. *calf, 2s*   N. Y.
3124 ——— (S. R.) Index of such English Books, printed before MDC., as are now in the Archiepiscopal Library at Lambeth, 8vo. *bds. 4s 6d*   1845
3125 ——— Dark Ages, a series of Essays intended to illustrate the State of Religion and Literature in the 9th, 10th, 11th, and 12th Centuries, 8vo. *bds.* 12s   1845
3126 MALLEMANS (——) Pensées sur le sens literal des 18 premiers Versets de l'Evangile de St. Jean, 12mo. *old red morocco, 3s*   *Par.* 1718
3127 MALTBY'S (Edw. *Bp. of Durham*) Illustrations of the Truth of the Christian Religion, 8vo. *calf, 4s 6d*   *Camb.* 1802
3128 ——— Sermons in the Chapel of Lincoln's Inn, 8vo. *hf. bd. calf, neat, 5s*   1831
3129 MAMACHIUS (Tho. M.) de Animabus Justorum in Sinu Abrahæ, ante Christi mortem, expertibus Beatæ Visionis Dei, 2 vols. 4to. LARGE PAPER, *vellum, very scarce,* £1. 11s 6d   *Romæ*, 1766
3130 [MAN'S (Dr. ———)] Critical Notes on some Passages of Scripture, comparing them with the most Ancient Versions, and restoring them to their Original Reading or True Sense, 1747—Objections to a Pamphlet lately published, intituled "Critical Notes, &c." by E. Langford, 1747—A continuation of the Objections, &c. by E. Langford, 1748—in 1 vol. 8vo. *bds. 3s*
3131 MAN OF SIN; (The) or, a Discourse of Popery; by no Roman, but a Reformed Catholick, 4to. *calf, scarce, 4s*   1677
3132 MANDER'S (Harry) Parochial Letters on subjects of the greatest importance, 12mo. *hf. bd. calf, very scarce, 2s 6d*   1729
3133 MANGEY'S (Tho.) Remarks upon Nazarenus; wherein the Falsity of Mr. Toland's Mahometan Gospel, &c. are set forth, 8vo. *sewed, 1s*   1718
3134 MANN'S (Nich.) True Years of the Birth and Death of Christ, 8vo. *calf, 2s*   1733
3135 MANNING'S (H. E. *Archdeacon of Chich.*) Sermons preached before the University of Oxford, 8vo. *bds. 6s*   *Oxford*, 1844
3136 ——— Sermons, 2 vols. 8vo. *cloth bds.* £1. 1s   1842-6
Either volume may be had separately.
3137 ——— (Owen) Sermons on important subjects, 2 vols. 8vo. *bds. 5s*   1812
3138 MANT'S (Rd. *Bp. of Down and Connor*) Sermons preached before the University of Oxford, &c. 8vo. *bds. 4s 6d*   *Oxford*, 1816
3139 ——— Sermons for Parochial and Domestic use, 3 vols. 8vo. *neat,* 16s   *ib.* 1813-14
3140 ——— Book of Psalms, in an English Metrical Version, founded on the basis of the authorized Bible Translation, and compared with the original Hebrew, with Notes critical and illustrative, 8vo. *bds. 4s*   *ib.* 1824
3141 ——— Clergyman's Obligations considered, with particular reference to the Ordination Vow, 12mo. *bds. 3s 6d*   *ib.* 1830

3142 MANT'S (Rd. *Bp. of Down and Connor*) The Church and her Ministrations; in a series of Discourses, 8vo. *bds. 7s*   1838
3143 MANTON'S (Tho.) Practicall Commentary, or an Exposition, with Notes, on the Epistle of James, 4to. *calf*, 10s 6d   1653
3144 —————— Practical Commentary, or Exposition of the general Epistle of James; abridged and edited by the Rev. T. M. Macdonogh, 8vo. *bds. 5s*   1844
3145 ————— CXCVI. Sermons on the Hundred-and-nineteenth Psalm, folio, *portrait, calf*, £1. 10s   1681
3146 —————— new edition, with the Life of the Author by Wm. Harris, D.D., 3 vols. 8vo. *bds*. £1. 1s   1842
3147 MANUAL of Devotions for the Holy Communion, compiled from various sources, 18mo. *bds. 2s 6d*   1843
3148 MANUALE Pastorum, ad uniformem Administrationem Sacramentorum, &c. nunc denuo recognitum, ad usum Episcopatus Iprensis, 4to. *calf, 7s 6d*   *Ipris*, 1693
3149 MARCA (Petrus de, *Archiep. Paris*) de Concordia Sacerdotii et Imperii, seu de Libertatibus Ecclesiæ Gallicanæ libri octo: edidit Steph. Baluzius, folio, LARGE PAPER, *calf*, £1. 1s   *Paris*. 1663
3150 —————— another copy, folio, *calf*, 16s   *ib.* 1669

Written by desire of the King of France, who charged him to keep a certain medium, which should not prejudice the liberties of the Gallican Church, nor lessen the reverence due to the Holy See. It is an answer to a work by Optatus Gallus.

3151 MARCH'S (John, *Vicar of Newcastle*) Sermons, 8vo. *portrait, calf*, 2s 6d   1693
3152 ————— the same, with a Preface by Dr. John Scot, and an Assize Sermon, 8vo. *portrait, calf*, 3s   1699
3153 MARCHANT (Petrus) Tribunal Sacramentale et Visible Animarum in hac vita mortali, 2 vols. folio, *calf*, £1. 1s   *Colon. Agrip.* 1672
3154 MARÉCHAL (Bernard) Concordance des Saints Peres de l'Eglise Grecs et Latins, où l'on se propose de montrer leurs sentimens sur le dogme, la morale, et la discipline, &c. 2 vols. 4to. *neat*, 12s   *Paris*. 1739
3155 MARIANA.—L'Antimariana, ou Refutation des Propositions de Mariana, &c. sm. 8vo. *neat*, 3s   *ib.* 1610
3156 MARKLAND'S (Dr. Abr.) Sermons at the Cathedral Church of Winchester, 2 vols. in 1, 8vo. *calf*, 4s   1729
3157 ———— (J. H.) Remarks on the English Churches, and on the Expediency of rendering Sepulchral Memorials subservient to pious and christian uses, 12mo. *plates, bds*. 4s   *Oxford*, 1842
3158 [MARKS'S (Rd.)] EVENING MEDITATIONS; or, a series of Reflections on various passages of Holy Scripture and Scriptural Poetry, for every day in the year, 12mo. *bds*. 2s   1838
3159 MARLORATI (Augustini) Novi Testamenti Catholica Expositio Ecclesiastica, ex universis probatis theologis excerpta, 2 vols. in 1, folio, *vellum*, £1. 4s   *Genevæ*, 1561

Contains Erasmus's Latin version of the New Testament, together with various expositions collected from the Fathers of the Church, as well as from later interpreters, both Lutheran and Reformed. Marloratus has also introduced some observations of his own.

3160 MARSH'S (Herb. *Bp. of Peterborough*) Comparative View of the Churches of England and Rome, 8vo. *bds.* 5s   *Camb.* 1814

3161 ———— Course of Lectures, containing a Description and Systematic Arrangement of the several branches of Divinity, with an account both of the principal Authors, and of the progress which has been made at different periods in Theological Learning, *seven parts*, in 1 vol. 8vo. *calf gilt, very scarce*, £1. 1s   *ib.* 1809-23

3162 ———— new edition, 8vo. *calf gilt*, 16s   .   1838

> The reprint of these Lectures contains only the first XXII., and are comprised in the first four parts of the original edition. The remaining three parts, which have not been reprinted, consist of XIV. Lectures. "On the Authenticity and Credibility of the New Testament, and on the Authority of the Old Testament."

3163 MARSHALL'S (Benj.) Chronological Treatise upon the Seventy Weeks of Daniel, 8vo. *calf*, 3s   .   1725

3164 ———— (Dr. Nath.) Penitential Discipline of the Primitive Church, for the first four hundred years after Christ; together with its Declension, impartially represented, 8vo. *bds.* 6s   *Oxford*, 1844

3165 MARTENE (Edmund.) de Antiquis Monachorum Ritibus, libri quinque, collecti ex variis Ordinariis, Consuetudinariis, Ritualibusque MSS., &c. 2 vols. 4to. *calf*, 14s   .   *Lugduni*, 1690

3166 ———— de Antiquis Ecclesiæ Ritibus lib. III. ex variis insigniorum Ecclesiarum Pontificalibus, Sacramentariis, Missalibus, Breviariis, Ritualibus, sive Manualibus, &c. collecti; acced. Tractatus de Antiqua Ecclesiæ Disciplina in divinis celebrandis officiis, &c. 4 vols. in 2, folio, *very fine copy, calf gilt*, £4. 4s   *Venetiis*, 1783

> "A work of the highest authority on the Ancient Rites of the Church. The most valuable collection of records relative to the occasional offices of the Western Churches."—PALMER'S *Origines Liturgicæ*.

3167 ———— ET URSINI DURAND, Thesaurus Novus Anecdotorum, 5 vols. *Lutet. Par.* 1717—Veterum Scriptorum et Monumentorum, Historicorum, Dogmaticorum, Moralium, amplissima Collectio; opera et studio D. Edmundi Martene, et D. Ursini Durand; 9 vols. *ib.* 1724-33—together 14 vols. folio, *fine copy, French calf*, £16. 16s

> MARTENE and DURAND, two learned Benedictines, following in the footsteps of the immortal Mabillon, have with incredible labour collected into fourteen volumes folio, an immense number of Ecclesiastical Documents, which, but for their industry, might have been lost entirely. Some idea of their value may be formed from the following selection:—"*Epistolæ Pontificum Imperatorum, Regum, Principum, Abbatum, &c.; Chronicon Normannicum sive Britannicum; Vitæ Sanctorum et Martyrum; Evrardi Passio S. Thomæ Cantuariensis Archiepiscopi; Bertrandi Vita S. Edmundi Archiepiscopi Cantuariensis; Historia Canonizationis S. Edmundi; S. Edmundi Miracula; Bedæ Homiliæ; Abælardi Theologia Christiana et Expositio in Hexaemeron; Rodulfi de Coggeshale Chronicon Anglicanum et Libellus de Motibus Anglicanis; Calendarium Anglicanum; Ferrerii Historia Monasterii Kenlos in Scotia; Miracula S. Anselmi; Concilia et Statuta Synodalia; Acta Concilii Basiliensis; duplex Historia Concilii Tridentini; S. S. Patrum Opuscula inedita, &c. &c.* A list of the entire contents of these volumes will be found in *Dowling's Notitia*, p. 4-9, and p. 90-101.

3168 [MARTENE (Edm.) et DURAND (Ur.)] Voyage Litteraire de deux Religieux Benedictins de la Congregation de Saint Maur, où l'on trouvera.—I. Quantité de Pieces, d'Inscriptions, et d'Epitaphs, servantes à éclaircir l'Histoire, et les Généalogies des Anciennes Familles. II. Plusieurs Usages des Eglises Cathédrales et des Monastéres, touchant la Discipline et l'Histoire des Eglises des Gaules. III. Les Fondations des Monastéres, et une infinité de recherches curieuses et interessantes, &c. 2 vols. 4to. *plates, scarce, calf*, £1. 11s 6d . . *Par*- 1717-24
3169 ———— the same, 2 vols. in 1, 4to. *fine copy, calf gilt*, £1. 18s *ib.* 1717-24

This is an account of the journies made by the Authors in search of Ecclesiastical documents, with a view to a new edition of the *Gallia Christiana*, the result of which were the *Thesauri Scriptorum et Monumentorum*.

3170 [MARTHE (———— Saint)] Lettres sur divers sujets de Morale et de Pieté, 10 vols. 18mo. *old calf gilt*, £1. 1s
Par. 1735, & *Amst.* 1782
3171 MARTIN'S (John) Sermons on the Character of Christ, 8vo. *bds.* 2s 6d . . 1793
3172 ———— (S.) Dissertation on the Nature, Effects, and Consequences of the Blasphemy against the Holy Ghost, &c. 8vo. *calf*, 2s 6d . . 1766
3173 ———— another copy, 1766—Two Discourses on the Danger of Self-Confidence, and the Scripture Doctrine of Justification, 1760 —in 1 vol. 8vo. *calf*, 3s . ——
3174 MARTYROLOGIUM.—Le Martyrologe Romain pour chaque jour de l'année, selon la Reformation du Calendrier, mis en lumiere par le Commandement du Pape Gregoire XIII., 8vo. *neat*, 3s 6d
Lyon, 1716
3175 MARVELL'S (Andrew) Rehearsal Transprosed; or, Animadversions upon a late book intituled "A Preface, shewing what grounds there are of Fears and Jealousies of Popery," 2 vols. 12mo. (*the 2nd very scarce,*) *calf, neat*, 6s . 1672-74
3176 MASCARON (Jules, *Evêque d'Agen*) Recueil des Oraisons Funebres, 12mo. *neat*, 3s . *Par.* 1741
3177 ——————— 12mo. *calf*, 3s 6d . *ib.* 1745
3178 MASON (John) The Lord's Day Evening Entertainment, containing 52 Practical Discourses, 4 vols. 8vo, *rough calf, scarce*, 10s 1752
3179 ——————— the same, 4 vols. 8vo. *calf*, 12s . 1754
3180 ——————— Self-knowledge: a treatise shewing the Nature and Benefit of that important Science, 8vo. *bds.* 3s 1813
3180*MASSEY'S (Edmund) Sermons and Tracts on various subjects, (9 tracts in 1 vol.) 8vo. *calf*, 2s 6d 1721-25
3181 MASSILLON, Œuvres, 13 vols. 8vo. *portrait, very neat*, £2. 12s 6d
Par. 1821
3182 ——————— autre exemplaire, 3 vols. 8vo. *sewed*, £1. 1s *ib.* 1843
3183 ——————— Petit Caresme, 12mo. *calf*, 3s 6d *ib.* 1757
3184 ——————— Petit-Carême; avec le Sermon sur la Passion de J. C. par Bourdaloue, &c. 12mo. *neat*, 3s 6d *ib.* 1820
3185 ——————— autre exemplaire, 18mo. *portrait, neat*, 4s *ib.* 1823

3186 MASSILLON's Sermons on the Duties of the Great, &c., translated by Dr. W. Dodd, 8vo. *bds. 3s* . 1776
3187 ——— ——— Sermons, with the Life of the Author, selected and translated by W. Dickson, 3 vols. 8vo. *hf. bd. calf, 12s.* *Edinb.* 1816
3188 MASTERS's (Robert) History of the College of Corpus Christi and the B. Virgin Mary (commonly called Bene't) in the University of Cambridge, two parts in 1 vol. 4to. *fine copy, calf, neat, (the plates of arms wanting) 8s* . *Cambr.* 1753
3189 MASTRICHT (Pet. Van) Novitatum Cartesianum Gangræna, seu Theologia Cartesiana detecta, 4to. *vellum, 5s 6d* *Amst.* 1677
3190 MATTHÆI PARIS, Monachi Albanensis, Angli, Historia Major, à Gul. Conquæstore, ad ultimam annum Henrici tertii, folio, *vellum,* £1. 1s . *Tiguri,* 1589
3191 ——— ——— Historia Major : cum Rogeri Wendoveri, Will. Rishangeri, authorisque Majori Minorique Historiis collati, cui accesserunt Vitæ Offarum, et XXIII. Abbatum S. Albani, cum variis Lectionibus, Glossariis, et Indicibus, edente Willielmo Wats, 2 vols. folio, *portrait, old calf gilt,* £1. 11s 6d *Lond.* 1640
3192 ——— ——— Editio Altera, edente W. Wats, folio, *calf,* £1. 10s *Paris,* 1644
3193 MATHER's (Nathaniel) Twenty-three select Sermons at Pinners-Hall and in Lime-Street, 8vo. *old red morocco, gilt leaves, 4s* 1701
3194 ——— ——— (Sam.) Vindication of the Holy Bible, 8vo. *calf, 3s* 1723
3195 MATTHEWS's (S. B.) Sermons intended to explain and enforce the leading truths of the Gospel, 8vo. *bds. 2s* *Aylesbury,* 1821
3196 MAUGUIN (Gilb.) Veterum Auctorum qui IX. Sæculo de Prædestinatione et Gratia, scripserunt Opera et Fragmenta, 2 vols. 4to. *calf, neat, 14s* . *Lut. Par.* 1650
3197 [MAURICE's (Dr. Henry)] Vindication of the Primitive Church, and Diocesan Episcopacy : in answer to Mr. Baxter, 8vo. *calf, 6s* 1682
3198 ——— ——— Defence of Diocesan Episcopacy, in answer to Mr. David Clarkson, 8vo. *calf, 6s* . 1700
3199 MAWER (Dr. John) The Nature and Design of the Lord's Supper, 8vo. *1s* . *York,* 1736
3200 MAXIMUS (S. *Episc. Taur.*) Opera, jussu Pii Sexti P.M. aucta, atque adnotationibus illustrata, et Victoris Amedio Sardiniæ Regi, D. D. folio, *new in calf gilt,* LARGE PAPER, £3. 3s *Romæ,* 1784
3201 MAXIMI TYRII Dissertationes, *Gr. et Lat,* recensuit et Notulis illustravit Jo. Davisius, 8vo. *calf, 6s* *Cantab.* 1703
3202 MAXWELL's (F. K.) Sermons at the Asylum for Female Orphans, 8vo. *bds. 2s* . 1809
3203 MAY's (Nath.) Sermons on the History of Joseph, 12mo. *bds. 2s* *Berkhamstead,* 1793
3204 ——— ——— (Wm.) Twenty practical Sermons on several subjects, 8vo. *calf, 3s* . . 1757
3205 MAYNARD's (Dr. Edw.) Sermons before the University of Oxford, and before the Hon. Society of Lincoln's-Inn, 2 vols. 8vo. *calf, 3s 6d* 1737

3206 MEAD'S (Matt.) Almost Christian discovered: or the False Professor tried and cast, 12mo. *bds.* 1s . 1825
3207 MEDE'S (Joseph) Works, (with his Life by J. Worthington) folio, *very scarce, calf,* £2. 10s . 1677
3208 MEDLEY'S (John, *Bp. of Fredericton)* Sermons, 12mo. *bds.* 7s 1845
3209 MELANCTHONIS (Philippi) Opera omnia, edidit cum Præfatione C. Peuceri, 4 vols. folio, *hogskin, lettered contents, scarce,* £5. 5s
Witteb. 1562-64
3210 ———— Examen eorum, qui audiuntur ante Ritum publicæ ordinationis, qua Commendatur eis ministerium Evangelii, sm. 8vo. *in the original stamped hogskin binding,* 7s *ib.* 1587
3211 ———— De P. Melancthonis Ortu, totius Vitæ Curriculo, et Morte, narratio diligens et accurata Joach. Camerarii, sm. 8vo. *in the original hogskin binding,* 5s 6d *Lipsiæ,* 1566
3212 ———— Observations upon the handwriting of Philip Melancthon, illustrated with fac-similes; also a few specimens of the autograph of Martin Luther, with explanatory remarks, by S. L. Sotheby, imp. 4to. *hf. bd. morocco,* £2. 12s 6d . 1839
Only 250 copies were printed of this highly interesting work. It is illustrated with 33 plates of fac-similes, comprising many hundred specimens of the various styles of writing adopted by Melancthon in his Common-place Book; his marginal annotations on printed works, his epistolary correspondence, and other documents preserved in the British Museum, the Royal and National Libraries at Munich, and other collections.
3213 MELVILL'S (Henry) Sermons, 8vo. *hf. bd. calf, neat,* 6s 1834
3214 ———— Sermons preached at Cambridge, in November, 1839, 8vo. *bds.* 4s 6d . . 1840
3215 ———— Sermons on certain of the less prominent facts and references in Sacred Story, vol. 2, 8vo. *bds.* 10s 1845
3216 MEMORIAL. A seasonable Memorial in some historical notes upon the Liberties of the Presse and Pulpit, &c. 4to. 3s 1680
3217 MENASSEH BEN ISRAEL, Conciliator, sive de Convenientia locorum S. Scripturæ, quæ pugnare inter se videntur, 4to. *vellum,* 6s
Amst. 1633
3218 MENDHAM'S (Joseph) Account of the Indexes both Prohibitory and Expurgatory of the Church of Rome, 8vo. *bds.* 4s 6d 1826
3219 ———— Clavis Apostolica; or a Key to the Apostolic Writings, 12mo. *bds.* 2s . 1821
3220 MENOLOGIUM Græcorum, jussu Basilii Imperatoris Græcè olim editum, nunc primum Græce et Latine prodit, studio et opera Annibalis Tit. S. Clementis Presb. Card. Albani, 3 vols. in 1, folio, *numerous plates, hogskin,* £4. 14s 6d . *Urbini,* 1727
3221 MERBESIUS (Bonus) Summa Christiana, e Sacris Literis, SS. Patrum Monumentis, Conciliorum Oraculis, Summorum denique Pontificum Decretis fideliter excerpta, 2 vols. folio, *calf gilt,* £1. 10s
Venet. 1770
3222 ———— aliud exemplar, 2 vols. folio, *calf,* £1. 10s *Par.* 1683
3223 MERCATORIS (Marii) Opera, cum Notis Jo. Garnerii, folio, *hogskin,* £2. 2s . *ib.* 1673
3224 ———— Opera, cum Notis Steph. Baluzii, 8vo. *calf,* 6s *ib.* 1684
3225 MERRICK'S (James) Annotations on the Psalms, 4to. *calf, scarce,* 9s—*bds. uncut,* 8s . *Reading,* 1768

[58, GREAT QUEEN STREET,

3226 MERRICK's (James) Psalms, translated and paraphrased in English Verse, 4to. *calf*, 8s . 1765
3227 ———— (Marshal Montagu) Marriage, a divine institution, and the high sacred Emblem of the mystical union between Christ and his Church, in two Sermons, 4to. 1s 1754
3228 METHODII (S.) Convivium Virginum, Græce et Latine, a Petro Possino, folio, *vellum, very scarce*, £1. 10s Paris. 1657
3229 MEULEN (Gerh. Vander) Veritas Religionis Christianæ reformatæ asserta, 4to. *calf*, 3s 6d . Lugd. Bat. 1667
3230 MICHAELIS (J. G.) Observationes Sacræ, in quibus diversis Sacris Scripturæ utriusque fœderis locis selectioribus ex Ling. Ebrææ, aliarumque Orientalium indole, priscorum item populorum ritibus et institutis lux adfunditur, etc. 12mo. *calf gilt*, 4s Trajecti, 1738
3231 ———— Exercitationes Theologico-Philologicæ, 8vo. *bds*. 2s 6d
   Lugd. Bat. 1757
3232 ———— Introduction to the New Testament, translated from the German, and augmented with Notes, by Bp. Herbert Marsh, 6 vols. 8vo. *hf. bd. calf*, £1. 16s Camb. 1793—1801
3233 ———— the same, 6 vols. in 4, 8vo. *fine copy, calf gilt by Mackenzie*, £2. 8s . Lond. 1802
3234 ———— another copy, 6 vols. 8vo. *calf gilt*, £3. 3s ib. 1823
3235 MIDDLETON's (Dr. Conyers) Treatise on the Roman Senate, 8vo. *calf, fine copy*, 3s . . 1747
3236 ———— Letter to Dr. Waterland, containing some Remarks on his Vindication of Scripture, in answer to [Tindal's] Christianity as Old as the Creation; together with the Sketch of another Answer [by Dr. Middleton] 1731—A Reply to the Letter to Dr. Waterland [by Z. Pearce, Bp. of Rochester] 1732—A Defence of the Letter to Dr. Waterland, [by Dr. Middleton] 1732—A Reply to the Defence, [by Bp. Pearce] 1732—Some Remarks on a Reply to the Defence, &c. [by Dr. Middleton] 1732—*in one vol.* 8vo. *bds.* 6s . . ——
3237 ———— A Popish Pagan, the Fiction of a Protestant Heathen [*i. e.* Dr. C. Middleton] a Conversation between a Gentleman of the States of Holland, a Deist by Profession, and a Doctor of Heathen Mythology, translated from the Dutch, 8vo. *calf, scarce*, 4s 1743
3238 ———— An Examination of a late Introductory Discourse to a larger Work, [by Dr. C. Middleton] concerning Miraculous Powers, by Tho. Comber, 1747—A Vindication of the Free Inquiry into the Miraculous Powers, &c. from the Objections of Dr. Dodwell and Dr. Church, by Conyers Middleton, D.D., 1751—Cursory Animadversions upon a late Controversy concerning the Miraculous Powers, &c. [by Ralph Heathcote, D.D.] 1752—in 1 vol. 4to. *hf. bd. calf*, 4s 6d . . ——
3239 ———— Free Answer to Dr. Middleton's Free Inquiry into the Miraculous Powers of the Primitive Church, by Will. Dodwell, 8vo. *sewed*, 1s 6d . . 1749
3240 ———— Letter to Dr. C. Middleton, occasioned by his late Free Inquiry, 8vo. *hf. bd. calf*, 2s 6d . 1749

3241 MIDDLETON's (Dr. Conyer) Vindication of the Miraculous Powers which subsisted in the three first centuries of the Church, in Answer to Dr. Middleton's Free Inquiry, by Tho. Church, M.A. 8vo. *calf*, 3s . 1750
3242 ———— Examination of Dr. Middleton's Free Inquiry, &c. by Z. Brooke, B.D. 8vo. *hf. bd.* 3s . Camb. 1750
3243 ———— another copy, 8vo. *tree-marbled calf extra, gilt leaves*, 6s ib. 1750
3244 ———— Two Questions previous to Dr. Middleton's Free Inquiry impartially considered, 1752—An Examination of the Bishop of London's Discourses on Prophecy, by C. Middleton, D.D., 1750—SHERLOCK's (Tho. *Bp. of London*) Appendix to the second Dissertation annexed to the Discourses on Prophecy, &c. 1749—RUTHERFORTH's (Dr. T.) Defence of the Bp. of London's Discourses on Prophecy, in a Letter to Dr. Middleton, *Camb.* 1750—*in one vol.* 8vo. *calf*, 4s 6d .
3245 ———— (T. F. *Bp. of Calcutta*) Doctrine of the Greek Article applied to the Criticism and the Illustration of the New Testament, 8vo. *bds.* 8s . 1808
3246 ———— the same, revised by the Rev. James Scholefield, 8vo. *bds.* 10s . Camb. 1828
3247 ———— with Prefatory Observations and Notes by H. J. Rose, B.D., 8vo. *bds.* 12s . 1841
3248 MILBOURNE's (Luke) Legacy to the Church of England, vindicating her Orders from the Objections of Papists and Dissenters, explaining the nature of Schism, and warning the Laity against Impostors, 2 vols. 8vo. *calf, scarce*, 8s 1722
3249 MILL's (W. H., D.D., *late Principal of Bishop's Coll. Calcutta*) Sermons preached in Lent, 1845, and on several former occasions, before the University of Cambridge, 8vo. *bds.* 12s Camb. 1845
3250 MILLAR's (Robert) History of the Propagation of Christianity, and the Overthrow of Paganism, 2 vols. 8vo. *calf*, 6s 1731
3251 MILLER's (James) Sermons on various subjects, 8vo. *bds.* 2s 1759
3252 MILNE's (Dr. Colin) Sermons, 8vo *hf. bd. calf*, 2s 6d—*calf*, 3s . 1780
3253 ———— (James) Sermons delivered in St. Andrew's Chapel, Banff, 8vo. 2s . Edinb. 1806
3254 ———— (Wm.) Retrospect of the first Ten Years of the Protestant Mission to China, 8vo. *bds.* 4s 6d Malacca, 1820
3255 [MILNER's (————)] Scripture Religion, or a Short View of the Faith and Practice of a True Christian, 8vo. *calf*, 3s 1706
3256 ———— (Jo.) Animadversions upon M. Le Clerc's Reflections upon the Saviour and his Apostles, the Primitive Fathers, and Dr. Hammond, 8vo. *calf*, 2s 6d . Camb. 1702
3257 ———— (Dr. John) Inquiry into certain Vulgar Opinions concerning the Catholic Inhabitants, and the Antiquities of Ireland, 8vo. *bds. very scarce*, 8s . 1810
3258 ———— Treatise on the Ecclesiastical Architecture of England, 8vo. *plates, bds.* 7s . 1810

3259 MILTON's (John) Tetrachordon: Expositions upon the foure chief places in Scripture which treat of Marriage, 4to. *sewed, 2s* 1645
3260 ———— ΕΙΚΟΝΟΚΛΑΣΤΗΣ, in Answer to a Book intitled Εικών Βασιλικὴ, sm. 4to. *calf, 3s* 1649
3261 ———— Pro populo Anglicano defensio, contra Cl. Anonymi, alias Salmasii defensionem regiam, 1651—Hon. Reggius de Statu Ecclesiæ Britannicæ hodierno, *Dantisci*, 1647 — *in one vol.* 4to. *vellum, 8s*
3262 ———— Poetical Works, with Notes by Tho. Newton, Bp. of Bristol, 4 vols. 8vo. *plates, calf gilt*, £1. 8s 1766-70
3262* ———— Poetical Works, with Notes of various Authors, and a Life of the Author, chiefly from Documents in the State Paper Office, by the Rev. J. H. Todd, 6 vols. 8vo. *calf extra*, £3. 10s 1826
3263 ———— Life, by Charles Symmons, D.D., 8vo. *portrait, bds. 4s 6d* 1810
3264 ———— Some Account of his Life and Writings, derived principally from documents in the State Paper Office, by the Rev. J. H. Todd, 8vo. *bds. 5s* 1826
3265 MINUCIUS Felix Octavius, cum integris observatiouibus N. Rigaltii, recensuit Jo. Davisius, præmittitur F. Balduini Dissertatio, sm. 8vo. *calf, 2s 6d* Cant. 1707
3266 ———— aliud exemplar, 24mo. *calf, 1s 6d* ib. 1643
3267 ———— Octavius, Cant. 1643—Introductio ad Sapientiam [Per Anonymum] *ib.* 1643—*in one vol.* 24mo. *calf, 1s 6d*
3268 ———— Octavius, ex recensione Jo. Davisii, cum ejusdem notis, accedit Commodianus Ævi Cyprianici Scriptor, 8vo. *calf, 4s 6d* Cant. 1712
3269 ———— Octavius, and Tertullian's Apology for the Primitive Christians, rendered into English, 8vo. *frontispiece, calf, 4s 6d* 1708
3270 MISCELLANEA Sacra, or a New Method of considering so much of the History of the Apostles as is maintained in Scripture, 2 vols. 8vo. *calf, 6s* 1725
3271 MISSALE Chaldaicum ex Decreto S. Congregationis de Propaganda Fide editum, 4to. *beautifully printed in red and black, calf extra*, £2. 10s *Romæ, ex ejusdem S. Cong. Typog.* 1767
3272 ———— Romanum, ex Decreto SS. Concilii Tridentini restitutum, S. Pii V. jussu editum, Clementis VIII. et Urbani VIII. auctoritate recognitum, folio, *printed in red and black, plates and vignettes, sealskin binding, with clasps, gilt and tooled edges, 18s* Antv. 1650
3273 MISSIONARIES. Thirty-four Conferences between the Danish Missionaries and the Malabarian Bramans, concerning the Truth of the Christian Religion, translated out of High Dutch by Mr. Philipps, 8vo. *calf, 3s 6d—calf, neat, 4s* 1719
3274 MITCHELL's (Dr. Patrick) Presbyterian Letters, addressed to Bishop Skinner, of Aberdeen, on his Vindication of Primitive Truth and Order, 8vo. *bds. 2s 6d* 1809
3275 MOLESWORTH's (J. E. N.) Passover, a Sermon, with an Appendix, 8vo. *1s 6d* 1824

3276 MOLINÆUS (Carolus) Omnia, 5 vols. folio, *calf*, £4. 4s *Paris*. 1681
3277 MOLINOS (Mich. de) Spiritual Guide, translated from the Italian, 18mo. 2s . . N. P. 1688
3278 MONASTICON Hibernicum, or the Monastical History of Ireland, containing all the Abbies, Priories, Nunneries, and other regular Communities which were in that kingdom; the several regular Orders, &c. 8vo. *with a map of Ireland, and plates, calf, very scarce*, 12s. . 1722
3279 MONCRIEFF'S (Alex.) Duty of National Covenanting explained in several Sermons, preached July 1744. *Edinb*. 1779—ARTHUR (Mich.) The two Witnesses prophesying: a Sermon. *Glasgow*, 1779—RAMSAY's (James) Public Confession of Christ, a Sermon. *ib*. 1780—WAYTOCK's (Geo.) Defence of Covenanting, against the attacks of Patr. Hutchinson. *ib*. 1780—BOSTON's (Tho.) Collection of Sermons. *Edinb*. 1772—MURRAY's (J.) Lawfulness of Self-defence, an Evening Lecture, *Glasg*. 1780—An Address to the Protestant Interest in Scotland, 1778—BISSET's (Jo.) Sermon at the Moderation of a Call to a Minister, *Aberdeen*, 1778—A Letter to the Lord Chancellor, on the Mode of Swearing upon the Gospels: by a Protestant; *in one* vol. 12mo. *hf. bd.* 3s 6d ——
3280 MONSELL's (Cha. Hen.) Temporal Punishment of Sin, and other Sermons, 12mo. *bds.* 6s . *Oxford*, 1845
3281 MONTAGU's (Rich. *Bp. of Norwich*) Appello Cæsarem: a just Appeale from two unjust Informers, 1625—A Gagg for the New Gospel? No: a New Gagg for an Old Goose, who would needes undertake to stop all Protestant's mouths for ever, with 276 places out of their owne English Bibles, &c. 1624—Immediate Addresse unto God alone, a just Treatise of Invocation of Saints, occasioned by a falsé Imputation of M. Ant. de Dominis, 1624, *in one vol.* 4to. *scarce, vellum*, £1. 1s . ——
3282 ———— Analecta Ecclesiasticarum Exercitationum, folio, *very scarce, sewed*, 10s . 1622
3283 ———— aliud exemplar, folio, *calf*, 15s 1622
3284 ———— de Originibus Ecclesiasticis Commentationes, 2 vols. in 1, folio, *vellum*, £1. 8s . 1636-40
3285 ———— ΘΕΑΝΘΡΩΠΙΚΟΝ: seu de Vita Jesu Christi Domini Nostri Originum Ecclesiasticarum libri duo, 2 vols. in 1, folio, *fine copy, very rare, vellum*, £1. 16s . 1640
3286 ———— Acts and Monuments of the Church, before Christ incarnate, 1642—Ecclesia Restaurata, or, the History of the Reformation of the Church of England, by Peter Heylin, 1661—*in one vol.* folio, *old red morocco, gilt leaves*, £1. 10s . ——
3287 MONTANUS (Bened. Arias) Commentaria in Duodecim Prophetas, sm. folio, *calf*, 7s 6d . *Antv*. 1583
3288 MOORE's (Cha.) Sermons, selected from his MSS. 2 vols. 8vo. *bds.* 6s . . 1818
3289 ———— (John, *Bp. of Ely*) Sermons on several subjects, 2 vols. 8vo. *portrait, calf*, 4s 6d . 1716

[58, GREAT QUEEN STREET,

3290 MOORE's (John, M.D.) View of Society and Manners in France, Switzerland, Germany, and Italy, 4 vols. 8vo. *fine copy, old calf gilt*, 12s . . 1780-81
3291 ———— (Sam.) ΘΕΟΣΠΛΑΓΧΝΙΣΘΕΙΣ, or, the Yearnings of Christ's Bowels towards his languishing Friends, sm. 8vo. *portrait by Marshall, neat, scarce,* 5s . 1648
3292 MORAVIANS. The History of the Moravians, from their first Settlement at Herrnhaag, to the present time, translated from the German, 1754—A candid Narrative of the Rise and Progress of the Hernhuters, or Moravians, by H. Rimius, 1753—A Supplement to the Candid Narrative, &c. 1755—*in one vol.* 8vo. *hf. bd.* 3s 6d ————
3293 MORE's (Hannah) Spirit of Prayer, 12mo. *bds.* 1s 6d   1825
3294 ———— (Hen.) Theological Works, folio, *calf. neat,* £1. 1s 1708
3295 ———— another copy, folio, *calf,* 18s   .   1708
Contaioing the Mystery of Godliness—The Mystery of Iniquity—Expositions of the Epistles to the Seven Churches in Asia—A Discourse of the Grounds of Faith—Ao Antidote against Idolatry—Divine Hymns.
3296 ———— Immortality of the Soul, so farre forth as it is demonstrated from the knowledge of Nature and the light of Reason, sm. 8vo. *hf. bd. calf gilt,* 3s 6d   .   1659
3297 ———— Explanation of the Grand Mystery of Godliness, folio, *calf,* 8s   .   .   1660
3298 ———— Modest Inquiry into the Mystery of Iniquity, folio, *calf,* 7s 6d   .   .   1664
3299 ———— (Sir Tho.) History of King Richard the Third, (edited by S. W. Singer) 8vo. *portrait, calf gilt,* 7s 6d   Chiswick, 1821
3300 ———— Memoirs of his Life, with his History of Utopia, translated into English, by Fred. Warner, LL.D., 8vo. *calf,* 4s   1758
3301 ———— Life of Sir Thos. More, by Sir James Mackintosh, 12mo. *portrait, bds.* 4s 6d   .   1844
3302 MOREHEAD's (R.) Series of Discourses, on the Principles of Religious Belief, as connected with Human Happiness and Improvement, 2 vols. 8vo. *bds.* 5s   .   Edinb. 1811-16
———— Thirty-four occasional Sermons, 8vo. *bds.* 3s   *ib.* 1825
3304 MORER's (Thos.) Sermons on several occasions, 8vo. *calf,* 2s   1708
3305 MORGAN's (Hector Davies) Survey of the Platform of the Christian Church, &c. comprising the substance of an Essay on the Christian Priesthood, 8vo. 1s 6d   .   Oxford, 1816
3306 MORICE's (Will.) Common Right to the Lord's Supper asserted, in a Diatribe and Defence thereof, folio, *old calf gilt,* 12s   1660
3307 MORINUS (Jo.) Exercitationes Ecclesiasticæ et Biblicæ, primæ quæ est de Patriarcharum et Primatum Origine : alterius, de Hebræi Græcique Textus Sinceritate libri duo, folio, *old calf gilt,* £1. 4s
Par. 1669
3308 ———— Commentarius de Sacris Ecclesiæ Ordinationibus, folio, *calf, very scarce,* £1. 16s   Antverpiæ, 1695
"The Treatise on Sacred Ordinations is exceedingly valuable. It contains a History of the Schism of the Greeks, and a collection of Rituals of the Greeks, Latins, Syrians, as well as Maronites and Nestorians, Jacobites and Eutychians, together with the Rites of Ordination of the Copticks in Egypt, &c."
Vide *Dupin.*

3309 MORINUS (Jo.) Exercitationes Ecclesiasticæ de Patriarcharum et Primatum Origine, etc. folio, *calf*, 8*s* *Par.* 1669

3310 MORLAND's (Israel) Short Description of Sion's Inhabitants, as also of the Inhabitants of the Bloody City and Harlot-Church, 4to. *calf, scarce*, 4*s* 6*d* . 1690

3311 MORLEY's (George, *Bp. of Winton*) Several Treatises, written upon several occasions, wherein his judgment is fully made known, concerning the Church of Rome and most of those doctrines which are controverted betwixt her and the Church of England, 4to. *large paper, calf*, 8*s* . . 1683

<small>Contains an examination and refutation of Maimbourg's assertion, that the Duchess of York became a Roman Catholic, from a conference she had with two English Bishops, &c. Bp. Morley was chaplain to the Royal Family whilst on the continent.</small>

3312 ——— Vindication of himself from divers False, Scandalous, and Injurious Reflexions made upon him by Mr. Richard Baxter, in several of his Writings, 4to. *calf*, 5*s* . 1683

3313 ——— (John) Discourses, Doctrinal and Practical, 8vo. *hf. bd. calf*, 3*s* 6*d* *Ipswich*, 1815

3314 MORNING EXERCISES, at Cripplegate, St Giles's, and Southwark, opened by several Ministers of the City of London, (Owen, Manton, Baxter, Bates, Jenkyns, Alsop, Vincent, Burgess, &c.) 6 vols. 4to. *fine copy, uniform in size, new in brown calf, carmine edges, very neat*, £8. 8*s* . 1676-90

3315 ——— at Cripplegate ; or several Cases of Conscience practically resolved by sundry Ministers, Sept. 1661, 4to. *old blue morocco, gilt leaves, presentation copy from Dr. S. Annesley, the editor*, 18*s* . . 1661

<small>This volume contains a Sermon by Abp. Tillotson, ("Wherein lies that exact righteousness which is required between man and man?") not included in any edition of his works.</small>

3316 MORRIS's (Joseph) Sermons on various subjects, with the Author's Life, 2 vols. 8vo. *calf*, 4*s* . 1743-57

3317 MORTON (Tho. *Bp. of Durham*) Apologiæ Catholicæ, in qua Paradoxa, Hæreses, Blasphemiæ, Scelera, quæ Jesuitæ, et Pontificii alii Protestantibus impingunt, fere omnia, ex ipsorum Pontificiorum testimoniis apertis diluuntur, Libri duo, de Notis Ecclesiæ, *Lond.* 1606—MATTHÆI SUTLIVII de Recta Studii Theologici ratione liber I. cum brevi de Concionum ad Populum formulis, libello, *Hanov.* 1604—2 vols. in 1, sm. 8vo. *new in stamped calf, old style, very rare*, 18*s* . . —

<small>The former of the above works is dedicated to Abp. Bancroft.</small>

3318 ——— Antidotum adversus Ecclesiæ Romanæ de Merito propriè dicto ex condigno Venenum, 4to. *rare, calf, gilt leaves*, 8*s* 6*d* *Cantab.* 1637

3319 MORUS (Alex.) Ad Esaiæ caput liii de Perpessionibus et Gloria Messiæ notæ ac diatribæ, 4to. *vellum*, 3*s* *Amst.* 1658

3320 MOSHEMIUS (Jo. Laur.) Institutiones Historiæ Christianæ majores, Sæculum primum, 4to. *sprinkled calf gilt*, 14*s* *Helmst.* 1739

3321 MOSHEMII Elementa Theologiæ Dogmaticæ; edita à Chr. Ern. de Windheim, 2 vols. sm. 8vo. *calf, neat, 6s*　*Norimb.* 1781

3322 ——— Dissertationes ad Historiam Ecclesiasticam pertinentes, 2 vols. sm. 8vo. *portrait, vellum, scarce, 8s*　*Atonæ,* 1767

3323 ——— de Rebus Christianorum ante Constantinum Magnum Commentarii, 4to. *calf gilt, scarce, £1. 1s*　*Helmst.* 1753

3324 ——— Commentaries on the Affairs of Christians before the time of Constantine the Great, translated, with Notes by Vidal, 3 vols. 8vo. *bds. £1. 1s*　.　1813-35

3325 ——— Historiæ Ecclesiasticæ antiquæ et recentioris libri IV. 4to. *calf,* 12s　.　*Helmst.* 1753

3326 ——— Ecclesiastical History, antient and modern, from the birth of Christ, to the beginning of the present century; translated by Arch. Maclaine, 2 vols. 4to. *calf,* 18s　.　1765

3327 MOSHEIM'S Ecclesiastical History, ancient and modern, translated by Maclaine, and continued by Cha. Coote, with a Dissertation on the state of the Primitive Church, by Bp. Gleig, 6 vols. 8vo. *calf gilt, £1.* 16s　.　1826

3328 ——— Institutes of Ecclesiastical History, ancient and modern, a new and literal translation from the original Latin, with copious additional Notes, original and selected, by James Murdoch, D.D.; edited, with additions, by Henry Soames, M.A. 4 vols. 8vo. *bds. £2. 2s—calf gilt, £2.* 16s　.　1845

3329 MOSIS Choronensis Historia Armenicæ Libri III. Accedit ejusdem Scriptoris Epitome Geographiæ, *Armenicè et Latine,* præmittitur Præfatio quæ de Literatura, ac Versione Sacra Armeniaca agit; et subjicitur Appendix, quæ continet Epistolas duas Pauli ad Corinthios, *Arm. Gr. et Lat.* Notis illust. Gul. et Geo. Whiston, 4to. *calf, very scarce, £1.* 10s　1736

3330 MOSS' (Dr. Robert, *Dean of Ely*) Sermons and Discourses, 8 vols. 8vo. *fine copy, old calf gilt, £1. 1s*　.　1736-38

3331 MOSSOM'S (R. *Bp. of Londonderry*) Preacher's Tripartite; the first, to raise Devotion, in Meditations upon Psalm xxv.; the second, to administer comfort, by Conference with the Soul in particular cases of Conscience; the third, to establish truth and peace, in several Sermons against the present Heresies and Schisms, folio, *calf,* 5s　.　1657

3332 ——— another copy, folio, *brown calf, neat, title reprinted, 7s 6d* 1657

3333 MOTTERSHEAD'S (Jos.) Religious Discourses on various subjects, 12mo. *calf,* 4s　.　*Glasgow,* 1759

3334 MOUCHON (Pierre) Sermons sur divers textes de l'Ecriture Sainte, 2 vols. in 1, 8vo. *hf. bd. calf, neat,* 4s　*Genève,* 1798

"Sa logique fort et pressant ne l'abandonne jamais, le genre persuasif est plus familier pour lui que le genre onctueux touchant."

3335 MOUNTAGUE'S (Hon. Walter) Miscellanea Spiritualia; or Devout Essaies, 4to. *engraved title by Marshall, hf. bd. calf, neat,* 7s 1648

3336 MOUNTAIN's (J. H. B.) Twenty-one Sermons on various subjects, 12mo. *bds.* 2s . 1835
3337 MOURAVIEFF's (A. N.) History of the Church of Russia, translated by the Rev. R. W. Blackmore, 8vo. *bds.* 14s   Oxford, 1842
3338 MOYER LECTURES.—1719-20. WATERLAND's (Dr. D.) Eight Sermons in defence of the Divinity of our Lord Jesus Christ, 8vo. *calf*, 4s . . Camb. 1720
3339 ———— KNIGHT's (Dr. James) Eight Sermons in defence of the Divinity of our Lord Jesus Christ, and of the Holy Spirit, 8vo. *calf*, 2s 6d . . 1721
3340 ———— 1728-29. FELTON's (Dr. Henry) Christian Faith asserted against Deists, Arians, and Socinians, 8vo. *calf*, 4s   1732
3341 ———— 1729-30. TRAPP's (Joseph) Doctrine of the most Holy and Ever-blessed Trinity briefly stated and proved; with Discourses on the Parable of Dives and Lazarus, 8vo. *calf*, 2s 6d
    1731
3342 ———— 1730-31. BROWNE's (John) Divine Authority of the Christian Religion, and the Natural Deity of Jesus Christ asserted, 8vo. *calf*, 3s . . 1732
3343 ———— 1733-34. WHEATLEY's (Cha.) Nicene and Athanasian Creeds, explained and confirmed by the Holy Scriptures, 8vo. *calf*, 5s . . 1746
3344 ———— 1737-38. BERRIMAN's (John) Critical Dissertation on 1 Tim. iii. 16, wherein the common reading of that text is proved to be the true one, 8vo. *calf*, 4s 6d . 1741
3345 ———— 1740-41. RIDLEY's (Glocester) on the Divinity and Operations of the Holy Ghost, 8vo. *bds.* 3s 6d   1802
3346 ———— 1764-65. DAWSON's (Benj.) Illustration of several Texts of Scripture, particularly those in which the Logos occurs; with two Tracts on an Intermediate State, 8vo. *calf*, 4s 6d—*bds.* 3s
    1765
3347 MOYSEY's (C. A.) Lectures on the Gospel according to St. John, 2 vols. 8vo. *bds.* 5s . Oxford, 1821-22
3348 MUDGE's (Z.) Sermons on different subjects, 8vo. *calf*, 3s   1739
3349 ———— Essay towards a new English Version of the Book of Psalms, from the original Hebrew, 4to. *calf*, 7s   1744
3350 MUNKHOUSE's (Dr. Rd) Occasional Discourses on various subjects, with copious annotations, 3 vols. 8vo. *portrait, bds.* 6s   1805
3351 ———— Sermons on various subjects, chiefly practical, 8vo. *bds.* 3s—*calf gilt, marbled leaves*, 4s 6d . 1813
3352 MUNTON's (Anth.) Sermons preached in Newcastle-upon-Tyne, 8vo. 2s 6d . Newc. 1756
3352*MURATORI (L. A.) Liturgia Romana Vetus tria Sacramentaria complectens, Leonianum scilicet, Gelasianum, et antiquum Gregorianum: accedunt Missale Gothicum, Missale Francorum; duo Gallicana, et duo omnium vetustissimi Romanæ Ecclesiæ rituales libri, 2 vols. in 1, folio, *fine copy, pannelled calf gilt, carmine edges*, £2. 16s
    Venet. 1748

3353 MURET'S (——) Rites of Funerals, ancient and modern, in use throughout the known world, translated by P. Lorrain, 12mo. *hf. bd. calf,* 2s . 1683
3354 MURRAY'S (James) Sermons to Doctors in Divinity; to which is subjoined, Lectures to Lords Spiritual; or, an Advice to the Bishops, and a Sermon on Self-Defence, &c. 12mo. *bds.* 2s
Glasgow, 1798
3355 MUSCULUS (Wolfg.) Comment. in Genesim, Psalmos, Jesaiam, Matthæum, et Joannem, 5 vols. folio, *not uniform,* £1. 11s 6d
Basil. v. y.
3356 ——— —— Common-places of Christian Religion, for the use of suche as desire the knowledge of godly truthe, translated out of Latine into Englishe (by John Man); hereunto are added, two other treatises made by the same author, one of Othes, and another of Usurye, folio, 𝔅lack letter, *calf,* 18s   *Lond.* 1563
3357 MUSCUT'S (James) Sermons on several subjects, 8vo. *calf,* 2s 6d
Camb. 1760
3358 NÆVIUS (Jo.) Eremus Augustiniana floribus honoris et sanctitatis vernans, 4to. *hf. bd.* 4s . [*Lovan.*] 1635
3359 NALSON'S (Val.) Twenty Sermons on various subjects, most of them preached in the Cathedral of York, 8vo. *calf, scarce,* 3s   1737
3360 NANCE'S (Dr. Jo.) Sermons, plain, brief, and explanatory, on the Lord's Prayer and Ten Commandments, 12mo. *bds.* 3s   1829
3361 NANTES.—The History of the famous Edict of Nantes: containing an Account of all the Persecutions that have been in France from its first publication to this present time, 2 vols. 4to. *calf,* 12s 1694

"It was a wonderful pleasure to Queen Mary to see this book made English, and was the only book to which she ever granted her license."—*Dunton's Memoirs.*

3362 NAPIER'S (John, *Lord of Marchiston*) Plain Discovery of the whole Revelation of St. John; whereunto are annexed certain Oracles of Sybilla, agreeing with the Revelation, &c. 4to. *scarce,* 6s   ———

"This curious and learned work, which produced a great sensation when first published, has been translated into the French, Dutch, and German languages."
Lowndes.

3363 NAPLETON'S (Dr. John) Sermons for the use of Schools and Families, 8vo. *calf,* 3s . *Hereford,* 1802
3364 NARE'S (Dr. Edw.) Discourses on the Three Creeds, and on the homage offered to our Saviour on certain occasions during his ministry, as expressed by the Greek term προσκυνεω, preached before the University of Oxford, 8vo. *hf. bd. calf, neat,* 4s   1819
3365 ——— —— Remarks on the Version of the New Testament edited by the Unitarians, &c. 8vo. 3s 6d . 1814
3366 ——— (Rob.) Discourses preached before the Hon. Society of Lincoln's Inn, 8vo. *bds.* 3s 6d . 1794
3367 NEAL'S (Dan.) History of the Puritans, or Protestant Non-Conformists, from the Reformation to the death of Queen Elizabeth, 4 vols. 8vo. *hf.bd. calf,* 18s . 1732-38
3368 ——— —— another copy, 4 vols. 8vo. *calf,* £1. 4s   1732-38
3369 NEALE'S (J. M.) Hierologus; or, the Church Tourists, 12mo. *bds.* 4s . . 1843

3370 NEAL'S (J. P.) and LE KEUX'S (J.) Views of the most interesting Collegiate and Parochial Churches in Great Britain ; with Historical and Architectural Descriptions, 2 vols. 4to. LARGE PAPER, INDIA PROOFS, *hf. bd. uncut*, £2. 2s   1824
3371 NEANDER's (Aug.) History of the Christian Religion and Church during the three first Centuries, vol. 1, 8vo. *bds.* 6s   1831
3372 NECKER ( ) Of the Importance of Religious Opinions, translated from the French, 8vo. *hf. bd. calf*, 2s 6d   .   1788
3373 NECTARIUS, (*Patr. Hierosil.*) Confutatio Imperii Papæ in Ecclesiam, 1702—The Book of Psalms, with the argument of each Psalm, and a Preface [by P. Allix.] 1701—*in one* vol. 8vo. *calf*, 9s ——
3374 NEEDHAM's (Rob.) Six Sermons preached at S. Marie's in Cambridge, 8vo. *calf*, 2s   .   1679
3375 NELSON's (Rob.) Companion for the Festivals and Fasts, with Life, &c., by Wm. Kirke, 12mo. *frontispiece, calf*, 2s   1715
3376 ——————— Companion for the Festivals and Fasts of the Church of England ; with Collects and Prayers for each Solemnity, 8vo. *frontispiece*, 4s   .   1752
3377 NEMESII de Natura Hominis, Liber unus. Gr. et Lat. *Antv.* 1565 —Alphabetum Græcum ; addita sunt Th. Bezæ Scholia, in quibus de Germana Græcæ Linguæ pronuntiatione disseritur, *R. Steph.* 1554. 2 vols. in 1, 12mo. *calf*, 5s   .   ——
3378 NESSE's (Chr.) Protestant Antidote against the Poyson of Popery, 12mo. *calf*, 4s   .   1679
3379 NEVE's (Tim.) Seventeen Sermons on various subjects, 8vo. *bds.* 3s
Oxford, 1798
3380 NEW TESTAMENT, translated out of Greeke by Theod. Beza, Englished by L. Tonson, *a perfect copy of the first edition, dedicated to Sir F. Walsingham, very rare*, 12mo. *blue morocco, gilt leaves*, £5. 5s   *Lond. by C. Barker*, 1576
3381 ——————— with Moral Reflections upon every Verse by Father Quesnel, translated by Russell, 4 vols. 8vo. *calf, very scarce*, £2. 5s   1719
3382 NEWCOME'S (Peter) History of the Abbey of St. Alban, exhibiting the Life of each Abbot, and the principal events relating to the Monastery, 2 parts, in 1 vol. 4to. *plates, hf. bd. calf gilt*, 10s 6d 1793-95
3383 ——————— (Wm. *Abp. of Armagh*) English Harmony of the Four Evangelists, with Notes and Indexes, 8vo. *map, hf. bd. calf, neat*, 7s 6d   .   .   1327
3384 ——————— Attempt towards an improved Version, a Metrical arrangement, and an Explanation of the Twelve Minor Prophets, 4to. *calf*, 12s   .   .   1785
3385 ——————— Observations on our Lord's Conduct as a Divine Instructor, and on the Excellence of his Moral Character, 4to. *calf*, 7s 6d
1782
3386 ——————— Observations on our Lord's Conduct, &c., 1782—The Question concerning Literary Property determined by the King's Bench, in the cause between A. Millar and R. Taylor, 1773, *in one vol.* 4to. *calf*, 9s   .   ——
3387 ——————— Harmony of the Gospels ; in which the Original Text is disposed after Le Clerc's manner ; with Wetstein's various readings and notes, &c. folio, *bds.* 10s 6d   *Dublin*, 1778

[58, GREAT QUEEN STREET,

3388 [NEWCOME'S (Mrs. —)] Enquiry into the evidence of the Christian Religion, 8vo. *calf*, 1s 6d . Camb. 1728
3389 NEWCOURT'S (Rich.) Repertorium Ecclesiasticum; an Ecclesiastical, Parochial History of the Diocese of London, containing an Account of the Bishops of that See; also of the Deans, Archdeacons, &c.; and lastly, of the several Religious Houses, 2 vols. folio, *portrait, calf,* £2. 12s 6d . 1708-10
3390 NEWLIN'S (Tho. *Magd. Coll. Oxon.*) Eighteen Sermons on several occasions, 8vo. *calf*, 6s . Oxford, 1720
"There is a zeal and pathos in them which rank them among the most useful Sermons and elegant compositions in the language."—*Clapham.*
3391 NEWMAN'S (J. H.) Works, viz., Parochial Sermons, Lectures on Justification, Sermons chiefly on the Theory of Religious Belief, and on Subjects of the Day, together 9 vols. 8vo. *calf extra, lettered contents,* £5. 15s 6d 1840-4
3392 ——— Parochial Sermons, 6 vols. 8vo. *cloth bds.* £3. 3s 1844
3393 ——— Lectures on Justification, 8vo. *cloth bds.* 10s 6d 1840
3394 ——— Sermons, chiefly on the Theory of Religious Belief, preached before the University of Oxford, 8vo. *cloth,* 9s 6d 1843
3395 ——— Sermons, chiefly bearing on Subjects of the Day, 8vo. *cloth bds.* 12s . 1844
3396 ——— Selections from the first four volumes of Parochial Sermons, 12mo. *bds.* 6s . 1841
3397 ——— Essay on the Development of Christian Doctrine, 8vo. *bds.* 12s . . 1846
3398 ——— (Tho.) Sermons on Happiness, and other subjects, 2 vols. 8vo. *calf*, 5s . . 1760
3399 NEWSON'S (John) Brief Explication of the Christian Religion, by question and answer, with Eight Sermons. 8vo. *bds.* 2s ——
3400 NEWTON'S (Benj.) Sermons on several occasions, 2 vols. 8vo. *port. calf*, 4s . . 1736
3401 ——— (Tho. *Bp. of Bristol.*) Works, with some Account of his Life, and anecdotes of several of his friends, written by himself, 3 vols. 4to. *portrait, calf,* £1. 11s 6d . 1782
3402 ——— Dissertations on the Prophecies, which have remarkably been fulfilled, and at this time are fulfilling in the world, 3 vols. 8vo. *half bd. calf, neat,* 16s . 1786
3403 NEW YEAR'S GIFT, complete: composed of Prayers and Meditations, &c. 18mo. *front. calf,* 3s . 1693
3404 NICHOLLS'S (Benj.) Book of Proverbs explained and illustrated, 12mo. *bds.* 1s 6d . 1842
3405 ——— (Dr. Wm.) Practical Essay of the Contempt of the World, sm. 8vo. *calf,* 2s . 1698
3406 ——— Commentary on the Book of Common Prayer, with the additional notes of Bp. Andrews, Bp. Cosins, &c. folio, *very scarce, calf, cut in the margins,* £1. 11s 6d . 1712
3407 ——— Paraphrase on the Psalter, or Psalms of David, 8vo. *calf, neat,* 5s 6d . . 1716
3408 ——— Conference with a Theist; containing an Answer to all the most usual objections of the Infidels against the Christian Religion, 2 vols. 8vo. *calf,* 6s . 1723

3409 NICHOLSON's (Will. *Bp. of Gloucester,*) Plain, but full Exposition of the Catechism of the Church of England, 4to. *calf, 5s* 1661
3410 ——— another edition, 4to. *calf, neat, 6s* 1662
3411 ——— new edition. 8vo. *bds. 6s* *Oxford*, 1844
3412 NICOLE (Pierre) Instructions Theologiques et Morales sur les Sacremens, 2 vols. 12mo. *hf. bd. calf, neat, 3s 6d* *Par.* 1767
3413 ——— Instructions Theologiques et Morales sur le Symbole 2 vols. 12mo. *hf. bd. calf, neat, 5s 6d* . *ib.* 1781
3414 NICOLL's (Dr. Alex.) Sermons, 8vo. *bds. 5s* *Oxford*, 1830
3415 NICOLSON's (Wm. *Abp. of Cashel*) Letters on various subjects, literary, political, and ecclesiastical, to and from him, including the Correspondence of several eminent Prelates, from 1683 to 1727; illustrated with literary and historical Anecdotes, by John Nichols, 2 vols. 8vo. *bds. 4s 6d* . 1809
3416 NILUS (S. *Asceta*,) Epistolarum Libri IV. *Gr. et Lat.* interprete L. Allatio, folio. *calf, £1. 4s* . *Romæ*, 1668

Dr. Parr's copy, with his book-plate.

3417 NISBET's (Alex.) Brief Exposition of the First and Second Epistles general of Peter, sm. 8vo. *neat, 14s* . *Edinb.* 1658
3418 NISBETT's (N.) Triumphs of Christianity over Infidelity displayed, or the Coming of the Messiah the true Key to the right understanding of the most difficult passages in the New Testament, 8vo. *hf. bd. calf, 3s* . 1802
3419 NOEL's (G. T.) Sermons, intended chiefly for the use of Families, 8vo. *hf. bd. calf, 4s 6d* . 1827
3420 ——— another copy 2 vols. 12mo, *bds. 7s* . 1830
3421 ——— — Sermons, 2 vols. 8vo. *hf. bd. calf gilt, 8s* 1826-27
3422 NOESSELTUS (Jo. Aug.) Opuscula ad Interpretationem Sacrarum Scripturarum, et ad Historiam Ecclesiasticam, 3 vols. in 1, sm. 8vo. *calf, neat, 8s* . *Halæ*, 1785-1817
3423 NOLAN's (Frederick) Inquiry into the Integrity of the Greek Vulgate, or received Text of the New Testament, 8vo. *calf gilt, 6s — bds. 4s* 1815

" To the biblical inquirer, it will present not only a new and wide field of most curious and happy research, but a mine of the most valuable information: to the classical inquirer it will be a most interesting work, as it involves so many points, both with respect to manuscripts and editions, which to him must be highly important. Of a volume that displays so much labour in investigation, so much originality in deduction, and so much sound principle in design, we can in common justice say no less, than that, whatever be the issue of the controversy which it has, we think very seasonably, revived, it reflects honour on the age and nation in which it was produced."—*Brit. Crit.*

3424 ——— The Time of the Millenium investigated, and its Nature determined on Scriptural ground, 8vo. *bds. 3s* 1831
3425 NOLDIUS (Chr.) Concordantiæ Particularum Ebrœo-Chaldaicarum, J. G. Tympius recensuit, *best edition*, 4to. *vellum, port. 16s* *Jenæ*, 1734
3426 NORDEN's (Jo.) Poore Man's Rest; founded upon Motives, Meditations, and Prayers, expressing to the Inward Man true consolation, 𝔅𝔩𝔞𝔠𝔨 𝔩𝔢𝔱𝔱𝔢𝔯, 24mo. *calf, 4s 6d* . 1615

[58, GREAT QUEEN STREET,

J. LESLIE'S CATALOGUE. 209

3427 [NORMAN'S] Lay-Nonconformity justified, in a Dialogue between a Gentleman of the town, and his Dissenting Friend in the country, 1728—Lay-Nonconformity further justified, in a Second Dialogue, 1718, *in one* vol. 8vo. *calf*, 2s

3428 NORRIS's (John, *of Bemerton*) Two Treatises concerning the Divine Light, sm. 8vo. *hf. bd. calf*, 2s . 1692

3429 ———— Letters concerning the Love of God, 8vo. *calf*, 2s 6d 1695

3430 ———— Account of Reason and Faith, in relation to the Mysteries of Christianity, 8vo. *calf*, 4s 6d . 1697

3431 ———— Treatises upon several subjects, 8vo. *calf*, 3s 6d 1698

3432 ———— Christian Blessedness, or Discourses upon the Beatitudes, 8vo. *neat*, 3s . 1740

3433 ———— Practical Discourses on the Beatitudes, 4 vols. 8vo. *not uniform, calf*, 10s . 1694

3434 ———— Collection of Miscellanies, consisting of Poems, Essays, Discourses, and Letters, 8vo. *calf*, 3s . 1692

3435 ———— the same, 8vo. *old calf gilt*, 3s 6d . 1706

" Norris is a fine writer for style and thought."—*Waterland.*

3436 NOVATIANUS (*Presb. Rom.*) Opera quæ extant, edita notisque illustrata per Ed. Welchman, 8vo. *calf*, 8s *Oxon.* 1724

3437 NOVUM TESTAMENTUM, Theod. Bezæ interprete, 12mo. *fine clean copy, in the original vellum wrapper*, 6s
Lond. T. *Vautrolerius*, 1687

3438 NOWELL (Alex.) Catechismus; sive Prima Institutio Disciplinaque Pietatis Christianæ, accedit J. G. Vossii Disputatio theologica de Sacramentorum vi et efficacia, 8vo. *hf. bd. calf*, 5s 6d *Oxon.* 1795

3439 ———— Life, chiefly compiled from Registers, Letters, and other authentic evidences, by Ralph Churton, 8vo. *plates, bds.* 6s . . *Oxford*, 1809

3440 NUTBROWNE MAID (The), from the earliest edition of Arnold's Chronicle, (edited by Thomas Wright) Black letter, 16mo. *hf. bd. morocco*, 5s . 1836

3441 NYE's (Stephen) Discourse concerning Natural and Revealed Religion, 8vo. *calf*, 1s 6d . 1696

3442 O'BEIRNE's (Tho. Lewis, *Bp. of Ossory*) Sermon before the Association for discountenancing Vice, 8vo. *calf*, 2s *Dublin*, 1798

Presentation copy from the Association to Mrs. Hannah More: it afterwards belonged to W. Wilberforce, Esq., as appears by his book-plate.

3443 ———— Sermons, with three Charges and a circular Letter to the Clergy of the Diocese of Ossory, 8vo. *bds.* 2s 6d 1799

3444 ———— Sermons and Charges, 3 vols. 8vo. *hf. bd. calf, neat*, 9s
1799-1821

3445 OBERLIN (John Fred.) Memoirs of J. F. Oberlin, Pastor of Waldbach in the Ban de la Roche, 8vo. *portrait and plates, bds.* 5s 1829

3446 ———— another copy, 8vo. *bds.* 4s 6d . 1830

3447 O'BRIEN's (James Tho., *Bp. of Ossory, &c.*) Charge at his Primary Visitation in September, 1842, 8vo. *sewed*, 3s 1843

3448 ODE (Jacobus) Commentarius de Angelis, 4to. *vellum, scarce*, 8s
Trajecti ad Rh. 1755

3449 O'Donnoghue's (H. C.) Christian Faith, stated and explained, in a course of Practical Lectures, 12mo. *hf. bd. calf*, 2*s* 1817
3450 Œcumenii Commentaria in Acta Apostolorum, in omnes Pauli Epistolas, et in Epistolas Catholicas omnes. Accesserunt Arethæ Cæsareæ Capp. Episcopi Explanationes in Apocalypsin, *Gr. et Lat.* Ed. Jo. Heutenio et Fed. Morello, 2 vols. folio, *vellum*, £2. 2*s*
Lut. Par. 1630-31
3451 Oelrichs (Jo.) Primæ Lineæ Institutionum Homileticarum, in usum Prælectionum ductæ, sm. 8vo. *sewed*, 1*s* 6*d* *Bremæ*, 1769
3452 —— — Commentarius de Scriptoribus Ecclesiæ Latinæ priorum VI. Sæculorum ; curavit A. H. L. Heeren, 8vo. *calf gilt*, 8*s*
Lips. 1791
3453 Office de la Semaine Sainte, a l'usage de Rome, en Latin et en François, 12mo. *ruled with red lines, plates, old red morocco, with morocco linings, gilt and marbled leaves,* 7*s* 6*d*
Par. 1675
3454 Ogden's (Dr. Sam.) Sermons on the Ten Commandments, 8vo. *bds.* 2*s* . . *Camb.* 1777
3455 ——— —— Sermons on the efficacy of Prayer, on the Articles of the Christian Faith, on the Ten Commandments, and on the Lord's Supper ; with the Author's Life by S. Hallifax, 2 vols. sm. 8vo. *fine copy, old calf gilt,* 7*s* . *Camb.* 1786
3456 ——— ——— another copy, 8vo. *calf gilt,* 6*s* . 1814
3457 Ogilvie's (Dr. James) Sermons on various subjects, 8vo. *calf gilt,* 3*s*—*hf. bd. calf*, 2*s* . 1786
3458 ——— ——— the same, large paper, 8vo. *calf*, 4*s* 6*d* 1786
3459 ——— ——— (Dr. John) Sermons on several subjects, 12mo. 1*s* 6*d* 1768
3460 Oldfield's (Josh.) Essay towards the improvement of Reason, in the pursuit of Learning and Conduct of Life, 8vo. *calf*, 2*s* 6*d* 1707
3461 Oldisworth's (Giles) Stone rolled away, and Life more abundant ; an Apologie urging Self-denyal, New-Obedience, Faith, and Thankfulnesse, 4to. *scarce, hf. bd. calf,* 6*s* . 1663
3462 [——— —— (Wm.)] Essay on the Nature, Extent, and Authority of Private Judgment in matters of Religion, 1711—A Vindication of the Bp. of Exeter, occasioned by Mr. Benj. Hoadley's Reflections on his Lordship's two Sermons of Government, 1709— in 1 vol. 8vo. *calf*, 2*s* 6*d* . . ——
3463 ——— —— Dialogue between Timothy and Philatheus, in which the principles of a late whimsical book, entitled, "The Rights of the Christian Church," are stated and answered, 3 vols. 8vo. *calf*, 6*s*
1709
3464 Oldmixon's (John) History of England during the reigns of Hen. VIII., Edw. VI., Mary, and Elizabeth, including the History of the Reformation of the Churches of England and Scotland, folio, *calf,* 12*s* . . 1739
3465 Olearius (Jo. Gottf.) Bibliotheca Scriptorum Ecclesiasticorum, cum præfatione J. F. Buddei, curante J. G. Oleario filio, 2 vols. in 1, 4to. *vellum,* 5*s* . *Jenæ,* 1711
3466 ——— —— Observationes Sacræ ad Evangelium Matthæi, 4to. *vellum,* 6*s* . . 1713
Mentioned with great approbation by J. B. Carpzov.

[58, great queen street,

3467 OLIVA (Jo. Paulus) IN SELECTA SCRIPTURÆ LOCA ETHICÆ COMMENTATIONES, (in Genesim, in Canticum Canticorum, in Esdram, de Cyro Regno, et Stromata ex Divinis Scripturæ,) 6 vols. folio, RARE, *hogskin*, £3. 3s . *Lugduni*, 1677-9

3468 OPTATUS (S. *Milev. Episc.*) de Schismate Donatistarum Libri VII. quibus accessere, ad eam spectantibus Historia Donatistarum, una cum Monumentis Veteribus, opera et studio Lud. Ellies Dupin, folio, *calf*, £1. 16s . *Lutet. Par.* 1700

3468* ——— aliud exemplar, folio, *hogskin*, £1. 16s *ib.* 1700

3469 ORAISONS Funèbres de Bossuet, Fléchier, et autres Orateurs, avec un Discours préliminaire et des Notices par M. Dussault, 4 vols. 8vo. *portraits and plates, calf extra*, £1. 15s *Par.* 1820-26

3470 ORDINANCE of the Lords and Commons for keeping of scandalous persons from the Sacrament of the Lord's Supper, the enabling of Congregations for the choyce of Elders, &c. 4to. 2s 1645

3471 ——— All the several Ordinances and Orders made by the Lords and Commons concerning Sequestring the Estates of Delinquents, Papists, Spyes, &c. 4to. *sewed*, 2s 1650

3472 ORIGENIS Opera omnia, quæ Græce vel Latine, tantum extant et ejus nomine circumferuntur, ex variis Editionibus et Codicibus MSS. collecta, recensita, Latine versa, atque Annotationibus illustrata, cum copiosis Indicibus, Vita Auctoris, et multis Dissertationibus, opera et studio D. Caroli Delarue, *best edition*, 4 vols. folio, RARE, *fine copy, calf*, £15. 15s . *Par.* 1733-59

3473 ——— Commentaria in S. Scripturam, *Gr. et Lat.;* edidit P. D. Huetius qui præfixit Origeniana, opus quo Origenis narratur vita, &c. 2 vols. folio, *fine copy, old red morocco, gilt leaves*, £3. 3s *Rothomagi*, 1668

3474 ——— aliud exemplar, 2 vols. in 1, folio, *vellum*, £2. 2s *Coloniæ*, 1685

3475 ——— idem, 2 vols. folio, LARGE PAPER, *calf, neat*, £3. 10s *Lut. Par.* 1679

3476 ——— Hexapla, Hebraice, Græce et Latine, *Editio Benedictina*, Notis illustrata, studio et labore B. de Montfaucon, 2 vols. folio, *fine copy, calf*, £2. 15s *Par.* 1713

3477 ——— de Oratione, una cum Anonymi Scholiis in Orationem Dominicam, &c. *Gr. et Lat.;* ed. Gul. Reading, 4to. *calf*, 6s 1728

3478 ——— Philocalia, de Obscuris S. Scripturæ locis, a SS.PP. Basilio Magno et Gregorio Theologo, ex variis Origenis Commentariis excerpta; Zachariæ Scholastici de Mundi Opificio Disputatio; Anastasius de Hominis ad Imaginem Dei Creatione, et celebres Opiniones de Anima), *Gr. et Lat.* opera et studio Jo. Tarini, 4to. *vellum*, 8s . *Par.* 1619

3479 ——— Contra Celsum Libri VIII. Ejusdem Philocalia, *Gr. et Lat.* Gul. Spencerus recognovit et annotationes adjecit; accedunt notæ D. Hoeschelii et Jo. Tarini, *best edition*, 4to. *calf*, 10s *Cant.* 1677

3480 ——— aliud exemplar, 4to. *title and first four leaves slightly damaged, calf*, 6s . *ib.* 1658

3481 ORIGEN against Celsus, translated by J. Bellamy, 8vo. *calf, very scarce*, 12s . . N. D.

3482 OROSIUS (Paulus) Adversus Paganos Historiarum Libri septem; illustrati opera et studio F. F. Marcodurani, sm. 8vo. *hf. bd.* 12s
Mogunt, 1615
From the collection of the late Duke of Sussex.

3483 ———— The Anglo-Saxon Version of the Historian Orosius, by Ælfred the Great; with an English translation from the Anglo-Saxon, (by Daines Barrington), 8vo. *calf, scarce*, 18s   1773

3484 ORR's (John) Fourteen Sermons on various subjects, 8vo. *calf*, 2s 6d
1739

3485 ORTHODOX CHURCHMAN'S MAGAZINE; or, Treasury of Divine and Useful Knowledge, 15 vols. 8vo. *portrait, calf*, £1. 8s   1801-8

3486 ORTHODOXOGRAPHA Theologiæ Sacrosanctæ ac syncerioris Fidei Doctores Numero LXXVI. Ecclesiæ Columina Luminaque clarissima, Authores partim Græci partim Latini, quorum quidem nulli hactenus visi, (cura Joannis Heroldi editi,) folio, *fine copy, pigskin, rare*, £1. 11s 6d   *Basil*. 1555

3486* ORTON's (Job) Exposition of the Old Testament, with Devotional and Practical Reflections, 6 vols. 8vo. *calf*, £1. 10s
Shrewsbury, 1791

3487 OSIANDRI (Jo. Adam) Commentarius in Pentateuchum, librum Judicum, et Josuam, 3 vols. folio, *portrait, vellum*, £1. 11s 6d
Tubingæ, 1676

3488 OSTERVALD (J. F.) Douze Sermons sur divers textes, 8vo. *calf, neat*, 3s   .   .   *Genève*, 1725

3489 · ———— Grounds and Principles of the Christian Religion explained in a Catechetical Discourse; to which is added, a Liturgy used in the Church of Neufchatel every Saturday evening: rendered into English by H. Wanley, and revised by Geo. Stanhope, D.D. 8vo. *interleaved in* 4to. *with a few MS. notes, rough calf*, 3s   1704

3489* ———— another copy, 8vo. *calf*, 2s 6d   .   1704

3490 OTES's (Samuel) Explanation of the General Epistle of Saint Jude, folio, *fine copy, calf*, 12s   .   1633

3491 OTTER's (Wm. *Bp. of Chichester*) Pastoral Addresses, 8vo. *bds.* 4s
1841

3492 OUTRAM's (Dr. Wm.) Sermons upon Faith and Providence, and other subjects, sm. 8vo. *calf*, 2s   .   168

3493 OVERALL's (Jo. *Bp. of Norwich*) Convocation-Book, MDCVI., concerning the Government of God's Catholick Church and the Kingdoms of the whole world, *portraits of Bp. Overall and Abp. Sancroft*, 4to. *calf, scarce*, 15s   .   1690

3494 ———— another copy, 4to. (*wanting the portrait of Bp. Overall*) *calf*, 14s   .   .   1690

3495 ———— new edition, 8vo. *portrait, bds.* 8s   *Oxford*, 1844

" What gave this book much consequence on its arrival was, that the celebrated Dr. W. Sherlock became, through it, reconciled to take the oaths at the Revolution."—*Chalmers*.

3496 OVERTON's (John) The books of Genesis and Daniel defended against Count Volney and Dr. Francis; also the Sonship of Christ against Jo. Gorton and the Rev. Mr. Evans, 8vo. *portrait, hf. bd. calf*, 3s   .   .   1820

3497 OVERTHROW of the Protestants' Pulpit-Babels, convincing their preachers of lying and rayling to make the Church of Rome seeme mysticall Babell; particularly confuting W. Crashawe's Sermon at the crosse, by I. R., Student in Divinity, 4to. *hf. bd. vellum, rare,* £1. 8s . N. P. 1612
From the library of the late Duke of Sussex.

3498 OWEN's (Cha.) Validity of the Dissenting Ministry; or, the Ordaining Power of Presbyters evinced from the New Testament and Church History, 8vo. 3s 6d . 1716
The late Duke of Sussex's copy.

3499 ———— (Dr. Henry) Intent and Propriety of the Scripture Miracles considered and explained, in a series of Sermons at the Boyle Lecture, and XVI. Sermons on various subjects, 3 vols. 8vo. *calf, very neat,* 10s 6d . 1783-97

3500 ———— (J. *Minister of the Gospel*) Plea for Scripture Ordination; or, Ten Arguments from Scripture and Antiquity proving Ordination by Presbyters without Bishops to be valid; with an Epistle by Mr. Daniel Williams, sm. 8vo. *calf,* 2s 6d 1707
From the library of the late Duke of Sussex.

3501 ———— (Dr. John) Display of Arminianisme, 4to. *calf,* 3s 6d 1642
Owen's first performance.

3502 ———— Vindiciæ Evangelicæ; or, the Mystery of the Gospell vindicated, and Socinianisme examined, in confutation of a Catechisme by J. Biddle, and the Catechisme of V. Smalcius, commonly called the Racovian Catechisme, 4to. *hf. bd. calf,* 6s *Oxford,* 1655
"Contains a learned and most important narrative of the progress of Anti-Trinitarianism."—*Orme.*

3503 [————] Discourse concerning Liturgies, and their Imposition, 4to. 1s 6d . . 1662

3504 [————] Animadversions on a Treatise entitled "Fiat Lux;" or, a Guide in Differences in Religion, 12mo. *scarce,* 4s 1662

3505 ———— Mortification of Sin in Believers, 1668—An humble Testimony unto the goodness and severity of God in his dealings with sinful churches and nations, 1681—in 1 vol. 12mo. *calf,* 3s 6d

3506 [————] Truth and Innocence vindicated, in a Survey of a Discourse concerning Ecclesiastical Polity, &c. sm. 8vo. *calf,* 3s 1669

3507 ———— another copy, *slightly wormed at the end,* 2s 1669

3508 ———— Exercitations concerning a Day of Sacred Rest, &c. sm. 8vo. *calf,* 3s . 1671

3509 ———— Brief Declaration and Vindication of the Doctrine of the Trinity, &c. 12mo. *calf,* 1s . 1676

3510 ———— Reason of Faith; or, an Answer unto that Enquiry, wherefore we believe the Scripture to be the Word of God, 1677—Causes, Ways, and Means of understanding the Mind of God, 1678—in 1 vol. 12mo. *hf. bd. calf,* 3s 6d . 1677

3511 ———— Doctrine of Justification by Faith, explained, confirmed, and vindicated, 4to. *calf,* 5s . 1677

3512 ———— Causes, Waies, and Means of Understanding the Mind of God, &c. sm. 8vo. *hf. bd. calf,* 2s 6d . 1678

3513 ———— Brief Instruction in the Worship of God; and Discipline of the Churches of the New Testament, 12mo. 2s 6d 1688

3514 OWEN's (Dr. John) Enquiry into the Original, Nature, Institution, Power, Order, and Communion of Evangelical Churches, 4to. *calf,* 4s . 1681
3515 ———— de Natura, Ortu, Progressu, et Studio veræ Theologiæ, 4to. *calf,* 4s 6d . *Bremæ,* 1684
3516 ———— editio altera, 4to. *vellum,* 5s *Franeq.* 1700
This work has never been translated into English.
3517 ———— Meditations and Discourses concerning the Glory of Christ, applyed unto unconverted sinners, 1691—A Treatise of the dominion of Sin and Grace, 1688—2 vols. in 1, sm. 8vo. *calf,* 2s
3518 ———— Guide to Church-Fellowship and Order, 24mo. 2s 1692
3519 ———— on Communion with God, 8vo. *calf,* 3s 1700
3520 ———— Gospel Grounds and Evidences of the Faith of God's Elect, sm. 8vo. 1s 6d . 1695
3521 ———— another copy, 12mo. 1s . 1718
3522 ———— Works, viz. Declaration of the Glorious Mystery of the Person of Christ, God, and Man—Of Communion with God—Of Indwelling Sin in Believers—Of Temptation—Of Mortification of Sin in Believers—The Death of Christ, &c. folio, *portrait, calf,* £1. 1s . 1721
3523 ———— Complete Collection of his Sermons, with several Tracts now first published, and his Latin Orations at Oxford, also his Life and Funeral Sermon, by D. Clarkson, folio, *portrait inserted, calf,* 16s 1721
3524 ———— the same, *large paper, fine copy, vellum,* £1. 11s 6d 1721
3525 ———— Discourse of the Work of the Holy Spirit in Prayer; Gospel Grounds and Evidences of the Faith of God's Elect—Eshcol, a Cluster of the Fruit of Canaan: and a Treatise of the dominion of Sin and Grace, sm. 8vo. *calf,* 3s *Glasgow,* 1757
3526 ———— Dissertation on Divine Justice, or the Claims of Vindicatory Justice asserted, against Socinus and his followers, &c. translated from the Latin by R. Hamilton, *Edinb.*—An humble Testimony unto the goodness and severity of God in his dealings with sinful Churches and Nations, 1796—2 vols. in 1, 12mo. *calf,* 2s 6d . . ——
3527 ———— Meditations and Discourses on the Glory of Christ, in his Person, Office, and Grace, 8vo. *calf,* 2s 6d 1684
The last work of Owen.—It was committed to the press on the very day he died.
3528 OXFORD. Reasons of the Judgement of the University of Oxford, concerning the Solemne League and Covenant, the Negative Oath, the Ordinances concerning Discipline and Worship, approved in Convocation, 4to. *sewed,* 2s . [*London?*] 1647
3529 ———— English Prize Poems, 12mo. *calf gilt,* 4s *Oxford,* 1828
3530 PAGET's (Fra. E.) St. Antholin's; or Old Churches and New, a Tale for the Times, 12mo. 3s 6d . 1842
3531 ———— Tales of the Village, *second series,* 12mo. *bds.* 2s 1841
3532 PAKINGTON's (Lady) Art of Contentment, edited by the Rev. W. Pridden, 12mo. *bds.* 2s 6d . 1841
3533 PALAIRET (Elias) Observationes Philologico-criticæ in Sacros Novi Fœderis libros, 8vo. *vellum,* 4s 6d *Lugd. Bat.* 1752

3534 PALEY's (Dr. Wm., *Archd. of Carlisle*) Works, with additional Sermons, and an Account of the Life and Writings of the Author, by the Rev. Edm. Paley, 4 vols. 8vo. *portrait, calf gilt*, £2. 10s . . 1838
3535 —————— Principles of Moral and Political Philosophy, 2 vols. 8vo. *calf*, 4s 6d . . 1790
3536 —————— Horæ Paulinæ, or the Truth of the Scripture History of St. Paul evinced, by a comparison of his Epistles with the Acts, and with each other, 8vo. *calf*, 4s 1796
3537 —————— View of the Evidences of Christianity, 8vo. *calf, neat, marbled leaves*, 5s . 1825
3538 —————— Natural Theology; or Evidences of the Existence and Attributes of the Deity, collected from the appearances of Nature, illustrated by a series of plates, and Explanatory Notes by James Paxton, 2 vols. 8vo. *hf. bd. calf gilt*, 8s *Oxford*, 1826
3539 —————— Sermons and Tracts, 8vo. *calf*, 5s 1808
3541 —————— another copy, 8vo. *bds.* 4s . 1815
3542 —————— Posthumous Sermons, edited by the Rev. Edmund Paley, 2 vols. 8vo. *bds.* 6s . 1825
3543 PALLADII, Divi Evagrii Discipuli, Lausiaca quæ dicitur Historia; et Theodoreti, Episcopi Cyri, Θεοφίλης, id est, Religiosa Historia, 4to. *olive morocco, gilt leaves, rich borders of gold*, £1. 4s
Par. *apud Bernardum Turrisanum, in Aldina Bibliotheca*, 1555
Dedicated to Cardinal Pole. Upon the title is the Aldine anchor.
3544 PALMER's (Wm.) Origines Liturgicæ, or Antiquities of the English Ritual, with a Dissertation on Primitive Liturgies, *second edition*, 2 vols. 8vo. *plates, calf gilt*, £1. 1836
3545 —————— third edition, 2 vols. 8vo. *bds.* 10s—*hf. bd. calf*, 14s 1839
3546 —————— fourth edition, 2 vols. 8vo. *bds.* 18s—*calf gilt*, £1. 5s 1845
3547 —————— Supplement to the three first editions, 8vo. 2s 6d 1845
3548 —————— Treatise on the Church of Christ, designed chiefly for the use of Students in Theology, 2 vols. 8vo. *bds.* 18s 1839
3549 —————— new edition, 2 vols. 8vo. *bds.* £1. 1s 1842
3550 —————— Letters to N. Wiseman, D.D. on the Errors of Romanism, with an Examination of Mr. Sibthorp's Reasons for his Secession from the Church, 8vo. *bds.* 12s *Oxford*, 1842
3551 PAOLINI (Stefano) Dittionario Giorgiano e Italiano, composto da S. Paolini con l'aiuto del M. Niceforo Irbachi Giorgiano, *Roma*, 1629
—Grammatica Linguæ Persicæ, auctore Ignatio a Jesu, *ib.* 1661, in one vol. 4to. *uncut*, 5s . ——
3552 PAREUS's (David) Commentary upon the Divine Revelation of the Apostle John, translated by Elias Arnold, folio, *calf*, 10s 6d 1645
3553 PARK's (J. R., M.D.) New Exposition of the Apocalypse, so far as the Prophecies are fulfilled, 8vo. *bds.* 3s 1832
3554 PARKER SOCIETY—A complete set of the Publications issued by this Society during the first four Years, 16 vols. 8vo. and 1 vol. 18mo. *cloth bds. new*, £5. 5s . V. Y.
3555 —————— BECON's (Thos.) Early Works: comprising News out of Heaven; a Christmas Banquet; a Potation for Lent; the Pathway unto Prayer, &c. edited by the Rev. John Ayre, imp. 8vo. *bds.* 10s . . 1843

PARKER SOCIETY PUBLICATIONS—*continued.*

3556 — BECON's (Thos.) Catechism and other Pieces, edited by the Rev. John Ayre, imp. 8vo. *bds.* 10s   1844

3557 — CRANMER (Archb.) on the Sacrament of the Lord's Supper, edited by the Rev. Edmund Cox, imp. 8vo. *bds.* 10s   1844

3558 — COVERDALE's (Myles, *Bp. of Exeter*) Writings and Translations, edited by the Rev. George Pearson, 8vo. *bds.* 10s   1844

3559 — EDWARD VI.—The Two Liturgies A.D. 1549 and 1552, with other Documents, set forth by authority, in the Reigns of Edward VI. viz. the Order of Communion, 1548—The Premier, 1553—The Catechism and Articles, 1553—Catechismus Brevis, 1553; edited by the Rev. J. Ketley, 8vo. *bds.* 10s   1844

3561 — FULKE's (William) Defence of the Translations of the Scriptures against the Cavils of Gregory Martin, edited by the Rev. C. H. Hartshorne, 8vo. *bds.* 9s   1843

3562 — GRINDAL's (Edmund, *Abp. of Cantab.*) Remains, edited by the Rev. William Nicholson, 8vo. *bds.* 10s   1843

3563 — HOOPER's (John, *Bp. of Gloucester, &c.*) Early Writings, edited by the Rev. Samuel Carr, 8vo. *bds.* 10s   1843

3564 — HUTCHINSON's (Roger) Works, comprising, the Image of God, or the Layman's Book; Three Sermons on the Lord's Supper, &c. edited by John Bruce, Esq. F.S.A., 8vo. *bds.* 10s   1842

3565 — PHILPOT's (John, *Archdeacon of Winchester*) Examinations and Writings, edited by the Rev. R. Eden, 8vo. *bds.* 9s   1842

3566 — PILKINGTON's (James, *Bp. of Durham*) Works, edited by the Rev. James Scholefield, 8vo. *bds.* 12s   1842

3567 — RIDLEY's (Nicholas, *Bp. of London*) Works, edited by the Rev. H. Christmas, 8vo. *bds.* 12s   1841

3568 — SANDYS's (Edwin, *Archbp. of York*) Sermons and Miscellaneous Pieces, edited by the Rev. John Ayre, 8vo. *bds.* 5s   1841

3569 PARKER (Matth. *Archiep. Cant.*) De Antiquitate Britannicæ Ecclesiæ et privilegiis Ecclesiæ Cantuariensis, cum Archiepiscopis ejusdem LXX. Recensente Sam. Drake, adjectis annotationibus, etc. folio, *plates, fine copy, calf,* £1. 10s   1729

3570 —————— another copy, folio, *plates, calf,* £1. 5s   1729

3571 [—————— (Sam. *Bp. of Oxon.*)] Reproof to the Rehearsal transposed, in a Discourse to its Author, 8vo. *old calf gilt,* 3s 6d   1673

3572 —————— Demonstration of the Divine Authority of the Law of Nature, and of the Christian Religion, 4to. *calf,* 2s 6d   1681

3573 —————— Religion and Loyalty, 8vo. *calf,* 2s 6d   1684

3574 —————— de Rebus sui Temporis Commentariorum Libri quatuor, 8vo. LARGE PAPER, *calf,* 5s   1726

3575 —————— History of his own Time, faithfully translated by Tho. Newlin, 8vo. *calf,* 5s   1727

3576 —————— History of his own Time, with two original journals of the Expeditions to Spain and France, during the reign of K. Charles I. and an Account of Parker's Life, and Conversion from Presbytery to Popery, 8vo. *calf,* 3s 6d   1728

3577 —————— History of the Tories Chronicle, from the Restoration of Charles II. in 1660 to 1680, 8vo. *calf,* 3s   1730

[58, GREAT QUEEN STREET,

3578 PARKER's (Dr. Wm.) Several Discourses on special subjects preached before the University of Oxford, and upon other occasions, 2 vols. 8vo. *calf, neat,* 5s . *Oxford,* 1790
3579 PARKHURST's (John) Hebrew and English Lexicon, without points, with an Hebrew and Chaldee Grammar, 8vo *calf gilt,* 14s 1823
3580 ———— Greek and English Lexicon to the New Testament, with a plain and easy Greek Grammar, royal 8vo. *calf,* 15s 1826
3581 ———— new edition, with additions by Hugh James Rose, revised by J. R. Major, D.D., 8vo. *bds.* 21s 1845
3582 PARKIN's (Chas.) Remarks upon Dr. Stukeley's Origines Roystonianiæ, wherein the Antiquity and Imagery of the Oratory, lately discovered at Royston, are truly stated and accounted for, 4to. *plates, sewed,* 7s . 1744
3583 PAROCHIAL LETTERS from a beneficed Clergyman to his Curate, 8vo. *bds.* 3s 6d . . 1829
3584 PARR's (Elnathan) Works, (an Exposition upon the Epistle to the Romans, the Grounds of Divinity, and Abba Father, a playne direction concerning Private Prayer) folio, *scarce, calf,* 10s 6d 1632
3585 PARRY's (Joshua) Seventeen Sermons on practical subjects, 8vo. *bds.* 3s . *Bath,* 1783
The author was a dissenting minister at Cirencester. The *Monthly Review* characterises the above-mentioned sermons as " very sensible and animated"—and says that they " breathe a warm and affectionate spirit of rational piety and Christian benevolence."
3586 ———— (Rich.) Fig-tree dried up, or the story of that remarkable transaction considered in a new light, 4to. *sewed,* 1s 1758
3587 ———— Harmony of the Four Gospels, so far as relateth to the History of our Saviour's Resurrection, with notes, 4to. *sewed,* 1s 6d
 1765
3588 ———— (Tho. *Bp. of Antigua*) Practical Exposition of St. Paul's Epistle to the Romans, with an Appendix, 12mo. *bds.* 4s 1832
3589 ———— Paul, Philemon, and Onesimus, or Christian Brotherhood, being a practical Exposition of St. Paul's Epistle to Philemon, in a Discourse preached in Antigua, 12mo. *bds.* 2s 1834
3590 PARSONS's (Robert) Book of Christian Exercise appertaining to Resolution, that is, showing howe that we should resolve ourselves to become Christians indeede: by R. P., perused and accompanied nowe with a Treatise tending to Pacification: by Edmund Bunny, 12mo. *calf,* 6s . [*Lond.*] 1585
" Altered to the Protestant use."—*Ant. a Wood.*
3591 ———— Christian Directory, being a Treatise of Holy Resolution, put into modern English, by George Stanhope, D.D., 8vo. *calf,* 4s
 1703
3592 ———— the same, 8vo. *calf,* 3s . 1716
3593 ———— the same, 8vo. *calf,* 3s 6d . 1742
This is accounted the best of Father Parsons's works.
3594 PARTRIDGE's (Sam.) Sermons, altered and adapted to an English Pulpit, from French writers, 8vo. *hf. bd. calf, scarce,* 5s—*bds.* 3s 6d
 1804
3595 — ———— Three Discourses preached in the Parish Church of Boston, 8vo. *bds.* 2s . *Boston,* 1808

3596 [PASCAL (Blaise)] Les Lettres Provinciales, ou Lettres escrites par Louis de Montalte a un Provincial de ses amis et aux Jesuits, sur la Morale et la Politique de ces Peres ; *French, Latin, Spanish, and Italian*, 8vo. *old calf gilt, 8s* . *Cologne,* 1684
3597 PATRES APOSTOLICI. Scripta Genuina Græca Patrum Apostolicorum, Græce et Latine, edita a C. F. Horneman, 3 vols. in 1, 4to. *vellum, 9s* . *Hauniæ,* 1828
3598 ———— SS. Patrum Apostolicorum Barnabæ, Hermæ, Clementis, Ignatii, Polycarpi, Opera genuina, una cum Ignatii et Polycarpi Martyriis versionibus antiquis ac recentioribus, Var. Lect. selectisque Variorum Notis illustrata, cura Ric. Russell, 2 vols. 8vo. *stained, rich calf gilt, old style, very scarce,* £1. 8s *Lond.* 1746
3598* ———— idem, 2 vols. 8vo. *fine copy, calf,* £1. 15s *ib.* 1746
3599 ———— Opuscula Patrum Selecta, 2 vols. in 1. sm. 8vo. *calf, neat,* 6s . . *Berol.* 1826-27
CONTAINING—Augustini et Clementis Alex. Tractatus Varii.
3600 ———— Thesaurus Patrum, Floresque Doctorum ; hoc est Dicta, Sententiæ et Exempla ex SS. Patribus probatissimis Scriptoribus collecta et per locos communes distributa, cura et opere plurimorum rebus sacris addictorum. Item, Introductio ad SS. Patrum Lectionem, auctore A. B. Caillau, 6 vols. 8vo. LARGE AND FINE PAPER, *vellum,* £2. 2s . *Mediolani,* 1830
3601 ———— Collectio Selecta S.S. Ecclesiæ Patrum ; complectens exquitissima Opera tum dogmatica et moralia, tum apologetica et oratoria; accurantibus D. Caillau, Missionum Gallicarum Presbytero, &c. 12 vols. 8vo. *sewed,* £1. 10s *Par.* 1829
Contains the Apostolic Fathers, also Irenæus, Minutius Felix, Clemens Alexandrinus, Hippolytus, Tertullian, Origen, &c. with copious Indexes.
3602 PATTRICK'S (George) Sermons, with a Help to Prayer, and the Life of the author, 8vo. *port.* 4s 6d . 1801
3603 PATRICK'S (Symon, *Bp. of Ely*) The Book of Job Paraphrased, 8vo. *calf, 3s* . . 1679
3604 ———— The Book of Psalms Paraphrased, 2 vols. 8vo. *calf, 7s* 1680
3605 ———— The Proverbs of Solomon Paraphrased, 8vo. *calf, 2s 6d— fine copy, 3s* . . 1683
3606 ———— Mensa Mystica : or, a Discourse concerning the Sacrament of the Lord's Supper, 8vo. *calf, 2s 6d* 1684
3607 ———— the same, with Aqua Genitalis : a Discourse concerning Baptism, 8vo. *calf, neat, 3s* . 1717
3608 ———— Paraphrase upon Ecclesiastes and the Song of Solomon, 8vo. *portrait, calf, neat, 4s* . 1685
3609 ———— Jesus and the Resurrection, justified by Witnesses in Heaven and in Earth, 2 vols. in 1, 8vo. *portrait, calf, 6s* 1703
3610 ———— Grief disarmed, or a Consolatory Discourse on the death of Friends, 12mo. *bds. 2s* . 1830
3611 ———— Treatise of Repentance and of Fasting, edited by F. E. Paget, 18mo. *bds.* 3s 6d . *Oxford,* 1840
3612 ———— Discourse concerning Prayer, &c., 18mo. *morocco, gilt leaves, 5s* . . *ib.* 1840

3613 PATRICK'S (Symon) Parable of the Pilgrim: a new and compressed edition, with an introduction, and some account of the author, by the Rev. Tho. Chamberlain, 18mo. *portrait, bds. 2s*   1840
3614 ——— —— Work of the Ministry; edited by the Rev. W. B. Hawkins, 18mo. *bds. 2s* . 1841
3615 ——— —— Treatise of the Necessity and Frequency of Receiving the Holy Communion; edited by the Rev. W. B. Hawkins, 18mo. *bds. 2s* (pub. at *3s 6d*) . 1841
3616 PATRICK, LOWTH, AND WHITBY'S Commentary on the Scriptures of the Old and New Testament, 6 vols. folio, *fine copy, rough calf,* £5. 15s 6d . 1732, &c.
3617 ——— —— another copy, 6 vols. folio, *calf gilt, neat,* £7. 7s 1732, &c.
3618 ——— —— the same, with ARNALD on the Apocrypha, 7 vols. 4to. *portraits, calf,* £5. 5s . 1809
3619 ——— —— another copy, to which is added, Lowman on the Revelation; revised and corrected by the Rev. J. Pitman, 6 vols. royal 4to. *calf gilt, very scarce,* £10. 10s . 1822
3620 PATTERNE (A.) of Popish Peace, or a Peace of Papists with Protestants, beginning in articles, leagues, oathes, and a marriage; and ending in a bloody massacre of many thousand Protestants, 18mo. 3s . . 1644
3621 PAUL'S (S.) CATHEDRAL. Frauds and Abuses at St. Paul's, 1712 —Fact against Scandal, in answer to a late malicious libel, entitled, Frauds, &c. 1713 – An Answer to a pamphlet entitled Frauds, &c. 1713—*in one vol. 8vo. calf, 3s 6d* . ———
3622 ——— —— (Father) History of the Council of Trent, translated by Brent, folio, *calf,* £1. 1s . 1640
3623 ——— —— History of the Council of Trent, translated by Brent, with a Life of the author, and a History of the Inquisition, *best edition,* folio, *scarce, fine copy, calf,* £1. 16s . 1676
3624 PAULINUS (S. *Patr. Aquileiensis*) Opera ex editis ineditisque primum collegit, et notis illustravit Jo. Fra. Madrisius, folio, *neat, rare,* £3. 3s . *Venet.* 1737
3625 ——— —— aliud exemplar, folio, LARGE PAPER, *bds.* £3. 3s *ib.* 1737
3626 ——— —— (S. *Episc. Nolanus*) Opera, cum Notis Variorum ac Dissertationibus, 2 vols. in 1, 4to. *calf*, 18s   *Par.* 1685
3627 PAUWELS (Jos.) Tractatus Theologicus de Casibus Reservatis in Diocesibus Antverpiensi, Buscoducensi, Cameracensi, Coloniensi, Gandavensi, Leodiensi, Mechliniensi, Namurcensi, Ruræmundensi, 8vo. *calf, 4s 6d*   *Lovanii,* 1750
3628 PAVILLON (Nic. *Evêque d'Alet*) Apologie de la Resolution du fameux Cas-de-Conscience contenue dans les ecrits suivants, I. Les Imaginaires. II. Les Visionaires. III. De la Foi Humaine. IV. Jugement Equitable. V. Lettre de N. Pavillon, Evêque d'Alet, a M. Hardouin de Perefixe, Arch. de Paris, 8vo. *neat, 3s 6d* *Cologne,* 1704
3629 PAYNE'S (John) Evangelical Discourses, 8vo. *bds. 2s*   1763
3630 ——— —— (Dr. Wm.) Practical Discourse of Repentance, 8vo. *calf,* 2s 6d . . 1693

3631 PAYNE'S (Dr. Wm.) Discourses upon several subjects : with a Preface giving some account of his Life, &c. 8vo. *calf, 2s 6d*   1698
3632 PAZZI—La Vie toute celeste de la Vierge Extatique S. Marie Madelene de Pazzi, Religieuse de l'ordre de N. Dame du Mont Carmel, 12mo. *neat, 3s*   *Douay,* 1671
3633 PEARCE'S (Zachary, *Bp. of Rochester*) Reply to the Letter of Dr. Waterland, setting forth the many falsehoods by which he endeavours to weaken the authority of Moses, 8vo. 1s   1752
3634 PEARSON'S (Edw.) Discourses to Academic Youth, 8vo. *calf, 3s*   *Cambr.* 1798
3635 ―――― (Jo. *Bp. of Chester*) Opera Posthuma Chronologica, &c. viz. de Serie et successione primorum Romæ Episcoporum Dissertationes duæ : quibus præfiguntur Annales Paulini, et Lectiones in Acta Apostolorum, edidit H. Dodwellus, 4to. *calf, 6s*   1688
3636 ―――― Exposition of the Creed, folio, *portrait by Loggan, calf, neat, 7s 6d*   1692
3637 ―――― another copy, *with Index,* folio, *portrait, calf, 8s*   1710
3638 ―――― the same, *with Index, fine large copy, calf, neat, 9s* 1741
3639 ―――― new edition, revised and corrected by the Rev. E. Burton, D.D., 2 vols. 8vo. *bds.* 10s—*calf gilt,* 17s   *Oxford,* 1843
3640 ―――― The True Faith of a Christian : in a very short Abridgment of Bp. Pearson's Exposition of the Apostles' Creed, by Cha. Lambe, 8vo. *calf,* 2s   1713
3641 ―――― Minor Theological Works, now first collected, with a Memoir of the Author, Notes, and Index ; by Edward Churton, M.A., 2 vols. 8vo. *fine portrait, bds.* £1.—*calf gilt,* £1. 7s   *Oxford,* 1844
3642 ―――― — (Dr. Wm.) Sermons on several occasions, preached at the Cathedral of York, 8vo. *calf,* 2s 6d   1718
3643 PECOCK'S (Reynold, *Bp. of Chichester*) Life, being a Sequel to the Life of Dr. John Wiclif; collected and written by John Lewis, 8vo. *calf, neat, scarce,* 7s 6d   1744

Only 250 copies printed.

3644 ―――― new edition, 8vo. *bds.* 6s   *Oxford,* 1820
3645 PECKARD'S (Peter) Observations on the Doctrine of an Intermediate State between Death and the Resurrection, with remarks on the Rev. Mr. Goddard's Sermon on that subject, 1756—Further Observations in answer to Dr. Morton's Queries, 1757, 8vo. *sewed,* 1s 6d
3646 PEGORIER (Cesar)Systeme de la Religion Protestante, 4to. *hf. bd. calf,*2s 6d—*calf,* 3s   *Rotterdam,* 1718
3647 PEIRCE'S (James) Remarks on Dr. Wells's Letters to Mr. P. Dowley, and to a Dissenting Parishioner ; with his several Defences of those Remarks, and some Considerations on the 6th Chapter of the Abridgment of the London Cases, &c. 12mo. *calf,* 3s   1711
3648 ―――― — Tracts ; (the same as the above, with the exception of the first,) 8vo. *calf,* 3s   1714-18
3649 ―――― Fifteen Sermons on several occasions, and a Scripture Catechism, 8vo. *calf,* 3s   1728

3650 Pierce's Tracts, viz. An Enquiry into the present Duty of a Low-Church-Man; in a Letter from a Dissenter in the Country, to a Low-Church-Man in the City—Useful Ministry a Valid one, a Sermon preached at a Meeting of the United Ministers of Devon and Cornwall—Presbyterian Ordination prov'd Regular, an Ordination Sermon—Defence of the Dissenting Ministry and Presbyterian Ordination—Letter to Dr. Bennet, concerning the Non-Jurors' Separation—The Curse Causeless, a Sermon—Dissenters' Reasons for not writing in the behalf of Persecution—Reflections on Sherlock's Vindication of the Corporation and Test Acts—Interest of the Whigs, with relation to the Test Act,—in 1 vol. 8vo. *calf*, 5s 1712-18

3650* ————— Vindication of the Dissenters, in answer to Dr. William Nichols's Defence of the Church of England, 8vo. *calf*, 3s 6d 1718

3651 Pelagii (S. Monachi) Epistola ad Demetriadem, cum aliis aliorum, Epistolis, et D. Whitby Tractatus de Imputatione Divina Peccati Adami, recensuit et notas addidit J. S. Semler, 8vo. *hf. bd. calf, uncut*, 7s 6d . *Halæ Magd.* 1775

3652 Pelletier (Claude le) Traité dogmatique et moral de la Penitence, 12mo. *neat*, 2s 6d . *Par.* 1728

3653 Pelling's (Edw.) Discourse of the Sacrament of the Lord's Supper, wherein the Faith of the Catholick Church concerning that Mystery is explained, 8vo. *calf*, 2s . 1685

3654 —— —— Practical Discourse upon the Blessed Sacrament, 8vo. *calf*, 2s 6d . . 1692

3655 —— —— Three Practical Discourses, I. Upon the Blessed Sacrament—II. Upon Prayer—III. Upon Charity, 8vo. *calf*, 3s 1694

3656 —— —— Practical Discourse of Patience, 8vo. *calf*, 2s 1693

3657 —— —— Practical Discourse upon Humility, 8vo. *calf*, 1s 6d 1694

3658 —— —— Practical Discourse concerning God's Love to Mankind, 8vo. *calf*, 2s . 1694

3659 —— —— Practical Discourse concerning the Redeeming of Time, 8vo. *calf*, 1s 6d . . 1695

3660 —— —— Practical Discourse concerning Holiness, 8vo. *cf.* 2s 6d 1695

3661 —— —— Discourse concerning the Existence of God, 8vo. *calf*, 2s 6d . . 1696

3662 Peltius (Jo.) Harmonia Remonstrantium et Socinianorum, *Lugd. Bat.* 1633—Happeruschim, hoc est Examinis Commentationum Rabbinicarum in Mosen Prodromus; authore Wilh. Schickardo, *Tubing.* 1624—Perspectiva Politica regno Poloniæ elaborata; authore Andrea de Pilca, *Dantisci*, 1652—in 1 vol. 4to. *calf*, 3s 6d v. y.

3663 Pemble's (William) Works, folio, *calf*, 10s *Oxford*, 1659
Containing Expositions of Ecclesiastes and Zechariah, on Justification, &c. Ant. à Wood calls Pemble "a famous preacher, a skilful linguist, a good orator, and an ornament to society." Bp. Wilkins classes his sermons amongst the best of the time.

3664 Penn's (Granville) Christian's Survey of all the primary events and periods of the world, from the commencement of History to the conclusion of Prophecy, 12mo. *bds.* 1s 6d . 1812

3665 —— —— Prophecy of Ezekiel concerning Gogue, the last tyrant of the Church, his Invasion of Ros, his Discomfiture, and final fall, 12mo. *hf. bd. morocco, very neat*, 3s . 1814

3666 PENN'S (James) Sermons, 8vo. *calf, 2s* . 1769
3667 PERALDUS (Guil.) Summa Vitutum ac Vitiorum, Notis illustrata, studio et opera Rod. Clutii, 2 tom. in 1, 4to. *calf, 4s*
Mogunt. 1618
3668 PERCEVAL'S (Hon. A. P.) Original Services for the State Holidays, with Documents relating to the same, 8vo. *bds. 3s 6d* 1838
3669 ——————— Sermons at the Chapel Royal, St. James's, 8vo. *bds. 10s 6d*
1839
3670 ——————— Collection of Papers connected with the Theological Movement of 1833, 8vo. *sewed, 4s* . 1843
3671 ——————— Three Sermons preached in times of public anxiety, 12mo. *bds. 1s* . . 1845
3672 PERCY'S (Tho.) Key to the New Testament, giving an Account of the several books, their contents, authors, &c. 12mo. *calf, 2s* 1773
3673 —————— another copy, *interleaved,* 12mo. *2s* 1773
3674 —————— the same, 12mo. *calf, 3s* . 1779
3675 —————— another copy, 12mo. *calf, 3s* . 1821
3676 PEREIRA (Antonio) Traité du pouvoir des Evêques, traduit du Portugais, 8vo. *French calf gilt, 3s* . 1772
From the library of the late Duke of Sussex.
3677 PERITSOL (Abr.) Itinera Mundi, sic dicta nempe Cosmographia, Latinâ Versione donavit et Notas passim adjecit Thomas Hyde, acced.—BOBOVIUS (Alb.) de Turcarum Liturgia, Perigrinatio Meccana, Circumcisione, &c. ; in 1 vol. 4to. *vellum, 3s Oxon.* 1690
3678 —————— idem, acced. Misnæ Pars : ordinis primi Zeraim, tituli septem, Lat. vertit et Commentario illustravit Gul. Guiseus— Accedit Mosis Maimonidis præfatio in Misnam, E. Pocockio interprete, *Oxon.* 1690—in 1 vol. 4to. *vellum, 4s 6d* 1690-91
Brunet speaks of the former as "Ouvrage recherchée des savans, et dont les exemplaires sont peu communes."
3679 PERKINS'S (W.) Warning against the Idolatrie of the last times, and an Instruction touching Religion or Divine Worship, sm. 8vo. *vellum, 3s 6d* . *Camb.* 1601
3680 PETAVIUS (Dion.) Opus de Theologicis Dogmatibus ; auctius in hac nova editione Libro de Tridentini Concilii Interpretatione, Lib. II. Dissertationum Ecclesiasticarum, Diatribâ de Potestate Consecrandi, Lib. VIII. De Pœnitentia Publica, et Notulis Theoph. Alethini, 6 vols. in 3, folio, *fine copy, calf, £7. 7s Antv.* 1700
3681 —————— idem, 6 vols. in 3, folio, *calf, £6. 6s Venetiis,* 1721-4
"The Dogmata Theologica of Petavius," says Gibbon, "is a work of incredible labour and compass ; the volumes which relate solely to the Incarnation are divided into 16 books, the first of bistory, the remainder of controversy and doctrine." The part relating to the Trinity is likewise very copious.
3682 —————— Opus de Doctrina Temporum, cum Præfatione et Dissertatione de LXX. Hebdomadibus, Jo. Harduini, 3 vols. in 2, folio, *portrait, vellum, £1. 16s* . *Antv.* 1703
3683 —————— idem, 3 vols. in 1, folio, *fine copy, Dutch prize vellum, gilt, £2. 10s* . . *ib.* 1703
3684 —————— aliud exemplar, 3 tom. folio, *portrait, hf. bd. uncut, £2.*
ib. 1705
3685 —————— idem, 3 vols. folio, *neat, £2. 2s Veronæ,* 1734

[58, GREAT QUEEN STREET,

3686 PETAVIUS (Denys) de la Penitence Publique, et de la Preparation à la Communion, 4to. *fine copy, old red morocco, gilt leaves*, 14s
Par. 1644
3687 PETERS's (Cha.) Critical Dissertation on the Book of Job. 8vo. *bds.* 5s . . 1757
" Contains a large portion of critical learning, and throws much light on all the subjects it investigates. It is altogether a valuable book."—*Orme.*
3688 ———— Sermons, 8vo. *calf, scarce*, 4s . 1776
" The erudition of Mr. Peters was uncommon, and his piety was unaffected, yet neither his erudition nor his piety could shelter him from Warburton's most illiberal abuse."—*Polwhele.*
3689 PETIT's (J. L.) Remarks on Church Architecture, 2 vols. 8vo. *plates, bds.* 15s . 1841
3690 PETRÆ (Vincentius, *Card.*) Commentaria ad Constitutiones Apostolicas, seu Bullas singulas Summorum Pontificum, secundum Collectionem Cherubini, 5 vols. in 2, folio, *hogskin*, £2. 12s 6d
Venetiis, 1729
3691 PETRONII Arbitri Satyricòn, cum Notis Variorum, curante P. Burmanno, 2 vols. 4to. BEST EDITION, *vellum*, £1. 8s *Amst.* 1743
3692 PETTO's (Sam.) Voice of the Spirit; or, an Essay towards a Discoverie of the Witnessings of the Spirit, &c. 12mo. *neat*, 3s 1654
3693 PFANNERUS (Tobias) Systema Theologiæ gentilis purioris, 4to. *vellum, very scarce*, 4s 6d . *Basil.* 1679
3694 PHALARIDIS Epistolæ, *Gr. et Lat.* ex MSS. recensuit, Versione Annotat. et vita authoris donavit C. Boyle, 8vo. *front. calf*, 2s 6d
Oxon. ——
3695 PHELIPEAUX (Jean) Discours en forme de Méditations sur le Sermon de Notre Seigneur sur la Montagne, 12mo. *calf*, 3s 6d
Par. 1730
3696 PHENIX: (The) or, a Revival of scarce and valuable pieces, (viz.—An Account of Origen and his Opinions—A Design to Harmonize the Bible—Dr. Barlow's Account of the Conference at Hampton Court, 1603—Naunton's Fragmenta Regalia—Dr. Colet's Sermon on the Convocation—A Discourse of the Troubles begun at Frankfort, about the Book of Common Prayer, Ceremonies, &c.—Calvin's Common Prayer Book—Brief Enquiry touching a better way to Refute Papists, &c.)—2 vols. 8vo. *fine copy, calf, scarce*, 16s
1707-8
3697 PHILASTRIUS (*Episc. Brixiensis*) Hæreseωn Catalogus : cui adjectus est, Eruditissimus Libellus Lanfranci Archiepiscopi Canthuariensis de Sacramento Eucharistiæ adversus Berengarium, [*Basil.* 1528?]
—BULLINGER (Hen.) Antiquissima Fides et vera Religio-Christianam Fidem mox à primis mundi exordiis ad hæc usq. tempora durasse, H. Bullingeri Apodixis ; e Germanico in Latinam linguam traducta per Diethelmum Cellarium, *Tiguri*, 1544 ; 2 vols. in 1, small 8vo. *calf*, 8s . ——
3698 ———— de Hæresibus Liber, cum Notis J. A. Fabricii, sm. 8vo. *calf*, 4s . *Hamb.* 1721
3699 PHILIPS's (Tho.) Sermons, 12mo. *bds.* 2s . 1836
3700 PHILIPPS's (J. Thomasius) Dissertatio Historico-philosophica de Atheismo, sive Historia Atheismi, 8vo. *calf*, 2s 1716

3701 PHILIPPS's (J) Account of the Religion, Manners, and Learning of the People of Malabar; in several Letters written by some of the most learned men of that country to the Danish Missionaries, 12mo. *plates, calf, 3s* . 1717

3702 —— —— Greek of the First Epistle of St. Paul to the Thessalonians explained, 1751—A Letter concerning a new edition of Spenser's Faerie Queene, to Gilbert West, Esq., 1751—De Anima, medica prælectio in Theatro Coll. Reg. Med. Lond. habita a Fra. Nicholls, M.D., 1750—in 1 vol. 4to. *calf, 2s 6d* 1750-51

Of the first of the above tracts, Orme speaks thus:—"This work contains the Greek text, but no translation; the notes are very considerable: they are philological, critical, and theological . . . . It is exceedingly scarce."

3703 [—— ——] Study of Sacred Literature fully stated and considered, in a Discourse to a Student at a Foreign University, 8vo. *bds. 3s* 1750

3704 PHILO Judæus. The Sentiments of Philo, concerning the Λογος, or Word of God; together with large Extracts from his writings compared with the Scriptures on many other doctrines, by Jacob Bryant, 8vo. *sewed, 3s* . *Camb.* 1797

3705 PHILOSTORGII Cappodocis Historia Ecclesiastica, a Constantino M. ad sua usque tempora, Libri XII. *Gr. et Lat.* Editi a Jac. Gothofredo, una cum Supplementis et Dissertationibus, 4to. *hf. bd. russia, uncut, 8s* . *Genevæ,* 1643

3706 PHILPOT's (Jo.) Trew Report of the Dysputacyon had and begonne in the Couuocacyon Hows at London among the clargye there assembled the xviij. daye of October, in the yeare of our Lord, M.D.LIIII. 𝔅lack letter, sm. 8vo. *hf. bd. neat, excessively rare,* £4. 4s *Imprinted at Basil by Alexander Edmonds,* ——

Archdeacon Philpot acknowledged this, in 1555, upon his examination, to have been written by him. He takes a very large part in the "disputacyon," and in one place declares that in the Eucharist he denies only "that gross and carnall presens," which, however, he contradicts soon after in another affirming "the masse is no sacrament at all, neyther is Christ in any wise present in yt."

3707 ——— (Tho.) Antiquitas Theologica et Gentilis; or, two Discourses: the first, concerning the Original of Churches and their Endowments: the second, concerning the Religion of the Gentiles, 18mo. *very scarce, 5s* . 1670

From the library of the late Duke of Sussex.

3708 PHOTII Myriobiblon, sive Bibliotheca Librorum quos legit et censuit Photius Patriarcha Constantinopolitanus, Græcè edidit et Notis illustravit, D. Hœschelius, Latinè vero reddidit et Scholiis auxit A. Schottus, folio, *title and last leaf inlaid, otherwise a fine copy, old calf gilt,* £1. 10s . 1613

3709 -——— Epistolæ, *Gr. et Lat.* cum Notis R. Montacuti, Episc. Norvicem, folio, *calf,* 16s . *Lond.* 1651

3710 PIANEZZA's (Charles, *Marquis of)* Truth of the Christian Religion, with an Account of the Author, of his Treatise, and the Translation of it; by Tho. Wise, 8vo. *frontispiece, tree-marbled calf gilt, very neat, 5s 6d* . . 1703

3711 PICOT (Pierre) Sermons sur divers sujets, 8vo. *tree-marbled calf extra, gilt leaves, 9s* . *Genève,* 1823

[58, GREAT QUEEN STREET,

3712 PICTET (B.) Huit Sermons prononcez à Genève, sur ces paroles de S. Paul, *Éprouvez toutes choses*, 12mo. 3s 6d Londres, 1704
3713 ——— —— Theologia Christiana, small 8vo. *vellum, 3s 6d* Lugd. Bat. 1734
3714 PIERCE's (John) Fifteen Sermons upon several occasions, 8vo. *calf, scarce, 3s* . . 1731
3715 ——— — -·(Sam. Eyles) Companion for the Lord's Table, 8vo. *calf, neat, 3s* . 1809
3716 ——— —— (Tho. *Pres. of S. Mary Magd. Coll. Oxon.*) Decade of Caveats to the people of England, of general use in all times, but most seasonable in these, 4to. *calf, 3s* . 1679
3717 ·—— — Law and Equity of the Gospel; or, the Goodness of our Lord as a Legislator, 4to. *calf, 5s 6d* . 1686
3718 PIETAS Romana et Parisiensis; or, a faithful relation of the Charitable and Pious Works eminent in Rome and Paris, sm. 8vo. 3s Oxford, 1687
3719 PILKINGTON's (Matthew) Remarks upon several passages of Scripture; rectifying some errors in the printed Hebrew text; pointing out several mistakes in the versions; and shewing the benefit of a more correct Translation, 8vo. *hf. bd. uncut, 3s* Camb. 1759
3720 PINKE's (Wm. *Magd. Coll. Oxon.*) Triall of a Christian's sincere Love unto Christ, 18mo. 2s . Oxford, 1657
3721 PIRIE's (Alex.) Dissertation on the Hebrew Roots, 12mo. *bds*. 2s Edinb. 1807
3722 PIRRUS (Don Rocchus) Sicilia Sacra Disquisitionibus et Notitiis illustrata, folio, *calf neat*, £1. 10s Lugd. Bat. s. a.
3723 PISCATORIS (Joannis) Commentarii in omnes Libros Vet. et Nov. Testamenti, 5 vols. in 3, folio, *fine copy, new in calf, carmine edges, old style by Hayday*, £2. 12s 6d Herbornæ, 1646
3724 PITT's (Joseph) Faithful Account of the Religion and Manners of the Mahometans, 12mo. *hf. bd*. 3s . 1738
3725 PIUS VII.—I. Statement of Facts presented to the Sovereign Pontiff, P. Pius VII.—II. A Letter to the Cardinal Litta, of the Propaganda Fide, 4to. LARGE PAPER, *not published, bds*. 8s 1818
3726 PLANTEVIT DE LA PAUSSE (Joan. *Episc. Lodovensium*) Florilegium Rabbinicum, complectens præcipuas Veterum Rabbinorum Sententias, versione Latina et Scholiis illustratas, &c. folio, *rare, fine copy, in old red morocco, with the author's arms on the sides*, £1. 1s Lodovæ, 1644
3727 PLATINA (Jo. Bapt.) de Vitis Maximorum Pontificum Historia. —Raphaellis Volaterrani. historia de Vita quatuor Pontificum. Platyne de falso et vero bono dyalogus: contra Amores dyalogus: de Vera Nobilitate dyalogus: de Optimo Cive dyalogus: Panegyricus in laudem Rev. Card. Niceni, et patriarche Constantinopolitani. Diversorum academicorum panegyrici in Platyne parentalia, folio, *calf, rare*, 18s . Venetiis, 1581
3728 PLATON's (*Abp. of Moscow*) Present State of the Greek Church in Russia; or, a Summary of Christian Divinity; translated, with a preliminary Memoir of the Ecclesiastical Establishment in Russia, and an Appendix on Russian Dissenters, by Rob. Pinkerton, 8vo. *hf. bd. russia, scarce*, 6s . Edinb. 1814

3729 LATT's (Tho. Pell) Letter to the Rev. E. B. Pusey, D.D. on certain Defects in a popular system of Theology, and on the Tracts for the Times so far as opposed to them, 8vo. *sewed*, 1s 6d   1840
3730 PLAYFERE's (Dr. Tho.) Whole Sermons, sm. 8vo. *calf*, 5s 6d   1623
3731 ——— the same, sm. 8vo. *calf*, 8s   .   1633
3732 PLOT.—A Letter written upon the discovery of the late Plot, 1678— The unreasonableness and impiety of Popery, in a second Letter, &c. 1678—An exact account of the Romish Doctrine in the case of Conspiracy and Rebellion, by Ezerel Tonge, D.D., 1679—sm. 4to. *sewed*, 1s 6d   .   1678-9
3733 ——— No Protestant Plot ; or the present pretended Conspiracy of Protestants against the King and Government, discovered to be a Conspiracy of the Papists, 2 parts, 4to. *hf. bd. calf*, 2s 6d   1681-82
3734 PLUCHE's (Abbé de la) History of the Heavens, considered according to the Notions of Poets and Philosophers, compared with the Doctrines of Moses, translated by J. B. de Freval, 2 vols. 8vo. *plates, calf*, 5s   .   1740
3735 ——— Truth of the Gospel demonstrated, from the Dispensations of Prophecy, 2 vols. 8vo. *frontispiece*, 6s   1751
3736 PLUMPTRE's (James) Four Discourses on the Amusement of the Stage, with Notes, 8vo. *bds.* 2s   .   1809
3737 POCOCK's (Edw.) Theological Works, containing his Porta Mosis, and Commentaries on Hosea, Joel, Micah, and Malachi, with his Life, &c. edited by Leonard Twells, 2 vols. folio, *portrait, calf*, £1. 15s   .   .   1740
3738 POLHILL's (Edward) Speculum Theologiæ in Christo ; or a View of some Divine Truths practically exemplified in Jesus Christ, &c. 4to. *calf, neat*, 9s   .   .   1678
3739 POLI (Reginaldi) de Summo Pontifice Christi in terris Vicario, ejusque Officio et Potestate, Liber verè singularis, et eruditionis, et puri Sermonis nomine, 12mo. *rare, fine copy, new in calf gilt*, 10s 6d   *Lovanii, apud J. Foulerum Anglum*, 1569
3740 ——— Phillips's (Thos.) History of the Life of Cardinal Reginald Pole, 2 parts in 1 vol. 4to. *portrait, hf. bd. uncut*, 10s   *Oxford*, 1764
3741 ——— Review of Mr. Phillips's History of the Life of Reginald Pole, by Gloucester Ridley, 8vo. *calf*, 3s 6d   1766
3742 POLI (Matth.) Synopsis Criticorum aliorumque S. Scripturæ Interpretum et Commentarium, 5 vols. folio, *fine copy, calf, gilt leaves*, £5. 15s 6d   .   *Lond.* 1669
3743 ——— idem, cura J. Leusden, *editio optima*, 5 vols. folio, *fine copy, vellum, scarce*, £8. 18s 6d   *Ultrajecti*, 1684
3744 POLWHELE's (Rd.) Discourses on different subjects, 2 vols. 8vo. *bds.* 4s   .   .   —
3745 POLYDORI VIRGILII Historia Anglicæ Lib. XXVII. folio, *in the original binding*, 12s   .   *Basil.* 1570
3746 ——— idem. *ib.* 1570—J. P. MAFFEII, Historiarum Indicarum Lib. XVI. accessit Ignatii Loiolæ Vita, *Colon.* 1589, in 1 vol. folio, *in the original stamped binding, with clasps*, £1. 1s   ———

3747 [POMMERAYE (J. F.)] Histoire de l'Eglise Cathedrale de Rouen, Metropolitaine et Primatiale de Normandie, 4to. *calf, very scarce,* £1. 1s . *Rouen,* 1686

3748 PONTIFICALE Romanum, Clementis VIII. primum, nunc denuo Urbani VIII. auctoritate recognitum, 12mo. *calf, gilt leaves,* 4s 6d *Lutet. Par.* 1664

3749 ———— idem, 12mo. *fine copy, morocco, gilt leaves,* 16s *Coloniæ,* 1682

3750 POOLE's (Matthew) Nullity of the Romish Faith, or a Blow at the Root of the Romish Church, sm. 8vo. *neat,* 4s *Oxford,* 1667

3751 ——— Dialogue between a Popish Priest and an English Protestant, wherein the principal points of both Religions are fully examined, 18mo. 4s . 1667
From the library of the Duke of Sussex.

3752 ———— another copy, 18mo. 3s . 1680

3753 POPE JOAN ; or, an Account collected out of the Romish-Authors, certifying that there was a She-Pope, who sate in that (the Roman) See, and ruled the same, sm. 4to. *bds.* 4s 1689

3754 POPE's (Rd. T. P.) Authentic Report of the Discussion between the Rev. R. T. P. Pope and the Rev. Tho. Maguire, in Dublin, 18mo. *bds.* 3s . 1827

3756 ———— Roman Misquotation; or certain passages from the Fathers, adduced in a work entitled "The Faith of Catholics," brought to the test of the originals, 8vo. *bds.* 5s 6d 1840

3757 POPERY absolutely destructive to Monarchy, proved by several examples, 12mo. *neat,* 2s 6d . 1673

3758 ———— A Free Examination of the common Methods employed to prevent the Growth of Popery, 8vo. *calf,* 3s 1766

3759 PORSON's (Rich.) Tracts and Miscellaneous Criticisms collected and arranged by the Rev. T. Kidd, 8vo. *bds.* 4s 6d 1815

3760 [PORTAL's (————)] Scripture account of Sacrifices, 8vo. 2s 6d 1755

3761 PORTER's (Edm.) ΘΕΟΣ ΑΝΘΡΩΠΟΦΟΡΟΣ; or God Incarnate, shewing that Jesus Christ is the onely, and the Most High God, 1655—Trin-Unus-Deus; or the Trinity and Unity of God, 1657— Sabbatum ; the Mystery of the Sabbath discovered, 1659—*in one vol.* sm. 8vo. *calf,* 3s 6d .

3762 PORTEUS's (Beilby, *Bp. of London*) Sermons on several subjects, 2 vols. 8vo *portrait inserted, bds.* 5s 1783-94

3763 ———— Lectures on the Gospel of St. Mathew, 2 vols. 8vo. *calf, neat,* 5s 6d . . 1807

3764 ———— the same, 2 vols. 8vo. *calf, neat,* 5s 6d 1815

3765 ———— Works, with his Life by the Rev. R. Hodgson, 6 vols. 8vo. *port. bds.* £1. 1s . . 1823

3766 PORT ROYAL. Histoire General de Port-Roïal depuis la Reforme de l'Abbaïe, jusqu'à son entiere destruction, 10 vols. 12mo. *calf gilt,* £1. 15s . *Amst.* 1755-57

3767 ———— Gemissements d'une Ame vivement touchée de la destruction du Saint Monastere de Port Royal des Champs -Quatrieme gemissement d'une ame vivement touchée de la Constitution de Clement XI. du 8 Sept. 1713, 4 parts in 1 vol. 12mo. *calf,* 2s 1714-24

3768 POTT's (J. H., *Archd. of London*) Discourses on the Rule of Life, a Charge, with Supplementary additions, 8vo. *bds.* 2s 6d   1823
3769 ——— (John) Preacher's Plan: or Jonah's Commission opened, in a course of Sermons. 8vo. *calf, scarce,* 2s 6d   1758
3770 POTTER's (Dr. Chr.) Want of Charitie justly charged on all such Romanists as dare affirme that Protestancie destroyeth Salvation, sm. 8vo. *hf. bd. calf,* 4s   *Oxford,* 1633
3771 ——— (John, *Abp. of Canterbury*) Discourse of Church-Government, wherein the right of the Church, and the Supremacy of Christian Princes are vindicated and adjusted, 8vo. *calf, fine copy, from the Duke of Sussex's collection,* 7s   1707
3772 ——— the same, 8vo. *calf,* 7s . 1711
3773 ——— another copy, 8vo. *calf,* 8s . 1724
3774 ——— Discourse of Church-Government, with Notes by the Rev. J. C. Crosthwaite, 8vo *bds.* 12s . 1839
3774* ——— Theological Works, 3 vols. 8vo. *calf, scarce,* £1. 11s 6d   *Oxford,* 1753
3775 P[OTTER's] (T.) Sober Guess concerning several dark Prophecies in the Revelation, especially the XIth Chapter, 12mo. *hf. bd.* 3s 6d   *Lond.* ——
3776 POULLE's (L'Abbé) Sermons, 2 vols. 12mo. 4s   *Par.* 1781
3777 POWELL's (Dr. Wm. Sam.) Discourses on various subjects, published by T. Balguy, D.D. 8vo. *hf. bd. calf, neat,* 5s—*calf,* 6s   1776
"Dr. Powell's Discourses should never be passed over. Permit me to recommend them to your perusal."—*Hey's Lectures.*
3778 POYNDER's (John) Popery in alliance with Heathenism, 8vo. *bds.* 2s . 1835
3779 PRADI (Hieron.) et Joannis Bapt. VILLALPANDI in Ezechielem Explanationes, et Apparatus Urbis ac Templi Hierosolymitani Commentariis et Imaginibus illustratus, 3 vols. fol. *hogskin,* £2. 10s   *Romæ,* 1596-1604
"This is a work of extreme rarity, and the best commentary on the Prophet Ezechiel that was ever written."—*Horne.*
3780 PRAYERS and Hymns, translated from the German (by Miss Ellis Cornelia Knight), 8vo. *bds.* 2s   1832
3781 ——— Preces Selectæ, or a Selection of Prayers for the use of Harrow School, 18mo. *roan,* 2s . 1843
3782 PREACHER (The), containing Sermons by eminent living Divines, 3 vols. 8vo. *hf. bd. calf,* 7s 6d   1831-32
3783 PREACHING. The method of good Preaching, being the Advice of a French Reformed Minister to his Son, 4to. *hf. bd. calf,* 2s 6d . 1701
3784 PREDESTINATION. A collection of Tracts concerning Predestination and Providence, and the other points depending on them, 8vo. *frontispiece, calf,* 12s . *Camb.* 1719
"A very valuable collection of Tracts."—*Wordsworth's Eccl. Biog.*
3785 PRESBYTERIANS. English Presbyterian Eloquence; or Dissenters' Sayings, ancient and modern, 8vo. 1s 6d   1720
3786 PRESERVATIVE against Popery, in several select Discourses upon the principal heads of Controversy, &c. (edited by Bp. Gibson) 3 vols. folio, *calf,* £10. 10s . 1738

3787 PRESTON'S (Dr.) Abridgment of Dr. Preston's Works, by Will. Jemmatt, M.A., thick 12mo. *calf*, 8s . 1648
3788 PRICÆI (John) Commentarii in varios Novi Testamenti . Hic accesserunt Annotationes in Psalmos, &c. folio, *calf*, 8s libros 1660
This work contains "many valuable observations, particularly illustrating the modes of diction which occur in the sacred classics, from profane writers."
Dr. Harwood.
3789 PRICE'S (Dr. Richard) Sermons on the Christian Doctrine, as received by the different denominations, &c. 8vo. *calf*, 3s 1787
3790 ——— the same, 1787—A Discourse on the Love of our Country, 1789—An Address at the Interment of Dr. Price, by A. Kippis, D.D., *in one vol.* 8vo. *calf*, 4s
3791 ——— Discourse on the Love of our Country, delivered to the Society for Commemorating the Revolution, 8vo. 1s 1790
3792 PRICHARD'S (Rees, *Vicar of Landovery*) Divine Poems, *Welsh*, 8vo. *calf gilt, old style, curious and scarce*, 10s . 1721
3793 PRIDDEN'S (W.) Australia, its History and present Condition, 12mo. *map, bds.* 4s . . 1843
3794 PRIDEAUX'S (Dr. Humphrey) History of the Orders of the Church of England, made out against the Objections of the Papists, 4to. *hf. bd. calf, neat*, 5s 6d . 1688
3795 ——— Original and Right of Tithes, with the draught of a Bill prepared anno 1691, for the restraining of Pluralities, 8vo. *calf*, 3s 6d . . 1710
3796 ——— True Nature of Imposture fully displayed in the Life of Mahomet, 8vo. *calf, neat*, 3s 6d . 1713
3797 ——— another copy, 8vo. *calf gilt*, 4s . 1808
3798 ——— Ecclesiastical Tracts, viz.—I. The Validity of the Orders of the Church of England. II. The Justice of the Law which gives the successor in any Ecclesiastical Benefice all the profits from the day of avoidance. III. An Award of King Charles I., shewing that personal Tithes are still due by the law of the land, 8vo. *fine copy, calf, neat*, 5s . 1716
3799 ——— Directions to Churchwardens for the faithful discharge of their Office, 12mo. 2s . 1713
3800 ——— the same, 12mo. 2s . 1723
3801 ——— the same, 12mo. 2s . . 1730
3802 ——— Old and New Testament connected in the History of the Jews and neighbouring nations, from the declension of the Kingdoms of Israel and Judah, to the time of Christ, 4 vols. 8vo. *plates, rich calf gilt, old style*, £1. 14s . 1725
3803 ——— another copy, 4 vols. 8vo. *plates, fine copy, old calf gilt*, £1. 8s . . 1749
3804 ——— the same, 4 vols. 8vo. *portrait and plates, calf, neat*, £1. 10s . . 1808
3805 ——— another copy, 4 vols. 8vo. *portrait, calf gilt*, £1. 11s 6d
Oxford, 1820
3806 ——— the same, 2 vols. 8vo. *plates, bds.* 18s *ib.* 1839
3807 ——— Life, with several Tracts and Letters, never before published, 8vo. *bds.* 2s 6d . . 1748

3808 PRIDEAUX'S (John, *Bp. of Worcester*) Doctrine of Prayer; to which are added certain Godly Prayers, from early editions of the book of Common Prayer, and the Treatise of St. Athanasius, on the use and virtue of the Psalms, by Sidney W. Cornish, D D., 18mo. *bds.*
Oxford, 1841

3809 PRIERIANUS (Silvester) Egregium vel potius divinum opus in Johannem Capreolum, 4to. Black letter, *with illuminated capitals, original stamped calf binding*, 8s *Cremone*, 1497

3810 PRIESTLEY'S (Dr. Joseph) Essay on the First Principles of Government, including Remarks on Dr. Brown's Code of Education, and on Dr. Balguy's Sermons on Church Authority, 8vo. *calf*, 2s 1771

3811 ―――― Discourses on the Evidence of revealed Religion, 8vo. *bds.* 3s . . 1794

3812 PRING'S (Johu) Kingdom Sermons : or Sermons on the Accidents of the Kingdom of Christ, 8vo. *bds.* 6s . 1834

3813 ―――― Second Series, 8vo. *bds.* 6s . 1838

3814 PRITIUS (Jo. Geo.) Introductio in lectionem Novi Testamenti, auxit novasque Dissertationes passim adjecit C. G. Hofmann, 8vo. *bds.* 6s
Lips. 1764

3815 PROPHECY (The Spirit of), wherein is proved the Divine Authority of the Scripture, and Christian Religion, &c. 8vo. *calf, (from the Duke of Sussex's collection),* 2s . 1687

3816 PROPHETS. The general Delusion of Christians touching the ways of God's revealing himself to, and by the prophets, evinced from Scripture and primitive Antiquity, 8vo. *calf*, 4s 6d 1713

3817 PROPOSITIONS et moyens pour parvenir a la reunion des deux religions en France, 4to. *large paper, old red morocco, gilt and marbled leaves*, 18s . . 1677

3818 PROSPERUS (S. *Aquitanus.*) de Gratia Dei, et Libero Arbitrio hominis et Prædestinatione Sanctorum, 12mo. *calf*, 5s 6d *Par.* 1760

3819 ―――― Opera omnia, cum vita ejus et S. Asterii Episcopi Amaseæ Homiliæ, 2 vols. 4to. *vellum*, £2. 2s *Bassani*, 1782

3820 PROTESTANT SYSTEM (The) : containing Discourses on the Principles of Natural and Revealed Religion, compiled from the works of Protestant Dissenters, 2 vols. 8vo. *calf*, 8s 1758

3821 PROTESTANTS. The Protestant Principle of appealing to the Holy Scriptures, subversive of Protestant Doctrine, 12mo. *bds.* 3s 6d
1834

3822 ―――― ―――― An impartial Survey and Comparison of the Protestant Religion as by Law established ; with the main Doctrines of Popery, 8vo. 2s . 1685

3823 PROVERBS. The Proverbs of Solomon translated by Bernard Hodgson, LL.D., Principal of Hertford Coll. 4to. *bds.* 1s 6d
Oxford, 1788

3824 PROVINCES-UNIES. Divers abus et nullités du decret de Rome du 4 Oct. 1707, au sujet des affaires de l'Eglise Catholique des Provinces-unies, 1708—Justification de la Memoire de M. Pierre Codde, Archeveque de Sebaste, Vicaire Apostolique dans les Provinces-Unies, contre un decret de l'Inquisition du 14 Jan. 1711—*In one* vol. 12mo. *neat*, 2s 6d . ―――

[58, GREAT QUEEN STREET,

3825 PSALMS (The Book of) collected into English Meeter by T. Sternhold, J. Hopkins and others, with the Music, sm. 4to. *bds*. 3*s* 6*d*
[*Circa*, 1599]
3826 ———— the same, *large paper*, 4to. *bds*. 5*s* [*ib*. 1599]
3827 ———— another copy, black letter, sm. 4to. *bds*. 3*s* 1641
3828 ———— The Book of Psalms in Metre; close and proper to the Hebrew: smooth and pleasant for the Metre; newly translated by William Barton, 12mo. *very scarce, neat*, 7*s* 6*d* 1696
3829 ———— A Version of the Psalms of David, fitted to the tunes used in Churches. By the Hon. Sir John Denham, K. B. 8vo. *scarce, calf*, 3*s* . 1714
3830 ———— the same, 8vo. LARGE PAPER, *fine copy*, 4*s* 6*d* 1714
3831 ———— The whole Book of Psalms: with the usual Hymns and Spiritual Songs, (Old Version) with all the ancient and proper tunes sung in Churches, with some of later use, composed in three parts, Cantus, Medius, Bassus. By John Playford, 8vo. *front. cf.* 4*s* 1697
3832 ———— the same, 8vo. *calf*, 5*s* . 1717
3832*———— An Essay towards a New English Version of the Book of Psalms, from the original Hebrew. By Z. Mudge, 4to. *calf*, 7*s* 1744
3833 ———— A new English translation of the Psalms from the original Hebrew, reduced to Metre by Bp. Hare, with notes, illustrations, and a preliminary dissertation, by Tho. Edwards, 8vo. *calf*, 4*s* . *Camb*. 1755
3834 ———— A new translation of the Psalms from the original Hebrew, with notes, and a Dissertation on the last prophetick words of Noah, by Wm. Green, 8vo. *calf*, 4*s* 6*d* . *ib*. 1762
3835 ———— The Psalms translated or Paraphrased in English verse, by James Meyrick, 4to. *calf*, 8*s* . *Reading*, 1765
3836 ———— The Psalms translated or Paraphrased in English verse, by James Merrick, M.A. *Reading*, 1765.—Annotations on the Psalms, by James Merrick, M.A. *ib*. 1768—Notes Critical and Explanatory on the Psalms and Proverbs, by H. Dimock, *Gloucester*, 1791— together 3 vols. 4to. *fine copies, uniformly bound in Russia, by Baumgarten*, £3. 3*s*
3837 ———— Hymns, and Anthems used in the Chapel of the Foundling Hospital. (Engraved throughout with Musical notes.) 8vo. *hf. bd*. 5*s* . . 1774
3838 ———— The Book of Psalms, in an English Metrical Version, with Notes, by the Right Rev. Richard Mant, Bp. of Down and Connor, 8vo. *bds*. 6*s* . *Oxford*, 1824
3838*———— A New Translation of the Book of Psalms and Proverbs, with Explanatory Notes by W. French, D.D., and George Skinner, M.A., 2 vols. in 1, 8vo. *calf gilt*, 9*s* . *Camb*. 1830-31
3839 ———— A course of Psalms adapted to the Services of the United Church of England and Ireland: selected from the New Version, by the Rev. J. T. Barrett, D. D., with the Psalms and Hymns in the Morning and Evening Services, pointed for chaunting, 18mo. *cloth*, 1*s* 6*d* . . 1844
3840 PSALTERIUM Romanum, decreto S. Concilii Tridentini restitutum, fol. *in the original stamped calf binding, with brass clasps and bosses*, 18*s* . *Antv*. 1655

3841 PSALTERIUM Beate Virginis Marie. LITERIS GOTHICIS, *sine loco aut impressoris nomine*, sm. 4to. *bds. fine copy*, 7s 6d
[*Argent*. 1475]
From the Library of Dr. Kloss of Frankfort. The present edition, which is rubricated by hand, is not mentioned by Panzer.

3842 PUBLIC CHARACTERS of the year 1828, 8vo. *bds*. 7s   1828

3843 PUFFENDORFF's (Sam) History of Popedom, the Rise, Progress, and Decay thereof, sm. 8vo. *hf. bd. calf*, 2s 6d   1691

3844 PUGIN's GLOSSARY OF ECCLESIASTICAL ORNAMENT AND COSTUME. Setting forth the Origin, History, and Mystical Signification of the various Emblems, Devices, and Symbolical Colours, peculiar to CHRISTIAN DESIGN of the MIDDLE AGES, with especial reference to the DECORATION of the SACRED VESTMENTS and ALTAR FURNITURE formerly used in the English Church. *Illustrated by* SEVENTY PLATES, *all splendidly printed in gold and colours by the new litho-chromotographic process, and about 50 wood-cuts in the letter-press*. Containing Examples of the Ecclesiastical Costume of the Roman, English, French, and German Bishops, Priests, and Deacons; Frontals, Curtains and Dossells of Altars; the embroidering of the Orphreys and Hoods of Copes, Stoles, Maniples, and Chasubles; Apparels of Albes; Patterns of Diapering for Ceilings, Walls, and precious Stuffs; Bordures and Powderings; Floriated Crosses; Emblems of the Holy Trinity; the Five Wounds and Passion of our Blessed Lord, the Four Evangelists, of our Blessed Lady, the Mysteries of the Rosary; Monograms of the Holy Name; Examples of the Nimbus; Conventional Forms of Animals and Flowers for Heraldic Decoration; Altar and Church Linen, Funeral Palls, &c. The whole drawn, coloured, adapted, and described from ancient Authorities, by A. WELBY PUGIN, Architect, royal 4to. *half morocco, richly gilt*, £7. 7s   1844

3845 PULLER's (Dr. Timothy) Moderation of the Church of England; edited by the Rev. Robert Eden, 8vo. *bds*. 10s 6d   1843

3846 PUSEY's (Dr. E. B.) Remarks on the prospective and past benefits of Cathedral Institutions, 8vo. *bds*. 3s   1833

3847 PYLE's (Tho.) Paraphrase, with short and useful Notes on the Old Testament, with a Paraphrase on the Acts of the Apostles, the Epistles, and Revelation of St. John, 7 vols. 8vo.*calf*, £1. 11s 6d
1717-37

3848 —— —— Ninety-six Sermons on plain and practical subjects, 3 vols. 8vo. *calf*, 12s   1785
" Characterized by perspicuity, and manly sense."—*Chalmers*.

3849 —— —— CLIV. Popular Sermons, 5 vols.8vo. *bds*. 12s
Norwich, 1789-95

3850 PYNCHON's (William). Time when the First Sabbath was ordained, not in the time of Adam's innocency, but after his fall, &c., 4to. *calf*, 1s 6d   1654

3851 —— —— Covenant of Nature made with Adam described, 4to. *calf*, 3s   1662

3852 QUARESMII (Francisci) Historica, Theologica, et Moralis, Terræ Sanctæ Elucidatio, 2 vols. folio, *maps and plates, vellum*, £1. 11s 6d
Antv. 1639

[58, GREAT QUEEN STREET,

3853 QUARLES (Fra.) Boanerges and Barnabas, Judgment and Mercy, or, Wine and Oil for Wounded and Afflicted Souls, 12mo. *hf. bd. calf, neat*, 3s 6d . 1674
3854 QUICK's (John) Synodicon in Gallia Reformata : or, the Acts, Decisions, Decrees, and Canons of the National Councils of the Reformed Churches in France, 2 vols. folio, *calf*, £1. 8s 1692
3855 ———— another copy, 2 vols. in 1, folio, *calf*, £1. 4s 1692
3856 ———.———— another copy, 2 vols. in 1, *large paper, calf gilt*, £1 16s 1692
3857 QUIETISTS. Refutation des principales Erreurs des Quietistes contenues dans les livres censurez par l'Archevêque de Paris, 16 Oct. 1694, 12mo. *neat*, 3s 6d . *Par*. 1695
3858 QUINCY's (Sam.) Twenty Sermons on various subjects, preached at St. Philip's, Charles-town, 8vo. *calf*, 2s 6d *Boston, N. E.* 1750
3859 RABADAN's (Mahomet) Mahometism fully explained : written in Spanish and Arabic in 1603, translated by M. Morgan, 2 vols. 8vo. *plates, calf*, 5s . 1723-25
3860 RABANUS MAURUS (Abbas Fuldensis postea Archiep. Moguntini,) Opera omnia ; a Jac. Pamelio olim collecta et nunc primum in lucem edita, 6 vols. in 3, folio, *fine copy, vellum*, £3.
Colon. Agrip. 1626

" At the head of the Latin writers may justly be placed Rabanus Maurus, whose last office was that of Abp. of Mentz. He was the common preceptor of Germany and France; with whom no one in this (IXth) century can be compared, either for genius or extent of learning, or the multitude of books he composed. Whoever acquaints himself with the opinions of Rabanus Maurus, learns all that the best of the Latins thought and believed for about four centnries ; for his writings were in the hands of all the learned."—*Mosheim*.

3861 [RACINE (L'Abbé)] Abrégé de l'Histoire Ecclesiastique contenant les évenemens considerables de chaque siecle, avec des réflexions, 15 vols. 12mo. *fine copy, calf, neat*, £1. 15s *Cologne*, 1752-62
3862 RADBERTUS (S. Paschasius, *Abbas Corbeiensis*) Opera (edente J. Sirmondo), folio, *vellum, scarce*, £1. 16s *Lutet. Par.* 1618
3863 ———— another copy, folio, *neat*, £1. 11s 6d *ib.* 1618

Containing his Commentaries on Matthew, Ps. xliv., and the Lamentations ; his treatise de Corpore et Sanguine Domini ; his Epistle to Frudegardus ; his Life of Adelhard, and his treatise concerning the Passion of SS. Rufious and Valerius.
Paschasius Radbert is said to have been the first promulgator of the doctrine of Transubstantiation, and to have been compelled to resign his Abbacy on that account. His treatise made a great noise on its publication, and drew forth various answers, the chief of which were by Ratrsm, John Scot, and the learned Archbishop of Mentz, Rabanus Maurus, who denounces Radbert's theory as *an error and a novelty*.

3864 RAINBOW's (Edw. *Bp. of Carlisle*) Life, with a Sermon preached at his funeral by Tho. Tully, 12mo. *very scarce*, 6s 1688
3865 RAINOLDES.—The Summe of the Conference between John Rainoldes and John Hart, touching the Head and the Faith of the Church ; with a Defence of such things as Thomas Stapleton and Gregorie Martin have carped at therein, &c. 4to. *bds. scarce*, 14s
Lond. 1584

3866 RAINOLD, or *Reynold* (Jo. *President of Corpus Christi Coll. Oxon.*) Summa Colloquii Jo. Rainoldi cum Jo. Harto de Capite et Fide Ecclesiæ. Hen. Parræo Gloucest. Episcopo, interprete, folio, *fine copy, vellum,* 16s . *Oxon.* 1610

3867 ———— Defence of the Judgment of the Reformed Churches, that a man may lawfullie not only put awaie his wife for her adulterie, but also marrie another, wherein both Robert Bellarmin and a namelesse author are confuted, 4to. *hf bd. morocco, very neat,* 5s . 1609

3868 ———— second edition, 4to. *hf. bd. calf, neat,* 6s 1610

3869 ———— Prophesie of Haggai, interpreted and applyed in sundry Sermons, sm. 4to. *hf. bd. calf, very neat,* 5s 1649

3870 RAITHIUS (Balth.) Vindiciæ Versionis S. Bibliorum Germanicæ M. Lutheri labore editæ, a malevola censura non Pontificiorum solum, sed etiam aliorum Sciolorum, &c. 4to. *bds.* 5s 6d *Tubingæ,* 1676

3871 RAMSAY's (And. Mich. *Chevalier*) Philosophical Principles of Natural and Revealed Religion, unfolded in a geometrical order, 2 vols. 4to. *bds. uncut,* 6s . *Glasgow,* 1748-49

A curious work. The author maintains the doctrine of Metempsychosis, and denies the eternity of future punishment. He not only contends that these were the sentiments of Fenelon, but that they are agreeable to the teaching of the Church.

3872 RANDALL's (John) St. Paul's Triumph; or, Cygnea illa et dulcissima Cantio, that swan-like and most sweet song of Master J. Randall, in eleven Sermons upon Rom. viii. 38, 39; [published] by Will. Holbrook, 4to. *neat,* 5s . 1640

3873 RANDOLPH's (Dr. Tho.) Vindication of the Doctrine of the Trinity, from the exceptions of an Essay on Spirit, &c. 8vo. *hf. bd. uncut,* 4s *Oxford,* 1754

3874 ———— Vindication of the Worship of the Son and of the Holy Ghost against the exceptions of Mr. Theophilus Lindsey, 8vo. *sewed,* 1s 6d . . *ib.* 1775

3875 ———— Letter to the Remarker on the Layman's Scriptural Confutation, wherein the Divinity of the Son of God is farther vindicated, &c. 8vo. *sewed,* 1s 6d . *ib.* 1777

3876 ———— View of our Blessed Saviour's Ministry, and the Proofs of his Divine Mission arising from thence; together with Charges, Dissertations, Sermons, Theological Lectures, and Life, 2 vols. 8vo. *calf* 8s—*fine copy, calf,* 9s . *ib.* 1784

3877 ———— another copy, 2 vols. 8vo. *tree-marbled calf gilt,* 14s *ib.* 1784

3878 ———— Prophecies and other Texts cited in the New Testament, compared with the Hebrew and the Septuagint, with Notes, 4to. *sewed,* 3s—*hf. bd. calf,* 4s . *ib.* 1782

"This valuable and beautifully printed tract is now rarely to be met with, and only to be procured at *seven* or *eight times* its original price."—*T. H. Horne.*

3879 RAPIN's (Paul de) History of England; translated, with additional notes and continuation, by N. Tindal, 21 vols. 8vo. *calf, plates, and folio vol. of maps, hf. bd. calf,* £5. 5s 1757-59

3880 RAPHELIUS (Geo.) Annotationes in S. Scripturam, Historicæ in Vetus, Philologicæ in Novum Testamentum, ex Xenophonte, Polybio, Arriano, et Herodoto, 2 vols. 8vo. *portrait, calf,* 10s 6d—*vellum,* 10s 6d . *Lugd. Bat.* 1747

"Raphael affords an excellent example to those who would make collections from pure Greek Writers, with a view of illustrating the New Testament. The whole collection forms an excellent and valuable work on the Scriptures."
Michaelis.

3881 RAPIN's (René) Salvation every Man's great Concern, translated by Geo. Stanhope, D.D. 8vo. *portrait of the translator, calf,* 3s
1728

3882 RAY's (John) Three Physico-theological Discourses, concerning—I. The Primitive Chaos; II. The general Deluge; III. The Dissolution of the World, and future Conflagration, 8vo. *plates, calf,* 2s
1693

3883 ———— the same, 8vo. *portrait and plates, calf,* 3s 6d 1713
3884 ———— the same, 8vo. *portrait and plates, calf,* 3s 1732
3885 ———— Persuasive to a Holy Life, 8vo. *calf,* 2s 6d—*sewed,* 1s
1719

3886 ———— Wisdom of God manifested in the Works of Creation, 8vo. *fine copy, calf,* 6s . 1743

3887 RAYNAUDI (Theoph. *Soc. Jesu.*) Opera omnia, cum Indicibus, 20 vols. in 10, folio, *fine copy, hogskin,* EXTREMELY RARE, £10. 10s
Lugduni, 1665, *et Cracoviæ,* 1669

CONTAINING :

Vol. I. Christus Deus Homo.
II. De Attributis Christi.
III. Moralis Disciplina.
IV. De Virtutibus et Vitiis.
V. Theologia Naturalis.
VI. Eucharistica.
VII. Marialia.
VIII. Hagiologium Lugdunense.
IX. Hagiologium Exoticum.
X. Pontificia.
XI. Critica Sacra.
XII. Miscella Sacra.

Vol. XIII. Miscella Philologica.
XIV. Opuscula Moralia.
XV. Heteroclita Spiritualia Cœlestium et Infernorum.
XVI. Heteroclita Spiritualia et Anomala Pietatis Terrestriam.
XVII. Ascetica.
XVIII. Polemica.
XIX. Indices generales.
XX. Apopompæua, admodum rara continens.

3888 READING's (Will.) CXVI. Sermons preached out of the First Lessons at Morning and Evening Prayer, for all Sundays in the year, *best edition,* 4 vols. 8vo. *fine copy, new calf gilt, old style,* £2. 2s . 1755

3889 ———— the same, 4 vols. 8vo. *fine copy, old calf,* £1. 18s
1755

3890 ———— another copy, 4 vols. 8vo. *calf,* (vol. 2 *stilted*), £1. 5s
1755

Recommended by Bp. Mant and Dr. Doyley in their Commentary on the Bible.

3891 ———— History of our Lord and Saviour Jesus Christ, with suitable Meditations and Prayers : also the Lives of the Apostles and Evangelists, and the Life of the Blessed Virgin Mary, 8vo. *plates, new in calf gilt, old style,* 6s 6d 1726

3892 REAY's (Wm.) Sermons on several subjects, with a recommendatory Preface by T. Church, D.D., 8vo. *calf,* 2s 6d 1755

3893 REEVES's (William) Apologies of Justin Martyr, Tertullian, and Minutius Felix, in Defence of the Christian Religion; with the Commonitory of Vincentius Lirinensis concerning the Primitive Rule of Faith : with a Prefatory Dissertation about the Right Use of the Fathers, 2 vols. 8vo. *calf, neat, very scarce*, 16s   1709

When this volume was given to the world, Mr. Reeves was Rector of Cranford, in Middlesex, and esteemed an able and spirited preacher. The translation of these interesting documents of primitive antiquity is generally perspicuous and faithful. The Notes contain a good deal of learning, and frequently illustrate the meaning where it is obscure.

3894 REGINALDUS (Antonius) De Mente S. Concilii Tridentini, circa Gratiam se ipsa efficacem. Accesserunt Animadversiones in XXV. Propositiones Lud. Molinæ, autore Jac. le Bossu, et Alternæ Epistolæ Petri Soto, Ruardi Tapperi, et Judoci Ravestein de Gratiæ et Liberi Arbitrii concordia, folio, *old calf gilt*, 18s   *Antv.* 1705

3895 —————— (Gul. *Anglus*) Calvino-Turcismus, id est Calvinisticæ perfidiæ, cum Mahumetana collatio, et dilucida utriusque Sectæ confutatio, edente Gul. Giffordo, sm. 8vo. *hogskin*, 14s   *Col. Agr.* 1603

Written against the Calvinistic doctrines, and in defence of the Roman Catholic Religion, by Father William Reynolds, professor of divinity at Rheims, and brother to Dr. John Reynolds, the Protestant divine. Of these two brothers it is related by Anthony Wood, " that after warm disputes on religion, they turned sides. William, originally a zealous Protestant, became a Catholic ; and John, originally a Catholic, became a decided Protestant, and even a high Calvinist and a Puritan."

3896 REGNIER (L'Abbé) Tractatus de Ecclesia Christi, 2 vols. 8vo. *neat*, 6s   *Par.* 1789

3897 RELANDUS (Hadr.) De Religione Mohammedica libri duo, 12mo. *port. and plates, calf*, 3s   *Traj. ad Rh.* 1717

3898 —————— De Spoliis Templi Hierosolymitani, in Arcu Titiano Romæ conspicuis : Notas, etc. adjecit E. A. Schulze, 12mo. *plates, bds.* 2s   *ib.* 1775

3899 RELIGIO Bibliopolæ; in imitation of Dr. Brown's Religio Medici, [by John Dunton] 12mo. 2s   1691

3900 RELIGION of Jesus, or Divines Mysteries made manifest, by one of the Legal Profession, (S. W.) 8vo. *cloth*, 2s 6d   [1838]

3901 RENAUDOTIUS (Eusebia) LITURGIARUM ORIENTALIUM Collectio, in qua continentur Liturgiæ Copticarum Tres, S. Basilii, S. Gregorii Theologi, S. Cyrilli Alexandrini ; Divi Marci, S. Jacobi, S. Joannis Evangelistæ, Matthæi Pastoris, S. Joannis Patriarchæ, S. Ignatii, &c. *Gr. et Lat.* accedunt Dissertationes de eorum origine et auctoritate, de Liturgiis Alexaudrinis, de Linguâ Coptica, de Patriarcha Alexandrino, etc. opera et studio EUSEBII RENAUDOTII, 2 vols. 4to. RARE, *fine copy, calf*, £4. 4s   *ib.* 1706

3902 —————— idem, 2 vols. in 1, 4to. *calf*, £3. 13s 6d   *ib.* 1706

The best collection of Greek and Oriental Liturgies that have ever been brought together. The author was assisted in the compilation by Dr. Pocock, the celebrated Orientalist.

3903 —————— Historia Patriarcharum Alexandrinorum Jacobitarum usque ad finem Sæculi XIII. cum Catalogo sequentium Patriarcharum, etc. 4to. *calf, scarce*, 18s   *Par.* 1713

3904 RENÉ (Theodoric de S.) Remarques historiques donnés à l'occasion de la Sainte Hostie miraculeuse, conservée pendant plus de 400 ans dans l'Eglise Paroissiale de St. Jean en Grêve à Paris, 2 vols. 12mo. *old red morocco, gilt leaves,* 9s . *Par.* 1725

3905 RENNELL'S (Dr. Tho. *Dean of Winchester*) Discourses on various subjects, 8vo. *bds.* 3s . 1801

3906 ———— second edition, 8vo. *calf extra,* 7s 1801

3907 ———— (Tho. *Vicar of Kensington*) Remarks on Scepticism, especially as it is connected with the subjects of Organization and Life, being an Answer to the Views of M. Bichat, Sir T. C. Morgan, and Mr. Lawrence, 8vo. *sewed,* 1s 6d 1821

3908 ———— Sermons on various subjects, 8vo. *calf gilt, marbled leaves,* 7s 6d . . 1831

3909 RENNEVILLE (Constantin de) The French Inquisition; or the History of the Bastille in Paris, 8vo. *calf* 4s . 1715
The author was a prisoner in the Bastille for eleven years.

3910 REVELATIO Admirabilis de Statu alterius Sæculi, divini apprime timoris eruditoria, *woodcut frontispiece, representing* " *Sanctus Petrus de Lucenburgo," s. a. aut. l.*—Consolatio Desolatorum, etc. *two curious woodcuts, Parisiis,* 1531—2 vols. in 1, sm. 8vo. *calf, neat,* 8s . .. ———

3911 REYNELL'S (W. H.) Sermons, or practical Discourses, 8vo. *bds.* 3s . . 1810

3912 REYNER'S (Edw.) Treatise of the Necessity of Humane Learning for a Gospel-Preacher, sm. 8vo. *hf. bd. calf, neat, scarce,* 4s 1663

3213 REYN (Lud. de) Speculum Abominationum, sive Epitaphia omnium Hæresiarcharum, a temporibus Apostolorum adusque modò Prosâ preeunte, metro expressa, &c. 8vo. *neat,* 4s *Ipris,* 1701

3914 ———— Antidotum adversus Hæresum Venena, sive Praxis peculiaris multiplex Convincendi Heterodoxos Romanæ Ecclesiæ adversariis, 8vo. 4s . *Audomari,* 1716

3915 REYNOLDS'S (Edward, *Bp. of Norwich*) Treatise of the Passions and Faculties of the Soule of Man, 4to. *calf,* 4s 1640

3916 ———— Whole Works, now first collected, with his Funeral Sermon by B. Rively, and his Life by Alex. Chalmers, 6 vols. 8vo. *portrait, calf, neat, scarce,* £2. 15s . 1826

3917 ———— another copy, 6 vols. 8vo. *calf gilt,* £3. 10s 1826

3918 ———— (John) Three Letters to the Deist, 8vo. *calf,* 2s 1725

3919 RHÆTORFORTIS (Sam.) Exercitationes Apologeticæ pro Divina Gratia, adversus J. Arminium, etc. 18mo. *vellum,* 3s *Franck.* 1660

3920 RHENFERDIUS (Jac.) Dissertationes Philologicæ de Decem Otiosis Synagogæ, 4to. *calf,* 2s 6d . *ib.* 1686

3921 ———— Dissertationum philologico-theologicarum de Stylo Novi Testamenti Syntagma, 4to. *vellum,* 4s *Leovardiæ,* 1701

3922 RIBADENEIRA (Petrus) Bibliotheca Scriptorum Societatis Jesu, ad 1642, editorum concinnata, et illustrium virorum elogiis adornata a Phil. Alegambe, folio, *stamped hogskin, with clasps,* 18s *Antv.* 1643
" Opus rariis obvium."—*Vogt.*

3923 RIBADENEIRA (Petrus) Illustrium Scriptorum Religionis Societatis Jesu Catalogus, 8vo. *vellum*, 5s *Antv.* 1608
3924 ———— Appendix Schismatis Anglicani, in qua nonnullorum martyriis ac de iis rebus agitur, quæ à primæ hujus N. Sanderi partis publicatione in Angliæ regno contigerunt, sm. 8vo. *morocco extra, gilt leaves, very scarce*, 14s *Col. Agr.* 1610
3925 RICAUT's (Paul) Present State of the Greek and Armenian Churches, 8vo. *calf*, 5s 6d . 1679
3926 ———— another copy, 8vo. *new in calf gilt, very neat*, 7s 1679
3927 RICHARD of Devizes (The Chronicle of), concerning the Deeds of Richard the First, King of England, also Richard of Cirencester's Description of Britain, translated and edited by J. A. Giles, LL.D., 8vo. *hf. bd. morocco, uncut*, 8s 6d 1841
3928 ———— the same, LARGE PAPER, *hf. bd. morocco, uncut*, 14s 1841
3929 RICHARDSON's (James) Athanasian Creed vindicated, 8vo. *sewed*, 1s 6d . *York*, 1822
3930 ———— (John, *Bp. of Ardagh*) Choice Observations and Explanations upon the Old Testament, with some further and larger Observations upon the whole Book of Genesis, folio, *calf*, 12s 1655
From the library of the late Duke of Sussex.
3931 ———— Canon of the New Testament vindicated, in Answer to the Observations of J. T.[oland] in his Amyntor, &c. *calf*, 3s 1701
3932 ———— the same, 8vo. *calf*, 3s 6d 1719
3933 ———— (Joannis) Prælectiones Ecclesiasticæ XXXIX; olim habitæ in Sacello Collegii Emmanuelis apud Cantabrigienses, 2 vols. 8vo. *calf*, 7s . 1726
Recommended by Bishop Watson.
3934 RICHELIEU (*Le Cardinal de*) Traitté qui contient la methode la plus facile et la plus assurée pour Convertir ceux qui se sont separez de l'Eglise, folio, *fine copy, ruled with red lines, in old red morocco, gilt leaves*, 18s . . *Par.* 1651
3935 ———— Les principaux Poincts de la Foy de l'Eglise Catholique, defendus contre l'escrit addressée au Roy par les quatre Miuistres de Charenton, 4to. *engraved title, fine copy, calf, gilt leaves*, 7s 6d *ib.* 1629
From the collection of the late Duke of Sussex.
3936 [RICHIE's (James, M.D.)] Criticism upon modern notions of Sacrifices, being an Examination of Dr. Taylor's Scripture Doctrine of Atonement, 8vo. *calf*, 2s 6d . 1761
3937 RICHMOND's (Rich.) Sermons and Discourses on several subjects and occasions, 4to. *bds.* 2s . 1764
3938 RIDGLEY's (Dr. Tho.) Body of Divinity; wherein the Doctrines of the Christian Religion are explained and defended; being the substance of several Lectures on the Assembly's larger Catechism, 2 vols. folio, *portrait, calf*, £1. 4s 1734
3939 RIDLEY (Gloucester) De Syriacarum Novi Fœderis Versionum indole atque usu Dissertatio, 1761—Massey de Sacra Vernacula Epistola, 1733—*in one* vol. 4to. *hf. bd. calf*, 4s ———
3940 ———— (Sir Thomas) View of the Civill and Ecclesiasticall Law, 4to. *calf*, 2s . *Oxford*, 1634

3941 RIGAUD'S (S. P.) Historical Essay on the first publication of Sir Isaac Newton's Principia, 8vo. *bds. 3s*   Oxford, 1838
3942 RINGER'S (Tho.) Twelve Discourses upon Texts of Holy Scripture, with a Rural Hymn in the Latin tongue, 8vo. *calf, 2s*   1734
3943 RITSON'S (Joseph) Pieces of Ancient Popular Poetry, from authentic MSS. and old printed copies, 8vo. *cuts, bds. 4s*   1833
3944 RIVET (Gul.) Libertatis Ecclesiasticæ Defensio, sive, adversus Potestatem quam Romanus Pontifex sibi arrogat, dissertatio, sm. 8vo. *2s*   *Genevæ*, 1625
3945 ROBERTS'S (Fra.) Clavis Bibliorum : the Key of the Bible, (Old Testament), sm. 8vo. *calf, 4s*   1649
3946 ———— Clavis Bibliorum : the Key of the Bible, unlocking the richest treasury of the Holy Scriptures, folio, *calf, 12s*   1675
3947 ———— (Wm.) Thoughts upon Creation, &c. 8vo. *plates, old calf gilt, 3s*   1782
3948 ———— Thoughts upon Creation, &c. *plates*, 1782—Poetical Attempts, 1784—in 1 vol. 8vo. *old calf gilt, 4s*
3949 ROBERTSON'S (J. C.) How shall we Conform to the Liturgy of the Church of England, 8vo. *bds*. 10s 6d   1844
3950 ROBERTSONI (Jac.) Clavis Pentateuchi, sive Analysis omnium Vocum Hebraicarum in Pentateucho Moseos occurentium, una cum Versione Latina et Anglica ; cum Notis criticis et philologicis adjectis, 8vo. *calf, very scarce*, £1. 1s   *Edin*. 1770
3951 [ROBERTSON'S (John, M.D.)] True and antient manner of Reading Hebrew without Points, and the Art of Hebrew Versification, 8vo. *calf, 3s*   1747
3952 ———— (W.) Attempt to explain the words Reason, Substance, Person, Creeds, Orthodoxy, Catholic-Church, Subscription, and Index Expurgatorius, &c. 12mo. *calf, 3s*   1767
3953 ROBIN HOOD.—A Collection of all the ancient Poems, Songs, and Ballads, now extant, relative to that celebrated English Outlaw, with historical Anecdotes of his life, by Joseph Ritson, 2 vols. in 1, small 8vo. *wood-cuts by Bewick*, LARGE PAPER, *morocco extra, gilt leaves*, 16s   1832
3954 ROBINSON'S (Dr. Edw.) Greek and English Lexicon of the New Testament : edited by S. T. Bloomfield, D.D. 8vo. *bds*. 10s   1837
3955 ———— (Ralph) Safe Conduct ; or the Saint's Guidance to Glory, a Sermon at the funerall of Mrs. Thomasin Barnardiston, late wife of Mr. Sam. Barnardiston, Merchant, 4to. *sewed*, 1s   1654
3956 ———— (Robert) Ecclesiastical Researches, 4to. *bds*. 8s   *Camb*. 1792
"The author, with indefatigable diligence, has examined the records of the ancient Christian churches, and has brought from obscurity many curious facts which have been little if at all known."—*Monthly Review*.
3957 ———— (Tho.) Scripture Characters ; or, a Practical improvement of the principal Histories of the Old and New Testament, 4 vols. 8vo. *calf*, 10s   1804
3958 ROBSON'S (Cha.) Greek Lexicon to the New Testament, on the basis of Dr. Robinson's, 12mo. *bds*. 9s   1840

240　　J. LESLIE'S CATALOGUE.

3959 ROCHEFOUCAULT (François, *Card. de la*) Considerations sur un livre intitulé, Raisons pour le desadueu faict par les Evesques de ce Royaume, &c. mis en lumiere soubs le nom de M. François Cardinal de la Rochefoucault; contre les Vrais Schismatiques de ce temps; par Timothée Francois, Catholique, sm. 8vo. *calf*, 3s　*s. l.* 1628

3960 ———— Maxims and moral Reflections, (translated by Lockyer Davis), 12mo. *bds.* 2s　.　1775

3961 ———— another copy, 12mo. *portrait, bds.* 2s　　1802

3962 RODOTA (Pietro Pompilio) dell'Origine, Progresso, e Stato presente del Rito Græco in Italia osservato dai Greci, Monaci Basiliani, e Albanesi, 3 vols. 4to. *vellum*, £1. 12s　.　1758

　　A very curious work, and learnedly illustrates the use of the Græco-Roman Ritual in Italy, and also contains much historical information with regard to the state of the Latin Church under the Greek Emperors.

3963 RÖELL (Herm. Alex.) Explicatio Catecheseos Heidelbergensis, 4to. *vellum*, 4s 6d　.　*Traj. ad Rh.* 1728

3964 R[OGERS'S] (Danniel]) Treatise of the two Sacraments of the Gospell, 4to. *calf*, 6s　.　1635

3965 ———— (F. N.) Practical Arrangement of Ecclesiastical Law, 8vo. *bds.* 18s　.　.　1840

3966 ———— (John) Discourse of the Visible and Invisible Church of Christ, 8vo. *hf. bd. calf*, neat, 4s 6d　.　1719

3967 ————— Review of a Discourse of the Visible and Invisible Church, being a Reply to Mr. Sykes's Answer to that discourse, 8vo. *calf*, 6s　　1721

3968 ———— Necessity of Divine Revelation, and the Truth of the Christian Revelation asserted, in eight Sermons, 8vo. *calf*, 3s　1727

3969 ———— the same, 8vo. *calf*, 3s　.　1729

3970 ———— the same 8vo. *calf*, 4s　.　1749

3971 ———— Vindication of the Civil Establishment of Religion, 8vo. *calf*, 4s　.　.　1728

3972 ———— Twelve Sermons on several occasions, 8vo. *calf*, 3s　1735

3973 ———— Seventeen Sermons, with two Tracts—I. Reasons against Conversion to the Church of Rome: II. Persuasive to Conformity, addressed to the Dissenters, 8vo. *calf*, 3s　1747

3974 ———— Nineteen Sermons on several occasions, with the author's Life, and an Elogium, by Jo. Burton, D.D. 8vo. *calf*, 3s　1735

3975 ———— XIX. Sermons, with the Author's Life by Jo. Burton, —XVII. Sermons, with two Tracts against Conversion to the Church of Rome; and a Persuasive to Conformity, 2 vols. 8vo. *calf*, 5s 6d　.　1735-36

3976 ———— Sermons, complete, with his Life, &c., by Jo. Burton, D.D. 4 vols. 8vo. *calf*, 10s 6d　.　1742, &c.

3977 ———— the same, 4 vols. 8vo. *rich calf gilt, carmine edges*, £1. 8s　　1742, &c.

3978 ———— Sermons, 4 vols.—A Discourse of the Visible and Invisible Church—A Vindication of the Civil Establishment of Religion— in all 6 vols. 8vo. *calf*, 18s　.　1735-52

3979 ———— the same, 6 vols. 8vo. *a fine set, old calf gilt*, £1. 8s　　1728-84

3980 ROGERS's (Nehemiah) True Convert; or, an Exposition upon the XVth chapter of St. Luke's Gospell, 4to. *calf, very scarce, 9s* 1632
3981 ——— ——— Wild Vine; or, an Exposition on Isaiah's parabolicall Song of the Beloved, 4to. *hf. bd. calf, neat, 5s* 1632
3982 ——— ——— (Richard) Seven Treatises : containing such direction as is gathered out of the Holy Scriptures, leading and guiding to true happinesse, &c. 4to. *calf, 9s* . 1630
3983 ROLLES's (Sam.) Burning of London in 1666 commemorated and improved, in CX. Discourses, 1667—London's Resurrection; or, the Rebuilding of London encouraged, directed, and improved, in Fifty Discourses, 1688—2 vols. sm. 8vo. *calf, 7s* ———
3984 ROMAN CATHOLIC CONTROVERSY—A Papist misrepresented and represented; or, a twofold Character of Popery, by J. L. 1685— The Doctrines and Practices of the Church of Rome truly represented; in answer to the above, [by Edw. Stillingfleet, D.D.] 1686 —Reflections upon the Answer to the Papist misrepresented, &c. —A Papist not misrepresented, &c. [by W. Sherlock, D.D.] 1686 —Remarks upon the Reflections, &c. [by Abednego Seller,] 1686— Papists protesting against Protestant Popery, in answer to a Papist not misrepresented, 1686—An Answer to the last, [by W. Sherlock, D.D.] 1686—An amicable accommodation of the difference between the Representer and the Answerer, 1686—An Answer to the last, [by W. Sherlock, D.D.], 1686—A Reply to the Answer, 1686—A View of the whole Controversy between the Representer and the Answerer, [by W. Clagett, D.D.] 1687—in 1 vol. 4to. *calf, neat, 9s* . ———
3985 ——— ——— Sure and Honest Means for the Conversion of all Hereticks, and wholesome Advice for the Reformation of the Church; writ by one of the communion of the Church of Rome, and translated from the French [by Abp. Wake], 1688—The Primitive Fathers no Papists, in answer to the Vindication of the Nubes Testium, &c. [by Mr. Gee, Rector of S. Benedict, Paul's Wharf,] 1688—An Abridgement of the Prerogatives of St. Ann, [published by Dr. Claget,] 1688—A true Account of the Conference between A. Pulton, Jesuit, and Tho. Tenison, D.D. 1687—Mr. Pulton considered in his sincerity, reasonings, and authorities, by Tho. Tenison, D.D. 1687—The pamphlet entituled "Speculum Ecclesiasticum" considered, [by H. Warton,] 1688—The Enthusiasm of the Church of Rome demonstrated, in some Observations on the Life of Ignatius Loyola, [by the same,] 1688—A Letter to a Lady, furnishing her with Scripture Testimonies against Popery, 1688— in 1 vol. 4to, *calf, neat, 18s* . ———
3986 ROMISH MASS-BOOK faithfully translated into English, with notes and observations thereupon, plainly demonstrating the Idolatry and Blasphemy thereof, 12mo. *front. calf, scarce, 6s* 1683
From the library of the late Duke of Sussex.
3987 ROSCOE's (W.) Life and Pontificate of Leo the Tenth, 2 vols. 8vo. *portrait and vignettes, bds.* £1. 1s 1846
3988 ——— ——— Life of Lorenzo de Medici, called the Magnificent, 8vo. *portrait and vignettes,* 10s 6d . 1846

3989 ROSE's (Hugh James) State of the Protestant Religion in Germany; in a series of Discourses preached before the University of Cambridge, 1825—An Appendix to 'the same, 1828—The Commission and consequent duties of the Clergy; in a series of Discourses preached before the University of Cambridge, 1828 — PUSEY's (Dr. E. B.) Historical Enquiry into the probable causes of the Rationalist character lately predominant in the Theology of Germany, *ib.* 1828, *in one* vol. 8vo. *bds.* 10s 6d ———

3990 ——— (John, *Rector of St. Martin Outwich.*) Sermons, 8vo. LARGE PAPER, *bds.* 3s . [1796]

3991 ——— Sermon preached at the Consecration of the Church of St. Martin Outwich, London, 8vo. LARGE PAPER, *bds.* 2s 1799

3992 ROSENMULLER (Jo. Geo.) Scholia in Novum Testamentum, 5 vols. 8vo. *bds.* £1. 11s 6d . *Norimb.* 1815

3993 ——— (E. F. C.) G. H. L. FULDNER; et J. V. D. MAURER, Commentationes Theologicæ, 4 vols. 8vo. *cloth*, 12s *Lips.* 1825

3994 Ross' (Alex.) View of all Religions in the World, with a Discovery of all known Heresies, 8vo. *portraits*, *calf*, 4s 1683

3995 ROSWEYDUS (Heribertus) Lex Talionis XII Tabularum Cardinali Baronio ab Isaaco Casaubono dicta, retaliante H. Ros-Weydo. 12mo. *neat*, 4s . . *Antv.* 1614

3996 ROTHERAM's (John) Essay on Faith, and its connection with good works, 8vo. 3s . 1768

3997 ——— another copy, 8vo. *bds.* 2s 6d *Newcastle*, 1772

3998 ROTOMAGUM. Sanctæ Rotomagensis Ecclesiæ Concilia ac Synodalia Decreta, cum Notis Angeli Godin, 4to. *calf*, 9s *Rotomagi*, 1677

3999 ROUS. — Mella Patrum, nempe, omnium, quorum per prima nascentis et patientis Ecclesiæ tria Secula, usque ad pacem sub *Constantino* divinitus datum, scripta prodierunt; collegit, et Ecclesiæ in Terris Militanti, in Cœlis conversanti dicavit FRANC. ROUS, Etonensis Præpositus, sm. 8vo. *calf, very scarce*, 14s 1650

4000 ——— Treatises and Meditations, dedicated to the Saints throughout the three Nations, folio, *calf*, 9s 1657

4001 ROUTH (M. J. *Coll. S. Magd. Oxon. Præses.*) Reliquiæ Sacræ, sive Auctorum fere jam perditorum secundi tertiúque seculi Fragmenta: accedunt Epistolæ Synodicæ et Canonicæ Nicæno Concilio antiquiores, notis illust. 4 vols. *very scarce*—*Oxon.* 1814-18, Ejusd. Scriptorum Ecclesiasticorum Opuscula, notis illust. 2 vols. *ib.* 1832 —together 6 vols. 8vo. *bds.* £5. ———

4002 RUBEUS (Theodosius) Horarium Universale perpetuum in universo terrarum orbe, Singulis Anni diebus Lucis diurnæ tempora, et temporum vices juxta quatuor Horarum genera, determinans. Ecclesiasticarum etiam functionum, Officii Divini, Celebrationis Missarum, Acquisitionis Indulgentiarum, et observantiæ Jejuniorum in Horis, et Minutis terminos definiens, folio, *vellum*, £1. 10s *Romæ*, 1637

4003 RUBRICÆ generales Missarum Solemnium et Divinorum Officiorum, ex variis Ritualibus Ecclesiæ Leodiensis excerptæ, 8vo. *neat*, 4s 6d
Leodii, 1769

4004 Rudd's (A. B.) Sermons on Practical subjects, 2 vols. 8vo. *bds.* 3s
  Shrewsb. 1789
4005 Ruinart (Theod.) Acta primorum Martyrum sincera et selecta, folio, *vellum,* 18s . . *Amst.* 1713
4006 Ruperti (*Abbatis Monast. Tuitiensis*) Opera, 2 vols. folio, *portrait, calf,* £1. 15s *Mogunt.* 1631
  Rupert was Abbot of the Benedictine Monastery of S. Heribert at Duytz.—" His writings" says Bp. Cosin " have been with most men of great account and authority ;" and Mosheim calls him " the most famous expositor of the Scriptures among the Latins of the XIIth Century ; a man generally of a sound judgment, and not destitute of imagination and taste."
4007 Russell's (J. F.) Judgment of the Anglican Church on the Sufficiency of Holy Scripture, and the Authority of the Catholic Church ; with notes, 8vo. *bds.* 5s . 1838
4008 Russen's (David) Fundamentals without Foundation : or, a true picture of the Anabaptists, in their rise, progress, and practice, 8vo. 2s . . 1703
4009 Rust's (— *Bp. of Dromore*) Choice and Useful Treatises : the one Lux Orientalis ; or an Enquiry into the opinions of the Eastern Sages concerning the præexistence of Souls : the other, a Discourse of Truth, 8vo. *frontispiece by Faithorne, calf, neat,* 5s 1682
4010 Rymer's (Tho.) General Representation of Revealed Religion, 8vo. *calf,* 3s 6d . . 1723
4011 Sacy (M. De) Histoire de l'Ancien et du Nouveau Testament, avec des explications édifiantes, tirées des Saints Pères, 4tc. *with numerous plates after Raphael and other great mascers, purple morocco, gilt leaves,* 21s . *Par.* 1811
4012 Sage's (Bp.) Fundamental Charter of Presbytery, as it hath been lately established in the Kingdom of Scotland, examined and disproved, 8vo. *new, pannelled calf gilt, scarce,* 16s 1697
4012*————— another copy, 8vo. *calf,* 13s 1697
4013 ————— Principles of the Cyprianic Age, with regard to Episcopal power and Jurisdiction, 8vo. *very scarce, hf. bd. calf,* 12s 1717
  From the library of the late Duke of Sussex.
4014 St. George's (Dr. Arthur) Blessings of Christian Philosophy ; being a Treatise on the Beatitudes, in a familiar Dialogue, 8vo. *calf,* 3s . . *Dublin,* 1737
4015 ————— the same, 8vo. *calf,* 3s . *Lond.* 1738
4016 ————— Archdeacon's Examination of Candidates for Holy Orders, 12mo. *bds.* 1s 6d . 1799
4017 St. John's (Dr. Pawlet) XIV. Sermons on Practical subjects, 8vo. *calf,* 5s . 1737
4018 ————— (Theoph.) Practical Sermons on several important subjects, 2 vols. 8vo. *bds.* 5s . 1803-10
4019 Sales (François de, *Evesque et Prince de Genève*) Œuvres, avec sa Vie par N. Talon, 2 vols. folio, *fine copy, French calf, gilt leaves,* £1. 15s . . *Par.* 1641
4020 ————— Traicté de l'Amour de Dieu, sm. 8vo. *neat,* 4s *Lyon,* 1617
4021 ————— A Treatise of the Love of God, a new translation, 8vo. *bds.* 5s 6d . 1835
4022 ————— La Morale de B. François de Sales, tirée mot à mot de tous ses escrits, par F. le Goulx, 12mo. *neat,* 3s *Par.* 1664

4023 SALES (François de S., *Evêsque et Prince de Geneve*) Constitutions et Instructions Synodales, mises en ordre, et augmentées par Jean d'Aranton d'Alex, son successeur dans l'Evesché de Geneve, 18mo. *neat, 2s 6d* . . *Bruxelles,* 1675

4024 ———— Introduction à la Vie Devote; revue par le Pere Brignon, sm. 8vo. *port. neat, 3s 6d* . *ib.* 1728

4025 SALGADO's (James, *a converted Spanish Priest*) Slaughter-house, or a brief description of the Spanish Inquisition, 12mo. *plates, 2s 6d*

Dedicated to King Charles II.

4026 ———— Short Treatise of the Last Judgment, 4to. *sewed, 2s* 1684

4026*SALLUSTIUS, cum Notis Variorum et Havercampi, 2 vols. 4to. *russia, gilt leaves, £1. 10s* *Amst.* 1742

4027 [SALMON (—)] Traité de l'Etude des Conciles, et de leurs collections, 4to. *calf, 8s* . *Par.* 1724

4028 ———— Essay concerning Marriage, 8vo. *calf, 2s* 1724

4029 SALTER's HALL. An authentic account of several things done and agreed upon by the Dissenting Ministers lately assembled at Salter's Hall, sm. 8vo. *sewed, 1s* . 1719

4030 SALVIANI (Massiliensis) Opera, curante C. Rittershusio, cum Vita descripta à Georgio F. sm. 8vo. *vellum, 6s* *Norib.* 1623

4031 ———— et Vincentii Lirinensis Opera, S. Baluzius ad fidem Veterum Codicum MSS. emendavit, notisque illustravit, 8vo. *fine copy, new in calf gilt, old style,* 10s *Par.* 1684

4032 ———— aliud exemplar, 4to. *neat,* 10s 6d *Pedeponti,* 1743

4033 SALVIAN. A Treatise of God's Government, and of the justice of his present Dispensations in this world; translated from the Latin by B. T[esdale], Presbyter of the Church of England; with a Preface by the Rev. Mr. Wagstaffe, 8vo. *calf, 6s* 1700

Salvian was a Priest of Marseille, and flourished in the Vth Century.

4034 SAMWAIES' (Peter) Devotion digested, in several Discourses and Meditations upon the Lord's most Holy Prayer, &c. 12mo. *calf, 4s 6d* . . 1652

4035 SANCHEZ (T.) de S. Matrimonii Sacramento Disputationes, 3 vols. in 1, folio, *hf. bd. uncut,* £1. 11s 6d *Lugduni,* 1739

4036 SANCROFT's (Wm. *Abp. of Canterbury*) Life, compiled principally from original and scarce documents: with an Appendix, containing Fur Prædestinatus, Modern Policies, and three Sermons by Abp. Sancroft; also a Life of Henry Wharton, and two letters of Dr. Sanderson, by George D'Oyly, DD., 2 vols. 8vo. *portrait, calf gilt, marbled leaves,* 14s—*bds.* 9s 1821

4037 SANCTO Jacobo (Philippus à) Sanctorum Patrum Bibliotheca Maxima Lugdunensi XXVII. voluminibus comprehensa, in epitomen redacta, 2 vols. folio, *hf. bd. neat,* 21s *Aug. Vind.* 1719

From the library of the late Duke of Sussex.

4038 SANDERCOCK's (Edw.) Sermon on the Parables of our Saviour: occasioned by an objection in [Tindal's] Christianity as Old as the Creation, 8vo. *sewed, 2s* . 1733

4039 SANDERSON'S (Robert, *Bp, of Lincoln*) Twelve Sermons, ad Clerum, ad Magistratum, ad Populum, whereunto are now added, two Sermons more, one at St. Paul's Crosse, the other at a Visitation, 4to. *calf,* 6s 6d . 1637

4040 ———— XXXIV. Sermons, with a large Preface, whereunto is added, another Sermon, folio, *portrait, calf,* 16s 1674

4041 ———— XXXVI. Sermons, with Life of the Author by Isaac Walton, folio, *portrait, new in pannelled calf, richly gilt, carmine edges,* £1. 11s 6d . 1689

4042 ———— Sermons, with his Life by Isaac Walton, and an Introductory Essay, by the Rev. R. Montgomery, 2 vols. 8vo. *bds.* 8s— *new in bds.* 10s 6d—*calf gilt,* 15s . 1841

4043 ———— Several Cases of Conscience, discussed in ten Lectures, in the Divinity School at Oxford, small 8vo. *calf, gilt back,* 6s 1660

4044 ———— Life, by Izaak Walton, with some short Tracts, or Cases of Conscience, written by the said Bishop, sm. 8vo. *portrait, calf,* 5s 6d 1678

4045 ———— the same, 8vo. *fine copy, but without the portrait, calf,* 5s . . 1678

4046 ———— Dialogue between Isaac Walton and Homologistes: in which the character of Bp. Sanderson is defended against [Archdeacon F. Blackburne], the Author of the Confessional, [by Tho. Towerson, D.D.], 8vo. *sewed,* 1s 6d . 1768

The Church of England is generally considered to be indebted to Bp. Sanderson for those beautiful additions to her Liturgy, the Prayer for all Sorts and Conditions of Men, and the General Thanksgiving.

4047 SANDERUS (Nic.) de Origine ac Progressu Schismatis Anglicani, ab anno Henrici VIII. quo primo cogitare cepit de repudianda legetima uxore serenissima Catherina, usque ad hunc 27 Elizabethæ, editus et auctus per Ed. Rishtonum, sm. 8vo. *calf,* 7s 6d
Col. Agr. 1585

4048 ———— de Visibili Monarchia Ecclesiæ Libri VIII. et de Clave David, seu de Regno Christi, Libri VI., folio, *vellum, (suppressed),* £1. 5s . *Wiceburgi,* 1592

4049 SANDYS'S (Edwin, *Abp. of York*) Sermons, with Life by J. D. Whitaker, 8vo. *calf gilt,* 9s . 1812

"Sandys, whose sermons are perhaps superior to any of his contemporaries."
Birch's Life of Tillotson.

4050 ———— (George) Paraphrase upon the Divine Poems, folio, *calf,* 9s 1638

4051 ———— Paraphrase upon the Song of Solomon, [in metre], 4to. 2s 1641

4052 SANKEY's (R.) Sermons preached in the Parish Church of Farnham, Surrey, 12mo. *bds.* 3s . 1841

4053 SARAVIA's (Hadrian) Treatise on the different degrees of the Christian Priesthood, 18mo. *bds.* 2s . *Oxford,* 1840

4054 SARPI (Paolo) Historia Concilii Tridentini Libri VIII., folio, *fine copy, russia,* 15s . *Aug. Trinob. Lond.* 1620

Published under the name of "*Petrus Suavis Polanus*" a Latinization of his fictitious name *Pietro Soave Polano,* which is an anagram of *Paolo Sarpio Veneto.*

4055 SARPI (Paolo) Historiæ Concilii Tridentini libri VIII. ex Italicis Latini facti, 4to. *vellum*, 8s . *Franc.* 1621
4056 ———— Histoire du Concile de Trente, traduite par Amelot de la Houssaie, avec des Remarques, 4to. *fine copy, old calf gilt*, 10s 6d *Amst.* 1713
4057 ———— Histoire du Concile de Trente, traduite en François par S. F. Le Courayer, 2 vols, folio, *calf*, £1. 11s 6d *Londres*, 1736
4058 ———— Treatise of Ecclesiastical Benefices and Revenues, translated by Tobias Jenkins, with the Life of Father Paul, by Mr. Lockman, 8vo. *calf*, 5s . *Westminster*, 1736
4059 ———— Opere Varie, 2 tom. folio, LARGE PAPER, *hf. bd. yellow morocco*, 15s . *Helmstat.* 1750
4060 SARTHIANO (B. Albertus à) Opera omnia, adnotationibus illustrata a Fra. Haroldo Hiberno. Quibus præmittuntur Gesta Beati B. Alberti ab eodem collecta, et conscripta. Opus posthumum, edidit Patr. Duff. folio, *very scarce, calf, neat*, 18s *Romæ*, 1688
4061 SAURIN (Jacques) Sermons sur divers textes de l'Ecriture Sainte, 12 vols. 8vo. *hf. bd. russia, neat*, £1. 16s *La Haye*, 1776
4062 ———— Sermons, translated by Robinson, Hunter, and Sutcliffe, 7 vols. 8vo. *calf gilt*, £1. 1s . 1800-1806
4063 SAUSSAYE (J. G. Ch. de la) Sermons, (avec son Eloge prononcé par M. Delprat) 8vo. LARGE PAPER, *portrait, hf. bd. calf, neat*, 7s 6d . *La Haye*, 1817
4064 SAVAGE'S (John) Rome's Conviction; or a Vindication of the original institution of Christianity, in opposition to the Usurpations of the Church of Rome, 8vo. *calf*, 4s . 1683
4065 SCACCHI (Fortunati) Sacrorum Elæochrismatum Myrothecia tria, in quibus exponuntur Olea, atque Unguenta Divinos in Codices relata, folio, *vellum gilt, fine copy*, 18s *Amst.* 1701
4066 SCANDRET'S (J.) Sacrifice the Divine Service, 18mo. *bds*. 3s 6d— *morocco, gilt leaves*, 6s . *Oxford*, 1840
4067 SCHELHORNII (J. G.) Amœnitates Historiæ Ecclesiasticæ et Literariæ, quibus Variæ Observationes, Scripta item quædam Anecdota et rariora Opuscula, diversis utriusque historiæ capitibus elucidandis inservientia, exhibentur, 2 vols. sm. 8vo. *hf. bd. vellum, scarce*, 14s . . *Franc.* 1737
4068 SCHELSTRATE (Eman. à) Acta Orientalis Ecclesiæ contra Lutheri Hæresim Monumentis, Notis, ac Dissertationibus illustrata; una cum Epistola Chr. Ranzovii adversus Lutheranorum Errores, 2 vols. in 1, folio, *calf gilt, very neat*, £2. 12s 6d *Romæ*, 1739
4069 SCHETELIGII (Chr. Hen.) Bibliotheca Disputationum Theologico-Philologico-Exegeticarum in V. et N. Testamentum, 3 parts in 1 vol. 4to. *hf. bd. vellum*, 6s *Hamb.* 1736
4070 SCHICKARDUS (Wilh.) Jus Regium Hebræorum, cum notis J. B. Carpzovii, 4to. *vellum*, 5s . *Lipsiæ*, 1674
4071 SCHMIDIUS (Erasmus) Novi Testamenti Græci, hoc est Originalis Linguæ, Tamæion, aliis Concordantiæ, folio, *vellum*, 15s *Witteb.* 1638
4072 ———— aliud exemplar, 2 vols. in 1, 8vo. *calf, neat*, £1. 1s *Glasg.* 1819

[58, GREAT QUEEN STREET,

4073 SCHLEUSNERI (Jo. Fried.) Novus Thesaurus Philologico-criticus: sive Lexicon in LXX. et reliquos Interpretes Græcos, ac Scriptores Apocryphos Veteris Testamenti, 3 vols. 8vo. *portrait, calf, neat,* £2. 2s . . *Glasguæ,* 1822
4074 ———— another copy, 5 vols. 8vo. *calf gilt,* £1. 16s
                                                                      Lips. 1820
4075 ———— idem, et Novum Lexicon Græco-Latinum in Novum Testamentum, 2 vols.—together 5 vols. 8vo. *calf gilt,* £3. 13s 6d
                                                          Glasguæ, 1822-24
4076 ———— idem, 5 vols. 8vo. *hf. bd. calf gilt,* £3. 3s *ib.* 1822-24
4077 ———— Novum Lexicon Græco-Latinum in Novum Testamentum, 4to. *portrait, calf gilt, marbled edges,* £1. 15s (pub. at £3. 3s in bds.) . *ib.* 1824
4078 SCHMIDT (Sebast.) Tractatus de Circumcisione, *Argent.* 1661— Ejusdem Tractatus de Paschate, *Franc.* 1685—Jo. Conr. Dürrii Compendium Theologiæ Moralis, *Alt.* 1675—in 1 thick vol. 4to. *vellum,* 5s . V. Y.
4079 SCHOENEMANN (C. T. G.) Bibliotheca Historico-Literaria Patrum Latinorum, a Tertulliano Principe usque ad Gregorium M. et Isidorem Hispalensem, 2 vols. 8vo. *calf gilt,* £1. 4s *Lipsiæ,* 1792-94
4080 SCHŒTTGENIUS (Chr.) Novum Lexicon Græco-Latinum in Novum Testamentum : nunc primum post Jo. Tob. Krebsium, recensuit G. D. Spohn, 8vo. *hf. bd. neat,* 5s . *ib.* 1790
4081 SCLATER'S (W.) Original Draught of the Primitive Church, in answer to Lord King, 8vo. *calf, scarce,* 8s 1717
4082 ———— another copy, 8vo. *calf,* 9s . 1727
4083 ———— Exposition, with Notes upon the I. and II. Epistle to the Thessalonians, 4to. *calf,* 10s . 1638
4084 SCOBELL'S (Edward) Sermons on the Lord's Prayer, and on other subjects, 8vo. *bds.* 3s . 1815
4085 SCOT'S (Dr. David) Key to the Psalms, Proverbs, Ecclesiastes, and Song of Solomon, in which all the Hebrew words are explained, &c. 8vo. *bds.* 7s . *Edinb.* 1828
4086 ———— Elements of Hebrew Grammar, and Extracts from the Hebrew Bible, 8vo. *bds.* 4s 6d . *ib.* 1834
4087 SCOTT'S (Daniel) New Version of St. Matthew's Gospel, with select Notes, and a Review of Dr. Mills' Notes on this Gospel, 4to. *bds.* 4s . 1741

The author was compiler of the Appendix to Stephens's Thesaurus.

4088 ———— (Dr. James) Sermons on interesting subjects, 8vo. *calf, neat,* 4s . . 1816
4089 ———— (Dr. John) Practical Discourses upon several subjects, 2 vols. 8vo. *calf,* 4s 6d . 1739
4090 ———— Christian Life, from its beginning to its consummation in Glory; with Forms of Prayer, 5 vols. 12mo. *calf,* 15s *Edinb.* 1754

"Dr. Scott's Christian Life is one of the finest and most rational Schemes of Divinity that is written in our tongue or any other."—*Spectator.*

4091 ———— Works, viz. :—The Christian Life, 5 vols.—Practical Discourses, 2 vols.—Sermons upon several occaasions, 1 vol.—together 8 vols. 12mo. *portrait, fine copies, calf, neat,* £1. 4s 1700, &c.

4092 SCOTT's (Tho.) Essays on the most important subjects in Religion, 12mo. *calf,* 3s . 1819
4093 [――― ――― (W.)] Essay towards pointing out the Eloquence and Action proper for the Pulpit, &c. by Philagoretes, 8vo. *hf. bd. calf,* 2s 6d . . 1765
4094 SCRIPTORES VETERES.—ANGELI MAII SCRIPTORUM VETERUM NOVA COLLECTIO, E VATICANIS CODD. EDITA, 10 vols. royal 4to. *calf gilt,* £17. 17s . *Romæ,* 1825-38

CONTENTS.—Tom. I. Eusebii Questiones ad Stephanum, et ad Marinum Eusebii, Apollinarii, et Photii Comm. in Lucam —Photii Patriarchæ Questiones ad Amphilochium—Anastasius Sinæits de Vitæ termino—Chronicon breviatam ex Eusebii opere de temporibus—Theodori Mopsuesteni Prologi et Comm. in Amosum, Zachariam, etc.—Polychronius in Danielem—Catena in Danielem ex Basilio, Cyrillo, etc.—Chronici Paschalis et S. Hyppolyti in Proverb. Supplementa—Aristidis Oratio adv. Demosthenem de Immunitate, etc.—Leontii et Joannis Monachi Index libri II. sacrarum rerum—Operis prædicti Specimen, id est, titulus primus de hominis creatione.

Tom. II.—Diodori |Siculi, Dionis Cassii, Eunapii, et Dexippi Excerpta—Jamblichi, et Menandri Fragmenta—Appiani, Polybii, Dionysii Halicarnassensis, Dionis Excerpts—Petrus Magister de Scientia Politica—Eubulus vel Proclus de Aristotelis dictis adv. Platonia rempublicam—Basilii Imperatoris, et aliorum Opuscula.

Tom. III. Ephræmii Byzantini Vitæ Cæsarum—Ejusdem Catalogus Patriarcharum Byzantinorum—Methodius Monachus de vitando schismate—Victorinus in Pauli Epist. ad Galatas, Philippenses, et Ephesios—Ejusdem Opusculum pro religione Christ. contra philosophos physicos — Ferrandi Diaconi adv. Arianos, etc. Epistola—Reliquiæ tractatus antiquissimi in Lucæ Evangelium ; Fragmenta varia, etc.—Julii Paridis, et Januarii Nepotiani Epitome Valerii Maximi—Præcepta artis musicæ, ex S. Augustino—Sermones veteres quatuor —Thomæ Magistri Orstiones—Sibyllæ libri addendi.

Tom. IV. Synodus Constant. sub. Luca patriarcha, imp. Manuele Comneno— Codicia Arabici vel a Christianis scripti, vel ad Christ. religionem pertinentea —Codices Arabici a Mahometanis Scripti—Codices Persici, et Turcici—Assemanni Frammenti Storici.

Tom. V. Inscriptiones Christianæ—Catalogus Cod. Syrisc. CII. Assemaniano editio addendus—Appendix ad Cat. Cod. Hebraic. Biblioth. Vaticanæ—Catalogus Cod. Æthiop. Copt. Armen. et Slavicorum Bibl. Vat. Codices Indici, et Sinici Bibl. Vat.—Assemanni sulla nazione dei Copti, etc.

Tom. VI. Theodori Mopsuesteni Comment. in Prophetas XII. Minores, etc.— Theoriani Disputatio cum Nersete patriarcha Armeniorum—Excerpta ex Epistolis Nersetis—Attonis Vercellensis Sermones, etc.—Remigii Comment. in Oseam.—S. Petri Damiani Iter Gallicum ; et alia varia.

Tom. VII. Patrum doctrina de Verbi incarnatione—Leontii et Joannis sacrarum rerum liber— Leontius Hierosol. adversus Monophysitas—S. Ambrosii, Anastasii, Eulogii, S. Gregorii, S. Nicetæ, Justiniani I. Imp. et aliorum Opuscula, et Fragmenta varia—Hieronymus Donatus de Processione Spiritus Sancti— Marini Prefazione alla sua inedita opere delle iscrizione antiche doliari—Tipuciti Conspectus universus, cum specimine Suppl. Basilicis Juris Civilis libris faciendorum.

Tom. VIII. Eusebii Pamphili Chronicorum Canonum liber prior, etc.—S. Gregorii Nysseni, et S. Cyrilli Alexandrini Opuscula et Fragments.—S. Silvestri Papæ I. Fragmentum.

Tom. IX. Photii Patriarchæ Quæstiones Amphilochianæ— Seduli Scoti, et aliorum Commentarii—Alcuini Comment. in Apocalypsin—Leontius Hierosol. contra objectiones Nestorianorum—Nicolai, Anastasii, Cyrilli, et aliorum Fragmenta.

Tom. X. Ebediesu Metropolitæ Sobæ et Armeniæ, Collectio Canonum Synodicorum et Chaldaicis Bibl. Vat. Codicibus sumpta, et in Latinam linguam translata ab Aloysio Assemano—Gregorii Abulpharagii Bar-Hebræi Ecclesiæ Antiochenæ Nomocanon, Latine, interprete Aloysio Assemano — Canones selecti Ecclesiæ Armeniorum— Ebediesu Liber Margaritæ, seu de Veritate Chiistianæ religionis, Syriacè et Latinè.

[58, GREAT QUEEN STREET,

4095 SCRIBONIUS (Jo. Marius) Prophetia sive Epistola Canonicæ S. Judæ Apostoli de hæreticis nostræ tempestatis, 4to. *in the original stamped calf binding, 3s 6d* . *Camberii,* 1634

The present copy contains a plate of the arms of Albert Prince of Arenberg, &c. who gave it "domni professæ Soc. Jesu Antverpiæ."

4096 SCRIPTURAL ESSAYS, adapted to the Holydays of the Church of England, 2 vols. 12mo. *bds. 2s 6d* . 1816

4097 SCRIPTURE RELIGION: or a short View of the Faith and Practice of a true Christian, &c. with suitable Devotions, 8vo. *calf, 1s 6d* . 1701

4098 SCRIVENER (Matth.) Apologia pro S. Ecclesiæ Patribus, adversus J. Dallæum. Accessit Apologia pro Ecclesia Anglicana adversus nuperum Schisma, 4to. LARGE PAPER, *fine copy, calf, 8s* 1672

4099 SCROPE'S (Dr. John) Enquiry concerning the Sacrament of the Lord's Supper, 12mo. *calf, 1s* . *Oxford,* 1761

4100 SCUDERY'S (Georges de) Curia Politiæ; or, the Apologies of severall Princes justifying to the world their most eminent actions, folio, *many portraits, calf, 5s 6d* . 1654

4101 SECKENDORF (Vitus Ludov.) Commentarius Historicus et Apologeticus de Lutheranismo, folio, *front. vellum,* £1. 10s *Lips.* 1694

4102 ———— another copy, folio, LARGE PAPER, *port. and front. hf. bd.* £1. 8s . . *ib.* 1694

" This work, which is very valuable on many accounts, and particularly curious for several singular pieces and extracts that are to be found in it, still holds its reputation, and is referred to by all writers on the Reformation."—Chalmers.

4103 SECKER'S (Tho. *Abp. of Canterbury*) Works, with his Life by Bp. Porteus, 6 vols. 8vo. *portrait, hf. bd. calf, neat,* £2. 2s 1811

4104 ———— Eight Charges, with Instructions to Candidates for Orders, and a Latin Speech intended to have been made in Convocation, 8vo. *bds. 3s 6d* . 1771

4105 ———— Lectures on the Catechism of the Church of England; with a Discourse on Confirmation, 12mo. *calf, 1s 6d* 1777

4106 ———— Lectures on the Catechism of the Church of England; with a Discoure on Confirmation, 8vo. *hf. bd. calf, neat, 5s* 1804

4107 SEDGWICK'S (Obadiah) Fountain opened, and the Water of Life flowing forth for the refreshing of thirsty Sinners, in several Sermons at Covent-Garden, 4to. *hf. bd. calf, neat, 7s* 1657

4108 SEED'S (Jeremiah) Discourses on several important subjects, with eight Sermons at Lady Moyer's Lecture, and his Posthumous Sermons, 4 vols. 8vo. *calf, 14s* . 1766

" His posthumous Sermons are chiefly on the Evidences of Christianity, the satisfaction of Christ, and the virtue of Benevolence, and they contain the same refined taste and delicacy of sentiment, and the same zeal for religion, as those published in his lifetime."

4109 SEGNERI (Paolo, *della Comp. di Gesu*) Quaresimale, 6 vols. 8vo. *port. sewed, 7s 6d* . *Padova,* 1815-16

4110 ———— Opere, viz.—Prediche e Panegirici, Opere Instruttive e Polemiche, ed Opere Ascetiche, 3 vols. in 4, 8vo. *port. sewed,* £3. 3s . *Milano,* 1837-38

4111 SELDEN (Joannes) de Synedris ct Præfecturis Juridicis Veterum Ebræorum, liber tertius et ultimus, 4to. *calf*, 4s   1655
 " A work of prodigious learning, in which every thing is recorded with relation to the Sanhedrim or Juridical courts of the Jews, both before and after the promulgation of the Mosaic law."—*Aikin's Life of Selden.*
4112 ———— de Jure Naturali Gentium juxta disciplinam Ebræorum, libri VII. 4to. *calf*, 5s 6d   *Argent.* 1665
4113 ———— Opera omnia, collegit ac recensuit D. Wilkins, 3 vols. in 6, folio, *fine copy, portrait, calf,* £6. 6s   1726
 CONTENTS:—VOL. I. Dedicatio, Præfatio, et Vita Seldeni—de Anno Civili Reipublicæ Judaicæ—de Jure Naturali et Gentium—de Synedris—Indices.
 VOL. II.—De successionibus in bona defunctorum, et de successionibus in Pontificatum Ebræorum—De Diis Syris—Eutychii Ecclesiæ suæ Origines— —Uxor Hebraica—Analecta Anglo-Britannica—Janus Anglorum—Dissertatio ad Fletam—Judicium de X. Scriptoribus Anglicanis—Mare Clausum—Vindiciæ de Scriptione Maris Clausi—Marmora Arundelliana—Notæ in Eadmerum— Epistolæ et Poemata.
 VOL. III.—His English Tracts, viz.—England's Epinomis—Origin of Duels— Titles of Honour—History of Tythes—of the Number 666—Notes on Drayton's Polyolbion, Speeches, Table Talk, &c.

4114 ———— Memoirs, and Notices of the Political Contest during his time. by Geo. W. Johnson, 8vo. *port. bds.* 3s   1835
4115 SELLON'S (Walter, *a Methodist preacher*) Doctrine of General Redemption considered, and the Arguments against it answered, 8vo. *sewed*, 1s   1807
4116 ———— (Wm.) Sermons on various subjects, 8vo. *bds. very scarce,* 4s 6d   1792
4117 ———— Sermon before the President, &c. of the Magdalen Charity, 1767—A Sermon before the Governors of the Middlesex Hospital, 1759—A farewell Sermon at St. James's, Clerkenwell, 1766—A Sermon at the Assizes at Guildford, 1759—A Sermon preached at Clerkenwell, St. Giles, and St. Andrew, Holborn, 1763 —A Sermon at the Orphan Hospital, 1763—in 1 vol. 4to. *hf. bd. calf*, 2s 6d   ——
 " Mr. Sellon wrote his sermons in short hand, and I believe only one person (his wife's sister) understood his cypher. His mode of delivery, though stiff, was, upon the whole, pleasing. Though there was a preciseness even in his speech, yet he had a sweet voice, was deliberate and distinct, so that not a single word was lost even at the end of a sentence; and he had much animation, or at least earnestness. In a word, he was an excellent preacher."—R. W.

4118 SENS, *Diocese de*—Defense de la Discipline qui s'observe dans le diocese de Sens, touchant l'imposition de la penitence publique, pour les pechez publics, 8vo. *neat*, 3s   *Sens*, 1673
4119 SEPTCHENE'S (M. le Clerc de) Religion of the Ancient Greeks Illustrated by an Explanation of their Mythology, 8vo. *bds.* 2s 6d   1788
4120 SERARIUS (Nic.) de Lutheri Magistro Libri duo, in quibus cum utilia plura, tum vero insunt duo hæc: I. Tota Diaboli cum Luthero disputatio ad Verbum. II. Disputationis ejusdem dispunctio, et ad ipsius Diaboli argumenta omnia responsio, sm. 8vo. *vellum*, 6s 6d
Mogunt. 1604
4121 SERGROVE'S (T. S.) Lectures on Popery, 2 vols. in 1, 8vo. *calf gilt,* 7s   ——

4122 [SERLE's (Ambrose)] Christian Remembrancer ; or, Short Reflections upon the Faith, Life, and Conduct of a Real Christian, 12mo. *calf*, 2s . . 1793

4123 SERMONS choisis de divers auteurs, avec un fragment de la vie de M. Jaquelot, et une Oraison Funèbre de la Reine Marie, sm. 8vo. *old red morocco, richly tooled, gilt leaves*, 6s
Lond. 1726
The Sermons are by Abp. Tillotson, Bezombes, Ostervald, Jaquelot, and Dr. Bentley. The funeral oration on Q. Mary was pronounced in Latin, by Græ̈vius, in the Cathedral of Utrecht.

4124 SERMONS on Humanity and Beneficence, 12mo. *bds*. 2s   1768
"These sermons have been erroneously attributed to Dr. Kippis."
Crit. Rev. xxv. 480.

SINGLE SERMONS, in volumes.

4125 ———— A Sermon before the Peers, by Seth [Ward] Bp. of Exon. 1666—A Sermon before the King, by J. Dolben, D.D. 1666 —A Sermon before the King, Jan. 30, by Geo. Stradling, D.D. 1675 —A Visitation Sermon by Jo. Templer, D.D. *Camb.* 1676—Moses and Aaron ; the King and the Priest, 1675—An Apology for the Mysteries of the Gospel, a Sermon by Seth [Ward], Bp. of Sarum, 1673—The Case of Joram, a Sermon before the Peers, on Jan. 30, by Seth, Bp. of Sarum, 1674—The divine Authority and Usefulness of the Holy Scriptures, a Sermon by R. Allestree, D.D. *Oxf.* 1673—A Sermon to those who had been Scholars of St. Paul's School, by W. Wyatt. M.A. 1679—A Sermon before the Lord Maior, &c. by Jo. Goodman, D.D. 1680—A Sermon on a Fast-day, by Geo. Topham, 1679—A Sermon before the Lord Maior, &c. by Rd. Meggott, D.D. 1674—A Sermon to those who had been Scholars of S. Paul's School, by Rd. Meggott, D.D. 1676—in 1 vol. 4to. *calf, neat*, 4s 6d

4126 ———— Nehemiah's Teares and Prayers for Judah's Affliction, a Fast Sermon before the House of Commons, by Jo. Greene, 1644— A two-edged Sword out of the mouth of Babes, a Fast Sermon before the House of Lords, by Stephen Marshall, 1646—A Fast Sermon before the Commons, by S. Marshall, 1647—Emmanuel : a Thanksgiving Sermon before the Commons, by S. Marshall, 1648 —England's Plus Ultra, a Thanksgiving Sermon before the Houses of Parliament, &c. by Joseph Caryl, 1646—The Oppressor Destroyed, a Sermon before the Lord Mayor in commemoration of the Victorie before Worcester, by J. Caryl, 1651—Reformation's Preservation, a Fast Sermon before the Commons, by Sidr. Simpson, 1643—A Sermon at Westminster before sundry of the House of Commons, 1643—The Glory and Beauty of God's Portion, a fast Sermon before the Commons, by Gaspar Hickes, 1644—The Life and Death of David, a Sermon at the Funeralls of Will. Strode, Esq., by Gaspar Hickes, 1645—The best Refuge for the most Oppressed, a Fast Sermon before the Commons, by Simeon Ash, 1642—Religious Covenanting directed, a Sermon before the Lord Mayor, &c. by Simeon Ash, 1646—The Excellency of the Solemn League and Covenant set forth, in a Speech made by Mr. Philip Nye to the House of Commons and Assembly of Ministers,

SERMONS—*continued.*

1646—The Church sinking saved by Christ, a Fast Sermon before the Lords, by S. Ash, 1645—God's incomparable Goodnesse unto Israel, a Fast Sermon before the Commons, by S. Ash, 1647—A sleeping Sicknes of the Distemper of the Times, a Fast Sermon before the Peeres, by Will. Jenkyn, 1647—The Stil-destroyer, a Sermon before the Lord Mayor, &c., by W. Jenkyn, 1645—A Sermon on Nov. 5, 1651, by W. Jenkyns, 1652—Stand still: or, a Bridle for the Times, a Discourse by Jo. Brinsley, 1647—Deliverance in the Birth, a Fast Sermon before the Peeres, by Sam. Bolton, *Camb.* 1647—England's Spirituall Languishing, a Fast Sermon before the Commons, by Tho. Manton, 1648—The Triumph of a good Conscience, a Sermon by Paul Amiraut, 1648—England's Deliverance from the Northern Presbytery, compared with its Deliverance from the Roman Papacy, a Sermon before the Parliament, Nov. 5, 1651—A Glasse for the Times, a Sermon by La. Seaman, 1650—A Voice from Heaven calling the People of God to a perfect Separation from Mystical Babylon, a Sermon before the Lord Mayor, &c. Nov. 5, 1653-1654—in 1 vol. 4to. *calf, neat,* 8s

4127 ———— Two Sermons: the first at Oxford, on Act Sunday, 1634; the second at Salisbury, at the Visitation of William [Laud], Abp. of Canterbury, 1634, by Tho. Lawrence, D.D. *Oxford,* 1635 — A Sermon at Whitehall, by Walter Curll, D.D., Deane of Lichfield, 1622—Labour forbidden and commanded, a Sermon by Edw. Rainbowe, 1635—Two Sermons by Edw. Gee, D.D. 1620—The Unmasking of the Hypocrite, a Sermon at Oxford, by Jo. Rawlinson, D.D. 1616—A Sermon preached at Barnstaple, upon occasion of the late happy Success of God's Church in forraine parts, by G. H., D.D. 1632—The Presentment of a Schismaticke, by Tho. [Morton], Bp. of Durham, in his Sermon at St. Paul's, June 19, 1642—The Flight of Time, discovered by the dim shadow of Job's diall, a Sermon at Bloxam, by R. M.[athew], 1634—The Convert's First Love, by Tho. Cooper, 1610—The Two Twins of Birth and Death, a Sermon by Samson Price, D.D., upon occasion of the Funeralls of Sir Will. Bryde, 1624—Christian Hospitalitie handled common-place-wise, by Caleb Dalechamp, *Camb.* 1632 – A Sermon concerning the Punishment of Malefactors, preached at Paule's Crosse, by Cha. Richardson, 1616—The Holy Citie Discovered, Besieged, and Delivered, a Sermon before Francis Lord Verulam, by Michael Wigmore, M.A. 1619—Lamentations for the Death of Prince Henry, two Sermons, by Daniell Price, 1613, (*imperfect*) – A Sermon or Publicke Thanksgiving for the Recovery of his Majesty, preached at Paul's Cross, by the B. of London, [Jo. King], 1619—Nicodemus for Christ; or, the religious moote of an honest Lawyer, an Assize Sermon, by Ant. Fawkner, M. A. 1634—Anthropophagus, the Man-eater: or a Caution for the Credulous, being a moral Discourse by E. S.[ymonds], B. D., a Sermon preached aboard of the Globe, by Will. Lesk, 1617—in 1 vol. 4to. *calf,* 10s 6d

[58, GREAT QUEEN STREET,

SERMONS—*continued*.

4128 ——— A Sermon preached on Palme-Sunday before King Henry VIII., by Cuthbert Tonstall, Bp. of Duresme, 1633—Two Sermons at St. Paule's Crosse, by Dr. Gouge, (*imperfect*)—A Sermon concerning the Punishing of Malefactors, (*title wanting*)—Tho. Drax's Churche's Security, &c. (*imperfect*)—A Sermon at Whitehall, Nov. 5, 1608, by Jo. King, D.D. Oxford, 1608—A Sermon before the King at Woodstocke, Aug. 28, 1614, by Will. Goodwin, *ib.* 1614—An Assize Sermon at Nottingham, by Will. Worship, D.D. 1614—A Sermon in St. Paul's, by Will. Walker, B.D. 1629—The Royall Passing Bell, a Sermon by H. Sydenham, (*title wanting*)—The Rich Man's Warning Peece, a Sermon by H. Sydenham, 1630—Waters of Marah and Meribah, by H. Sydenham, 1630—A Sermon at S. Paul's, by Doctor Westfield, 1641—Mysticall Babylon: two Sermons, (*imperfect*)—The Allegeance of the Cleargie, a Sermon—The Supper of the Lord, a Sermon—The Cape of Good Hope, five Sermons for the use of the Merchant and the Mariner, by Sam. Page, D.D. 1616—God be Thanked, a Sermon by S. Page, D.D. 1616—in 1 vol. 4to. *calf*, 10s 6d . . ———

4129 ——— Six Sermons by Edw. Chaloner, D.D. Oxford, 1629—Five Sermons preached before His Majesty, by B. [Layney,] Lord Bp. of Ely, 1662—The Danger of Hypocrisie, a Sermon, by W. Ashton, B.D. 1673—The Mark of the Beast; or, the present Degeneracy of the Church of Rome, a Sermon, by Edw. Pelling, 1682—in 1 vol. sm. 4to. *calf, neat*, 6s . ———

4130 ——— A Collection of occasional Discourses by Dr. W. Starkey (Assize), Heigham, Dr. F. Hutchinson (Assize), James Frost, J. Juxon (on Wichcraft, occasioned by a late attempt to discover witches by swimming), Leeke, Bp. Porteus (Letter on Sunday Schools), Dr. N. Forster, G. Rogers, Dr. R. Valpy (two Assize Sermons), Hurdis, and some other anonymous writers, 8vo. *hf. bd. calf*, 4s 6d . 1668-1793

4131 ——— — A collection of XI. Sermons on various subjects and occasions, by Bp. Stillingfleet, Bp. Beveridge, Dr. Meggott, and Abp. Tenison—In 1 vol. 4to. *calf*, 4s . 1678-91

4132 ——— A collection of Sermons by Bp. Blackall, Dr. Ab. Campbell, Dr. Tho. Manningham (Concio habita coram Præside et Sociis Coll. Sion), Bps. Fleetwood, Nicholson, Kennett, Atterbury, Abp. Wake, Abp. Dawes, Bps. Williams, Moore, Gibson, Dr. Z. Cradock, Bp. Moss, Dr. E. Sydall, and Jon. Bernard—in 1 vol. 4to. *calf*, 5s . . 1700-6

4133 ———— A collection of Sermons by Atterbury, Bennett, Bentley, Berriman, Bingham, Bisse, Blackall, Bradford, Brady, Brett, Burnett, Clarke, Dawes, Fleetwood, Friend, Hare, Hoadley, Ibbot, Kennett, Law, Lucas, Marshall, Milbourne, Nicholls, Nicholson, Rogers, Sacheverell, Sherlock, Smallridge, Stanhope, Stennett, Swift, Synge, Trapp, Wake, Walker, Waterland, Waugh, Wheatley, Whitby, and other celebrated English Divines, together 22 vols. 8vo. *calf*, £3. 3s . 1708-23

4134 SERMONS, chiefly relating to the Bangorian Controversy, in 1 vol. 8vo. *calf*, 8s

    CONTENTS:—COLLIER'S (A.) Justification by Faith, 1716—A short Letter to the Abp. of Canterbury [Dr. Wake], being a modest Defence of the Bp. of Bangor's [Dr. Hoadly] Sermon before the King, by a Divine of the Church of England, 1717—WILLIS's (Rd. Bp. *of Glouc.*) Sermon before the Lord Mayor, &c. 1717—SHERLOCK's (Tho.) Sermon before the Lord Mayor, &c. 1717—BENNET's (Dr. Tho.) Beneficence to our Saviour Christ, a Sermon, 1717—SNAPE's (Dr. A.) Sermon before the House of Commons, 1717—TRAPP's (Jo.) real Nature of the Church or Kingdom of Christ, a Sermon in answer to [Hoadly] Bp. of Bangor, 1717—BURNET's (G.) Letter to Mr. Trapp, occasioned by his Sermon, 1717—Reality without Existence; or, [Trapp's] Sermon proved to be unnatural. by a Gentleman of Oxford, 1717—HILLIARD's (S.) Nature of the Kingdom of Christ,&c. a Sermon, [1717]—INNES's (Dr. A.) Absolute Authority of the Church and Men's right of disputing for themselves reconciled, in two Discourses, 1717—WRIGHT's (John) Rights of the Christian Priesthood asserted, in an Ordination Sermon, 1717—LOVELING's (Benj.) Authority of Christian Princes, &c. not inconsistent with the true nature of Christ's Kingdom, a Sermon, 1717—HIND's (Tho.) Divinity of our Saviour proved from the Scriptures, a Sermon, *Oxford*, 1717—LAURENCE's (Jo.) Christian Religion the best Friend to Civil Government, an Assize Sermon, 1717—LAUGHTON's (Dr. Rd.) Sermon before the King, at King's Coll. Chappel, *Camb.* 1717—LUPTON's (Dr. W.) Sermon before the Sons of the Clergy, 1717—BRADFORD's (Dr. Sam.) Sermon before the King, 1708—CHANDLER's (Edw. Bp. *of Cov. and Lichf.*) Sermon before the Lords, Jan. 30, 1718—HOADLY's (Dr. Jo.) Sermon before the Commons, Jan. 30, 1718—FEUILLERADE's (Peter) Nature and Necessity of Faith, a Sermon, 1717—WHITCHCOT's (Dr.) True Notion of Peace in the Kingdom or Church of Christ, a Sermon, corrected by Jo. Jeffery, D.D. 1717

4135 ———— A collection of Sermons by Bp. Hoadley (Assize), Jo. Waller, Dr. P. Nourse, Bp. Blackall, Dr. R. Lambert, Jo. Tribbeko (on the Death of Prince George of Denmark), P. Stubbs (on the same), Dr. P. Bisse, Dr. Jos. Rawson (Concio ad Clerum, &c.) by Trimnell, Bp. Willis, Bp. Hare, Dr. Tho. Manningham, Abp. Dawes, Dr. H. Lambe, Dr. J. Adams, Dr. R. West (Assize), Dr. Tho. Synford, and Dr. Jo. Smith—in 1 vol. 4to. *calf*, 5s   1708-9

4136 ———— XX. Sermons by the following Divines:—W. Stonestreet, Dr. T. Lynford, Bp. Moore, W. Whitfield, Dr. Jo. Hancock, D. Waterland (Assize), H. Topping, Bp. Willis, Wm. Talbot, Bp. of Oxon. (at the Coronation of Geo. I.) Dr. N. Brady, Bp. Hoadly (Nov. 5.), Bp. Gibson (Assize), St. George, Bp. of Clogher, Dr. Tho. Linford, Bp. Trimnell, Dr. Jo. Turner, Abp. Boulter, Dr. E. Sydall—in 1 vol. 4to. *calf*, 4s   .   1709-15

4137 ———— Twenty-five Sermons preached at the Aniversary Meetings of the Charity Schools, from 1704 to 1728, 8vo. *calf*, 3s   1729

4138 ———— A collection of Sermons by Dr. Will. Stuart, Bp. Talbot, Dr. W. Barker (Assize), Dr. A. Laughton, Bp. Clagett, T. Payne, Bp. Hoadly (Jan. 30, &c.), B. Carter, Dr. W. Lupton, Dr. E. Waddington, Bp. Bradford (Jan. 30.), Bp. Kennett, Dr. Jo. Waugh (Jan. 30), and Dr. B. Ibbot—in 1 vol. 4to. *calf*, 5s
                                                                                     1717-19

4139 ———— XI. Sermons on various occasions, by Dr. Alured Clarke, Dr. T. Ford, E. Owen, Dr. Jo. Hey, James Johnson, T. Tweady, Dr. Webster, Dr. Jo. Rogers, &c. 8vo. *hf. bd. calf*, 3s   1724-90

SERMONS—*continued*.

4140 ———— XII. Sermons on various subjects and occasions, by James Parker, Bp. Clagett, (*with his autograph*), Dr. G. Fothergill, S. Chandler, G. Stephens, Bp. Sherlock, Dr. R. Bentley, H. Venn, Chishull (Visitation), G. Rogers, (Do.), and Lindsey (at the opening of the Chapel in Essex Street), 8vo. *hf. bd. calf*, 3*s* 1711-90

4141 ———— XIX. Sermons chiefly by Dissenters, viz. J. M. Ray, Davies, Some, Rogers, Gibbons, (on a great fire at Burwell,) Kingsbury, (at the ordination of Sir H. Trelawney, Bart.) Bostwick, Parsons, Craner, Doddridge, Hextal, Wright, Elliot, Tailer, and Bingham, 8vo. *half bd. calf*, 2*s* 6*d* 1725-82

4142 ———— against Popery, preached at Salters-Hall, in 1735, by several Ministers, 2 vols. 8vo. *calf*, 7*s* . 1735

4143 ———— another copy, (*the general title supplied in MS.*) 2 vols. 8vo. *calf*, 5*s* . . 1735

4143* ———— A collection of Sermons on various occasions by Dr. W. Webster, Bp. Warburton, Abp. Secker, Dr. P. Williams, S. Chandler, Bp. Keene, Bp. Ashburnham, Bp. Egerton, Bp. Hurd, Dr. B. Buckler, Dr. I. Weld, (Funeral Sermon on Dr. Jo. Leland), Howes, (Visitation), Dr. T. Knowles, J. M. Ray, Hallward, and W. Jones, 8vo. *hf. bd. calf*, 3*s* . 1742-95

4144 ———— A collection of XVIII. occasional Sermons by Goddard, Hurn, Daking, Jones, Barry, Turner, Hodson, Bp. S. Butler, Howman, Bp. Tomline, Stevenson, Dewhirst, Cobbold, Burnet, Hughes, Philipps, and White, 8vo. *hf. bd. calf* 2*s* 6*d* 1756-1803

4145 ———— A collection of occasional Sermons by Archdeacon Pott, Dr. S. Glasse, G. H. Glasse, Bp. Porteus, Abp. Markham, Bp. Horsley, Bp. Hurd, Archd. Paley, Bps. Lowth, Tomline, Hallifax, Dr. J. B. Leale, Bp. Randolph, Bp. Horne, Jo. Walters, Robert Holmes, and J. Lettice, *in one* vol. 4to. *hf. bd. calf*, 5*s* 1758-93

4146 ———— XXXV. preached at the Anniversary Meetings of the Charity Schools at St. Pauls, and on other occasions, including several before the House of Lords, by Bps. Horsley, Tomline, Horne, &c., Stinton, Raye, Plymley, Finch, Peters, Dupré, Jekyll, Watson, Coleridge, Butler, &c., *in one* thick volume, 4to. 5*s* . . 1789, &c.

4147 ———— CLXIV. Original Family Sermons, by Bps. Blomfield, Bethell, Davys, Sumner, Whately, Kaye, Jebb, Tomlinson, Skinner, Jolly, Copleston, Torry, McIlwain, &c., Drs. Burton, Chandler, Pusey, Russell, Barrett, Shuttleworth, Arnold, Wilberforce, H. Blunt, Molesworth, Raikes, J. K. Arnold, Berens, Dale, Tyler, Le Bas, Rodwell, Dealtry, Slade, &c. 5 vols. 12mo. *hf. bd. calf*, £1. 1*s* . . 1833-5

4148 ———— A course of Sermons (by Keble, Marriot, Richards, Dodsworth, Williams and Pusey), on solemn subjects, chiefly bearing on Repentance and Amendment of Life, preached in St. Saviour's Church, Leeds, during the week after its consecration; edited by Dr. E. B. Pusey, 8vo. *cloth bds.* 7*s* 6*d* . 1845

4149 SETHOS. The Life of Sethos, taken from private Memoirs of the Ancient Egyptians: translated from a Greek MS. into French, and now done into English, by Lediard, 2 vols. 8vo. *calf, 6s* 1732
4150 SEVERTIUS (Jacobus) Chronologia Historica Successionis Hierarchiæ illustrissimorum Archiantistitum Lugdunensis Archiepiscopatus, Galliarum Primatus, necnon Ecclesiæ et Diœceseos historia, folio, old green morocco, £1. 11s 6d . *Lugduni*, 1628
The following inscription is stamped on each side, " PRO CAPITULO PRIMATIALIS ECCLESIÆ SEU CANONICOR. COMITUM LUGDUNENSIUM."
4151 SEWEL'S (Wm.) History of the rise, increase, and progress of the people called Quakers, folio, *calf*, 14s . 1722
4152 —— — (W *of Exeter Coll. Oxon.*) Christian Morals, 12mo. *bds.* 4s . . 1840
4153 —— — Christian Politics, 12mo. *bds.* 5s 1844
4154 SHARP'S (Granville) Remarks on the uses of the definitive Article in the Greek text of the New Testament, containing many new proofs of the Divinity of Christ, 12mo. *bds.* 2s . 1803
4155 SHARP'S (John, *Abp. of York,*) Sermons on several occasions, 7 vols. 8vo. *port. new, in rich calf gilt*, £2. 2s 1729-35
4156 —————— another copy, with some Papers on the Popish Controversy, 7 vols. 8vo. *fine copy, calf,* £1. 1s . 1749
4157 —————— Theological Works, 5 vols. 8vo. *bds.* £1. 16s—*pannelled calf gilt*, £2. 12s 6d . *Oxford*, 1829
4158 SHELFORD'S (Rob.) Lectures, or Readings upon the 6th verse of the 22nd Chapter of the Proverbs, concerning the vertuous education of Youth, 16mo. *hf. bd. calf, neat,* 3s 6d . 1606
4159 SHEPHEARD'S (Wm.) Sermons on several religious and important subjects, 8vo. *calf,* 3s . *Sherborne*, 1748
4160 SHEPHERD'S (John) Critical and practical Elucidation of the Book of Common Prayer, with a Memoir of the Author, 2 vols. 8vo. *calf, neat,* 18s . . 1817
4161 —————— the same, 2 vols. 8vo. *calf gilt,* £1. 2s 1828
4162 —————— (R.) Notes Critical and Dissertatory, on the Gospel and Epistles of St. John, 4to. *bds.* 4s 6d . 1796
4163 —————— (*Archd. of Bedford*), Sermons on several occasions, 8vo. *bds.* 2s . . 1803
4164 —————— (Sam.) Sermons on various subjects, 2 vols. 8vo. *cf.* 6s 1790
4165 —————— (Tho.) Several Sermons on Angels, with a Sermon on the power of Devils in bodily distempers, sm. 8vo. *calf*, 2s 6d 1702
4166 SHERIFFE'S (Mrs.) Practical Reflections on the Psalms, 2 vols. 12mo. *bds.* 3s . . 1821
4167 SHERINGHAM (Rob.) de Anglorum Gentis Origine Disceptatio, 8vo. *calf, neat,* 3s . *Cantab.* 1670
4168 SHERLOCK'S (Dr. Richard) Principles of Holy Catholic Religion: or, the Catechism of the Church of England paraphrased, 18mo. *cloth,* 1s 6d . *Oxford,* 1841
4169 —————— Practical Christian: or the Devout Penitent; edited by the Rev. H. H. Sherlock, 18mo. *morocco, gilt leaves,* 6s *ib.* 1841
4170 —————— (Tho. *Bp. of Lond.*) Use and Intent of Prophecy, in the several Ages of the World: in Six Discourses delivered at the Temple Church; with three Dissertations, 8vo. *calf,* 3s 1725

4172 [SHERLOCK'S (Tho. *Bp. of Lond.*)] Discourse on Church Unity, and Continuation of the Defence of Dr. Stillingfleet's Unreasonableness of Separation, in answer to Baxter, Lob, &c. 2 vols. 8vo. *old calf gilt, 7s* . . 1681-82
4173 ———— Use and Intent of Prophecy, in the several ages of the World: in Six Discourses at the Temple Church, with IV. Dissertations, and an Appendix, 8vo. *fine copy, old calf gilt, 5s 6d* 1749
4174 ———— the same, 8vo. *calf, 2s 6d* 1755
4175 ———— Several Discourses at the Temple Church, 8vo. *calf, 3s 6d* 1754
4176 ———— Several Discourses at the Temple Church (including the six Discourses on Prophecy), 5 vols. 8vo. *new in calf gilt, carmine edges, old style, £1. 18s* . 1754-55
4177 ———— Discourses at the Temple Church, on several occasions, and on the Use and Intent of Prophecy, &c. 4 vols. 8vo. *calf gilt, marbled leaves, £1. 10s* . *Oxford*, 1812
4178 ———— Several Discourses preached at the Temple Church, 12mo. *calf, 1s 6d* . 1756
4179 ———— Several Discourses at the Temple Church, 3 vols. 8vo. *calf, 10s 6d* . 1756
4180 ———— Several Discourses preached at the Temple Church, 3 vols. 12mo. *6s* . *Edinb.* 1774
4181 ———— Several Discourses, &c. 3 vols. 12mo. *calf, 6s Lond.* 1775
4182 ———— (Dr. Wm.) Practical Discourse of Religious Assemblies, 8vo. *calf, 3s* . . 1682
4184 ———— the same, with a Preface by the Rev. H. Melvill, 12mo. *bds. 3s* . 1840
4185 ———— Case of Resistance of the Supreme Powers stated and resolved, 12mo. *calf, 2s* . 1690
4186 ———— Discourse concerning Divine Providence, 8vo. *calf, 2s 6d* 1702
4187 ———— Discourse concerning Divine Providence, 8vo. *calf, 3s* 1715
4188 ———— Scripture proofs of our Saviour's Divinity, Explained and Vindicated, 8vo. *calf, 3s* . 1706
4189 ———— Practical Discourse concerning Death, 8vo. *fine copy, old calf gilt, 3s* . . 1751
4190 ———— Practical Discourse concerning Death, 1751—A Discourse concerning the Divine Providence, 1753—A Discourse concerning the Happiness of Good Men, and the Punishment of the Wicked, in the next world, 1760—A practical Discourse concerning a Future Judgment, 1760, together 4 vols. 8vo. *hf. bd. calf, neat, 16s*
4191 ———— Sermons upon several occasions, 2 vols. 8vo. *fine copy, old calf gilt, 7s 6d* . 1755
4192 SHIPLEY'S (Jonathan, *Bp. of St. Asaph*) Works, (consisting of Sermons and Charges), 2 vols. 8vo. *port. calf, 8s 6d* 1792
4193 SHOREY'S (Wm.) XIV. Discourses on several occasions, 8vo. *calf, 2s* 1725

4194 SHORT's (T. V. *Bp. of Sodor and Man*) Sketch of the History of the Church of England to the Revolution, in 1688, 2 vols. 8vo. *hf. bd. calf, neat,* 12s . *Oxford,* 1832
4195 ———— the same, 8vo. *bds.* 10s . *ib.* 1838
4196 ———— another copy, 8vo. *calf extra,* 15s . 1840
4197 SHUCKFORD's (Sam.) Sacred and Prophane History of the World connected, from the Creation to the dissolution of the Assyrian Empire, 3 vols. 8vo. *calf gilt,* 15s . 1731
4198 ———— the same, with a Treatise on the Creation and Fall of Man, 4 vols. 8vo. *fine copy, old calf gilt,* £1. 4s   1728
4199 ———— the same, 4 vols. 8vo. *calf gilt,* £1. 10s   1808
4200 ———— another copy, 2 vols. 8vo. *calf gilt,* £1. 4s *Oxford,* 1810
4201 SHUTE's (Josias) Sarah and Hagar: or Genesis XVI. opened in XIX Sermons; published by Edw. Sparke, D.D., folio, *portrait by W. Marshall, hf. bd. calf,* 9s . 1649

"In his character were united every qualification of an excellent divine. He was frequently styled the English Chrysostom, and was particularly conversant in the writings of that Father."—*Granger.*

4202 SHUTTLEWORTH's (P. N. *Bp. of Chichester*) Sermons on some of the leading principles of Christianity, 8vo. *calf, marbled leaves, very neat,* 11s . 1827
Bp. Van Mildert's copy, with his book-plate.

4203 ———— Not Tradition, but Revelation, 12mo. *bds.* 2s 6d   1838
4204 SIBS's (Rich.) Bowels Opened; or a Discovery of the neare and deare love, union, and communion betwixt Christ and the Church, and consequently betwixt him and every believing soule, delivered in divers Sermons on the Canticles, 4to. *clean copy, hf. bd. calf, neat,* 8s . 1641
4205 ———— Glorious Feast of the Gospel, in divers Sermons upon Isaiah 25th chap. V. 6, 7, 8, and 9, 4to. *hf. bd. calf, neat,* 4s 6d   1650
4206 SIKES's (George) Evangelical Essays, being a Discovery of the everlasting Gospel Life of Christ, 12mo.1s 6d   1698
4207 SILVESTRI (F.) Compendium in Johannem Capreolum de Sententiis, 4to. Black letter, *with rubricated capitals, in the original stamped binding, (from the late Duke of Sussex's collection),* 8s
Cremonæ, 1497
4208 SIMEON's (Cha.) Helps to Composition, or 600 Skeletons of Sermons, several being the substance of Sermons preached before the University, 5 vols. 8vo. *hf. bd. calf,* £1. 15s . 1808
4209 ———— Works, including his SKELETONS OF SERMONS AND HORÆ HOMILETICÆ, or Discourses digested into one continued series, and forming a Commentary upon every Book of the Old and New Testament; to which are annexed, an improved edition of Claude's Essay on the Composition of a Sermon, and very comprehensive Indexes. Edited by the Rev. Thomas Hartwell Horne, 21 vols. 8vo. *cloth bds. contents lettered,* £5. 15s 6d   1837
4210 SIMONIS (Joh.) Lexicon Manuale Gæcum in quo omnium textus N. T. Vocabulorum significatus explicantur, 8vo. *bds.* 3s 6d
Halæ Magd. 1766

4211 SIMON (Richard) Histoire critique du Vieux Testament, *Rott.* 1685
—Histoire critique du texte du Nouveau Test. *ib.* 1689—Hist.
critique des principaux Commentateurs du N. T. *ib.* 1693,—together
3 vols. 4to. *fine copies, hf. bound russia,* £2. 10s ——

4212 ———— The New Testament according to the ancient Latin edition,
with Critical Remarks; translated by W. Webster, 2 vols. in 1,
4to. *calf,* 10s 6d . 1730

4213 SIMPSON's (David) Plea for Religion and the Sacred Writings;
addressed to the Disciples of Thomas Paine, &c., 8vo. *hf. bd. calf
gilt,* 5s . . 1829

4214 ———— (Sydrach) Two Books, viz.—I. Of Unbelief.—II. Not
going to Christ for Life and Salvation is an exceeding great sin, yet
it is pardonable, 4to. *calf,* 4s 6d . 1658

4215 SIM's (Joseph) XV. Sermons on various subjects, 8vo. *calf,* 3s 1772

4216 ———— (Tho.) Lay Helpers : or, a Plea for the Co-operation of the
Laity with the Clergy, 12mo. *bds.* 1s 6d . 1831

4217 SIMSONI (Edw.) Chronicon Historiam Catholicam, complectens ab
exordio Mundi ad natu Jesu Christi ad An. 71, seriem Historiarum
omnis ævi secundum tempora digesta; recensuit P. Wesseling,
folio, *vellum, gilt,* 16s . *Amst.* 1752
" Egregium et absolutissimum opus, summa industri omnigena editione magno
judicio multorum annorum vigilus productione."—E. REYNOLDS, *Episc. Norv.*

4218 SIRMONDUS (Jacobus, *Soc. Jesu*) Opera Varia, nunc primum collecta ;
accedunt S. Theodori Studitæ Epistolæ, aliaque Scripta Dogmatica,
cum notis, J. Sirmondi, 5 vols. folio, *old calf gilt, neat,* £4. 4s
Paris. 1696

4219 ———— aliud exemplar, 5 vols. folio, *hf. bd. uncut,* £3. 13s 6d
Venetiis, 1728

CONTENTS. Vol. I. Eusebii Cæsariensis Opuscula XIV.—Marcellini et Faustini
Libellus Precum—Rufini Palæstini Liber de Fide—Nota Sirmondi in XL Sermones novos S. Augustini.—Opuscula dogmatica veterum quinque Scriptorum ;
Lepori Presbyteri Libellus Emendationis ; Capreoli Carthaginiensis Epist. ;
Auctoris incerti Breviarium Fidei adversus Arisnos ; Isaac ex Judæo Liber
Fidei ; et Victorini Afri Liber contra Manichæos et de Principio Diei—Notitia
Provinciarum Civitatum, et Episcoporum Africæ—Prædestinatus—S. Valeriani
Episc. Cemeliensis Homiliæ XX et Epistola ad Monachos—Appendix Cod.
Theodosiani—Epistolæ aliquot veterum Conciliorum et Pontificum Romanorum
—Appollinaris Sidonii Opera—Ennodii Opera.
VOL. II. S. Aviti Viennensis Opera—Idatii Chronicon et Fasti Consulsres—
Marcellini Chronicon—Facundi Episc. Hermianensis pro Defensione trium
capitulorum Concilii Chalcedonensis Libri XII.—B. Eugenii Episc Tolet.
Opuscula—Dracontii Hexæmeron, etc.—Columbani Abbatis Epistola parænetica—D. Severini Episcopi Doctrina—Prosperi Aquitani Confessio—Theodulfi Episc. Aurelianensis Opera—Amolonis Epist. sd Gothescalcum—S.
Augustini Sententiæ de Prædestinatione, &c.—Servati Lupi Liber de tribus
Quæstionibus et Epistolæ II.—Rabani Moguntini tres Epistolæ.
VOL. III. Caroli Calvi et Successorum aliquot Franciæ Regum Capitula—
Anastasii Bibliothecarii Collectanea—Gofferini Abbatis Vindocinensis S. Priscæ
Cardinalis Opera—Petri Abbatis Cellensis Epistolarum Libri IX.—Alexandri III. Papæ ad Petrum Cellensem et alios Epistolæ LVI.
VOL. IV. Sirmondi de Ecclesiis Suburbicariis et alia Opuscula—Gelasii Epistolæ
—Flodoardi Presbyterii Historia Remensis Ecclesiæ.
VOL. V. Theodori Studitæ Epistolæ et Opuscula Græcè et Latinè.

4220 SISMONDI (J. C. L.) Historical View of the Literature of the South
of Europe; translated, with Notes, by Tho. Roscoe, 4 vols. 8vo.
bds. 18s . 1823

4221 [SKELTON's (Philip)] Ophiomaches : or, Deism Revealed, 2 vols. 8vo. *fine copy, old calf gilt*, 8s . 1749
4222 ———— Discourses Controversial and Practical, on various subjects, 2 vols. 8vo. 8vo. *calf,* 4s 6d . 1754
4223 ———— Complete Works, with Life by Burdy, edited by Lynam, 6 vols. 8vo. *calf, neat,* £1. 11s 6d . 1824
4224 SKINNER's (John, *Bp. of Aberdeen*) Course of Lectures delivered on the Six Sundays in Lent, 12mo. *scarce,* 1s 6d Aberdeen, 1786
4225 ———— Annals of Scottish Episcopacy, from 1788 to 1816, being the period during which he held the office of senior Bishop and Primus ; by the Rev. John Skinner, A. M., 8vo. *portrait, bds.* 12s Edinb. 1818
4226 ———— Primitive Truth and Order vindicated from modern misrepresentation ; with a Defence of Episcopacy, particularly that of Scotland, against the attack of the late Dr. Campbell, 8vo. *bds.* 6s Aberdeen, 1803
4227 SKURRAY's (Fra.) Sermons on Public subjects and occasions, 12mo. *bds.* 1s 6d . . 1817
4228 SLADE's (James) Annotations on the Epistles, 2 vols. 8vo. *calf,* 14s Camb. 1816
4229 ———— Annotations on the Epistles, 2 vols. 8vo. *bds.* 14s — *calf gilt,* £1. 3s . 1836
4230 ———— Plain Parochial Sermons, 3 vols. 12mo. *hf. bd. calf, neat,* 12s . 1832-35
4231 ———— System of Family Prayer for each Morning and Evening of the Week, 12mo. *bds.* 2s . 1837
4232 SLEIDAN's (John) General History of the Reformation of the Church from the errors and corruptions of the Church of Rome, begun in Germany by Martin Luther, with the progress thereof in all parts of Christendom from 1517 to 1556 ; translated from the Latin, with a continuation to the end of the Council of Trent, by Ed. Bohun, folio, *calf, six fine portraits,* £1. 1s 1689
4233 ———— de Statu Religionis et Reipublicæ Carolo V. Cæsare Commentarii : editio nova, à J. G. Boehmio multisque annotat. illust. a C. C. Am. Ende, 3 vols. 8vo. *bds.* 10s 6d Franc. 1785
4234 SMALLBROKE's (Richard, *Bp. of St. David's*) Vindication of the Miracles of our Blessed Saviour, in which Mr. Woolston's Discourses on them are examined, 2 vols. 8vo. LARGE PAPER, *fine copy, calf extra,* 18s . 1729
4235 SMALRIDGE's (George, *Bp. of Bristol*) Sixty Sermons preached on several occasions, folio, *portrait, calf,* 10s 6d Oxford, 1724
The English Cicero.
4236 [Smith (Elisha)] Cure of Deism : or, the Mediatorial Scheme by Jesus Christ the only true Religion, 2 vols. 8vo. *calf,* 6s 1736
4237 SMITH's (Fred.) Reason and Revelation considered as connected with Christian Faith and Experience, 12mo. *calf,* 2s 1811
4238 ———— (Haddon) Twelve Sermons on the most interesting subjects of the Christian Religion, 8vo. *calf,* 2s 1769
4239 ———— (John) Christian Religion's appeal from the groundless prejudices of the Sceptick to the bar of Common Reason, folio, *calf,* 4s 6d . 1675

4240 SMITH's (John, *of Campbelton*) View of the Last Judgment, 8vo. *calf, neat, scarce*, 4s 6d . *Edinb.* 1783
4241 ———— Summary View and Explanation of the Writings of the Prophets, 12mo. *calf*, 2s 6d . *ib.* 1787
4242 ———— the same, revised by the Rev. P. Hall, 12mo. *bds.* 4s 1835
4242* ———— (J. B.) Manual of the Rudiments of Theology, 12mo. *bds.* 5s . 1837
4243 ———— (Dr. John Pye) Principles of Interpretation as applied to the Prophecies of Holy Scripture, 8vo. *sewed*, 1s 6d 1829
4244 ———— (Joseph) Modern Pleas for Schism, Infidelity, and Heresy reviewed, 8vo. *calf*, 2s . 1717
4245 ———— Unreasonableness of Deism, or the certainty of a Divine Revelation evinced, 8vo. *calf*, 2s 6d 1720
4246 ———— (Sam.) Great Assize; or Day of Jubilee, delivered in four Sermons on Rev. xx.: with two Sermons on Cant. i. 6, 7, 12mo. *calf, neat*, 4s 6d . . 1757
4247 ———— (Sydney) Sermons, 2 vols. 8vo. *bds.* 7s 6d 1809
4248 ———— Three Letters to Archdeacon Singleton, on the Ecclesiastical Commission, 8vo. *sewed*, 2s . 1837-9
4249 ———— (Tho.) Miscellanea, in quibus continentur, Responsio ad nuperas D. Simonii in libro super Fide Græcorum de dogmate Transubstantionis cavillationes—Dissertatio in qua integritas I. Epist. Joannis, cap. v. vers. 7. vindicatur—Defensio superioris Dissertationis contra exceptiones D. Simonii, Commentarius in II. S. Petri Epistolam, 8vo. *hf. bd. calf, neat*, 3s 6d . 1690
4250 ———— De Græcæ Ecclesiæ hodierno Statu Epistola, *Lond.* 1678 —Septem Asiæ Ecclesiarum et Constantinopoleos Notitia, *Traj. ad Rh.* 1694—in 1 vol. 8vo. *vellum*, 4s 6d ———
4251 ———— (William) Morning Watch; or a Spiritual Glass opened, by one who travels for Israel's Freedom, 4to. *hf. bd. calf*, 2s 1660
4252 ———— History of the Holy Jesus, with the Lives and Deaths of the Holy Evangelists and Apostles, 18mo. *frontispiece and woodcuts, calf*, 2s . 1705
4253 ———— Domestic Altar: a Six Weeks course of Morning and Evening Prayers, for the use of Families, 8vo. *calf gilt*, 5s 1818
4254 SMYTH's (Edw.) St. Paul against Calvin; or a full Exposition of the ninth Chapter of his Epistle to the Romans, 12mo. *calf, neat*, 2s 6d . . 1809
4255 ———— (Dr. Wm.) Future World demonstrated by Rational Evidence, 8vo. *calf*, 2s 6d . 1688
4256 ———— (*Professor* Wm.) Evidences of Christianity, 12mo. *bds.* 5s . 1845
4257 SOAMES's (Henry) Anglo-Saxon Church, its History, Revenues, and general Character, 8vo. *bds.* 5s 6d 1838
4258 SOBRINI (Sebast.) Divina Christianæ Religionis Institutio et Propagatio, adversus hujus temporis Libertinus, 4to. 5s *Matriti*, 1791
4259 SOCIETIES for the Reformation of Manners (An account of the) 12mo. *sewed*, 1s . [1786]

4260 SOCINUS — Anti-Socinus, hoc est, Solida Confutatio Errorum quos olim Ariani, Ebionitæ, Samosateniani, Pelagiani, et Tritheitæ horribili audaciâ propugnârunt; et nuper demum Servetus, Ochinus, Blandrata, Socinus, corumq; complices ab inferis revocârunt, etc. 8vo. *vellum*, 4s 6d . *Franc.* 1612

4261 SOCRATIS Scholastici et Hermiæ Sozomeni Historia Ecclesiastica, *Gr. et Lat.* cum annotationibus H. Valesii, folio, *bds. uncut*, £1. 1s *Par.* 1686

4262 ———— History of the Church from 306 to 445, with some account of the Life and Writings of the Author, 8vo. *bds.* 7s 1844

4263 SOLOMON. A Poetical Translation of the Song of Solomon, with a preliminary Discourse and Notes, by Ann Francis, 4to. *calf*, 3s . . 1781

" Her version is elegantly executed."—*Horne.*

4264 ———— Solomon's Song, translated by the Rev. Bernard Hodgson, Principal of Hertford College, 4to. *sewed*, 3s *Oxford*, 1786

4265 SOMERVILLE'S (Tho.) History of Political Transactions, and of Parties, from the Restoration to the Death of King William, 1792—The History of Great Britain during the Reign of Queen Anne, 1798—2 vols. 4to. *calf extra, by Mackenzie*, £1. 16s ———

" On the whole the best history of the reign of William III. we as yet have."
Professor Smyth's Lectures.

4266 SONGS and Carols, from a MS. in the Sloane Collection in the British Museum, (Ed. by Tho. Wright) 𝔅lack letter, 16mo. *hf. bd. morocco*, 5s . . 1836

4267 SONNIUS (Fra.) Demonstrationum ex Verbo Dei, de Septem Sacramentis Ecclesiæ, sm. 8vo. *vellum*, 1s 6d *Antv.* 1576

4268 SOUL.—The Soule's Humiliation, 4to. *calf*, 3s 6d 1640

4269 [SOUTH'S (Dr. Robert)] Tritheism charged upon Dr. Sherlock's new notion of the Trinity, 4to. 4s . 1695

4270 ———— Twelve Sermons upon several occasions, 8vo. LARGE PAPER, *old blue morocco, gilt edges*, 12s . 1692

4271 ———— Twelve Sermons upon several subjects and occasions, 8vo. LARGE PAPER, *portrait, old blue morocco, gilt leaves*, 12s 1698

4272 ———— Sermons on several occasions, including his Posthumous Discourses and Life, *new edition*, 5 vols. 8vo. *calf gilt*, £3. 10s *Oxford*, 1842

This edition comprises all that is contained in the eleven volumes of the old editions.

4273 SOUTHGATE'S (Rich.) Sermons preached to Parochial Congregations, with a Biographical Preface by Geo. Gaskin, D.D. 2 vols. 8vo. *portrait, bds.* 4s—*calf gilt*, 5s 6d . 1798

4274 SPANHEMII (Friderici) Dubia Evangelica, 3 vols. in 2, 4to. *best edition, calf*, 9s . *Genevæ*, 1639

4275 ———— Opera, 3 vols. folio, *fine copy, portrait and maps, vellum*, £2. 2s . *Lugd. Bat.* 1701-3

CONTENTS.—TOM. I. Geographia, Chronologia, et Historia Sacra atque Ecclesiastica utriusque temporis.
TOM. II. Miscellanea ad Sacram Antiquitatem et Ecclesiæ Historiam pertinentia.
TOM. III. Theologica Scripta omnia, exegetico-didactico-elenctica.

[58, GREAT QUEEN STREET,

4276 SPARKE's (Edw.) Scintillula Altaris; or, a Pious Reflection on Primitive Devotion, as to the Feasts and Fasts of the Christian Church, orthodoxally revived, sm. 8vo. *plates, new in sprinkled calf gilt*, 8s
1652
4277 ———— Primitive Devotion in the Feasts and Fasts of the Church of England, 8vo. *plates, calf*, 6s . 1700
4278 SPARROW's (Ant. Bp. *of Norwich*) Collection of Articles, Injunctions Canons, Orders, Ordinances, and Constitutions Ecclesiastical, with other publick Records of the Church of England, chiefly of the times of Edward VI., Queen Elizabeth, and King James, 4to. *frontispiece by Hollar, representing the arms of the English Sees, new in calf extra, very scarce*, £1. 4s . 1661
4279 ———— the same, enlarged, 4to. *fine copy, new in sprinkled calf*, £1. 5s . 1671
4280 SPAULDING's (Josiah) Universalism confounds and destroys itself; or different Schemes of Future Punishment, 8vo. *bds*. 2s 6d
1805
4281 SPEARMAN's (Rob.) Letters to a Friend concerning the Septuagint Translation and the Heathen Mythology, 8vo. *bds*. 6s
Edinb. 1759

The author was one of the ablest of the Hutchinsonians. His work "contains some sensible remarks on the quotations from the LXX. in the New Testament. He considers all mythology to have been derived from Revelation."—*Orme*.

4282 SPEEDY PASSAGE to Heaven; or a perfect Direction for every true Christian to walke in the right Path, &c. containing an explanation of the Tenne Commandments, the Creede, and our Lord's Prayer, with divers other Godly Prayers, both for Morning and Evening, 𝔅𝔩𝔞𝔠𝔨 𝔩𝔢𝔱𝔱𝔢𝔯, 12mo. *hf. bd. calf*, 4s 6d 1612
4283 SPELMAN's (Sir Henry) Works, viz.—Concilia, Decreta, Leges, et Constitutiones in Re Ecclesiarum Orbis Britannici, 2 vols. 1639-64— Glossarium Archaiologicum, continens Latino-Barbara, Peregrina, Obsoleta, et Novatæ Significationis Vocabula, Scholiis et Commentariis illustrata, *portrait*, 1687—English Works published in his life-time, with his Posthumous Works relating to the Laws and Antiquities of England; and the Life of the Author, by Edmund [Gibson], Bishop of London, *portrait*, 1727 —4 vols. folio, *fine copies, uniformly bound in dark blue morocco, richly tooled borders, gilt leaves*, £8. 8s . ——
4284 ———— English Works, edited by Edmund [Gibson], Bishop of London, folio, *calf, portrait*, £1. 11s 6d 1727
4285 ———— Reliquiæ Spelmannianæ: his Posthumous works relating to the Laws and Antiquities of England, with his Life, folio, *port. calf*, 9s . *Oxford*, 1698
4286 ———— Two Tracts—I. De non Temerandis Ecclesiis, by Sir H. Spelman—II. The Poor Vicar's Plea for Tythes, by Tho. Ryves, D.C.L., 8vo. *new in marbled calf gilt*, 7s 1704
4287 ———— De non Temerandis Ecclesiis: Churches not to be violated, 18mo. *bds*. 2s . . *Oxford*, 1841

4288 SPELMANNI (H.) Concilia, Decreta, Leges, Constitutiones, in Re Ecclesiastica Orbis Britannici, ab Initio Christianæ ibidem Religionis ad introitum Normannorum A.D. 1066, folio, *calf*, £1. 10s   1639
" An elaborate and most valuable work."—*Lowndes*.

4289 SPENCER's (Benj.) Chrysomeson, a Golden Meane, or a Middle Way for Christians to Walk by, folio, *frontispiece*, 12s   1659

4290 ———— another copy, folio, *calf, marbled leaves*, 14s   1659

4291 ———— (John) Things New and Old; or a Storehouse of Similies, Sentences, Allegories, Apophthegms, Adagies, Apologues, divine, moral, and political, &c. folio, *calf, scarce*, £1. 1s   1658

4292 ———— Discourse concerning Prodigies, 4to. *hf. bd. calf, very neat*, 3s 6d   .   .   *Camb*. 1663

4293 —— —— Dissertatio de Urim et Thummim, in Deuteron. 33, v. 8. 8vo. *calf*, 3s   .   *ib*. 1669

4294 ———— idem, 8vo. *calf*, 3s 6d   .   *ib*. 1760

4295 SPICILEGIUM Romanum (edente Angelo Maio) 10 vols. 8vo. LARGE PAPER, *French calf gilt*, £11. 11s
Romæ, Typis Collegii Urbani, 1839-44

CONTENTS.—Vol. I.   Virorum illustrium CIII. qui sæculo XV. extiterunt vitæ, auctore coævo, *Vespasiano Florentino*.

Vol. II.   *Ang. Politiani* Interpretatio Poetica librorum IV. Iliadis.   *Jac. Sadoleti* Card. Tract. de Christiana Ecclesia, et alios ad Clem. VII.   *Alcandri senioris* Card. Epistolæ. *Cosmæ Hieros*. Comment. ad Carmina S. Greg. Naz.   *Nonni* ad duas ejusdem orationes.   *Libanii* Dictiones IV.   *Jo. Philoponi* Prologus ad Nicomachi Arithm.

Vol. III.   SS. MM. Cyri et Joannis Laudes et Miracula LXX. scriptore *S. Sophronio*, interpretibus Bonifacio Consiliario et Anastasio Bibliothecario.   S. *Petri Alexandrini* Vita, eodem Bibliothecario interp.   Fragmenta Theologica priscorum auctorum, ex Codd. Arabicis et Syiracis.   *Henrici VIII. R.A*, Epistola adversus Lutherum.

Vol. IV.   Patrum Ecclesiasticorum *Serapionis, Joh.Chrysostomi, Cyrilli Alex., Theodori Mopsuesteni, Procli, Diodarhi, Sophronii, Joh. Monachi, Paulini, Claudii, Petri Damiani*, Scripta varia.   Item ex *Nicetæ* Thesauro excerpta, Biographi Sacri Veteres, et *Asclepiodoti* Militare Fragmentum.

Vol. V.   *Apponius* in Canticum.   *Fausti, Faustini, Arnobii, S. Cyrilli, Laurentii* Episcopi, et *Alberici Diaconi* Sermones   Epistolæ Veteres, et Codicum ampla notitia.   *Stephanus* in Prognosticum Hippocratis. *Eustathius* ad Hymnum S. Joh. Damasceni. *Zonaræ, Pradromi*, et *Nicetæ* Specimina. *Choricii Rhetoris* scripta.

Vol. VI.   Pontificum Rom. Vitæ.—Collectiones Canonicæ. *Innocentii* III. Sermones et Dialogus.   Rei Liturgicæ, et Historiæ Ecclesiasticæ, ac Gnomicorum fragmenta.   *Sfortiæ Pallavicini* Card. Tractatus de Principe erudito.

Vol. VII.   *S. Germani I. Patr. Const*. de Hærisibus et Synodis. *Photii* item *Patr*. Syntagma Canonum.

Vol. VIII.   *Sedulii Scoti, Aug. Card. Valerii, Ant. M. Gratiani, Card. Joh. Commendoni* et *P. Bembi, A. S. Sannazarii, Jul. Valerii, Ant. Galatei, J. C. Capacii, Onuphrii Panv. Procli Lycii. S. Augustini Episc. Hippon*. Opuscula.

Vol. IX.   Græca vetera *Eusebii Alex. S. Joh. Damasceni, Photii*.   Latina vetera *Priscilliani, Sedulii, Claudii Taur., Odorumni*, Chronicon Palat., Fragmenta Sacra, Glossarium Latinitatis.   Recentiora *Poggii, Vespasiani, Ponrinii*, et Catalogus Ecclesiarum Rom.

Vol. X.   Synodus Cpolitana, *Constantinus Diaconus, Severus Ant. Leontius, Nicephorus Patr. Nicolaus I. Patr. Photius* ad Armenios, et minora alia.   *Poggii* Epistolarum centuria et Oratio.   *

[58, GREAT QUEEN STREET,

4296 SPINOLA — Vita P. Caroli Spinolæ Soc. Jesu, pro Christiana Religione in Japonia Mortui; Italiæ scripta a P. Fabio Ambrosio Spinola, Latine reddita a P. Herm. Hugone, sm. 8vo. *portrait, 3s 6d*
Antv. 1630

4297 SPITTLEHOUSE'S (John) Answer to one part of the Lord Protector's Speech; or a Vindication of the Fifth Monarchy-men, &c. 4to. 2s . . 1654

4298 SPOTSWOOD'S (John, *Abp. of St. Andrews*) History of the Church and State of Scotland, from A.D. 203 to the end of the reign of James VI. folio, *fine impression of the portrait by Hollar, calf,* 18s . . 1655

4299 —————— the same, with an Appendix, containing the Succession of the Archbishops and Bishops in their several Sees, untill the year 1676; also the several Orders of Monks and Friers, &c. in Scotland, before the Reformation, folio, *best edition, portrait, calf,* £1. 5s . . 1677

4300 SPRAT'S (Tho. *Bp. of Rochester*) Sermons on several occasions, 8vo. *calf,* 3s . *In the Savoy,* 1710

4301 —————— another copy, 8vo. *calf,* 3s . 1722

"I have heard it observed, with great justness, that every book Dr. Sprat wrote is of a different kind, and that each has its distinct and characteristic excellence."
Dr. Johnson's Life of Sprat.

4302 SQUIRE'S (Dr. Sam.) Indifference to Religion inexcusable, 8vo. *calf,* 2s 6d . . 1758

4303 STACK'S (Dr. Rd.) Lectures on the Acts of the Apostles, 8vo. *bds.* 2s . . 1805

4304 STACKHOUSE'S (Tho.) Complete body of Speculative and Practical Divinity, folio, *calf,* 9s . 1734

4305 —————— the same, 3 vols. 8vo. *fine copy, calf gilt,* 16s
Edinb. 1787

4306 —————— New and practical Exposition of the Apostles' Creed, folio, *calf,* 6s . 1747

4307 —————— History of the Holy Bible, with Dissertations on the most remarkable Passages, and a Connection of Profane History all along, 2 vols. folio, *plates and maps, rough calf,* 16s . 1742-44

4308 —————— another copy, 2 vols. folio, *plates and maps, calf,* 18s . . 1755-56

4309 —————— another copy, 2 vols. folio, *plates and maps, calf,* 16s
1762-71

"This work has always been highly esteemed for its utility and the variety of illustration which the author has brought together from every accessible source."
Horne.

4310 —————— Works, viz.—The History of the Bible, and a Complete Body of Divinity, 9 vols. 8vo. *fine copy, calf, neat,* £1. 10s 1767-76

4311 —————— Fair State of the Controversy between Mr. Woolston and his Adversaries, 8vo. *calf,* 3s . 1730

4312 —————— Defence of the Christian Religion from the several Objections of Modern Anti-scripturists, 8vo. *calf,* 3s . 1731

4313 STAFFORD'S (John) Scripture Doctrine of Sin and Grace considered, in twenty-five plain and practical Sermons on the Epistle to the Romans, sm. 8vo. *hf. bd.* 2s . 1774

4314 STAGE.—The Stage Condemned, and the encouragement given to the immoralities and profaneness of the Theatre by the English Schools, Universities, and Pulpits, censured, &c. 8vo. 3s   1698

4315 STANHOPE'S (Hon. Alex.) Spain under Charles II. ; or, Extracts from the Correspondence of the Hon. Alex. Stanhope, British Minister at Madrid, 1690-1699 ; selected by Lord Mahon, 8vo. *bds. 4s 6d* . . 1844

4316 ——— (Dr. Geo.) Paraphrase and Comment upon the Epistles and Gospels, 4 vols. 8vo. *calf, £1. 4s* . 1732

4317 ——— the same, 4 vols. 8vo. *fine copy, calf, £1. 10s*   1775

4318 STANIHURSTI (Gul. Soc. Jesu) Dei Immortalis in Corpore Mortali patientis Historia Moralis Doctrinæ Placitis et Commentationibus illustrata, sm. 8vo. *vellum, 9s*
               Typis Ducalis Monasterii Campidonensis, 1670
           Stanihurst was uncle to Abp. Usher.

4319 STANLEY'S (Tho.) History of Philosophy: containing the Lives, Opinions, Actions, and Discourses of the Philosophers of every Sect, folio, *portraits, calf, 18s* . 1701

4320 STAPFERUS (Jo. Frid.) Institutiones Theologiæ Polemicæ, 5 vols. 8vo. *vellum, £1. 1s* . *Tiguri.* 1743

4321 STAPLETONI (Thomæ) Antidota Apostolica, contra nostri temporis Hæreses, sm. 8vo. *engraved title, fine copy, new, calf gilt, old style, 16s* . *Antverpiæ*, 1595

4322 ——— Tres Thomæ, seu Res Gestæ S. Thomæ Apostoli, S. Thomæ Archiep. Cantuar. et Martyris, et Thomæ Mori Angliæ quondam Cancellarii, 12mo. *rare, fine copy, calf gilt, old style, £1. 1s* . *Coloniæ*, 1612

4323 ——— Promptuarium Catholicum, ad instructionem Concionatorum contra Hæreticos nostri temporis, supra omnia Evangelia totius Anni, 8vo. *fine copy, calf gilt, old style, scarce, 18s* ib. 1613
          The last three volumes are uniformly bound.

4324 STATUTA Synodalia per Nicolaum Episcopum Harlemensem ædita anno 1564, *wood-cut title*, 4to. *calf, neat, 5s*   *Harlemi*, 1564

4325 STAVELEY'S (Tho.) Romish Horseleech ; or, an Impartial Account of the intolerable charge of Popery to this Nation, in an historical remembrance of some of those prodigious sums of money heretofore extorted from all degrees, during the exercise of Papal power here; with an Essay on the Supremacy of the King of England, 8vo. *neat, 4s* . . 1674

4326 ——— another copy, 8vo. *sewed, 2s*   1769

4327 STAYNOE'S (Tho.) Instructions for the Good Education of Children; with his Funeral Sermon by Dr. Adams, 8vo. *calf, 2s 6d*   1717

4328 STEBBING'S (Dr. H.) Treatise on the Operations of the Holy Spirit, being the substance of Dr. Wm. Clagett's Discourse upon that subject, with Additions, 8vo. *calf, 2s 6d*   1719

4329 ——— Polemical Tracts ; or, a collection of papers in defence of the Church of England, with an Exposition of the Church Catechism, &c. folio, *calf, 7s* . *Camb.* 1727

[58, GREAT QUEEN STREET,

4330 STEBBING's (Dr. H) Defence of Dr. Clarke's Evidences of Natural and Revealed Religion, in answer to Tindal's Christianity as Old as the Creation, 8vo. *calf,* 1s 6d   1731

4331 ———— Letters to Foster on the subject of Heresy; with Foster's Replies and Stebbing's Rejoinders—A critical Dissertation on Titus iii. 10, 11, wherein Mr. Foster's Notion of Heresy is confuted, and the Power of the Church to censure Hereticks is vindicated, by Tipping Silvester, &c., in 1 vol. 8vo. *hf. bd. calf, neat,* 2s 6d   1735-37

4332 ———— Brief Account of Prayer, and the Sacrament of the Lord's Supper, and other religious duties appertaining to the Christian Worship; with a Discourse on Speech and the abuses of it, 8vo. *calf,* 2s   1739

4333 ———— Collection of Tracts in Defence and Explanation of Christianity, 8vo. *port. bds.* 3s   1766

4334 ———— Sermons, 12mo. *hf. bd. calf,* 3s   1833

4335 STEELE's (Sir Rd.) Romish Ecclesiastical History of late years, sm. 8vo. *front.* 3s   1714

4336 ———— the same, 8vo. *tree-marbled calf extra,* 6s   1714

4337 STEFFE's (John) Five Letters concerning an Intermediate State, the Characters and Definitions given of Man, and the Christian Sabbath, 8vo. *hf. bd. calf, neat,* 2s 6d   1757

4338 STENNETT's (Jos.) Advice to the Young; or, the Reasonableness of an early Conversion to God demonstrated, sm. 8vo. *calf,* 3s   1695

4339 ———— [Poetical] Version of Solomon's Song of Songs, together with the XLV. Psalm, 12mo. *old red morocco,* 3s   1700

4340 ———— (Dr. Samuel) Discourses on Personal Religion, 2 vols. 8vo. *calf,* 5s   1769

4341 ———— another copy, 8vo. *bds.* 3s   Edinb. 1801

" Earl Mansfield, L.C.J. of the K.B. is said to have declared these sermons so excellent, that everybody should read them."—*MS. Note.*

4342 ———— Discourses on Domestick Duties, 8vo. *calf,* 3s   1783

4343 STEPHEN—Life of St. Stephen Harding, Founder of the Cistercian Order, 12mo. *sewed,* 2s 6d   1844

4344 STEPHEN's (Tho.) Guide to the Morning and Evening Service of the Church of England, 18mo. *bds.* 1s 6d   Edinb. 1835

4345 ———— Confession of Faith of the Church of England in the Thirty-nine Articles, 18mo. *bds.* 1s 6d   *ib.* 1836

4346 ———— History of the Church of Scotland from the Reformation to the present time, 4 vols. 8vo. *portraits and plates, bds.* £2. 10s   1843-44

4347 ———— (J.) Principles of the Christian Religion compared with those of all other Religions and Systems of Philosophy, 8vo. *calf,* 2s   1777

4348 ———— (Tho.) Three Sermons preached before the Justices of Assize, at Bury-St.-Edmunds: with Sacred Hymns upon the Gospels for the Hyemal Quarter, sm. 8vo. *calf,* 2s 6d   Camb. 1661

4349 STEPHENS's (Wm.) Sermons on several subjects, 2 vols. 8vo. *Oxford,* 1737, together with the following, not included therein — The Personality and Divinity of the Holy Ghost proved from Scripture and the Ante-Nicene Fathers, *ib.* 1721—The Catholic Doctrine concerning the two Natures of Christ, *ib.* 1722 — The Divine Persons one God by an Unity of Nature, 1722 — The several Heterodox Hypotheses concerning the Persons and Attributes of the Godhead, a Visitation Sermon, 1725—in 2 vols. 8vo. *calf,* 5s ——
Several of the sermons in the 2 vols. published in 1737, were in all probability composed by Bp. Conybeare, the Editor.

4350 STEPHENSON's (J. A.) Christology of the Old and New Testament: an Historical Development of the Predicted Occurrences of Holy Scripture, 2 vols. 8vo. *bds.* 5s 6d . 1838
4351 STERNE's (Lawrence, *Preb. of York*) Sermons, 7 vols. in 4, 12mo. *calf,* 6s . . 1771, &c.
4352 —— —— Sermons, 8vo. *portrait, calf,* 3s 6d 1787
4353 STEVENS's (B. B.) Discourses on the Festivals and Fasts of the Church of England, 8vo. *bds.* 2s 6d 1817
4354 —————— (Joseph) Parable of Dives and Lazarus explained and applied, in several Sermons, sm. 8vo. *calf, scarce,* 2s 1697
4355 —— —— (Dr. Wm.) Sermons, 3 vols. 8vo. *port. bds.* 5s 1801
4356 —— —— History of the Scottish Church, Rotterdam: to which are subjoined, Notices of the other British Churches in the Netherlands; and a brief View of the Dutch Ecclesiastical Establishment, 8vo. *plates, bds. scarce,* 8s . *Edinb.* 1833
4357 —— —— Conference upon the Miracles of our Blessed Saviour, wherein all the Objections proposed in Mr. Woolston's six Discourses are considered, 8vo. *calf,* 3s . 1730
4358 STEWARD's (Tho.) XV. Sermons upon several practical subjects, with a Charge given at an Ordination, 8vo. *calf,* 2s 1734
4359 STILLINGFLEET's (Edw. *Bp. of Worcester*) Rational Account of the Grounds of the Protestant Religion: being a Vindication of the Abp. of Canterbury's Relation of a Conference, &c. from the pretended Answer of T. C. folio, *calf,* 12s 1665
4360 —— —— new edition, 2 vols. 8vo. *bds.* 17s *Oxford,* 1844
4361 —— —— Six Sermons; with a Discourse concerning the True Reason of the Sufferings of Christ, wherein Crellius's Answer to Grotius is considered, 8vo. *calf,* 4s 6d . 1669
4362 —————— another copy, folio, *calf,* 8s . 1673
4363 —————— Catholicks no Idolators; or, a full Refutation of Dr. Stillingfleet's unjust Charge of Idolatry against the Church of Rome, (by T. G.) 8vo. *calf, very scarce,* 8s 1672
4364 —— —— Discourse concerning the Idolatry practised in the Church of Rome, and the hazard of Salvation in the Communion of it, 8vo. *calf,* 4s . . 1672
4365 —— —— Defence of the Discourse concerning the Idolatry practised in the Church of Rome, in answer to a book entituled, Catholicks no Idolators, 2 vols. 8vo. *ruled with red lines, old red morocco, gilt leaves,* 12s . . 1676
4366 —————— Letter to a Deist, in answer to several Objections against the Scriptures, 8vo. *calf,* 2s 6d . 1677

[58, GREAT QUEEN STREET,

J. LESLIE'S CATALOGUE. 269

4367 STILLINGFLEET's (Bishop) Fifty Sermons preached upon several occasions, folio, *portrait, calf,* 18s . 1707
4368 ———— Origines Britannicæ; or, the Antiquities of the British Churches, with a Preface concerning some pretended Antiquities relating to Britain; in Vindication of the Bp. of St. Asaph, folio, *calf,* 10s 6d . 1685
4369 ————— new edition, 8vo. *bds.* 7s . 1837
4369* ———— another copy, with Lloyd's Historical Account of Church Government, edited by the Rev. T. Pantin, 2 vols. 8vo. *bds.* £1.
Oxford, 1842
4370 ————— Origines Britannicæ, &c. 1685—INETT's (Dr. John) Origines Anglicanæ; or, a History of the English Church, beginning where Bp. Stillingfleet has ended his History of the British Church, 2 vols. 1704-10—together 3 vols. folio, *fine copies, uniformly bound in dark blue morocco, gilt leaves, old style,* £5. ——
4371 ———— Origines Sacræ; or, a Rational Account of the Grounds of the Christian Faith, 4to. *calf,* 6s . 1680
4372 ———— Origines Sacræ: or, a Rational Account of the Grounds of Natural and Revealed Religion, folio, *calf, portrait,* 9s—*fine copy, calf,* 10s 6d . Camb. 1702
4373 ———— new edition, 2 vols. 8vo. *bds.* 12s Oxford, 1817
4374 ———— another copy, 2 vols. 8vo. *calf gilt,* £1. 1s *ib.* 1836
"One of the ablest defences of revealed religion that had then appeared in any language."—*Chalmers.*
4375 ———— Discourse about Church Unity; being a Defence of Dr. Stillingfleet's Unreasonableness of Separation; in answer to several late Pamphlets, but principally to Dr. Owen and Mr. Baxter, 8vo. *hf. bd.* 3s 6d . . 1681
From the library of the late Duke of Sussex.
4376 ———— the same, with additions, 2 vols. 8vo. *calf, not quite uniform,* 6s 1681-2
4377 ———— Discourse concerning the Doctrine of Christ's Satisfaction; with an Answer to the Socinian Objections, 8vo. *calf,* 3s 6d 1696
4378 ———— Discourse in Vindication of the Doctrine of the Trinity; with an Answer to the late Socinian Objections against it, 8vo. *calf,* 3s . . 1697
4379 ———— Ecclesiastical Cases relating to the Duties and Rights of the Parochial Clergy stated and resolved, according to the Principles of Conscience and Law, 8vo. *calf,* 4s . 1698
4380 ———— the same, with a second part relating to the Exercise of Ecclesiastical Jurisdiction; two Speeches in the House of Lords, (I. The Case of Exeter College—II. The Case of Commendams); and a Discourse of the Antiquity of London, 2 vols. 8vo. *calf,* 12s
1698-1704
4381 ———— the same, 2 vols. 8vo. *fine copy, calf, neat,* 14s
1698-1704
4382 ———— (James) Sermons, preached in the Cathedral Church of Worcester, 8vo. *portrait, bds.* 3s . 1819

4385 STOCK's (Joseph, *Bp. of Killala*) Book of Job: metrically arranged according to the Masora, and newly translated into English, with Notes critical and explanatory, and the authorized English version, 4to. *bds. scarce*, 8s . *Bath*, 1805

"Of all the versions of the different books of Scripture we know, this is the most remarkable for the novelty of the rendering, yet keeping close in the track of the original."—*Brit. Crit.* See also *Horne's Introduction.*

4386 STOCKDALE's (Percival) Eight Sermons, 8vo. *port. bds.* 2s   1788
4387 STONEHAM's (Matthew) Two Sermons of Direction for Judges and Magistrates, 16mo. *hf. bd. calf, neat*, 3s . 1608
4388 STONHOUSE's (James) Friendly Advice to a Patient; and Spiritual Directions for the Uninstructed, 12mo. 1s
4389 STOUGHTON's (John, *Emman. Coll. Camb.*) XV. Choice Sermons, preached upon select occasions, 1640 — Seven Sermons preached upon severall occasions, 1640—in 1 vol. 4to. *calf*, 6s   1640

"They are indeed so plain as that the simple may understand them; and yet not so uopolished, as that the friendly and judiciously curious may scorn them."

4390 STRADLING's (Geo. *Dean of Chichester*) Sermons and Discourses upon several occasions, with the Life of the Author, 8vo. *calf*, 3s   1692
4391 ———— the same, *with a portrait*, 8vo. *calf*, 3s 6d   1692
4392 STRAFFORD (Thomas Wentworth, *Earl of*) His Tryal upon an Impeachment of High Treason; collected and published by John Rushworth, folio, *portrait, calf,* 10s 6d . 1680
4393 STRAIGHT's (John) Select Discourses on moral and religious subjects, 2 vols. 8vo. *hf. bd. calf*, 3s 6d . 1741
4394 STRODE's (George) Anatomie of Mortalitie, 4to. *calf*, 3s—*vellum*, 2s 6d . . 1632
4395 STRONG's (Tho. Linwood) Six Discourses before the University of Oxford, 8vo. *calf, neat*, 4s . 1821
4396 ———— (Will.) Voice from Heaven, calling the People of God to a perfect Separation from mystical Babylon, a Sermon at St. Pauls, Nov. 5, 1653, 4to. *sewed*, 2s . 1654
4397 STRUENSEE (*Count* Jo. Fred.) A faithful Account of his Conversion and Death, published by D. Munter: with the History of Count Enevold Brandt, from the time of his imprisonment to his death, (by D. Hee;) translated from the German by Wendeborn, 8vo. *two portraits, calf*, 4s 6d   1774

"This work contains a good summary of the evidences of Christianity."
Dean Rennell.

4398 STRUTT's (Joseph) Common-Place-Book; or, a Companion to the Old and New Testaments, 8vo. *hf. bd. calf*, 6s   1813
4399 ———— Common-Place Book to the Holy Scriptures, 8vo. *hf. bd. calf, neat*, 10s . 1824
4400 STRYPE's (John) Memorials of Thomas Cranmer, Abp. of Canterbury, wherein the History of the Church and the Reformation of it, during the Primacy of the said Archbishop, are greatly illustrated, folio, *portraits, calf,* 18s . 1694
4401 ———— History of the Life and Acts of Edmund Grindal, Archbishop of Canterbury, folio, *portrait, calf*, 12s   1710

[58, GREAT QUEEN STREET,

4402 STRYPE'S (John) Life and Acts of Matthew Parker, first Abp. of Canterbury in the reign of Q. Elizabeth, under whose Primacy and Influence the Reformation of Religion was happily effected, and the Church of England restored and established upon the principles whereon it stands to this day, folio, *portrait, calf*, 16s   1711

4403 ———— Life and Acts of Dr. John Whitgift, Abp. of Canterbury, folio, *portrait, calf*, 18s   .   1718

4404 ———— Memorials of Tho. Cranmer, Abp. of Canterbury, *port.* 1694—The Life and Acts of Matthew Parker, Abp. of Canterbury, *portrait*, 1711—The Life and Acts of John Whitgift, Abp. of Canterbury, *portrait*, 1718—Ecclesiastical Memorials relating chiefly to Religion and the Reformation of it under Henry VIII, Edward VI., and Q. Mary, 3 vols. *portrait*, 1721—The Life and Acts of Abp. Grindal, 1710—together 7 vols. folio, *calf, neat and uniform*, £8. 8s   .   .   ———

4405 ———— Works, complete, viz.—Lives of Archbishops Cranmer, Parker, Grindal, Whitgift, Bp. Aylmer, Sir J. Cheke, and Sir T. Smith; Ecclesiastical Memorials, and Annals of the Reformation, with General Index; to which are added, Lewis's Life of Wiclif and Peocok; in all 29 vols. 8vo. uniformly bound in 25, *tree-marbled calf gilt, lettered contents*, £18. 18s   Oxford, 1821-28

4406 ———— the same, ON LARGE PAPER, 29 vols. royal 8vo. *uniformly bound in rich blue morocco, gilt leaves, and broad borders of gold, a fine set*, £   .   ib. 1821-28

4407 STUART'S (Moses) Hebrew Chrestomathy, 8vo. *bds.* 5s   ib. 1834

4408 ———— Commentary on the Epistle to the Hebrews, 8vo. *bds.* 6s   1837

4409 ———— Commentary on the Epistle to the Romans, with a translation and various excursus, 8vo. *bds.* 5s 6d   1838

4410 ———— Grammar of the New Testament Dialect, 12mo. *bds.* 5s   1838

4411 ———— Commentary on the Apocalypse, 2 vols. royal 8vo. *bds.* £1. 8s   .   .   1845

4412 STUBBS'S (Ph.) Divine Mission of Gospel Ministers: a Sermon before the Lord Mayor, &c. 8vo. *hf. bd. morocco, very neat*, 2s   1711

4413 STUKELEY—Remarks upon Dr. Stukeley's Origines Roystonianæ, wherein the antiquity and imagery of the Oratory lately discovered at Royston in Hertfordshire, are truly stated and accounted for, by Charles Parkin, 4to. *plates, sewed*, 3s   1744

4414 STURGES'S (Jo.) Considerations on the Present State of the Church-Establishment, in Letters to the Bp. of London, 8vo. *hf. bd. calf, neat*, 1s 6d   .   .   1779

4415 STURMY'S (D.) Theological Theory of a Plurality of Worlds, 8vo. 1s   1711

4416 STURT'S (John) Orthodox Communicant, by way of Meditation on the Order for the Administration of the Lord's Supper, 12mo. *Entirely engraved on copper, with a border to each page, and many plates, old red morocco, gilt leaves*, 12s   1721

4417 SUICERI (Jo. Casp.) Thesaurus Ecclesiasticus e Patribus Græcis, ordine alphabetico exhibens quæcunque Phrases, Ritus, Dogmata, Hæreses, et hujusmodi alia spectant, 2 vols. folio, *vellum*, £3. 10s
Amst. 1682
4418 ———— *editio optima,* 2 vols. folio, *calf, scarce,* £4. 4s   *ib.* 1728
4419 SULPICIUS SEVERUS cum Notis Variorum et Horni, 8vo. *fine copy, old calf gilt,* 6s   .   *Amst.* 1665
4420 SUMME of a Disputation between Mr. Walker, Pastor of St. John Evangelist's, Watling Street, and a Popish Priest, calling himselfe Mr. Smith, but indeed Norrice, assisted by other Priests and Papists, sm. 4to. 4s 6d   .   1624
4421 SUMNER's (Cha. R. Bp. *of Winchester*) Ministerial Character of Christ, practically considered, 8vo. *bds.* 5s   1824
4422 ———— (John Bird, Bp. *of Chester*) Evidence of Christianity, derived from its nature and reception, 8vo. *bds.* 5s 6d   1824
4423 ———— Sermons on the Christian Faith and Character, 12mo. *bds.* 2s 6d   .   1826
4424 ———— Sermons on the Principal Festivals of the Christian Church; to which are added, three Sermons on Good Friday, 12mo. *hf. bd. calf,* 4s   .   .   1828
4425 ———— Practical Exposition of the Gospels of St. Matthew and St. Mark, in the form of Lectures, 8vo. *bds.* 6s 6d—*hf. bd. calf gilt,* 8s—*calf gilt,* 10s 6d   .   1831
4426 ———— Practical Exposition of the Gospel of St. Luke, in the form of Lectures, 8vo. *bds.* 6s 6d   .   1832
4427 ———— the same, 8vo. *calf gilt,* 10s 6d   .   1833
4428 ———— another copy, 8vo. *bds.* 7s   .   1834
4429 ———— Practical Exposition of the Gospel according to St. John, in the form of Lectures, 8vo. *bds.* 6s—*new in calf gilt,* 12s   1835
4430 ———— Practical Exposition of the Acts of the Apostles in the form of Lectures, 8vo. *bds.* 8s   .   1838
4431 ———— Charges addressed to his Clergy in 1829, 1832, 1835, and 1838, 8vo. *bds.* 4s   .   1839
4432 SUPERVILLE (Dan. de) Mélange de Sermons, 8vo. *calf,* 3s 6d
Rott. 1711
4433 SURENHUSIUS (Guilielmus) Mischna; sive totius Hebræorum juris, rituum, antiquitatum, ac legum oralium systema, cum Maimonidis et Bartenoræ commentariis; Latinitate donavit ac notis illustravit G. Surenhusius, 3 vols. folio, *hf. bd. uncut,* £4. 4s
Amst. 1698-1700
"This is a very beautiful and correct work, necessary to the library of every critic and divine. He who has it need be solicitous for nothing more on this subject."—*Dr. A. Clarke's Succession of Sacred Literature.*

4434 SURIN's (F.) Foundations of the Spiritual Life; drawn from the book of the Imitation of Jesus Christ: translated and adapted to the use of the English Church (by Dr. Pusey), 12mo. *front. bds.* 4s   .   .   1844
4435 SUSPIRIUM Sanctorum; or Holy Breathings: a series of Prayers for every day in the Month; by [Lady Charlotte Bury], 8vo. *bds.* 4s 6d   .   1826

4436 SUTTON's (Dr. Chr.) Godly Meditations upon the most holy Sacrament of the Lord's Supper, 12mo. *hf. bd. calf, neat,* 4s 6d 1635
4437 ———— Godly Meditations upon the most holy Sacrament of the Lord's Supper. [Edited by the Rev. J. H Newman.] 18mo. *bds.* 3s . . *Oxford,* 1839
4438 ———— Disce Mori, Learn to Die, 18mo. *bds.* 3s 6d—*morocco, gilt leaves* 6s . . *ib.* 1840
4439 SWADLIN's (Thomas) King Charles, his Funeral, 4to. *scarce, calf,* 3s 1661
A series of sermons at the anniversary of King Charles's Martyrdom, from 1648 to 1659.

4440 SWAINE's (Edw.) Shield of Dissent : or, Dissent in its bearings on Legislation; with Strictures on Dr. Brown's Work on Tribute, 12mo. *bds.* 2s . . [1839]
Presentation copy to the late Duke of Sussex, with a letter from the author.

4441 SWAN's (Cha.) Sermons on several subjects, with notes, 8vo. *bds.* 2s 6d . . 1823
4442 ———— (John) Redde Debitum, or, a Discourse in defence of three chiefe Fatherhoods, 4to. *calf,* 3s 6d . 1640
4443 ———— Speculum Mundi, or, a Glasse representing the face of the World, 4to. *fine impression of the engraved title by Marshall, hf. bd. calf,* 4s . *Cambr.* 1643
From the library of the late Duke of Sussex.

4445 SWINDEN's (Tobias) Enquiry into the Nature and Place of Hell, 8vo. *calf,* 2s 6d . . 1727
4446 SWINNOCKE's (George) Works, viz., The Door of Salvation opened by the Key of Regeneration, 1664—Heaven and Hell epitomized, and the true Christian characterized, as also an Exhortation with motives, means, and directions to be speedy, and serious about the work of Conversion, 1663—The fading of the Flesh, and flourishing of Faith, 1662—*in one* vol. 4to. *calf, scarce,* 7s   ————
4447 ———— The Fading of the Flesh, 4to. *title page wanting, hf. bd.* 2s . . 1662
4448 SYDENHAM's (Hen.) Five Sermons preached upon several occasions, 4to. *vellum,* 2s 6d . . 1637
4449 SYKES (Dr A. A.)—Remarks on a Book entitled, Christianity as Old as the Creation, &c. [By Dr. J. Chapman.] *Camb.* 1732— A Dissertation on the Eclipse mentioned by Phlegon; by A. A. Sykes, D.D. 1732—A Defence of the Dissertation on the Eclipse ; by the same. 1733—Phlegon examined critically and impartially, by Jo. Chapman, *Camb.* 1734—A Second Defence of the Dissertation, &c., by A. A. Sykes, D.D. 1734—Remarks on Christianity as old as the Creation, continued, [By Dr. J. Chapman.] *Camb.* 1733— Plegon re-examined, in answer to Dr. Sykes's Second Defence, by Jo. Chapman, *ib.* 1735—*in one* vol. 8vo. *calf,* 4s   ————
4450 ———— Dissertation on the Eclipse mentioned by Phlegon, 1732 —A Defence of the same, 1733—A Second Defence, 1734—*in one* vol. 8vo. *calf,* 3s . . ————

4451 SYLLOGE Confessionum sub tempus Reformandæ Ecclesiæ editarum, videlicet, Professio Fidei Tridentina, Confessio Helvetica, Confessio Augustana, Saxonica, et Belgica: subjiciuntur Catechismus Heidelbergensis et Canones Synodi Dordrechtanæ, 8vo. *bds.* 4*s* 6*d*
Oxon. 1804

4452 SYLVESTER'S (Matth.) Christian's Race and Patience described, in several Sermons from Heb. xii., 2 vols. 8vo. *portrait, calf, scarce,* 5*s* 6*d* . 1702-8

" His genius was elevated, his fancy rich and copious, and he possessed great depth of thought."—*Calamy.*

4453 SYMMONS'S (Cha. *Clare Hall*) Sermons, 8vo. *bds.* 2*s*—*calf,* 3*s* 6*d*
1789

" Evidently the production of an elegant and improved mind."—*Monthly Review.*

4454 SYNGE's (Edw. *Abp. of Tuam*) Charitable Address to all who are of the Communion of the Church of Rome, *Dublin,* 1730—The Abp. of Tuam's Defence of his Charitable Address, in reply to Dr. Nary, *ib.* 1729—The Abp. of Tuam's answer to two objections lately made against his Charitable Address, *ib.* 1728—The Abp. of Tuam's Observations on Dr. Nary's Rejoinder, [*ib.* 1731—The Abstruse Philosophy of Transubstantiation considered, *ib.* 1730—*in one* vol. sm. 8vo. *calf,* 4*s* . ——

4455 ———— Works, 4 vols. 12mo. *calf,* 5*s* . 1744

4456 ———— A Gentleman's Religion, with the Grounds and Reasons of it, 12mo. *bds.* 2*s* . *Oxford,* 1800

4457 SYMMONS'S (Edw.) Militarie Sermon, preached at Shrewsbury, to His Majesties Army under Prince Rupert, 4to. *sewed,* 1*s* 6*d ib.* 1644

4458 SYMONS'S (J.) Enquiry into the design of the Christian Sabbath, 12mo. 1*s* 6*d* . 1784

4459 SYMONDS'S (John) Observations upon the Expediency of revising the present English Version of the Gospel and Acts, 4to. *bds.* 4*s* 6*d*
Camb. 1789

4460 ———— Observations upon the Expediency of revising the present English Version of the Epistles and Gospels of the New Testament, 2 vols. 4to. *bds.* 7*s* 6*d* . *ib.* 1789-1794

4461 ———— the same, 2 vols. in 1, 4to. *hf. bd. calf,* 8*s* 6*d ib.* 1789-94

4462 ———— (Jos.) The Case and Cure of a Deserted Soule, sm. 8vo. *calf, scarce,* 3*s* . 1639

4464 TABLEAU de la Doctrine des Peres et Docteurs de l'Eglise, 2 vols. 8vo. *vellum,* 6*s* . *Lyon,* 1785

4465 TALBOT'S (Wm. *Bp. of Durham*) Twelve Sermons on several subjects and occasions, 8vo. *calf,* 3*s* . 1725

4466 TALE of the Basyn, and the Frere and the Boy, two early Tales of Magic, printed from MSS. in the Library at Cambridge, with a Preface by T. Wright, 𝔅lack letter, 16mo. *hf. morocco,* 3*s* 6*d* 1836

4467 TAMAGNINUS (J. B.) Celebris Historia Monothelitarum, atque Honorii Controversia scrutiniis octo comprehensa, 8vo. *calf,* 2*s* 6*d*
Par. 1678

4468 TATE'S (Nahum) Miscellanea Sacra: or Poems on Divine and Moral Subjects, sm. 8vo. *calf,* 3*s* 6*d* . 1698

[58, GREAT QUEEN STREET,

4469 TATIANI Oratio ad Græcos, et Hermiæ Irrisio Gentilium Philosophorum, *Gr. et Lat.* recensuit Notisque Variorum suas adjecit W. Worth, 8vo. *vellum, 8s* . *Oxon.* 1700
4470 TAVERNER'S (Rd.) Postils on the Epistles and Gospels, edited by Edw. Cardwell, D.D., 8vo. *bds.* 10s 6d *Oxford*, 1841
4471 TAYLOR'S (Hen.) Considerations on Ancient and Modern Creeds with a Treatise on the Soul, 8vo. *bds.* 2s 6d 1788
4472 [―――― (Isaac)] Natural History of Enthusiasm, 8vo. *bds.* 3s 1829
4473 ―――― another copy, 8vo. *calf gilt,* 5s 6d 1831
4474 ―――― (Bp. Jeremy) Whole Works, with his Life and a Critical Examination of his Writings, by Bp. Heber, 15 vols. 8vo. *portrait, rich calf gilt, lettered contents,* £8. 18s 6d 1839
4475 ―――― Of the Sacred Order and Offices of Episcopacy, by Divine Institution, Apostolicall Tradition, and Catholike Practice, 4to. *hf. bd. calf, very neat* 4s 6d . *Oxford*, 1642
Published by command of King Charles I.
4476 ―――― Discourse of the Liberty of Prophesying, shewing the unreasonableness of prescribing to other Men's Faith, and the iniquity of persecuting differing opinions, *engraved title by Marshall,* 4to. *calf,* 4s 6d . 1647
"The most curious, and perhaps the ablest of all his compositions,—his admirable Liberty of Prophesying."—*Bp. Heber.*
4477 ―――― Unum Necessarium, or the Doctrine and Practice of Repentance, 8vo. *engraved title by P. Lombart, calf,* 5s 1655
4478 ―――― Great Exemplar of Sanctity and Holy Life, described in the History of the Life and Death of Jesus Christ, folio, BEST EDITION, *fine impressions of the frontispiece and plates, by Faithorne, calf,* 10s . 1653
4479 ―――― Antiquitates Christianæ: or the History of the Life and Death of the Holy Jesus, by Bp. Taylor, and the Lives of his Apostles, by W. Cave, D.D., folio, *plates, calf, gilt back,* 18s 1684
4480 ―――― Ductor Dubitantium, or the Rule of Conscience in all her General Measures, &c., folio, *portrait, calf,* 18s 1671
4481 ―――― another copy, folio, *portrait, calf,* £1. 1s 1696
4482 ―――― The Worthy Communicant, or a Discourse of the Nature, Effects, &c., of the Lord's Supper, sm. 8vo. *portrait, calf,* 3s 1667
4483 ―――― the same, with a Sermon never before printed, sm. 8vo. *front. calf,* 3s . 1678
4484 ―――― Contemplations of the State of Man in this Life, and in that which is to come, 8vo. *calf,* 2s . 1692
4485 ―――― the same, 8vo. *calf, portrait,* 2s 6d . 1707
4486 ―――― the same, 8vo. *calf, portrait,* 3s . 1718
4487 ―――― another copy, 8vo. *portrait, calf,* 3s 1734
4488 ―――― Discourses on various subjects, 3 vols. 8vo. *sprinkled calf gilt,* £1. 1s . 1807
4489 ―――― another copy, 3 vols. 8vo. *calf gilt,* £1. 1s 1817
4490 ―――― (John, *of Norwich*) Hebrew Concordance adapted to the English Bible; disposed after the manner of Buxtorf, 2 vols. folio, *calf,* £4. 4s . . 1754

4491 TAYLOR's (John, *of Norwich*) Paraphrase with Notes on the Epistle to the Romans, 4to. *calf, 8s* . 1754
An exposition upon Arian principles, but contaiuing many valuable philological observations.

4492 ———— (Dr. ——) Summary of the Roman Law, taken from Dr. Taylor's Elements of the Civil Law ; with a Dissertation on Obligation, 8vo. *calf, 3s 6d* . 1772

4493 ———— (Dr. John, *Preb. of Westminster*) Sermons on different subjects; published by Sam. Hayes, A.M. 2 vols. 8vo. *bds. 3s* 1800
These sermons are generally attributed to Dr. Sam. Johnson.

4494 ———— (Joseph) Court of Guard for the Heart, 18mo. *sewed, 1s 6d* . 1626

4495 ———— (Matthew) England's Bloody Tribunal ; or Popish Cruelty displayed, containing a complete account of the most pious English Protestant Martyrs, &c. 4to. *plates, calf, 9s* ——

4496 ———— (Nathaniel) Preservative against Deism, 2 vols. in 1, 8vo. *calf, 2s 6d* . 1698

4497 ———— Baptism of Iufants vindicated by Scriptures and Reasons, 12mo. *vellum, 2s* . 1683

4498 ———— (Dr. Tho.) Parable of the Sower and of the Seed, in five Sermons, 4to. *calf, frontispiece, 4s 6d* 1634

4499 TEATE's (Faithfull) Ter Tria. or, the Doctrine of the Three Sacred Persons, Father, Son, and Spirit; principal Graces, Faith, Hope, and Love; Main duties, Prayer, Hearing, and Meditation, 12mo. *calf, neat, 3s 6d* . 1669

4500 ———— another copy, *English and German*, 12mo. *neat, 5s*
Leipsig, 1699
"Contains some passages of brilliant thought, and not infelicitous expression, intermixed with much quaint singularity."—*Brydges's Restituta.*

4501 TELLERUS (Guil. Abr.) Notæ Criticæ et Exegeticæ in Gen. xlix., Deut. xxxiii., Exod. xv., Jud. v., 12mo. *sewed, 1s 6d Halæ,* 1766

4502 TELLEZ's (Balth. *of the Society of Jesus*) Travels of the Jesuits in Ethiopia, &c. containing a Description and History of that Empire, 4to. *map, calf, scarce, 9s* . 1710

4503 TEMPLER's (Dr. John) Treatise relating to the Worship of God, 8vo. *calf, 2s 6d* . 1694

4504 TERRY's (Isaac) Sixteen Sermons upon select subjects, 8vo. *calf, 3s bds. 2s* . *Canterbury,* 1746

4505 TERTULLIANI (Q. Sept. Florentis) Opera Omnia, ad vetust. exemp. fidem locis quam plurimis emendata, N. Rigaltii Observationibus et Notis illustrata; cum Indice Glossario Stili Africani, folio, *calf,* £1. 15s . *Lut. Par.* 1641

4506 ———— idem; edente N. Rigaltio, cum ejus et aliorum Annotationibus: accedunt Novatiani Tractatus de Trinitate, folio, *calf,* £2. 2s . *ib.* 1664

4507 ———— idem, acced. Novatiani Tractatus de Trinitate et Cibis Judaicis, et Tertulliani Carmen de Jona et Ninive, *best edition,* fol. *calf,* £2. 12s 6d . *ib.* 1675

4507* ———— aliud exemplar, folio, *calf,* £2. 10s . *ib.* 1675

4508 ———— another copy, folio, *slightly stained,* £2. 2s . *ib.* 1675···

[58, GREAT QUEEN STREET,

4509 TERTULLIANI (Q. Sept.) Opera Omnia, juxta correctionem Pamelii, De la Cerda, aliorumque doctissimorum Catholicorum Virorum fideliter castigata; cum Scholiis et Indicibus, folio, *vellum*, £2. 10*s*
Venet. 1701
4510 ———— De la Chair de Jesus-Christ, et de la Resurrection de la Chair, de la traduction de Louis Giry, 12mo. *calf*, 3*s*   *Par.* 1661
4511 ———— Prescription against Hereticks; and the Apologeticks of St. Theophilus, Bp. of Antioch, to Autolycus, against the malicious calumniators of the Christian Religion; translated with Notes, by Joseph Betty, 8vo. *frontispiece, hf. bd. calf*, 12*s*   *Oxford*, 1722
4512 ———— Address to Scapula Tertullus, pro-consul of Africa, translated by Sir David Dalrymple, 12mo. *bds.* 4*s* 6*d*   *Edinb.* 1790
4513 TERTULLIAN, translated by the Rev. C. Dodgson—Vol. I. containing the Apologetic and practical Treatises, 8vo. *bds.* 7*s*   *Oxford*, 1842
4514 ———— Ecclesiastical History of the 2nd and 3rd Centuries, illustrated from the Writings of Tertullian, by John [Kaye] Bishop of Lincoln, 8vo. *hf. bd. calf*, 10s 6*d*   1826
4515 ———— third edition, 8vo. *cloth*, 14*s*   . 1845
4516 THACKERAY's (F.) Researches into the Ecclesiastical and Political State of Ancient Britons under the Roman Emperors, with Observations upon the principal Events and Characters connected with the Christian Religion during the first five Centuries, 2 vols. 8vo. *bds.* 9*s*   . 1843
4517 THEODORETUS (*Episcopus Cyri*) Dialogi tres contra quasdem Hæreses et contra Hæreticos Liber, *Græcè*, 4to. *vellum*, 5*s*   *Romæ*, 1547
4518 ———— et Evagrii Scholastici Historia Ecclesiastica Item Excerpta Historiis Philostorgii et Theodori Lectoris, *Gr. et Lat.* Ed. H. Valésius, folio, *calf.* £1. 1*s*   . *Par.* 1673
4519 ———— Opera omnia, ex recensione I. Sirmondi, denuo edidit, Græca e Cod. locupletavit, antiquiores editiones adhibuit, versionem Latinam recognovit et Variantes Lectiones adjecit J. L. Schulze, 10 vols. 8vo. *French calf gilt*, £5. 5*s*   *Halæ*, 1769-74
4520 THEODORET's History of the Church, in five Books, from 322 to 427: a new Translation, with a Memoir of the Author, 8vo. *bds.* 7*s*
1843
4521 THEOLOGICA Germanica, in qua continentur, Articuli de Fide, Evangelio, Virtutibus et Sacramentis: quorum Materia jam nostra tempestate controverti solet, *Aug. Vind.* 1531—Catalogus Sanctorum, congestus a Petro de Natalibus, Episc. Equilino, 𝕭𝖑𝖆𝖈𝖐 𝖑𝖊𝖙𝖙𝖊𝖗, 1521—2 vols. in 1, folio, *in the original binding*, 14*s* ————
4522 THEOPHILI (*Presbyteri et Monachi*) Diversarum Artium Schedula, with a French Translation by Chevalier De l'Escapolier, and an Introduction by J. M. Guichard, 4to. *sewed*, 18*s*   *Par.* 1843
4523 THEOPHYLACTI (*Archiep. Bulg.*) In D. Pauli Epistolas Commentarii, studio et cura Aug. Lindselli, Episc. Herefordensis, *Gr. et Lat.* folio, *fine copy, vellum*, £1. 5*s*   *Lond.* 1636
4523*———— ———— Opera omnia, Gr. et Lat. curis B. de Rubeis et B. Finetti edita. Accedunt Euthymii Zigabeni Commentarii in Psalmos, Gr. et Lat. 4 vols. folio, *very scarce, fine copy, vellum*, £9. 9*s*
Venetiis, 1754-63

4524 THERESA (S.) La Vie de Sainte Therese, écrite par elle-mesme : traduction nouvelle par M. l'Abbé Chanut, 8vo. *frontispiece, neat,* 4s . . *Par.* 1691
4525 ———— La Vie de Sainte Therese, écrite par elle-mesme, de la traduction de M. Arnauld d'Andilly, 8vo. *neat, 3s 6d ib.* 1702
4526 ———— Le Chemin de la Perfection, tiré des Œuvres de Sainte Therese, de la traduction de M. Arnauld d'Andilly, 12mo. *calf, 2s ib.* 1697
4527 ———— L'Esprit de Sainte Thérese, recueillé de ses Œuvres et des ses Lettres, avec ses Opuscules, 8vo. *frontispiece, neat,* 4s *Lyon,* 1779
4528 THIRLWALL (T.) Diatessaron, seu integra Historia D. N. Jesu Christi Latine ex quatuor Evangeliis confecta, 12mo. *calf, neat, 2s* 1802
4529 THOMÆ WALDENSIS, Carmeletæ Anglici, Doctrinale Antiquitatum Fidei Catholicæ Ecclesiæ, ad vetera exemplaria recognitum et Notis illustratum a Rev. Patre E. Buonaventura Blanciotti, 3 vols. folio, *port. fine copy, hf. bd. morocco, marb. leaves,* £5. 5s *Venet.* 1757
4530 THOMAS's (John, *Bishop of Rochester*) Sermons and Charges, published by G. A. Thomas, with a Life of the Author, 2 vols. 8vo. *hf. bd. calf,* 5s 6d . 1796
4531 THOMASII (Cardinalis) Institutiones Theologicæ Antiquorum Patrum, quæ aperto Sermone exponunt breviter Theologiam sive theoreticam sive practicam ; recensuit notisque auxit A. F. Vezzosi, 4 vols. 4to. *fine copy, calf gilt, rare,* £3. 13s 6d *Romæ,* 1769
CONTENTS :—Tertullian de Præscriptionibus—Gregorius Nazianzenus de Moderatione in Disputat. et de Theologiâ, Gr. et Lat.—Vincentius Lirinensis Commonitorium—Cypriani Testimonium ad Quirinum, lib. III.—Basilii M. Ascetica, Gr. et Lat.—Epiphanii Ancoratus Expositio Fidei, et Anacepbaleoris, Gr. et Lat—Augustini Catecheses duæ, Euchiridon, de Civitate Dei, libb. XI-XIV et XXIX-XXII., de Agone Christiano, et de Hæresibus—Gennadius de Ecclesiasticis Dogmatibus—Theodoreti Hæreticorum Fabularum libb. V. Gr. et Lat. Fulgentius de Fide ad Petrum.—Isidori Hispan. Sententiarum libb. III.
4532 ———— (Jac.) Dissertatio Philosophica de Plagio Literario, *port.* 4to. *calf, 3s* . 1679
4533 THOMASSIN (Louis) Ancienne et Nouvelle Discipline de l'Eglise touchant les Benefices et les Beneficiers, 3 vols. folio, *calf,* £1. 15s *Paris,* 1725
The best work on Ecclesiastical discipline ever published.
4534 THOMPSON's (Henry) Pastoralia : a Manual of Helps for the Parochial Clergy, 12mo. *calf, 3s* . 1830
4535 THOMSON's (Andrew) Lectures, expository and practical, on select portions of Scripture, 2 vols. 8vo. *bds.* 4s *Edinb.* 1816
4536 THORNDICII (Herbert) de Ratione ac Jure finiendi Controversias Ecclesiæ Disputatio, folio, (*slightly wormed*) *calf, very scarce,* £2. 8s . . *Lond.* 1670
4537 THORNDIKE's (Herbert) Discourse of the Right of the Church in a Christian State, 12mo. *very scarce, hf. bd.* 10s 6d 1649
4538 ———— another copy, *calf,* 9s . 1649
4539 ———— Government of Churches, a Discourse pointing at the Primitive Form, edited by the Rev. David Lewis, M.A. 12mo. *cloth,* 4s . 1841
4540 THORNTON's (Henry, M.P.) Family Commentary on portions of the Pentateuch, in Lectures, with Prayers adapted to the subjects, 8vo. *bds.* 5s 6d . 1837

4541 THUANI (J. A.) Historia sui Temporis, cura Buckley, 7 vols. folio, *fine portrait, calf, £4. 4s* . 1733

" Chancellor Hardwicke is said to have been so fond of this admirable work, as to have resigned his office, and the seals, on purpose to read it."—*Clarke.*

" Sir Robert Filmore, of Kent, was intimately acquainted with Camden, who told him that he was not suffered to print many things in his Elizabeth, which he sent over to his correspondent Thuanus, who printed it all faithfully in his annals without altering a word."—*Weale's M.S. Collectanea.*

4542 TIDCOMBE's (Jerem.) Sermons on various subjects, 8vo. *bds.* 2s 1757

4543 TILLEMONT (S. Lenain de) Memoires pour servir à l'Histoire Ecclesiastique de six premiers Siécles ; *best edition,* 16 vols. *Par.* 1693-1712—Histoire des Empereurs et des autres Princes qui ont régné durant les six premiers Siécles, de leurs guerres contre les juifs, des ecrivains prophanes, et des personnes les plus illustres de leur temps, 6 vols. *ib.* 1706-38—together 22 vols. 4to. *French calf gilt,* £9. 9s

4544 TILLOTSON's (John, *Abp. of Canterbury,*) Works, 3 vols. folio, *portrait, calf,* £1. 10s . 1735

4545 —— —— Sermons preached upon several occasions, 2 vols. in 1, 8vo. *with the autograph of John Locke, calf,* 4s 1688

4546 —— —— Six Sermons at St. Lawrence Jury, 8vo. *portrait, calf,* 4s 6d . 1694

" Liber Jo. Locke ex dono Reverendissimi authoris."

4547 —— —— the same, 1694, and Sermons concerning the Divinity and Incarnation of our Blessed Saviour, 1693—2 vols. in 1, 8vo. *old red morocco, gilt leaves,* 8s

4548 —— —— Rule of Faith : or, an Answer to the treatise of Mr. I. S.[argeant], entituled Sure-footing, &c. With a reply to Mr. I. S. his 3d Appendix, by Edw. Stillingfleet, 8vo. *calf,* 3s 6d 1676

4549 —— —— A Twofold Vindication of the late Abp. of Canterbury, (Dr. Tillotson) and of the Author of the History of Religion. (*i. e.* Sir Robert Howard) and a word in Defence of the eminent Bp. of Salisbury, 8vo. *calf,* 2s . 1696

4550 —— —— Life, compiled chiefly from his original papers and letters, by Tho. Birch, 8vo. *hf. bd. calf,* 4s . 1752

4551 TILLY's (William) Acceptable Sacrifice ; being a full collection of Scripture-Devotions, taking in the whole Book of Psalms, sm. 8vo. 4s . *Oxford,* 1719

" The Duke of Sussex employed Dr. Busfield and others for many months to procure this copy for his royal mother. She lived a few weeks after receiving it, and perused it with much attention."—*M.S. note on fly-leaf.*

4552 —— —— Sixteen Sermons, preached before the Univ. of Oxford, 8vo. *calf,* 2s 6d . 1737

4553 TITELMANNUS (Franciscus) Elucidatio in omnes Epistolas Apostolicas, una cum textu, 8vo. *old stamped binding,* 3s *Antv.* 1528

4554 TITTMANNUS (J. A. H.) Institutio Symbolica ad Sententiam Ecclesiæ Evangelicæ, 8vo. *bds.* 3s . *Lips.* 1811

4555 TODD's (Hen. John) Vindication of our authorised translation and translators of the Bible ; in answer to Mr. John Bellamy, and Sir J. B. Burges, 8vo. *bds.* 2s 6d . 1819

4556 TODD's (Henry John) Observations on the Metrical Version of the Psalms, made by Sternhold, Hopkins and others ; with notices of other Metrical Versions, 8vo. *bds.* 2s 6d . 1822
4557 ———— (W. G.) History of the Ancient Church in Ireland, 12mo. *maps, bds.* 4s 6d . . 1845
4558 TOLAND's (John) Christianity not Mysterious, 8vo. *calf,* 3s 1696
4559 TOLERATION disapproved and condemned, 4to. *hf. bd.* 3s 6d
 Oxford, 1670
4560 ———— discussed ; in two Dialogues, sm. 8vo. *calf,* 2s 6d 1670
4561 TOMLINE's (George, *Bp. of Winchester*) Elements of Christian Theology : with notes, and a Summary of Ecclesiastical History, by Henry Stebbing, D.D., 2 vols. 8vo. *bds.* £1. 1s 1843
4562 ———— Abridgment of his Elements of Christian Theology, for the use of Families, by S. Clapham, 8vo. *calf,* 5s 6d *Camb.* 1832
4563 TOMLINSON's (Rob.) Attempt to rescue the Holy Scriptures from the ridicule they incur with the inconsiderate, occasioned by incorrect translations, by a new translation of the various controverted passages, with notes, &c., 8vo. *bds.* 3s 6d 1805
4564 TONSTALL (Cuthebert) de Veritate Corporis et Sanguinis D. N. Jesu Christi in Eucharistia, 4to. LARGE PAPER, *fine clean copy, in the original binding,* 18s . *Lutetiæ,* 1554
4565 ———— A Letter written by Cuthbert Tunstall, late Bp. of Duresme, to Reginald Pole, Cardinall, being then at Rome, and sometime Abp. of Canterbury, sm. 4to, *bds.* 14s
 Lond. imprinted by H.(enry) B.(ynneman), N. D.

This rare tract has escaped the researches of Ames and Herbert, and shews Tunstall to have had a better feeling to the Reformation than is generally supposed. It was published under the auspices of Abp. Parker.

4566 TOPLADY's (A. M.) Collection of valuable Tracts, viz., Church of England vindicated from the charge of Arminianism — Absolute Predestination — Caveat against unsound Doctrines, Letter to J. Wesley, Clerical Subscription no grievance, — Joy in Heaven, Dying Avowal of Religious Sentiments, &c., 8vo. *neat,* 4s 1806
4567 TOWNSEND's (G.) Œdipus Romanus ; or, an attempt to prove, from the principles of reasoning adopted by the Rt. Hon. Sir W. Drummond, in his Œdipus Judaicus, that the Twelve Cæsars are the twe. signs of the Zodiack, 8vo. *bds.* 3s 1819
4568 ———— Sermons on some of the most interesting subjects in Theolog. 8vo. *hf. bd. calf, very neat,* 7s . 1830
4569 ———— (Jo) Character of Moses established for Veracity as an Historian, recording Events from the Creation to the Deluge, 2 vols. in 1, 4to. *plates, fine copy, calf gilt,* £1. 1s *Lond.* 1814-15
4570 TOWNSON's (Dr. John) Practical Discourses : a selection from his unpublished Manuscripts, with a Memoir by Archdeacon Churton ; edited by John [Jebb], Bp. of Limerick, 8vo. *hf. bd. calf, neat,* 7s . . 1830
4571 ———— (Tho.) Discourses on the Four Gospels, with an Inquiry concerning the Hours of St. John, and of the Romans, &c., 4to. *calf,* 5s . . *Oxford,* 1778
4572 ———— new edition, 8vo. *bds.* 6s (pub. at 10s 6d) *Dublin,* 1831

4573 Townson's (Dr. Tho.) Discourses on the Evangelical History, from the Interment to the Ascension of our Lord: with an account of the Author, 8vo. *bds.* 3s 6d . *Oxford,* 1793

4574 Tracts. A Collection of Theological Tracts, 6 vols. 8vo. *neat,* £1. 15s

Contents.—Vol. I.—Sermons, chiefly preached before the University of Oxford. Parker (W.) The Nature and Reasonableness of the Inward Call and Outward Mission to the Ministry—An Ordination Sermon, 1754—The Mosaick History of the Fall—Two Sermons, 1750—Cleaver (Wm) The Time of our Saviour's Coming, 1743—Dodwell (Wm.) The Importance of the Christian Faith illustrated, 1752—Webber (Dr. F.) The Jewish Dispensation, 1751—Tottie's (Dr. Jo.) Sermon at the opening of St. Martin's Church, Worcester, 1772—Hopkins' (Jo.) Attempt to restore the true reading of Neh. iv. 23, 1771—The Reasonableness of Subscription, 1771—Horne (Bp.) The Providence of God manifested, an Assize Sermon, 1775.

Vol. II.—Rotheram (Jo.) The Force of the Argument for the Truth of Christianity—A Sketch of the one great Argument formed from the several concurring Evidences for the Truth of Christianity, 1754—An Apology for the Athanasian Creed, 1762—On the Origin of Faith, 1763—On the Wisdom of Providence, 1762—The Influence of Religion on Human Laws, an Assize Sermon, 1763—Griffiths (Dr. Tho.) Sermon on Act Sunday, 1773—The Difficulties of the Ministerial Office in the Present Age, a Sermon, 1773—The Use of Reason in Religion, a Sermon, 1773—Weare's (Tho.) Trust in God, in time of Scarcity recommended, 1767—Gratitude to God for the Restoration, 1764—The Necessity and Means of Religious Knowledge, 1763—Hawkins's (W.) Regal Rights consistent with National Liberties, a Sermon, 1795.

Vol. III.—The Tryal of the Witnesses of the Resurrection of Jesus, 1729—A Dissertation on the Message from St. John the Baptist to our Saviour, &c. 1788—[Dr. Napleton's] Considerations on the public exercises for first and second Degrees in the Univ. of Oxford, *n. p.* 1773—Massillon's Sermons on the Duties of the Great; inscribed to George Prince of Wales, by W. Dodd, LL.D. 1769—Adams's (Dr. W.) Essay in answer to Mr. Hume's Essay on Miracles, 1767—The Nature and Obligation of Virtue, 1768—False Zeal reproved, 1777—A Fast Sermon at Shrewsbury, 1777—A Test of True and False Doctrines, 1770—Perseverance in well-doing, 1777.

Vol. IV.—Sermons and Tracts. Blair's (Dr. Hugh) Sermon for the Sons of the Clergy, 1796—Robertson's (Dr. Wm.) Sermon before the Society in Scotland for Propagating Christian Knowledge, 1775—Collett's (J.) Discourses delivered in the Abbey Church, Bath, 1774—Stone (Edw.) On the Nature of Truth and Falsehood, 1797—Cappe's (N.) Fast Sermon to a Congregation of Dissenters, 1777—Bruce's (G.) Personal Religion, a necessary qualification in a Minister of the Gospel, 1744—Wilson (Sam.) Industry and Liberality recommended; a Sermon, 1739—Elworthy (John) The Influences of the Spirit, a Visitation Sermon, 1753—Berkeley's (G.) Inquiry into the Origin of Episcopacy, a Sermon at the Consecration of Bp. Horne, 1795—Cappe's (N.) Sermon at York, on the King of Prussia's Victory, 1758—Burleigh's (Rd.) Assize Sermon, 1777—Denham (W.) The Love of God to Mankind, a Sermon, 1742—Duncan (Dr. Jo.) The Interests of Truth and Virtue, a Visitation Sermon, 1775.

Vol. V.—The Duties of Man in connection with his Rights, 1793—[Adam's (Dr.)] Pastoral Advice before Confirmation, 1775—Leechman (Wm.) The Nature, Reasonableness, and Advantages of Prayer, 1745—A Short Discourse on the Sabbath, 1788—Turnor's (Tho.) Sermon before the Sons of the Clergy, 1731—Warren's (Dr. R.) Two Discourses on the Death of Abp. Dawes, 1724—Stock's (T.) Sermon on the Anniversary of the Restoration, 1782—Tucker's (Dean) Six Sermons on important subjects, 1772—Ellis' (W.) The Due Method of Keeping the Sabbath, 1784—The Use and Abuse of the things of the World, 1712—Payne's (Tho.) Defence of Church Musick, 1738—Berriman's (Wm.) Family Religion recommended, 1735.

Vol. VI.—Bennet's (Tho.) Discourse of Schism, 1702—A Defence of the Discourse of Schism, 1703—Cicero's Cato Major, *Philadelphia, printed and sold by B. Franklin,* 1744.

4575 TRACTS. A Letter to Protestants converted from Romanism, by Joseph Blanco White, 1827—Historic Doubts relative to Napoleon Buonaparte, [By Abp. Whateley] 1821—Observations relative to the Divine Mission of Joanna Southcott, 1807—An Appeal to the Public on the condition of the Parochial District of Trinity Church, Kingswood, 1823—A Visitation Sermon at Bedminster, by Will. Shaw. D.D .1810—in 1 vol. 8vo. *hf. bd. calf*, 3s 6d

4575* ———— STANHOPE'S (Dr. Geo.) Meditations and Prayers for sick persons, 1783—CAMPBELL'S (Dr. George) Nature and Duty of Allegiance, a Fast Sermon, 1778—SYNGE'S (Abp. Edw.) Answer to all the excuses which men ordinarily make for not coming to the Holy Communion, 1783—HORT's (Abp.) Instructions to his Clergy, 1773—OWEN's (Henry) Directions for young Students in Divinity, 1773—STONEHOUSE'S (James) Explanation of the Sacrament of the Lord's Supper—SYNGE'S Discourse of Confirmation, 1768—A Short Discourse on the Sabbath, 1787—GORE's (Rob.) Sermon at the Ordination of the Rev. Ph. Taylor, 1770—CRADOCK'S (Dr. Z.) Two Sermons, 1742. —BENSON'S (Joseph) Defence of the Methodists, 1793—Seasonable Reflections on the approaching Fast, 1794—A Letter to the Rev. Dr. Priestley, by an Undergraduate, 1787—MANN's (Bp.) Exposition of the Catechisms, 1787 &c. 2 vols. 12mo. *neat*, 3s 6d

4576 ———— Essays on Rhetoric, abridged from Dr. Blair's Lectures, 1784—The Temper, character, and duty of a Minister of the Gospel, by W. Leechman, 1749—The Nature, Reasonableness, and Advantages of Prayer, 1749—Reflexions on the sources of Incredulity with regard to religion, 1750—*in one* vol. 12mo *bds*. 2s 6d

4577 TRACTS FOR THE TIMES. An Essay on the Oxford Tracts, 12mo. *bds.* 2s . . 1839

4578 TRANSUBSTANTIATION, (An Essay on) by a Country Divine, 1687, with a Preliminary Dissertation by Tho. Stephen, 18mo. *bds.* 2s 6d
Edinb. 1835

4579 TRAPP's (John) Annotations upon the Old and New Testament, 5 vols. folio, *with brilliant impression of the portrait, fine copy, russia extra, gilt leaves, rare*, £12. 12s . 1662, &c.
A Puritan Minister, and Vicar of Weston-upon-Avon. Born 1601, died 1669. This book is of the most extreme rarity, and but seldom seen complete. Mr. Horne, in speaking of the New Testament part, which he says contains "many judicious observations," observes, that " the same author also wrote Commentaries on some parts of the Old Testament," which he had not seen. The truth is, that they are so seldom seen that few know them. Mr. Bickersteth says, that " they contain many useful remarks, with much quaintness of wit." And Granger, " that his character for strictness of life, and as a preacher, was such, that he was, on the foot of his merit, offered very considerable benefices, which he refused to accept, as his condition was equal to his wishes."

4580 ———— (Jos.) Preservative against unsettled notions and want of Principles in Religion, 2 vols. 8vo. *calf*, 4s 6d   1715-22
4581 ———— another copy, 2 vols. 8vo. *calf*, 5s . 1722
4582 ———— Popery truly stated and briefly confuted, in several Sermons, 8vo. LARGE PAPER, *calf*, 3s . 1726
4583 ———— another copy, 12mo. 1s 6d . 1727
4584 ———— The Church of England defended against the Calumnies and False Reasonings of the Church of Rome; in answer to a Popish book, entitled "England's Conversion and Reformation compared," 8vo. *calf*, 3s—the same, *on large paper, calf*, 5s 1727

4585 ———— Preservative against Unsettled Notions, and want of Principles in Religion, 2 vols. 1722—Popery truly stated and briefly confuted, 1726—Sermons on Moral and Practical subjects, 2 vols. 1752—together 5 vols. 8vo. *portrait, calf*, 10s

4586 TRAPP's (Jos.) Explanatory Notes upon the Four Gospels, with three Discourses, 8vo. *calf, 3s* . 1748
4586* ———— the same, 8vo. *calf, 4s* . 1775
4587 ———— another copy, 8vo. *hf. bd. russia, 5s* Oxford, 1805
"The design of this very useful work, is to take notice only of difficult texts, to correct the authorized version, and to explain the diction of the sacred writings."
Horne.
4588 TRAVIS's (George, *Archd. of Chester*) Letters to Edward Gibbon, Esq., [on the disputed passage, 1 Jo. v. 7.] 8vo. *bds. 4s 6d* 1785
4589 ———— the same, 8vo. *bds. 5s—calf gilt, 8s* 1794
4590 TREBECK's (Andrew) Sermons preached at the Royal Chapel at St. James's, 8vo. *calf, 2s* . 1713
4591 TRENT. REVISION du Concile de Trente, contenant les nullités d'icelui : les Griefs du Roy du France et autres Princes Chrestiens de l'Eglise Gallicane, et autres Catholiques, [par Guillaume Ranchin] 8vo. *vellum, rare, 10s* [*Genève,*] 1600
4592 ———— Catechismus Concilii Tridentini Pii V. Pontif. Max. jussu promulgatus, 24mo. *sewed, 3s 6d—calf gilt, 6s* *Par.* 1830
4593 ———— SS. et Œcumenici Concilii Tridentini Paulo III. Julio III. et Pio IV. Pont. Max. celebrati Canones et Decreta, 24mo. *sewed, 2s 6d—calf gilt, 5s* . *ib.* 1837
4594 ———— Le Catechisme du Concile de Trente, 12mo. *fine copy, old red morocco, gilt leaves, 8s 6d* *ib.* 1686
4595 ———— another copy, 12mo. *neat, 3s 6d* *ib.* 1686
4596 TRINDER's (W. M., M.D.) Practical Sermons preached at Hendon, 8vo. *bds. 2s 6d* . 1793
4597 TRINITY.—A plain Account of the Trinity from Scripture and Reason, wherein it is proved that the belief of this doctrine as imposed by Church Authority is a human invention, 8vo. *hf. bd. calf, 2s* . . 1739
4598 ———— The Trinitarian Controversy reviewed; or, a Defence of the Appeal to the Common Sense of all Christian People, 8vo. *calf, 3s* . 1760
4599 TROMMIUS (A. B.) Concordantiæ Græcæ Versionis vulgo dictæ LXX. interpretum, ed. B. Montfaucon, 2 vols. folio, *calf, £2. 2s*
Amst. 1718
4600 ———— idem, 2 vols. folio, *fine copy, French calf, £2. 10s*
ib. 1718
4601 TROY's (Dr. Jo. Tho. *titular Abp. of Dublin*) Pastoral Instruction on the Duties of Christian Citizens; with Observations on a late publication entitled "The Roman Catholic Claims to the Elective Franchise, &c. by C. F. Sheridan," *Dublin,* 1793—M'Kenna's Review of the Catholic Question, &c. *ib.* 1792—Presbytero-Catholicon; or, a Refutation of the modern Catholic Doctrines propagated by several Societies, 1791—Declaration of the Catholic Society of Dublin, &c. *ib.* 1791—in 1 vol. 8vo. *hf. bd. calf, 4s* ———
4602 TRYON's (Tho.) Knowledge of Man's self the surest Guide to the true Worship of God, in opposition to Tradition, Custom, and Bigotry, 8vo. *port. 4s 6d* . 1703
4603 TURBERVIL's (Henry) Manual of Controversies, demonstrating the Truth of the Catholick Religion, 18mo. *4s* 1686
From the collection of the late Duke of Sussex.

4604 TUCKER's (Abraham) Light of Nature pursued, 9 vols. 8vo. *calf, neat,* £1. 10s . *Lond.* 1768-77
4605 ———— another copy, 4 vols. royal 8vo. *calf gilt,* £1. 11s 6d
Cambridge, U. S. 1831
Published under the name of "Edward Search, Esq." "The Light of Nature," says Sir J. Macintosh, "is a work, which after much consideration, I think myself authorized to call the most original and profound that has ever appeared on Moral Philosophy."
4606 [————] Freewill, Foreknowledge, and Fate, a fragment, 8vo. *bds. scarce,* 3s 6d . 1763
4607 TURNAMENT.—The Turnament of Totenham and the Feest; two early Ballads, printed from a MS. in the Public Library at Cambridge; with a Preface by T. Wright, black letter, 16mo. *hf. bd. morocco,* 5s . 1836
4608 TURNER's (Dr. John) Vindication of the Rights and Privileges of the Christian Church, in answer to a late book intitled "The Rights of the Christian Church asserted," 8vo. *calf,* 2s 6d 1707
4609 ———— (Rob.) Discourse of the pretended Apostolical Constitutions, wherein the Evidence brought by Mr. Whiston to prove them genuine is confuted, 8vo. *calf,* 3s 6d . 1715
4609*TURTON's (Dr. Tho.) Thoughts on the admission of persons without regard to their religious opinions to certain degrees in the Universities of England, 8vo. *bds.* 3s *Camb.* 1835
4610 ———— Natural Theology considered with reference to Lord Brougham's Discourse on that subject, 8vo. *bds.* 4s *ib.* 1836
4611 TUSON's (F. E.) Sermons designed chiefly for Parochial and Family use, 12mo. *bds.* 3s . 1843
4612 TWELLS's (Dr. Leonard) Vindication of the Gospel of St. Matthew, against a late tract entitled "A Dissertation or Inquiry concerning the Canonical Authority of the Gospel according to Matthew," 8vo. *calf,* 4s . . 1732
4613 ———— Critical Examination of the late new Text and Version of the New Testament, wherein the Editor's corrupt text, false version, and fallacious notes, are detected and censured, 3 parts in 1 vol. 8vo. *complete, calf,* 5s 6d . 1743
4614 Two RECTORS (The), by the author of "Body and Soul," 12mo. *bds.* 3s . 1825
4615 TWYSDEN's (Roger) Historical Vindication of the Church of England in point of Schism, as it stands separated from the Roman, and was reformed 1 Elisabeth, 4to. *new in stamped calf, old style,* 14s . . 1657
4616 ———— another copy, 4to. *calf,* 10s . 1675
4617 TYMME's (Tho.) Silver Watch-bell: the sound whereof is able (by the grace of God) to win the most profane worldling, &c. black letter, 12mo. *calf,* 5s . . 1638
4618 ———— Chariot of Devotion, black letter, 12mo. *calf,* 4s 6d
1618
4619 TYNDALE (Will.)—The Works of the English Reformers, W. Tyndale and John Frith; edited by Tho. Russell, 3 vols. 8vo. *large paper, calf gilt, marbled leaves,* 18s . 1831

4620 TYPING's (Wm.) Discourse of Eternity, (*two leaves wanting*) 1646
—The Father's Counsell, by W. T. 1644—The Preacher's Plea,
1646—in 1 vol. 18mo. *bds. 2s*

4621 [UDALL's (Ephraim)] Good Workes, if they be well handled; or, certaine Projects about Maintenance for Parochiall Ministers, Provision for Lecturers, Erection of new Churches in the great out Parishes about London, 4to. *sewed, 2s* . 1641

4622 UGHELLUS (Ferdinandus) Italia Sacra, sive de Episcopis Italiæ, et Insularum adjacentium, Rebusque ab iis præclare gestis, deducta serie ad nostram usque ætatem. Editio secunda, aucta et emendata, cura et studio N. Coleti, 10 vols. in 9, royal folio, BEST EDITION, *fine copy, vellum,* £8. 8s *Venetiis*, 1717-22

4623 UGOLINI (BLATII) THESAURUS ANTIQUITATUM SACRARUM, complectens selectissima clarissimorum Virorum Opuscula, in quibus veterum Hebræorum Mores, Leges, Instituta, Ritus, Sacra et Civiles, illustrantur. Opus ad Illustrationem utriusque Testamenti et ad Philologiam Sacram et Profanam utilissimum maximeque necessarium; cum Indicibus locupletissimis, 34 vols. folio, *plates, hf. bd. russia, cloth sides, fine copy,* £34. . *ib.* 1744-69

"This valuable work, a library in itself on the subjects of which it treats, contains not only a republication of various important Treatises (nearly 500), but many not to be found elsewhere. The principal authors in this collection, are—Abarbanel, Alphen, Allmann, Arnold, Bartolocci, Bertram, Biel, Bonfrerius, Braun, Buxtorf, Calmet, Calovius, Cappell, Carpzov, De Veil, Deylinger, Doederlein, Epiphanius, Fleury, Gomar, Goodwin, Hare, Haremberg, Harduin, Hottinger, Huet, Jablonski, Kircher, Lampe, Lamy. Lightfoot, Lowth, Lyser, Maimonides, Mill, Michaelis, Osiander, Petavius, Pfeiffer, Prideaux, Reland, Reiske, Schmid, Schoettgen, Selden, Spencer, Walch, Witsius, Wolf, &c., with very copious Indices. " Many other books treating of Jewish Antiquities have been published; but those who have a taste for such sort of reading, will find this collection far more useful to them than any other of the kind."—*Bp. Watson.*

4624 UMFREVILLE's (Cha.) Discourses on Divine Revelation, the Trinity, the Creed of St. Athanasius, and the Methodists, 8vo. *neat, 2s* 1759

4625 UNIGENITUS.—Hexaples, ou les Six Colomnes sur la Constitution Unigenitus, 12mo. *neat, 4s* . 1715

4626 ————— Refutation du Memoire publié en faveur de l'Appel des quatre Evêques, addressé a l'Evéque de Mirepoix, avec le temoignage de l'Eglise Universelle en faveur de la Bulle Unigenitus, 3 vols. in 1, sm. 8vo. *neat, 4s* . *Brux.* 1718

4627 UPHAM (Edw.) The Mahávansi, the Rájá-Ratnácari, and the Rájá-Vali, forming the Sacred and Historical Books of Ceylon; also, a collection of Tracts illustrative of the Doctrines and Literature of Buddhism: translated from the Singhalese, 3 vols. 8vo. *bds. 14s* 1833

4628 URSINUS's (Zacharias) Summe of Christian Religion, by way of Catechisme; Englished by Henry Parry, folio, *calf, 7s* 1633

4629 USUARDI Martyrologium, quo Romana Ecclesia, ac permultæ aliæ utuntur; jussu Caroli Magni conscriptum; cum additionibus ex Martyrologiis Romanæ Ecclesiæ, et aliarum, potissimum Belgii; opera Joannis Molani; eodem auctore, de Martyrologiis, et Indicibus Sanctorum Belgii, sm. 8vo. *vellum, 7s 6d* *Antverpiæ*, 1583

4630 USHER'S (James, *Abp. of Armagh*) Works, now first collected, arranged, and edited, from the original and hitherto unpublished MSS. in Trinity College, Dublin, by C. R. Elrington, D.D. 21 vols. 8vo. *Dublin, University Press*, 1842-44
This important publication is now rapidly advancing towards completion. Fourteen volumes have already appeared (price 12s each). An elaborate Life of the learned Prelate will be added by the editor, together with copious indexes, &c.
As nearly the whole impression has already been subscribed for in Ireland, early application is recommended to those desirous of obtaining the work.

4631 ——— Body of Divinity; or, the Summe and Substance of Christian Religion explained, by way of Question and Answer; with a Tract intituled "Immanuel; or, the Mystery of the Incarnation of the Son of God, folio, *portrait, calf*, 9s 1648

4632 ——— De Græcâ Septuagint interpretum Versione, Syntagma 1655—Chronologia Sacra: ed. Tho. Barlow, *Oxon*. 1660—De Romanæ Ecclesiæ Symbolo Apostolico vetere, aliisque fidei formulis, *ib*. 1660—in 1 vol. sm. 4to. *vellum*, 5s

4633 ——— De Græcâ LXX. interpretum versione Syntagma: cum Libri Estheræ editione Origenicâ, et vetere Græcâ alterâ, &c, 1655 —De textus Hebraici Vet. Testamenti certitudine, contra Lud. Capelli Criticam, Epistola A. Bootii ad Jac. Usserium, *Par*. 1650—in 1 vol. sm. 4to. *calf*, 4s

4634 ——— Chronologia Sacra; ed. Tho. Barlow, *Oxon*. 1660—De Romanæ Ecclesiæ Symbolo Apostolico vetere, &c. *ib*. 1660—in 1 vol. 4to. *calf*, 3s

4635 ——— Power communicated by God to the Prince, and the Obedience required of the Subject; published by Rob. Sanderson, Bp. of Lincoln, 8vo. *portrait, calf*, 4s 1683

4636 ——— Answer to a Challenge made by a Jesuite in Ireland, wherein the Judgement of Antiquity in the points questioned is truly delivered, &c.; with a Sermon before the King at Wansted, 1625—An Answer to the Ten Reasons of Edm. Campion; also the Summe of the Defence of those Reasons, by John Duræus, with a Reply to it, written in Latine, by Will. Whitaker, D.D., translated by Rd. Stocke, 1606—The Peace of Rome proclaimed unto all the world, by her famous Cardinall Bellarmine; whereto is prefixed, a serious Dissuasive from Popery, by Jos. Hall, 1609— in 1 vol. 4to. *calf*, 18s . v. y.
From the late Duke of Sussex's library.

4637 ——— Annales Veteris et Novi Testamenti, a prima mundi origine deducti, una cum rerum Asiaticarum et Ægyptiacarum Chronico, folio, *vellum*, 12s . *Veronæ*, 1741

4638 ——— His Life and Death, published in a Sermon at his funeral, and now reviewed, by Nicholas Bernard, D.D. sm. 8vo. *port. calf*, 4s . 1656

4639 ——— His Life and Death, by N. Bernard, D.D. *port*. 1656— A Sermon at the Funeral of Dr. BROWNRIG, late Lord Bishop of Exeter, with his Life and Death, by Dr. Gauden, *port*. 1660—The Life of Dr. HAMMOND, written by John Fell, D.D. Dean of Ch. Ch. in Oxford, 1661—*fine copies*, in 1 vol. sm. 8vo. *calf*, 7s ———

4640 USHER'S (James, *Abp. of Armagh*) Life, with three hundred Letters between the said Lord Primate and most of the eminent persons in his time; collected and published by Rd. Parr, D.D. folio, *port. calf*, £1. 1s 1686
4641 ———— another copy, *new in tree-marbled calf gilt, very neat*, £1. 10s . 1686
4642 VALPY'S (Dr. R.) Address from a Clergyman to his Parishioners, 8vo. *hf. bd. calf, neat*, 2s 6d . 1823
4643 VANCE'S (Wm. Ford) Sermons, 8vo. *bds.* 3s 1829
4644 VAN-ESPEN, Jus Ecclesiasticum Universum, antiquæ et recentiori Disciplinæ præsertim Belgii, Galliæ, Germaniæ, et vicinarum Provinciarum accommodatum, 5 vols. folio, *old French calf*, £4. 4s *Lovanii*, 1753
4645 ———— idem, editio novissima, omnibus anteactis longe præstantior, et nitidior, plurimis Tractatibus hactenus ineditis, Litteris, et Monumentis passim suo loco positis, præsertim vero selectis adnotationibus J. P. Gibert nuperrime aucta et illustrata, 10 vols. in 2, folio, *fine copy, new in vellum*, £4. 4s *Venetiis*, 1769

"It would be useful to consult some good author that comprehenda all that concerns the universal canon law, of which sort there is none better than Van-Espeo."—*Dupin.*

4646 VAUGHAN'S (E. T.) Expository Sermons, preached in the Parish Church of St. Martin, Leicester, 12mo. *bds.* 3s 1843
4647 ———— (Henry) Nine Sermons on the Fruits of the Spirit: with three Miscellaneous Discourses, 8vo. *bds.* 3s 6d 1837
4648 ———— (Sir Will. *Knt.*) Church Militant, historically continued from the yeare of our Saviour's Incarnation 33, untill the present, 1640, [a poem] 12mo. *calf*, 3s 1640
4649 VELTHUSEN (J. C.) Exercitationes Critica in Jobi, cap. xix. 23—29, 12mo. *sewed*, 5s *Lemgoviæ*, 1772
4650 VENDIUS (Erasm.) Ecclesiæ Catholicæ Trophæa illustria ex recentibus Anglicorum Martyrum, Scoticæ proditionis, Gallicorumque Furorum Rebus gestis graviss. Virorum Fide notatis; sm. 8vo. *fine copy, French calf, gilt leaves*, £1. 1s *Monachii*, 1573

Contains an account of the English Martyrs, Sir Thomas More, Bishop Fisher, John Houghton, Prior of London, &c.

4651 VENEMA (Hermannus) Dissertationes V. ad Librum Geneseos, 2 parts in 1 vol. 4to. *vellum*, 5s *Leovard.* 1747-50
4652 ———— Commentarius ad librum Elenctica Propheticum Malachiæ, 4to. *hf. bd. calf*, 4s 6d . *ib.* 1759
4653 ———— Dissertationes ad Vaticinia Danielis emblematica, 4to. *hf. bd. calf*, 5s . *ib.* 1745

"Quum istæ erudité atque adcuratè conscriptæ sint, ac Danieli multam lucem præbent."—*Walch.*

4654 VENN'S (Henry) Sermons on various subjects, 8vo. *calf*, 2s 6d 1759
4655 VENNING'S (Ralph) Mysteries and Revelations, or the explication and application of severall extra-essentiall and borrowed names, &c. in the Scriptures, 12mo. 4s . 1647

4656 VERON'S (Jhon) Fruteful Treatise of Predestination, and of the devyne Providence of God, as far forth as the Holy Scriptures shal lead us, and an Answer made to all the vain and blasphemous obiections that the Epicures and Anabaptistes of our time canne make, set forth Dialoge-wise, Black letter, sm. 8vo. *hf. bd. calf, neat, very scarce*, 10s . *Lond. by Jhon. Tisdale*, N. D.

4657 VERSTEGAN'S (Rd.) Restitution of decayed Intelligence, in Antiquities; concerning the most noble and renowned English nation, sm. 4to. *plates, fine copy, neat*, 8s . *Antwerp*, 1605

4658 VERT (Dom Claude de) Explication simple, litterale et historique des Cérémonies de l'Eglise, 4 vols. 8vo. *old calf gilt*, £1. 4s
Par. 1720

4659 VICCARS (Jo.) Decapla in Psalmos: sive Commentarius ex decem Linguis MSS. et impressis, etc. folio, *fine copy, old blue morocco*, 12s . . 1639

4660 VIDA'S (Hieron. Bp. *of Alba*) Poems on divine subjects, translated from the Latin, with large Annotations, by Tho. Morell, 8vo. *portrait, calf*, 4s . . 1732

4661 VIGOR (Simon) de l'Etat et Gouvernement de l'Eglise, 8vo. *fine copy, in old crimson morocco, gilt leaves*, 7s *Troyes*, 1621

4662 VILLEGAS'S (Alfonso) Lives of the Saints, translated out of Italian into English, and diligentlie compared with the Spanish, whereunto are added, the Lives of sundry other Saints, out of F. Ribadeneira, Surius, &c.; the 3rd edition, set forth by Iohn Heigham, 4to. *calf, marbled leaves, very rare*, £1. 1s [*S. Omers*] 1630

4663 VILLERS (Cha. de) Précis Historique sur la presentation de la Confession d'Augsbourg a l'Empereur Charles V.; ouvrage posthume, suivi du texte de la Confession, 12mo. *sewed*, 2s *Strasbourg*, 1817

4664 ———— Essai sur l'esprit et l'influence de la Reformation de Luther, 8vo. *hf. bd. calf, uncut*, 3s 6d *Par.* 1808

4665 ———— Essay on the spirit and influence of the Reformation of Luther, translated, with Notes, by James Mill, 8vo. *new in calf gilt*, 6s . . 1805

4666 ———— the same, translated by B. Lambert, 8vo. *portrait of Luther, hf. bd. calf*, 4s 6d . 1806

4667 VILTHIERY (Girard de) La Vie des Religieux et des Religieuses, ou les obligations de ceux qui embrassent la vie monastique prouvées, 12mo. *neat*, 3s 6d . *ib.* 1724

4668 VINCENT'S (Nath.) More excellent Way to edifie the Church of Christ; a Discourse concerning Love, sm. 8vo. *calf*, 2s 6d 1684

4669 VINCENT'S (Dr. W. Dean *of Westminster*) Sermons on Faith, Doctrines, and public Duties, with a Life of the Author by Archdeacon Nares, 8vo. *bds.* 4s . 1817

4670 VINCENTIUS Lirinensis Commonitorium, *Latin and English*, 2 parts in 1 vol. 12mo. 4s *Oxon.* 1836-37

4671 ———— another copy, 12mo. *vellum*, 6s *ib.* 1836-37

4672 ———— Against Heresy, 18mo. *morocco, gilt leaves*, 5s *ib.* 1841

4673 VINTRINGA (Campegius) Archisynagogus Observationibus Novis illustratus: quibus Veteris Synagogæ Constitutio tota traditur; inde deducta Episcoporum Presbyterorumque primæ Ecclesiæ origine, 4to. *hf. bd. vellum*, 5s . *Franeq.* 1685

[58, GREAT QUEEN STREET,

4674 VITRINGA (Campegius) De Decem-viris Otiosis ad Sacra necessaria Veteris Synagogæ curanda deputatis, *Franeq.* 1687—Jac. Rhenferdii Specimen Animadversionum in Decem-Viros Otiosis, etc. *ib.* 1688—Ejusdem Dissertationes de Decem Otiosis Synagogæ, in 1686—*in one* vol. 4to. *vellum,* 8s

"Full of learning, and of every thing relating to the synagogue. There is a great deal of research displayed in it."—*Orme.*

4675 ———— de Synagoga Vetere libri tres, quibus de Sacris Synagogarum agitur, tum præcipue formam regiminis et ministerii earum in Ecclesiam Christianam translatam esse demonstratur, &c. 4to. *calf,* 6s . *ib.* 1726

4676 ———— Commentarius ad Canticum Mosis, cum prolegomenis; edente Herm. Venema, *Harlingæ,* 1734—Commentarii ad librum Zachariæ, edente H. Venema, *Leovard.* 1734—in 1 vol. 4to. *vellum,* 4s 6d

4677 ———— Doctrina Christianæ Religionis, per Aphorismos Summatim descripta, 10 vols. 4to. *sewed,* £1. 10s *Arnhem.* 1761-9

4678 VOICE from the Font, 18mo. *frontispiece, bds.* 2s 1838

4679 VOLUSENUS (Florentius) [*vulgo Wilson, aut Wolsey*] de Animi Tranquillitate Dialogus, sm. 8vo. *calf,* 3s *Edinb.* 1751

4680 VOSSIUS (Ger. Jo.) Harmonia Evangelica de Passione, Morte, Resurrectione, ac Adscensione Jesu Christi Servatoris nostri, 4to. *calf,* 3s . . *Amst.* 1656

From the library of the late Duke of Sussex.

4681 ———— Opera omnia, Etymologica, Rhetorica, Theologica, Grammatica, et Historica, 6 vols. folio, *calf, russia backs,* £2. 2s *Amst.* 1695-1701

"The works of G. J. Vossius are not among the number of those which are current for a while, and afterwards confined to the narrow bounds of a library, or abandoned to the mercy of the dust and worms; but will be esteemed as long as there are learned men or persons of good judgment in the world."

Works of the Learned, 1702.

4683 VOX ECCLESIÆ; The Judgment of the Bishops of the Church of England against the Ecclesiastical Commission, 8vo. *sewed,* 2s 1839

4684 WADDINGTON'S (Geo.) Present Condition and Prospects of the Greek, or Oriental Church, 12mo. *hf. bd. calf,* 4s 1829

4685 ———— History of the Church, from the earliest ages to the Reformation, 8vo. *calf,* 9s . 1833

4686 WADESWORTH'S (James) Copies of certaine Letters which have passed between Spaine and England, in matter of Religion, between Master James Wadesworth, a late Pensioner of the Holy Inquisition in Sivill, and W. Badell, a Minister in Suffolke, 4to. *rare,* 5s 1624

4687 WAITE'S (Dr. T.) Sermons, explanatory and practical, on the XXXIX. Articles, 8vo. *bds.* 5s 6d . 1826

4688 WAKE'S (W. *Abp. of Cant.*) Sermons and Discourses on several occasions, 8vo. *new in calf gilt,* 7s 6d . 1690

4689 ———— Practical Discourse concerning Swearing, especially Perjury and Common-Swearing, sm. 8vo. 2s 6d 1696

4690 ———— Authority of Christian Princes over their Ecclesiastical Synods asserted; with particular respect to the Convocations of the Clergy of the Realm and Church of England, 8vo. *calf,* 12s 1697

4691 WAKE's (W. *Abp. of Cant.*) State of the Church and Clergy of England in their Councils, Synods, Convocations, Conventions, &c. historically deduced from the Conversion of the Saxons to the present times, folio, *calf, gilt back, very scarce,* £2. 15s   1703

4692 ———— Principles of the Christian Religion explained, in a brief Commentary on the Church Catechism, 8vo. *neat,* 2s 6d   1720

4693 ———— Genuine Epistles of the Apostolical Fathers, St. Barnabas, St. Ignatius, St. Clement, St. Polycarp, the Shepherd of Hermas, and the Martyrdoms of St. Ignatius and St. Polycarp; with a preliminary Discourse, 8vo. *frontispiece, neat,* 5s

Manchester, 1799

4694 ———— another copy, 8vo. *bds.* 7s   .   1840

4695 WAKEFIELD's (Gilbert) Evidences of Christianity, 8vo. *bds.* 2s 1793

4696 WAKIUS (Jo. Conr.) Expositio atque Illustratio Hoseæ, sm. 8vo. *vellum,* 2s   .   .   Ratisb. 1711

4697 WALÆUS (Antonius) Loci Communes S. Theologiæ; ejusdem Tractatus de Sabbatho, 4to. *calf,* 6s   Lugd. Bat. 1640

Upon the title is the autograph of "Jo. Prideaux," Bp. of Norwich, with the date 1640.

4698 WALCHIUS (C. G. F.) Breviarium Theologiæ Symbolicæ Ecclesiæ Lutheranæ, 8vo. *bds.* 2s 6d   .   Goett. 1765

4699 WALKER's (George) Doctrine of the Holy Weekly Sabbath, in divers Sermons, 4to. *calf,* 3s   .   1641

4700 ———— (Geo. *of Nottingham*) Sermons on various subjects, 2 vols. 8vo. *fine copy, old calf gilt,* 7s 6d   1790

4701 ———— (Dr. James) Sermons on various subjects and occasions; with a Sermon on Redemption, by the late Rev. James Ramsay, 1829:—A Sermon at Dundee, the Sunday after the Funeral of Bp. Strachan, *Edinb.* 1810—in 1 vol. 8vo. *hf. bd. calf, neat,* 7s 6d ——

4702 ———— (J.) Attempt towards recovering an Account of the Numbers and Sufferings of the Clergy of the Church of England, Heads of Colleges, Fellows, Scholars, &c. who were sequestered, harassed, &c. in the late times of the Grand Rebellion, folio, *fine copy, calf, scarce,* £1. 16s   .   1704

4703 ———— another copy, *slightly stained, calf,* £1. 10s   1714

4704 ———— the same, folio, LARGE PAPER, *wormed at the end, calf,* £1. 11s 6d   .   .   1714

4705 [———— (Obad.)] Vulgar Errours in Practice censured; also the Art of Oratory, composed for the benefit of Young Students, sm. 8vo. 3s   .   .   1659

4706 ———— Of Education, especially of Young Gentlemen, 12mo. *calf,* 2s 6d   .   Oxford, 1687

4708 ———— Two Discourses concerning the Spirit of Martin Luther, and the Original of the German Reformation, also concerning the Celibacy of the Clergy, 4to. *sewed,* 2s   .   ib. 1687

4709 ———— An Answer to [his] Discourse concerning the Celibacy of the Clergy, [by Geo. Tully], 4to. *hf. bd. calf, neat,* 4s 6d

ib. 1688

From the collection of the late Duke of Sussex.

4710 WALKER's (Tho.) Vindication of the Discipline and Constitutions of the Church of Scotland for preserving Purity of Doctrine, 8vo. *calf,* 3s . Edinb. 1774
4711 WALL's (W.) History of Infant Baptism; with his Defence of it against the Reflections of Gale and others, 3 vols. 8vo. *calf gilt,* £1. 4s . 1819
4712 ———— History of Infant Baptism; together with Gale's Reflections and Dr. Wall's Defence; *new edition,* revised by the Rev. H. Cotton, 4 vols. 8vo. *calf gilt,* £2. 2s—*bds.* £1. 10s
Oxford, 1844
4713 [WALLACE's (Dr. Rob.)] Various Prospects of Mankind, Nature, and Providence, 8vo. *bds.* 2s . 1751
4714 [WALMSLEY's (—)] General History of the Christian Church, from her Birth to her final triumphant state in Heaven; chiefly deduced from the Apocalypse, 8vo. *neat,* 6s—*calf gilt,* 7s 6d Dublin, 1812
Published under the name of Signior Pastorini.
4715 WALTER's (Henry) Lectures on the Evidences in favour of Christianity, and the Doctrines of the Church of England, 12mo. 1s 6d
Camb. 1816
4716 WALTONI (Brian) In Biblia Polyglotta Prolegomena, Prefatus est J. A. Dathe, 8vo. *vellum,* 6s . Lips. 1777
4718 ———— idem, recognovit Dathianisque et Variorum Notis suas immiscuit Fra. Wrangham, 2 vols. royal 8vo. LARGE AND TINTED PAPER, *calf gilt,* £1. 11s 6d . Cantab. 1827
4719 ———— Memoirs of his Life and Writings; with Notices of the Authorized English Version of the Bible, and Dr. Watson's own Vindication of the London Polyglot, by Henry John Todd, 2 vols. 8vo. *portrait, bds.* 5s 6d 1821
4720 WALTON's (Izaac) Lives of Dr. John Donne, Sir Henry Wotton, Richard Hooker, Mr. George Herbert, and Dr. Robert Sanderson, 2 vols. 12mo. *bds.* 4s . Oxford, 1805
4721 ———— another copy; to which is now first added, Love and Truth; with Notes, and the Life of the author, by Tho. Zouch, D.D. 2 vols. 8vo. *portraits, bds.* 6s—*calf gilt,* 7s 6d York, 1817
4722 ———— (Jonathan) Sermons, 2 vols. 8vo. *bds.* 6s 1822
4723 WAPLE's (Edward) Book of the Revelation paraphrased, with Annotations on each Chapter, 4to. *calf,* 3s . 1715
4724 WARBURTON's (Wm. *Bp. of Gloucester*) Works, with his Life and Letters to Bishop Hurd, 13 vols. 8vo. *portrait, fine copy, calf gilt,* £5. 5s . 1811
4725 ———— another copy, 13 vols. in 7, 8vo. *calf gilt,* £5. 5s 1811
4726 ———— Julian; or a Discourse concerning the Earthquake, &c. that defeated the Emperor's attempt to rebuild the Temple at Jerusalem, in which the reality of a Divine Interposition is shewn, 8vo. *calf, neat,* 3s 6d . 1751
4727 ———— Principles of Natural and Revealed Religion explained in a course of Sermons at Lincoln's Inn, 8vo. *old calf gilt,* 6s 1753
4728 ———— Doctrine of Grace, or the Office and Operations of the Holy Spirit vindicated from the insults of Infidelity, and the abuses of Fanaticism, 8vo. *calf,* 3s . 1763

4729 WARBURTON's (Wm. *Bp. of Gloucester*) Letters from a late eminent Prelate (Warburton) to one of his friends (Rd. Hurd, Bishop of Worcester), 8vo. *calf, neat*, 6s   1809
       Bishop Van Mildert's copy, with his book-plate.
4730 ———— another copy, 4to. *calf*, 6s
4731 ———— Tracts by Warburton and a Warburtonian, [Bp. Hurd] not admitted into the Collections of their respective Works, 8vo. *hf. bd. calf*, 5s 6d   1789
4732 ———— another copy, *with portrait of Dr. Parr inserted*, 8vo. *bds.* 5s   1789
4433 ———— Divine Legation of Moses demonstrated, in five books, 4 vols. 8vo. *hf. bd. calf*, £1. 4s   1766, &c.
4734 ———— the same, with two additional books, 5 vols. 8vo. *calf*, £1. 10s   1755-88
4735 ———— another copy, with additions, 6 vols. 8vo. *hf. bd. morocco*, £1. 11s 6d   1766-88
4736 ———— Remarks on several occasional Reflections, in Answer to Drs. Middleton, Pococke, the Master of the Charter-House, and Dr. Rd. Grey, &c. serving to justify several passages in the Divine Legation, &c. 1744 Four Queries concerning the Miracles wrought in the first Ages of the Church, 1748—Remarks on the Pamphlets lately published against Dr. Middleton's Introductory Discourse, &c. 1748—*in one* vol. 8vo. *hf. bd. calf*, 3s
4737 WARBURTONIAN LECTURES, 1769-72—HURD's (Bp.) Introduction to the Study of the Prophecies concerning the Christian Church, and in particular concerning the Church of Papal Rome, in twelve Sermons, 8vo. *calf*, 4s—*hf. bd. morocco*, 3s 6d   1772
4738 ———— another copy, 2 vols. in 1, 8vo. *calf*, 4s   1788
4739 ———— 1773-6—HALLIFAX (Bp.) On the Prophecies concerning the Christian Church; and in particular concerning the Church of Papal Rome, 8vo. *calf, neat*, 4s   1776
4740 ———— 1781-5—APTHORP (East) On Prophecy, 2 vols. 8vo. *calf gilt*, 8s   1786
       These discourses " display much knowledge of the subject, much learning, and no small share of ingenuity."—*Brit. Crit.*
4741 ———— 1823—DAVISON (John) on Prophecy, in which are considered its Structure, Use, and Inspiration, 8vo. *bds.* 12s   1845
4742 ———— another copy, 8vo. *calf*, 7s   1824

4743 WARD's (Dr. John) Dissertations upon several Passages of the Sacred Scriptures, 2 vols. 8vo. *bds.* 4s   1761-74
4744 ———— (Richard) Theological Questions, Dogmatical Observations, and Evangelical Essays on the Gospel of St. Matthew, folio, *calf, scarce*, 18s   1640
4745 ———— (Seth, *Bp. of Salisbury*) Life, with a brief account of Bishop Wilkins, Mr. Lawrence Rooke, Dr. Isaac Barrow, Dr. Turbevile, and others, written by Dr. Walter Pope, sm. 8vo. 3s   1697

[58, GREAT QUEEN STREET,

4746 WARD's (Tho.) England's Reformation, from the time of King Henry the VIIIth to the end of Oates's Plot, a Poem, 4to. *calf, 4s* . *Hamburgh*, 1710
4747 ———— another copy, 2 vols. 12mo. *plates, hf. bd. calf, 4s* 1747
4748 WARDEN's (John) System of Revealed Religion digested under proper heads, and composed in the express words of Scripture, 4to. *large paper, calf, 14s* . 1769
4749 WARNEFORD's (John) Sermons on several subjects and occasions, 2 vols. sm. 8vo. *calf, 3s 6d—bds. 2s 6d* *Oxford*, 1776
4749* - ———— the same, 2 vols. in 1, sm. 8vo. *calf, 3s* *ib.* 1776
4750 WARNER's (Ferd.) System of Divinity and Morality, in a series of Discourses on Natural and Revealed Religion, compiled from the Works of eminent Divines of the Church of England, 4 vols. 8vo. *calf, 12s* . . 1756
4751 WARREN's (John, *Queen's Coll. Camb.*) Sermons on several subjects, preached in the Cathedral Church of Exeter, 2 vols. 8vo. *calf, 4s* . 1739
4752 ————— (Dr. Robert) Practical Discourses on various subjects, 2 vols. 8vo. *calf, scarce, 6s* . 1723
4753 ————— Impartial Churchman: or, a Fair and Candid representation of the excellency of the Church of England, 8vo. *portrait, calf, 2s* . 1728
4754 WATERLAND's (Archdn.) Works, with a Review of his Life and Writings, by Bishop Van Mildert, 6 vols. 8vo. *calf gilt, £4.* *Oxford*, 1843
4755 ————— Works, the original editions, viz. — Doctrine of the Holy Trinity, 1734 — Moyer Lectures, 1740 — Vindication of Christ's Divinity, 1719 — Second Vindication of ditto, 1723—A farther Vindication of Christ's Divinity, 1724—A Review of the Doctrine of the Eucharist as laid down in Scripture and Antiquity, 1737—Critical History of the Athanasian Creed, 1728—An Answer to Dr. Whitby's Reply, being a Vindication of the Charge of Fallacies, Mis-quotations, &c. respecting his book intitled, Disquisitiones Modestæ, 1720—The Case of Arian Subscription considered, with Supplement, 1721-22—The Scriptures and the Arians compared, in their accounts of God the Father, and God the Son, 1722—A rational Enquiry into the proper methods of supporting Christianity, so far as it concerns the Governors of the Church, by Henry Stebbing, 1720—Remarks on Dr. Clarke's Exposition of the Church Catechism, 1730—The Nature, Obligation, and Efficacy of the Christian Sacraments considered, 1730—The Doctrinal use of the Christian Sacraments considered, 1737 —Christianity vindicated, 1732—A Discourse of Fundamentals, 1735 —Sermon at St. Paul's on the Anniversary Day of Thanksgiving for the Restoration, 1723 —A Letter to Dr. Waterland concerning the Nature and value of Sincerity, 1734 — The Sacrament Sacrifice explained, 1738 — Distinctions of Sacrifice, 1740 —Scripture vindicated in Answer to Tindal's Christianity as Old as the Creation, *three parts*, 1730-3 —Sermons on several important subjects of Religion and Morality, 2 vols. 1776—together 12 vols. 8vo. *calf, £2. 2s*

4756 WATERLAND'S (Dr. Dan.) Vindication of Christ's Divinity, being a Defence of some Queries relating to Dr. Clarke's Scheme of the Holy Trinity, 8vo. *calf*, 4s . *Camb.* 1719
4757 —————— the same, 8vo. *calf*, 4s *ib.* 1720
4758 —————— Reply to Waterland's Defence of his Queries, &c. by a Clergyman in the country [Dr. Sam. Clarke?] 8vo. *calf*, 4s   1722
4759 WATSON'S (Alexander) Sermons on Doctrine, Discipline, and Practice, 8vo. *bds.* 6s . 1843
4760 —————— (Rd. *Bp. of Landaff*) Works; viz.—A Collection of Theological Tracts, *large paper*, 6 vols —Miscellaneous Tracts, 2 vols. —Two Apologies for Christianity and the Bible, in answer to T. Paine —together 9 vols. 8vo. *fine set, russia gilt*, £3. 10s
  1791—1816
4761 —————— A Collection of Theological Tracts, 6 vols. 8vo. *fine copy, tree-marbled calf gilt*, £2. 8s . 1791
  Intended as a library for candidates for Holy Orders.

4762 —————— Apology for Christianity, in a series of Letters to Edward Gibbon, Esq. 8vo. *calf*, 2s . *Dublin*, 1777
4763 —————— Sermons on public occasions, and Tracts on Religious subjects, 8vo. *calf*, 3s . *Cambr.* 1788
4764 —————— Chemical Essays, 5 vols. 12mo. *fine copy, old calf gilt*, 7s 6d . 1787, &c.
4765 —————— Anecdotes of his Life, written by himself at different intervals, and published by his Son, 4to. *portrait, calf*, 6s 1817
4766 —————— Imitations and Evidences of a Future State, 8vo. *new in sprinkled calf gilt, very neat*, 5s 6d . 1792
4767 —————— (Tho. *Pastor of Stephens, Walbrook*) Christian's Charter, shewing the Priviledges of a Believer (with God's Anatomy upon Man's Heart, a Sermon before the Commons), 1655—Art of Divine Contentment, 1657—The One Thing necessary, a Sermon before the Lord Mayor, &c. 1656—*in one* vol. sm. 8vo. *calf*, 6s ——
4768 —————— Art of Divine Contentment, sm. 8vo. 2s   1654
4769 —————— Practical Divinity, consisting of 176 Sermons on the Lesser Catechisms of the Assembly of Divines, &c. folio, *portrait, calf*, 14s . . 1692
4770 WATTS'S (Dr. Isaac) Sermons and practical Works, with his Life, and Extracts from his Correspondence, 3 vols. 8vo. *hf. bd. calf*, 8s
  1806
4771 WAYNFLETE—Chandler's (R.) Life of Wm. Waynflete, Bishop of Winchester, and Lord High Chancellor in the reign of Henry VI. royal 8vo. *plates, calf*, 7s 6d . 1811
4772 WEBB'S (F.) Sermons, 4 vols. 12mo. (*two sermons in the 4th vol. neatly supplied in MS.*) 4s . 1767-72
  "Mr. Webb, formerly a Dissenting Minister, but now of the Custom-house. This gentleman, it seems, although such a master of composition, thought proper to quit the pulpit for the sake of a good place in the revenue. His sermons are bought up greedily by the clergy, but Dr. Trusler is now labouring to supersede them."—[*Macgowan's*] *Letter to Blackett*, 1772.

4773 WEBSTER'S (James) Sacramental Sermons, and Discourses at the Lord's Table, 4to. *calf*, 3s . *Edinb.* 1705

4774 WEBSTER'S (James) Discourses on several subjects, preached at the Cathedral Church of Winchester, 8vo. bds. 2s *Winchester*, 1787
4775 ———— (Will.) Complete History of Arianism, from its origin in 306 to 1666; to which is added, the History of Socinianism; translated from the French of Maimbourg and Lamy, &c. 2 vols. 4to. *calf*, 8s . . 1735
4776 ———— Tracts, consisting of Sermons, Discourses, and Letters, 8vo. *calf*, 3s . 1745
4777 ———— Two Discourses on Prayer, and on the Sacrament; with three Sermons, 8vo. *calf*, 2s . 1753
4778 WEEKLY PACQUET of Advice from Rome; or, the History of Popery, a deduction of the Usurpations of the Bishops of Rome, and the Errors and Superstitions by them from time to time brought into the Church, 3 vols. in 1, 4to. *wants title, calf*, 9s
1678-81

A weekly publication, suppressed about 1680 by the King's Bench, but continued under other titles.

4779 WEEMSE'S (John) Works, viz.—An Exposition of the Morall Law or Ten Commandments—The Christian Synagogue—The Portraiture of the Image of God in Man—Observations, Naturall and Morall—An Exposition of the Laws of Moses, Ceremonial and Judiciall—Exercitations Divine—A Treatise of the Foure Degenerate Sons, viz. the Atheist, the Magician, the Idolater, and the Jew—together 4 vols. 4to. *calf*, £1. 1s . 1632-6

"These works contain much valuable biblical information, especially the author's Christian Synagogue and Exercitations."—*Lowndes*.

4780 WEEVER'S (John) Ancient Funerall Monuments within the united Monarchie of Great Britain, Ireland, and the Isles adjacent, as also the Death and Buriall of certaine of the Blood Royall, the Nobilitie and Gentrie of these Kingdomes entombed in forraine Nations, &c. folio, *fine copy in blue morocco, richly tooled, gilt leaves*, £2. 10s
1631
4781 WELDON'S (Rob.) Doctrine of the Scriptures concerning the Originall of Dominion, 4to. *hf. bd. calf*, 5s . 1648

"In this book," says Ant. à Wood, "the author shews himself well read in all sorts of Learning."

4782 WELLS's (Edw.) Help for the more easy Understanding of the Old and New Testaments, 6 vols. 4to. *calf, scarce*, £3. 3s
Oxford, 1724-28
4783 ———— Rich Man's great and indispensible Duty to contribute liberally to the Building, Repairing, and Adorning of Churches, 8vo. *sewed, scarce*, 2s . 1715
4784 ———— new edition, edited by the Rev. I. H. Newman, 18mo. *bds*. 2s—*morocco, gilt leaves*, 5s 6d *Oxford*, 1840
4785 ———— Controversial Treatises against the Dissenters, sm. 8vo. *calf*, 3s . . 1716
4786 WELLES's (John) Soule's Progresse to the Celestial Canaan or Heavenly Jerusalem, by way of Godly Meditation and Holy Contemplation, 4to *calf, neat*, 4s . 1639
4787 WELSH'S (Dr. David) Elements of Church History, Vol. 1, comprising the External History of the Church during the first three Centuries, 8vo. *bds*. 12s . *Edinb.* 1844

4788 WELTON'S (Dr. Rd.) Substance of Christian Faith and Practice represented in XVIII. practical Discourses, 8vo. *port. calf*, 2s 6d
1724
4789 WERENFELS (Sam.) Sermons sur des Verités importantes de la Religion, avec des Considerations sur la reünion des Protestants, 8vo. *calf*, 2s 6d . Basle, 1715
4790 ——— — another copy, 8vo. *vellum*, 3s Amst. 1716
4791 ——— —— Opuscula Theologica, Philosophica, et Philologica, 2 vols. 4to. *port. hf. bd. calf, uncut*, 7s Genevæ, 1739
4792 WERNINCK'S (Dr. J.) Sermons on practical subjects, translated from the works of the most eminent French and Dutch Protestant Ministers in Holland, 8vo. *bds*. 3s—*calf gilt*, 6s 1823
4793 WESLEY'S (John) Explanatory Notes upon the New Testament, 2 vols. 8vo. *calf, neat, port*. 10s 6d . 1831
4794 [——— (Sam.)] Letters from a Country Divine to his Friend in London, concerning the Education of Dissenters in their Private Academies; with a Defence of the said Letter in Answer to the "Defence of the Dissenters' Education," 1704—Wesley's Reply to Palmer's Vindication of the Learning, Loyalty, and Christian Behaviour of the Dissenters, towards the Church of England, 1707 —together, *three tracts*, 8vo. *scarce*, 6s ———

Samuel Wesley was the Father of the leader of the Wesleyan Methodists, and was educated a dissenter; he conformed to the Established Church, and wrote these letters to a friend, by way of justifying his conformity, but not with a view to publication. Palmer, who got great credit among his own people by abusing Wesley in his Vindication of the Dissenters, subsequently *conformed*, and published a Sermon in 1709, styling himself a *Presbyter of the Church of England.*

4795 WEST'S (Gilbert) Observations on the History and Evidences of the Resurrection of Jesus Christ, 8vo. *calf*, 3s . 1747
4796 ——— —— the same, with [Lord Lyttleton's] Observations on the Conversion and Apostleship of St. Paul, 8vo. *fine copies, old calf gilt*, 4s . . 1747-49
4797 ——— —— (Matthew) Sermons on various subjects, 2 vols. 8vo. *bds*. 4s . . Dublin, 1819
4798 ——— —— (W.) Nature, Design, &c. of Prayer, illustrated in seven practical Discourses on the Lord's Prayer, 8vo. *calf*, 3s 1758
4799 WESTMACOT'S (W.) Historia Vegetabilium Sacra; or, a Scripture Herbal, 18mo. *calf, very scarce*, 3s . 1695
4800 WESTON'S (Hon. Edw.) Family Discourses; [edited by his Son], 8vo. *bds*. 2s . Camb. 1776
4801 ——— —— (Steph. *Bp. of Exeter*) Sermons on various subjects, 2 vols. 8vo. *port. calf*, 3s . 1747

" The style of these sermons is strong and impressive."—*Bp. Sherlock.*

4802 ——— —— (W.) Enquiry into the Rejection of the Christian Miracles by the Heathens, 8vo. *calf*, 2s . Camb. 1746
4803 WESTONIIS (Edvardiis, *Londinensis*) Theatrum Vitæ Civilis ac Sacræ, sive de Moribus Reipub. Christianæ Commentarius, folio, *in Spanish binding*, 12s . Brugis, 1626
4804 WHALEY'S (Nathl.) Eight Sermons on several occasions, sm. 8vo. 2s
1695

[58, GREAT QUEEN STREET,

4805 WHARTONI (Hen.) Anglia Sacra ; sive Collectio Historiarum partim Antiquitas partim recentio Scripturam, de Archiepiscopis Angliæ à prima Fidei Christianæ susceptione ad Ann. 1540, 2 vols. folio, *calf, very scarce*, £2. 15s . 1691
4806 —— —— Defence of Pluralities, or Holding two Benefices with Cure of Souls, as now practised in the Church of England, small 8vo. *calf, scarce*, 3s 6d . 1692
4807 WHAT is the Church of Christ? 12mo. *bds*. 2s 1843
4808 WHATELY's (Rd. *Abp. of Dublin*) Essays on some of the Peculiarities of the Christian Religion, 8vo. *bds*. 4s *Oxford*, 1825
4809 —————— the same, 8vo. *bds*. 5s . *ib*. 1827
4810 [——————] View of the Scripture Revelations concerning a Future State, 12mo. *bds*. 3s . 1829
4811 —————— Errors of Romanism traced to their origin in Human Nature, 8vo. *bds*. 5s . 1830
4812 —————— (Will.) Prototypes ; or, the Primarie Precedents out of the Booke of Genesis, folio, *portrait inserted, calf*, 12s 1640
4813 WHATLEY's (Steph.) Parallel of the Doctrines of the Pagans with the Doctrine of the Jesuits ; and that of the Constitution Unigenitus, issued by Clement XI., with the 101 Propositions of Father Quesnel thereby condemned, 8vo. *calf, fine copy*, 4s 1726
4814 WHEARE's (D.) Method and Order of Reading both Civil and Ecclesiastical Histories, with an Appendix by N. Horseman, and Mr. Dodwell's Invitation to Gentlemen to acquaint themselves with Antient History, 8vo. *calf*, 2s 6d . 1698
4815 WHEATLAND's (——) Twenty-six Sermons on various subjects, 8vo. *calf*, 3s . . 1739
4816 WHEATLIB's (Wm.) Caveat for the Covetous ; in a Sermon preached at Paul's Cross, 16mo. *hf. bd. calf, neat*, 5s . 1616
4817 WHEATLEY's (Charles) Rational Illustration of the Book of Common Prayer, 8vo. *frontispiece, calf*, 6s . 1728
4818 —————— the same, 8vo. *frontispiece, calf*, 6s 1729
4819 —————— another copy, 8vo. *calf*, . 1759
4820 —————— another copy, 8vo. *bds*. 5s . 1825
4821 —————— new edition, 8vo. *bds*. 7s 6d – *calf gilt*, 11s *Oxf*. 1839
4822 —— —— Bidding of · Prayers before Sermon, no mark of disaffection to the present government; or, an Historical Vindication of the 55th Canon ; shewing that the form of Bidding Prayers has been prescribed and enjoined ever since the Reformation, and constantly practiced by the greatest divines of our Church, 8vo. *new edition*, 2s . 1845
4823 WHICHCOTE's (Dr. Benj.) Several Discourses, 4 vols. 8vo. *portrait, calf*, 10s . . 1702-19
4824 —————— another copy, 4 vols. 8vo. *portrait, old calf gilt*, 12s 1702-7
4825 —————— Select Sermons, 12mo. *calf*, 2s *Edinb*. 1742
4826 —————— the same, with a recommendatory Preface by Dr. Wishart, 12mo. *bds*. 1s 6d . *Bath*, 1773
4827 [——————] Moral and Religious Aphorisms, 8vo. *calf*, 3s 6d *Norwich*, 1703

4828 WHIG.—The Independent Whig, 8vo. *calf*, 2s 6d   1722
4829 WHISH's (M. R.) Modern Infidelity and National Reformation; three Sermons, 8vo. *neat*, 2s   *Bristol*, 1819
4830 WHISTON's (WILLIAM) WORKS, collected; viz.—Theory of the Earth, *plates*, 1708—The Accomplishment of Scripture Prophecies; eight Sermons at Boyle's Lecture, 1708—Sermons and Essays, with Novatian de Trinitate, 1709—Historical Preface to Primitive Christianity revived; with an Appendix concerning the Author's prosecution at, and banishment from, the University of Cambridge, 1711—Primitive Christianity revived, containing the Epistles of Ignatius, Greek and English; the Apostolical Constitutions, Gr. and English; an Essay on them; and an Account of the Primitive Faith concerning the Trinity and Incarnation, and the Recognitions of Clement, 5 vols. 1711-12—A collection of small Tracts, containing a Reply to Dr. Allix—Remarks on Dr. Grabe's Essay, 1712—Three Essays, viz.—The Council of Nice vindicated from the Athanasian Heresy; a collection of Ancient Monuments relating to the Trinity and Incarnation; and the Liturgy of the Church of England reduced nearer to the Primitive Standard, 1713—An Argument to prove that, either all Persons solemnly set apart for the Ministry are real Clergymen; or else, there are now no real Clergymen, 1714—Vindication of the Sibylline Oracles, 1715—Several Papers relating to Mr. Whiston's Cause before the Court of Delegates, 1715—New Method for discovering the Longitude, by W. Whiston and H. Ditton, 1715—St. Clement and St. Irenæus's Vindication of the Apostolical Constitutions, &c. 1716—An Account of a surprizing Meteor seen March 16, 1716; and an Account of another surprizing Meteor, 1719, (in 1 vol.)—Astronomical Principles of Religion, 1717—Scripture Politicks, 1717—Humble Address to the Princes of Europe for the Admission of the Christian Religion into their dominions, 1716—An Account of Mr. Whiston's Prosecution at, and Banishment from, Cambridge, 1718—A Commentary on the three Catholick Epistles of St. John, 1719—Letter to the Earl of Nottingham concerning the Eternity of the Son of God and of the Holy Spirit, *(first and second editions)* 1719-21—A second Letter to the Bp. of London concerning the Primitive Doxologies, 1719: Letter of thanks to the Bp. of London for his late Letter against the use of new forms of Doxology, N. D.: Letter to the Earl of Nottingham, 2nd edition, 1721: (in 1 vol.)—The Longitude and Latitude found by the Inclinatory or Dipping Needle, 1721—The Newe Attractive, shewing the nature and manifold Varieties of the Loadstone found out and discovered by Rob. Norman, 1720—An Essay towards restoring the true Text of the Old Testament, 1722, (with a Supplement, 1723)—The literal Accomplishment of Scripture Prophecies, 1724—The Calculation of Solar Eclipses without Parallaxes, 1724—A collection of authentic Records belonging to the Old and New Testament, 2 vols. 1727-28—Six Dissertations, 1734—The Eternity of Hell Torments considered, 1740—Primitive New Testament, according to the Greek MSS.

[58, GREAT QUEEN STREET,

WHISTON'S WORKS—*continued.*
of Beza, in the University Library Cambridge; with the single sheet on the Resurrection, from Beza's double copy of the IV. Gospels, 1745—Sacred History of the Old and New Testament, from the Creation till the days of Constantine the Great, 6 vols. 1745-46—Memoirs of his Life and Writings, by himself, *two parts, with portrait,* 1753—together 28 vols. 8vo. *rich pannelled calf gilt, carmine edges, and lettered contents,* £12. 12s

The most complete set of Whiston's Works that has occurred for many years.

4831 ——— View of the Chronology of the Old Testament, and of the Harmony of the Four Evangelists, 4to. *calf,* 3s   Camb. 1702

4832 ——— Essay on the Revelation of St. John, so far as it concerns the past and present times, 4to. *calf,* 3s   *ib.* 1706

4833 ——— another copy, *with the autograph and book-plate of Bp. Burnet,* 4to. *calf,* 5s   .   *ib.* 1706

4834 ——— Sermons and Essays upon several subjects, 8vo. *calf,* 3s
1709

4835 ——— Primitive Christianity revived; containing, the larger Epistles of Ignatius; the Apostolical Constitutions, with an Essay on them; and an Account of the Primitive Faith concerning the Trinity and Incarnation, 4 vols. 8vo. *calf,* £1. 4s   1711

4836 ——— Essay towards restoring the true text of the Old Testament: and for vindicating the citations made thence in the New Testament, 8vo. *hf. bd. uncut,* 4s 6d   .   1722

4837 ——— Sacred History of the Old and New Testament, from the Creation till the days of Constantine the Great, 6 vols. 8vo. *calf,* £1. 1s   .   .   1745

4838 ——— Memoirs of his Life and Writings, written by himself, 8vo. *port. calf,* 7s   .   1753

4839 WHITAKER'S (E. W.) Six Sermons, 12mo. *calf,* 2s   Egham, 1793

4840 ——— (John) Origin of Arianism disclosed, 8vo. *bds.* 6s   1791

4841 WHITBY'S (Dan.) Endeavour to evince the Certainty of Christian Faith in general, and of the Resurrection of Christ in particular, sm. 8vo. *calf,* 3s   .   Oxford, 1671

4842 ——— another copy, 8vo. *hf. bd. vellum,* 3s   *ib.* 1671

4843 ——— The Protestant Reconciler, humbly pleading for condecention to Dissenting Brethren in things indifferent; *with the second part,* earnestly persuading the Dissenting Laity to joyn in full communion with the Church of England, 2 vols. in 1, 8vo. *calf,* 8s
1683

"Part I. of this work was burnt by the hands of the University Marshall, at Oxford, in the school quadrangle. Part II. was published to stop the clamours of the people against the first."—*Ant. à Wood.*

4844 ——— Discourse of the Necessity and Usefulness of the Christian Revelation; by reason of the Corruption of the Principles of Natural Religion among Jews and Heathens, 8vo. *calf,* 3s   1705

4845 ——— Sermons on the Attributes of God, 2 vols. in 1, 8vo. *calf,* 4s 6d   .   1710

4846 WHITBY'S (Dan.) Paraphrase and Commentary on the New Testament, 2 vols. folio, *portrait, calf, neat,* £1. 8s . 1709-10
4847 ———— another copy, 2 vols. folio, *calf,* £1. 4s 1718
4848 ———— another copy, 2 vols. 4to. *portrait, calf,* £1. 5s
Edinb. 1807

" Divines of every denomination concur in pronouncing Dr. Whitby's Commentary to be, upon the whole, the best on the New Testament that is extant, in the English language. It is inserted in almost every list of books that we have seen recommended to students."—*Horne.*

4849 ———— Discourse concerning, I. Election and Reprobation. II. The Extent of Christ's Redemption. III. The Grace of God. IV. The Liberty of the Will. V. Perseverance, 8vo. *calf,* 5s 1710
4850 ———— another copy, 8vo. *calf,* 5s—*fine copy, old calf gilt,* 6s 1735
4851 ———— another copy, 8vo. *bds.* 4s 6d . 1816
4852 ———— the same, 8vo. *bds.* 4s 6d . 1817
4853 ———— Tractatus de Imputatione divina Peccati Adami posteris ejus universis in reatum, 8vo. *neat,* 2s 6d . 1711
4854 ———— Dissertatio de S. Scripturarum Interpretatione secundum Patrum Commentarios, 8vo. *calf, scarce,* 6s 1714
4855 ———— The Guilt of Adam's Transgression not imputed to his Posterity: a Treatise concerning Original Sin, translated by H. Heywood, 8vo. *calf,* 5s . 1739
4856 ———— Sermons on several occasions, 8vo. *calf,* 2s 6d 1720
4857 WHITE'S (Francis) Orthodox Faith, and Way to the Church explained and justified: in answer to a Popish Treatise entituled, White died Blacke; wherein T. W. P. in his triple accusation of D. White, is proved a trifler, &c., 4to. *very scarce, fine copy, calf, gilt leaves, arms on the sides,* 15s 1617

The author of this book was afterwards Bp. of Norwich and Ely, successively. " White died Black," was "a libelling and despitefull Treatise," against a book written by his deceased brother, John White, D.D., entitled "A way to the Church." The present copy belonged to John Duke of Newcastle, and subsequently to the late Duke of Sussex, as appears by their book-plates.

4858 ———— Reply to Jesuit Fisher's Answere to Certain Questions propounded by King James. Hereunto is annexed, a Conference of the Bp. of St. Davids, [Laud], with the same Jesuit, folio, *fine copy, portrait, and engraved title, hf. bd. calf,* £1. 4s 1624

From the library of the late Duke of Sussex.

4859 ———— (John) Way to the true Church, wherein the principall motives perswading to Romanisme, are familiarly disputed, &c., in answer to a Popish Discourse concerning the Rule of Faith, 4to. *rare,* 9s . . 1616
4860 ———— Commentary on the Three First Chapters of Genesis, folio, *hf. bd. calf, neat,* 9s . 1656

" The author is usually called the Patriarch of Dorchester; he was a constant preacher, and by his wisdom and ministerial labours, Dorchester was much enriched with knowledge, piety, and industry."—*Fuller.*

4861 ———— Free and Candid Disquisitions relating to the Church of England, 8vo. *calf,* 3s 6d . 1750

4862 WHITE'S (John) Letter to a Gentleman dissenting from the Church of England, concerning the lives of Churchmen and Dissenters, 1743—A Second Letter, wherein the Pleas of Dissenters against Communion with the Church are refuted, 1745—The Third and last Letter, wherein the design of the Second is farther pursued and completed, 1745 - The genuineness of Lord Clarendon's History of the Rebellion vindicated, and Mr. Oldmixon's slander confuted, by Jo. Burton, D.D. *Oxf.* 1744—*in one* vol. 8vo. *hf. bd. cf.* 4s ——

4863 —— —— Three Letters to a Gentleman dissenting from the Church of England, 1748—Defence of the three Letters, &c. 1746-8—Letter to Samuel Chandler, in vindication of some passages in the Three Letters, &c., 1749—Appendix to the Controversy, 1750—*in one* vol. 8vo. *old calf gilt,* 5s 6d ——

4864 —— —— (Dr. Jos.) Diatessaron sive integra historia Domini Nostri Jesu Christi, Græcé, ex IV. Evangeliis inter se collatis, 8vo. *russia, neat,* 5s . . Oxon. 1800

4865 —— —— (Sam.) Commentary on the Prophet Isaiah, wherein the literal sense is briefly explained, 4to. *calf,* 5s 1709

4866 —— —— (Tho.) Institutionum Sacrarum peripateticis inædificatarum ; hoc est Theologiæ, super fundamentis in Peripateticâ Digbæanâ jactis, extructæ, pars theorica, 2 vols. 12mo. *calf,* 4s 1652

4867 —— —— another copy, 2 vols. in 1, *calf,* 4s . 1652
The author styles himself "Thomas Anglus, è generosâ Albiorum in Oriente Trinobantum Prosopoia oriundus." He was a Roman Catholic.

4868 —— —— (*Preb. of Lichf.*) Twenty Sermons on various subjects, 8vo. *calf,* 3s . . 1771

4869 WHITFIELD (George) Memoirs of his Life, compiled by the Rev. John Gillies, D.D., 8vo. *portrait, bds.* 3s . 1772

4870 —— —— (P.) Dissertation on the Hebrew Vowel-points, shewing that they are an original and essential part of the language, 4to. *hf. bd. calf,* 3s . Liverpool, 1748

4871 —— —— Christianity of the New Testament, 8vo. 3s 6d *ib.* 1757

4872 WHITLOCKE'S (Sir Bulstrode) Essays, Ecclesiastical and Civil, 8vo. *calf,* 2s . . 1706

4873 WHITTAKER'S (Jo. Wm.) Historical and Critical Enquiry into the Interpretation of the Hebrew Scriptures, with remarks on Mr. Bellamy's New Translation, 8vo. *bds.* 3s Camb. 1819

4874 —— —— Justification by Faith, a course of Sermons before the University of Cambridge, 8vo. *bds.* 2s 1825

4875 WHITTY's (John) Sermons on the Lord's Prayer and the Lord's Supper, 2 vols. 8vo. *hf. bd. calf,* 6s . 1772

4876 WHOLE DUTY OF MAN, with Private Devotions; new edition, with a Preface by the Rev. W. B. Hawkins, sm. 8vo. *bds.* 4s 6d 1842

4877 WIGANDUS (Jo. *Episc. Pomezaniensis*) De persecutione Piorum, exiliis Piorum, exiliis Facinorosorum, martyriis Piorum, Pseudomartyriis, fuga Ministrorum verbi, Constantia, Apostasia, Patientia, *Franc. ad M.* 1580—De arguendis falsis Dogmatibus et Doctoribus, aliisq ; peccatis et peccatoribus, juxta verbum Dei, *s. l.* 1580—2 vols. in 1, sm. 8vo. *neat,* 4s 6d . ——

4878 WIGHT's (Tho.) History of the Rise and Progress of the Quakers in Ireland, from 1653 to 1700, revised and continued to 1751, by John Rutty, 8vo. *calf,* 4s . 1800

LINCOLN'S INN FIELDS.]

4879 WICLIFFE'S (John) LAST AGE OF THE CHURCH, *now first printed from a manuscript in the University Library, Dublin.* Edited with Notes, by JAMES HENTHORN TODD, D.D. *Fellow of Trinity College,* &c. square 12mo. *hf. bd· morocco,* 5s Dublin University Press, 1840
One of the most beautiful little volumes which have issued from the Irish press; the preface and notes of the learned editor abound with interest, in the former of which, he urges the great importance and necessity of the works of Wycliffe being collected and published, before his opinions can be determined, or his real merits fixed as a reformer, and further urges the danger of delay as the chances of their destruction are every day becoming greater. " What nobler, what more imperishable monument, could the gratitude of England, raise to her first reformer, than a complete and uniform edition of his extant writings?"

4880 ———— The History of the Life and Sufferings of John Wicliffe, with a Collection of Papers and Records, by John Lewis, 8vo. *calf,* 4s 6d . . 1720

4881 WILBERFORCE'S (Rob. Isaac) Church Courts and Church Discipline, 8vo. *bds.* 5s . . 1843

4882 ———— The Five Empires : an Outline of Ancient History, 12mo. *bds.* 4s . . 1840

4883 ———— Rutilius and Lucius, or Stories of the Third Age, 12mo. *bds.* 3s . . 1842

4884 —— —— (Samuel, *Bp. of Oxford*) Sermons, 12mo. *bds.* 6s 1845

4885 —— —— (Wm.) Family Prayers, edited by his Son R. I. Wilberforce, 12mo. *sewed,* 2s . 1834

4886 W[ILCOCKS] (T[homas])—A very Godly and Learned Exposition upon the whole Booke of Psalmes, 𝔅lack letter, sm. 4to. *very scarce, two leaves wanting, neat,* 7s . Lond. 1591

4887 WILFORD'S (John) Memorials and Characters, together with the Lives of divers Eminent and Worthy Persons, from 1600 to the present time, folio, *calf,* 14s . 1741

4888 WILKINS (David) Leges Anglo-Saxonicæ Ecclesiasticæ et Civiles; accedunt Leges Edvardi Latinæ, Guilielmi Conq. Gallo-Normannicæ, et Henrici I. Latinæ; subjungitur H. Spelmanni Codex Legum veterum Statutorum Regni Angliæ, ab ingressu Guil. I. ad an. 9 Henr. III. præmittitur Dissertatio Epistolaris Guil. Nicolsoni Episc. Derrensis de Jure Feudali Veterum Saxonum. Cum Codd. MSS. contulit, Notas, Versioncm, et Glossarium adjecit D. Wilkins, folio, *hf. bd. calf,* £1. 18s . 1721

4889 —— —— (John, *Bp. of Chester*) Sermons preached before the King ; with a Discourse concerning the Bounty of Providence, sm. 8vo. *portrait,* 3s . 1680

4890 —— —— Discovery of a New World, with a Discourse concerning a New Planet, sm. 8vo. *engraved title by W. Marshall, calf,* 4s 1640

4891 ———— Principles and Duties of Natural Religion, two books ; with his Funeral Sermon, by Bp. Lloyd, 8vo. *portrait, calf,* 2s 6d 1699

4892 ———— the same, 8vo. *portrait, calf,* 3s 1734

4893 ———— Discourse concerning the Gift of Prayer; with Ecclesiastes, a Discourse concerning the Gift of Preaching, 8vo. *calf,* 3s 6d . . 1704

4894 ———— another copy, 8vo. *calf,* 4s . 1718

[58, GREAT QUEEN STREET,

4895 WILLAT'S (Tho.) Apology for the Church of Christ and the Church of England ; with a Vindication of the Doctrines of the late Hon. and Rev. W. B. Cadogan, 8vo. *hf. bd. neat*, 2*s* 6*d*   Henley, 1798

4896 WILLET'S (Dr. And.) Catholicon, that is a general preservative or remedie against the Pseudo-Catholike Religion, gathered out of the Catholike Epistle of St. Jude, &c. 12mo. *hf. bd. calf, scarce*, 12*s*
Camb. 1602
From the library of the late Duke of Sussex.

4897 ———— —— Synopsis Papismi, that is, a General View of Papistrie ; wherein the whole Mystery of Iniquity, and Summe of Antichristian doctrine is set downe, which is maintained by the Synagogue of Rome against the Church of Christ, &c. BEST EDITION, with Life by Peter Smith, D.D., folio, *calf, very scarce*, £2. 16*s*   1634

4898 ———————— Hexapla, that is, a Six-fold Commentarie upon Genesis and Exodus, wherein six severall translations are compared, 2 vols. in 1, folio, *best edition, calf*, £1. 1*s*—*old calf*, 18*s*   1632-33

4899 ———————— Hexapla, or Six-fold Commentary on Exodus, Leviticus, and Romans, 3 vols. folio, *hf. bd. calf*, £1. 18*s*   1620-33

4900 ———————— Hexapla, or Six-fold Commentarie upon Leviticus, folio, *calf*, 18*s*   .   1631

4901 WILLIAMS'S (Dr. Dan.) Practical Sermons on several important subjects, with some account of his Life, 3 vols. 1738-50—Tractatus selecti ex Anglicis Latine versi, quibus præfixa est Narratiuncula de Auctoris Vita, &c. 1760—together 6 vols. 8vo. *old calf gilt*, 14*s*   .   .   ——

"His pulpit discourses were admirably adapted to answer the great end of preaching—usefulness to the souls of men."—*Wilson's Dissenters*.

4902 ———————— (Isaac) Gospel Narrative of our Lord's Nativity harmonized, with Reflections, sm. 8vo. *bds.* 8*s* 6*d*   1844

4903 ———————— Gospel Narrative of our Lord's Passion harmonized, with Reflections, 12mo. *calf gilt*, 6*s*   .   1842

4904 ———————— Gospel Narrative of our Lord's Resurrection harmonized, with Reflections, sm. 8vo. *bds.* 8*s*   .   1845

4905 ———————— Thoughts on the Study of the Holy Gospel, intended as an Introduction to a Harmony and Commentary, sm. 8vo. *bds.* 5*s* 6*d*   .   .   1842

4906 ———————— (John) Concordance to the Greek Testament, with the English Version to each word ; the principal Hebrew Roots corresponding to the Greek words of the Septuagint, and Notes, 4to. *calf, scarce*, 10*s*   .   .   1767

4907 ———————— another copy, *large paper*, 4to. *calf*, 14*s*   1767

"Compiled with great pains and accuracy."—*Monthly Review*.

4908 ———————— Concordance to the Greek Testament, 1767—RANDOLPH'S (Thos.) Prophecies and other Texts, cited in the New Testament, compared with the Hebrew and the Septuagint, with Notes, *Oxford*, 1782—Harmonia quatuor Evangeliorum juxta Sectiones Ammonianas et Eusebii Canones, *Græcè, Oxon.* 1805—*in one vol.* 4to. *calf*, 18*s*   .   .   ——

4909 WILLIAMS—Scrinia Reserata: a Memorial offered to the great deservings of John Williams, D.D., *Abp. of York, and Lord Keeper*, containing a series of remarkable transactions of his Life, in relation both to Church and State; written by Jo. Hacket, Bp. of Litchfield and Coventry, folio, *portrait, calf, scarce*, £1. 18s   1693

4910 —— —— (W. *Queen's Coll. Camb.*) Truth exhibited between extremes, and the Progress of Error in the British and Foreign Bible Society traced, with Sermons on different subjects, 8vo. *hf. bd. calf, neat*, 2s   *Guildford*, 1819

4911 WILLINGTON (James)—Memoirs of a Protestant, condemned to the Gallies of France for his Religion, written by himself, and translated by James Willington, [*i. e.* Oliver Goldsmith] 2 vols. 12mo. *calf*, 7s   .   1758

<small>This is believed to be Goldsmith's first publication. The present copy belonged to his late Royal Highness the Duke of Sussex.</small>

4912 [WILLIS's (—— *Bp. of Winton*)] Address to those of the Roman Communion in England, occasioned by the late Act of Parliament for the further preventing the Growth of Popery, 12mo. *calf*, 2s 6d   .   1700

4913 WILLYMOTT's (Dr. Wm.) Collection of Devotions for the Altar, with a Preparatory Confession of Faith, and the necessity of such Confession, extracted from Bishop Pearson, 2 vols. 8vo. LARGE PAPER, *morocco, gilt leaves*, by C. Lewis, £2. 2s   1720

4914 WILSON's (Dan. *Bp. of Calcutta*) Sermons, 8vo. *bds*. 3s 6d   1818

4915 —— —— Apostolical Commission, a Sermon at the Cathedral Church of St. John, at an Ordination, 4to. 1s   *Calcutta*, 1833

4916 —— —— (Thos.) Commentary on the Epistle of St. Paul to the Romans, folio, *imperfect, hf. bd. calf, scarce*, 6s   1653

4917 —— —— (*Bp. of Sodor and Man*) Short and Plain Instruction for the better understanding of the Lord's Supper, 12mo. *calf, neat*, 2s   .   1749

4918 —— —— (Dr. Wm.) XXXIX Articles, illustrated by Extracts from the Liturgy, Homilies, Nowell's Catechism, and Jewell's Apology, and confirmed by passages of Scripture, 8vo. *bds*. 3s   *Oxford*, 1821

4919 —— —— Illustration of the Method of explaining the New Testament, by the early opinions of Jews and Gentiles concerning Christ, 8vo. *hf. bd. calf*, 5s— *bds*. 4s   .   *Camb*. 1797

<small>" A refutation of Priestley's History of Early Opinions. It would be injustice to the ingenious writer of this Reply, not to allow him, unequivocally, the praise of having written, in a correct and perspicuous style, a learned and well digested work, and having conducted his part of the controversy with unity and candour."—*Analytical Review*.</small>

4920 WILTON's (Sam.) Review of some of the Articles to which Subscription is required of Protestant Dissenting Ministers, 8vo. *bds*. 2s   .   1774

4921 WIMBLEDON's (R.) Sermon, no lesse fruitefull than famous, preached at Paul's Crosse on the Sunday of Quinquagesima, 1388, and found out hid in a wall, 1 mo. Black letter, *hf. bd. calf, neat*, 10s   1617

4922 WINBOLT's (Tho.) Sermons on various subjects, preached at Southgate Chapel, 2 vols. 8vo. *bds*. 2s 6d   .   1800

4923 WINDER's (Hen.) Critical and Chronological History of Knowledge, chiefly Religious, from Adam to Christ, 2 vols. 4to. *calf*, 5s
1745-46
4924 ——— another copy, 2 vols. in 1, 4to. *calf*, 6s 1745-6
4925 WINKLE's (Benj.) French Cathedrals, from drawings taken on the spot by R. Garland, Architect, with an Historical and Descriptive account, 4to. *plates, cloth bds.* 18s . 1837
4926 WINSLOW (Benj. Davis) True Catholic Churchman, in his Life and in his Death : the Sermons and Poetical Remains of the Rev. B. D. Winslow, with the Sermon preached on the Sunday after his decease, by the Rt. Rev. G. W. Doane, sm. 8vo. *bds.* 5s
Oxford, 1842
4927 WINSTANLEY's (Wm.) England's Worthies ; select Lives of the most eminent persons, from Constantine the Great to the Death of Oliver Cromwell, late Protector, sm. 8vo. *frontispiece, calf, old style*, 7s . . 1660
4928 ——— Christian Calling, 8vo. *bds.* 2s 1754
4929 WINTLE's (Thos.) Daniel, an improved Version attempted, with a Preliminary Dissertation, and Notes Critical, Historical, and Explanatory, 4to. *hf. bd. calf, neat*, 8s . 1807
" A very valuable translation."—*Horne.* The author availed himself of the MS. collections of Secker, and the notes of several other learned Oriental Scholars.
4930 WISHART's (Dr. Wm.) Discourses on several subjects, 12mo. *bds.* 2s . . 1753
4931 WITSIUS's (Herman) Economy of the Covenants between God and Man, comprehending a complete body of Divinity, translated by W. Crookshank, with a Life of the Author, 2 vols. 8vo. *portrait, hf. bd. calf, marbled edges*, 9s . ———
4932 WITHERBY's (Tho.) Attempt to remove prejudices concerning the Jewish Nation, by way of Dialogue, 8vo. *hf. bd. calf*, 3s 1804
4933 WITTY's (John) Essay towards a Vindication of the vulgar Exposition of the Mosaic History of the Fall of Adam, 8vo. *calf*, 2s 6d . . 1705
4934 ——— First Principles of Modern Deism confuted, 8vo. *calf*, 3s . . 1707
4935 WODENOTE (Theoph.) Hermes Theologicus : or, a divine Mercurie dispatcht with a grave Message of new Descants upon old Records, 18mo. *engraved title, new in sprinkled calf gilt*, 4s 6d · 1649
4936 WODROW's (R.) History of the Sufferings of the Church of Scotland, from the Restoration to the Revolution, with his Life and Notes by R. Burns, D.D., 4 vols. 8vo. *calf gilt*, £1. 11s 6d
Glasgow, 1828
4937 WOGAN's (Will.) Essay on the proper Lessons for Sundays, and chief Festivals, 4 vols. 8vo. *calf*, £1. 10s 1754
4938 ——— another copy, 4 vols. 8vo. £1. 1s—*fine copy, calf*, £1. 11s 6d . . 1764
4939 WOIDII (C. G.) Notitia Codicis Alexandrini, cum variis ejus Lectionibus omnibus, curavit, notasque adjecit G. L. Spohn, 8vo. *bds.* 4s 6d
Lips. 1788

4940 WOLLASTON'S (William) Design of part of the Book of Ecclesiastes; or the Unreasonableness of Men's restless contentions for the present enjoyments, represented in an English Poem, 8vo. *calf, rare,* 7s 6d . . 1691
Rigidly suppressed by the author, who destroyed every copy he could lay his hands on soon after publication.

4941 ———— Religion of Nature delineated, 4to. *calf,* 3s 6d 1726

4942 WOLSELEY'S (Sir Charles, *Bart.*) Reasonablenesse of Scripture Belief, 1672—The Unreasonableness of Atheism made manifest, 1669—*in one* vol. 8vo. *calf,* 4s . ————
"This treatise, I think, is the justest account of the truth of Christianity of any I have ever yet read, and is recommended as such by the learned and judicious Dr. Scott."—*MS. Note.*

4943 WOLSEY (Tho. *Cardinal*) Life of Cardinal Wolsey, by Richard Fiddes, D.D., folio, *fine copy, portrait and plates, calf, neat,* 12s . . 1724

4944 ———— another copy, folio, *portraits and plates, calf,* 12s 1726

4945 WOOD'S (Anthony à) Athenæ Oxonienses; an exact History of all the Writers and Bishops who have had their education in the University of Oxford, from 1500 to 1695; with the Fasti, or Annals of the said University, 2 vols. folio, *fine copy, calf,* £1. 1s
1721

4946 ———— (Lubbridge) Five Discourses relating to Christian Practice, 8vo. *neat,* 2s . *Reading,* 1747

4947 ———— (Tho.) Mosaic History of the Creation, illustrated by discoveries derived from the present state of Science, &c. 8vo. *port. bds.* 5s . . 1818

4948 ———— Parish Church; or Religion in Britain, 8vo. *bds.* 4s 1825

4949 WOODBRIDGE'S (Benj.) Method of Grace in the Justification of Sinners, being a reply to a book written by W. Eyre, entitled Vindiciæ Justificationis Gratuitæ, 4to. *hf. bd. calf,* 3s 1656

4950 WOODFORD'S (Sam.) Paraphrase upon the Psalms of David, 4to. *frontispiece, hf. bd.* 4s 6d . 1667

4951 WOODHOUSE'S (J. C. *Dean of Lichfield*) Annotations on the Apocalypse, intended as a Sequel to Elsley and Slade, 8vo. *bds. very scarce,* 12s . . 1828

4952 WOOLFREY (Mary Anne) Church and the Widow! an Exposure of the Case of M. A. Woolfrey, 8vo. *sewed,* 1s 6d 1838

4953 WOOLSTON'S (Tho.) Old Apology for the Truth of the Christian Religion against the Jews and Gentiles revived, 1732—Six Discourses on the Miracles, 1732—The Christian Religion not founded on Allegory, 1724—The Miracles of Jesus vindicated, 1733—A Discourse on our Saviour's miraculous power of Healing, 1742— in 3 vols. 8vo. *old calf gilt, neat,* 7s 6d ————

4954 WORDSWORTH'S (Dr. Chr.) Christian Institutes: a series of Discourses and Tracts, arranged systematically, and illustrated with Notes, 4 vols. 8vo. *bds.* £2. 16s—*calf gilt,* £3. 10s 1842

4955 ———— Ecclesiastical Biography; or Lives of eminent Men connected with the History of Religion in England, from the commencement of the Reformation to the Revolution, 4 vols. 8vo. *bds.* £2. 15s—*calf gilt,* £3. 10s 1839

4956 WORDSWORTH'S (Dr. Chr.) Sermons, 2 vols. 8vo. *bds.* 7*s* 6*d*. 1814
4957 ―――――― Six Letters to Granville Sharp, Esq. respecting his Remarks on the use of the Definite Article in the Greek Text of the New Testament, 8vo. *bds.* 3*s* 1802
4958 ―――――― Who wrote Icôn Basilikè? considered and answered, in two Letters to the Archbishop of Canterbury, 1824—Documentary Supplement, 1825 — King Charles the First, author of Icôn Basilikè, further proved, in a Letter to the Archbishop of Canterbury, *Camb.* 1828—*in one* vol. 8vo. *bds.* 5*s*
4959 ―――――― (C. *late Master of Harrow School*) Theophilus Anglicanus, or Instruction for the Young Student, concerning the Church and the Anglican branch of it, 8vo. *bds.* 8*s* 1845
4960 WORK for an excellent Scholar: containing an Examination of several mistranslated Texts of Scripture, 4to. 2*s* 1703
4961 WORTHINGTON'S (H.) Great Duty of Resignation to the Divine Will, 18mo. 2*s* . 1714
4962 ―――――― (Hugh, *of Leicester*) Discourses on various subjects, evangelical and practical, 8vo. *bds.* 4*s* . 1785
4963 ―――――― (John, *Preb. of Lincoln*) Select Discourses: treating—I. Of Self-resignation to the Divine Will. II. Of Christian Love. III. Of the Resurrection, and a Reward to come, 8vo. *calf*, 5*s* 1725
4964 ―――――― (John, *Master of Jesus Coll. Camb.*) Miscellanies, viz.— Observations on the Millennium, &c.; Dissertatio de Ecclesiæ in Terris Futura Fælicitate; de Voce Merachépheth, Gen. i. 2; and Epistles to Mr. Hartlib, with the Author's Character by Abp. Tillotson, 8vo .*calf*, 5*s* . 1704
4965 ―――――― (Rd.) Sermons: to which is affixed a short Discourse on the Divinity of Christ, 8vo. *bds.* 3*s* *Warrington*, 1793
4966 [―――――― (Dr. Wm.)] Scripture Theory of the Earth, throughout all its Revolutions, from the Creation, to the final Renovation of all things, 8vo. *bds.* 3*s* . . 1773
4967 ―――――― Impartial Enquiry into the case of the Gospel Demoniacks, 8vo. *bds.* 3*s* 6*d* . 1777
4968 ―――――― Farther Enquiry into the case of the Gospel Demoniacks, occasioned by Mr. Farmer's letters on the subject, 8vo. *bds.* 2*s* 6*d* 1779
4969 ―――――― Essay on the Scheme and Conduct, procedure and extent of Man's Redemption; with a Dissertation on the Design of the Book of Job, 8vo. *calf*, 4*s* 6*d* . 1748
4970 WOTTON'S (Wm.) Reflections upon Ancient and Modern Learning, with a Defense thereof, in answer to Sir W. Temple, and a Dissertation on the Epistles of Themistocles, Socrates, Euripides, and the Fables of Æsop, by R. Bentley, D.D., 8vo. *calf*, 4*s* 1705
4971 WRANGHAM'S (Fra. *Archdeacon of Cleveland*) Sermons practical and occasional; Dissertations, Translations, including new versions of Virgil's Bucolica, and of Milton's Defensio Secunda, Seaton poems, &c., 3 vols. 8vo. *cloth*, 7*s* 6*d* . 1816
4972 WRIGHT (Tho.) St. Patrick's Purgatory: an Essay on the Legends of Purgatory, Hell, and Paradise, current during the Middle Ages, 8vo. *bds.* 4*s* . 1844

4973 WREN's (Matth. *Bp. of Ely*) Increpatio Bar Jesu : sive Polemicæ Adsertiones locorum aliquot S. Scripturæ, ab imposturis perversionum in Catechesi Rocoviana, 4to. *vellum, scarce, 7s—calf, 6s* 1660

> Wren was Chaplain to King Charles I. and successively Bp. of Hereford, Norwich, and Ely. During the Great Rebellion his property was seized, and he was committed to the Tower, where he remained 18 years before he was brought to Trial. During this time he wrote the above work. He was restored to his Bishoprick in 1660, and died at Ely house, in 1667, aged 81.

4974 WYNARD's (Montagu John) Sermons on Christian Duties, 8vo. *hf. bd. calf, 5s* . . 1832

4975 XERES's (John) Address to the Jews, containing his Reasons for leaving the Jewish and embracing the Christian Religion, 8vo. *calf, 3s 6d* . . 1710

4976 XIMENES.—Histoire du Cardinal Ximenes, par Esprit Fléchier Evêque de Nismes, 4to. *portrait, calf, 5s* Par. 1693

4977 YORK. The Churches of York, by W. Monkhouse and F. Bedford, jun., with Historical and Architectural Notes by the Rev. Joshua Fawcett, 4to. *fine lithographic plates, bds.* £1. *4s* York, ——

4978 YOUNG's (Arthur) Historical Dissertation on Idolatrous Corruptions in Religion, from the beginning of the world, 2 vols. 8vo. *calf, 6s* 1734

4979 ——— (Edward, *Dean of Sarum*) Sermons on several occasions, 2 vols. 8vo. *calf, 5s* . 1720

4980 ——— Works, containing his Night-Thoughts, and other pieces, 6 vols. 12mo. *portrait, fine copy, old calf gilt, 6s* 1774-78

4981 ——— (Will. Toy) Seventy Sermons on the Doctrines and Duties of Christianity, consisting partly of Discourses, altered and abridged from the Works of eminent Divines, 2 vols. 8vo. *calf, 6s* Birmingham, 1807

4982 YOUNGE's (B.) Cause and Cure of Ignorance, Error, Enmity, Atheism, Prophanesse, &c., sm. 8vo. *uncut, 2s* 1648

4983 ZACCARIA (Fra. Ant.) Bibliotheca Ritualis, cum Supplementis, 2 vols. in 3, 4to. *very scarce, neat,* £3. *3s* Romæ, 1776-81

4984 ZANCHIUS (Hier.) de Operibus Dei intra spacium sex dierum creatis opus, 4to. *calf, 5s* . Hanov. 1597

4985 ——— In D. Pauli epistolam ad Ephesios Commentarius, 4to. *vellum, 5s* . Neustadii, 1600

4986 ZEIGELBAUER (N.) Historia Rei Litterariæ Ordinis S. Benedicti, recensuit, auxit, jurisque publici fecit O. Legipontius, 4 vols. in 2 folio, *fine copy, hogskin binding,* £3. *3s* Augustæ Vind. 1754

> The Literary History of that learned body, THE BENEDICTINES, is divided into —1st. Their rise, progress, and vicissitudes, including particulars of their schools, libraries, &c. 2nd. Their literary history proper, containing a complete account of the progress of literature, the arts and sciences from the time of St. Benedict, and their cultivation of each. 3rd. Biographical, in which both the lives and works of the various members are described. 4. Bibliographical, in which the numerous productions of this body are given in classes, with critical accounts of each.

4987 [ZIMMERMAN (J.)] De Miraculis, quæ Pythagoræ, Apollonio Thyanensi, Francisco Assisio, Dominico et Ignatio Loyolæ tribuuntur libellus, 8vo. *calf gilt, 3s* Edinburgi, [Genevæ], 1762

4988 ZOLLIKOFER's (G. J.) Sermons on the Evils that are in the World, and other topics; translated by the Rev. W. Tooke, 2 vols. 8vo. *calf, 8s* . . 1804
4989 ——— Sermons on the Dignity of Man, and on the Evils that are in the World, &c., together 4 vols. 8vo. *bds.* 10s 1802-4

"Zollikofer's Sermons, which are in the highest estimation in Germany, have lately been known in this country by a translation of great purity and elegance. In these sermons the aim is to explain the nature and grounds of Christian morality, and to reconcile it with the best dictates of philosophy; to reveal man to himself: and they discover a talent seldom possessed—a knowledge of the human heart."—*Chalmers.*

4990 ZOPFIUS (Jo. Hen.) Introductio ad Lectionem cursoriam Veteris Testamenti, 12mo. *calf, 3s* . *Lips.* 1763
4991 ZYPÆUS (Franciscus) Juris Pontificii Novi Analytica enarratio, 8vo. *neat, 3s* . *Coloniæ Agr.* 1624

ADDENDA.

4992 ABBOT's (Geo.) Exposition upon the Prophet Jonah, contained in certaine Sermons, preached in St. Marie's Church in Oxford, small 4to. *calf, scarce, 9s* . 1600
4993 ADAMS's (Thos.) Exposition upon the Second Epistle general of St. Peter, revised and corrected by Sherman, royal 8vo. *bds.* 15s 1839
4994 AQUINATIS (S. Thomæ) Summa totius Theologiæ, 2 vols. 4to. *vellum, 16s* . *Venetiis,* 1586
4995 ——— aliud exemplar, folio, *calf, £1. 4s* *Antverp.* 1624
4995*———— idem. folio, *fine copy, hogskin, with clasps, £1. 10s*
Lugduni, 1737
4996 ——— Summa Theologica, cum Commentariis Thomæ de Vio Card. Cajetani, et Elucidationibus Litteralibus P. Seraphini Capponi a Porrecta, Ord. Prædicatorum, cui etiam accedunt in fine ejusdem S. Thomæ Questiones Quolibitales, et peculiares quidam alii Tractatus, 10 vols. in 7, royal folio, *slightly wormed, in the original Spanish binding, £4. 4s* . *Romæ,* 1773
4997 BABINGTON's (Gervase, *Bp. of Exeter*) Certain plaine, briefe, and comfortable Notes upon Genesis, Exodus, and Leviticus, gathered and laid down for the good of them that are not able to use better helps, and yet careful to read the word, and right hartily desirous to taste the sweet of it, 2 vols. sm. 4to. 𝕭lack letter, *fine clean copies, calf, neat,* 16s . 1596-1604
4998 BELLARMINI (Roberti) Disputationes de Controversiis Christianæ Fidei, adversus hujus temporis Hæreticos, 3 vols. folio, *stamped calf, £3. 13s 6d* . *Ingold.* 1588-93
4999 BELLARMIN's Notes of the Church, examined and confuted, 4to. *calf, scarce, 7s 6d* . 1688

5000 BERNARDI (Sancti Claravallensis Abbatis primi, melliflui Ecclesiæ Doctoris) Opera omnia, edente J. Picardo, folio, *calf*, £1. 1*s*
Antv. 1616

5000*BERNARD's (Richard) Thesaurus Biblicus, seu Promptuarium Sacrum, together with the Bible's Abstract and Epitome, folio, *calf*, 7*s* . 1644

5001 THE HOLY BIBLE, translated from the Latin Vulgate, and first published at the English College at Douay, revised according to the Clementin edition of the Scriptures; together with the Rhemish New Testament, and Annotations upon the whole, 5 vols. sm. 8vo. *neat*, 15*s* . *Edinb.* 1796-7

5002 ———— containing the authorized Versions of the Old and New Testaments, with 20,000 emendations, derived from ancient and modern Versions, original and scarce MSS. &c. 8vo. *bds.* 10*s* 1841

5003 ———— Histoire du Vieux et du Nouveau Testament, *enrichie de plus de* 400 *figures en taille-douce*, 2 vols. royal folio, *brilliant impressions of the plates, calf*, £2. 10*s* *Amst.* 1700

5004 ———— Commentary upon the Holy Bible from Henry and Scott, with Observations and Notes from other Writers, 6 vols. sm. 8vo. *bds.* 18*s* . *Religious Tract Society*, 1832

5004*BIDDING PRAYER (Form of), with Introduction and Notes, 18mo. *bds.* 3*s* 6*d* . *Oxford*, 1840

5005 BILSON's (Thos.) True Difference betweene Christian Subjection and Unchristian Rebellion, 4to. *fine copy, in the original binding, calf, gilt leaves*, 14*s* . 1585

5006 ———— Survey of Christ's Sufferings for Man's Redemption, and of his descent to Hades or Hell for our Deliverance, folio, *(wants part of the first leaf in the preface) calf*, £1. 1*s* 1604

5007 BREVIARIUM Ecclesiæ Rotomagensis, 4 vols. 12mo. *fine copy, old red morocco, gilt leaves*, £1. 10*s* *Rotomagi*, 1777

5008 BROWNISTS—The Rasing of the Foundations of Brownisme, wherein all the Writings of the principal Masters of that Sect, and their contrarie Arguments are deliberately examined and clearly repelled, 4to. *bds.* 5*s* . *Lond. by J. Windet*, 1588

5009 BULLINGER's (Henry) C. Sermons upon the Apocalips of Jesu Christe, sm. 4to. 𝕭lack letter, *stained, wanting a leaf in the Index, and the title supplied in MS. calf*, 12*s* 1571

5010 BURROUGHS's (Jeremiah) Exposition, with Practical Observations upon the first Seven Chapters of the Prophecy of Hosea, 2 vols. 4to. *very scarce*, 14*s* . 1650-52

5011 BUTLER's (Joseph, *Bp. of Durham*) Works, containing his Analogy of Religion and Sermons, 2 vols. 8vo. *bds.* 11*s*—*calf gilt*, 18*s*
Oxford, 1844

5012 CALVINI (Joan.) Institutio Christianæ Religionis, sm. 8vo. *calf*, 5*s* 6*d* . *Genevæ*, 1618

5013 CAVE's (W.) Dissertation concerning the Government of the Ancient Church by Bishops, Metropolitans, and Patriarchs, 8vo. *rich calf gilt, old style*, 9*s* . 1683

5014 ———— Primitive Christianity, or the Religion of the Ancient Christians in the first ages of the Gospel, 8vo. *calf gilt*, 8*s* 6*d* 1728

5015 CHINESE—The Domestic Habits, Customs, Amusements, Games, &c. of the Chinese, *illustrated with numerous coloured drawings by a Native, and descriptive letter-press in the Chinese language, bound up in two vols.* imp. 8vo. *bds.* £4. 14s 6d

5016 COMMON PRAYER (The Book of), with the Psalter, sm. 4to. *title inlaid, bds.* 3s   .   Lond. by C. Barker, 1608

5017 ———— another copy, sm. 4to. *title inlaid, and defective in the Kalendar, bds.* 5s   .   *ib.* R. Barker, 1614

5018 ———— sm. 4to. *soiled, bds. cut rather close,* 4s 6d
              Norton and Bill, 1621

5019 ———— sm. 4to. *bds.* 3s   R. Barker, 1633

5020 ———— 8vo. *ruled with red lines, title inlaid, calf,* 3s
             J. Bill and C. Barker, 1665

5021 ———— 4to. *bds.* 2s 6d   Camb. by J. Field, 1666

5022 ———— sm. 8vo. *ruled with red lines, bds.* 3s   In the Savoy, 1761

5023 ———— another copy, Oxford, 1701—New Testament, Lond. 1696—Sternhold and Hopkins's Psalms, *ib.* 1701—*in one* vol. 8vo. *old morocco, gilt leaves,* 9s   .   ————

5024 ———— *with portrait of Queen Anne, and plates,* Oxford, 1703—Brady and Tate's Psalms, Lond. 1701—*in one* vol. 8vo. *old morocco, gilt leaves,* 10s 6d   .

5025 CONCILIORUM NOVA ET AMPLISSIMA COLLECTIO, AB INITIIS ÆRÆ CHRISTIANÆ AD ANNUM MDIX., in qua præter ea quæ P. Labbæus et G. Cossartius et novissime Nich. Coleti in lucem edidere ea omnia insuper suis in locis optime disposita exhibentur quæ J. D. Mansi evulgavit. Editio novissima ab eodem Patre Mansi curata, locupletata et perfecta, 31 vols. folio, *extremely scarce, vellum,* £48.
                Florentiæ, 1759-98

5026 CRACKANTHORPE's (Dr. Rich.) Vigilius Dormitans, Romes Seer overseene; or, a Treatise of the Fift Generall Councell held at Constantinople, Anno 553, wherein is proved that the Pope's Apostolical Constitution and definitive sentence in matter of Faith was condemned as hereticall by the Synod, and the exceeding Frauds of Cardinall Baronius and Binius are clearly discovered, folio, *calf, scarce,* 15s   .   .   1631

5027 CRANMER's (Abp.) Remains, collected and arranged by Henry Jenkins, M.A. 4 vols. 8vo. *bds.* £2. 10s—*calf gilt,* £3. 3s
                 Oxford, 1834

5028 ———— Short Instruction into Christian Religion, being a Catechism set forth by Abp. Cranmer, 1548; together with the same in Latin, by Justus Jonas in 1549, *with fac-similes of the curious wood-cuts,* 8vo. *bds.* 14s 6d—*calf gilt,* 17s 6d   *ib.* 1829

5029 CYPRIANI (S.) Opera, jam quartam à mendis per D. Erasmum repurgata, 8vo. *margin of the title cut off, otherwise a fine clean copy, in the original stamped binding,*   Lugduni, 1535

5030 DIODATI's (John) Pious and learned Annotations upon the Holy Bible, plainly expounding the most difficult places thereof, folio, *vellum,* 12s   .   1651

5031 DOWLING's (J. G.) Introduction to the Critical Study of Ecclesiastical History, 8vo. *bds.* 9s   .   1838

5032 ELISABETH.—Duo Edicta Elizabethæ Reginæ Ang. contra Sacerdotes Soc. Jesu, et alumnos Seminariorum, quæ à Gregorio XIII. Pont. Max. Romæ et Remis pro Anglis sunt instituta. Una cum Apologia D. Guil. Alani pro iisdem Sacerdotibus Soc. Jesu, et aliis Seminariorum Alumnis, &c. 12mo. *rare, fine clean copy, bds.* 12s *August. Trev.* 1583

5033 ENGLISHMAN's Greek Concordance to the Old and New Testament, royal 8vo. *bds.* (pub. at £2. 2s) £1. 8s . 1839

5034 EUCHOLOGIUM—A Collection of Greek Services and Prayers, 4to. *hf. bd.* £1. 5s . *Romæ,* 1754

5035 EVANS's (R. W.) Biography of the Early Church, 2 vols. 12mo. *bds.* 4s 6d . . 1837-9

5036 FAIR WARNING, the second part ; or, XX. Prophecies concerning the Return of Popery, by Abps. Whitgift, Laud, Bancroft, Bps. Sanderson, Gauden, Mr. Hooker, and others, sm. 4to. *bds.* 5s 6d 1663

5037 GALLANDII (AND.) BIBLIOTHECA GRÆCO-LATINA VETERUM PATRUM, ANTIQUORUMQUE SCRIPTORUM ECCLESIASTICORUM, 14 vols. folio, *excessively rare, fine clean copy, in the original binding,* £50. *Venetiis,* 1765-81

An elaborate account of this invaluable work will be found in the Bibliotbeca Patristica of Walcbius, and also in Dowling's Notitia, pp. 192-209, where a detailed list of its contents is given. Very few copies have appeared for sale in this country, and the work is of equal rarity on the continent, where it is sought after with much eagerness, and sells at a very high price.

5038 GILL's (John) Exposition of the Old and New Testament, 9 vols. 4to. *maps and plates, fine copy, calf gilt,* £9. 19s 6d 1810

5039 HALL's (Tho.) Practical and Polemical Commentary upon the 3rd and 4th chapters of the latter Epistle of St. Paul to Timothy, folio, *calf, very scarce,* 14s . 1658

5040 HILDERSAM's (Arthur) CLII. Lectures upon Psalm LI., preached at Ashby-de-la-Zouch, folio, *calf, scarce,* 16s 1642

5041 HUGHES's (Geo.) Analytical Exposition of the whole Book of Genesis, and of the 23rd Chapter of Exodus, folio, *calf, very scarce,* £1. 1s . . 1672

5042 HUTCHINSON's (Geo.) Exposition of the Prophecies of Obadiah, Jonah, Micah, Nahum, Habakkuk, and Zephaniah, 12mo. *scarce,* 8s . . 1654

5043 JOHNSON's (John) Unbloody Sacrifice and Altar, unvailed and supported, Vol. 1, 8vo. *calf, scarce,* 10s 1724

5043*JUSTINI (St. Martyris) Opera Omnia, Græcè et Latinè, necnon Tatiani adversus Græcos Oratio ; Athenagoræ Legatio pro Christianis ; S. Theophili Antiocheni tres ad Autolycum Libri ; Hermiæ Irrisio Gentilium Philosophorum, etc. *Editio Benedictina,* folio, *with a few MS. notes, interlineations, and corrections, hf. bd. russia, uncut, gilt top,* £2. 15s. . *Paris,* 1742

5044 ——— Apologia pro Christianis, Gr. et Lat. Annotationis adjecit C. Ashton, 8vo. *hf. bd. uncut,* 7s *Cantab.* 1768

5045 KING's (Lord) History of the Apostles' Creed, with Critical Observations on its several Articles, 8vo. *fine copy, calf,* 5s 6d 1703

5046 LEIGH's (Edw.) Annotations upon all the New Testament, philological and theological, folio, *calf, scarce,* 8s . 1650

[58, GREAT QUEEN STREET,

5047 LE QUIEN (R. P. Michaelis) Oriens Christianus in quatuor Patriarchatus digestus; quo exhibentur Ecclesiæ, Patriarchiæ, cæterique Præsules totius Orientis, 3 vols. folio, *fine copy, calf, very scarce,*
Par. 1740
5048 LIBRARY OF THE FATHERS of the Holy Catholic Church, anterior to the division of the East and West; translated by Members of the English Church, 21 vols. 8vo. *(all published) bds. £8. 8s*
Oxford, 1838-45
5049 MANTON'S (Thos.) CXC. Sermons on the CXIXth Psalm, folio, *fine clean copy, but imperfect in the index, rough calf,* 18s   1681
5050 MORI (Thomæ) Lucubrationes, viz.—Utopiæ Lib. II. Progymnasmata, Epigrammata, Epistolæ, &c. quibus additæ sunt due aliorum Epistolæ, de Vita, Moribus et Morte Mori, sm. 8vo. *fine clean copy, in the original binding, calf,* 14s   *Basil.* 1563
5051 PEARSON'S (Bp.) Exposition of the Creed, 2 vols. 8vo. *portrait, fine copy, old calf gilt,* 12s   *Oxford,* 1797
5052 SECKER'S (Abp.) Works, containing his Sermons, Lectures on the Catechism, Discourses on War and Rebellion, with his Life by Bp. Porteus, 11 vols. 8vo. *fine copy, calf gilt,* £3. 3s   1796, &c.
5053 WADDINGI (Lucæ, *Hiberni*) Annales Minorum, seu trium ordinum a S. Francisco institutorum, locupletior et accuratior Jos. M. Fonseca; accesserunt Syllabus J. M. de Ancona confectus, et Continuatio ad A.D. 1664, a Jo. de Luca et J. M. de Ancona, 19 vols. folio, *uncut,* £15. 15s   *Romæ,* 1731-45

MANUSCRIPTS.

5054 COUNCILS.—Histoire des Conciles, 4to. *A MS. of upwards of* 340 *pages, very neatly written, calf, gilt back, very neat,* 8s
5055 DODSON (Jeremy) Concio ad Clerum Londinensem habita in Ecclesia parochiali S^{ti.} Alphagii, Maiæ 13, 1690, small 4to. *calf,* 5s
5056 FELL'S (John, *Bp. of Oxford*) Sermons in his own hand-writing, 4 thick vols. 8vo. *calf, neat,* £1. 11s 6d
5057 HARRIS, THE HISTORIAN. The Historical Common-place Book of Dr. William Harris, author of the Lives of James I., Charles I., Oliver Cromwell, Charles II., etc. containing, *inter alia, some of his materials for a* HISTORY OF JAMES II., which it was his intention to publish. MANUSCRIPT, *in his own handwriting,* folio, *in vellum binding,* £1. 10s

In addition to the historical matter contained in this volume there are many private memoranda of the author; the following are certainly curious:—
" Dec. 11, 1764. If I dye before the publication of Charles II., I desire my MS. may be sent to Mr. Hollis, (his friend Thomas Hollis, the republican, who had lent him many books,) if he survives, to be disposed of as he shall think proper. All his letters I hereby order shall be sought out and returned without perusal to him. Let my policy of insurance be made over immediately in the name of Mrs. Harris, by an indorsement from the office of Exon. I desire Mrs. Harris constantly to have a will by her in due form, otherwise the lawyers may run away with her effects: and that Mr. How, or in case he dies, Mr. Stokes may have the management of her affairs. But never employ Mr. Gidley. Part with no writings without having a receipt for them on your book. *This book I give to Molly Freeman, and desire her very carefully to preserve. If Mrs. Macauley desires* ANY MINUTES FOR THE LIFE OF JAMES II. CONTAINED IN THIS BOOK, *let them be transcribed and sent her.* Will. Harris, Nov. 10, 1767." There are other testamentary directions.

MANUSCRIPTS—*continued.*

5058 S. LAURENTII JUSTINIANI, Veneti, liber de officio pastorali. MANUSCRIPT ON VELLUM, of the fifteenth century, small folio, *in neat half-morocco binding,* £2. 2s

> Lorenzo Giustiniani, of one of the noblest families of Venice, was consecrated bishop of that city by Eugenio IV. 1431-35, and seems to have said "nolo Episcopari" in earnest, for Cave says he was so appointed "postquam nullas non preces, nullas non artes, ut onus impositum excuteret, adbibuisset. Vir infucata erga Deum pietate, prodiga in pauperes charitate, et ingenti religionis zelo, merito celebrandus." Venice was erected into a patriarchate by Nicolas V. in 1450, and Giustiniani was the first who filled that high dignity. He died in 1450, and was canonized by Clement VII. in 1524.
> There is no piece under the above title included in the editions of his printed works, unless it be his treatise "de regimine et institutione Prælatorum." It is certain, however, that this MS. remained in his family, from the following inscription in the hand-writing of his celebrated Nephew, the Historian of Venice, "liber hic est mei Bernardi Justiniaoi, oratoris, procuratoris, nepotis Beati Justiniani suctoris hujus libri, qui est de officio pastorali." This is the autograph of one who was a pupil of Guarino, of Filelfo, and of George of Trebisond, who was repeatedly ambassador from the Republic, and who was a member of the Council of Ten, and at last Procurator of St. Mark, the second dignity of the state.
> We may consider this author as almost belonging to the English series, for the present head of his family, Prince Giustiniani, is the nearest heir to an earldom in this country, the Scotch Peerage of Newburgh, and the title is at present assumed by a younger branch, on the ground that Prince Giustiniani, as an alien, is incapable of inheriting English honours.

5059 MARSDEN AND FAIRFAX. Devotional Pieces.
    i. The anatomie of the bodie of a beleever in the resurrection further exemplified in a discourse upon that texte used at the buriall of the dead: John xi. 25: by Mr. Raphe Marsden.
    ii. "A Rich dewry, or jonter, made mee bye my maker, my husband, (the Lord of Hosts is his name,) and my redeemer the holy on of Israel, the God of the whole earth shall he be called: Isaiah, liv. 4. And delivered me bye his survant, my dear loveing husband, as my only, and alone suficient porcion to rest on."
    By Mary Cholmley, daughter of Sir H. Cholmley, wife of Henry Fairfax, second son of Thomas, first Lord, and brother of Ferdinando, second Lord Fairfax.
MANUSCRIPT, neatly written, 12mo. £1. 1s

> This Manuscript belonged to Bryan Fairfax, son of the above Henry and Mary Fairfax, as appears from his name at the commencement. He has also prefixed this note to the second tract. "The hand-writing and hart-enditeing of the most Vertuous and Pious Mrs. Mary Fairfax, wife to the truely religious Mr. Henry Fairfax, of Newton-Kyme."

5060 MARSHALL.—A Literal Translation of the Book of Psalms from the original Hebrew; with a Comment, Criticism, and Annotations to which is added, an Attempt to Explain many of the difficult Texts in the Revelation of St. John. By the Rev. William Marshall, Rector of Willingaledoe in Essex, and Chaplain to the Duchess Dowager of Douglas. THE ORIGINAL UNPUBLISHED MANUSCRIPT, *prepared for the press,* 3 vols. folio, *containing upwards of* 1000 *closely written pages, in vellum binding,* £2. 2s

[58, GREAT QUEEN STREET,

MANUSCRIPTS—*continued.*

5061 MAZARIN. Lettres et Mémoires du Cardinal Mazarin à Messieurs de Tellier et de Lionne: contenans le sécret de la négociation de la paix des Pyrenées, dans les conférences tenues à Saint Jean de Luz en 1669: avec plusieurs lettres du mesme, très curieuses, éscrites au Roy et à la Reine pendant son voyage. MANUSCRIPT, *very neatly written*, large and thick folio, *in calf binding*, £2. 2s

These letters contain Mazarin's account of the celebrated negociation between himself and Don Luis de Haro at St. Jean de Luz, where these two prime ministers of France and Spain completed in person the long pending treaty of Westphalia. This transaction is very properly considered the chef-d'œuvre of Mazarin's policy, and he himself appears to have considered it somewhat in that light, for he wrote this account of the conferences for the King's instruction, and with a view of initiating him into politics. One of his historians justly says, " il n'existe pas de meilleures leçons diplomatiques; ce qui se passait dans ces conférences y est développé avec une netteté, une précision qui met en quelque façon le lecteur en tiers avec les deux plénipotentiaires."
This MS. may be considered an official copy, as it was procured for Sir Robert Southwell, Secretary of State to William III. and ancestor of the late Lord De Clifford, by William Blathwayt, Secretary at War to James II., and afterwards to William III., whose letter to Sir Robert, dated Whitehall, 23 Jan. 1685, accompanies this volume: in it he says, " Mazarin's letters are in a good forwardness, and will be sent you entire and bound from hence."

5062 ——— Some remarks on Cardinal Mazarin's Negociation of the Pyrenean Peace in 1659. Chiefly for what then related to England; and as now appears from his owne letters, printed in two parts, in 1690 and 1693. By Sir Robert Southwell, Knt. MANUSCRIPT, *neatly written*, folio, £1. 11s 6d

5063 MISCELLANEA THEOLOGICA: a Collection of seven Treatises of various authors. MANUSCRIPT on paper, *chiefly written by Robert Stocktun, an English student at Padua, in the year* 1447, 4to. *in vellum binding*, £1. 1s

This Manuscript appears to have belonged in 1520 to Robert Whetley, a monk, to whom it was given by Richard Janson; in 1574 it was given by William Beopor, Esq. to John Bidlake, who has inserted some indexes of its contents, which are
i. S. Gregorii Papæ I. libellus de proprietatibus vocabulorum et animalium.
ii. Lotharii diaconi, postea Innocentii Papæ III., de miseria hominis, sive de contemptu mundi liber.
iii. Petri Brunicheli opus abbreviatum.
iv. S. Augustini Hipponensis liber Soliloquiorum.
At the end of this we read, " Scriptus a fratre Robarto Stocktun, anno Domini 1447, in florentissimo gingnasio Padua nomine."
v. Quædam excerpta sive dicta Beati Isidori.
vi. Beati Bernardi liber de templo spirituali et qualiter in nobis debeat edificari.
vii. Ejusdem libellus de miseria hominis.

5064 ——— A large and curious Collection of Treatises, some of them unpublished. MANUSCRIPT, written in the latter part of the fifteenth century, thick 4to. *in very fine internal condition*, £2, 12s 6d

This Manuscript formerly belonged to the Monastery of *Rubea Vallis*, (Roode-Clooster) a house of Canons regular, near Brussels, and was, not improbably, written for the use of its monks. A short notice of its contents follows:
i. Petri de Rosenhaym Roseum memoriale, sive compendium singulorum librorum

MANUSCRIPTS—*continued.*

utriusque Testamenti versibus heroicis compositum ; una cum concordia quatuor evangelistarum.
ii. Regulæ Juris Canonici. Dat. Romæ, 5 non. Martii, anno pontificatus Bonifacii VIII. quarto, 1298.
To these are added the names of the chief commentators on the Canon Law.
iii. Quæstiones et responsiones de Sanctissima Trinitate.
iv. Disputatio de anima, sub modo dialogi, extracta ex dictis SS. Hieronymi et Augustini.
v. Hugonis de Sancto Victore tractatulus de anima.
vi. Sancti Augustini episcopi Hipponensis liber soliloquiorum.
vii. Jacobi de Voragine, de ordine prædicatorum, Archiepiscopi Januensis, tractatus super libros beati Augustini.
viii. Vita ancillæ Christi S. Mariæ de Oegines, edita a venerabili viro magistro Jacobo de Vitriaco, primo Aconensi episcopo, postea vero episcopo Tusculano et sedis Apostolicæ Caıdinali, ad Fulconem episcopum Tholosanum dicata.
At the end is a curious note by the scribe, stating that when he wrote this copy he was not aware that the monastery already possessed the work at the end of the life of St. Gudild, with many additions by a canon regular of Contimpré, near Cambray, who had sent his work to Ægidius, Prior of the monastery of Oignies.
ix. S. Basilii Cæsariensis, cognomento Magni. liber de modo studendi atque rectè beatèque vivendi, e Græco in Latinum traditus per Leonardum [Bruoi] Aretionm ad [Linum] Colucium [Pierium Salutatum de Stignano, Florentiæ Cancellarium.]
x. Arnoldi de Nova Villa tractatus " de consumacione seculi et tempore antichristi, qui alias intitulatur de misterio cymbalorum ecclesie et fuit editus in aula summi Pontificis Bonifacii, videlicet octavi sibique presentatus ac per ipsum eximie commendatus."
xi. Tractatulus de adventu Christi.
xii. " Gesta inclita Tyrii Appollonii Regis "
xiii. Lotharii Diaconi Cardinalis, postea Innocentii Papæ III., libri iii. de vilitate humanæ conditionis, sive, de miseria hominis.
xiv. S. Anselmi Archiepiscopi Cantuariensis libellus de quatuordecim beatitudinibus, septem quæ pertinent ad corpus et septem quæ ad animam. [imperf.]
xv. Vita Santæ Hermenildis virginis de stirpe Karolidarum apud Meldricem quiescentis.

5065 ORAISONS et Sermons diverses, *very neatly written,* sm. 8vo. *old red morocco, gilt leaves, 6s* . Cent. XVII.

5066 ORDO Cantus et lecture sororum ordinis Sancta Salvatoris in horis diurnis pariter et nocturnis observandus, MS. ON VELLUM, OF THE END OF THE XV. CENTURY. 8vo. *calf, neat, old style, wooden boards,* £2. 12s 6d

The name of the writer appears from the explicit, which reads thus " Hic explicit ordinarium Sororum Vatzstinensium Sancti Salvatoris ordinis. Orate Deum pro Scriptrice, Sororis Christina filia Johannis"

5067 THE POPISH PLOT. Letters from the Privy Council to Lord Norreys, (James Bertie, Lord Norreys of Rycote, afterwards created Earl of Abingdon,) Lord Lieutenant of Berkshire, to cause the houses of all Papists or reputed Papists to be searched for arms in consequence of a conspiracy against the life of the King, (Charles II.) Dat. 30 Sept. 1678. THE ORIGINAL MANUSCRIPT, WITH FOURTEEN AUTOGRAPH SIGNATURES, £1. 10s

Signed by
" Finch, C." *i. e.* Heneage Finch, *Lord Chancellor,* the First Earl of Nottingham.

[58, GREAT QUEEN STREET,

MANUSCRIPTS—*continued*.
"Danby," *i. e.* Sir Thomas Osborne, Earl of Danby, Lord High Treasurer, the first Marquess of Carmarthen, and Duke of Leeds.
"Anglesey," *i. e.* Arthur Annesley, first Earl of Anglesey.
"Lauderdale," *i. e.* John, Duke of Lauderdale.
"Bath," *i. e.* John Granville, first Viscount Granville, and Earl of Bath.
"Craven," *i. e.* William Craven, first Earl of Craven.
"Carbery," *i. e.* Richard Vaughan, second Earl of Carbery.
"St. Alban," *i. e.* Henry Jermyn, Earl of St. Alban.
"Berkeley," *i. e.* George, Lord Berkeley, first Viscount Dursley, and Earl of Berkeley.
"N. Duresme," *i. e.* Nathaniel, third Lord Crewe, Bishop of Durham.
"H. Coventry," *i. e.* the Hon. Henry Coventry, *Secretary of State*.
"G. Carteret," *i. e.* Sir George Carteret, Bart. first Lord Carteret of Hawnea.
"J. Ernle," *i. e.* Sir John Ernle, Knt. *Chancellor of the Exchequer*.
"Robert Southwell," *i. e.* Sir R. S. *Clerk of the Council*.

5068 PROPHETARUM MINORUM fragmenta. Coptice et Latinè. MANU-SCRIPT, *evidently prepared for the press*, in the hand-writing of DR. DAVID WILKINS, the Editor of the Coptic Pentateuch and New Testament, sm. 4to. *beautifully written,* £2. 2s ——

At the sale of the family papers of Lords Fairfax, little or no care seems to have been taken to preserve them in order, in consequence many of the more curious manuscripts are incomplete, part having fallen to one purchaser, part to another. This has been the case with these curious and valuable fragments of the unpublished part of the Old Testament in Coptic. It is probable that the entire work existed in the Collection, but the following fragments are all that the publisher has been able to find. The MS. contains:—

    Daniel, ch. viii. ver. 1 to ch. xi. ver. 15.
    Bel and the Dragon, complete.
    Hosea, ch. iv. ver. 6. to ch. vii ver. 14.
    Amos, complete.
    Micah, complete.
    Joel, as far as ch. ii. ver. 22.
    Zephaniah, complete, except part of one verse.
    Haggai, complete.
    Zecharish, as far as ch. i. ver. 9.

5069 SERMONS: apparently the production of a Court preacher in the reign of King James I. One appears to have been preached before Prince Charles, Nov. 3, 1613. They contain a temperate and judicious defence of the constitution and usages of the Church of England, sm. 8vo. *rough calf,* 12s   Cent. XVII.

5070 VENETIAN RELATIONS, etc. i. Relatione della Republica di Venetia fatta dal Marchese de Bedmar, Ambasciadore Cattolico presso la serenissima Republica de Venetia.

This account of Venice relates to one of the most extraordinary periods of its history. The author, Alfonzo de la Cueva, Marquez de Bedmar, one of the most intriguing men of his time, was sent, in 1607, by Philip III. of Spain, as his ambassador to Venice. In 1618 he was said, in concert with Don Pedro de Toledo, Governor of Milan, and the Duke of Ossuña, Viceroy of Naples, to have conspired against the Republic to which he was accredited; Spanish soldiers were to be introduced by stealth, the arsenal fired, the strong posts seized, the nobles murdered *en masse*, and Venice itself brought under the Spanish yoke. The plot, however, was discovered, or said to be discovered, by the Venetian Senate, and several hundreds fell victims to their vengeance. Five months after the commencement of the executions, either a tardy gratitude or a profane mockery was offered to Heaven; and the Doge

MANUSCRIPTS—*continued.*

and Nobles returned thanks for their great deliverance, by a solemn service at St. Mark's. Bedmar, whose office was respected by the Senate, escaped by their connivance, and took refuge at Milan. He was afterwards, in 1622, created Cardinal by Gregory XV. and appointed Governor of the Low Countries. THIS WORK HAS NEVER BEEN PRINTED.

ii. Relazione della corte di Roma, fatta nel Senato Veneto alli 22 di Nov. 1623 dal Cavaliere Raniero Zeno.

This is a curious picture of the state of Rome, after the death of Gregory XV. and the election of Urban VIII. The author was the head of the noble house of Zeno, and is here stiled Cavaliere, a title usually given to a noble on his return from an embassy, and accompanied by the distinction of a golden star embroidered on his robe.

iii. Instruttion data dal Marchese di Bedmar, già Ambasciadore Cattolico in Venetia, à Don Luigi Bravo, suo successore, circa il modo col quale si dovera governare nella sua ambascieria.

This work, which may be called a continuation of the first, IS ALSO UNPUBLISHED.

MANUSCRIPT on paper, *very neatly written,* folio, *in russia binding. (From the* FAIRFAX COLLECTION, *with the autograph of Bryan Fairfax*), £2. 12s 6d

PAINTINGS.

** *The measurement given is exclusive of the frames.*

THE INFANT JESUS, attended by the VIRGIN MARY, JOSEPH, and ST. JOHN; *a splendid old painting on canvas, in a rich gilt frame,* 4 ft. 2 in. by 3 ft. £30.

THE CRUCIFIXION, by GUIDO; *in the finest preservation; in gilt frame* 2 ft. 6 in. by 2 ft. £25.

PORTRAIT OF DRYDEN, by Sir Godfrey Kneller, *in rich gilt frame,* 2 ft. 4 in. by 2 ft. £8. 8s

A PAIR. Landscape and Cattle, by BERGHEM, *two charming cabinet pictures, in richly gilt frames,* £24.

In ~~October~~ *March* *will be published, in* 8 *vols. folio, illustrated with* 250 *copperplates, including Facsimiles of all Hollar's Engravings, and a multitude of Wood-cuts,*

PRICE £31 10s. Hf. Bnd. MOROCCO, UNCUT,

A NEW EDITION OF

𝔇ugdale's 𝔐onasticon 𝔄nglicanum;

A HISTORY OF THE

ABBEYS, AND OTHER MONASTERIES,

HOSPITALS, FRIARIES, AND

CATHEDRAL AND COLLEGIATE CHURCHES,

IN ENGLAND AND WALES,

AND ALL SUCH SCOTCH, IRISH AND FRENCH MONASTERIES
AS WERE IN ANY MANNER CONNECTED WITH THE
RELIGIOUS HOUSES IN ENGLAND.

THIS NEW EDITION OF THE MONASTICON will be reprinted from that edited in 1817, by MESSRS. CALEY, ELLIS AND BANDINEL, and upon which those eminent Antiquaries were employed from the year 1812 to 1830. From the mode of publication then adopted, the work crept slowly through the press during a period of thirteen years, and consequently it was found impossible to keep up an exact uniformity of paper and typography. The great improvements which have taken place in the manufacture of paper, the brilliancy of the ink now employed by our great printers, and the very superior skill of the copperplate printers of the present day, will enable the proprietors to place before the public, at the comparatively low price of £31 10s., a work in every way superior to that for which the former subscribers paid no less than £141 15s. The limited impression of 350 copies, to which the last edition was confined, has in no way injured the copperplates, the greater part of which were executed by the late JOHN CONEY, from sketches made by him expressly for the work. The numerous typographical errors, which unfortunately are to be met with in the impression of 1817—30, will be carefully corrected in the present reprint;* which otherwise will be *paginatim*, to facilitate reference from the labours of other antiquaries and professional men, who have availed themselves of the valuable information contained in the enlarged edition of the Collections of SIR WILLIAM DUGDALE.

It would be quite out of place, as well as unnecessary, to dwell at any length upon the value of this imperishable monument of the indefatigable industry of the original compiler. To the ANTIQUARY and HISTORIAN the Monasticon affords the most ample information respecting our venerable and wealthy Religious Houses. A receptacle for a mass of biographical and historical information, its value is greatly enhanced by the numerous AUTHENTIC CHARTERS preserved in its pages. In this particular, the labours of SIR HENRY ELLIS and the REV. DR. BANDINEL have enriched the work from LEIGER BOOKS, CHARTULARIES, ROLLS, AND OTHER NATIONAL DOCUMENTS, and thus rendered it indispensable to those professional men, who on questions respecting REAL PROPERTY, practise in the highest Courts of the Country, the PRIVY COUNCIL, and the COURT OF CHANCERY. Hence it will be seen that, *acknowledged and admitted as it is, as evidence in all doubtful points as to the distribution of property, and in tracing landed possessions from their earliest proprietors*, the Monasticon is indispensable to EVERY LAWYER employed in the higher walks of his profession.

* The revision of this new Edition has been entrusted to an eminent Antiquary.

To the Clergy the work possesses an interest, not only of an antiquarian and historical character, but one which has a more solid claim to their notice. By its means they are frequently enabled to settle, without employing the costly machinery of the Law, disputed questions respecting the property of the Church; and a reference to the very copious Index, added by the editors to the work, will show at once that there is scarcely a single parish which is not mentioned in its pages. The numerous ground plans, sections, and full descriptions of the Ecclesiastical Edifices of the Middle Ages, have enabled the Architect, in many cases, to restore those buildings to their original grandeur; whilst it is admitted on all hands, that the great improvement of the National Taste in this respect, during the last ten years, is mainly attributable to the inimitable plates by John Coney, which adorn the pages of Dugdale's Monasticon.

Thus the Clergy, the Lawyer, the Antiquary, the Historian, the Architect, and the Topographer, as well as the possessor of real property, and the descendant of a noble line of Ancestors, will find the Monasticon Anglicanum one of the most interesting and indispensable works, that has ever issued from the press of this country. Feeling convinced that their efforts to place the new edition within the reach of all, by reducing the price to *less than one-fourth of its original cost*, will meet with the encouragement of the learned public, the present proprietors have determined upon reprinting a limited impression, the copies of which will be delivered *complete*, before the close of the present year, in the order in which they are subscribed for; and a list of the patrons of this noble undertaking will be prefixed to each copy, the subscriber's own name being printed in red ink, to mark his copy to his latest posterity.

To those who may prefer to receive the volumes at an interval of every three months, upon signing an undertaking to purchase

4 DUGDALE'S MONASTICON ANGLICANUM.

the entire work, the eight volumes will be delivered, half-bound in morocco, within two years, upon the quarterly payment of four guineas, commencing from the day of publication. As, however, no volume will be issued till the whole eight are printed, such subscribers will be entitled to receive their copies, in the numerical order in which their names appear in the subscription list.

Anticipating the same success which attended the publication of the former edition, every copy of which had been appropriated before the first part was sent to press, an early application is recommended. Subscribers' names received by

JOHN LESLIE, BOOKSELLER, 58, GREAT QUEEN STREET, LINCOLN'S INN FIELDS.

Lightning Source UK Ltd.
Milton Keynes UK
UKHW011040091221
395376UK00002B/524